W9-CDG-910

FREEDOM'S CAP

THE UNITED STATES CAPITOL

AND THE

COMING OF THE CIVIL WAR

GUY GUGLIOTTA

 HILL AND WANG

A DIVISION OF FARRAR, STRAUS AND GIROUX   NEW YORK

Hill and Wang
A division of Farrar, Straus and Giroux
18 West 18th Street, New York 10011

Copyright © 2012 by Guy Gugliotta
Distributed in Canada by D&M Publishers, Inc.
Printed in the United States of America
First edition, 2012

A portion of Freedom's Cap originally appeared, in slightly different form, in Smithsonian.

Library of Congress Cataloging-in-Publication Data
Gugliotta, Guy.
    Freedom's cap : the United States Capitol and the coming of the Civil War / Guy
Gugliotta. — 1st ed.
        p.   cm.
    Includes bibliographical references and index.
    ISBN 978-0-8090-4681-2 (alk. paper)
    1. United States Capitol (Washington, D.C.)—History.   2. Washington (D.C.)—
Buildings, structures, etc.   3. United States—History—1849-1877.   I. Title.

F204.C2G84 2012
975.3—dc23

                                                                    2011025750

Designed by Abby Kagan

www.fsgbooks.com

1   3   5   7   9   10   8   6   4   2

FREEDOM'S CAP

CONTENTS

PROLOGUE   3

1. "CONGRESS HOUSE"   9

2. PLANTING THE SEED   31

3. JEFFERSON DAVIS LOSES ONE AND WINS ONE   48

4. THE CONTEST   69

5. THOMAS U. WALTER IN CHARGE   88

6. SHARKS IN THE WATER   107

7. JEFFERSON DAVIS RETURNS   126

8. ENGINEER IN CHARGE   145

9. WALTER HAS A NEW IDEA   163

10. THE ALIEN MENACE   185

11. "A LIVELY OLD MAN WITH A VERY RED NOSE"   206

12. BLEEDING KANSAS   226

13. A NEW HOUSE OF REPRESENTATIVES   253

14. THE FEUD   274

15. MEIGS UNDER SIEGE   296

16. SWAN SONG   318

17. TYING OFF LOOSE ENDS   340

18. FREEDOM'S CAP   365

    EPILOGUE   395

    NOTES   413

    SELECTED BIBLIOGRAPHY   455

    ACKNOWLEDGMENTS   461

    INDEX   465

PROLOGUE

Army captain Montgomery C. Meigs was not a timid man. Bearded and burly, he stood over six feet tall and weighed close to two hundred pounds. Downturned lips and a pair of dark, glittering eyes gave his broad face an intimidating, challenging cast. None of this was an illusion. Meigs at thirty-nine was just beginning to realize his potential, which was considerable. He was intelligent, ambitious, capable, imposing, and arrogant. He had graduated fifth in his class at West Point in 1836, and would have done better, he wrote later, but the commandant marked him down 100 points because "I had many demerits."[1] His mother had once described Meigs as "high-tempered, unyielding, tyrannical towards his brothers; very persevering in pursuit of anything he wishes."[2] That was when he was six. Not much had changed.

When he arrived at his office in the U.S. Capitol building on January 11, 1856, he had an awkward task to perform. Meigs was an engineer by profession and on this Friday had served for nearly three years as superintendent in charge of transforming the cramped, crowded, hard-used U.S. Capitol building into a magisterial seat of government, with new marble wings for the Senate and House of Representatives and a spectacular central dome made of cast iron. Late the previous fall, just before the snow started, his men had finished tearing down the Capitol's old wooden dome, a rotting, leaking, copper-sheathed fire hazard, and had covered the hole with a temporary roof—a wooden frame draped in waterproof canvas. It kept the Rotunda dry, and already the lawmakers, lobbyists, and hangers-on who thronged the building during the day had pretty much forgotten it was there.

He had done all this quickly, and, he thought, elegantly. What he had done next, however, had never been tried before, as far as he knew—at least not on any kind of big building. From a base on the floor of the Capitol Rotunda, he had erected a wooden tower made of four large timbers strapped together. It stretched upward through the center of the new roof and beyond. On top of the tower—the highest point in the city of Washington—he had mounted a derrick and a boom that was able to swing 360 degrees. When a multiton piece of cast iron was ready for installation, teamsters would put it in a wagon and bring it to the base of the building, where it would be winched to the top of the new Senate wing. Then the new boom would drop a hook, grab the piece, lift it all the way up to the dome, and swing it around so the ironworkers could easily bolt it into place. There would be no manhandling and virtually no need for scaffolding. The construction team would use a ladder to climb the tower and work from a catwalk below the boom. It was not even that complicated.[3]

Meigs, utterly certain of his technical brilliance, embraced his engineering challenges with joy, but in many ways, building the Capitol was a thankless job. Meigs had already spent significant time and talent dodging contractors' kickbacks, refusing employment to party hacks and thieves, lobbying Congress for extra money, and fending off political dustups.

This year was shaping up to be even nastier. At least 100 of the 234 House members in the incoming Congress were Know-Nothings—anti-Catholic, anti-immigrant nativists who kept their affiliation secret from outsiders.[4] They were going after Meigs for hiring foreigners—many of them Catholic—to paint the Capitol's murals, carve its stone, and design its ornaments. Meigs was a Democrat, and immigrants were an important Democratic constituency, but politics, if you were to ask him, had nothing to do with his hiring practices. Skilled stonemasons, artisans, and artists, many of them undesirables or fugitives from failed revolutions in France, Germany, and Italy, were washing up at U.S. ports by the shipload. Meigs wanted the best; the job deserved the best; and he did not care where the best came from, what language they spoke, or what god they worshipped. Immigration was a spigot that belched experts. He would have been a fool not to hire them.

He had learned to ignore the political carping. Much harder to deal with was the tension over slavery. There was nothing Meigs could do about it, but the growing rancor was crippling the government. The wheels were turning ever more slowly, and Meigs, who needed new money every year to continue building the Capitol, had to have a Congress that was willing to act on his legislation. But right now it was impossible to get Congress to act on anything. President Franklin Pierce, a Democrat, had submitted his annual message to Congress, but the new House had refused to let it be formally read or debated until a Speaker was elected, and the failure to do so for a hundred ballots—and counting—was because different factions distrusted the aspirants' positions on slavery.

Pierce's message talked a lot about foreign affairs, but most of what he said was shadowed by the slavery question. There was a dispute with Great Britain over possible isthmian canal routes across Central America, where southerners were hoping to create a new slave state. The previous year, U.S. diplomats had called on Spain to sell Cuba to the United States and threatened to take Cuba by force if Spain refused. The idea, once again, was to make Cuba a slave state.

Closer to home, in the western reaches of the Louisiana Purchase, rival gangs of proslavery and abolitionist thugs had been dueling for almost two years over the future—slave or free—of what would come to be called "Bleeding Kansas." There was no resolution in sight, and with a Speakerless House, the government had all but ground to a halt.

Meigs had his own views about slavery. Although he had been born in Augusta, Georgia, his mother had forced his father to move back to Philadelphia because she could not stand the idea of raising her family in a slave state. On the other hand, Meigs was a good Democrat, and Democrats—especially southern Democrats—were slavery's biggest supporters.

Ultimately, however, Meigs did not have to have an opinion about slavery. As an Army officer, he was never asked for one and he never offered one. More important, keeping quiet was critical for Meigs because his boss was Secretary of War Jefferson Davis, of Mississippi.

Everybody knew Davis as a formidable public figure, one of the most outspoken slavery and states' rights advocates in Washington. What everybody had not known—at least at first—was that he was also the political guiding spirit of the Capitol project, a role he had assumed as a senator when it was launched in 1850 and had eagerly resumed as a member of Pierce's cabinet.

Davis had hired Meigs in 1853 and had supported him unfailingly in making elaborate changes to the new Capitol's design, in planning the sumptuous décor that Meigs wanted for the new wings and in substituting more durable—and more expensive—materials everywhere in construction. Meigs wanted the Capitol to last. So did Davis.[5]

Davis was not only Meigs's mentor, but also, as Meigs said in his diary, "my superior and my friend."[6] When Meigs finalized his plan for building the Dome with a boom derrick, he had described the apparatus in numbing detail in a long letter to Davis, probably because he knew that Davis—who, like Meigs, loved gadgets and innovation—would read every word. The previous day, Meigs and his family had eaten supper at the Davis home.

Anyone who opposed Davis took a risk. He was an eloquent, even an inspiring advocate. In private, he was an intimidating infighter—a feuder and grudge holder, capable of towering rages. He was a loyal ally, but a vicious enemy. Meigs, who had never experienced the bad Davis, knew he could not have had a finer protector. But he also knew he had to keep the faith. Once a person got on Davis's bad side, he seldom got off.

Worrying about Davis is what had brought Meigs to the task that currently lay before him. Two months earlier he had received a letter and a photograph from Thomas Crawford, an American sculptor based in Rome. The photograph depicted the statue of a woman. Crawford called her *Freedom Triumphant in War and Peace*, and she was absolutely exquisite, an elegantly draped "light and beautiful figure,"[7] Meigs wrote in his diary. She was to be placed atop the new dome. *Freedom* would stand—literally—at the pinnacle of American democracy. Meigs needed to have Davis approve the design.

The statue was not the hard part. Davis, like Meigs, was a cultured man. How could he not like the statue? The problem, Meigs knew, was the narrow, floppy cloth hat that *Freedom* wore. It was a "liberty cap," the symbol from classical antiquity of a manumitted slave, which had been revived during the American and French revolutions.

Davis did not like liberty caps. He had made that clear some time ago. Liberty caps had little meaning in the United States, Davis had told Meigs:

"He says it is the sign of a freedman," Meigs wrote in his diary, "and that we were always free, not freedmen, not slaves just released."[8]

If Meigs agreed with this bit of oblique sophistry, he left no record of it. Nor did he comment on, or, apparently, even think about what could become a much larger and potentially far more incendiary problem: the irony of using a freed slave as the symbol of liberty in a nation that was holding four million people in bondage. Meigs was smitten with the statue, as he wrote in his diary, but pessimistic about its future: *Freedom*, he noted in his diary, had "the inevitable liberty cap, to which Mr. Davis will, I do not doubt, object."[9]

Now he was sending Davis the photograph. He had tactfully made his own position clear in an accompanying note without mentioning the liberty cap. The statue's "strongly marked lines and shadows," he had said, "will, I think, give it a striking effect, even at the height of 300 feet, at which it is to stand."[10] He handed the envelope to a messenger.

1

"CONGRESS HOUSE"

In 1850, the city of Washington was almost sixty years old. It had a population of 40,001, of whom 26 percent were classified as "colored" and 5 percent were slaves.[1] Congress had 233 House members and sixty-two senators from thirty-one states. Democrats held a plurality in the House and a solid Senate majority, but the president was a Whig. He was General Zachary Taylor, "Old Rough and Ready," hero of the Battle of Buena Vista in the recently concluded Mexican War. The most important political question facing Taylor and the Congress was how to divide up the immense piece of territory that the United States had won in this unequal struggle. How many new states would there be? How would their boundaries be drawn? How many of them would be free, and how many slave? None of these questions had easy answers, and slavery was a topic so poisonous that it threatened disunion or even civil war. Stalling, a favorite congressional tactic to avoid unpleasant tasks, would not work. Prospectors had discovered gold in the new territory of California; ninety-five thousand fortune hunters, speculators, settlers, and former Mexican citizens were already there, and more were on the way.[2] California needed to become a state, and quickly. The problem of the "Mexican Cession" would not wait.

Debate began as soon as the 31st Congress convened in December 1849, and lawmakers, lobbyists, diplomats, townspeople, tourists, vendors, and vagrants converged every day on the U.S. Capitol, Washington's largest and tallest building. It commanded the city, even defined it, for the luminaries who worked there eclipsed most of the lesser-known transients who held the presidency. Congress was always the best show in town, and visitors to the Capitol could climb the steps of the eastern entrance, walk into the cavernous Rotunda, and choose: the Senate on the right-hand, or northern, side, or the House of Representatives on the south side. On any given day they had a chance to hear, among others, Clay, Webster, and perhaps even the ailing Calhoun.

The East Front of the United States Capitol, around 1846, by John Plumbe, Jr. The East Portico (center) opened onto the second-floor Rotunda. The House of Representatives was on the left (south) side of the building, with the Senate on the right (north) side. (Library of Congress)

Or even speak with them. An interesting mix of formality and informality reigned in the Capitol. Lawmakers—especially senators—dressed elegantly, for the most part, and those visitors who watched the debates from the Senate and House galleries were expected to dress well themselves—and to behave accordingly. Apart from debates, however, the public mingled freely with their elected officials. No senator or House member had an office of his own—they were all men—and all of them conducted the majority of their official and personal business at their chamber desks or out in the hallways, where they chatted with constituents, visitors, lobbyists, news reporters, and whoever else might be in the building.

But by 1850, the Capitol had many defects. Walls were cracking, roofs sagged, timbers rotted. The Senate sweltered in the summer but was so cold in winter that the inhabitants wrapped themselves in quilts or blankets. Sam Houston, wearing a multicolored Indian poncho, a cougar skin vest, and a Mexican sombrero, would whittle wooden hearts during debate, sending pages to deliver them to pretty ladies seated in the gallery.[3] Older senators, in particular, stayed close to the hickory stoves and had to be pried away when debate began.[4] In the House, the acoustics were so bad that members could not hear each other unless they stood next to whoever was speaking or found one of the sweet spots that allowed them to eavesdrop on a colleague in conversation halfway across the room. Serious people had suggested more than once that the bedlam imposed on the House by its peculiar physics was a key reason why members always seemed to be at each other's throats.[5]

Yet the worst flaw was that the Capitol was not big enough. In addition to Congress, it also housed the Supreme Court, the Library of Congress, the vice president's office, and the office of the commissioner of public buildings. It was crowded and cramped—more so every year. Committees needed more meeting rooms. Maybe the Senate heating and the House acoustics could be fixed, although this was doubtful. But there was no fix for the space problem. The country was only going to get bigger, and the government had to keep pace.

The Capitol began in 1790 as the centerpiece of a plan hatched by President George Washington and Secretary of State Thomas Jefferson to transform a ten-mile-square chunk of farmland and bucolic wilderness on the border between Maryland and Virginia into a federal district. With impressive wooded bluffs and flatland thickets, it would straddle a lovely stretch of the Potomac riverfront below Great Falls. In time, it was thought, the new capital would flourish as a commercial metropolis linking North and South to promote national unity and economic prosperity.[6]

Washington, D.C., in 1790 was mostly undeveloped woodland with some farms.
Georgetown and Alexandria, Virginia, became part of the federal district, and
George Washington's home was just across the Potomac River in Mount Vernon.
(Kiplinger Washington Collection)

Certainly, the site had drawbacks. The weather in summer was dreadful, and would-be residents risked losing loved ones to dysentery, malaria,
yellow fever, smallpox, diphtheria, typhoid, cholera, and other deadly dis-
eases. And there was nowhere to buy much of anything beyond basic
foodstuffs, lumber, hand tools, plug tobacco, whiskey, and tack for the
horses.

Yet these shortcomings were no worse on the Potomac than in most
places. Disease was ubiquitous, and the District, green and pretty in
1790, probably seemed at the time to be healthier than Philadelphia, the
biggest city in the United States and the temporary seat of government.
And anyway, Philadelphia was relatively close by for those who needed
to send away for a book, a set of wineglasses, or the dress for a daughter's
wedding.

Washington and Jefferson must have known that the capital's early development would be attended by political carping, sectional controversy
between North and South, and a callous disregard for the city's needs. But
they probably would not have predicted that these headaches would per-

sist in one form or another for six decades. Before 1850, the story of the U.S. Capitol and the city it commanded is in many respects one of grand conception, questionable judgment, and spotty execution. Every good idea was matched by a corresponding mistake—caused by indifference, bad taste, or a ruinous compulsion to do it on the cheap. The Capitol should have been a source of pride to the lawmakers who worked there, but just as often it was a source of irritation.

The French-born engineer Pierre Charles L'Enfant, hired by Washington to design the city, divided the District into a grid, with public plazas and squares connected by wide diagonal avenues.[7] The city's principal building, and the center of the grid, would be called "Congress House" and was to be built at the city's highest point, on "Jenkins Hill," so named by L'Enfant after the farmer who owned it even though no one named Jenkins had ever lived there. And when Jefferson reviewed and edited L'Enfant's plan before publication, he crossed out the words "Congress House" wherever they appeared and instead inserted the word "Capitol," endowing the building with the primacy it would never relinquish.[8]

From the foot of Jenkins Hill, on the Capitol's West Front, L'Enfant drew the Mall, a large open space intended as a park, stretching more than a mile to the Potomac. The "President's House" would be placed above the Mall's northwest corner, away from the river. Along the northern edge of the Mall, although it was not part of L'Enfant's vision, engineers would eventually dig a canal to facilitate the economic boom that was expected to accompany the city's development. The Capitol and the executive mansion would be connected by a wide boulevard, named Pennsylvania Avenue as a sop to the northerners who had lobbied hard to keep the capital city where it was. These opponents had been worried about locating the country's new center of gravity between two southern slave states, but President Washington, whose family home at Mount Vernon overlooked the Potomac, ultimately prevailed.[9]

L'Enfant's plan was grandiose, even vainglorious, for a "city" that had 3,210 inhabitants when it became the capital in 1800.[10] This was a blessing in that the city's basic design was majestic and arresting and never changed, enabling both the city and the federal government to expand, consolidate, and ultimately dignify the surroundings simply by creatively filling in the blanks. L'Enfant, who was fired in 1792 for being temperamental and dogmatic, would surely have felt vindicated had he returned two centuries later to view his handiwork.

But the plan was also a curse. The city had a difficult youth as it tried to cope with its emptiness, and the pretensions forced upon it by L'Enfant attracted frequent and often derisive attention from visitors. Alexis de Tocqueville decided that the limitless horizons reflected a national nervousness. This feeling of inferiority, he remarked in his 1835 opus *Democracy in America*, caused "people living cramped lives in tiny houses" to "conceive their public monuments on a gigantic scale." Thus, "they have erected a magnificent palace for Congress" and have "given it the pompous name of the Capitol."[11]

And it was not just foreigners who regarded "Washington City" with contempt. The capital chronically suffered from inattention and outright neglect. Many lawmakers saw no reason to spend taxpayer money for improvements in a hot, disagreeable town where they bivouacked in boardinghouses during legislative sessions and bolted for the hinterlands as soon as the gavel dropped. Government was generally regarded as a necessary evil, not an investment to be encouraged with displays of decadent European-style architecture.

With L'Enfant gone, President Washington in 1792 was left with a plan for a new city but nothing to put in it. Construction of the Capitol and the President's House were top priorities. Both were big government projects that would dwarf anything else that was going on along the Potomac. The federal government, at the beginning and forever, would be the District's chief source of income.

Late in 1792, Washington sponsored a contest to design the Capitol, but he saw nothing he liked. Early the next year, however, he allowed a late entry by William Thornton, a physician, amateur architect, and part-time resident of the West Indies. Thornton's design captivated both Washington and Jefferson, an architectural savant in his own right. At the center was a massive Corinthian-style eastern portico and a rotunda surmounted by a low dome. Wings on either side offered a more traditional Georgian treatment, but the overall effect was both handsome and imposing. Nothing like it existed in the United States at the time. Thornton won the $500 first prize. The building was to be finished by 1800, when the government would depart Philadelphia for good.[12]

Bad blood followed immediately. Stephen Hallet, an immigrant from France like L'Enfant and the only trained architect in the 1792 competition, had tried but failed to land the Capitol job. In recognition of his

The dome and the eastern portico of Dr. William Thornton's design for the new Capitol anticipated the coming neoclassical style, while the façade reflected popular Georgian motifs. Thornton—a physician by profession—won President Washington's $500 prize for the plan. (Architect of the Capitol)

efforts, Hallet was awarded $500 and asked to evaluate Thornton's plan, which he of course contemptuously dismissed as expensive and unbuildable. After more discussions, the president kept Thornton's design for the exterior but adopted Hallet's plan for the interior and put him in charge of construction. This ill-advised arrangement benefited neither man.

And the pattern would repeat. Architects and engineers, anxious to leave their mark on the most important structure in the country, would undercut rivals and routinely overpromise results in order to win the contract. Once hired, they would move forward unimpeded as long as their patrons lingered in office and liked what they saw. But anyone who ran afoul of the boss could expect to be quickly sacked. L'Enfant needed only five months to fall out of favor. Hallet, never Washington's first choice, lasted nine months.

The president's interest in the project, however, never wavered. Washington chose the cream-colored sandstone of Aquia Creek, Virginia, for the exterior, and personally laid the cornerstone in a Masonic ceremony on September 18, 1793.[13] And it was Washington who installed a new

Board of Commissioners to oversee the project and who made Thornton—his man—a member.

Construction limped toward the deadline. Washington left office and John Adams succeeded him. Washington died on December 14, 1799. Two more building supervisors came and went. Workmen focused on finishing the Capitol's northern wing, to be used by the Senate, and ended up with a temporary building, which became known as "the Oven," on the south side for the House. The center section was left vacant for the moment, since it served no legislative function. On April 24, 1800, Adams transferred the seat of government, and in November, the Senate met on Capitol Hill for the first time. The House occupied the Oven in 1801.

The original Capitol offered only a hint of what it might in time become. The Senate—what would be the Senate wing in 1850—was built to last. The chamber was on two levels, a semicircle located on the East Front, as it would be in 1850. But the main floor was the first, not the second, while the Library was located on the West Front, but on the second story. The building was finished in sandstone on three sides, but the fourth side was naked brick. It awaited the arrival of the as yet unbuilt central section and the Rotunda.

On the south side of the empty space was the oval House chamber, which looked like a cross between a brick igloo, a beehive, and a Dutch oven. This was one reason it acquired its name. The other was that it was horribly ventilated and had a tendency to bake the members during the hot months. A narrow covered passage connected the House with the Senate across the empty lot.[14]

It was left to Jefferson, who became president in 1801, to complete the Capitol, or at least to set the process firmly in motion. With Washington, he had overseen the original design, and as vice president under Adams, he had served as presiding officer in the Senate's new home. Nobody had a bigger stake in the success of the new building.

In 1803, Jefferson invited the British-born architect Benjamin Henry Latrobe to supervise construction—to transform the Oven into a permanent House of Representatives chamber. Latrobe thus seemed to have everything: he was handpicked by the president, all but guaranteed a permanent position, and apparently impervious to outside attack.[15]

Congress could not stand him. It criticized him constantly for insubordination and wastefulness. This, too, would become a permanent feature of Capitol construction, enduring long after Latrobe was gone.

Congress's homespun populism warred incessantly with its equally ingrained compulsion to always have the "biggest and best." Lawmakers wanted a fabulous building, but they also wanted to look humble to their constituents by refusing to pay for it. This did not work in 1803, and it would never work. Latrobe, in particular, had to spend excessive amounts of money and time fixing shoddy mistakes made by predecessors—leaky roofs, junky masonry, and timbers consumed by dry rot.[16]

He also feuded publicly and incessantly with Thornton, now a Jefferson-appointed official, over proposed changes to Thornton's original design. Jefferson wanted his two favorites to get along, but they loathed each other.[17] To build the U.S. Capitol was—potentially—to fulfill the dream of a lifetime. No one who controlled the project was interested in sharing the glory or taking someone else's advice.

It took Latrobe four years to build the south wing and the House of Representatives. He put the chamber on the second floor and the gallery on the third. The chamber was racetrack-shaped, with semicircular colonnades on either side of the Speaker's desk. It was, by most accounts, a beautiful room. But by all accounts, the acoustics were terrible. The House appointed a committee to figure out what to do about the din, and it decided to hang draperies to soak up the sound. This did not work.[18]

Latrobe continued. Ceilings in the Senate wing sagged, pieces of plaster fell off, and timbers and wooden columns were cracked and rotting. The Supreme Court, meanwhile, had no permanent headquarters, and while it kept its records in the Capitol, it heard cases in several nearby locations, including a tavern.[19] Latrobe decided to put the Senate on the second floor, and redesign its chamber. The Supreme Court would take over the old first-floor Senate space down below.

Latrobe over the years learned nothing about cultivating Congress. He underestimated expenses and missed deadlines, and by early 1809, when Jefferson departed, his fate appeared to be sealed. His new second-floor Senate chamber opened in early 1810, but funding ran out in 1811. Congress failed to make a new appropriation, and Latrobe was out of a job.

And then came the War of 1812, mooting whatever plans anyone had for Capitol construction. Instead, on the night of August 24, 1814, British troops entered Washington, made their way to Capitol Hill, and set fire to the building, destroying Latrobe's Hall of the House, the new Senate, and most of the Library. The President's House was also torched. Jefferson's successor, President James Madison, escaped to Virginia.

Smoke eddies from the Capitol windows after the British raided Washington and burned the building on August 24, 1814. The House and Senate were gutted; the Rotunda had not yet been built. Painting by George Munger. (Kiplinger Washington Collection)

In the aftermath of this debacle, Washington-haters in Congress urged colleagues to move to another city, but the effort failed. In the end, lawmakers authorized borrowing $500,000 to restore the gutted buildings exactly where they had been. The exteriors of both the Capitol and the President's House were in decent shape, and both could be renovated completely for $460,000. Up until the war, Congress had spent $1,215,111 on public buildings in Washington, and they did not want to start again from scratch.[20] Here was one instance where the cheap alternative worked in the District's favor.

Latrobe had abandoned Washington during the war, but he petitioned Madison to be reinstated, and against the odds he was invited back. He redesigned the interiors of both the gutted Capitol buildings. The new House Chamber would be a half-domed semicircle with a marble colonnade, an arrangement Latrobe insisted would finally silence the complaints about ventilation, lighting, and acoustics. The Senate would be enlarged, and committee rooms would replace the Library of Congress, which would move into the Capitol's still-to-be-built center section. The plans were all approved, and Latrobe went to work.

He did not last long. He had no friends in Congress, and Madison had always kept him at arm's length. When Madison appointed Samuel Lane, a disabled veteran and crony of Secretary of State James Monroe, to oversee construction, Latrobe's already fading sun began to set. Latrobe and Lane never got along, but Latrobe fought him to a draw until Monroe took office as president the following year. During a meeting with Lane and Monroe at the President's House in late 1817, Latrobe's wife recalled, Latrobe attacked Lane, "seized him by the collar, and exclaimed, 'were you not a cripple I would shake you to atoms, you poor contemptible wretch.'" Monroe, astounded and furious, turned to Latrobe: "'Do you know who I am, sir?'" he asked. Latrobe went home and wrote his resignation.[21]

Even before Latrobe's departure, Monroe had been angling for a replacement. He had focused on Boston's Charles Bulfinch, a sophisticated Harvard graduate with an upper-class family background and a city full of monuments to his architectural prowess, including the Massachusetts Statehouse and its golden dome. Bulfinch also ran Boston as chair of the Board of Selectmen, a testament to his political savvy and easy confidence in dealings with the rich and powerful. It was an almost perfect résumé, and Bulfinch had enhanced it further as host and chief greeter for Monroe's visit to Boston in the summer of 1817. Monroe hired him at the end of the year, and he arrived in Washington in January 1818.[22]

Bulfinch's job was to finish off Latrobe's House and Senate chambers and to build the Capitol's center section. The Capitol at that moment consisted of two buildings—still unfinished, but well along—with nothing in between. The task in constructing the central section was not only to retain the large ceremonial Rotunda conceived by Thornton but also to provide Congress with new committee rooms. Accomplishing both goals posed a problem.

The Rotunda was a given. Congress in 1817 had commissioned the artist John Trumbull to provide the Capitol with four large historical paintings of the American Revolution with life-size figures. These gigantic canvases—*The Declaration of Independence, The Surrender of Burgoyne, Surrender of Lord Cornwallis at Yorktown*, and *George Washington Resigning His Commission*—could only be displayed in a gigantic setting like the Rotunda.[23] To find new space for committee rooms, Bulfinch decided to use the Capitol's geography. He would put the rooms in a lower fourth story that he would build for the central section on the West Front, where Capitol Hill began to spill downward toward the Mall. The addition would protrude beyond the existing western boundary of the Senate and House.[24]

Progress came quickly. Bulfinch's Rotunda plan was approved in March 1818, and the next year, the House and Senate moved back into the building they had abandoned for five years after the British invasion. Throughout this part of his tenure, Bulfinch enjoyed a cordial and even warm relationship with Monroe, his cabinet, and Congress. Like Latrobe, he moved more slowly than advertised, and also as with Latrobe, things frequently ended up costing more than Bulfinch had predicted. But appropriations marched out of Congress each year with handsome regularity. Bulfinch's social credentials undoubtedly contributed to his success, as did his political acumen, but his chief advantage, of course, was that he was Monroe's man.

The effectiveness of this rule became apparent once Congress was reinstalled in the Capitol. The new accommodations played to generally favorable notices, but the House quickly ascertained that the acoustics in its new chamber were worse than ever. Everything from historic speeches to procedural announcements bounced off the smooth, arched ceiling to settle all but unheard somewhere in the chamber's nether reaches. Latrobe likely would have been pilloried for this, but Bulfinch simply offered three bad solutions: raise the floor (which would do nothing to compensate for the curved ceiling); close off the chamber with a glass partition (in which case nobody in the gallery would be able to hear); or put in a flat glass ceiling (too unsightly). In the end, the House did nothing, hoping the Chamber would improve with use.[25] It did not.

Bulfinch also understood the corollary to the basic rule: to stay in good grace, always do what the boss wants. Charged with building a dome for the Rotunda, Bulfinch made a model of what it might look like and showed it to the president, the cabinet, and Congress. The design was approved, "but there was one universal remark," Bulfinch wrote much later. "The dome is *too low*." A bit later he prepared drawings of a number of domes, including one that was "of a greater height than the one I should have preferred." This was the United States, so of course that was the one everybody liked, and there was "even a wish expressed that it might be raised higher."[26] Bulfinch managed to quash this last extravagance. In the end he built both an inner and an outer dome. The inner dome, of stone, brick, and wood, was well proportioned and thus attractive to anyone who stood in the Rotunda below. The outer dome was made of wood and covered with copper sheathing. It towered above the more elegant inner dome and, at least at first, gave the Capitol the impressive presence that Congress thought it needed. The novelty quickly wore off, however, and by 1850 the dome had long been an object of ridicule. It swelled skyward like a thumb that had been whacked with a hammer, and was so tall that it gave the rest of the Capitol a stubby appearance—a tasteless statement of outsized aspirations.

The Rotunda opened in 1824, and the Eastern Portico—the Capitol's central entrance—was completed in 1826. Bulfinch managed to weather the transition to John Quincy Adams in 1824, probably because he had a good relationship with Secretary of State Henry Clay and because Adams was a fellow Bostonian, but Andrew Jackson got rid of him three months after taking office in 1829. There was nothing personal in the decision, Jackson told Bulfinch, but the Capitol was finished, so the job was over.[27] Also, Jackson detested Adams and Clay, whom he had accused of forging a "corrupt bargain" to deny Jackson the presidency in 1824. Bulfinch stood no chance.

The Capitol he left behind was the same one that greeted lawmakers in 1850. Considering the number of engineers, architects, builders, politicians, and British soldiers who had laid hands upon it, the building looked surprisingly handsome. It was imposing—351 feet 7½ inches long at its base and 282 feet 10½ inches wide, with the Senate and House chambers on either side of the East Portico. The elegant Rotunda was the biggest indoor space in the country, at 70,000 square feet.[28] The exterior Aquia sandstone was grand and impressive, as long as it was periodically painted to keep it from eroding in the weather. This precaution, unfortunately, would not be faithfully carried out. When Bulfinch left, Congress had 48 senators and 213 House members from twenty-four states. The Capitol had cost $2,432,851.34, but it was a huge building, and on the day Bulfinch left, it was huge enough.[29] And at that moment, it was in good repair.

Attitudes toward the District of Columbia began to change—not all at once and not always dramatically, but Congress began to take steps toward transforming the capital into both a fitting seat of government for a great nation and, perhaps not incidentally, a fitting showcase for the elected officials who worked there.

This effort began inauspiciously in 1832 when Congress appropriated $5,000 for a centennial statue of George Washington and hired sculptor Horatio Greenough to create it. Congress left it up to Greenough to decide on a design for the statue, which in hindsight was probably a bad mistake. Washington arrived nine years later. He weighed 20 tons and was half-dressed, wearing a Roman toga. Congress originally installed him in the Rotunda, but Greenough did not like the lighting and had him moved outdoors to a pedestal in front of the East Portico two years later. Washington's departure from his original spot was later ascribed either to the inability of the Rotunda to support his bulk or to Greenough's phenomenal misjudgment of public taste for an unclothed icon.[30] In the first half of the nineteenth century, George Washington was the only unquestioned hero the United States had. Nudity did not become him.

The Washington Monument Society fared better. Formed as a nonprofit fund-raising organization in 1833, the Society limped along for years trying to get enough money to build a monument to the first president, eventually settling on the obelisk that the architect Robert Mills first proposed in 1836. Finally, in 1847, Congress offered to donate any piece of public land the Society chose. A site on the Mall west of the Capitol and south of the President's House was staked out, and the cornerstone was laid with great fanfare in a Masonic ceremony on July 4, 1848.[31]

The biggest change, however, was in the way Congress began to regard its own place of business. This adjustment, too, began slowly. After Jackson got rid of Bulfinch, the Capitol languished for more than twenty years without a full-time architect, and very little happened to the building except that it got older.

Gas lighting was installed. More history paintings were commissioned and hung in the Rotunda. Mills, the Washington Monument architect, earned $30 for designing the Capitol's mahogany toilet seats.[32] In the mid-1830s, Congress bought a fresh spring on a farm three miles north of the Capitol and built a private aqueduct to pipe in drinking and cooking water. This meant that the Capitol could at last have its own restaurants. Up to then the only source of sustenance in the building was the so-called Hole in the Wall, a Senate hideaway tucked in a tiny room behind the Post

Office and close to the Rotunda. Senators coming off the floor could grab a ham sandwich and "other simple eatables," according to the Senate doorkeeper, Isaac Bassett. More important, "the supply of liquor was quite liberal." The Senate, as Bassett had cause to know, paid for the Hole in the Wall out of the Senate contingency fund, listing it under the heading "horse hire."[33]

A couple of whiskeys probably went down very well on cold winter days. The Senate chamber was served by fire grates in a lobby behind the vice president's desk and by two hickory stoves on either side of the chamber entrance. But the air was dank, cold, and smoky, and "it was a common sight to behold the revered dignity of the Senate wrapped head and all in . . . big shawls, and comfortably retaining them in the chamber."[34]

It was no surprise that little was done about either the Senate's draftiness or the Capitol's other shortcomings. Ever since Washington and Jefferson had huddled with L'Enfant, the executive had been approving the designs and making the rules for Capitol construction. Congress could raise a certain amount of stink if the plans involved something or someone it simply could not stomach, but the political drive had always emanated from the president. Jackson did not particularly care about the Capitol, and neither, apparently, did his successors.

But by the 1840s, Congress was under no illusions about its building. The House commissioned a study by the Army's Bureau of Topographical Engineers on the possibility of building an "Extension" for "the better accommodation of the sittings of the House of Representatives." At that point the nation consisted of twenty-six states, with Florida and Texas looming on the horizon. Fourteen years after Bulfinch's departure, space was at a premium, and Chief Engineer Colonel John James Abert, in his report delivered early in 1844, spoke of the growing need for more committee rooms, rooms for the clerk of the House, and space for public documents.[35]

Also important, of course, was the House chamber's enduring flaw. Army lieutenant A. A. Humphreys, who did the Engineers' actual survey, summarized the acoustical mysteries of the House chamber in exquisite detail: "A person speaking in this hall, from some positions, even in a low voice, can be heard with perfect distinctness in a few other positions, although distant," Humphreys said. "In other positions in the hall, a speaker will exhaust himself in vain efforts to make himself heard, and his auditors find themselves also exhausted in efforts to hear him."[36] Despite Bulfinch's optimism, House acoustics had not improved with age.

The arched ceiling and colonnades of the beautiful but baffling House of Representatives produced echoes and dead spots that made normal discourse all but impossible. Lawmakers loved how it looked but hated to work there. (Architect of the Capitol)

Humphreys wanted simply to abandon the chamber and build a new square room in the proposed Extension, for a total cost of $296,248.86. Abert seconded the idea, but he recommended not one, but two new extensions—for symmetry. The House piece would go up first, and the Senate side could be delayed "until increased accommodations for the Senate and the Supreme Court may render it necessary." Abert also raised another unpleasant subject: "Viewing the present Capitol from any point, it evidently wants length, having in its present condition a disproportionate height. To increase its length, would therefore relieve it from this defect, and increase its beauty." Fifteen years had done nothing to make the dome look any better.[37]

In May 1844, the House Committee on Public Buildings and Grounds offered its conclusions on the Abert report. Here the main purpose of the remodeling was stated baldly: to remedy "the defects of the sound in this

Hall."[38] The committee said it could do the job for only $55,000 simply by converting the Library into a new House chamber. Abert was uninterested in this plan, worrying that the conversion would not work and would create an unnecessary fire hazard. New construction was needed.[39]

And there the proposal died. It was an election year, never a good time for new projects. Florida was admitted to the union the day before James K. Polk took office in early 1845, and by the time the new Congress met in December, Texas had also been admitted, infuriating Mexico and making another war all but inevitable. Congress had little time to prepare or pay for a Capitol Extension.

Interest revived immediately almost as soon as the Treaty of Guadalupe Hidalgo was signed in February 1848. There were now twenty-nine states in the union, and Wisconsin was waiting in line. More important, Mexico had ceded 525,000 square miles of land to the United States—55 percent of its prewar territory—in exchange for a payment of $13 million. The Mexican Cession included all of what would become California, Nevada, and Utah, as well as most of Arizona, about half of New Mexico, a third of Colorado, and a slice of Wyoming. A flood of new congressmen and senators would soon descend on Washington.

With the end of the war, the House Committee on Public Buildings and Grounds hired the Savannah-based architect Charles B. Cluskey to survey Washington's public buildings and make recommendations. Cluskey had moved north a few years earlier in hopes of getting more commissions in public architecture, so he had an obvious interest in finding fault with the Capitol. The report was predictably devastating.

Cluskey noted that the Capitol "should compare with any other [building] of like character in the world," but it was "in many respects, very defective, and its general condition is very bad." He succinctly condemned the House chamber as "a perfect Babel of sounds," suggested a new glass ceiling to kill the worst of the echoes, and recommended extensions, either on the wings or on the Eastern Front, both to increase the size of the building and to provide a way out of the House's acoustical dilemma.

The Aquia sandstone used on the exterior facing and for some interior surfaces needed to be painted more often. It absorbed four to five pounds of water per cubic foot, depending on the weather, creating "continual dampness" throughout the building as it continued "mouldering away" with the change of seasons.

Plaster walls and ceilings needed patching. The brick floors of hallways between committee rooms of the Senate and House on the Capitol's third floor created "continual dust." Wooden roofing was rotting, the copper sheathing over the dome and the Eastern Portico was a mess, chimneys were broken, mounds of garbage were piled in every nook and cranny. The roof platforms "should be taken up," and the basement was packed with junk.[40]

Cluskey's report clearly had an effect. In December, Secretary of the Interior Thomas Ewing said in his annual report that painting and renovation of the Capitol were under study. He was especially worried about the porous sandstone, predicting that if it were not protected from atmospheric moisture, "this noble edifice would become a mound of sand."[41] Whether Ewing had made his own assessment or had simply put his department's stamp on Cluskey's work, the two reports marked a sea change in the Capitol's fortunes. The executive was still making the pronouncements and still controlled the building, but Congress for the first time had taken the lead in demanding changes and recommending construction. Congress, apparently, had finally decided that the United States had become too powerful to conduct its business in a tumbledown Capitol.

Washington, D.C., itself was also beginning to feel intolerably behind the times. Charles Dickens, during an 1842 visit, had dismissed the city in his *American Notes* with a couple of sneering sentences: it is "sometimes called the City of Magnificent Distances, but it might with greater propriety be termed the City of Magnificent Intentions"; Washington had "spacious avenues, that begin in nothing, and lead nowhere; streets, mile-long, that only want houses, roads and inhabitants; public buildings that need but a public to be complete; and ornaments of great thoroughfares, which only lack great thoroughfares to ornament."[42]

By 1850 there were some improvements. The brand-new Smithsonian Institution was on the northern edge of the Mall, and the stub of the rising Washington Monument poked up from the Mall's flatlands directly in front of the Capitol's West Front Portico. Albeit unpaved, Pennsylvania Avenue had several blocks of handsome homes, and all the good hotels—

Willard's, Brown's, Kirkwood House, the National, the St. Charles, and the Washington—stretched along it from the foot of Capitol Hill almost to the President's House, better known by this time as the White House.

Unfortunately, the hoped-for transformation from country village to commercial juggernaut had never materialized, and the symbol of this failure—and the defining feature of the midcentury downtown—was the ill-maintained and virtually useless Washington Canal, a fetid ditch dammed up with silt and filled with sewage, garbage, and other unmentionables.[43] Eventually this eyesore would be paved over and renamed Constitution Avenue, but in 1850 the canal effectively cut off a large southwestern chunk of the city to create an urban hellhole known as "the island."[44] The Mall itself was part of the island, noted principally for its mosquito-infested standing water, its feral dogs, and Washington's two slave markets.

And the admirable features of Pennsylvania Avenue, or simply "the Avenue," as it was known, were offset, depending on the season, by choking clouds of dust and knee-deep mud holes. The strip of zoned land between the Avenue and the Washington Canal to the south was known familiarly as "Murder Bay," a maze of alleyways, saloons, clapboard sheds, and shanties. It was peopled by whores and their pimps, delinquent youths, muggers, gunmen, and other marauding lowlifes.[45] There were "great gaps" between the houses along the Avenue, noted Virginia Clay-Clopton, the wife of Alabama senator Clement Clay. "The greatest contrasts in architecture existed, hovels often all but touching the mansions of the rich." Across from the fancy hotels, sprawling open-air markets sold foodstuffs and pigs wallowed in the leavings.[46] The St. Charles Hotel, at Northwest Third Street and Pennsylvania Avenue, encouraged guests to keep their slaves "well-cared for" in basement pens outfitted with iron doors, iron wall rings, and chains.[47]

Vast areas of the city were still unpopulated, but its center was bursting at the seams, and the shortcomings of earlier decades, largely ignored as minor discomforts, had become objects of community disgust. Population during the 1840s grew by 42 percent.[48] Crime, in the early years largely confined to petty thievery and the burglary of homes abandoned by lawmakers during the summer, intensified. Armed robbery, stabbings, and shootings could turn nighttime travel into a harrowing and sometimes fatal adventure.[49]

City services were virtually nonexistent. Houses had no numbers, neighborhoods were connected by rutted tracks. The Avenue had gas lamps, but these were lighted only on moonless nights. There was no sewage system, no garbage collection, and no running water. As the city began to fill up, fires became more common, but the engine companies were staffed by rival gangs of thugs suspected of deliberately lighting the blazes to encourage mayhem and enable their own vandalism and theft. Not infrequently the firefighters set off false alarms on Sunday evenings so they could watch panicked church congregations bolt for the doors.[50]

And lots of open space offered lots of places to hide things. Many residents emptied their privies in open fields and stagnant ponds. The hotels flushed sewage directly into vacant lots. Sewage from the White House and the cabinet offices spilled into a marsh above the canal. Residents pulled dead animals off the roadside into bramble thickets where they could rot in peace, out of sight but unfortunately not out of mind. Carcasses, garbage, sewage, horse droppings, and slaughterhouse offal combined to create a fearful stench. In dry times, clouds of dust choked unfortunate pedestrians. Wisconsin congressman Charles Billinghurst, confronting this phenomenon for the first time, wrote of winds "lifting the sand and dust of the streets and fouling the whole atmosphere, sometimes for hours." Pedestrians covered their faces with handkerchiefs, but even so, he confessed, he had on occasion been "nearly suffocated and blinded."[51]

The city had always had what seemed like a disproportionate number of poor people. In an area that began with virtually no local population, the labor force, both skilled and unskilled, had to be imported. By the 1830s, large numbers of immigrant laborers also began to arrive. The only business to speak of in the city was government, and government's most labor-intensive enterprise was construction. The earliest projects—the Capitol, the President's House, and the principal streets—were built by transient free labor brought mostly from the North, and by contractors who used slaves. When each building "season" ended in late autumn, or when government funding ran out, or when projects were completed, workers were laid off and had to fend for themselves.

So the unemployed idled away the off-season in ramshackle houses on the island, waiting for spring. This confusion was muddled further by the large number of freedmen in town—8,158, according to the 1850 census, or more than 20 percent of the total population.[52] The free blacks worked as laundresses, handymen, freelance carpenters, draymen, and hack drivers, turning casual labor into a respected profession and crowding out many of the idle whites who needed jobs during downtime. Freedmen and immigrants worked just as well as free whites, and more cheaply, while contractors with slaves worked even more cheaply per capita than that, pulling down the wages for everyone.

Still, the percentage of slaves actually living in the city dwindled steadily, and the decline, coupled with the large number of freedmen, suggested that a free black could make a living in Washington and that slavery, by 1850, was not popular.[53] Washingtonians, however, were not audibly involved in the debate over slavery's future. The city was surrounded by slave states and straddled two worlds, and the District's prosperity, perhaps even its continued existence, depended upon the ability of the politicians to resolve their disputes.[54] Washington had to end up on the winning side of the slavery debate.

At the dawn of 1850, that outcome was far from clear. Zachary Taylor, like Jackson, was a crusty popular hero, a slave owner and a westerner. He had been born in Virginia but lived in southern Louisiana. He was bowlegged, with a short, thick physique and a leathery complexion from a lifetime outdoors. He neither smoked nor drank, but he chewed tobacco and was reputed to be an expert at hitting a spittoon.[55] He rarely wore a uniform, and during battle sat sidesaddle on his horse, "Old Whitey," watching his troops through a spyglass. Taylor was sixty-four when he took office and had the aura of a simple, homespun grandfather. This, too, was part of his attraction.

Taylor had never been involved in politics before he joined the Whig Party to become its candidate. He said virtually nothing regarding his views on slavery, but he owned 118 slaves, making him one of the top two thousand slave-owning planters in the country, according to his biographer Holman Hamilton.[56] His background gained him all the southern support he needed, and with erstwhile Democrat and Free-Soil candidate Martin Van Buren stealing northern antislavery votes from Democrat Lewis Cass of Michigan, Taylor won a comfortable victory.

"Old Zack" was a political amateur, scorned as an unlettered, slave-owning hayseed in the antislavery North and regarded by Washington's pundits, at least at first, as little more than chum for the sharks on Capitol Hill.[57] Some of this criticism was justified. Taylor was not much of a public speaker, and his letters frequently displayed a reluctance to lift pen from paper. This habit, along with an affinity for commas and ampersands and a disdain for full stops, gave his correspondence a disconcerting stream-of-consciousness it did not entirely intend.

But anyone who thought Zachary Taylor was a blank slate made a grave error, for no one could mistake his meaning when he wanted to be understood. "No man of ordinary capacity can believe for a moment that if we annex the whole or any part of Mexico to the U. States that Congress will ever permit a state made from it to enter our union with the features of slavery connected with it," he wrote in a July 27, 1847, letter from Mexico to his confidant and former son-in-law Jefferson Davis. But "we of the South must throw ourselves on the Constitution" and defend slavery there "to the last, and when arguments will no longer suffice, we will appeal to the sword, if necessary to do so, I will be the last to yield one inch."[58]

Taylor's views—opposing slavery in new states while upholding it in the South where it already existed—would never change. His position remained largely unknown during the 1848 campaign, but by the beginning of 1850 he had made it crystal clear. Many onetime political allies had already branded him a turncoat, and his refusal to moderate his position was stripping the gray shades from the slavery debate and replacing them with either-or choices that Congress did not want to make. "Northern members were determined not to be driven from their 'free soil' position, while the representatives from the South clamorously insisted upon being allowed the right of carrying their slaves into all the territories of the United States," wrote the journalist Lawrence Gobright. "The issue had been fairly joined; neither side was disposed to yield anything."[59]

2

PLANTING THE SEED

Early in April 1850, the Washington architect Robert Mills received a letter from Jefferson Davis, the junior senator from Mississippi, a Mexican War hero and a rising star among the congressional defenders of slavery and states' rights. Davis was playing an important role in the increasingly rancorous debate over the future of the Mexican Cession, but in this letter he had something else on his mind. He asked Mills to prepare for him a set of drawings and estimates for an enlargement of the U.S. Capitol by adding new wings to either end of the existing building.[1] Davis's power base was the Senate Committee on Military Affairs, which he chaired, but he also served on the Public Buildings Committee and had an abiding interest in the fortunes of Washington, D.C.

For Mills, the letter was a godsend. Mills was one of the leading architects in the country. Only two years earlier he had watched the cornerstone being laid for the Washington Monument, the greatest achievement of his career. But the triumph had been fleeting, and he had come on hard times. The preceding year, all but broke, he had taken a job as an assistant on the Smithsonian Institution building, only to be fired within two months for complaining about the fireproofing.[2] At sixty-eight, his career was on the ebb when he could least afford it. Now Davis—just maybe—was coming to his rescue.

Deliverance, if that is what it was, had not, however, arrived altogether unplanned. Mills was an old Washington hand, and on February 25, he had played a long shot. He had submitted a letter to Congress—a peti-

tion—proposing an enlargement of the Capitol, and he had prevailed on
Maryland senator James A. Pearce, a longtime booster of the capital city,
to insert it for the record and speak in favor of it on the Senate floor.
Davis, apparently, was interested.

Mills's petition had two themes, and he made the Mexican Cession the
inspiration for both. The first was obvious. The Mexican War had handed
the United States so much more territory that the country would soon be
filling up with new states, which would flood Washington with new senators and congressmen. The second theme, though also obvious, needed a
dose of hyperbole to help it along. Three weeks before Mills offered the
petition, Senator Henry Clay of Kentucky had introduced eight compromise measures intended to resolve the sectional crisis precipitated by
the Mexican Cession. Mills spied an opportunity. It was winter, and the
weather was cold and miserable. Senators, when they were not busy denouncing each other, spent their days coughing, wheezing, blowing their
noses, spitting, and stamping their feet by the fire grates behind Millard
Fillmore, the vice president, who was presiding over the debate and complaining about the noise and the interruptions. Now might be a good time
to remind senators that if they were going to hate each other while they
conducted such important business, they did not have to make it worse by
enduring damp, dungeonlike conditions.

In the House, Mills had a much easier sell. The acoustics were so bad
in the chamber that members could hardly be heard at all, even on good
days, and now, with the onset of the compromise debate, they were
screaming vile insults at one another and even greater offense was being
taken. Things had reached such a pass, Mills said in his petition, that "one
of the most distinguished members of your House" several years ago had
told him "that except that [the] Hall underwent a change so as to render
it better capable of conveying the correct sense of what was spoken by
Members to the ear of every Member present, he should fear consequences
to follow of the most disastrous character, even of the breaking up of the
Union."[3] Build a new House chamber, he suggested; avoid civil war.

The proposal was both clever and faintly cloying, reflecting a personal
style that Mills had cultivated during six presidencies and nine Congresses
over twenty years as the city's quasiofficial public architect: a hustler's ex-
aggeration linked to a Uriah Heepish obsequiousness, offering spectacular solutions to all problems in "your honorable body" without unduly
interfering in Congress's momentous public business.

As a sales pitch, the petition was like many Mills efforts—just a little too much and not quite right. That the House loathed its chamber was no secret, but there were plenty of ways the union could fall apart without blaming it on the building. And flattering congressional egos, while never a bad idea, had to be handled delicately, not slathered on with a trowel. Finally, submitting the petition as a teaser—"I have a plan, details to follow"—implied a climate of congressional expectation that did not exist. Proposals to repair, renovate, or enlarge the Capitol came and went, and were generally greeted with indifference.

But Mills in February 1850 had nothing to lose. He was trying to gauge the level of congressional interest in what he hoped would be an immense project, and if he got a nibble, he would have the best chance of becoming the architect who would build it. And if he got the job, he would cement his place in history and be fixed financially for the rest of his days. The potential was enormous, the risk minimal.

Still, Mills's pseudobrassiness diminished him. He was an eminent man with a list of architectural credits that could compete with any in the country. But like all the architects who had worked on the Capitol before him—L'Enfant, Hallet, Latrobe, and even Bulfinch—he served as an appendage of the power broker who protected him. When the patron was gone, a new one was needed. It was a career requisite that Mills had generally handled adroitly, beginning as a Jefferson disciple, then shifting to Calhoun, his fellow South Carolinian, then shifting again to Andrew Jackson, Calhoun's bitter enemy.

Between Jackson's arrival and his departure in 1837, Mills built a new Treasury after the old one burned down. He designed the U.S. Patent Office and the General Post Office, and in 1836 he submitted his first proposal for a Washington Monument at the west end of the Mall. Members of Congress complained bitterly that the new, larger Treasury would interfere with their unrestricted view of the White House, but Jackson, according to the Washington historian Constance McLaughlin Green, deliberately chose the site so he would not have to look at the Capitol, and especially its inhabitants.[4]

Even as Jackson's accomplice, however, Mills had good relations with legislators. He had moved permanently to Washington the year after Bulfinch departed and immediately took note of the House chamber acoustics. He proposed a redesign: turn the Speaker's chair around and put it on the other side of the chamber, make new desks and rearrange them, construct a new visitors' gallery, raise the floor level, and change the drapes and the filthy carpets.[5] In 1832 the House finally endorsed the design and paid Mills a thousand dollars for it. He did the job during the summer, and most members reported "general satisfaction." Specific satisfaction, unfortunately, proved elusive. The acoustics were just as bad.[6] Undaunted, Mills in 1836 suggested to the House that they bump the Library of Congress from its elegant digs on the West Front and use the space for a new chamber.[7] The plan went nowhere, yet Mills may have been the first person with any expertise to figure out that the existing House chamber was a lost cause.

With Jackson's help and protection, Mills nimbly navigated the political shoals during his early years in Washington. He lost no luster when the House refurbishment proved a failure. And it was not his fault that the Washington family refused his plan to put the remains of George and Martha in a crypt two floors below the Rotunda. But Mills was Jackson's man; once Jackson left, Mills had no protection, and it cost him. In September 1837, only six months after Jackson departed, the House started investigating Mills for "extravagance." The next year the House restored its chamber to the configuration it had had before Mills's remodeling job, and in 1842 the Tyler administration booted him out of his Treasury office.[8]

Mills endured, mostly by doing small jobs and by trying to realign himself with Calhoun. In 1837 he fireproofed the House Post Office and modified heating and ventilation for the House. In 1839 he supervised the recoppering of the Capitol dome. In 1843 he designed a pedestal for Greenough's statue of Washington after it was moved out of the Rotunda and into the yard. But these were housekeeping chores, none of which was going to restore Mills's prestige. Drawing pictures of toilet seats for the Capitol did not help, either, nor did building six desks in 1845 for senators from new states, including one known as the "throne of the King of Texas" for Sam Houston. Mills's fee for that job was five dollars. Without a patron, architects did what they had to do to survive.

In early 1846, in a move that previewed what he would try four years later, Mills probed the congressional psyche by submitting two sets of plans for an enlargement of the Capitol to the Senate Committee on Public Buildings. The first called for a new addition to the East Front of the existing building. "By this arrangement the Capitol assumes the form of the Greek Cross," he wrote. This would cure one long-standing visual defect by putting the dome in the geographic center of the building. A new eastern projection would balance Bulfinch's Western Front, thus enhancing the Capitol's symmetry.

A new House chamber would be built in this eastern projection. The Senate would take over the West Front from the Library. The Library would move to the old House chamber, and the Supreme Court would move upstairs and occupy the old Senate chamber. The current Supreme Court, on the first floor, would become a law library. The new Senate would hold a hundred senators, the new House three hundred congressmen; the new Court would be much more spacious, the new Library would hold two hundred thousand books, and the Rotunda would serve as the second-floor vestibule for all four destinations. This design, Mills said, offered a "compact form," and would cost only $480,000.[9]

Plan two, however, was something different altogether—simpler, but much more ambitious. Leave the old Capitol intact and add two "ample wing buildings" to the north and south, Mills said, "furnishing extensive accommodations, both for the Senate and House of Representatives." This would "double the accommodations of the present Capitol building," offering "new chambers for both houses and 36 rooms for each body on the three floors, plus spacious corridors and fine staircases." The Library would stay where it was but would be much enlarged. The Supreme Court would move to the old Senate chamber, and the accursed House chamber would be used for something else as yet unspecified. The wings plan would cost $592,497.[10]

Although the Topographical Engineers three years earlier had been first to suggest solving the House acoustical dilemma by adding a wing to the southern end of the building and putting a new chamber in it, their proposal had been motivated by expediency rather than by any broader concerns. The Engineers wanted to fix the acoustics in the House. They offered only a passing glance at the need for more government workspace in a rapidly expanding nation. And the Engineers' only concession to the aesthetic possibilities inherent in new wings was that the Senate ought to have one, too, for "symmetry," even though it was not yet necessary.

Mills's proposal offered much more, and in his letter he defined the arguments that would dominate the debate over the "Capitol Extension" for the next five years. The eastern projection, which would come to be known as the Eastern Front, or the Eastern Extension, focused, as had the Engineers, on curing the evils of the House chamber. At the same time, however, Mills's design also sought to improve the Capitol's architectural coherence. Mills would make a better Capitol—roomier, more pleasing, more substantial.

The second plan, however, was visionary. Wing extensions of the size Mills proposed were unnecessary if the goal was simply to build a better House of Representatives. But if the United States was going to double in size, why not double the size of its greatest building? And why not add "spacious corridors and fine staircases" so that people would know that the greatest building served the greatest nation? Unlike many of Mills's proposals over the years, this one showed foresight, thought, and attention to detail and was uncluttered by needless pandering. And implicit in it, for anyone who thought about it in detail, was the ultimate promise: if this plan went forward and was executed properly, the result would be spectacular. Mills could be a wheedling, irritating man, but here he had planted the seed of greatness. It was his idea, and it would take root.

There was no public reaction from Congress, but Mills nonetheless returned to the committee a month later with a second letter. This one was a full-dress proposal for his Eastern Front "Greek Cross" plan. It is not clear why Mills decided to forget about a wings design, but he may have abandoned it simply because Congress had shown no interest. Still, there is little doubt that Mills always preferred an Eastern Extension. In 1849, Robert Dale Owen, chairman of the Smithsonian Building Committee, a former congressman and the son of the British-born utopian Robert Owen, praised Mills's Greek Cross plan in his *Hints on Public Architecture* as the only solution to the House dilemma.[11] Mills thought he had the right idea, and he was still promoting it—and very effectively—three years after he invented it. But he was thinking small.

So in February 1850 he tried again. The stars were not as favorably aligned as they had been in 1846. He was a Democrat now trying to impress a Whig administration. Calhoun, his patron, was almost dead from tuberculosis. And Mills was too old to move elsewhere or start over. Enlarging the Capitol was his last roll of the dice.

At first, the proposal must have seemed hopelessly ill-timed. The weeks after Mills submitted it produced one thunderous political moment after another. The compromise debate, which the historian David Potter more than one hundred years later called "one of the classic and inevitable set pieces" in American history, had begun in earnest.[12] On March 4, 1850, Calhoun left his deathbed to denounce Clay's plan. Unable to read the speech himself, he sat rigidly while Senator James M. Mason of Virginia read it for him.[13] On March 7, Daniel Webster rose to speak in favor of the compromise, "not as a Massachusetts man, not as a Northern man, but as an American . . . I speak today for the preservation of the Union. 'Hear me for my cause.'"[14] On March 11, the antislavery senator William H. Seward of New York argued the existence of a "higher law" than the Constitution and demanded that the compromise be rejected.[15] And on March 31, Calhoun died. Who had time to think about the Capitol?

But four days later, Jefferson Davis wrote to Mills, requesting that he make a wings design. This simple act would turn out to be the first step in a project that in fifteen years would convert the smoky, mildewed Capitol—largely untouched since Bulfinch had "finished" it in 1829—into a national showpiece. And from this day in April 1850, Davis would cultivate and promote the project with unflagging enthusiasm and relentless single-mindedness. From April 1850 until the day he abandoned Washington to become president of the Confederacy eleven years later, Davis would be the new Capitol's political champion, benefactor, and shepherd. Without him the modern Capitol, recognized throughout the world as an enduring symbol of republican democracy, would never have existed.

Mills's motives in this transaction were transparent. He needed a new job, he wanted a new patron, and he wanted to cement his historical legacy. Davis's motives, however, remain a puzzle. From one vantage point, his interest in the Capitol was unsurprising. First as a House member, then as a senator, he had taken an interest in the city of Washington and its public buildings since he first arrived five years previously. He had played a significant role in setting up the Smithsonian Institution as a scientific research facility and was a member of its Board of Regents. He had lobbied hard to create buildings for a national botanical garden at the foot of the Capitol's West Front and had served on various committees interested in cleaning up and beautifying the Mall. The question that lingers, however, is why he cared.

Two other senators who would provide crucial support for the Capitol project, Pearce of Maryland and Virginia's Robert M. T. Hunter, chairman of the Public Buildings Committee, were staunch allies of the city, but their states embraced the District of Columbia, and they had a vested interest in anything that would help the District shed its image as a national eyesore. Davis, by contrast, lived on a Mississippi River island about twenty miles south of Vicksburg, and, like most of his Senate colleagues, he headed home the moment Congress adjourned. And although he was rich, he lived small in Mississippi. Brierfield, his plantation house, was modest when compared to many of the Deep South's legendary stately homes. He had no reputation as an aesthete.

Given this context, Davis's approach to Capitol enlargement seemed even more anomalous, for his purpose was clear from the moment he became involved in it. He wanted the best. He had no thought of drifting into a stopgap renovation project: there would be no lowering of the House chamber ceiling, no musical chairs to see which tenant fit best into which space, no grafting of a new House of Representatives onto the Capitol's eastern façade. Davis was the first member of Congress from either house to show any more than a passing interest in a north-south extension, and he never backtracked. The wings design was more adventurous and therefore more difficult to pull off, but what made it more attractive was that by doubling the size of the current building, the United States could make a statement about national strength, confidence, and potential. From the beginning, and for most of the next eleven years, Davis drove the project. He prevailed on Congress to fund it when it was reluctant to do so; he bullied those who opposed him until they succumbed; he courted allies and cajoled presidents. He did it early on, when no one else cared, and he continued even as his own world began to crumble.

What Davis demonstrated repeatedly throughout this period was an ability to champion the contradictory ideals of states' rights and unionism. He was willing to dissolve the union to protect slavery, but at the same time he was convinced, as few of his colleagues were, of the greatness and potential of the United States. He was a lifelong Democrat and admirer of Andrew Jackson, the great unionist. He had met Jackson at the Hermitage when he was a boy, and remembered the visit fondly for the rest of his life.[16] At the same time, however, he would on countless occasions assert his reverence for John C. Calhoun, Jackson's sworn enemy and the country's leading voice for slavery and states' rights.[17] The day in April when he wrote to Mills about the north-south Capitol extension was the

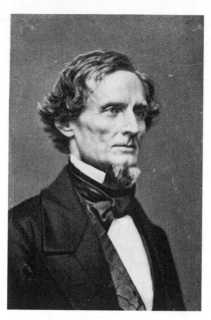

Jefferson Davis of Mississippi. Just under six feet tall, lean and athletic with icy blue eyes, he was a formidable debater and a relentless political advocate. As a U.S. senator and as secretary of war under President Franklin Pierce, he was the driving political force in favor of building a new U.S. Capitol. (Library of Congress)

same day the Senate put him on the committee that escorted Calhoun's remains home to South Carolina.[18] Nothing was more national than the U.S. Capitol. Nothing was more sectional than the burial of Calhoun.

There is no single event that illustrates how Davis came to embody these competing tendencies. Yet there are trends in his life that, taken together, suggest reasons he was able to move comfortably in two different worlds.

His childhood was unusual. Born in Kentucky in 1808, the youngest of ten children, he was the favored baby of the family. First Samuel, his father, and later his eldest brother, Joseph, a wealthy and successful attorney and cotton planter, wanted so badly to give him a good education that they sent him away to boarding school before he was eight and kept him away for nearly half of the first twenty years of his life. His brother Joe pulled him out of Kentucky's Transylvania University before he could graduate and sent him to West Point. Calhoun, then the secretary of war, signed his appointment.

At Transylvania, Davis had excelled in the classics and history, but at

West Point, the first four-year engineering college in the country, he struggled. He knew barely enough arithmetic to pass the entrance exam.[19] And while he managed to finish in the top half of his class in his first year, he declined every year after that, graduating twenty-third in a class of thirty-three in 1828.[20]

Davis was probably lucky to graduate at all. He was almost thrown out three times; his academic standing was indifferent; and he resented anyone in authority. With 137 demerits as a senior, he was one of the worst-behaved cadets in the entire corps, finishing 163rd out of 208.[21] While the army's best students went to the Corps of Engineers and the Corps of Topographical Engineers after graduation, Davis was sent to the infantry—to build forts, fight Indians, and protect settlers on the frontier. He was twenty-one years old when he left West Point, just a hair under six feet tall, lean and wiry with curly brown hair, high cheekbones, and icy blue deep-set eyes. According to one classmate, "his figure was very soldier-like and rather robust; his step springy, resembling the tread of an Indian 'brave' on the warpath."[22] Very quickly he was in the wilderness at Fort Crawford, in the Michigan Territory. There was little excitement but, he confessed in a letter to his sister Lucinda, "I know of nothing else that I could do which I would like better."[23]

Purpose came into his life in the spring of 1832 when Sarah Knox Taylor, the nineteen-year-old daughter of Colonel Zachary Taylor, the commanding officer at Fort Crawford, moved to Michigan to join her father. Soon Davis and Sarah, known as Knox, fell in love. Taylor was not pleased. "I will be damned if another daughter of mine shall marry into the Army," he wrote in a letter to a friend.[24] When Davis early in 1833 asked Taylor for his permission to marry Knox, Taylor refused.

Davis's fortunes went downhill from there. He had never been particularly fond of superior officers and did not make a habit of cultivating them or showing them deference. Not long after Taylor dampened Davis's marriage hopes, both men were assigned to sit on a court-martial with a third officer whom Taylor detested and a fourth officer who had come from St. Louis. The newcomer had forgotten to bring his dress uniform, required at military trials, but asked to be allowed to participate anyway. Taylor refused, but Davis and the third officer overruled him. Taylor was furious. Not only could Davis not marry Knox, Taylor said, but henceforth he was forbidden to visit her at the Taylor home. Davis, equally furious, thought about challenging Taylor to a duel, but a friend talked him out of it. If Davis ever wanted to be part of Taylor's family, the friend offered, shooting the patriarch was not a good plan.[25] Davis, with an exalted sense of southern honor and an evil temper, issued and accepted challenges through a good part of his life. He never fought a duel, but it was not for lack of trying.

This crisis fortunately subsided in the spring, when Davis received orders sending him to join a new regiment of dragoons. Whether this was a clever gambit by Taylor to rid himself of an unwanted pest or deus ex machina is not known, but it gave Davis—without prejudice—a timely escape. And it did not end Davis's romance. He and Knox considered themselves engaged.

Davis spent most of the next two years—his last two years in the regular army—building and maintaining forts or making tough, physically punishing treks into the hinterlands of what would later become Oklahoma. He endured this duty without notable incident until Christmas Eve 1834, when simmering resentment toward his immediate superior erupted into a nasty quarrel after he failed to show up for morning roll call. Three days later charges were filed against him for "conduct subversive of good order and Military discipline."[26] Davis was later acquitted of criminal behavior after an eight-day trial, but the court found him guilty of what was, at bottom, disrespect. It was an even-handed verdict that rebuked both officers: Davis had behaved badly, but not badly enough to be put before a court-martial and sent to jail. In March 1835 he went home to Mississippi on leave. On April 20 he resigned his commission. His reputation was intact, but at that point he held no particular fondness for the army, and he had taken a fearful physical beating for the previous two years. It was time to move on.

But at twenty-seven, Davis had little to offer. He was vain, cocksure, and immature, and he had managed to incur the wrath of almost every superior officer he had ever encountered, including the man he hoped would become his father-in-law. But it was during this period that Davis's unionism probably began to grow. Beginning with his peripatetic schooling and extending through the army years, Davis by 1835 had probably seen as much of the United States as any man his age in the country, and not merely as a visitor. He had lived there: in the South, in the mid-Atlantic, in the Midwest, and in the Southwest. He had met people from all over the country and had a sense of the vastness and potential of the United States. He had found that the skills he had disdained at West Point—engineering, map reading, the building trades—had served him well on the frontier. By the age of twenty-seven he had been everywhere, had met people from all parts of the country, and had as much education and life experience as it was possible for anyone his age to have in the United States in 1835.

Davis as a young man had no love for the army or its discipline, but he probably resigned for a simple reason. As he wrote in a short autobiography decades later, he was "anxious to fulfill a long-existing engagement with a daughter of Colonel Zachary Taylor."[27] Knox had written to him late in 1834, announcing to Davis that she had told her father she intended to marry Davis with or without permission. Davis, enraptured when he received this news, replied to "my dear Sarah, my betrothed" that "whatever I may be hereafter, neglected by you I should have been worse than nothing."[28]

The couple did not elope, as folklore had it at one time, but were married in Louisville on June 17, 1835, at the home of Knox's aunt with a large contingent of Taylor relatives on hand. The colonel was not present, but he no longer opposed the marriage. His daughter wanted Davis, and there was nothing he could do about it. And not only was Davis out of the army, but his brother Joe, who owned more than a hundred slaves, wanted to set him up as a planter on his own vast holding.

This idyll did not last long. The newlyweds went to Mississippi to stay with Joe at his Hurricane plantation and take a look at the land he was giving to Jefferson below Vicksburg. By August, however, the "sickly season" had arrived in the Delta swamp, and Davis and Knox decided to spend it with Davis's sister in the hills of Louisiana. Soon after their arrival, both were stricken with malaria. Knox died on September 15. She and Davis had been married for just under three months.[29]

The death of Sarah Knox Taylor was a defining moment for Davis. During his largely rootless early life, Knox had been the only thing he had cared about. He had waited three years to have her, and now she was dead. He was devastated. He spent most of the next eight years at Brierfield, his 900-acre Mississippi River plantation.

After Knox's death, nobody would ever again describe Davis as a devilish, immature prankster or a ringleader in schemes to flout authority.

Indeed, instead of flouting authority, Davis was becoming authority. By October 1836, he owned thirty-six slaves.[30] Those meeting him for the first time during these years and beyond would remark on his intelligence and charm, but he also had acquired a standoffishness that could turn instantly to coldness or icy rage, depending on the circumstances. And he was developing political skills. During his eight years in Mississippi, he spent hours debating current events, philosophy, and the Constitution with his brother Joe and reading the books in Joe's ample library, adding intellectual polish to his other gifts.[31] In 1840, he went to a Warren County Democratic Party meeting and ended up being named as a delegate to the Mississippi state Democratic convention. He was also a delegate two years later, and in 1843 he agreed at the last minute to run for the Mississippi House of Representatives when the party lost faith in its first candidate. Davis closed strongly but lost to a Whig heavyweight in a Whig district. The race, however, marked him as a comer and won him stature in the Democratic Party.[32]

Soon after the election, Davis met Varina Howell of Natchez, Mississippi, then seventeen years old, the daughter of a friend of Joseph Davis who was spending Christmas with Joe and his family at Hurricane. Varina was witty, smart, and engaging—an avid student of Latin, the English classics, and French—and could hold her own in any conversation.[33] She immediately caught the attention of Jefferson, and for most of the next two months the two were inseparable. Varina was at first impressed that Davis was twice her age and had "an uncertain temper." She also presciently noted that Davis had "a way of taking for granted that everybody agrees with him when he expresses an opinion, which offends me."[34] It would offend her more than once in the coming years, and she would not be the only one.

But Davis had his good qualities as well, including, Varina told her mother, "a peculiarly sweet voice and a winning manner." Davis, she also noted much later, although he was thirty-six when she met him, "looked about thirty; erect, well-proportioned and active as a boy. He rode with more grace than any man I have ever seen, and gave me the impression of being incapable either of being unseated or fatigued."[35]

They became engaged in January 1844, just before Varina returned home. A few days later Davis went to the state Democratic convention,

where he became an at-large party elector for the 1844 presidential election. Instructed by his Warren County constituents to support Van Buren,
Davis instead gave an impassioned speech in favor of Calhoun. He would
acquiesce on Van Buren, he said, but he wanted the convention to know
his preference for a rock-solid southern rights man.[36] Davis had established his states' rights credentials.

In the end, the national Democratic Party chose James K. Polk as the
candidate, and Davis, as an elector, was on the road campaigning for him
all over the state until Election Day. Polk won, and shortly afterward, on
a riverboat trip, Davis ran into Zachary Taylor by accident. Taylor approached Davis "cordially" and extended his hand, and "an entire reconciliation took place."[37] The two men, who had not seen each other for
more than a decade, became fast friends. In the coming years, Taylor, simple and straightforward—and a rock-bottom unionist—would ask for
Davis's trust and counsel, both in battle and in politics. Davis, reserved,
unyielding, and skeptical of practically anyone in authority not himself,
gave Taylor unconditional respect and absolute loyalty.

Davis and Varina were married on February 26, 1845, in Natchez. On
June 28, Davis was invited to give a eulogy in Vicksburg for Andrew Jackson, who had died earlier that month. Davis lauded Jackson's "moral firmness" and "high sense of duty" and repeated Jackson's maxim that "the
Union it must be preserved."[38] A bit over a week later, state Democrats
selected him to run for U.S. Congress. Davis won handily on November 4 but delayed his departure for Washington so he could make a wel-
coming speech for the distinguished visitor John C. Calhoun. This went
well, as Varina recounted later, as Davis finished "with States rights sails
all set, and Mr. Calhoun at the helm."[39] At the dawn of his political career,
Davis had Jackson and Calhoun in harmony.

There is no record of how Davis felt about the bedlam in the House
chamber during what would be his very brief sojourn as a congressman.
By February 1846, war with Mexico had become inevitable. Congress the
previous year had passed a joint resolution offering statehood to independent Texas, and on December 29, 1845, Texas was admitted to the union.
Mexico, infuriated, sent troops northward, and in early May 1846 they
crossed the Rio Grande from Matamoros. Zachary Taylor, now a general
commanding a small force intended to protect U.S. interests, fought and
defeated the Mexicans on May 8 and 9, driving them back across the river.
On May 13, Congress declared war.

Varina Howell Davis, a Natchez, Mississippi, teenager when she met her future husband, became one of Washington's leading hostesses during the 1850s. She was intelligent and charming, did not suffer fools, and was never shy about expressing her opinions. (Library of Congress)

Davis was already halfway out the door. In a June 3 letter to the editor of the Port Gibson *Correspondent*, Davis let Mississippi know he would welcome the opportunity "to command a Warren [County] regiment" in the conflict with Mexico.[40] On June 18, the Mississippi militiamen elected him to command the First Mississippi Volunteers with the rank of colonel. He left Washington on July 4 and joined the regiment in New Orleans on July 17, 1846.

Davis's decision to leave Congress caused serious trouble with Varina, who made him promise not to go, only to have him break the promise almost immediately. "I have cried until I am stupid," she told her mother, "but you know there is 'no use crying, better luck next time.'"[41] The war marked the beginning of a rocky two-year period in the Davises' marriage, caused mostly by Varina's refusal to submit to her husband's will.

Taylor was already in Mexico, encamped north of the city of Monterrey, when Davis reached the border. By late August he had joined Taylor, who was assembling a 6,500-man force to attack Monterrey, where 10,300 Mexican defenders awaited them. The battle began on September 19 and lasted four days. The centerpiece for Davis was the September 21 assault on a Mexican strongpoint called La Tenería—"The Tannery." Two regiments of volunteers, Davis's Rifles and the First Tennessee under Colonel William Campbell, approached the fort and stopped to await orders. Receiving none, the two regiments decided, independently and at virtually the same moment, to assault the breastworks, charging the fort and driving the Mexicans out. Two days later, after hard fighting, Taylor and the Mexican commander concluded an agreement giving Taylor control of Monterrey in return for allowing the Mexicans to withdraw. The two sides agreed on an eight-week armistice.[42] Shortly thereafter, Davis asked for, and was granted, a sixty-day leave.

Davis used the intermission, in part, to cement his reputation. As the first high-ranking Mississippian to return from the front, he was the toast of the state. Davis's main personal task, however, was to try to mend fences between Varina and his brother Joseph. Varina had learned that his brother Joe had never deeded Brierfield to Jefferson and suspected that Joe wanted to keep the Howell family—including Varina herself—from inheriting the estate should anything happen to her husband.[43] She distrusted Joseph and grew to hate him. Davis did not succeed in resolving the dispute, and back on the Rio Grande in December, he wrote Varina that rancor did not become her: "To rise superior to petty annoyances, to pity and forgive the weakness in others which galls and incommodes us is a noble exhibition of moral philosophy and the surest indication of an elevated nature."[44] Davis in the coming years would repeatedly demonstrate his own inability to follow this advice, proving effortlessly capable of holding petty grudges for years.

Davis rejoined Taylor on Christmas Day and found the general upset because U.S. Army commander General Winfield Scott had taken most of his troops for a major offensive against Mexico City. Taylor suspected that Polk, a Democrat, was determined to keep Taylor out of the limelight, even though Scott was a Whig, because Taylor's politics were unknown.[45] Davis adopted Taylor's views and developed an intense, almost irrational contempt for Scott in later years.

Taylor, hearing that a large Mexican army was advancing northward, brought his forces together at Saltillo in early February. Two weeks later, he confirmed that a Mexican army of twenty thousand was approaching.

Early in the morning of February 23, Davis and the Mississippi Rifles moved six miles south from Saltillo to the Buena Vista hacienda, where fighting had already begun, with U.S. forces in retreat. Davis brought the Rifles forward until they came within range, then ordered them to slow down and "advance firing." The shock of their attack stalled the Mexican advance. During the action a musket ball hit Davis in the ankle, driving shards of brass from his spur and pieces of sock into the wound. He wrapped the foot with a handkerchief and remained in the saddle.

Reinforcements arrived just in time. A body of Mexican lancers estimated at two thousand men was massing for a cavalry charge. Davis, with little time to prepare a classic "hollow square" defense, deployed his men in a V, with an Indiana regiment on the right and the Rifles on the left. He positioned himself at the vertex and placed his one cannon at the far end of the Mississippi line. The Mexican advance began at a gallop, then slowed to a trot and finally to a walk. The lancers were about fifty yards away when Davis's soldiers opened fire. The Mexican charge broke. Fighting continued for the rest of the day, but the Mexicans withdrew overnight.[46]

For Davis, the war was over. He and the Mississippi Rifles had fought with courage and tenacity, and the regiment had taken nearly a hundred casualties—out of a total strength of about four hundred men. Taylor, in his official report, was effusive in his praise for Davis's "distinguished coolness and gallantry at the head of the regiment." This, he said, "entitled him to the particular notice of the government."[47]

And he got it, almost immediately. In a letter dated May 19, 1847, Polk offered Davis a commission as a brigadier general in the regular army. On June 20, Davis thanked Polk but declined the offer. On August 10, Mississippi governor Albert Brown appointed Davis to fill out the term of a recently deceased Mississippi senator, noting that the people "expect me to offer you this commission, and it gives me sincere personal pleasure to gratify that expectation." Five days later, Davis accepted the appointment.[48]

3

JEFFERSON DAVIS LOSES ONE AND WINS ONE

On September 23, 1850, the Senate considered amendments to the humbly named Civil and Diplomatic Appropriations Bill providing yearly funding for embassies, lighthouses, and other federal facilities. Most of the add-ons were earmarks, small bits of federal largesse distributed to favored communities in favored states for breakwaters, beacons, dredging, and other amenities.

Senator Jefferson Davis of Mississippi interrupted the annual gift giving to present an amendment providing $200,000 to enlarge the U.S. Capitol. This initiative favored nobody in particular, thus triggering a spirited discussion by suddenly parsimonious senators who scoffed at Davis's estimate. What Davis contemplated would cost twice as much, one senator said, or could even surpass $2 million, said another. Davis finally offered a halfhearted defense: the original estimate was for "the exterior of the building, as I stated when I introduced it."[1] This was an outright lie. He had said nothing about the exterior of the building.

Then he stopped playing games. Yes, he acknowledged, it would cost more than $200,000. How much it cost would depend on how much extension Congress wanted to build. But no matter how much Congress spent, it would not be enough: "If this Union continues together, and this continues to be the seat of Government, I have no idea that any plan which may now be suggested will finally answer all the wants of the country." Eventually, he said, "I think it likely" that Congress may have to "cover the whole square with buildings."[2]

It was an extraordinary statement, particularly from Davis, who had spent much of the year as an implacable defender of slavery and southern rights and a bitter opponent of all who would extend the reach of the federal government to trump the prerogatives of individual states. Making Washington more powerful, or even making Washington *look* more powerful, was not something that advanced his agenda.

Yet on this day, at the very end of one of the most contentious sessions in congressional history, he was a different person. Colleagues knew Davis wanted to enlarge the Capitol—to make more office space and to give the House a better place to work. But on this day Davis was not talking about construction money or giving Congress more room. On this day Davis, the defender of states' rights, was talking about the inevitability of national greatness.

He would espouse these competing visions repeatedly for the next decade, even as it became increasingly clear that they were tearing the country asunder. Davis's nationalism would build the modern U.S. Capitol; Davis's sectionalism would try to destroy it.

By mid-1850, Davis had become an important man, someone to be heard and heeded. He had been in the Senate since 1847 and been elected to a new six-year term. He had reconciled with his wife after a difficult two years and been named to the Smithsonian Board of Regents. He had become chairman of the Senate Committee on Military Affairs, and in the Senate chamber had sat next to the ailing but still magisterial John C. Calhoun, one of his idols.[3]

His biography accounted for part of his success. When he first entered the Senate chamber on crutches, a wounded veteran of the Battle of Buena Vista, he commanded everyone's attention. The journalist Benjamin Perley Poore years later recalled an imposing man, who stood straight, had "square shoulders and a muscular frame" and a "high forehead . . . shaded by masses of dark hair, in which the silvery threads began to show."[4] He and Taylor were heroes of the Mexican War—and Taylor, in 1847 already a putative presidential candidate, was Davis's ex-father-in-law. Davis had outstanding credentials. And he looked like a senator.

Talent also helped. Davis had an agile mind and prepared extremely well. He seemed able to speak knowledgeably on almost any topic, whether it be the advisability of building a U.S. mint in San Francisco (a good idea) or to recruit more westerners for the mounted cavalry (they were better riders, and thus able to "tame the terror of those predatory Indians which infest the borders of Texas").[5] The Senate doorkeeper Isaac Bassett fittingly described Davis as "a rapid, impetuous and direct speaker."[6] And regardless of the subject, he almost always had something to say.

But there was something else. Davis seethed. He had little or no sense of humor, and as an advocate for states' rights, slavery, or dozens of other subjects, he was a cold and cutting debater, arrogant, glib, occasionally sneering, and needlessly overbearing, coming up to the line of outright rudeness and frequently crossing it. He never suffered a slight quietly, and he held grudges for years. He may have had grand visions, but he could also be a small, petty man. To his Senate colleagues he must have seemed like a volcano, ready to erupt at any moment. This was not necessarily a bad quality for a senator to have, especially in the kinetic atmosphere of the slavery debate. The lesson with Davis was that it was perhaps better to leave him alone or agree with him than to risk humiliation, or worse.

By 1850, Davis's ability to negotiate the divide between unionism and southern sectionalism had been apparent for several years, and it gave him more depth than many of his colleagues—from both the South and the North. By the late 1840s, many southerners already regarded conciliation with the North as a forlorn hope and had begun talking openly about leaving the union. Many northerners regarded this attitude as treasonous, but beyond issues relating to slavery—of which, admittedly, there were many—they, too, were often reluctant to assert the existence of anything resembling a "national will" or a "national interest." This indifference was particularly notable whenever someone like Davis suggested spending taxpayer money to clean up the Mall, build a national botanical garden, or otherwise improve the city of Washington, which had neither voice nor vote in Congress.

Davis had no difficulty articulating the small, sectional view—political bread and butter for virtually every southern lawmaker. But during the decade leading up to the Civil War, he also repeatedly demonstrated an ability to see beyond parochial concerns and embrace a larger perspective. His vision could encompass the grandiose: a Capitol building worthy of a great nation; a Smithsonian Institution that served as a world-famous font of research and scientific knowledge. Or it could focus on the lethally mundane: he would be instrumental in replacing the U.S. Army's outdated muskets with modern, more accurate rifles, helping union forces prepare for the brutal war that would ultimately destroy his homeland.

Davis never reconciled the conflict between unionism and states' rights, but the evidence also suggests he was never particularly troubled by his competing loyalties. He certainly knew the issues, and he explored them in depth in a long exchange of letters with Zachary Taylor that began in the summer of 1847, virtually the moment Davis returned wounded from Mexico to convalesce at Brierfield. The general, secure in his victories at Monterrey and Buena Vista and growing conscious of his national potential, was passing along gossip and seeking advice and counsel from his more politically experienced subaltern. Davis's side of the correspondence has not survived, but references in Taylor's letters show that the two men exchanged ideas on virtually every twist and turn of national politics.

Taylor held nothing back. While he and Davis were in Mexico, Representative David Wilmot of Pennsylvania, who had served with Davis on the House Smithsonian Committee when both were congressmen, had introduced legislation prohibiting slavery in any territory obtained in the war. This "Wilmot Proviso" never became law, but the South hated it, and it served for years in Congress as a lightning rod for sectional strife. Taylor told Davis the Proviso ought to be ignored. Slavery, he said in several letters, would never catch on in the territories, and the North would never permit slavery to be established in any new states. The South, he said, should concentrate on keeping slavery in the states where it existed. If the North failed to respect southern rights, "the Union in that case will be blown to atoms." Keeping the union together, for Taylor, was the most important thing, and he was willing to rise above "sectional prejudices" to ensure it.[7]

Davis did not share Taylor's views and would never share them. He regarded the Wilmot Proviso as anathema, believed in the spread of slavery, and asserted that Congress and the federal government had no right to prohibit slavery in any state. He was not a unionist like Taylor.

Except when it suited him. And it suited him frequently.

He donned the unionist hat during a stormy debate in early 1848, arguing in favor of raising ten additional regular army regiments. He criticized Calhoun for dismissing the proposal as "mere braggadocio," pointing out that Calhoun himself had made a series of belligerent moves as secretary of state during the run-up to the Mexican War. He had the details at hand. This elicited some short replies from a clearly irritated Calhoun about needlessly provoking Mexico, which prompted Davis, in sudden indignation, to exclaim: "What! Shall a foreign power dispute our territorial limits—refuse to settle the boundary by negotiation—seize by force, territory rightfully ours, and our executive stand powerless by?" Then, for good measure, he jumped on Daniel Webster for describing the war as "odious."

"'Odious' for what?" Davis asked. "On account of the skill and gallantry with which it has been conducted? Or is it because of the humanity, the morality, the magnanimous clemency which has marked its execution? 'Odious!'" The public is celebrating our victories, he said. "Where is the odium?"[8]

And this was the final piece of Davis's public persona. He was willing to take on the Senate's icons—to be impolite, to be unpleasant, to interrupt them, to throw their words back at them. Colleagues knew Davis by the company he offended—by the senators he opposed, the senators he insulted, and the senators he provoked. If he could do that to the lions and survive, it made him a lion, too.

As a loyal Democrat he campaigned perfunctorily for Michigan senator Lewis Cass in 1848 and helped put Mississippi in the Democratic column. But he had conflicting loyalties. Taylor's success as a candidate was based in part on his silence about his views on slavery. He was a slave owner, which spoke for itself and helped him greatly in the southern states. Had the South known what Taylor had told Davis, voters would have abandoned him in droves. But Davis, albeit a good Democrat, never broke faith. In late January 1849, only five weeks before Taylor's inauguration, he wrote a letter to his friend John J. Crittenden, the Whig governor of Kentucky and a close Taylor adviser, to ask him to look after "the Genl." At that point Davis knew that Henry Clay was going to return to Congress as a Whig senator, and he feared that Clay would not support Taylor's administration. He urged Crittenden, an old Washington hand, to "talk fully with Genl. Taylor [as] he knows very little of our public men personally and will have very little opportunity to observe them after his arrival."[9]

Davis was right about Clay. When the senator from Kentucky stepped forward on January 29, 1850, to present his eight compromise proposals,

Congress had no viable plan to escape the dilemma of the Mexican Cession. Instead, the only thing on the table was a relatively simple proposal by Taylor: allow immediate statehood for California without slavery, and encourage citizens of New Mexico to form a territorial government with a view toward entering the union as a free state. These positions, from which Taylor never deviated, caused widespread consternation in the South, which by the end of 1849 deepened to outright fury when Taylor refused to disavow the Wilmot Proviso. This was political brinkmanship—intended or not—and Taylor, a poor speaker and an even poorer salesman, needed someone to help him make his case. There was no one. In a letter to Davis he had commented on the indifference of his cabinet, noting that "there is not one among them who stands so conspicuous above the others as even to aspire to the presidency."[10]

So Clay stepped into the breach. His proposals boiled down to five main themes: annex California as a free state; set up territorial governments elsewhere in the Mexican Cession without reference to slavery; fix the Texas boundary by giving a big piece of Texas to New Mexico, compensating Texas by having the federal government assume the state's public debt; abolish the slave trade in Washington, D.C.; and strengthen fugitive slave laws.

Davis challenged Clay the moment Clay had spoken. His two "great objections," he told the Senate, were that the proposals mandated federal government interference in the Texas boundary and D.C. slavery questions. Davis also refused to concede that slavery had no future in California. Slaves could work in the mines or help with plantation crops: "We, sir, have not asked that slavery should be established in California. We ask only that there should not be any restriction." Still, in the interests of sectional comity, he would not insist that slavery be unrestricted in the Mexican Cession, but would accept the extension of the Missouri Compromise line to the Pacific Ocean: slavery would be prohibited above 36 degrees 30 minutes north latitude.

Davis's presentation was impressive, once again, because of his knowledge of the issues raised and his ability on short notice to state his views clearly and incisively. But it was also notable for its mocking and belligerent tone—surprisingly so at such an early moment in the debate, when personal animosities and frustrations had not yet had a chance to mature. Davis began with sardonic irony: Congress had been looking for "something that would heal the existing dissensions," but instead this "honorable and distinguished senator" was "raising new barriers" with a set of measures that "augments the existing dangers."

Then he offered a personal rebuke: "A representative from one of the slaveholding states [Kentucky] raises his voice for the first time in disregard of this admitted right." Then he questioned Clay's competence: "We are called on to receive this as a measure of compromise!" he said. "Is a measure in which we of the minority are to receive nothing, a measure of compromise?" And he closed with a veiled threat: "I can never consent to give additional power to a majority to commit further aggressions upon the minority in this union."

Taken aback by Davis's zeal, Clay somewhat stuffily attempted to dismiss what he termed a "premature" and "in my opinion, unnecessary discussion" and promised to engage Davis "at a proper time."

To which Davis responded: "Now is the time."

Clay: "I choose not to give way now."

Davis: "The senator asked me to name my time; and I say now."

The exchange continued, with Davis repeatedly badgering Clay to debate him "now," and sneering that Clay "several times has regretted this premature discussion; but pray, sir, who introduced it?" Did Clay intend to fire "a mere volley of blank cartridges . . . in order that he might come up under cover of the smoke, and make a charge upon us before we saw him?"[11]

It was a vintage Davis performance, opening with a cold and quick dismissal of his opponent's arguments, offering little or nothing as an alternative, and finishing by suggesting his adversary was mounting a sneak attack. He had already gone after Calhoun and Webster. Now he had challenged Henry Clay.

The great compromise marked the last time that Calhoun, Clay, and Webster appeared together in the Senate, and it would be one of the last and one of the greatest debates ever hosted in the semicircular chamber designed by Benjamin Latrobe. The room was carpeted in red and dominated by the vice president's desk on a raised platform on the east side, beneath a red canopy surmounted by a gilt eagle. Rembrandt Peale's "porthole portrait" of Washington hung high on the east wall above the eagle. A colonnade behind the vice president created a lobby and walkway where senators, who had no offices except for their chamber desks, could stretch their legs, confer, and, during the winter, warm their hands at fireplaces set in the wall. Desks—one for each of the sixty-two senators—were arrayed in tiers before the vice president on either side of a central aisle. Senate debates had proved to be such an enduring public attraction that Bulfinch had added a semicircular balcony that extended the length of the chamber's west side. When the crush of spectators overwhelmed this gallery, senators habitually invited lady visitors to join them on the Senate floor and sit at their desks.

Light came from windows on the Capitol's east façade behind the vice president and from skylights in the roof. Heating was often insufficient, and ventilation was inadequate in almost every season. In contrast to the chaos in the House, however, senators could hear one another. Behavior was ordinarily civil, and the entire montage had received generally favorable reviews from distinguished visitors over the years. The English novelist Frances Trollope was impressed with how elegantly turned out the senators were in their formal suits, adding, however, as had Dickens and many others, "I wish I could add that they do not spit."[12]

The old Senate chamber, too cold in winter, too hot in summer, and roughly used by its tobacco-chewing tenants, was nevertheless an elegant room. Visitors packed the makeshift gallery for the opportunity to see and hear the likes of Clay, Webster, and Calhoun. (Architect of the Capitol)

Besides chewing tobacco, many senators took snuff, and when the compromise debate began, an official Senate snuffbox rested on the vice president's desk. Henry Clay, for one, was an inveterate snuff user; when speaking, the Senate doorkeeper Isaac Bassett recalled, he would frequently stop in the middle of a sentence and, to the amusement of colleagues and visitors alike, ask one of the pages to "bring me a pinch of stuff." This became so tedious that at one point Bassett asked Clay why he did not have his own snuffbox. "I have my box on my table at my hotel," Clay told Bassett. "If I bring it with me, I am constantly using it."[13]

And this, of course, was another reason why the Senate played to packed houses. "A debate on any political principle would have had no such attraction," said the Washington hostess and chronicler Margaret Bayard Smith. "But the personalities are irresistible. It is a kind of moral gladiatorship."[14] Anyone could read about the debates in the newspaper, but only those in the chamber could laugh about Henry Clay's snuff breaks and see him live—tall, rail-thin, and hawklike, dressed all in black with a high white collar, lank gray hair framing his long face, as his piercing voice rose in cadence with his excitement.[15]

On February 13, 1850, Davis rose in the Senate chamber to "lift the glove" that Clay had thrown down and make his formal reply to the compromise proposals. He was "grievously disappointed" in Clay, lamenting that the Kentuckian had not used his "power and influence" and "eloquence" on behalf of "the weak" and the "cause of the Constitution." Had he done so, Davis reflected, with a quick reference to Clay's advancing years, "the evils by which we are surrounded might perhaps have been removed, and the decline of that Senator's sun been even more bright than its meridian glory."

Still, though Davis sprinkled his address—spread over two days—with more personal jabs, his main purpose was to articulate southern opposition to the compromise. Davis's basic position on slavery—a position he would maintain for the rest of his life—was that the Constitution protected the right of any U.S. citizen to bring his property, including "slave property," into U.S. territories. The Clay package offered little, he said. Instant annexation of California simply affirmed the Wilmot Proviso without putting it into law and upset the balance of slave and free states in the Senate, leaving the South marooned, never to have a majority in either

House. "Denying the title of Texas to one-half her territory" did not improve the political balance, either, even if the federal government sought
to bribe Texas by paying its debts. The fugitive slave provisions looked
nice, he acknowledged, but, he noted presciently, no northern state would
ever comply with them. And finally, he dismissed Clay's Washington,
D.C., proposals by claiming that they abolished slavery in the District. In
fact, they called for abolition of the slave trade—not the same thing. Davis
nevertheless pressed on: abolishing District slavery, he said, would mean
that a resident southerner could not move into town with "a species of
domestics to which he is accustomed and attached."

It could probably be argued that Davis's floor speech, coming only two
weeks after Clay introduced the compromise, did as much to polarize the
debate over slavery as any speech during the run-up to civil war. He helped
crystallize the hard-line southern position and rejected out of hand any
effort to finesse the dilemma. The only compromise Davis was willing to
entertain was the Missouri line. If that would not work, the only solution,
by his lights, was for the North to roll over: open up new lands to slavery,
maintain sectional parity in the Senate, and curb abolitionist fury. Both
sides wanted a way out, but neither could find one. And Davis asserted in
1850 that it was not the South's job to find a solution. "We are unable to
pass any measure, if we propose it, therefore I have none to suggest," he
finished. "We are unable to bend you to any terms which we may offer; we
are under the ban of your purpose; therefore from you, if from anywhere,
the proposition must come."[16]

These words, in their hopelessness and their readiness to fix blame,
might as well have been uttered in 1860. Seeing them a decade earlier, it is
difficult to understand how Davis acquired a reputation as a moderate.
While it was not his custom to preach disunion, he had, with this speech,
at this moment, placed himself irrevocably on the side of those who did,
and had willingly identified himself as one of their spokesmen, if not their
principal spokesman. One searches the record during the ensuing years
for some change in viewpoint, some frisson of doubt, some hope for conciliation not based on winning or losing. But it never comes. In a rare
moment of self-knowledge later in the compromise debate, Davis acknowledged—but not without a hint of pride—that "if I have one defect
which stands out more prominently than the rest, I fear it is that I adhere
to my own opinion when others believe that arguments enough have been
offered to warrant a change."[17] For Davis, backtracking was weakness.

What may have saved him from being irrevocably lumped together with the most militant southern rights advocates, however, was his remarkable ability, even during this tension-filled time in 1850, to change the subject and put himself at the center of a new endeavor completely unrelated—or at least so it seemed—to the Mexican Cession. This was what happened when he asked Robert Mills to produce a plan to redesign and enlarge the U.S. Capitol with north and south wings. Unlike the compromise debate, this was not a congressional main event, but it was not a sideshow, either. Davis never undertook anything frivolously, and overcoming congressional inertia to get the money to build a new Capitol was not going to be easy.

He also benefited from his colleagues' bad behavior, which, with the debate becoming more contentious by the day, soon eclipsed his own. Two weeks after he asked Mills for the Capitol design, Senator Henry S. Foote, Davis's Mississippi colleague, pulled a gun on Senator Thomas Hart Benton on the Senate floor. An incensed Benton, seeing the drawn gun, stood up on a nearby desk, flung open his coat, and yelled: "I disdain to carry arms; let him fire! Stand out of the way, and let the assassin fire."[18] Senator Daniel S. Dickinson, of New York, quietly suggested to Foote that he hand him the revolver, and Foote did so.

The day after Benton-Foote, the Senate created a select committee of thirteen, chaired by Clay, to evaluate all the compromise proposals thus far offered and decide what to do. On May 8 it issued its report, embracing a plan first suggested by the ubiquitous Foote—that all the Clay proposals be rolled into a single legislative package to be voted once, up or down. This tried-and-true maneuver, a congressional evergreen even then, was designed to get lawmakers to vote for things they did not like by mixing them with other things they did like.[19] Thus, a tough fugitive slave law would become a price an antislavery northern senator might be willing to pay if, in return, he could abolish the slave trade in Washington, D.C. The effectiveness of this approach, soon dubbed the "Omnibus Bill," depended, of course, on the ability of Clay as floor leader to muster the votes to pass it. Omnibus legislation risks everything on one throw.

What Clay was trying to pull off was complicated, but tempers also ran hot and tension remained high because of President Taylor's insistence that California statehood be considered without reference to any of the other outstanding questions. During most of the Compromise debate, the president and Clay had preserved at least the appearance of comity, but this began to unravel in mid-May when Taylor made it clear that he opposed Clay's package. On May 21, a furious Clay rose to issue a ringing denunciation of Taylor: "Here are five wounds—one, two, three, four, five—bleeding and threatening the well-being, if not the existence, of the body politic," he said. "What is the plan of the president? Is it to heal these wounds? No such thing. It is only to heal one of the five, and to leave the other four to bleed more profusely than ever, by the sole admission of California, even if it should produce death itself."[20] The outburst was colorful, but it solved nothing and probably made the situation worse. Taylor did not like to be pushed around, and he had no history of backing away from hard-won convictions. Clay had ensured in this speech that Taylor would never seek reconciliation. Also, as Clay certainly realized, even if the Senate passed the Omnibus Bill, Taylor would probably kill it with a veto as soon as it reached his desk. It was not in Clay's interest to antagonize Taylor. But he had done so, and now the two most powerful Whig leaders in the country were at each other's throats. The party had started to unravel.

Amid these fireworks, Senator Robert M. T. Hunter of Virginia, chairman of the Committee on Public Buildings, on May 28 submitted a report on Robert Mills's proposal to enlarge the U.S. Capitol—the original petition introduced by Maryland's James A. Pearce in February. Documents Hunter submitted along with the report showed that Mills had taken a month to produce a coherent wing plan, and that he had prepared it specifically for Davis, who had requested it. The committee had apparently examined it for nearly another month before Hunter presented it.

The Hunter report made no mention of Mills's favored Eastern Extension. It had either been dismissed outright, per Davis's wishes, or had been considered in the Public Buildings Committee and discarded. In either case, what Hunter presented was what Davis wanted. Mills's report and design had been addressed to Davis. It had been, and still was, Davis's initiative.

The report again affirmed that Congress, or at least the Senate, was ready to make a change, and that repairs and modifications to the Capitol would not be enough. This was because the Mexican Cession had mooted all the old arguments. "A larger Senate chamber has become almost indispensable," Hunter said. "It is already too small for the present number of senators, and that number is increasing." The same was true for the House, which "besides being too small, has been proved by experience to be unfit for purposes of deliberation."

The solution was at hand: "By the addition of two wings of a suitable size—one to the north, and one to the south of the present building—we may afford ample accommodations for the two houses of congress and their officers." The library would be able to expand throughout the entire West Front. The beautiful but accursed House chamber would become a charming public room and a place to exhibit paintings and other "objects of art." The present Senate would become the new Supreme Court. Hunter noted that the Army Topographical Engineers had initially broached the concept of additional wings, but he made a generous bow to Mills for having modified this plan and made it his own. The "committee recommend the plan of Mr. Mills just referred to," Hunter said, but cautioned that it must first seek the opinion of its counterparts on the House Committee on Public Buildings and Grounds.[21]

Hunter also submitted Mills's drawings and the brief that accompanied them. These were dated May 1 and addressed to Davis. The wings, Mills said, would be stand-alone buildings 100 feet long and 200 feet wide, east to west. Each wing would be separated from the original Capitol by a "*spacious* court," so that the north and south ends of the central building would continue to receive their own light and ventilation.

The new Senate chamber would be bigger than the current chamber (increasing the diameter from 75 feet to 90 feet), would have a flatter ceiling to improve the acoustics, and would "accommodate 100 senators at their separate desks." The public would be able to enter the chamber from the east and west sides of the building, while the North Portico would be for senators only. The new House chamber, like the Senate, would have a 45-foot ceiling. Its diameter of 100 feet would ensure ample space, "capable of containing with comfort 300 members."[22]

Finally, Mills suggested, he would build a new and larger central dome to provide symmetry for the elongated Capitol. The dome "assumes the architectural character of that crowning St. Peter's Church, at Rome; St. Paul's, London; the church of the Invalids, Paris; and other like buildings." Here again, as in Mills's initial wings proposal in February, was another radical and potentially transformational proposal. The Topographical Engineers in 1843 had noted that their wings design, in addition to providing more room for lawmakers, would also have the felicitous consequence of making Bulfinch's grotesque dome look as though it belonged there. Mills was taking a giant step beyond that. Build his wings, he suggested, and the too-big Bulfinch dome would suddenly become too small. The new dome Mills now proposed would be 70 feet taller than the Bulfinch dome.[23]

He offered two estimates for the cost of the wings, depending on their size: $1,109,500 for wings measuring 240 feet by 100 feet, with another $380,000 for the dome; or $1,024,000 for wings 100 feet long by 200 feet wide, plus a new dome for $330,000.[24] Hunter, of course, went for the low end and left the dome—presumably—to be debated at a later date. He deposited his report unobtrusively into the Senate record, without discussion, conscious, perhaps, that the proposal faced an uphill struggle. The senators already had a relatively nice place to meet and a dedicated, fawning audience to watch them.

When Robert Mills awoke on the sweltering morning of July 4, 1850, he probably felt quite cheerful and optimistic. His Capitol Extension had received the endorsement of the Senate Committee on Public Buildings, the first time any of his comprehensive Capitol designs had made it that far. Furthermore, Senator Hunter had graciously inserted his name into the congressional record as the designer, an encomium that, if the Capitol Extension moved forward—and it might—would presumably give Mills the inside track on becoming the architect who built it. If that happened, his name would live in posterity as the man who designed—at either end of the Mall—the two buildings that defined Washington, D.C. The Masons had broken ground for the Washington Monument two years earlier, and the stubby beginnings of Mills's obelisk could easily be espied from the Capitol's West Front.

July 4 was the date of the Washington Monument Society's annual fund-raiser. After a spirited beginning, the flow of funds was starting to dwindle, but the event still drew a big crowd and a great many important people, including the president of the United States.

It was not a particularly good time for Zachary Taylor. He remained at loggerheads with Clay and virtually all of Congress's southern Whigs. Not only did he refuse to back off his demand that California be admitted to the union as a free state, but he continued to encourage officials in

New Mexico to draw up a free-state constitution and to assume that they would get a big chunk of Texas to augment the territory allotted to them in the Mexican Cession. This last part had enraged Texas, which had sent militia to the border. Taylor remained unmoved. On July 3, he had asked his secretary of war to order federal troops in New Mexico to resist any attempt to take over the disputed territory. The secretary tried unsuccessfully to get the president to change his mind, then told Taylor that he could never sign such an order. "Then I will sign it myself," Taylor said.[25]

The Monument fund-raiser began in the early afternoon and lasted for three hours. The journalist Benjamin Perley Poore said Taylor was there for all of it—what he called a "long, spread-eagle address by Senator Foote" followed by a "tedious supplementary harangue by George Washington Parke Custis," a descendant of the first president. One can only imagine the discomfort: blazing sun on a typical July day in Washington, the ceremony suffused by swamp gas from the fetid Mall ponds, with three hours of dreary speeches to endure. During this ordeal, Poore said, Taylor "drank freely of ice-water," then walked back to the White House, ate a basket of cherries, and drank several glasses of cold milk.[26] Taylor's biographer Holman Hamilton cites other accounts that say he may have eaten cucumbers, cabbage, or bread. Whatever he ate, it did not agree with him. That night he had cramps, and five days later he was dead.[27] Davis and Varina were with him at the end. According to Varina, Taylor's last words "were to Jeff . . . 'Apply the Constitution to the measure, Sir, regardless of consequences.' "[28] It was an anticlimactic finish for an unusual man at a key moment in U.S. history. Taylor would probably never have accepted Clay's package of legislation, but his death suddenly made a compromise possible.

On July 22, 1850, the Hunter report reached the House floor, along with an invitation to join the Senate in a joint committee to study plans to improve the Capitol. Representative John W. Houston, a Delaware Whig, introduced a resolution to convene the committee. What followed, recorded by official reporters from the *Congressional Globe*, was almost Dickensian. The reporters had recently begun using shorthand to transcribe the proceedings in both houses of Congress. The system worked almost flawlessly in the Senate, and by 1850 the *Globe* was producing verbatim transcripts of the debates there. The House, however, with its terrible acoustics, was a different story.

As soon as Houston offered his resolution, Illinois Democrat Samuel A. Richardson stood up "and said a few words which it was not possible to hear," the reporter wrote, paraphrasing the proceedings, "but which were understood to be in opposition to the resolution, and in general protest against these great projects for the improvements of the Capitol. He was opposed to the whole matter."

Houston pointed out that no money would change hands and no contracts would be let. The committee would simply meet for a discussion. Richardson was unswayed. Should the House consort with the Senate on this, the reporter wrote, still paraphrasing Richardson, "appropriations would be made for the construction of these buildings. And this was about all the House would know about the matter."[29]

Then South Carolina Democrat Joseph A. Woodward spoke. The House was horrible, the reporter paraphrased: "It was impossible for members to debate—it was impossible for them even to practice good manners here, because a member was not going to sit silent whilst another member was speaking, when he could not hear." The chamber was "an unmannerly Hall," and "order never could be maintained in it. Look at it! . . . It was not a Hall—it was a cavern—a mammoth cave, in which men might speak in all parts, and be understood in none." Woodward, for one, was willing to construct a new building, "even if the cost were five millions of dollars." The House was demoralized, the reporter paraphrased, "and the habit and bearing of the members would be improved if they had a Hall in which it was possible to hear." How could the House "hesitate a moment"? Woodward asked. "Men could not even keep their tempers here. They were obliged to get into a passion in order to speak loud enough to be heard at all. And hence it was that . . . debate which was in the worst taste was that which generally engaged attention."

Democratic representative Hugh White of New York was then recognized. Apparently having other things on his mind, he asked Speaker Howell Cobb whether the Senate's invitation could be informally set aside for the moment. To which Woodward replied (not paraphrased), "I cannot hear a word the gentleman says—not one word, sir." Which was followed by a chorus from what the reporter described as "members in other parts of the Hall. '*We* cannot hear a word'" (italics in the original).[30]

White tried again, but Mississippi Democrat Jacob Thompson interrupted him. He understood there was a proposal on the floor for a joint committee: "Is there some object upon which it is proposed to act?" he asked. White persisted, and Cobb finally agreed that the House would take up the resolution the following Monday. Thompson again interrupted, asking for an explanation of the resolution, but Houston refused. He had already explained it, he said, and had nothing to add. Cobb then called for yeas and nays on whether to postpone the discussion.

The motion was defeated. Debate continued in much the same vein. Finally Kentucky Democrat Richard H. Stanton, chairman of the House Committee on Public Buildings and Grounds and an important player in the Capitol debate, stood up for the last word. He endorsed the joint committee, and furthermore, he told Cobb, if it came to money, he sided with Woodward.

"This chamber was unfit for the purpose for which it had been built," the reporter paraphrased. "If for the purpose of hearing, he went into the area in front of the Clerk's table, the Speaker, as it was his duty to do, called him to order. If he advanced a few paces into the aisle, to hear something . . . there, also, he was called to order." As a result, "he was in ignorance of much that was going on in the Hall," and "it was his constitutional privilege to *hear*, just as much as it was to speak." Cobb then called for a vote on the resolution. It was approved unanimously.[31]

Mills had successfully negotiated his second major hurdle, and it had come surprisingly easily, given past attempts to enact Capitol improvement legislation. Obviously he had touched a nerve. Unlike the Senate, which had only been given an inkling of the Capitol plan so that Hunter and Davis could gauge its chances from behind the scenes, the House had embraced the joint committee with boisterous enthusiasm, shouting down the unfortunate Richardson in a raucous demonstration of exactly why it needed a Capitol Extension. Resentment, it seemed, had finally ripened into resolve. A new House of Representatives chamber was an idea whose time had come.

There also appeared to be progress in the compromise debate. Clouds began to lift immediately after Taylor's death. Fillmore as vice president had chaired the Senate debate for six months. He knew the players, he knew the arguments, and he knew his own mind. As president, he quickly signaled his willingness to support the compromise by appointing Daniel

Webster—a Clay ally—as his secretary of state and de facto congressional liaison. Clay's Omnibus, which had faced near-certain death by presidential veto three weeks earlier, now could become law—if it had the votes.

The package held seven provisions, but they dealt with the same five issues that Clay had brought forward in January: statehood for California; organization of the New Mexico and Utah territories; the Texas boundary; fugitive slaves; and abolition of the Washington slave trade. Opponents of the bill were ideological opposites: southern rights activists, led by Davis, and antislavery northerners, led by New York's William H. Seward and others. They tried with some success to corrupt the Omnibus with nuisance amendments and other delaying tactics, but on July 27, in what turned out to be a test vote, the Omnibus easily survived an attempt to kill it. Success seemed assured.

But four days later, in an effort to clean up the package before the final vote, floor manager James A. Pearce removed objectionable Texas boundary language from it with the intention of reinserting substitute language. Removal went off without trouble, but when Pearce—the same Pearce who had so generously brought Mills's Capitol memorial to the Senate's attention in February—tried to add the new language, he lost the vote. In very short order, the Omnibus fell apart. Without the full package, the legislation lost its cohesion, and supporters, unsure what the final product would look like, stood aside while opponents systematically stripped the bill of its provisions until nothing remained but Utah. Clay, exhausted and apparently defeated, left town for a rest. Davis and Seward were ecstatic.[32] In what amounted to a victory speech, Davis told his Senate colleagues on August 3 that if anyone blamed him for "any portion of the defeat of that bill," he would "feel highly honored." Indeed, he continued, "I glory in defeating it."[33]

But his celebration was premature. If the compromise could not pass as an Omnibus, perhaps it could succeed the hard way: piece by piece. Illinois senator Stephen A. Douglas, chair of the Committee on Territories and a first-term Democrat with only a few months' seniority over Davis, took it on. He was a tiny man—five feet three inches tall—known for his barrel chest and his very big voice. But Douglas was also a skilled, tireless legislator, and he had done his homework. By assembling sectional blocs of votes for each provision of the bill and working with his House counterparts, he hoped to find majorities to pass each provision of the compromise.

And he did. Davis was unremittingly contentious and nasty, picking fights and wasting time to slow the wheels of debate. Nevertheless, the compromise moved inexorably forward. Tension began to seep out of Congress, and Washington finally began to relax. "The whole difficulty is considered at an end, and a better and more fraternal feeling prevails," *The New York Herald* reported in early September.[34] Crittenden, Davis's longtime friend and Fillmore's attorney general, "waded through mud and a drenching rain" to congratulate Sam Houston: "My heart is lighter than it has been in a year," he said.[35]

House passage of the Texas boundary and California bills in August prompted a prolonged celebration throughout the city on Sunday night, September 8. Fireworks began at dusk. Lights blazed from the Capitol and along Pennsylvania Avenue. Crowds gathered at the National Hotel to hear the Marine Band give an impromptu concert and applaud speeches by Clay, Houston, Webster, Douglas and other heroes. "Everybody seemed delighted," the *New York Tribune* reported.[36] And finally, on September 16 and 17, with passage in the House and Senate of the bill abolishing the Washington, D.C., slave trade, it was over.

On Monday morning, September 16, 1850, with the D.C. vote still to be taken but with success assured, the Senate took a deep breath. There was plenty of bonhomie, but it had been a rough trip, and egos had been rubbed raw. Benton, who had loathed the Omnibus, opened the debate by congratulating himself for having been the first to recognize that the compromise had to be passed in pieces. Results showed "I was right in everything I said." Mississippi's Foote, inventor of the Committee of Thirteen and early proponent of the Omnibus, rose to say, "without egotism," that by combining the bills to "produce a free discussion," he had moved public opinion toward compromise. Douglas, whose contribution needed no amplification, urged an end to bickering and praised the compromise, which he asserted had "removed all causes of sectional discontent, and again united us together as one people."

Then Davis rose, and in short, clipped sentences, coldly dismissed the compromise and the colleagues who praised it so lavishly. "Whilst gentlemen are dividing the honors that result from the passage of these bills, either in a joint or a separate form, I have only to say that, so far as I am concerned, they are welcome to the whole," he said. "I do not represent that public opinion which required the passage of them." When the chair, hearing nothing useful, gaveled all to silence and called for yeas and nays on the D.C. slave trade, the measure passed 33–19. Davis voted nay.[37]

Four days later, senators were still hard at work, but without the drama. The session was coming to an end, and they were wrestling with the pre-recess crush of mundane measures that had languished during the long months of compromise debate, among them the Civil and Diplomatic Appropriations Bill. Davis's amendment for enlargement of the Capitol read as follows:

> For the extension of the Capitol by wings, according to such plans as may be adopted by the joint committee of both houses of Congress, $100,000 for each wing. This appropriation to be expended under the direction of the President of the United States, and he shall be authorized to appoint an architect to carry out the plan or plans which may be adopted as afore-said.[38]

Davis explained that the Committee on Public Buildings had had "this matter for some time under their consideration" and had looked at "various plans of different architects." The amendment, he said, offers "an estimate" that the committee thinks "will approach very nearly the amount required." There was no mention of "exterior" or "interior" costs. He described Mills's wings plan as "perhaps the one which will be adopted."[39]

Davis was not interested in the East Front alternative, and he gave his colleagues no clue that Mills and others had ever had such a design under consideration. He wanted wings, and to get the Senate to go along, he deliberately mush-mouthed the cost estimate. If Mills's May 1 submission was any guide, $200,000 was unlikely to accomplish much more than lay foundations.

Three days later, the amendment came to a vote. This time Hunter, the committee chairman, offered it. He wanted to strike out the word "wings" and substitute "addition." Perhaps he had talked to the House and discovered that Stanton's Committee on Public Buildings and Grounds was less than enthusiastic about wings. Or perhaps Hunter himself was a dissenter. There was no indication—at that point—of friction between Davis and Hunter, but underlings—Davis in this case—ordinarily did not manage

Senate legislation when there were chairmen—Hunter—available. Davis may have stolen a march on Hunter three days earlier. Davis, however, said nothing about the Hunter substitution except to note that there was no need to shift language around. Hunter, he said, could accomplish his object simply by eliminating the words "wing" or "wings."

Discussion of the cost estimate followed, and Davis made his case for a new Capitol that would be adequate for a great nation. If anyone shared his enthusiasm, however, it was not immediately apparent. Michigan's Lewis Cass, the ponderous Democrat who had lost to Taylor in 1848, sounded the final lament: "I know nothing as to the merits of the several plans proposed, but I think this to be the very worst building on the face of the earth for the purposes to which it is devoted, and I have no idea of voting for the erection of another like it."[40] But Cass did not prevail. Davis won a squeaker, 24–21.

A few days later Hunter returned with a new resolution, proposing to dip into the Senate contingency fund to offer a $500 prize to anyone who submitted a plan for the Capitol Extension that was chosen by the Senate and House Public Buildings Committees. This, too, was approved.

And finally, in one of its last acts before adjournment, the House on September 27 brought forward an amendment to its version of the Civil and Diplomatic Appropriations bill asking for $300,000 for a Capitol Extension. It failed to pass, but a scaled-back appropriation for $100,000—there was no mention of wings—was approved, and the Senate adopted the House version.[41] The money, as Davis had to know, was a pittance, but the project would go forward. He had won.

4

THE CONTEST

On October 7, 1850, Washington's *Daily National Intelligencer* printed a public notice at the top of column one on its front page. The Senate Committee on Public Buildings had decided to "invite plans accompanied by estimates" for an Extension of the U.S. Capitol building and to offer a $500 prize for the winning entry.

"The committee do not desire to prescribe any condition that may restrain the free exercise of architectural taste and judgment," the notice continued, but "would prefer" that the new Extension conform to the existing building, "to preserve the general symmetry of the entire structure, when complete." The notice warned that only "one plan can be adopted, but the committee reserve to themselves the right to form such plan by the adoption of parts of different plans submitted, should such a course be found necessary." If that happened, the committee would also divide the prize money among the contestants as it saw fit. Plans should be delivered to the Senate by December 1, and the entries would be examined by committee members from both houses of Congress. The notice was signed by all three members of the Senate committee: Chairman R.M.T. Hunter of Virginia, Jefferson Davis of Mississippi, and John H. Clarke of Rhode Island.[1]

As with most things Congress did in haste, the contest had flaws. Participants were given just seven weeks to redesign the most important building in the country, and even if someone managed to produce something brilliant, the committee guaranteed nothing. The prize was an insult, and the winning design would undoubtedly end up as an amalgam of entries. But the committee held all the trumps. For an architect, this was the most prestigious job in the country. Whoever made the final design and built the Capitol Extension would secure his reputation for all time. No sooner did the public notice appear than architects began pilgrimages to Washington, not only to see the building and assess the job, but also to line up political patrons and get them to make introductions and write letters on their behalf.

The most important person at the outset of the competition was Jefferson Davis. He had written the legislation for the Capitol Extension, and had undoubtedly thought up the contest. He had two goals. First, he wanted a new Capitol with north and south wings. He did not want either of the two talked-about alternatives: an Eastern Extension in which an addition would be grafted onto the east façade of the current Capitol, or a design in which a near-duplicate of the existing Capitol would be placed on the grounds in front of it. His second goal was to control the project.

He had obstacles to overcome. Hunter, in presenting the legislation, had, for whatever reason, opened the possibility that a non-wings design might be chosen. And the legislation had given power of the purse for building the Extension not to Congress but to the president of the United States. To make the contest work for him, Davis needed a certain amount of finesse, a quality which at this point in his political career hardly seemed a strong point. But aside from his reputation as an advocate, he was also an extremely clever bureaucrat, although it was not a skill he routinely displayed. If he could ensure that the winning entry would be a wings plan, then he could bring the design to the joint Senate-House committee, get it approved there, and send it to the White House. The president was neither a southerner nor a Democrat (Millard Fillmore was a Whig from New York) and therefore not someone Davis could cajole or intimidate. But what he could do was hand the president a bipartisan, Congress-endorsed design that Fillmore would be hard-pressed to ignore.

Davis's machinations would not work out. It would take eight months to design a plan for the new Capitol and select an architect to execute it, and Davis would not even be in town when the final decisions were made. Instead, President Fillmore, all but invisible while the Senate contest went forward, would assume control of the project and embrace it with enthusiasm. From the scrum of design contestants, he would choose Thomas Ustick Walter, a talented and successful onetime bricklayer and stonemason from Philadelphia, as his architect. Walter, ironically, would never produce a design of his own that Davis or Fillmore would accept. And Davis, although he had no role in the final result and no particular affinity for Walter, would, ironically, end up getting most of what he wanted.

Thomas U. Walter, at forty-six, was in the prime of his career. By his own estimate he had built "about 300 houses," nearly four dozen churches, nine banks, six prisons, four colleges, and sundry other buildings—some four hundred jobs in all. He had made his mark nationally before he turned thirty, winning an 1833 competition to design Philadelphia's Girard College for Orphans, a project he completed in 1847. The son of a bricklayer, Walter apprenticed with his father for seven years and partnered with him for two more years while he studied draftsmanship, painting, mathematics, and physics at the Drawing School of the Franklin Institute. He then joined William Strickland, one of Philadelphia's leading architects, as a draftsman before opening his own office in 1831. Strickland was one of the losers in the Girard competition.[2]

The architect Thomas Ustick Walter was at the top of his profession when President Fillmore hired him to design and build the new United States Capitol in 1851. Prodigiously gifted as an artist and draftsman, he was also skilled at cultivating the rich and powerful, a talent that served him well in Washington. (Architect of the Capitol)

Walter was a hardheaded, fire-eating Baptist who had made a fortune in the 1830s, lost it in the Panic of 1837, and recouped it by the early 1840s. He had married in his early twenties, been widowed in 1847, and remarried a year later.[3] He had fathered nine children by his first wife, of whom one had died, and had an infant daughter with his second wife, Amanda. He was a tall, "striking" man with "a large frame" and a formidable shock of thick, wavy white hair.[4] And despite his modest background, he was intelligent and well-spoken, easy to like and easy to befriend. He wrote well and drew exquisitely. His knowledge of national politics was superficial, but his ability to negotiate the Washington bureaucracy would turn out to be exceptional.

And he was a Whig. Walter arrived in Washington on September 28, 1850, for what would turn out to be the first of thirteen visits over the next eight months. His initial purpose was not entirely clear. Certainly he must have known about the pending Capitol Extension, but the final version of the legislation had not yet been approved by both Houses.

Most likely, Walter's primary objective was to meet Daniel Webster, Fillmore's secretary of state. Walter had spent several months in Venezuela in 1843 designing the harbor of La Guaira, the port city of Caracas, Venezuela, and had not been paid in full. He had been urging secretaries of state to press his case with the Venezuelan government ever since, and he would continue to do so—without success—for the rest of his life. Walter's contact in Washington was Whig congressman Joseph R. Chandler, a fellow Philadelphian, a board member of Girard College, and a longtime friend.[5]

Chandler took Walter to visit Webster, and apparently he made a good impression. On October 1, with Congress adjourned, Walter briefly returned to Washington. Three days later in his diary he noted that he had made "elevations of the Capitol," apparently intending to submit a contest design. But these brief entries also suggested that he was working simultaneously on about a dozen different projects, of which the Capitol was only one.[6]

That changed on October 17. Walter took an overnight train from Philadelphia, breakfasted in Baltimore, arrived in Washington, and went straight to the State Department to confer with Webster once again, probably regarding La Guaira. He spent the rest of the day at the Capitol, measuring and assessing it "in reference to the additions to the wings." He left that evening.

From that point until late November he worked on the Capitol drawings virtually to the exclusion of all else, every day except Sundays until he had completed his designs. Like many of the contestants, he planned to submit entries for both an Eastern Extension and north-south wings.[7]

When the contest began, Robert Mills appeared to have a head start on Walter and everyone else. But while his wings plan was the one Jefferson Davis had described on the Senate floor as "perhaps" the design that would be adopted, Mills was anything but overconfident. He also had disadvantages. He was a Democrat, and Fillmore, a Whig, was going to pick the winning plan and ultimately choose the architect. He was old—sixty-nine in early 1851—and might not live to finish the project. And Mills was familiar around town, which may not have been a good thing. Nobody remembered the Treasury Building or the General Post Office, and the Washington Monument was now notorious for having killed President Taylor. And finally, he probably suspected that his supposedly cozy relationship with fellow Democrat Davis might be an illusion.

Nothing, however, suggested that Walter had any more of an inside track than his competitors. Every one of more than a dozen contestants was a seasoned professional, and all of them had hedged their bets by submitting more than one design. Walter's principal drawing was an Eastern Extension that would be attached to the existing building. A new Eastern façade would keep Bulfinch's neoclassical motif, with the same sweeping staircase to the second floor. An indoor colonnade would connect the new front to the old building, and new House and Senate chambers would be placed in the new building on either side of the colonnade. Under this scheme the Capitol would become an immense square, with Bulfinch's library protruding from an unchanged Western Front.[8]

Mills prepared a wings plan that offered a slight variation on the design he had made for Davis. He also submitted a pair of duplicate Capitol plans. In each case the second Capitol was placed 300 feet east of the existing building. One design offered a 160-foot-wide link between the two façades, with the new Library placed inside. The second proposed a courtyard between the two with a 200-foot monument to the American Revolution marking the center.[9]

Other contestants were equally prolific, if not more so. William Elliot, another Washington architect, prepared twelve drawings, including several duplicate Capitols. Charles Anderson, of New York, presented a wings design with the wings projecting eastward to embrace the entire east plaza and create a forecourt in front of the East façade.[10]

Walter returned to Washington on November 22 and checked into the National Hotel on Pennsylvania Avenue, about midway between the Capitol and the White House. The next day he went with the Senate sergeant-at-arms, Robert Beale, to visit the executive mansion and began writing a rough draft of the long contest entry letter that would accompany his designs. On November 25, he returned to the White House, where he met Fillmore and the mayor of Washington, D.C.

Walter spent most of the next five days probably in much the same manner as his competitors—working vigorously on his presentation with occasional breaks to massage existing political contacts, make new friends, and present himself to official Washington as a cultured, confident professional. Walter's diary shows another meeting with Webster, an introduction to the Smithsonian Institution secretary, Joseph Henry, and "interviews with several members of Congress." On November 30, the day before the deadline, he delivered his entry package to the Capitol.[11] His chaperone and facilitator during this prolonged trip appears to have been Beale, a Virginian whose connection to Walter was not clear but who may have helped him gain the ear of Senator Hunter, also a Virginian and the person who was, at least nominally, running the contest.

Walter did not know it, but Hunter and Davis were at odds. The first hint of disagreement had arisen in September when Davis, apparently in Hunter's absence, had introduced the Capitol appropriation as if a wings design were a foregone conclusion. Hunter three days later took over floor leadership, eliminated any reference to the manner of enlargement in the proposal, and got it passed. The initial conclusion to be drawn from this byplay was that Hunter, facing an extremely tight vote, wanted to make the proposal as nonprescriptive and noncontroversial as possible, thereby broadening support not only in the Senate but also in the House.

But in three undated letters from Robert Mills, at least two of which were probably written between congressional adjournment and the end of 1850, it was clear that Hunter favored the Eastern Extension and was trying to put the brakes on Davis's two-wing proposal even as Davis was working to make it a fait accompli.

The first letter was Mills's attempt to convince Hunter to support an Eastern Extension. It was probably sent after Davis had asked Mills in early April 1850 to produce a wings design. At that time Mills probably understood that Davis fully intended to move ahead on a Capitol Extension and wanted to be on record with Hunter as favoring the Eastern Front. His favorite option, as he described it in the letter, was the Greek Cross plan he had first presented in 1846.

A wings design had many disadvantages, he told Hunter. The wings would "necessarily close all the windows opening on the north and south ends of the Capitol," and no one would be able to get to the new House chamber from the Rotunda except by walking through the Library, which would move to the old House chamber. A wings plan would also place the House and Senate so far apart that lawmakers would have almost no communication. Finally, construction would be a terrible nuisance for members of both Houses, and the whole job was expensive—$592,497.72. The Eastern Extension, by contrast, "possesses none of the objections" of the wings plan, Mills concluded. No windows would be obscured, the Senate would move to the West Front, displacing the Library, and the whole design could be built for $480,000.[12]

Mills sent his second letter to Davis, probably written close to the December 1 deadline for contest submissions, or even a bit later. Here Mills shifted emphasis to the duplicate Capitol. Perhaps uncertain of his reception from Davis, Mills fell into his old habits of being mealymouthed and didactic by turns. "Permit me to point out to you some of the *advantages* of the plan I have submitted for the Extension of the Capitol *East*" (emphasis in the original). Much of what he said was the same as what he had told Hunter: with an Eastern Extension there would be no noise, no blocking the carriage entrances with equipment, no long walks to get from one chamber to the other, and no "disturbing the deliberations of Congress." Also, the duplicate building, Mills asserted, would be placed on the spot where Washington originally intended to build the Capitol. At that time, the site had been too low, but over time the extra ground had been "made," presumably by gardeners, and the new building could easily be placed on the same level as the existing building. The cost of an Eastern Extension would be about the same as for wings, and if the new building were constructed of marble, the difference between it and the sandstone in the existing Capitol would not be as noticeable as it would be if new wings were attached to the old. Finally, he said, if the Capitol once again proved too small in the future, the space between the two buildings could be filled in to create "one grand and perfect design."[13]

This letter probably doomed Robert Mills. In it, he had made two catastrophic mistakes. He had first assumed that Davis would be impressed with his experience and knowledge of the Capitol's architectural history. But Davis had never been impressed with experience or age, by themselves, and he hated to be lectured by anyone.

Mills's second mistake was to believe that Davis had an open mind. Once Davis had asked Mills in April 1850 for a wings design, he had given no thought whatsoever to an Eastern Extension. He wanted wings. He did not care how much they cost, did not care how far apart the chambers were, did not care about the noise, did not care about the clutter, and did not care whether the north and south side windows were closed off. Davis was neither a flexible nor an adaptable man. He was an advocate, not a negotiator. Mills's arguments were beside the point.

Mills, however, thought he had done the right thing. In a third letter that he must have written to Hunter immediately after sending his note to Davis, Mills told the chairman that he had enumerated the advantages of the Eastern Extension, "as you propose," an indication that Hunter, with Mills as an ally, was openly in opposition to a wings plan. "I hope that Col. Davis will agree with you in giving this sanction to the [Eastern] Extension," he added.[14]

This was Mills's third, and worst, mistake. He had assumed that Senator Hunter was in charge, and so had sought Hunter as his chief ally. He also told Hunter that he had spoken with Stanton, chair of the House Committee on Public Buildings and Grounds, and believed Stanton would favor the Eastern Extension.[15] He undoubtedly thought that the two chairmen would ultimately gang up on Davis and make him come around.

That, of course, would never happen. It was Davis who had pushed the Capitol Extension in the first place, Davis who had introduced the appropriation, and Davis who had described a wings plan—Mills's wings plan—for the congressional record. Hunter had been trying to catch up for months, but it was Davis who still led the parade. Mills was right about Stanton's favoring an Eastern Extension, but wrong about Hunter's being the most important man in the Senate.

———

Walter stayed in Washington until December 4. He attended the opening of Congress on December 2, saw Henry a second time, had two meetings with Hunter, and visited the White House to see Fillmore and meet Treasury Secretary Thomas Corwin.[16] On December 3, the joint committee put all the contest entries—plans, drawings, and models—on display in the Library of Congress, where lawmakers and the public could examine them.

Walter, along with his competitors, would certainly have participated in all these events. But what set him apart from the other contestants was that he alone at this early date was lobbying his design not only with senators and House members, but also with Fillmore and his cabinet—especially Webster and Corwin. Mills had gotten in touch with Corwin, but he was interested primarily in gaining intelligence about what the Senate committee thought of his design. Walter, by contrast, from the very beginning of his Washington trips, had set out directly to cultivate the administration. This decision would turn out to be critical—perhaps even definitive—as the struggle to win the Capitol Extension job intensified in the coming months.

It is not clear from the available evidence whether Walter's strategy developed by chance or by design. It may simply have arisen from his relationship with Chandler and other prominent Whigs. It may have been because he had charmed Webster during their conversations about La Guaira. Or he may in fact have consciously realized that since the final decision on the Capitol Extension was Fillmore's, he should begin planning early for the endgame. Unlike Mills, Elliot, Cluskey, and others, he was not a Washingtonian and thus was probably less impressed by the aura of Congress—and the power of the Senate Democrats. Although Fillmore was an accidental president, he was nonetheless the president.

For most of the next two months, beginning in December 1850, the Senate and House public buildings committees examined contest entries, seeking consensus on the best design. Contemporary accounts describe a tedious, nerve-racking process that yielded no agreement in either chamber, let alone in the joint committee. Architects, to judge from Walter's experience, made frequent visits to Congress to explain their work, provide extra plans and designs, and visit with Capitol Hill power brokers. Diary entries show that Walter spent ten days in Washington, from December 11 to December 21, ostensibly to submit a perspective drawing of his plan to the two committees. On Friday evening,

December 13, he had dinner at Beale's house with Stanton, chair of the House committee, then met Stanton at the Library the following day to look at the design exhibits and to visit with Hunter, and, apparently for the first time, Davis. The two senators asked him to have his proposal printed up, which he did, and he delivered it to both committees on Monday, December 16, while he was making the rounds of Congress to press his case. This continued for three more days. On December 19 he met with the joint committee, and finally, after one more day of interviews, he went home.[17]

With the arrival of the new year, the committees began meeting "two or three times weekly" with the architects, but still could decide nothing. Charles Cluskey, one of the contenders, said no more than three members of the joint committee—composed of three senators and five House members—could agree on any plan.[18] In late January 1851, a briefing letter sent to Fillmore and signed simply "Washington" confirmed that the majority of the Senate committee favored a wings design, while most of the House committee members favored an Eastern Extension.[19]

Not surprisingly, the Senate contest ended in a muddle. The prize money was shared among five architects: William P. Elliot and Philip Harry got $125 each; Mills and Charles F. Anderson won $100 each; and Thomas McCleland, another local architect, won $50.[20] Walter received nothing, which came as no surprise. He had focused on the Eastern Extension, and Davis, a wings zealot, was overseeing the contest. By January 30, when the Smithsonian's Joseph Henry was invited by the Senate committee to take a look at the designs, there was nothing in play other than wings plans.[21]

On February 8, 1851, Davis issued a report outlining the committee's findings. After "exhaustive study and patient investigation," it said, the members had decided "to recommend the addition of wings, attached to the north and south ends of the Capitol, and placed at right angles to its axis." There were several reasons for this choice, but better hearing, speaking, ventilation, heating, and lighting were "paramount to all others." The committee also wanted to preserve the integrity of the original building, whose position had been "rendered sacred" by having been chosen by President Washington. New wings would create a forecourt on the Eastern Front, thus balancing the protruding center on the west side, where

Bulfinch had built the Library. The dome would then be restored to the Capitol's geographical center, as Washington intended. Finally, the report estimated the project would cost $1,291,000, less than "one-half the sum which would be required for the plan of duplicating the Capitol." The report included a plan for the proposed new Capitol, "combined from various sources, especially from the drawings submitted to the committee according to invitation publicly given." The design had been drafted by Robert Mills, "the architect in the employment of the government."

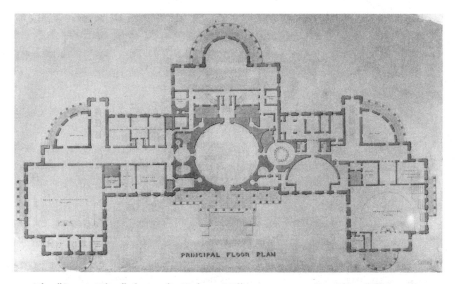

PRINCIPAL FLOOR PLAN

The "Senate Plan," drawn by Robert Mills, was sent to President Fillmore in early 1851 by Jefferson Davis, who hoped it would be used as the basis for the enlargement, or "Extension," of the Capitol. Like Davis, Fillmore favored new Senate and House wings on the north and south ends of the original building, but he wanted them detached and did not want the new chambers to be placed on the East Front. (Architect of the Capitol)

The report was signed by Davis and by Senator John H. Clarke, a Whig from Rhode Island, but not by Hunter. It was dated February 7, 1851.[22]

The report was a remarkable exercise in brass. It had been endorsed by two members of the Senate Committee on Public Buildings over the opposition of the committee chairman, while the House committee had apparently rejected it out of hand. Davis neglected to mention these unpleasant details. No individual design had been approved, and the prize money had been diced into insignificance. Four months after Congress had appropriated money for a Capitol Extension, held a contest, and picked its winners, there was no consensus, no architect, and no plan except for a notional drawing that had the approval of two senators. This was not a ringing bicameral, bipartisan endorsement.

On February 9, Davis sent Mills's composite to Fillmore along with the letter that Mills had written to Davis describing it.[23] Davis's accompanying note was short: "In communicating thus a paper directed to myself I offer as an apology the imperfections of the report of the committee," he wrote. "The plan submitted is little more than a suggestion, which a competent architect could fashion and execute."[24] This transparent slight made Davis's wishes quite clear: he wanted Mills's composite, but he did not want Mills to build it.

Davis did not know that Fillmore was himself inclined toward a wings design. He also did not know, but must have suspected, that Fillmore might be less than impressed with the Senate's non-contest and its non-result. Davis had given Fillmore almost nothing to work with, certainly nothing that he was obliged to consider seriously. If Fillmore cared, he would have to start over.

So he did. In the middle of February, the *Intelligencer* announced that Fillmore had summoned architects to his office for a meeting at noon on Thursday, February 20, to hear what they had to say about their respective plans. Fillmore had formally taken ownership of the project.

The meeting must have been quite an event. Cluskey, in a report written ten years later, said the architects were at the White House for "nearly four hours," while Walter in his diary said it lasted even longer.[25] A half-dozen architects attended, including all the heavyweights: Cluskey, Walter, Mills, Anderson, and Elliot. Several cabinet members also attended, along with the mayor of Washington, D.C., and "other citizens of judgment and taste."[26] Neither Cluskey nor any of the other contestants other than Walter appeared to have anything more than a passing acquaintance with Fillmore.[27] Walter, by contrast, had spent several days in mid-February working for the Treasury Department on a design for the San Francisco customs house and, accompanied by Representative Chandler, had gone to visit Fillmore once more on February 12, only eight days before the architects met with Fillmore at the White House.[28]

The president opened the meeting by telling the architects what they probably already knew. Notwithstanding the Davis report, the joint committee had failed to agree on a Capitol enlargement plan, and Fillmore wanted to hear what the architects had to say. In effect, a second contest was beginning, albeit without the fanfare of the first.[29]

"Each architect explained the peculiar features and advantages of his own design," Cluskey wrote later, "and throughout, they questioned each other on whatever was considered by any of them a defect in the plan under consideration." The tension among the participants, most of whom had known each other long enough to have developed years' worth of grudges and professional jealousies, can only be imagined. Walter brought forth his Eastern Extension plan, Cluskey said, but it was "rejected by the President." At the end of the session, Fillmore made no decision but asked the leading architects to stake out their plans at the Capitol itself so he could at least imagine how each one would fill the space. Cluskey said he, Mills, Elliot, and Anderson did so the following day.[30]

Cluskey's implication was that Fillmore had already eliminated Walter from the competition, but this was not the case. The day after the meeting, Walter staked out the shape of his Eastern Extension and went home to Philadelphia to work on the San Francisco customs house. Before leaving, however, he wrote a short note to Fillmore apologizing for not being able to show him the plan personally but advising him that "I have left the matter with Mr. Stanton, as it seems to be most appropriate that the chairman of the committee who have approved the plan, should explain its location."[31] In three months, Walter had apparently managed to develop a close enough relationship to Fillmore so that the president would not be offended in having Stanton greet him at the Capitol. And Stanton, chair of the House Committee on Public Buildings and Grounds, was hardly a nobody. That Walter knew Stanton well enough to ask him to serve as a stand-in would have told Fillmore a lot about Walter's stature in Congress.

The February 20 meeting had resolved nothing, but it had categorically shifted the focus of the Capitol project away from Congress and over to the White House. Perhaps seeking to strike a congressional balance, Fillmore summoned the House committee to outline its position.[32] This meeting took place in March, after which Stanton, the committee chairman, submitted a long letter to the editor of the *Intelligencer* describing the House's deliberations and the committee's decision to back the Eastern Extension. In virtually every respect the letter served as a counterweight to the Davis report, probably deliberately so. If Fillmore told Stanton that he would not approve an Eastern Extension, Stanton might simply have wished to put the House committee's thoughts on the historical record, making its case as publicly and loudly as possible. But if Fillmore was reconsidering, the letter unequivocally endorsed Walter's Eastern Extension as the House's preferred design and Walter, "a gentleman of great practical experience," as its preferred architect.[33]

Whatever Stanton's intention, the letter effectively put Walter on at least an equal footing with his prizewinning rivals, and perhaps moved him ahead of them. Walter was now squarely positioned in the spotlight for the next phase of the Capitol contest.

After the February 20 meeting, the architects shifted their attention to the White House, realizing belatedly that Fillmore was in charge. Mills on February 26 prevailed upon the Whig congressman John L. Taylor of Ohio to write the president "in my favor in relation to the appointment of Architect for the Capitol," noting, perhaps unnecessarily, that "the Senate Committee have accepted my plan."[34] Less innocuous was Charles Anderson's pompous March 14, 1851, advisory on why he was the best available architect: "Permit me to remark without presuming to dictate," Anderson said, "that to do justice to the Capitol it must be treated as a Roman structure," but "none of my competitors seem aware of the difference between Greek and Roman architecture."[35] As for Walter, his diary was silent on Capitol developments for nearly a month until March 19, when he took an overnight train from Philadelphia to Washington. He visited the Treasury Department the morning of March 20, probably to talk about the San Francisco customs house. Then he went to the White House for a noon meeting. The Pennsylvania congressman Henry D. Moore had advised Fillmore that Walter wished to see him, and Walter ended up conferring with Fillmore for two and a half hours about modifications to the Capitol design. He returned to Philadelphia the next day.[36]

This meeting appears to have been crucial, perhaps decisive. Moore's note suggests that Walter had sought the appointment, perhaps to present his Eastern Extension once again. It was also possible, however, that Fillmore had summoned Walter to enlist him as a consultant on how to choose the best wings extension. Beginning in March, Cluskey said much later, Walter was filling this advisory role. "The architects . . . were called together several times to examine plans," Cluskey said. At each of these meetings, Walter presented "new compilations or modifications of the plans" of the others, "evidently under the advice and direction of the president."[37] There was no evidence that Fillmore offered Walter the job on March 20, but Walter clearly had replaced Mills as the "house man," for he was now the one making the composites.

In Philadelphia he finished his design for the customs house, then, taking little more than a week, he produced Capitol designs for an Eastern Extension, a north-south wings design, and a north-south-east Extension, with estimates for all three. On April 7, he sent a letter to Fillmore apologizing for not finishing earlier. His infant daughter, Irene, he said, had "taken suddenly ill just after my return to Philadelphia and we have been under the most fearful apprehension . . . for many days."[38]

On Friday, April 11, with his daughter apparently improving, Walter brought his drawings to Washington, arriving late in the day. He delivered the customs house plans to the Treasury Department on Saturday, billing the government $250, then handed over the composites to Colonel Abert of the Topographical Engineers, the custodian of the Capitol plans. Then he got a telegram from Philadelphia saying that Irene was "much worse." He left for Philadelphia that night.[39]

The pace was intensifying as expectations began to rise that Fillmore would soon make a decision. The president, at least publicly, had remained noncommittal, and architects continued to send proposals, sketches, models, and designs and to ask for appointments.[40] Fillmore apparently called an architects' meeting the week after Walter's sudden departure and gave them Walter's drawings to study. According to Cluskey, these efforts, regardless of whether Walter was there to defend them, "on being examined by his competitors and their defects pointed out," were rejected as "manifestly inferior to the originals from which they were taken."[41]

After ten days in Philadelphia, Walter wrote in his diary that Irene was "improving," and again traveled to Washington. He stayed for four days and met with several architects.[42] This may have given him an inkling of what the competition was saying behind his back, because his friend the Philadelphia congressman Joseph Chandler on April 23 sent Fillmore a testimonial. He suspected that Fillmore was getting ready to appoint an architect for the Capitol and recommended Walter, whom he had known for twenty-four years. "I can with truth, and, I hope, with proximity, say that he is eminently skilled in his profession. An upright man, reliable in company, esteemed for the excellency of his private character."[43]

Walter was in town when Fillmore got this letter, but again he had to leave because of Irene. His diary entry from Philadelphia for April 27 said simply: "My daughter Irene departed this life at ½ past 8 o'clock aged 1 year and 8 months."[44]

But even then there was no respite. On April 29, the day of Irene's burial, Fillmore announced that he and his cabinet would inspect the drawings at the Capitol on May 1. Walter, his wife, Amanda, and his daughter Olivia arrived on April 30. Walter called on Fillmore at the White House and stayed for two hours.[45] It was not clear whether he was taking Amanda for a courtesy call or meeting with the president alone to plot Capitol strategy. But after spending two days in Washington, perhaps to show Olivia and Amanda the city, the family returned to Philadelphia, where Walter immediately started working on more drawings.

Once again, Fillmore sat back while chaos swirled around him. On May 2, architect A. B. Young sent a letter to Fillmore asking for his plans to be returned. With only two days' advance notice of the cabinet viewing, he had apparently rushed his designs over to the Capitol half-finished. He told Fillmore he needed to "put on them proper references and explanations to make them more intelligible to those not likely to fully understand them."[46]

But at least Young had had something ready for perusal. Cluskey had missed the showing altogether, he told Fillmore on May 2, because the announcement had not caught up to him until "this morning."[47] Also shut out was Mills, who tried to catch up on May 3, telling Fillmore he had belatedly brought his designs to the Capitol repository and stashed them there on a shelf: "I shall be happy to enter into some explanation of these plans, when the President is at leisure to hear them," he said.[48]

In fact, the free-for-all was drawing to a close. Walter was in Philadelphia working on two sets of plans, both wing designs, and by May 8 he had finished them. The second set, entitled "plan of wings with colonnades as suggested by Mr. Webster," was the one that mattered.[49]

The dilemma resolved by Webster was Fillmore's stipulation that he would not accept a wings plan if the wings closed off the windows at the north and south ends of the existing Capitol. This requirement prohibited the architects from grafting new additions onto the old building.

The alternative was to build detached wings—separate buildings that stood apart from the existing Capitol so that the old buildings continued to enjoy sunshine and fresh air on four sides. The difficulty here was remoteness—lawmakers needing to get from one chamber to the other would have to hike into and out of three buildings. The House's opposition to any wings plan was based in part on the lack of easy access between the two chambers. Detached wings would make it even worse.

But sometime in late spring, perhaps during Walter's May 1 meeting with Fillmore, Secretary of State Webster suggested a fix: Why not construct two covered, all-weather, colonnaded passageways connecting the new wings to the old Capitol? If done properly, this would give lawmakers indoor access to the opposite chamber and leave uncovered most of the north and south façades of the original building.

Walter's newest set of designs now reflected this insight, and he refined the plans through the rest of May. In accordance, once again, with Fillmore's preference, he placed both chambers on the western side of their respective wings so that lawmakers could look out the windows across the broad expanse of the Mall. He put a new Supreme Court on the first floor of the new north wing, below the Senate chamber. Committee rooms were on the third floor. The south wing offered a similar configuration, except that the much larger House chamber and its gallery occupied the entire western half of the second and third floors.

As Walter worked and time passed, his competitors began to realize that the game was over, or nearly so. Young, still completing his own design, asked Fillmore to "delay judgment" until the end of the month.[50] Anderson, in New York, said he, like Cluskey, had failed to get word in time to make the May 1 meeting and was sending his plans by railway express mail.[51]

The Virginia architect Thomas McCleland, however, was through being polite. On May 17, 1851, he wrote to Fillmore, saying he understood that the president had hired Walter to make "an entire new draught of the capitol." McCleland knew what that meant. But McCleland needed a job, and although "I have never for once thought of putting in a claim politically for services rendered," the time had come. He told Fillmore "that I was your firm supporter" from the beginning of the 1848 campaign, "and excuse me for saying that I believe it was mainly [due] to the stand I took in your support that gave you the state of New Jersey, where I resided at the time." McCleland said he would not have mentioned "such things" but "when I see very important structure and buildings put into the hands of really incompetent men that cannot compete with me as a draughtsman, and when I am wanting bread, it becomes necessary for me to do so, and it would be madness if I did not." And besides, he closed, "a very few years ago, Mr. Walters was merely a bricklayer, as you will find by making the inquiry."[52] Fillmore, who spent part of his youth as an indentured servant and taught himself to read in his spare time, probably found this faintly amusing.

On Saturday, May 31, Walter finished his last set of Capitol drawings, and on Monday, June 2, he took the train to Washington and let Fillmore know he had the plans with him. On June 3 he made revisions to the plans in accordance with Fillmore's wishes, and the following day he again met with the president for two hours, showing him five different treatments.[53] On June 9, Fillmore told Walter that he accepted the connecting corridors plan proposed by Webster. Two days later, Walter returned to the White House and spoke with Fillmore and Interior Secretary Alexander H. H. Stuart. Then he telegraphed Amanda: "recd. Commission as Architect of the Capitol." He was sworn in at 3:00 p.m. and left at 5:00 p.m. for Philadelphia.[54] Fillmore had made the politically Solomonic decision. As William C. Allen, former historian for the Architect of the Capitol, has pointed out, the president named the House's architect to execute the Senate's plan.[55] And Walter had made the right political calculation—at least for now. He was Fillmore's man.

On July 4, 1851, President Fillmore, cabinet secretaries, governors, Supreme Court justices, congressmen, senators, diplomats, and a large number of other officials gathered at the Capitol to lay the cornerstone for the Capitol Extension. The grounds "were filled to their utmost capacity," journalist Lawrence Gobright wrote. "The ladies were there in great force, enlivening and adding gaiety to the occasion, together with military companies and civil associations."[56] The Senate chaplain opened the ceremony, and Fillmore laid the hollow granite stone after Thomas U. Walter, the newly named Architect of the U.S. Capitol Extension, placed a jar containing commemorative coins, newspapers, and a statement by Secretary of State Daniel Webster inside it.[57] Webster gave the principal speech, a last great plea for national unity from an aging, ailing giant. The Capitol, he said, now stretched north and south—an additional cord binding the union: "Let it rise—let it rise—let it rise until it meet the sun in its coming."[58]

"Be it known that on this day the Union of the United States of America stands firm," he said. "And all here assembled, whether belonging to public life or to private life, with hearts devoutly thankful to Almighty God for the preservation of the liberty and happiness of the country, unite in sincere and fervent prayers that this deposit and the walls and arches, the domes and towers, the columns and entablatures, now to be erected over it, may endure forever! God save the United States of America!"[59]

Jefferson Davis was probably not in the audience that day. Congress had adjourned in March, and Davis had quickly left town for Mississippi. Had he attended, he would likely have been pleased, and somewhat bemused. He had done his best to force-feed a north-south Capitol Extension to Fillmore, but the president had seen his heavy-handed efforts for what they were: a power play that did not quite come off. So Fillmore showed Davis how it could be done. Davis had used Mills as a stalking horse, then cast him aside, finishing the Senate phase with a plan but no architect. Fillmore used all the architects as stalking horses, picked Walter, and tossed the others aside. Then his architect made the plan. Fillmore now owned the architect and the project.

But not for long. Davis would be back.

5

THOMAS U. WALTER IN CHARGE

On Thursday, June 19, 1851, Thomas U. Walter moved to Washington with his wife, Amanda, and three young daughters, Olivia, Ida, and Agnes, all of them under ten years old. With the death of his baby daughter Irene two months earlier, Walter had nine surviving children. Two grown sons, Robert and Thomas, were trying to make it on their own, with limited success. Horace, the third and youngest son, was a surly teenager about to get thrown out of boarding school. Three married daughters, Mary Ann, Helen, and Debby, were living in or around Philadelphia with husbands and children. Besides his wife and minor children, Walter supported his elderly father and two unmarried sisters, and he sent money to the older children pretty much whenever they asked for it, which was frequently.[1]

Walter's new job—to design and build two wings for the United States Capitol—was a formidable one. At 61,201 square feet, the Capitol was already one of the biggest buildings in the country, if not the biggest. The design approved by President Millard Fillmore would more than double the length of the current Capitol and increase the ground covered by the building to 153,112 square feet, which, as Walter noted in an early report, would be "652 square feet more than *three and a half acres.*"[2] Walter was in charge of all of it: drawing the plans, choosing the materials, assembling the labor force, and supervising construction. He was to be paid $4,500 per year, a considerable sum for the time. With additional income from investments and outside jobs, he intended to live well. So did his family.

As he contemplated his task, Walter was quite likely enthused but not overawed. There was no one in the United States in 1851 with a better résumé. Walter had apprenticed as a stonemason and bricklayer, studied at the Franklin Institute, trained under a leading professional, toured Europe, and run his own successful architectural firm for twenty years.[3] During his career, Walter had done business with most of the leading materials suppliers in the country, and if he needed to consult an expert, he knew where to find one.

The Capitol Extension's architectural and engineering challenges, however, were only half the battle. Walter would be trying to accomplish his task under the supervision and scrutiny of both the president of the United States and all 293 senators and House members in the U.S. Congress. Navigating this obstacle would require intelligence, tact, and Machiavellian political artistry. That Walter would never be able to satisfy everyone was a given. L'Enfant, Latrobe, and even Bulfinch had eventually foundered on this shoal. Now Walter would try to beat the odds.

Walter was fortunate in that he held a presidential appointment, which afforded him considerable protection from congressional whim. The president had hired him, and only the president could fire him. And although Fillmore had not won the presidency on his own, his administration still had more than twenty months to serve when Walter began work. Walter had enough time to succeed.

The design that Walter had drawn, and Fillmore had approved, placed the two new wings on either side of the old Capitol, the Senate wing to the north and the House wing to the south. Walter's original drawing had positioned the two new buildings so that they protruded forward of the old Capitol's East Front. This compensated for the western bulge in the old Capitol that Bulfinch had created in expanding the Library. A new Capitol with eastern protrusions would be aesthetically balanced on a north-south axis.

The disadvantage of this plan was that it would place the chambers on the east side of the new wings, punishing lawmakers with the noise, grit, dust, and bustle from the Capitol's courtyard and main commercial thoroughfare. So Fillmore and his cabinet instead insisted the chambers be placed on the west side of the new wings. They would overlook the Mall, giving Congress a glorious panoramic view.[4] There would be no eastern protrusions, and the east and west fronts of the new wings would line up with those of the old Capitol. The Library bulge would not be balanced.

Also, if the wings slid backward, their western sides would approach the edge of Capitol Hill where the cliff began to fall away into the Mall. Consequently, Walter would need much deeper foundation trenches to reach bedrock on the plunging west side. The two wings would be attached to the old Capitol with the covered connecting corridors that Webster had suggested and Fillmore had stipulated. Neither Walter nor Fillmore had given much thought to the interior. Chambers, committee rooms, offices, and corridors would be clean, elegant, and undecorated, with plenty of pristine white space for paintings should Congress want to commission artwork.

Congress was not in session when Walter began and would not reconvene until December. This gave him almost a whole construction season—spring, summer, and autumn—to get started without congressional scrutiny of his every move. It also gave him a chance to cultivate his executive patrons: Secretary of State Daniel Webster, aging but still formidable; Interior Secretary Alexander H. H. Stuart, Walter's immediate boss; and Fillmore himself, an interested observer and welcome facilitator.

Walter spent his first weekend in the District getting settled, then went to the Capitol at 5:30 a.m. Monday, June 23, put sticks in the ground, and wound them with twine to frame his design, finishing in time to meet with Webster at the State Department at 10:00 a.m.[5] His initial concern was to get ready for the July 4 cornerstone ceremony. Webster was giving the speech.

Walter had brought two of his Philadelphia assistants with him— Edward Clark and Clement West. Both men would serve with Walter for long periods in the coming years, and Clark would eventually succeed him as Architect of the Capitol Extension. Besides this pair, Walter quickly hired August Gottlieb Schoenborn, a young German immigrant trained as a stonemason and draftsman. Schoenborn in time would become Walter's chief assistant, and he would work at the Capitol for fifty-one years until his death in 1902.[6]

Work began in earnest after the ceremony. Walter met with Fillmore and Webster on July 11 and again three days later. His diary shows frequent visits to the White House over the next several months.[7] There were also frequent visits to the Capitol by Stuart and Fillmore, whose keen interest in the project was, according to Schoenborn, unmatched by any of the presidents who succeeded him.[8]

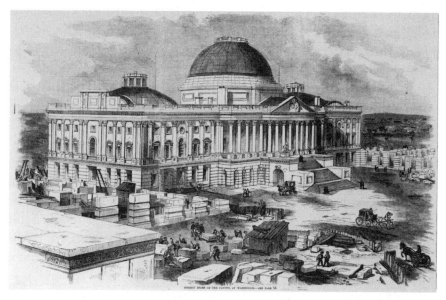

Thomas Walter began construction of the Capitol Extension in midyear 1851. Huge trenches were dug for the foundations, the grounds were churned to mud, and piles of stone, brick, and other materials began to collect in the front yard— conditions that would persist to some degree for well over a decade. (Architect of the Capitol)

Walter needed to make several important choices quickly, and in a long July 29, 1851, letter to Fillmore he outlined some of them. The most sensitive was the composition of his workforce. Should he hire federal employees and pay them himself, or do the job with contractors and let them worry about manpower? Prominent Washington citizens were already lobbying Fillmore to use federal employees working for day wages. This system, known as "day's work," would presumably lead to more local hires. Day's work would be the politically smart way to go.

But Walter was having none of it. He preferred a single contractor, he told Fillmore. Under that system, he explained, the contractor had an interest in hiring the best workers to do the best job in the shortest time. By contrast, federal employees tended toward corner cutting and sloth. "None of the overseers have any direct interest in advancing the work," Walter said. "Nor can they have anything like the pride in its execution that is felt by an honest and ambitious contractor." He also predicted that first-rate artisans of the kind he required would be unlikely "to abandon [their] business[es] for a mere per diem allowance." He was aware that the city fathers were pushing hard for day's work, he told Fillmore, but while their "petition certainly demands a most respectful consideration," he opposed it categorically.[9]

Walter lost the argument. Fillmore took the politically easy path and put the vast majority of Capitol Extension workers—hundreds of men at various times—on day's work. They were free white workers. Walter eventually did bid one large labor contract and several materials contracts, and the contractors may have used slaves to build parts of the Capitol Extension, though the evidence for this is minimal.[10]

Walter's other immediate concern was to choose the stone that would face the new Capitol wings, and on this he and the president agreed. The Aquia sandstone used in the original Capitol was "a weak and friable material, wholly unfit for a public building," he wrote Fillmore in the same July 29 letter, while granite was the wrong color and unsuitable for what Walter planned. "My own judgment," Walter told Fillmore, "is in favor of marble," as "white as can be obtained." Marble, he suggested, would be used for all but the bottom three feet of the building, which would be faced "with light-colored granite."[11] The trick was to find a marble source that could provide a sufficient quantity of stone—both in the specified color and in the proper sizes—to build both wings. Having to switch quarries in midproject courted catastrophe, since no two sources of stone were exactly alike.

When it was written, the July 29 letter may have seemed superfluous, since Walter, still enjoying his Congress-free honeymoon, could do no wrong. The available evidence suggests that he could see Fillmore and Stuart whenever he wanted, and if he did not pay them enough attention, they would seek him out. Momentous decisions—and these were momentous decisions—could probably have been handled more quickly and more simply in conversations with his bosses.

Still, by putting his thoughts on paper, Walter had created a public record that he might need in the future. He had probably learned this skill during bureaucratic battles in his professional past, and he practiced it routinely. This was a wise move, for he would soon learn that political infighting in Washington was more poisonous than anything he had ever experienced.

Even during the Congress-free opening months, Walter was not altogether among friends. The long competition to win the appointment as Capitol architect had left disgruntled losers, and at least three of Walter's rivals—Charles Anderson, Charles Cluskey, and Robert Mills—would eventually charge that Walter had stolen their ideas.[12] And in fact, Walter, at Fillmore's behest, had assembled composite designs from ideas submitted by all the contestants. The architects had known and accepted this condition as a price for entering the competition. To complain about it ex post facto was largely sour grapes. But not entirely. Keeping their names before their friends in Congress or the administration was simply good business. The architects were biding their time, waiting for Walter to run afoul of the administration or mess up the job so they could come to the rescue.

An early and dangerous adversary was William Easby, a wealthy Washington granite contractor and Whig stalwart appointed by Fillmore to the highly coveted and potentially lucrative job of commissioner of public buildings. The commissioner oversaw all the public works in Washington—including the original Capitol—and dispensed patronage accordingly. By virtue of his own presidential appointment, Walter did not have to answer to Easby. At the same time, Easby tended the old Capitol, the White House, the Mall, the Treasury, and all of Washington's other public buildings and grounds. He also supervised the Capitol police. Put simply, the two men were in each other's way.

Trouble with Easby began almost immediately, when Walter, on Fillmore's recommendation, hired Samuel Strong as his construction superintendent. Strong was a New Yorker and a militant Whig with twenty-eight years' experience as a stonemason and construction foreman. Fillmore had met Strong when Strong was building the New York City arsenal. As state comptroller at the time, Fillmore had handled Strong's accounts and had been impressed with his work. In mid-1851, with Walter in immediate need of someone to boss the Capitol Extension project and train its workforce, Fillmore said later, he regarded Strong as "eminently qualified" and "I so advised Mr. Walter." Fillmore had "no doubt" that Walter hired him "on that advice." Strong went to work July 22.[13]

Strong was clearly competent, but he was also a profane, bullying man, which did nothing to smooth relations between Walter's workers and Easby's Capitol employees. These had been less than friendly from the start.[14] Strong had also alienated many of his own employees by pushing them around, playing favorites and undercutting Walter. Very hard-edged, Strong was not the best choice either to handle difficult labor relations or to keep peace with someone as touchy as Easby, with whom he clashed frequently.

Apart from Easby, however, Walter by mid-1851 had handled the politics of the Capitol Extension about as adroitly as was possible. He had won the confidence of the Fillmore administration and had done his due diligence with the Democratic Congress during the Capitol competition. He was particularly close to Kentucky's Richard H. Stanton, chair of the House Committee on Public Buildings and Grounds, and he also had a cordial acquaintance with the Democratic senator Robert M. T. Hunter of Virginia, Stanton's Senate counterpart. He could nurture these relationships once Congress returned in December.

The one politician Walter had not seriously tried to cultivate was Jefferson Davis, the driving force behind the Capitol Extension. This omission would eventually cause Walter considerable anxiety and nearly cost him his job, for Davis did not like Walter, even though he barely knew him. Davis would never articulate the origins of his animosity, and Walter, at this point, had no idea that it existed. Yet it was palpable, and it could only have taken root during the Senate competition and its immediate aftermath. More than likely it was caused by the simple fact that Walter was Stanton's choice for Capitol architect, and Stanton had challenged Davis's preference for a wings extension. Stanton—and, by extension, Walter—could never be forgiven.

Fortunately for Walter, two years would elapse before he felt the full force of Davis's displeasure. When Congress adjourned in mid-March 1851, Davis had gone home to Mississippi, fully expecting to be back in December. His plan for the summer was to meet his Senate colleague and rival Henry S. Foote in a series of debates over who had best represented Mississippi during the recently concluded Clay-Douglas compromise of 1850. This idea had arisen after a brief but nasty Senate spat the previous September, when Davis had denounced the compromise and claimed that Mississippi did not support it. Foote, a leading compromise supporter and unionist, jumped to his own defense and made the opposite claim.[15] The summer debates probably would not resolve the matter, but they would provide rhetorical fireworks and captivating entertainment.

Davis and Foote were the state's two best orators; they held opposing views on almost everything; and they hated each other. The debates, however, never took place. Instead, the two senators would end up in a bigger battle—to see who would become governor of Mississippi.

The 1850 compromise had given unionism a boost in the South generally, and Foote, emboldened by the trend and his role in promoting the compromise, decided to run for governor as a unionist Whig against former governor John A. Quitman, a hard-line states' rights Democrat. Quitman was a miserable campaigner and public speaker, and by late spring his candidacy was in free fall. Davis was the natural choice to replace him. One delegate to the state Democratic Party convention in June found "three out of four voters" preferred Davis over Quitman, and "many said that in a choice between Foote . . . and Quitman, they would vote for Foote."[16]

At the party convention, Democratic stalwarts offered the candidacy to Davis, but he turned it down. When Quitman's campaign subsequently collapsed, forcing him to abandon the race in mid-September, however, Davis was left with no choice. The party needed him, and Davis agreed to run. On September 23, 1851, he resigned his Senate seat.

Davis had little or no desire to become governor of Mississippi. As Varina Davis noted much later in her memoirs, senator was "the office he preferred to all others."[17] The Senate offered the things he relished: national stature, rhetorical combat, and the opportunity to share the stage with the best-known men in the country. Running for governor, strictly as a matter of personal preference, was a political sacrifice.

The gubernatorial campaign did, however, have the unexpected benefit of allowing Davis to stay close to home while he recovered from an unexpected illness that by mid-1851 had left him totally incapacitated and suffering excruciating physical pain. This affliction, a facial neuralgia, would recur several times during his life, causing him weeks of agony and leaving him weakened and exhausted for months. It was an inflammatory condition that infected the cornea of his left eye and caused him great pain along the entire left side of his face. It was accompanied by chronic headaches, general weakness, and an inability to read, endure daylight, or even sleep. The disease may have been an outgrowth of the hardships he had suffered as a young man, either in the army or when he nearly died of the malaria that killed his first wife, Knox.[18] Stress also appeared to increase the chance of an attack.

Davis had campaigned eagerly for Quitman in the late spring, but by the time Democratic leaders sought him out in September, he was lying prostrate in the darkness at Brierfield. For the first three weeks after that he remained at home, orally editing speeches written by others on his behalf and read to him by Varina. By mid-October he felt well enough to travel and joined the campaign, wearing "goggle glasses" to shield his eyes.[19] He was behind by about seven thousand votes when he started, but by all accounts waged a tremendous campaign. He lost by 999 votes. He did not mind that he had failed to become governor. But he hated losing to Foote. He went home to Brierfield, retired from politics, and became a resident landowner. He was forty-three years old.

In Washington, Walter made great progress during the 1851 summer and fall construction season in preparing the foundations for the new wings. He sometimes had more than eight hundred men on the payroll—the largest workforce the project would ever use at one time. Walter had divided the men into two crews, one working primarily on the new Senate building, north of the existing Capitol, and the other working on the House building, on the south side. The bulk of the workers were unskilled ditchdiggers and laborers, but each crew also had contingents of stonemasons, carpenters, ironworkers, teamsters, and machinists. Washington in 1851 was underpopulated, underdeveloped, and virtually devoid of ambitious construction projects and, as Walter had warned, could not supply the requisite craftsmen. Skilled workers were either deliberately imported or simply flowed into the capital when they heard that Walter was hiring.[20]

Samuel Strong, as superintendent of the work, picked the shop foremen and the "sworn measurer," in charge of making sure that the project was getting the materials it paid for and for keeping a written record of deliveries.[21] Walter's $4,500 per year was the highest salary on the project by far. Strong probably earned well under half of that. Skilled artisans, hired on a day's-work basis, earned up to $2.25 per day during this early period, while laborers and watchmen started at $1.00 per day. Foremen, with Strong's approval, could raise wages for deserving workers.[22]

The crews started digging trenches in July, and by late November, Secretary Stuart was able to report to Congress that the work was being "diligently prosecuted" and that the foundations of the two new wings were almost finished.[23] On the east side, laborers dug fifteen feet down before reaching solid ground. On the west side, where the bluffs overlooked the Mall, excavators had to dig through an enormous layer of trash and wreckage that had been cleared away and buried on-site after the British torched the old Capitol in 1814. Cutting through this fill, described as "made ground," as opposed to virgin soil, meant that some of the West Front foundation trenches were forty feet deep.[24] The foundation, constructed primarily from Virginia gneiss, known as bluestone, or blue rock, was 8 feet 9 inches thick at the base of the foundation, tapering to 6 feet 9 inches at ground level.[25] Walter planned to finish laying the foundations of both wings by the end of the year, and to begin erecting the walls during the 1852 season.

Walter took his next big step on September 13, 1851. In another letter to Fillmore, he proposed to seek bids for six contracts: marble, brick, cement, lime, sand, and lumber. There was no reason, he added, to bother at this point with interior flooring, roofs, painting, and decoration. These would be needed later. Since the pending task for 1852 was simply to construct the shells of two buildings, Walter needed only basic materials.

But he had come to another pivotal moment, for the choice of marble for the Extension was as important as any decision he would ever make for the project. "I consider it desirable that all the marble for both buildings should come from the same quarry, so as to insure a uniformity of color," he told Fillmore.[26] Every other contract could be reconsidered and suppliers changed at any time, but the marble—the face that the new Capitol would present to the rest of the world—was forever. Walter had to get it right, and he wanted to take his time choosing it.

He advertised for bids in key newspapers around the country on September 19, and by the 6:00 p.m. deadline on Monday, October 20, he had received 103 offers on the six contracts, all collected in his temporary offices in two vacant committee rooms in the old Capitol. To prevent tampering, both he and Interior Secretary Stuart had stamped the unopened envelopes with their personal wax seals and placed them in Walter's safe. At 10:00 a.m., October 21, in the presence of Stuart and Attorney General John J. Crittenden, Walter opened them.[27]

For most of the contracts for materials, Walter had only three concerns: which bid was low, whether the bidder had a quality product, and whether the bidder could fulfill the contract as promised. He wanted to avoid speculators and jobbers. He knew, for instance, that he needed a steady supply of bricks—millions of bricks—and worried that the winning bidder would be a middleman with no idea how to set up the logistics for an undertaking of such immensity. Finding reliable people was crucial. Luckily, Walter was as well fixed as anyone to choose wisely, for he personally knew most of the country's leading contractors and could easily find out about anyone he did not know.

But the marble was different. Certainly there were issues of quality: it would be necessary to assess hardness, durability, and other properties to ensure that the stone would survive for several lifetimes. And quantity was a crucial question: whether the contractor's quarry held enough marble to build both new wings. These were serious but manageable concerns. Not so easy, however, were the two imponderables: color and appearance. Walter wanted very white, very elegant marble without streaks, and in this he apparently had Fillmore's support. With this as his guiding principle, it was important to Walter only that the best marble be offered, at a price low enough to be competitive with its chief rivals. Having the low bid, by itself, would ultimately mean next to nothing.

Samples accompanied twelve of the marble entries, and Walter put Strong and his stonemasons to work testing the specimens for strength. Then he and Amanda set off on a ten-day trip to visit quarries in Maryland, New York, Pennsylvania, Connecticut, and Massachusetts.[28] No available correspondence suggests why Walter chose these quarries and presumably ignored others, but the logical inference is that he had selected the marbles he liked best from the samples he had received and wanted to narrow the competition from there.

If that was the case, then it is equally likely that he chose his favorite during the trip. His preference, although he did not say so immediately, was for the nearly streak-free, fine-grained white marble of a recently opened quarry in western Massachusetts, near the town of Lee. On his return trip to Washington, he stopped in Philadelphia to visit members of his family, and he also took the opportunity to visit with John Rice, a longtime collaborator and, as would become clear later on, one of Walter's closest friends. Rice, surely not coincidentally, was also a principal in the firm of Rice, Baird & Heebner, the owners of the Lee deposit.

At this point in October, Walter almost certainly had made up his mind, but there is no indication that he either tried to force Fillmore to accept it or promised to get Rice the contract in return for financial considerations. In fact, the quarry trip was only the prelude to a long, detailed, and refreshingly transparent process that by any measurement was above reproach. Walter undoubtedly knew where he wanted to be at the end of the competition, but Rice, Baird & Heebner had to win the contract on their own.

Back in Washington on November 1, Walter submitted his trip report to Interior Secretary Stuart, and two days later, Stuart appointed a blue-ribbon commission to test the different marble specimens for strength, resistance to weathering, and reaction to temperature change. He named Walter to the commission, along with the landscape architect Andrew Jackson Downing, in town to beautify the Mall; the Smithsonian's Joseph Henry; Patent Office Commissioner Thomas Ewbank; and General Joseph G. Totten, commander of the Army Corps of Engineers.[29]

The commission held its first meeting on November 4, and the tests began. For the next seven weeks, working mostly at the Smithsonian, the commissioners froze and thawed samples to see how much water they absorbed and how quickly they weathered under extremes of temperature. They borrowed a metal press with a pressure gauge from the Washington Navy Yard and squashed one-and-a-half-inch cubes of marble until they disintegrated. Finally, they compiled their results in a table, signed an accompanying report on December 22, 1851, and sent these to Stuart. The commissioners gave each of the quarries an overall grade and told the administration they would recommend any of the top four finishers: Provest & Winter, of Washington, D.C., and Baltimore; Masterton-Smith, of East Chester, New York; James G. Wilson, of Hastings-on-Hudson, New York; and Rice, Baird & Heebner, with offices in Philadelphia and the quarry in Lee, Massachusetts.[30]

Very shortly, perhaps within days, Walter dropped Provest & Winter from his list because their quarry did not have enough stone. That left three finalists. Wilson had bid the job for $1,697,069; Masterton-Smith bid $1,008,052; and Rice, Baird & Heebner were low, at $895,365.[31] Walter at this point abandoned impartiality: "I am gratified to find that the marble from Lee . . . is stronger than any . . . marble heretofore used for building purposes, and is only exceeded (and that to a very trifling amount) by the coarse crystal marble of the East Chester quarries," he said in a December 27 letter to Stuart. He also noted that Fillmore and the cabinet had apparently reached a similar conclusion with "much unanimity." As expected, Walter added, the Lee marble's "exceeding beauty" would have made it a contender even if it had not performed well in the commission's tests, but its "performance and ease of workability" made it as attractive as "any marble in the world." The supply is "abundant," he finished; and, of course, Rice, Baird & Heebner had submitted the low bid.[32]

The newly opened Lee, Massachusetts, marble quarry offered a seemingly un-limited supply of the strong white stone preferred by Thomas Walter and Pres-ident Fillmore to bring simple neoclassical elegance to the Capitol Extension. (Architect of the Capitol)

Fillmore, perhaps nudged by Walter, liked the Lee marble, but he wanted to check with the bidders once again. Walter's original solicitation had asked the contractors to submit bids for the whole job—to include not only material and quarrying, but also transportation and finishing. Since then, probably at Walter's behest, the administration had agreed to bid a separate contract—what would become the only non-day's-work la-bor contract in the early part of the project—for finishing. Fillmore therefore wanted new estimates from the marble finalists that reflected this change.

After this second round, Masterton-Smith was high, agreeing to furnish stone at an average price of $1.47 per cubic foot; Rice, Baird & Heebner bid $1.0933, and Wilson bid $0.8167. The increase was of no consequence. Fillmore, the cabinet, and Walter all agreed that the Lee marble was best. Samples were then submitted to Congress, which had been in session for a month, and the members of the House and Senate public buildings committees "unanimously recommended" the Lee marble. The deal was done.[33] On January 13, 1852, Walter wrote to John Rice and John Baird in Philadelphia notifying them of their selection. Under the contract, they would furnish marble for the Extension of the Capitol for a price of $0.65 per cubic foot for all blocks smaller than thirty cubic feet, and $1.98 for anything larger.[34]

By the time it was achieved, however, this victory had already been eclipsed by other matters demanding immediate attention. The most important of these was to find funding to keep the project going, and Walter was slow to identify the need and even slower in meeting it.

The trouble began in mid-December when the Extension's initial $100,000 appropriation ran out. Davis and Stanton had won this piddling stipend more than a year earlier after considerable effort, especially on Davis's part, and all sides had understood at the time that it was little more than earnest money. Walter had managed to dig trenches and begin building foundations with it, but he had to have more cash—lots of it, and quickly—to keep going. And to get money, he needed Congress to vote it.

This appropriation was something the superintendent of the Capitol Extension had to request every year, and virtually every year Congress would use the funding debate as the occasion to criticize the work, make its preferences known, and deliver rebukes to the president for his mistakes. Congress did not control the project, but it controlled the money, and this prerogative made it virtually an equal partner in the enterprise.

Walter either did not understand this process or was not paying attention, but he soon found out that when the money ran out, the work stopped. Immediately. He had no choice but to lay off three hundred

workers because he could not pay them.[35] Many of the discharged workers petitioned their congressmen to be kept on the payroll. And since the
men were federal employees on day's work, the person responsible for
their hardship was Walter. They went to their elected representatives for
help, and their elected representatives went to Walter. Walter's labor woes
became congressional business.

Hoping to avoid a prolonged shutdown, Chairman Stanton, Walter's
ally, introduced a stopgap resolution on December 16, 1851, that would
allow Walter to continue to employ part of his workforce during the winter.[36] Colleagues greeted this initiative with little enthusiasm and no sympathy: "I can never consent to recognize . . . the principle that it is the
primary duty of this government to afford work to anybody," said Democrat Abraham W. Venable of North Carolina. The debate dragged on for
two days, going nowhere, before the resolution was finally tabled and
killed.[37]

Walter's performance during this affair did him no credit. He had to
have known that his funding was nearly exhausted, yet he had apparently
done no lobbying nor made any preparations either to warn the administration or to get Stanton and the Senate working on new money as soon
as Congress reopened on December 1. Instead, he had let his people be
laid off, apparently in the faint hope that Stanton's emergency appeal
would meet with congressional approval. Finally, as far as can be ascertained, he had done nothing to enlist Senate support.

Walter's path got no smoother as he stumbled toward the new year. In
fact, through no fault of his own, things got considerably worse. Shortly
after dawn on the morning of Christmas Eve, Capitol policeman John W.
Jones, apparently patrolling the West Front grounds, noticed smoke, or
perhaps flames, streaming from one of the second-floor windows of the
Library of Congress overlooking the Mall.

Capitol policemen were not allowed to hold keys to the main Capitol
building, but an alarmed Jones, with the assistance of a passerby, forced
open a door and ran to the Library's main reading room. There they found
a wooden library table on fire at the north end. Flames were starting to
climb up the shelving and engulf books in alcoves in the northeast corner.
At that point, Jones later told the *National Intelligencer*, a half-dozen buckets of water would have quenched the flames. But as Washington still had

no municipal water system, Jones's only recourse was to scoop water from outdoor fountains and raise the alarm. Unfortunately, Jones and his companion neglected to shut the library door when they ran outside. By the time they returned, the entire room was ablaze.[38]

Fire companies began to arrive. The pumper *Columbia* was first, and was carried up the eastern stairs and into the Rotunda itself. *Perseverance* started emptying the stone basin on the eastern side of the Capitol and sending water to *Columbia* to fight the flames. *Anacostia* and *Union* arrived next, and ultimately there were seven companies on hand.[39] According to the *Intelligencer*, the heroes of the day were the firefighters from *Anacostia*, who, by pulling down a blazing staircase leading up into Bulfinch's wooden dome, avoided the loss of the entire Capitol. A contingent of marines from their barracks near the navy yard kept order and organized a multitude of local residents, who passed buckets and did whatever else they could to help out.[40] The worst was over by 11:00 a.m., but firefighters were bathing the smoking embers until midafternoon, and several inches of water stood in the Rotunda by the time the fire was out.[41]

The Capitol had been saved, but losses were heavy. On Christmas Day, the Capitol librarian, John S. Meehan, wrote a short preliminary note to House Speaker Linn Boyd, explaining that about 35,000 of the Library's 55,000 volumes appeared to have been destroyed, along with "painting, statuary, medals, and other property" stored there or on display.[42] Gilbert Stuart's portraits of the first five U.S. presidents—Washington, Adams, Jefferson, Madison, and Monroe—were either damaged or destroyed. A number of other portraits were also lost. Additional losses included a statue of Jefferson, a bronze likeness of Washington, a bust of Zachary Taylor, and a bust of Lafayette.[43]

Since the fire had occurred in the old Capitol, Walter had no responsibility for what had happened. Public Buildings Commissioner Easby, who did, soon received a letter from Interior Secretary Stuart asking him to investigate. Easby formally requested Walter to do so in a note dated December 27. Walter replied in a note dated the previous day and included his already completed analysis. Stuart, it appeared, had asked Walter for help immediately after the fire, and had included Easby in the correspondence only as an afterthought. Easby could not have been pleased.[44]

According to Walter, a timber supporting one of the alcoves at the north end of the main reading room had apparently poked its way into a chimney flue extending upward and been ignited by sparks from a fireplace in the room below, which was used by the Senate Committee on Indian Affairs.[45]

The next task was to figure out what to do, and Stuart put Walter to work immediately. While no direct correspondence describes the sequence of events, Walter, in his annual report to Stuart nearly a year later, spoke of being instructed after the fire to prepare plans as soon as possible for a new Library to be rebuilt on the same site.[46]

A month later, Walter finished his report. The new Library would have three main rooms, extending 302 feet in length to occupy the entire West Front of the old Capitol. The design could not be fully implemented, however, until the new Senate and House wings were finished, allowing the old Capitol committee rooms to be dismantled and moved. He would start by redoing the old Library. The center of the main floor would essentially be an open space, lit by windows and skylights. Books would be shelved in three tiers of alcoves lining the Library walls on four sides, creating a gallery effect.

But that was not the most important thing. Given the "irreparable loss" suffered by the country because of the fire, Walter said, "I considered it an indispensable element in the design now presented, to use no combustible materials whatever in any part of the work." The entire Library, "the alcoves, cases, galleries, doors, window shutters, ceilings and the brackets that support them," would be made of cast iron, and therefore fireproof. He would build the bookshelves of thick glass or enameled iron, frame the roof in wrought iron, and set the floor in stone. "In a library thus constructed, fire will be out of the question, and the materials of which it is formed will not be subject to decay or deterioration." The whole job, he said, could be done for $72,500. The Senate approved the plan on February 12, and the House followed a month later.[47]

For Walter, the Library represented a "structural revolution."[48] Apprenticed as a stonemason and a disciple of neoclassical forms, he had never in his career built anything so extensive from iron. Clearly he, like Congress, had been badly traumatized by the Library fire and its fearsome consequences. Government had betrayed the public trust. The contents of the Library, second in size in the country only to that of

Harvard University, was priceless. Meehan forbade movable lamps, candles, and cigars in the reading room, but what use were such trivial rules when the committee chambers below the Library were heating up like pressure cookers, setting off fires in superannuated chimneys during predawn winter mornings when there was practically no one in the building? And what a disgrace, in 1851, to have to fight such a fire with buckets, simply because Congress had been too cheap to build a municipal water system. Given the circumstances, it came as no surprise that Walter got his money quickly and almost without congressional demur.

Even though Walter had had little experience with cast iron, he would certainly have known about it in 1851, for the United States was in the middle of its "cast-iron age." The Chinese, centuries before, had been the first to make things with it, but its wide use as a construction material only began in Britain toward the end of the eighteenth century, when the coke-fueled blast furnace sharply reduced production costs. Cast iron's first industrial application was in making parts for the newfangled steam engine, but by the end of the century, engineers were building cast-iron bridges and starting to frame buildings with it. In the early nineteenth century, the invention of the hot blast furnace cut production costs even further, and suddenly, like steel, aluminum, and plastic in times to come, cast iron was all the rage.[49]

In architecture it was a wondrous solution to many dilemmas. Cast iron was easy to shape, like wood, but could support a much heavier load. It could look just as imposing as stone but could be molded and bent to create much lighter structures. It was brittle and had little tensile strength, but it was ideal for framing, joists, studs, columns, ribbing for vaults, and other stationary load-bearing applications.[50] By the 1850s, builders, notably New York's James Bogardus, were using cast iron not only for girders and beams, but also to make façades for factories and commercial buildings.

And, of course, if not altogether fireproof, cast iron was definitely fire-resistant, and that was the decider for Walter and Congress. A library with stone walls, stone floors, an iron roof, iron fixtures, and iron shelves was the safest that could be built in 1851. Viewed simply as a utilitarian solution to an intractable problem, a cast-iron Library had all the charm of a three-story bank vault. But Walter, even without ever having used it before, saw immediately that he could do pretty much whatever he wanted with it. The key, as he might or might not have known in 1851, was to take advantage of cast iron's potential without going overboard. He would try it out on the Library and see what happened. What he probably did not know in 1851 was that the Library would be the dry run for the most important design of his career.

6

SHARKS IN THE WATER

By the beginning of 1852, Congress had been back in session for a month. The U.S. Capitol, with its horrible House chamber acoustics, its stuffy, stagnant air, its erratic heating and ventilation, and its tobacco-stained carpets and curtains, had never been a comfortable place to do the people's business. But this year the new Capitol Extension had made it more of a mess than usual. Trenches had been dug, foundations had been laid, and enormous quantities of earth had been loaded into carts and driven off. The front yard was littered with large chunks of stone, and the lawn was scarred, rutted, and alternately muddy or frozen, depending on the day. It was also evident that no one was trying to clean it up. And there was no respite indoors. Most of the workers who were building the new wings—several hundred of them—had been fired because there was no more money to pay them, and a significant number of them were now hovering in the Capitol's public areas, importuning lawmakers to enact a new appropriation so they could go back to work. And finally, the dank smell of the fire-gutted Library lingered heavily in the corridors. It was not a happy New Year.

Thomas Walter seemed curiously unaware of the precarious state of the Extension project—or his own precarious position as its head. Enjoying his stature as a favorite of Whig president Millard Fillmore, Walter, his wife, and his visiting sister, Anna, attended New Year's Day parties hosted by Fillmore, Interior Secretary Alexander H. H. Stuart, the secretary of the Treasury, the postmaster general, the secretary of state, the secretary of war, and the secretary of the Navy.[1]

The layoffs he clearly believed to be only temporary. Congress would surely soon ante up more cash to get things going again, and not much work could get done anyway during the winter months when the ground was frozen. But things were changing fast. When Congress reconvened, Walter would have a new, more complicated power broker to appease.

Both houses were now controlled by Democrats, who had no stake in Fillmore's future, Fillmore's Capitol Extension, or Fillmore's architect. In fact, if the Democrats allowed Fillmore's project to survive—and this was by no means certain—they would quite likely want to make it their own. They would want their own architect, their own contractors, perhaps even a new design. And to make things even tougher on Walter, 1852 was a presidential election year. Fillmore's chances of winning the Whig nomination were already dwindling to insignificance, and Whig chances of finding anybody who could win the election were not far behind.

Walter needed to make more friends of different political persuasions, but he had not done himself any favors. Instead, the Capitol at the dawn of 1852 was grimmer than ever—an immense eyesore with an unpleasant smell and nobody doing anything about it. Walter was not responsible for the Library fire, but the exhaustion of construction funds for the new wings and the layoffs that accompanied it had put him in an unwelcome spotlight. If anyone in Congress was looking for a whipping boy, Walter might as well have raised his hand.

But Walter was oblivious. On his estimates, Congress had unhesitatingly appropriated money to repair and rebuild the Library, and perhaps he thought that a quick appropriation for the Extension would follow after the holidays. If so, he was wrong. Instead of voting more money, Congress decided to challenge Walter's work. On January 5, Pennsylvania representative John A. McNair, a Democrat, introduced a House resolution calling for the appointment of a select committee to examine the foundations of the Extension in order to determine whether they were strong enough to support the new buildings.[2] The origin of McNair's discontent was unclear. He might simply have been intent on grabbing headlines and embarrassing a Whig administration and its Whig architect during an election year. More likely, McNair was trying to get Walter sacked so he could hand the architect's job to one of his own constituents, or to a crony who would let McNair in on the patronage that such an enormous job commanded.[3] Regardless, Walter was vulnerable, and McNair was simply the first shark to attack.

On its face, McNair's resolution to inspect the new wings' foundations seemed prudent, even though he offered no evidence of problems. The investigation could, if it was prolonged, stall construction and intensify worker resentment, but who could argue against safety? The resolution won approval by a vote of 107–28 a week after it was introduced.

But there was nothing innocent about the measure. Instead, it was the beginning of a classic, chaotic congressional floor fight rife with competing agendas, questionable motives, and outright blather. It would last for four months. The Capitol's foundation would be a recurring theme, not so much because anyone harbored any serious doubts about it but because it served as a convenient starting point. Democrats wanted to take the measure of Walter to see how vulnerable he was. They wanted to see if he had messed up contracts—contracts that could be relet to their friends; they wanted to see if he was cutting corners or taking kickbacks, so they could dump him quickly and name someone else; and they wanted to see who his friends were, and whether he had enough of them to handle the storm.

The upcoming debate would also serve as a convenient moment to argue the larger questions about the Capitol Extension—questions that there had been no time to raise during the tumult that had accompanied the 1850 compromise debate and its 1851 aftermath. Did the United States, the cradle of rock-solid republican values, need or want a fancy new seat of government? Congress's Protestant majorities were wary of European-style pretense and extravagance. And even if the government was getting bigger with each additional state, did it make sense to put new money into a building in a mid-Atlantic backwater like Washington? The time would soon come, many westerners thought, when Congress should strike the tents and move to St. Louis, say, or maybe Chicago, just beginning to turn into the monster it would become. And finally, there was the unspoken question that underlay almost everything that happened in Washington: Why should southerners spend money to construct a huge public building that they would never use? Disunion was coming, and if it did, the southern states would never be seen in Congress again.

Walter had no idea how bad these controversies could become. On January 16, four days after McNair's resolution passed the House and only three days after Walter had notified Rice, Baird & Heebner in Philadelphia that they had won the marble contract, he attended a meeting with Fillmore and McNair, probably at the White House. In addition to these two, Walter's brief diary entry records that Stuart, Chandler, Stanton, and Attorney General John J. Crittenden—all Walter allies—also attended.[4] It is not known who called the meeting. Perhaps McNair requested it so he could describe how his select committee intended to proceed. Or perhaps Fillmore summoned McNair to pressure him into dropping the investigation. If that was the case, it did not work.

Instead, the Senate decided to get involved. On February 5, Michigan senator Lewis Cass introduced a resolution calling for the project to be funded so the Extension workers could be put back to work, noting that Stanton had introduced a similar measure in the House. Cass's measure would be companion legislation.[5] Opposition was voiced immediately by Arkansas Democrat Solon Borland, reluctant to proceed because "a committee has been appointed by the other House" to study the foundations of the Extension to determine whether construction "should go on at all." It would thus be "improper," he said, to do anything until the House investigation.[6]

Borland did not prevail, and Cass's resolution was sent to the Committee on Public Buildings, a harmless outcome. But Borland had taken McNair's concern and raised the ante, suggesting that the House investigation sought to determine not only the safety of the foundation but whether the project itself should continue. As in McNair's case, it was difficult to determine Borland's motives. At least at first, he manifested none of the personal rancor against Walter that seemed to fuel McNair's opposition.

What distinguished him from McNair, however, was his militance as a southern rights activist and incipient secessionist. Although he never said so, his opposition to the Capitol Extension may well have stemmed from his belief that building new monuments to a federal government to which he had little fealty was a waste of money and effort.

But the issue on the Senate floor at that moment was neither southern rights nor the foundation of the Capitol Extension, but simply Cass's resolution to make relief payments to Walter's laid-off workers. The next day, Robert M. T. Hunter, Stanton's counterpart as chair of the Senate Committee on Public Buildings, announced that he was ready to consider the Cass resolution. Borland objected. McNair had told him that the foundations of the Extension were unsafe, and Borland did not want to spend any money on the project until the investigation was complete. Hunter said that workers' relief had nothing to do with the foundation, and Borland retreated, withdrawing his objection.[7] This meant that workers' relief could be debated. Whether it would be passed was another question. Congress, as would become quite clear as time passed, was not fond of paying people to do nothing.

Walter appeared remarkably unworried about the wrangling—or the work stoppage. Since it was still the off-season and his men could not work outside, he was not losing time, and the job itself was not suffering. His diary shows he spent a lot of time on the Library early in the year and met many times with McNair's investigators, but he betrays not the slightest hint of either outrage or irritation.[8]

Nor is there any mention in Walter's diary of a seemingly innocuous request from Texas senator Sam Houston asking Walter how much marble he had ordered in blocks smaller than 30 cubic feet, at $0.65 per cubic foot, and how much in larger blocks, which cost $1.98 per cubic foot. Walter replied on February 14 that he had received about four times as much marble in the larger blocks as he had in small blocks, and then he apparently thought no more about it.[9] He would have cause to remember the interchange later.

The showdown in the House began on March 12, 1852. Stanton, chiding his colleagues for refusing to fund the Capitol Extension, thereby missing "two months of fine weather," asked for a $500,000 appropriation to resume work and rehire the labor force. Stuart had asked for more money, he added, but $500,000 would suffice to carry the project to the end of the Fillmore administration in March 1853 and through the end of the fiscal year ending June 30.[10]

Stanton's challenge triggered an immediate response from members who demanded an update on the McNair investigation. Called on to respond, McNair promised that the select committee would report by the following week, then told his colleagues that "we have found the wall in dreadful condition—in a condition that has astonished us all." When the committee inspected it, he said, the members found "shells built up on the outside and small stones thrown in on the inside. There are no stones running through the wall to bind it. There are no headers, and there is no bond work."[11]

Stanton still had the floor, but he left McNair alone, and McNair continued. The foundation did not have enough mortar, he said, and what there was "has been in there about three months, and it is not yet set. Men with picks just dug out the inside, and threw out the stones with their hands, and threw out the sand or mortar, or whatever you call it, with a shovel. We have, as one member of the committee expressed it, realized our very worst anticipations."[12]

At this point McNair, having built up a significant head of steam, began attacking Walter for spending the initial $100,000 appropriation, "how, we know not." Walter had drawn the money in $20,000 chunks to be "expended or disbursed by him, I know not how." The whole matter "requires an inquiry."[13]

Had McNair stopped there, he might have cast enough doubt on the project to halt the new appropriation in its tracks. Instead, he kept going: "One of the best architects, perhaps, in the state of Pennsylvania was here," McNair said, "and he declared to me, when he looked at that wall and examined the formation of it, that he would venture his life the building would fall down if built upon it."[14]

The atmosphere in the chamber suddenly intensified. McNair, apparently, had initiated a private inspection of the works without clearing it with his colleagues on the select committee. Massachusetts Whig James H. Duncan, a member of the committee, demanded the name of the Pennsylvania architect and wanted to know whether he had come before the committee. McNair admitted that the committee had not seen him, and he said the architect was "a friend of Mr. Dimmick," referring to Representative Milo Dimmick, another Pennsylvania Democrat. He invited Dimmick to say the name of the architect.[15]

This, according to the official reporter, who obviously could hear nothing in the accompanying din, provoked "[Cries of 'No! No!']," to which Duncan responded: "As he is represented as a person of such high reputation, we want to know who he is."

This was followed by "[Cries of: 'Name! Name!']."

"He was introduced to me by Mr. Dimmick," insisted McNair, which elicited "[Loud cries of 'name!' 'Name!' and 'Oh, no, go on!']" Dimmick, if he was in the chamber, said nothing.

"Oh no," lamented Pennsylvania Democrat Thomas B. Florence with mock gravity. "The reputation of Pennsylvania may be at stake. [Cries of 'Order!' and laughter.]"

"Well," McNair said finally, "his name is Knowles."

The chamber erupted in laughter once more, apparently because Knowles, far from being "one of the best architects," was a complete stranger to the other members—and probably hoping to take over the project.

McNair pressed on, finally allowed to change the subject: "I wish gentlemen to know something about the disbursement of that money, before they judge whether everything is perfectly right . . ."

He was immediately interrupted by New York's David Seymour, who asked for the evidence of misuse of funds. McNair insisted, "I have knowledge that the money has been drawn by the architect. He has drawn it and there has been no return made by him for the disbursement . . ."

He was cut off again, this time by James Woodward of South Carolina, who wanted to know about the wall, not listen to a rant about Walter. McNair, finally chastened, sat down, only to be challenged by Thomas Florence, his fellow Pennsylvanian, who demanded to know if the select committee had taken a vote on the wall and whether the committee had had competent outsiders—apart from the mysterious Knowles—examine it. There had been no vote, McNair said, and then he admitted that outsiders had examined the wall—and found nothing wrong.[16]

After this incredible statement, Stanton reclaimed the floor to put the nails in McNair's coffin: "I was about to remark, when I was interrupted, that it had been the misfortune of all great men who had the genius and resolution to undertake works of this magnitude, to be harassed and annoyed by the criticism and censure of petty minds," he said. He did not mean to "allude to the gentleman from Pennsylvania," he added, but "I do allude to that description of meddlers who, from motives of disappointment at having failed to secure contracts on this work, come into this Hall to harass the House and, I had almost said, to lead intelligent and honorable members of Congress into dilemmas, of which, when they learn the whole truth, they will be ashamed."

Then Stanton, obviously much better prepared for the confrontation than the unfortunate McNair, sprang his own trap. The Committee on Public Buildings and Grounds, it turned out, had enlisted the help of a "Professor Johnson," a "scientific gentleman" well-known in Washington, to test the blue rock used in the Capitol Extension foundation. Johnson found that the weakest of the samples could endure a crushing weight of 1,152,000 pounds per square foot, whereas the maximum load the foundation would ever support would be 10,500 pounds per square foot. The blue rock was thus strong enough by two orders of magnitude. The walls, Stanton said, "are subjects of admiration to every scientific and practical man who has seen them. Such solidity, such strength, and such admirable skill in their construction, have never been manifested before in any work done in this city, and I doubt whether better work of the kind can be found in any part of the Union."

Then what the official reporter described simply as "a voice" yelled from the floor: "How many applicants for the contracts were from Pennsylvania?" Stanton did not know, he said, but he was finished talking about that, and wanted instead to discuss Walter's expenditures, which had been handled with complete transparency, he insisted. He invited anyone who had questions to visit Walter and look over the books. He finished with an ode to the Capitol Extension, and as for McNair, he said with a last rhetorical flick of the wrist: "I deem the investigation to be made by this committee as of very little importance."[17]

It was a bravura performance. While Stanton wanted new funding for the Capitol Extension, he had also succeeded in flushing McNair into the open. McNair had risen to the bait magnificently, and with only perfunctory coaxing had shown his colleagues everything he had, which was woefully little. Stanton had given McNair as much time as he needed to make a fool of himself, then had systematically dismembered his arguments. The House adjourned before taking a vote, but members returned the next day to distance themselves from the discredited McNair and continue the debate. At day's end, the resolution was voted and passed.

Now it was the Senate's turn to pass the $500,000 appropriation. The resolution was introduced on March 15, 1852, two days after House passage. Senator Borland had done his homework and had mustered a number of reasons why the funds should not be voted. Unlike McNair, he had not set himself up as the expert of record on the Extension, but simply as a concerned senator trying to defend the public trust. His strategy was to raise a long list of complaints about the Extension and wait to see which ones took root.

He began by apologizing for being the bearer of bad tidings. He had placed himself "in a very ungracious attitude before the Senate," he said, and "certainly before the *galleries*," which were packed with laid-off workers who had "beset" him.[18] He would not be moved.

Next, he complained about parliamentary procedure. Why had the bill not been sent to committee, to determine "what public necessity requires this appropriation of *half a million of dollars*?" Especially, he continued, changing the subject once again, since "it is neither proper nor necessary" to build an Extension. "Whoever will look around him will find, I think, the Chamber is not only large enough now, but likely to be so for years to come." And even if this were not the case, he added, the old Capitol could simply be enlarged, making it "ample, commodious, and comfortable" for "the next fifty years."[19]

Then he tried the McNair approach. Borland asserted, without citing any source, that the Extension to date had cost "five to ten times" as much as "any prudent private individual would have incurred." And he had learned from McNair, he said, that the work had been "unfaithfully and badly done."[20]

Walter was his next target. He was "a new officer of our government," Borland said, "a sort of presidential creation" responsible for spending the money allotted to the Extension and therefore suspect. At this point, North Carolina Whig senator George E. Badger interrupted to remind Borland that Walter, by law, had responsibility for disbursing the Extension funds. Borland asked Badger if he was satisfied with the way the money had been spent. Badger said he was not sure, and sat down.[21]

Borland then made his final point. He was worried, he said, about "the dangerous tendency of our system of government toward *centralism* and *consolidation*." There was a "school of politicians," he said, that would support any plan that would "concentrate and consolidate power here in this Federal head, at the expense of the sovereignty, the independence, the rights, and legitimate power of the several States."

"If . . . this Union of States shall ever be destroyed, this will be the cause," he said. "Towering up as a great central power, it will overshadow the States, and swallow up their sovereignty; and then nothing of the *Union* will be left but its *name*, while one great consolidated despotism will fill its place."[22] In his view, the new Capitol was a symbol of political dominance by the northern, antislavery majority.

It was another rhetorical masterpiece. Borland criticized the appropriation on philosophical grounds: he was against workers' welfare. Then he criticized it on procedural grounds: he wanted a committee review of the measure. Then he questioned the need for an enlarged Capitol and questioned the project's workmanship and cost. He then suggested that Walter was cheating the taxpayers. And finally he condemned the new Capitol as a federal encroachment on states' rights. He had sought to create a climate of doubt and uncertainty, and, as would soon be evident, he had succeeded, monopolizing the Senate floor for several hours without giving away his own agenda. What did he really want?

Stanton had disposed of McNair in time-honored House fashion: bludgeoning him to death with facts and information. Borland's diatribe was a textbook Senate finesse: throw up a smoke screen of possibilities to disguise the ultimate goal; plant doubts while professing ignorance; establish expertise without seeming to do so; take control of the debate if possible. The next day Borland introduced a resolution calling on the Senate Committee on Public Buildings "to make a thorough examination" of the work done on the Extension foundations and on the new wings generally. It passed unanimously. Using nothing but suspicion and innuendo, he had induced the Senate to launch a completely new investigation.[23]

Borland's presentation had shown that the new Capitol Extension had no serious Senate advocate. The Public Buildings Committee chairman, Hunter, was the project's natural Senate helpmate, but he had done nothing except cede leadership on the issue to someone who wanted to kill the Extension.

Hunter had never favored new wings for the Capitol, but he had always wanted an Extension. But now it seemed that he did not care enough to lead the fight, and no one else stepped forward. Most senators had supported the Extension in 1850—albeit by a narrow margin—and most would probably support it now, if one of their colleagues told them what to do. But Hunter was weak, and Davis, who could easily have matched Borland's invective, was gone. The Capitol Extension, lying dormant for four months for lack of funding, was now at risk of abandonment.

And Borland was just getting started. On March 24, he called on Fillmore to furnish copies of all available documents relating to the Capitol Extension. At a time when official records were kept in longhand, such a request represented an enormous effort by government clerks, especially since Walter had already offered to make his records available to any lawmaker who came to his office to look at them. Borland in part was asserting Senate prerogative—if the U.S. Senate wanted its own copies of something, the U.S. Senate should have them—but he was also deliberately goading the administration, which he blamed for attacking him in Whig-controlled newspapers: "I have been put before the public as throwing myself before the mouths of starving men," he intoned.[24] If the administration wanted to attack him in the newspapers, then it could copy all the paperwork and send it to him.

The next few hours saw Borland reprise many arguments he had made the previous week, but he also added a few new ones. He was outraged, he said, that Walter had signed contracts for $1.5 million in building materials when he was working with only a $100,000 appropriation. Then Borland questioned the design competition of 1851, noting that Fillmore had discarded both the House and Senate plans "and adopted—what? Nobody knows what. I have been utterly unable to discover that there is now any regular or determinate plan." This statement, patently absurd, triggered a prolonged back-and-forth between Borland and Fillmore's defenders, who accused Borland of implying that the president had done something illegal. Borland denied it.

Finally Hunter stepped forward to confirm that Fillmore had the power to design the Capitol Extension to his own specifications and had had no obligation to adopt plans submitted to him by either the Senate or House. Still, Hunter said, he had no objection to Borland's resolution calling for the records.[25]

And it passed. Once again, Borland had gotten what he wanted without revealing his true intentions. Having decided that attacking Walter was a dead end, he shifted his guns to Fillmore, a plausible tactic in a Democratic Senate during a presidential election year. Hunter, who knew that virtually everything Borland said was foolishness, nevertheless kept his mouth shut and gave his approval to Borland's request, effectively ensuring that it would pass.

Five days later, on March 29, 1852, Stuart presented the asked-for materials, together with a cover report from Walter. The packet, probably well over a hundred pages, included the plans for the Extension, all the contracts, the results of the previous year's marble tests, and Stuart's assurance that "no verbal agreements" had been made to supplement the contracts.[26] Once again, there is little suggestion in Walter's diary that he was at all upset with the Borland request, and he was able to comply with it in two days.

On April 4, Hunter submitted the Public Buildings Committee report requested by Borland, accompanied by analyses of the foundation made by the Army Corps of Engineers and the Topographical Engineers. The Corps report, dated March 25, 1852, deemed the blue rock foundation stone "excellent—probably no better could be obtained for foundations." The mortar, it said, could be better in some spots, but it is the same as that used in the original building. The quality of the work "we consider excellent," the report said, and it took note of "the accomplished architect in charge."[27] The Topographical Engineers' report, dated March 30, 1852, deemed the foundation stone "of an excellent and durable quality" and the stone and mortar to be better than that used in the original Capitol.[28]

Hunter let the $500,000 appropriations bill languish for another week, then brought it to the floor Friday morning, April 9, normally a time set aside for small "private bills" conferring honors, pensions, and other special favors to constituents. Borland objected, pointing out that important senators who opposed the bill were not in the chamber. Hunter acknowledged that this was true, but he wanted to bring it up anyway. Other senators agreed, as long as he limited debate to one hour. Hunter readily agreed, probably hoping that "private bill day," with senators anxious to reward important backers and contributors, would offer an opportunity to sneak the appropriation through quickly.[29]

But Borland did not go without a fight. He had decided that he wanted to pay back wages to the workers, but would not support the appropriation "because I do, in my conscience, believe it is for a purpose that is not only unnecessary, but improper." He then talked about the Corps and Topographical Engineers' reports. He did not disagree with them, he said, but "I should be uncandid if I did not say that my opinion is not changed." He had visited the works with another senator, who, "I believe, is better qualified by practical experience" than anyone else in town to examine the work. And, he said, he found wet mortar, and displayed it: "In one hour from the time it was taken out, it was in the condition you here see! Sand, sir, sand, and nothing else; save here and there a few detached and uncombined particles of a dirty lime!" Then he attacked Walter, but noted that both sets of engineers "say he is both accomplished and honest, and I shall not now controvert their opinion."[30]

He continued, sounding more like a filibusterer with each tick of the clock. There was no need for a bigger Capitol, and even if there was, he opposed it because he hated the design: "It will make a structure which I can call by no other name than *architectural monstrosity*, the like of which has never been seen in any civilized country on the face of the Earth," he said. "It will resemble, more nearly than anything which suggests a comparison, a mammoth brick-kiln, or some Mexican hacienda, which as every one knows, is the very burlesque of all architectural proportion."[31]

The chair then called for a vote on an amendment to pay off the workers and abandon the project. This went down hard, 11–30. Borland then rose and began complaining about contracts exceeding the money allotted by the appropriation. This triggered groans and cries of "Let's have a vote!" Borland conceded that the appropriation would pass overwhelmingly, but would not sit down.

Senators were seething. The test vote had already been taken. Borland had lost, and it was time for him to stop. Nonetheless, he forced his colleagues to take three more votes before the appropriation itself was voted and passed.

The Capitol Extension had survived another crisis, but this one was much more serious than McNair's inept effort, for it exposed the new Capitol as a project without a safe mooring in the Senate. Walter's status, so comfortable in 1851 while Congress was not in session, had also suddenly become tenuous. His executive branch patrons, Fillmore and Stuart, were lame ducks, and the Democrats smelled blood in November. The Capitol itself was in much the same fix. It had been Fillmore's project, and it would be up to the next president to decide how hard to push it. The Capitol Extension needed a new patron.

Walter had spent a good part of the five-month work stoppage firming up plans for the new Library, a separate job unaffected by the Extension's travails. He sent out for bids on the Library ironwork and received eight responses. Then in May he spent five days in Massachusetts and New York visiting foundries, and had dinner in New York City with Charles Fowler, a partner in Janes, Beebe & Co., ironworkers, the low bidder for the Library job at $59,872. Walter signed them up, beginning another close collaboration that would last more than a decade.[32] Fowler, like the marble broker John Rice in Philadelphia, would become one of Walter's closest friends.

Walter expected Library construction to move quickly, and it did. The cast iron, as advertised, proved to be light, easy to make, easy to shape, and easy to handle. Still, his early prediction that he would finish the job by July 1 was overly optimistic.

Work on the Capitol Extension, meanwhile, resumed immediately af-

ter final passage of the new appropriation, and Walter notified Stuart on
June 26 that he had received a bill of lading for the first shipment of marble from the Rice, Baird & Heebner quarry in Lee, Massachusetts. He said
he wished to contract Provest & Winter of Washington to cut, carve, and
set the marble once it had arrived from Lee.[33] Stuart forwarded the request to Hunter and Stanton, who concurred, and Walter notified the
company on July 3.[34] Alexander Provest, like Rice in Philadelphia and
Fowler in New York, would stay with the project to the end.

These were the last reasonably carefree days Walter would have for
some time. The next attack came on July 21. Commissioner of Public
Buildings William Easby, in a blistering letter to Fillmore, denounced
Walter for fraud, conspiracy, taking kickbacks from contractors, buying
substandard materials, and following shoddy construction practices. Fillmore forwarded the letter to Walter, asking him for an explanation.[35]

The accusations were largely unsubstantiated and, for the most part,
because of Walter's meticulous record keeping, easily refuted. The only
charge about which Walter had no direct knowledge was Easby's allega-
tion that Samuel Strong, Walter's construction supervisor, had told Easby
about plans to make a new brickwork contract in which the government
would end up paying $6.00 for each thousand bricks—higher than what
would be considered a normal price. Walter told Fillmore that he had
asked Strong for an explanation, and concluded by saying he was puzzled
by why Easby had decided to attack him, apparently choosing to ignore all
the little evidences of bad blood that had arisen between the two men the
previous year.[36]

It was clear that Easby was interested in getting Walter ousted from the
project and getting himself, or more likely a crony, to take Walter's place.
Easby, like Walter, was a Fillmore appointee, and probably destined for
involuntary retirement if a Democrat won the presidential election, which
seemed likely. But as a local quarryman, Easby was well positioned to get
a substantial piece of the Extension business once he left government, and
he probably saw a better chance if Walter was gone. It is noteworthy that
Easby's letter to Fillmore was written less than three weeks after Provest &
Winter, a local firm, got the marble finishing contract—and it was Provest
& Winter that bore the brunt of Easby's accusations.

Fillmore was apparently satisfied with Walter's explanation, but Walter was jittery. Easby's case was too tenuous to merit serious consider-

ation from Fillmore. Did Easby have other political connections of which Walter was unaware?

He did. On August 5, 1852, the Senate appointed a five-man "Select Committee to Investigate Abuses, Bribery and Fraud." Its brief was to investigate whatever needed investigating. The committee was chaired by Texas Democrat Sam Houston and included Senator Solon Borland. While the panel did in fact look at corruption in the Treasury Department and blackmail in the Navy, its main target, with Borland as lead investigator, was the Capitol Extension. On August 28, Borland called his first witness. It was William Easby.[37]

Easby's testimony reviewed most of the allegations he had made in his Fillmore letter, but in much more detail. There were also new accusations. Easby called attention to Walter's marble shipments, saying that he had purchased many more large, expensive blocks of marble than small, cheaper blocks. The effect of this practice, Easby said, was that Walter was paying Rice, Baird & Heebner far more than necessary, since most of the Extension could be built with small blocks. Rice, Baird & Heebner were thus cheating the government and probably kicking back significant sums to Walter for letting them do it. If allowed to continue, Easby continued, the "government will be defrauded out of $359,100."[38]

The Easby testimony, coming more than six months after Houston's request to Walter for information on marble blocks, suggests that Easby had Houston's ear and had been whispering in it for some time. Easby obviously had been trying to set Walter up for months.

Once again, however, Walter's record keeping and general probity rendered him a hard target to slander. Walter eventually told the committee that he had bought more large blocks of marble in his initial orders for the simple reason that lower layers—or "courses"—were always bigger, thicker, and stronger. And using big blocks on the lower layers of the new Capitol seemed an especially wise policy, he said, given that Congress "as evinced by their investigations of the last session," was demanding foundations "of unusual strength."[39]

Marble blocks were only one of Borland's concerns. The select committee had a broad mandate to conduct what at a later time would be termed a "fishing expedition" into the Capitol Extension, and for seven months it took testimony from losing contractors, disgruntled employees, crooked foremen, and public officials, among them Walter and (by mail)

Fillmore himself. Borland's conclusions were flawed because they were clouded by his desire to discredit Walter, the new Capitol, or both, but he gathered a massive amount of information. And he found a soft spot: Samuel Strong.

The testimony taken in mid-1852 and early 1853 was published by the committee in a Senate report in March 1853 and dealt with events that took place in late 1851 and 1852. The investigation painted the portrait of an enormous construction job, capably run for the most part, but with an undercurrent of petty corruption. Most striking was the workers' perception of Walter and Strong. Walter, it seemed, was regarded mostly as a benevolent but remote and somewhat disengaged presence. The day-to-day boss was Strong, who was seen as the overlord of a vast empire of patronage. Workers were divided between those who sought his favor and profited from it, and a much larger number who loathed him.

Among the witnesses were nine day laborers and low-level apprentices who testified to being hired at $2.25 per day—stonemasons' journeyman wages—and being forced to kick back anything from 75 cents to $1.00 to either the deputy superintendent Robert Strong, Samuel's brother, or the foreman Nathan Kingsley.[40] One apprentice described picking up his wages from Kingsley, who then escorted him to a nearby cellar where Robert Strong took his share. Kingsley made change. Kingsley essentially confirmed these accounts, describing the laborers as "apprentices."[41] Samuel Strong, meanwhile, at first professed no knowledge of his brother's and Kingsley's activities, but under close questioning acknowledged that Robert took the money as a fee to "teach them to lay brick."[42]

This practice, other witnesses testified, continued for months and so enraged the true journeyman masons that they struck the project and paid a visit to Walter to tell him they would not "work with common laborers." Walter, under the impression that the masons were refusing to work because their guild would not allow anyone but members to carve marble, told them to get out of his office or he would call the police.[43]

The smith shop foreman, Samuel Champion, a longtime devotee of Walter who had come from Philadelphia to work on the Extension, talked about having to fire one of his blacksmiths to make way for a Strong crony, who acted "more like the foreman," undermining Champion's authority.[44] He also recounted how Strong brought a wagon to work on Election Day and urged workers to use it to go to the polls and cast votes for the Whig candidate for mayor of Washington. A clerk said Strong fired him

on Election Day for passing out handbills before work on behalf of another candidate.[45] And two workers recalled Strong offering bonuses—in
one case $100—if they would "raise a mob" to burn McNair and Borland
in effigy. Strong would provide the dummy.[46]

Still, in many cases, it was difficult to tell where the cover-up ended
and the truth began. Nearly a dozen witnesses from the carpenters' shop
described how the two shop foremen there were stealing lumber from the
government—mostly mahogany—and using it to make writing desks,
candle stands, tables, bookcases, picture frames, tool chests, fancy boxes,
and other knickknacks, which they either kept for themselves or sold on
the outside. These stories would have been more convincing if they had
not been virtually identical.[47]

When Strong was asked about these abuses, he told committee investigators that he had instructed the carpenters "to make nothing" from
extra lumber except "government work," and that he had fired the deputy
foreman for refusing to follow these instructions.[48] At that point, the deputy amended his earlier testimony to say that all the extra jobs had been
done on Strong's orders. The shop foreman also initialed the amendment.[49]

Strong's downfall came in November 1852, and it, too, was part of a
confused sequence of events. Easby's charge in the Fillmore letter—that
Strong was looking to take over the brick contract and wanted to get Easby
to participate—had been repeated by Easby in his committee testimony.
Walter had promised Fillmore that he would find out about the contract,
and in his written testimony before the committee he described how he had
attempted to ascertain its history. Dissatisfied with the original contractor, Walter had moved the contract three times, finally finding a supplier
he liked. During this process he demanded a "chain of assignments"—a
list of those who had held the contract during the year. "This was withheld
for some time," Walter's testimony said, but he eventually got the list and
"I found out that on the 12th of January 1852," the entire contract had
been assigned to Samuel Strong. On November 18, 1852, the day after he
learned this, Walter accepted Strong's resignation.[50]

This seemed a straightforward conflict of interest, but there was more
to it. Strong, in his testimony, acknowledged that his name had been on
the contract, but he claimed he had not subsequently sold it but simply
passed it on and had "never received a farthing" from it—a contention
impossible to prove or disprove.[51] His recollection of the Easby encounter,
however, differed markedly from Easby's. Strong said that he had done

nothing to conceal his intention to resign from the Extension if he could induce Fillmore to allow him to have the brick contract at $5.00 per thousand. He asked Easby "to speak to the President in my behalf, as he had boasted of his intimacy with him." Easby agreed, and said that "if I would get it he would take an interest with me in the contract. The next day he told me that the President said I had better stay where I was and not resign. There the matter ended."[52] Instead of looking for a sweetheart deal, as Easby had claimed, Strong was dealing fairly all around—according to Strong—and Easby was the public official who wanted a piece of the action. Were these two enemies trying to discredit each other, or had there been another falling-out among thieves because Strong took over the brick contract and did not need Easby's help?

Congress adjourned on August 31, 1852, only a week after the Houston committee convened and three days after Easby's initial appearance. Between that time and the beginning of the new session on December 6, the committee did little, if anything, and most of the witnesses did not appear before the panel until the early months of 1853, when Congress was once again in session. Walter at first attended the sessions to listen to the accusations against him, but at one point he became so incensed at the testimony of some of the stonemasons that he lost his temper and had to leave.[53]

Walter was under no illusions. The Houston committee, as far as it pertained to Walter, was in reality a Borland committee with Walter in the gun sights. In his diary Walter referred to the "false" allegations against him, which was an accurate assessment, but beside the point.[54] Walter was in deep trouble. Senators did not like to be wrong, and if Walter could not be the villain, he would become the scapegoat.

Walter also understood finally that time was running out on Fillmore and Stuart and on their ability to ward off congressional tempests. Walter could feel the ground begin to shift, and his misgivings were borne out with the reopening of Congress and the arrival of the new year. On February 15, 1853, the Fillmore administration in its waning days asked for a $400,000 supplementary appropriation to fund the Capitol Extension through the end of the fiscal year. Borland immediately introduced an amendment to take away Walter's authority to disburse money for the Extension. He wanted to give the authority to Easby. Walter was "an irresponsible person," he said, and began waving pages of Houston committee testimony in the air and describing excerpts from it that were particularly damning to Walter.[55]

Hunter, perhaps worried that Borland's latest attack would kill the appropriation outright, agreed to the amendment, which was then passed. Hunter had once again abdicated his authority and had agreed with Borland, who had handed power of the purse to Walter's chief accuser. Borland immediately introduced another amendment to kill the appropriation, thus suspending the project until the work could be put "in proper hands." Hunter argued that the work should not be stopped, although he agreed with Borland that that management of the project should be transferred to someone else.[56]

At that point, however, several outraged senators stepped forward. Walter had not yet been found guilty of anything. He had not been allowed to see the charges against him, nor to present his own defense. "It was enough for me to hear that the character of this gentleman had been assailed, to induce me to rise at once to enter my protest," said Whig senator James Cooper of Pennsylvania. "If he has an opportunity to vindicate himself, he will do it," because it is impossible that someone of Walter's stature will have "bartered it so instantaneously as he must have done."[57] Support had arrived just in time. Borland lost his amendment 23–24.[58]

Debate continued the following day, but Borland was in full retreat, so much so that Hunter, in a humbling confession of weakness, acknowledged that he wished he had not voted to make Easby the Extension's disbursement officer. On February 28, undoubtedly thanks to Stanton, the House stripped out both the disbursement amendment and another proviso that Borland had managed to attach to the bill, then passed the appropriation. Walter had slipped through yet again.[59]

7

JEFFERSON DAVIS RETURNS

It was a chill, blustery day on March 4, 1853, when Franklin Pierce of New Hampshire took the oath of office as the fourteenth president of the United States. The handoff was surprisingly congenial, owing equally to the hospitality of outgoing president Millard Fillmore and the courteous, unaffected manner of Pierce, a Democrat, who, if nothing else, was almost universally regarded as a nice man.[1] The traditionally raucous event was unusually muted because Pierce's only child, Benjamin, eleven, had died just two months earlier, his skull crushed in a freakish train accident in Massachusetts. Pierce's wife, Jane, devastated by the loss, stayed in Baltimore during the inauguration. Also absent was vice president–elect William R. King, who was in Cuba, terminally ill with tuberculosis. He took the oath of office there, returned to his home in Alabama, and died in April, leaving Pierce without a vice president through the rest of his administration.

The inauguration ceremony would be remembered for several reasons. Fillmore was the last Whig ever to serve as president, his party irrevocably split over the question of slavery. Pierce was, at forty-eight, the youngest man to take office as president up to that time. And the inauguration was the first to take place while the Capitol Extension was being built.

Granted, there was still not much to see. The foundations were all but finished, and the walls of the lower floor were beginning to rise like redoubts before a medieval fortress. Pierce, as he stood at the East Portico surveying the multitude through a dreary swirl of wet snow, may also have wondered at the profusion of boulders and rocks lying about— granite and gneiss—as well as the towering piles of bricks. With the resumption of construction the previous year, Congress had been driven mad by the sounds of hammers, saws, and polishers shaping and finishing stone on the Capitol grounds. The masons had been forced to move their shop a quarter mile away on New Jersey Avenue.[2] But when it came time to set the stone, it had to be carted back to the Capitol and chiseled and hammered into position. By early 1853 a tourist could begin to imagine what the new Capitol might look like when it was finished, but the grounds would more and more take on the appearance of a quarry, and even the nearby vacant lots would be littered with leftovers and mistakes.

One of the invitees that March morning was Jefferson Davis. He had met Pierce during a foray to Washington in the 1830s, when, as a young ex–Army officer, he was deciding whether he wanted to remain a cotton planter like his brother Joseph or perhaps get into politics. Pierce at the time was a young senator from New Hampshire, a political prodigy of sorts, and the two men—Davis was only four years younger—got along well. There was no indication that they had kept up their acquaintance, but Pierce needed credibility with southern Democrats, and Davis—the principled "moderate"—was a natural fit. On March 7, 1853, three days after the inauguration, Pierce appointed Davis secretary of war. A bit over a fortnight after that, Davis shoved Pierce's interior secretary aside and took control of the Capitol Extension, reaffirming leadership of the project he had abandoned two years earlier.

Pierce, a compromise candidate, was a courtly, handsome, and popular man, and he took office at what appeared to be a propitious time. The U.S. economy was flourishing, and the tension that had gripped the country during the compromise debate of 1850 had abated, making Washington a more congenial place than usual. This would not endure. In 1852 *Uncle Tom's Cabin* was published and became an immediate sensation—good or bad, depending on where the reader lived—thus demonstrating that the passions over slavery boiled as virulently as ever. Pierce was unable to cope effectively with this danger, and he appeared to be easily led and not very bright, showcasing his incompetence by making some of the worst decisions ever to come out of the White House. He had a history of alcoholism but appeared to stay sober for most of his presidency. Still, by the time he left office in 1857, pro- and antislavery forces would be at each other's throats again and Pierce's reputation would be in tatters. History would dismiss him as the quintessential "doughface," a malleable northerner who, fatally influenced by his advisers, had sold out to the slave power. Nobody was closer to him than Jefferson Davis.[3]

Davis was destined to serve Pierce badly as a policy adviser. At the same time, however, he would serve the new U.S. Capitol magnificently. Fillmore and Walter had struggled for a year to keep Congress from killing off the project out of fecklessness or politics. By the time Davis left the War Department in 1857, the Capitol Extension could not be stopped. Davis fought the political battles, decided crucial architectural and engineering questions—albeit not always for the best—and kept the money coming. His ideological intransigence doomed him as a statesman, but his incorruptibility, tireless attention to detail, and skill as a political infighter made him a brilliant advocate and defender of the new Capitol. For four years, he kept opponents off balance and drove the project forward. On the day Pierce arrived, the Capitol Extension was still little more than an idea. When he left, it was well on its way to completion.

Davis's reemergence in Washington as a cabinet secretary, and his subsequent takeover of the Capitol Extension, were almost accidental events, for he had given no indication that he wanted to join the Pierce administration until he actually did so. After losing the 1851 Mississippi governor's election to Henry S. Foote, he and Varina returned to Brierfield, Varina said, "to put our home in order."[4] From Varina's standpoint, retirement from politics was a joy. She was only twenty-five years old, and she had appreciated her husband's time in Washington enough to write eventually about many of the great men she had met. But much of her early marriage had been marked by acrimonious disagreement and separation from Davis. At the beginning of 1852, for the first time, and just as she was maturing as an adult, she had her husband to herself. The Davises were rich: they owned 113 slaves in 1860, and the plantation earned $35,000 to $40,000 per year, substantial for the time.[5] Mail came twice a week; there were plenty of books to read; neighbors paid occasional visits; and every day Jefferson and Varina jumped on their "fast racing horses" and traversed the countryside until they found a "smooth road" where they could gallop.[6]

It quickly became apparent, however, that Davis did not intend to abandon politics. Only two months after the 1851 gubernatorial election, he attended the state Democratic convention in Jackson to mend fences, and he spent the early part of 1852 writing editorials in a "newspaper war" with Henry S. Foote, his erstwhile opponent.[7] He did not attend the national party convention in Baltimore in early June and thus missed a prolonged stalemate in which none of the heavyweights—James Buchanan, Lewis Cass, Stephen A. Douglas, or former New York governor William L. Marcy—could win the nomination, leaving Pierce to claim the prize on the forty-ninth ballot. Pierce offered the Democrats a unity candidate who could hold the party together, but apart from that, his credentials were thin.

The Whig convention, also in Baltimore, followed a similar script about two weeks later. Here the contenders were Daniel Webster, back for one last try; Fillmore, the incumbent president, supported by the southerners and blocked by fellow New Yorker and rival William H. Seward; and Winfield Scott, the commander of the U.S. Army, who was supported by the northerners. Scott won on the fifty-third ballot. Like Taylor four years earlier, he was at least nominally a southerner (from Virginia) and was a famous general who had never said anything of significance about slavery. The night the convention ended, jubilant Whigs serenaded Fillmore at the White House, then paid a visit to Webster, who finally appeared on his balcony in a dressing gown, said a few words without once mentioning Scott by name, and went back to bed. "The serenaders retired as if they had had a funeral sermon preached to them," wrote the journalist Benjamin Perley Poore years later.[8]

The Whigs were unraveling, and neither the southerners nor the northerners had much confidence in General Scott. Another ominous portent for the Whig cause came on June 19, 1852, when Henry Clay, who had been lying gravely ill in Washington's National Hotel during the convention, died two weeks after it ended. Webster, worn out and depressed, died at home in Marshfield, Massachusetts, on October 24. The Whigs were bereft of national leaders.

For Davis, however, undoubtedly keeping track of these events from Brierfield, the news was all good. Unlike in 1848, when his political obligation to support the Democrat Lewis Cass was compromised by his close personal relationship with Zachary Taylor, Pierce versus Scott offered the clearest possible choice. Pierce, a southern sympathizer and probably a drinking companion of Davis's from the old days in Washington, was good, while Scott, who had taken the field in the Mexican War only after

Taylor had won the crucial victories, was bad. Campaigning for Pierce, Davis lost no time making these views known to voters.

Pierce sent Davis a feeler on December 7, only a month after the election. He began by expressing sympathy for Davis's eye problems and "relief and joy" that all was now well: "You will not be surprised," Pierce continued, "that, under all the circumstances of our early acquaintance and present positions respectively, I much desire to see you, and to avail myself . . . of your advice. Can you gratify such desire without too great inconvenience? I wish to converse with you of the South, and particularly of the formation of my cabinet." Pierce made no overt promises, but wondered, "Do you propose to visit Washington soon? Can you come as far north as Boston?"[9]

There was no mistaking Pierce's meaning, but Davis, after mulling the invitation for three weeks, declined. Much later Varina attributed this initial reticence to "my entreaties," coupled with "Mr. Davis's unwillingness to embark again on a political life." Also, the couple now had their first child, Samuel, born in July.[10] However, given the gusto with which Davis was once again embracing the political life, Varina's disclaimer does not altogether ring true.

Pierce sent a second letter to Davis on January 12, 1853, telling him about the death of his son and wondering "how I shall be able to summon my manhood and gather up my energies for the duties before me."[11] Next was an invitation to attend the inauguration, and Davis made the trip. Once in Washington he called on Pierce, where he was, as he explained many years later, "induced by public considerations" to change his mind and enter the cabinet as secretary of war.[12] He gave no reason for his decision, but he undoubtedly knew full well that a personal invitation from Pierce would quite likely entail the offer of something besides a celebratory drink. Despite his eighteen-month Mississippi exile, he had never abandoned national politics, and both he and Varina, despite her protestations, were probably getting bored. Pierce appointed him on March 7, 1853. Davis rented a furnished house on Thirteenth Street, very close to both the White House and the red brick War Department, while Varina closed down Brierfield, hired an overseer to manage the plantation, and made a final round of visits to relatives. Then, with Samuel in tow, she headed north and joined Davis in midsummer.

———

The United States Army, when Davis joined the cabinet, had 13,821 men, most of them garrisoning forts and defending settlers in the sparsely populated western states and territories, or building dams, bridges, and harbors, or making surveys in the more developed East. Davis had ninety-two clerks, ten messengers, and five watchmen working for him. Perhaps the department's biggest asset was its library of ten thousand books.[13] Relations with Scott, still the Army commander, were strained from the beginning, and would get much worse in coming years. Scott's solution was to get away from Davis by shifting his headquarters to New York—an awkward arrangement, but one that Davis did not contest.

Davis as war secretary was wearing his unionist hat. He wanted to enlarge the regular army to create a more national and professional armed force less dependent on volunteers. He was interested in improving armament and equipment and in learning everything he could about innovations in tactics and weaponry. One of his enduring passions was to use camels as Army pack animals in remote outposts in the arid West, an idea that had first intrigued him during his Senate days. During his tenure at the War Department he would sponsor a camel-buying expedition to the Middle East and fact-finding trips to the Crimean War and elsewhere, and would host frequent get-togethers at his home for visiting scientists, referred to by Varina as the "savans."[14] The Smithsonian secretary, Joseph Henry; and Alexander Dallas Bache, head of the U.S. Coast Survey, were friends and frequent consultants for Davis's many projects.

It took a while for Davis's scientific inclinations to show themselves, but when they did, they would have a significant influence on the construction of the Capitol Extension. Even more distinctive would be his preference for more ornate artistic decorations than those envisioned by Fillmore. This "higher style" would help define the new Capitol in ways that Congress in 1852 could not even imagine.

One thing that old Washington hands would have noticed immediately, however, was that Davis worked hard and did not delegate. Scrawled notes could be found in the margins of everything from major policy documents to requests for a job as night watchman. The other thing immediately noteworthy about Davis was that while he held one of the biggest patronage jobs in the country, he had no particular interest in patronage. There would be no sweetheart contracts and no emptying the department of political opponents and filling it up with Democratic operatives and other favored friends. He had a soft spot for military veterans and his own old comrades in arms, and he could be extremely nasty to employees he did not like, but he tended to judge people on whether they pleased him, not on their politics.

When Pierce took office, the Capitol Extension appeared to be on firm financial footing. Up to that point, Congress had appropriated $1 million to fund the project through the end of the fiscal year on June 30.[15] The $400,000 that had been voted at the end of 1852 served the dual purpose of conveying the "sense of Congress" that the Capitol Extension was a worthy project while giving the administration time to master the inner workings of what was about to become a huge enterprise. Foundations— the theme for 1852—were important but largely invisible. Walls—the plan for 1853—were a different story.

The money may also have helped, perhaps for a moment, to conceal the fact that the project was under political siege. The Houston committee had reconvened with the return of Congress in December 1852, and in the months between the election and Pierce's March 4 inauguration it had gathered the vast majority of its evidence and vetted much of it on the Senate floor, building the image of a vast undertaking rife with tawdry corruption. Pierce's advance men must have known everything about the investigation, since Democrats were running it. The incoming interior secretary, Robert McClelland, must have been dreading the moment when he would have to sort out the mess.

But while McClelland might have been worried, Thomas U. Walter should have been desperate, for he was in serious danger of losing his job. During the hiatus between William Easby's opening testimony in August and the return of Congress on December 1, 1852, virtually nothing had happened, and Walter may have decided the crisis was past. He was still on good terms with Fillmore; he had sacked Samuel Strong, his corrupt construction supervisor; and he had the documentation to refute virtually every charge made against him up to that time. He was confident enough by year's end to ask the Fillmore administration to get him an additional $20,500 to finish refurbishing the Library. He wanted to gild the Library's finished metalwork in different shades of gold. The ornamental molding, pendants, and ceiling fixtures would be gold leaf bronze, and the bookcases, railings, and remaining iron would be done in light gold bronze.[16]

Had he better understood the threat posed by the Houston investigation, he might not have been so quick to dun Congress for the Library. The House, with Stanton pushing hard on Walter's behalf, succeeded in passing a funding bill on January 25. The Senate, however, used the request to hammer Walter once again during debate, passing the appropriation three weeks later over opposition from several senators, including the ubiquitous Senator Borland, Walter's leading accuser.[17]

By that time, Walter's fortunes were dimming. Between his December 28 letter and Senate passage of the Library funding, the Houston committee had been working in earnest. Easby was invited to visit the panel once more and delivered scathing testimony about the Extension project, charging that it was using bad materials, that contractors were overcharging, and that waste was rife. For the rest of the month, stonemasons testified about having to kick back part of their wages to Strong's brother, and in early February, the carpenters accused Strong of stealing lumber for private jobs. Virtually all of the testimony focused on the sins of Strong. Unfortunately for Walter, neither Easby nor Borland was particularly interested in Strong. They wanted Walter's head, and they heaped him with guilt by association.

By February 7, Robert Mills, for one, had seen and heard enough to believe that Walter was badly, perhaps fatally, wounded. He decided the time was right to try to shove him out of the way and take over. On March 1, only three days before Pierce's inauguration, the incoming president received three letters: one from sixteen senators, one from twenty House members, and one from Mills himself. The lawmakers' letters both said the same thing: Robert Mills, who "has had charge of all the public buildings erected in this city since his original appointment" under Andrew Jackson, should be made Architect of the Capitol. The Senate signatories, all Democrats, included President Pro Tempore David R. Atchison of Missouri, Stephen A. Douglas, and, not surprisingly, Borland. The House signatories included Speaker Linn Boyd of Kentucky.[18] No one replied to Mills, or to his supporters.

On March 9, Walter, unacquainted with either Pierce or McClelland, his new bosses, visited the White House, probably to pay his respects and to brief them on the progress of the Capitol Extension and on its administrative requirements. Legislation had left disbursing procedures somewhat ambiguous, and Walter suggested in a note to the new president, probably written after that first White House meeting, that Pierce and

McClelland allow him to continue handling finances until the administration figured out how it wished to proceed. But, Walter said, "should your Excy. conclude to relieve me from the charge of the disbursements, I shall consider it as a great favor."[19]

Walter has left only a sketchy record of these early contacts with Pierce, but this evidence suggests that he had made a good impression. Pierce and McClelland almost certainly talked with him about disbursement, and they may have told him that it would be a good idea if he did not handle the money any longer. But Walter's letter indicates that such a proposal—if it was made—had been presented to him more as a possibility than as an order. Seen in this light, Walter's eagerness to shed disbursement responsibility hardly seems feigned. He had kept immaculate books; his bidding procedures had been fair and transparent; and he had apparently taken no kickbacks. Yet Congress had still gone after him. Who needed the aggravation?

But then, on March 22, the Houston committee released its report, and it was blistering. The long cover letter—what at a later time would be called an "executive summary"—was written by Borland and deliberately aimed at Walter. It comprised only fifteen pages of the 120-page report, but it was, and remains, an extraordinary document. Borland used Easby's testimony almost verbatim in his own remarks, presenting the allegations as if they were the committee's conclusions. Walter had bought inferior stone, had mixed the small pieces of stone with cement, and had used granite instead of bluestone for part of the foundation, at far greater expense. He had made a *"private contract"* with Provest & Winter for the marble finishing work "at prices said to be about $100,000 above what others would have done it for." He had conspired with the marble suppliers to defraud the government by ordering many more large and more expensive stones than necessary: "The effect is that the cost of marble *is increased more than 200 per cent.*"[20]

Borland then went on to describe the kickbacks by the stonecutter apprentices, the lumber thefts by the carpenter's shop, the plans to burn Representative McNair and himself in effigy, and a whole list of transgressions by Strong. Borland—and Easby—did not, however, accuse Walter of direct responsibility. Instead, they were careful to characterize him either as an accomplice or, at best, a dupe of Strong, his superintendent. Borland wrote that when Easby went to warn Walter of Strong's perfidy, Walter "seemed to be under the control of Mr. Strong."[21] Borland compiled the charges against Walter almost exclusively from the testimony of jilted contractors, fired workers, and, in the case of the carpenters, outright thieves. The Houston committee did nothing to prove or disprove any of the most serious allegations. It never interviewed Rice, Baird & Heebner about kickbacks for shipping heavy marble, nor did it contact Provest & Winter—a local company—to talk with them about no-bid contracts. When documentation disproving the allegations was available—the two Army reports on the new foundations, the stonemasons' analyses, the interior secretary's letter categorically denying Provest & Winter's private contract—Borland ignored it. The report seemed to be a classic congressional hatchet job: target someone, cook the evidence to reflect a particular point of view, turn the target into a villain, and get rid of him.

But then, after burying Walter beneath a tidal wave of innuendo and half-truth, Borland—after a fashion—presented the defense case. Fillmore, he noted, had told the committee that he had been impressed with Strong's work in New York but had urged Walter to watch him closely. Borland wrote that Walter had fired Strong when he noticed irregularities. Also enclosed, Borland said, were affidavits from experts describing the work as well done (by the Corps of Engineers and Topographical Engineers) and the acknowledgment that experienced stonemasons had testified to the excellence of the materials.[22]

But after glossing over all this somewhat perfunctorily, Borland described Walter's defense dismissively as "a denial of all the allegations of fraud and impropriety made against him by other witnesses." He enclosed Walter's 123-page defense in an appendix to the report.[23] In summary, Borland concluded that "examination of the testimony in this case leaves no doubt in the minds of the committee that great irregularities and gross abuses and frauds have been practiced." And in doing so, Borland explained, "the public money has, so far, been expended in a wasteful and unwarranted manner, and, under existing contracts, will continue to be so expended, unless prompt and proper measures" are taken.[24] The best solution: get rid of Walter, and give the disbursement responsibility to "regular accounting officers of the treasury."[25]

Any close reader who chose to look beyond Borland's opening screed would soon find that the committee's report actually ended up refuting itself by including all the documentation that gave the investigation the lie. There was absolutely no hard evidence of bad contracts, bad stone, or shoddy workmanship in the foundation. In fact, all the reports were glow-ing, including one from Robert Mills, who, as the committee was finishing its deliberations, was trying his best to oust Walter and take his job. The committee, in the final analysis, had proved nothing.

The odds that Pierce read it closely, however, were remote, and, in a way, moot. He would have learned two things if he had read Borland's cover letter, neither of which had anything directly to do with the Capitol Extension. First, he would have seen that Walter had enemies in Congress, and second, that Walter was a Fillmore hire, so Pierce owed him nothing. Right or wrong, there was no reason to defend him. What president—especially a Democratic president who had no stake in the Capitol Extension—was going to risk perpetual disharmony with Congress by hanging on to a Whig appointee like Walter?

Pierce took action the day after the report came out, issuing an executive order making a radical change in the administration of the Capitol Extension project. The "public interests involved in the erection of the Wings of the United States Capitol" would best be served, Pierce said, "by exercise of a general supervision and control of the whole work by a skillful and competent officer of the Corps of Engineers or of the Topographical Corps." But since such officers were "immediately responsible" to the War Department, he continued, "I hereby direct that the present duty heretofore exercised over said work by the Department of the Interior be transferred to the War Department." The secretary of war, Pierce finished, will "designate to the President a suitable Officer" to take over the project.[26] Walter was out as building supervisor and disbursing officer, but, at least for the moment, he would stay on as the architect for the project. The Army officer would take the job left vacant after Strong's firing, and Walter would work for him, thus flipping the previous hierarchy.

This was not what Borland, Easby, or Mills had envisioned. Instead of pressing the inexperienced McClelland or the uninterested Pierce into swapping Walter for Mills or someone more congenial to their interests—whatever those might have been—they were going to get Davis and an Army engineer. Davis was the proverbial gorilla in the room. He knew as much about the project as they did; he was smart and understood Congress; he, not Congress, would control the designated Army officer; and he could invoke the power of the presidency whenever he felt like it. Easby, as he undoubtedly had feared, lost his job as commissioner of public buildings, and was replaced by Benjamin Brown French, who was an important Mason in Washington and a childhood friend of Pierce. He took over as commissioner at the end of June.[27] Davis, after sixteen days on the job, was in charge of the new Capitol Extension.

Most accounts of this event, the most important administrative change made during construction of the Capitol Extension, characterize the transfer as a Pierce initiative prompted by Borland's skewed and damning report the previous day.[28] Walter's position was untenable, regardless of guilt or innocence, and Congress could be expected to chew up any presidential appointee that took his place. Special legislation had given Fillmore—and succeeding presidents—the power to name the architect of the Capitol virtually by fiat and without confirmation by Congress. This ensured that congressional resentment would never altogether abate.

Given these circumstances, putting an Army officer in charge was an adroit move—and certainly not something one would have expected from Pierce, who was anything but adroit. Patriotism required that the designee be presumed honest, a privilege never enjoyed by Walter, and any officer who was chosen would almost certainly have impeccable professional credentials. West Point was the first four-year engineering college in the country, and its graduates were the best engineers available: officers and gentlemen by definition, as opposed to the thuggish Samuel Strong—or Thomas U. Walter, dismissed by some Washington power brokers as little more than a glorified stonemason. Congress would think twice before taking on the U.S. Army.

Davis in later years buttressed this view of the takeover, portraying himself in his memoirs, written more than a decade after the end of the Civil War, as the passive instrument of Pierce's wishes: "My advocacy, while in the Senate of an Extension of the Capitol, by the construction of a new Senate Chamber and Hall of Representatives, may have caused the appropriation for that object to be put under my charge."[29]

The available evidence, however, tells a much different story. The catalyst for the changeover was neither the Houston committee report nor Pierce. It was Interior Secretary Robert McClelland who called for a change, opening the door for Davis to seize control.

McClelland obviously knew of the Houston committee's investigation and of the uproar that it had caused. And he knew about Strong's transgressions and his heavy hand. He apparently did not intend to fire Walter, but he was looking to reorganize the project under a new construction supervisor and wanted someone as unlike Strong as he could find.

On Saturday, March 19—three days before the Borland report was published—McClelland wrote a letter to Jefferson Davis, asking for help: "Being impressed with the belief that the public interest connected with the Extension of the Capitol . . . would be promoted by the supervision of some well-qualified scientific person, I should be glad to have the services, for this purpose, of a competent officer of the Corps of Engineers," McClelland wrote. He did not want "to displace or dispense with the services of any of the officers now employed," he continued, "but to exercise a general supervising control over the whole work." He asked Davis, "if it can be accomplished without detriment to any other branch of the public service," to name the officer.[30]

This was followed on Monday, March 21, by an internal War Department memo, probably written by Davis himself, saying that "since the receipt of this [the McClelland] letter, the Extension of the Capitol has been turned over to the charge of the War Department. The Secretary desires the Chief Engineer to detail an officer for that duty." The note was signed on March 22 by Archibald Campbell, Davis's chief clerk. Pierce issued his executive order the next day, Wednesday, March 23.[31]

The conclusion to be derived from this correspondence was that Davis took the project from McClelland the moment McClelland asked him for an Army engineer to run it. Davis, the tireless bureaucrat, would have seen McClelland's note as soon as a messenger brought it by. If he had had time on Saturday he would probably have run it over to the White House then and shown it to Pierce. If not, he would have had to wait until Monday. Pierce never did business on Sunday. In either case, by the time Davis—or someone else—wrote the Monday memo, Pierce had already agreed to transfer the project. By the time Pierce announced it on March 23, the deal had already been closed for at least two days, and maybe four.

Davis, no matter what he might have claimed, was anything but a passive underling carrying out orders. Instead, given the sequence of events, it is clear that Davis actively sought control of the Capitol Extension and talked Pierce into making the switch.

Why did Davis want the job? Probably for several reasons. Given how closely—even obsessively—he monitored the things that mattered to him, it likely irritated him profoundly that McClelland wanted to take one of

Davis's men to oversee a project that Davis himself had invented three years earlier when he was in the Senate. Davis may well have had designs on the Capitol from the day Pierce brought him into the cabinet. McClelland's letter simply gave him an excuse to jump.

That McClelland had a good idea seems clear. The language in Pierce's executive order was obviously cribbed from the interior secretary's original letter to Davis, and Pierce's description of what the change was supposed to accomplish simply repeated McClelland's vision. The only difference between the McClelland letter and the Executive Order was that Davis had taken McClelland's job—deliberately, and on the same terms on which McClelland wanted to keep it.

So why did Davis, so many years later, disclaim any proprietary interest in the Capitol? Respect for Pierce may have contributed to his reticence. Davis was almost as fond of Pierce as he was of Zachary Taylor, and he may have wanted to give Pierce's legacy at least a hint of luster.

A more likely reason, perhaps, is that Davis, in the post–Civil War years, was working on his own image as the personification of the South's "Lost Cause." It could not have been convenient to acknowledge in his memoirs that he had aggressively sought a leading role in building the nation's most enduring monument to the power of the federal government.

The next task was to pick the new supervisor, and the War Department wasted no time. Following Pierce's announcement, General Joseph G. Totten, chief of the Army Corps of Engineers, on March 25 proposed Lieutenant William S. Rosecrans to take over at the Capitol. Rosecrans, Totten told Davis, "possesses the highest qualification for the duty." Totten's signature, however, was dated March 28. The delay, he said, was caused by difficulties in relieving Rosecrans, on duty in Rhode Island at the time. These, he said, now appeared to have been worked out.[32]

But not for long, for in a second note, also dated March 28, Totten changed his mind, withdrawing Rosecrans's name "after further consideration." Instead, he said, he now proposed Captain Montgomery C. Meigs, "as having more rank and . . . experience in construction." Meigs was already in Washington, having just completed a survey of possible sites for an aqueduct to bring running water to the capital—another project initiated because of the Library fire. "I did not name him in the first instance,"

Totten said, "because I feared that the labors connected with the introduction of water into the city might absorb too much of his time." But, he added, "I have since satisfied myself that he will be fully equal to the care and supervision of both operations."

Besides his availability in Washington, Meigs had also served a tour of duty as a Totten adjutant in the 1840s. The general's relationship with Meigs was a long and apparently a cordial and close one: "I do not hesitate to say that the whole country can afford no man with so fine a character and habits of life, of scientific attainments, and cultivated taste, as more fit to meet the duties and responsibilities involved in the proposed assignment."[33] At the bottom of the letter, also dated March 28, were the words "Let Col. [sic] Meigs be detailed," followed by Davis's signature.[34]

Totten had given Meigs as lovely a recommendation as a military superior could write, particularly for an engineer officer so obscure that Davis could not even remember his rank. But Totten was not finished. In two more letters, also dated March 28, he gently prodded Davis, first, to get Pierce to approve Meigs's aqueduct recommendations, and second, to put the Corps in charge of building the aqueduct and give Meigs the job.[35]

And Meigs got it all. On March 29, undoubtedly following further discussion with Davis, Totten ordered Meigs to begin work on the Washington Aqueduct, and on April 4, Davis ordered him to take control of the Capitol Extension.

Captain Montgomery C. Meigs had hit the jackpot. He had spent most of the previous ten years building forts in the wilderness, had missed out on the Mexican War, and by 1851 had five children and needed a $300-per-year allowance from his father, a prominent Philadelphia physician, to make ends meet.[36] Luckily for him, he had earned Totten's goodwill, and in 1852 he seemed to catch a modest break when the general plucked him from the nether reaches of upstate New York and sent him to Philadelphia, where he could at least be close to his family. At this point in his life, his biographer Russell F. Weigley has suggested, Meigs, still a first lieutenant, was probably drifting toward mediocrity.[37] The peacetime U.S. Army had little for him to do but build frontier garrisons and levees, and once he had mastered that, there was little else available on which to test his talents. His choices were to leave the service and make a lot of money running a mine or building railroads, or stay in the army, clear tree stumps from river channels, and go hunting after work.

Radical changes began November 1, 1852, the day Meigs and his family arrived in Philadelphia. Totten, unannounced, was waiting for him. Corps Captain Frederic A. Smith, assigned to do the surveys for the Washington Aqueduct, had suddenly dropped dead. Totten needed someone to finish the job, and he had picked Meigs. Orders arrived the following day, and Meigs began the survey November 3. He would live in Washington for the rest of his life.[38]

Meigs trusted Totten completely, and in his early years in Washington he consulted the general frequently and regularly for advice on a wide range of topics: the members of another commission to examine the Lee marble; the performance of a rock crushing machine; which books to borrow from the Corps' library; how big an engine to use in the Capitol's mortar mixer; what changes to make in the marble and marble finishing contracts. In the summer of 1854, Totten invited Meigs over to look at photographs of Roman ruins sent to him by his daughter, who lived in Italy.[39]

And Totten's loyalty to Meigs was absolute and unwavering. Meigs finished his aqueduct survey on February 12, offering three possibilities. The cheapest option was to draw the water from Rock Creek, in the middle of the District; another was to take the water from the Potomac at Little Falls; and the third, and most expensive, was to pipe the water from Great Falls, fourteen miles upriver from Washington, D.C. Meigs, in a pattern that would become almost a trademark, chose permanence over expedience and recommended Great Falls. Totten forwarded Meigs's report to Fillmore's War Department two days later, saying "I entirely concur" with Meigs's assessment and that he had "no hesitation" in endorsing it. It would be expensive—Meigs estimated $1,921,244—but would require almost no maintenance and would deliver an inexhaustible supply of water coming into town at 1,700 horsepower. Totten's only criticism of Meigs's report, he said, was that it had not put enough stress on the advantages of such a system for firefighting.[40] Like his recommendation to Davis a month later, this vote of confidence was just about perfect. Totten believed in Meigs's plan, staked his own reputation on it, and, seeing that Meigs was not yet fully attuned to the politics of public works, gave the plan an extra push by recalling the Library disaster.

The Washington Aqueduct, surveyed, designed, and built by army captain M. C. Meigs during the 1850s, was a jigsaw of tunnels, sluices, bridges, conduits, reservoirs, and valves leading from Great Falls, on the Potomac River between Virginia and Maryland, to Washington. It has been in continuous use since 1859. (Library of Congress)

In all, within five days in late March, Meigs took control of both the Aqueduct and the Capitol, as well as a smaller project adding wings to the U.S. Patent Office. Maybe Totten picked Meigs for the Capitol because he was having trouble springing Rosecrans from his current job. Or maybe he picked Meigs because, as he said in his letter to Davis, Meigs outranked Rosecrans, or maybe simply because Meigs was available. The only thing that sounds a truly false note in Totten's letter is his contention that Meigs was fully capable of handling all the jobs simultaneously. This was preposterous on its face. But Totten turned out to be right.

Davis may have known of Meigs before he was appointed to the Capitol Extension, but it is unlikely. And Meigs himself certainly had no idea that he could become superintendent of the Extension. No matter. Meigs got his Capitol marching orders as Engineer in Charge of the Capitol Extension from Davis on April 4, 1853. The mandate was clear and sweeping: "*You will consider yourself fully empowered to make such changes in the present administration as you may deem necessary* and to regulate the

Captain Montgomery Cunningham Meigs of the Army Corps of Engineers was thirty-six years old when Secretary of War Jefferson Davis appointed him to oversee construction of the Capitol Extension. Like many army engineers his age, he had spent most of his career in obscure frontier outposts, but he was also a highly regarded protégé of Corps commander General Joseph G. Totten. (Architect of the Capitol)

organization hereafter as your experience may dictate." This presumably meant that Walter was expendable, if Meigs decided to get rid of him. Meigs would be handling disbursement, using Treasury Department guidelines, Davis said, and in his only overt nod to the Houston committee, he asked Meigs to conduct another inspection of the Capitol foundations because of "public sentiment" that a "careful examination be made." If he found nothing wrong, he was to leave the foundations alone. If there were problems, he should fix them.

Davis's chief concerns, he told Meigs in the letter, were "the arrangements for warming, ventilation, speaking and hearing. The great object of the Extension of the Capitol is to provide rooms suitable for the meeting of the two houses of Congress." He wanted rooms with breathable air where lawmakers could hear each other. "These problems are of difficult solution and will require your careful study," Davis continued, urging Meigs to look at public meeting rooms elsewhere in the country. If Meigs needed books, he should buy them. He should "freely consult with this department and make your reports directly to this office."[41]

Davis's letter was at once a policy statement, a helping hand, and a warning. Meigs now understood that Davis knew a great deal about the Capitol and its shortcomings. Meigs also understood that Davis did not want half measures and did not intend to pinch pennies. Meigs could travel wherever he wanted and buy whatever books he needed to learn how best to carry out the instructions. He could organize the workforce to his own satisfaction and he would enjoy the War Department's unwavering trust and support. But Davis cautioned that the job was difficult, and above all, he wanted Meigs to get it right. He had given Meigs carte blanche, a compliment every bit as handsome as those that had been paid to him by Totten. But now he was Davis's man.

8

ENGINEER IN CHARGE

Captain Montgomery Cunningham Meigs was a month short of his thirty-seventh birthday when he became Engineer in Charge of the Capitol Extension in April 1853. The Washington Aqueduct was the project he had coveted. He had spent months picking the route, then surveying it and designing the structures. The Aqueduct was the essence of his West Point training: riding through the dense woods along the Potomac, moving tons of earth, laying pipe, diverting a river.

Now, finally, he had the Aqueduct; but he had also been handed the Capitol Extension, which was easily just as important, and probably more so. The new Capitol already had a design, a foundation, contractors, and a payroll of several hundred men. At the Capitol, Meigs would also have Congress looking over his shoulder—every day. Instead of the avuncular General Totten, he would answer to Jefferson Davis, a severe southerner about whom he knew nothing and whom he at first described in his diary simply as "the secretary," or "the secretary, Mr. Davis." Still, the presence of Davis told Meigs, if he needed telling, everything he had to know about the significance of the project. For the Aqueduct, he reported to the Army's chief engineer, an important man. But for the Capitol, he reported to the secretary of war.

If Meigs was intimidated, he did not show it. He was well qualified for the job, and not just because of his experience and training as a West Point engineer. Meigs had the right personality. He had a strict military bearing, and he radiated self-confidence, even outright arrogance, traits that would enable him to mingle easily and without fear with the large egos that surrounded him on Capitol Hill. He also had an impressive intellectual swagger. He was very smart, could think clearly, and mastered new subjects effortlessly. He read constantly, he could write cogently, and he could explain himself in words that laymen could understand. He was deeply interested in gadgets and self-improvement. He was fascinated by photography and its potential, and by 1853 he was a committed disciple of Pitman shorthand, which had only recently been introduced into the United States. Meigs had dreadful handwriting, and throughout his life he made no effort to improve it. He found that he could write faster in shorthand, and since he worshipped speed in all things, he used shorthand in his diary and in rough drafts of his letters, even though for most people the symbols were as indecipherable as his cursive.[1]

When Meigs was six years old, his mother had described him as "very inquisitive about the use of anything, delighted to see different mechanics at work, appears to understand their different operations when explained to him and does not forget them—uses knives, hammers all very dexterously, remembers the particulars of many incidents that occurred two or three years ago, and many things that I had not supposed he noticed. He seems to observe every thing that passes."[2] For Meigs at thirty-six, this long-ago cameo had become reality. He was seldom, if ever, taken aback.

Meigs was also aware of some of his weaknesses. He was envious, even jealous, of others' success and contemptuous of others' ignorance. He tried to control, or at least mask, these defects. He was also stubborn, irascible, quarrelsome, impatient, effortlessly overbearing, and incredibly ambitious, and these things he did not recognize at all. Resentment toward him, a frequent result of his imperious ways, was to him an annoyance. It did not cause him to back off. Lesser people, he decided, simply did not like it when he noticed their faults and took them to task.[3]

Then there were the intangibles. Meigs was scrupulously honest. At the Capitol he could easily spend $50,000 in a month, sometimes much more, and throughout his Army career he would handle billions of government dollars—the first person ever to do so, by some estimates. His enemies—and he had plenty—searched for the money he had squirreled away, but they searched in vain. As far as anyone could determine, he never stole a dollar, took a kickback, consorted with contractors, or partnered with a crony on an outside job. And he remained clean even though he needed money all the time. In 1853, as a brand-new captain, he made only $1,800 per year, and even with the $300 annual stipend his father sent him, he had to count every dollar he spent. He was proud, even pompous, about his honesty, but he hated his poverty and complained about it frequently in his diary: "I have superintended the work of some 4 or 500 men, and the expenditure of a good many thousands of dollars, in which I have saved a good amount," he wrote after a bit more than a year on the job. "I do not think that in these times I am paid half and ¼ as much as I fairly earn."[4]

Meigs knew that he, like any other trained engineer in the country, could make a relative fortune in the civilian world. But army life fit him like a glove. He never said so in so many words, but his actions and attitudes consistently reflected a military outlook. He spoke often of duty; he set rules for himself, lived by them, and required his subordinates to do the same. He was by-the-book, doctrinaire, and even dogmatic, a churchgoing Episcopalian who tried to take Communion every week. The army and his church had long ago answered any questions he may have had about his place in the cosmos or about how to behave.[5]

Finally—and this was an advantage Meigs had over many colleagues, and especially Walter—he was a blueblood. His family had settled as Puritan immigrants in Massachusetts in the seventeenth century, his great-uncle was a Continental Army hero, and his grandfather was a Yale professor and president of the Columbian Institute, the forerunner of George Washington University. He had an uncle who had served as governor of Ohio, and his father, Charles J. Meigs, was a renowned obstetrician and a leading citizen of Philadelphia.[6] And in 1842, during a first and relatively short stay in Washington, Meigs had met and subsequently married Louisa Rodgers, daughter of the War of 1812 naval hero Commodore John Rodgers.

When Meigs, Louisa, and their five children came to Washington in 1853, they moved in with her mother, the commodore's widow, who allowed them to live rent-free and contributed $600 per year for food and upkeep. Meigs did not have enough money to entertain, but he had a fine address at Northwest Fourteenth and H Streets and a guaranteed entrée into the capital's most exalted social circles. His standard of living he characterized as "mean, rather than profuse," but in exemplary Protestant fashion decided that "it is good for us to have this trial and to practice this self-denial."[7] Especially since, notwithstanding his penury, he could rub elbows with the elite.

The Meigs family had been Democrats since Jefferson, and Meigs went to West Point while Jackson was president, graduating fifth in his class in 1836. This may have made him attractive to Davis, although Meigs's politics, if he had any, were all but invisible. Other than party affiliation, however, he had nothing special to offer the Pierce administration. Much later, researchers looking for something significant in his background would discover that he had spent the summer of 1837 with then U.S. Army captain Robert E. Lee on a Mississippi River mapping and harbor improvement expedition in and around St. Louis.[8] This excursion became interesting only in hindsight, of course. Apart from that, he had spent his career in forgettable billets—dredging the Delaware River and building forts in Detroit and on the northern shore of Lake Champlain.

Now, however, the easy life was over. On April 5, the day after he formally took charge of the Capitol, Meigs had a cordial meeting with Walter, told him how he planned to run the project, and took a briefing on the plans and the financial records. Meigs then sent Davis a brief note informing him that he had told Walter to pay off the Extension's existing debts before he took financial control.[9] This was followed three days later by a longer letter in which Meigs complained that the Treasury Department would no longer accept Walter's vouchers. Such a procedure, he reminded Davis, was not acceptable in the army, where an engineer would take a new job only after his predecessor had settled the accounts.[10] He asked Davis for instructions. This was to be Meigs's lone bureaucratic hiccup. The problem came to nothing, and in future, as he became more confident, Meigs focused less on asking for Davis's opinions and more on informing him of news, plans, gossip, and the interesting discoveries and innovations he had made on the job. Still, Davis had told him to keep him informed about everything, and nothing was too trivial for the secretary.

On April 15, Meigs and Walter together went to visit Davis at the White House. Walter described the meeting in his diary as a "consultation" with the "Cap:Sec," an indication that he clearly understood, both from the venue and the participants, where Meigs derived his authority.[11] Meigs by this time had, on Davis's orders, begun an inspection of the Extension foundations. Like those who had gone before him, he had found nothing seriously wrong.[12] This result, which he formalized at the end of May, effectively eliminated the most enduring charge leveled by the

Houston committee against Walter. Everything else had either been dis-
proved by Walter's detailed documentation or laid at the feet of Samuel
Strong, Walter's disgraced and dismissed project superintendent.

So Walter apparently had a clean slate. It is likely that Davis needed
to hear about the inspection findings at the April 15 meeting in order to
make a decision about the Capitol architect. Neither Walter nor Meigs at
that moment recorded particular discomfiture with Walter's position, and
the meeting with Davis appeared to come off smoothly. Meigs, in typical
military fashion, had moved quickly to clear the air with Walter and was
ready to move on. As for Walter, his continuing role as the architectural
"house man" for official Washington probably settled any remaining
doubts. Besides the Capitol Extension, Walter was working on the Library
and on smaller jobs at the White House and the Patent Office. Even if he
was fired from the Extension, he would not go away. Walter's skills were
much in demand, and neither he nor Meigs nor Davis had a lot of time to
ruminate on his future.

Still, it would have been an agonizing three weeks for Walter between the release of Senator Borland's Houston committee report and the
April 15 meeting. Walter desperately wanted to stay on at the Capitol, and
he must have communicated his wish to Meigs almost immediately. Much
later, Meigs described his view of the transition in a letter to Walter, and
Walter never disputed the account. Meigs said he had immediately understood from his orders that Davis had "deprived you of all authority, ex-
cepting such as I might confide to you as my assistant."

Meigs also noted that Davis had offered to get rid of Walter—perhaps
even urged it. It is not clear from Meigs's letter whether Davis first made
this suggestion in April 1853, but Walter was never a Davis favorite, and
Davis in future would come close to ordering Meigs to fire Walter. Meigs
had "resisted" Davis's wishes, he told Walter later, "upon the ground that
you were faithfully acting as my assistant, (and a most laborious and skillful one) and that to remove you under the charges made against your
management of the work in debate, in the report of a senatorial committee . . . was to destroy your reputation and ruin you personally." Davis ultimately backed off, and a grateful Walter, Meigs recalled, "more than
once expressed to me your sense of the obligations you thus incurred."[13]

While there is no evidence that the complexities of the Meigs-Walter-
Davis relationship were vented at the White House on April 15, they were
certainly resolved to Walter's relieved satisfaction within the first few

months of Meigs's arrival. Walter, in a June 27, 1853, letter to his father-in-law, Richard Gardiner, expressed his satisfaction at "the thorough vindication" he had won from the Treasury Department on the handling of the Capitol monies and from "the Engineer in Charge [Meigs] on the excellence of the work and the firmness and solidity of every part of it."[14] And early in 1854, in another letter to Gardiner, Walter praised Meigs, calling him "as noble a man as the country can produce." Also, he continued, with Meigs in charge, "you have no idea what a luxury it has been to me, during the past year, to be able to devote myself to my legitimate professional duties" without having to worry about the administrative details.[15]

Walter, in this correspondence, finally appears to have understood how close he had come to getting the sack. He would not have known about Davis's personal vendetta—that Walter's close relationship with Richard Stanton had placed him permanently on Davis's blacklist. He may also not have been aware that Davis was unimpressed with Walter's professional credentials, an attitude he appeared to hold toward all architects.[16] Now that Davis had Meigs, his well-trained and well-connected West Point engineer, it did not really matter to him who drew the pictures.

Walter, however, certainly would have realized that in the transition between Fillmore and Pierce, he had become a political orphan. The Houston committee had undercut him badly, and now he was a residual, badly scarred Whig in a Democratic administration. Quite apart from any personal animosity or contempt Davis might have felt, Walter was expendable.

Given these drawbacks, it was in fact remarkable that Walter survived. One circumstance undoubtedly helped him, and, together with Meigs's intercession, may have saved him. This was the latest—and what would be the last—foundation inspection. Davis probably ordered it to clear the fog from the project and give Meigs a clean slate on which to begin work. But its other result was to vindicate Walter in all respects and to unmask the Houston committee report as a travesty. Davis could be an evil-tempered, mean-spirited grudge holder and a fearsome enemy, but in his own professional—as opposed to political—dealings, he was almost always fair. Quite simply, Walter had done nothing wrong, and there was no reason for Davis to fire him. The case was closed.

———

Meigs threw himself into the Capitol project, and within five weeks he had come up with fundamental alterations that would forever change the Walter-Fillmore plan. On May 17 he sent Davis the first draft of a proposal to move the new Senate and House chambers away from the West Front, where Walter had put them, and place them instead in the centers of their respective buildings. This was a radical departure from current construction practices, for it meant that there would be no windows, and therefore no natural ventilation or uninhibited sunshine in either space. There were nonetheless advantages to the new design. Having enclosed chambers would allow Meigs to configure them to optimize their acoustical properties without reference to outside noise or outdoor changes in temperature. Giving lawmakers—especially House members—rooms in which they could hear one another was a key goal in Davis's orders to Meigs. Also, by moving the chambers into the center of the new wings, Meigs would make the flow of traffic through the entire Capitol much easier and more coherent. There would be corridors, reception rooms, and offices on all sides of the new chambers, and senators and House members would be able to reach their desks without long pilgrimages to the western extremities of the two buildings.

To make his redesign a reality, Meigs proposed to roof the two chambers with glass and light them with skylights during the day and gas lamps—mounted between the ceiling and roof—at night. Fans would blow fresh air, heated during the winter, into the two chambers from outlets in the floor and ceiling. Exhaust fans in the basement would remove the stale air. The air would be entirely replaced every fifteen minutes.[17]

This design was destined to become a signature feature of the Capitol Extension, and it would be criticized for decades. For its opponents, the transgression could not have been more obvious. Under the Meigs plan, the clean, sunlit, breezy meeting halls of Fillmore and Walter would be replaced by murky interiors that depended for fresh air and light on an untested system of remote man-made devices. This would not only be a fundamental alteration in design, but would also change the very ambiance of Congress. The Fillmore-Walter chambers would have been wide open and boisterous. The Meigs-Davis chambers would be hushed and intimate.

It is tempting to regard the Meigs proposal as the first manifestation of an egomania that in coming years would drive him to make his presence felt in every brick of the Aqueduct and every alcove and archway of the

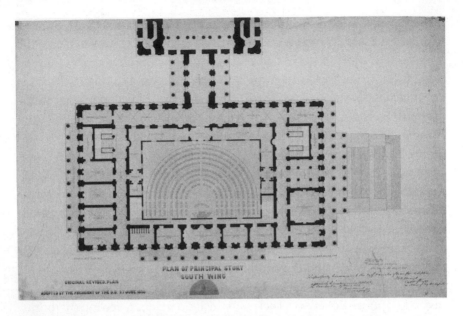

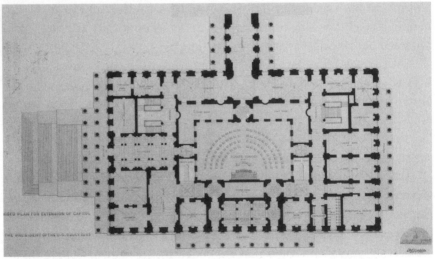

Meigs's plan to move the Senate and House chambers away from the outside windows remained controversial for years after the Capitol Extension was built. The design may have marked the first time anyone proposed artificially heating and cooling a public building of any size. (Architect of the Capitol)

new Capitol. Obsessed with creating a legacy for himself, Meigs sought opportunities—whether for good or ill—to put his stamp on the building, sometimes literally. He stuck copper plates bearing his name in the masonry of the Capitol and Aqueduct and had his name cast on iron fixtures used in the projects. He even had a flight of Aqueduct stairs built in the shape of the letters of his name. The chamber redesign could be seen as the first of these private adventures.[18]

There is substance to this view. Of the three principal actors who built the new Capitol—Davis, Meigs, and Walter—Meigs was the youngest and, at the beginning of the project, the only one with a scanty résumé. Ambition and a desire to be remembered for his accomplishments certainly drove him throughout his career. At the Capitol he studied architecture and art, in part so he could compete with Walter and make informed judgments about ornaments and statuary. His first request for money from Davis to purchase expensive art books came only ten days after he began work.[19] By the time he was finished he had made himself an expert in every facet of the project—from papier-mâché decoration to heating systems.

But if he was guilty of egomania, it was a vice he shared with both of his associates. All three men were infused with a desire to create a unique building—one that would win respect and glory not only for the United States but also for themselves. The tension inherent in this shared obsession is part of what caused the triumvirate to seek innovative and occasionally spectacular solutions to the unique problems posed by the Capitol. Davis had already made his mark by insisting on the rambling sweep of a north-south horizontal wing design. Walter had created the outer shell of the new building and designed a one-of-a-kind cast-iron Library of Congress. Now it was Meigs's turn.

And if his ideas were controversial, he could simply point out that he was following orders. Davis wanted "suitable" meeting rooms, and Meigs was eager to build them. His proposal, as explained in a detailed paper that appeared a year later in *The Civil Engineer and Architect's Journal*, used Davis's mandate—especially the acoustical constraint—as the guiding principle of the new design. For optimum public speaking, Meigs said, no room should have a ceiling higher than 30 to 35 feet. To offset echoes and reverberation, chairs and desks should have cushions, the floor should have thick carpeting, and walls should be hung with drapery to muffle sound. The "next essentials" to ensure good hearing "are a tranquil atmosphere and the absence of extraneous sounds," he continued. This could best be attained by getting rid of the windows, which, in cold weather particularly, had the effect of chilling the indoor air that touched them, creating "different densities" that distorted sound. "If we exclude external windows and light the room only from the roof, we get rid of this fruitful source of discomfort and indistinctness" and obtain a "pleasanter light, ample for all useful purposes," he said. And in the summer, there would be no open windows either to let in unwelcome outside sounds or let members' voices escape. Finally, piping air in from the ceiling and draining it through the floor would maintain a uniform atmosphere throughout the room, while noxious dust from the carpets, instead of swirling through the air to be inhaled by lawmakers, would be sucked away before it could do any harm.[20]

Meigs was well aware of the audacity of his proposal when he submitted it to Davis on May 17, and he suggested that "some persons of eminence in science" examine the plan to determine whether it would accomplish what he said it would.[21] Two days later he delivered the completed report to Davis, asking him to pass it on to the Smithsonian's Joseph Henry and Alexander Dallas Bache, head of the Coast Survey. Davis did so.[22] On June 8, Meigs, Henry, and Bache, with Davis's blessing, traveled to Philadelphia, New York, and Boston to examine churches and other public meeting houses. In Philadelphia, among other landmarks, the group visited Girard College—Walter's most important pre-Capitol design—and Robert Mills's "Circular Church," which Meigs dubbed the "worst room I have seen out of Washington."[23] On June 24, Henry and Bache endorsed the Meigs redesign, and Pierce formally approved it for both wings. Workmen would now have to dig new trenches and build new foundations. This would be expensive, but Davis did not care.[24]

Meigs was not finished. He also had new ideas for the exterior of the building. And these, too, would be expensive. For durability and permanence, he wanted to have much thicker marble facing for the outside walls of the new wings. Walter's original plan had called for blocks of between nine and eighteen inches in width; Meigs now wanted blocks between two and three feet wide. He informed Rice, Baird & Heebner of the plan in early August.[25] The company wanted to be paid more for bigger blocks, reminding Meigs that the original contract had stipulated the smaller dimensions. Protracted negotiations on a new contract began.

This Meigs proposal was as bold in its way as his interior redesign. It also showed how the politics, and the balance of power, of the new Capitol project were changing. Walter's early marble orders had caused trouble with the Houston committee the previous year because he had asked for more of the larger, costlier blocks than Easby and Senator Borland thought necessary. But Walter had been a civilian working for a parsimonious Whig administration and facing a hostile Congress. Meigs was working for Jefferson Davis, who had told him, in effect, to do whatever he thought best for the building, regardless of price. Meigs decided the best course was to increase the size of the "small" blocks by 162.5 percent and double the size of the large blocks.

Another Meigs change, also expensive, was both structural and aesthetic. Under the Walter-Fillmore plan, the façade of the Capitol, when completed, would have one hundred new marble columns, each of them 24 feet 3 inches tall and weighing 15.7 tons. Meigs decided that for durability—and because they looked better—these columns should be made of a single piece of marble instead of a series of drums fitted one on top of the other. Meigs asked Rice, Baird & Heebner about these "monoliths" early in his tenure, and at the end of July the company told him the Lee quarry could provide the columns in one or two pieces for $6.00 per cubic foot. Meigs replied on August 4. "This is not a very large item," he said. "I think that you ought to be willing to furnish them at a less price."[26]

It took Meigs and John Rice five months to reach a tentative agreement on both the facing blocks and the columns. Meigs outlined the basics for Davis at the end of the year. He did not mention prices, but he explained forcefully and without embellishment that the company—whose stone had proved to be as tough and stunningly beautiful as predicted—now held all the cards. For the facing blocks, Meigs said, he had two choices: buy smaller stones under the terms of the 1852 contract, or write a new contract and pay more for the larger blocks. Meigs wanted the new contract, and he also wanted it to include a deal for columns. As the contractors had dug deeper into the Lee quarry, he said, it had appeared that there was stone in sufficiently large blocks to provide the exterior monoliths. "The sandstone columns of the old building are generally in single blocks, and we ought not in this matter to be behind our ancestors," he told Davis. He "respectfully" suggested that the administration ask Congress for authorization to rewrite the contract. "If Congress refused," he finished, "the building will have to be constructed in an inferior manner."[27]

This, Meigs knew, would not be tolerated. Meigs had learned that he and Davis had the same grand vision of what the Capitol should be. Meigs knew what he wanted to do to implement the vision, and eight months into his relationship with Davis, he did not hesitate to ask for it. The written communications, which consisted mostly of Meigs making proposals and Davis facilitating them, rarely hinted at disagreements. But Davis was neither easygoing nor passive. There were undoubtedly discussions and arguments, but these must have taken place face-to-face. Once differences were settled, letters were exchanged for the record.

Meigs had one more change to make in Walter's original exterior design. Like his other moves, it would be fundamental. He wanted to add pediments—triangular gables—at the eastern porticoes of both new wings. In Walter's design these entrances had no pediments, making them architecturally subordinate to the grand central portico and staircase leading up to the central Rotunda, which did have a pediment. Meigs's plan, by adding pediments to the wings, made the side entrances more prominent. This gave the entire eastern façade a more horizontal, expansive appearance. The new pediments, also like Meigs's other initiatives, would be expensive, and not only because of the additional construction. Meigs intended to fill their recessed spaces, or tympana, with statuary.

On July 7, Meigs wrote to Massachusetts senator Edward Everett, a noted Harvard University classicist, describing his plans and asking him for names of American sculptors to provide the pediment statuary.[28] Everett, in Boston during recess, responded five days later. He had "no hesitation" in recommending two artists, both expatriates living in Italy. Hiram Powers, in Florence, was celebrated as the sculptor of the life-size nude statue *The Greek Slave*, on permanent display in England's Raby Castle and taken on tour in 1848. Thomas Crawford, in Rome, was working on a large equestrian statue of Washington for the state of Virginia. Powers, Everett's first choice, was "in some respects" America's "first living artist," he said, while he ranked Crawford second. Either, however, could do the work.[29]

On August 18 and 21, Meigs wrote virtually identical letters to the two men. He told them he had consulted with Davis and was prepared to offer both, as American sculptors, an unprecedented invitation to provide statuary for the new U.S. Capitol. He advised both sculptors to provide sketches as soon as possible but cautioned them to keep quiet about the proposal so Congress would not get wind of it and interfere. His plan was for Powers to do the tympanum for the Senate, or northern, pediment and Crawford the House pediment to the south. He suggested to Crawford that he consult with Powers so that their designs would "harmonize," and he urged both sculptors to try to please both scholars and "the less refined multitude."[30]

Powers replied in a brief and remarkable letter dated September 28. He had found Meigs's proposal "welcome and most interesting," but "I have not the time to prepare designs for the decorations of our capitol buildings."[31] Crawford, by contrast, accepted Meigs's offer immediately. A bit over three months after that, he had made models of his proposed statuary, which he arranged in a tableau he called *Progress of Civilization*, and sent Meigs photographs. The statuary consisted of thirteen human figures, dominated by a female *America*, who stood in the center of the pediment with an eagle by her side. To her left were figures from early America: an Indian chief, an Indian mother and child, a hunter, and a frontier woodsman. To her right, representing contemporary "Diversity of Human Endeavor," were a soldier, a merchant, two youths, a schoolmaster and student, and a mechanic.

Meigs described *Progress* in his diary as "a very fine composition," and he wrote to Crawford about it. He had shown the photograph to Davis, he said, and told him that he wished to hire Crawford and put his statues in the Senate pediment. Davis "approves it highly," he told Crawford. Pierce gave final approval to the statuary on November 30, and Meigs closed the deal for $20,000.[32] He dashed off a short note to Crawford the same day, urging him "from time to time" to let him know how the work was progressing.[33]

Crawford, only two years older than Meigs, quickly became a favorite because of his easygoing personality, his desire to please, and his remarkable ability to take advice without rancor or sarcasm and turn it into a statue with almost breathtaking speed. Meigs had quibbles. He told Crawford in a December 27 letter that his soldier looked a bit too much like George Washington, probably not a good idea.[34] Two days later, suspecting that Crawford had never seen an Indian, Meigs tactfully suggested that he visit the papal library, which had a book with useful pictures.[35]

Meigs had made an outstanding beginning. Not only had he boldly changed the design of the Capitol Extension, but he had cemented a cordial and respectful relationship with Davis and convinced him of the wisdom of his ideas. He had asked for and ultimately received the good wishes of the two most accomplished scientific minds in Washington in Henry and Bache. And he had made a comfortable and apparently seamless transition with Walter, retaining his expertise and winning his loyalty.

Davis's support was particularly welcome, for it gave Meigs an extremely effective ally in warding off attacks by Congress and other outside bureaucracies, and these were not long in coming. A bit over a month after taking charge, with Congress still in session, Meigs wrote a note to Davis asking whether the contracts with Rice, Baird & Heebner and Provest & Winter were illegal because they outran the yearly appropriations for those purposes. Borland had promoted this idea during the previous Congress in hopes of voiding the contracts and stopping the project.[36] A few days later, Easby, not yet ousted as commissioner of public buildings, told Meigs that under the terms of the contracts, he, as commissioner, was responsible for appointing certain key officials in the Capitol construction hierarchy.[37] This had been part of Borland's move to hand administrative control of the Extension to Easby. In 1852 both of these measures were jettisoned only after prolonged debate. This time Davis all but dismissed them out of hand. It would take more than nuisance legislation to engage Davis.

Meigs's debut was not, however, completely smooth. He fought with Provest & Winter, who complained about having to haul marble from their workshop on New Jersey Avenue to the Capitol, a considerable expense. Congress and the Supreme Court had banished the firm from the Capitol grounds because of the noise, a problem that should have been "foreseen," Meigs wrote in his diary. Since the contractors made the mistake, Meigs said, "they ought to suffer from their want of foresight."[38] This disagreement remained unresolved.

A much bigger headache arose when Meigs decided to transfer the brick supply contract to a low bidder who, in Walter's opinion, would never be able to fulfill it. This proved to be true, but the shortfall did not become immediately apparent because Meigs also decided to get rid of Walter's contract bricklayers and replace them with bricklayers on a day's-work basis.[39] One of the biggest differences in the project between the Walter and Meigs regimes was that while Walter was always looking for opportunities to use contractors, Meigs liked day's work, which gave him greater hands-on control of the workforce.

Unfortunately, however, his new government-paid bricklayers struck for higher wages during the summer, the height of the building season. Meigs, backed by Davis, would not negotiate. The bricklayers then formed a "society" and refused to work with anyone who did not belong to it. Davis told Meigs to stand fast: the "ulterior objective is to compel the Government to employ the members of the society and them only," Davis wrote. "The Department feels it a duty to resist a movement so improper in itself and so injurious to the public interest."[40]

Meigs then advertised in New York and Philadelphia to import strike-breakers, and on August 2 he telegraphed one of his recruiters that "bricklayers are flocking in here . . . I have 50 bricklayers, want only 20 more—board 3.00 per week."[41] The strike soon ended, and by late August, Meigs was laying more than fifty thousand bricks per day.[42] Then, as Walter predicted, the supply of bricks ran out, because the supplier did not know what he was doing. Meigs fired him, and over the next three months he traveled up and down the eastern seaboard negotiating deals for more than 4 million bricks—enough to keep the bricklayers working until December, when the weather shut them down, and to build a stock-pile for the spring.[43]

This months-long blunder offended Walter, who vented his frustra-tion in a long diary entry in September. "If my recommendation had been taken, we would have had a steady supply of the best hand-made bricks at $7.12 [per thousand] from Washington contractors—as it is, we get all sorts of bricks, hand-made, slush bricks, dry clay, pressed bricks, bricks large and small, good bad and indifferent and an uncertain supply at that." He predicted that the government would lose $30,000 for having gone with the low bidder. Still, he was charitable toward Meigs, who "has done his best, and gives me credit for having been right."[44]

Relations between Meigs and Walter were always complicated. They started—at least publicly—with respect and mutual admiration. Meigs had treated Walter delicately and admired his skill. Walter was grateful to Meigs, undoubtedly suspecting, probably correctly, that he owed him his job. Still, there was an undercurrent of competition and tension between the two men. Walter did not like being either ignored or interfered with. He kept his objections to himself, complaining in his diary about the bricks affair, and again in October, when Clement West, one of his top assistants, quit the project because Meigs would not allow draftsmen to augment their salaries with outside work.[45] On Meigs's side, at least during the opening months of the partnership, there is some reason to suspect that he, as the new arrival, may have been somewhat intimidated by Walter. As a professional builder himself, he not only respected Walter's abilities, but he also would have noticed that Walter, engaging and well connected, had many friends on Capitol Hill. He also would have felt the glow of Walter's genius when the new Library of Congress opened in August to spectacular reviews. Regardless, working in tandem, Meigs and Walter successfully navigated the transition to Franklin Pierce and forged a successful partnership by the end of 1853. Both could be satisfied that they had met, and triumphed over, serious professional challenges.

Like Walter two years earlier, Meigs in 1853 was able to negotiate his first months on the job without the burden of intense congressional scrutiny. But with the opening of the first session of the 33rd U.S. Congress in December, he, again like Walter, could expect to be second-guessed and called to account. Meigs's engineering and supervisory skills would be questioned, but these were assaults he could easily repel. The key contest would be a political one.

Meigs appeared to be in better shape than his predecessor. Walter had been a civilian and the ward of a weak Whig administration, with one congressional ally, Richard Stanton, chair of the House Committee on Public Buildings and Grounds. Meigs was only a junior Army captain—not even a field-grade officer—but he answered to the secretary of war, an energetic and powerful Democrat well known in Congress not only as a fierce advocate for slavery and southern rights, but also as a vindictive and ruthless infighter. If lawmakers decided to go after Meigs, their adversary would not be an Army captain. It would be Jefferson Davis.

Still, Meigs was vulnerable. Congress was always jealous of its prerogatives, and never more so than when it was defending its own house. And while Congress was away, and despite a total absence of relevant experience or personal reputation, Meigs had changed almost everything about the new Capitol. Without consulting anyone but Davis, he had discarded the entire interior layout and replaced it with a revolutionary design that might or might not work, and that featured windowless Senate and House chambers. He had decided—again, with Davis's help and without consulting Congress—that the marble facing on the exterior walls should be heavier, much heavier; that the porticoes of the new wings should be changed; and that the façade needed a hundred monolithic new marble columns. If all this were done, the cost of the Capitol Extension would go up like a rocket, and he wanted to present the plan to Congress—with Davis's blessing—as a fait accompli.

Walter, perhaps not surprisingly, was the first person to remark on the inevitable storm this would provoke, since he knew better than anyone that Meigs's changes were far more radical than anything he himself had tried in the nearly two years he had held the top job. In a letter to his father in Philadelphia, written three weeks before the December 5 congressional opening, Walter wryly recalled his own travails and predicted that "a general onslaught will be made on Meigs, and I shall have to bear my share."[46]

Davis, too, knew what was coming, but he prepared brilliantly. On December 1 he sent his first annual report to Congress as secretary of war. He introduced Meigs with unalloyed enthusiasm. He outlined the progress of the new construction, focusing on the need to fix the House acoustics. Meigs, with the endorsement of Henry and Bache, had produced the correct plan: "In view of the many unsuccessful attempts which have been made in our own and other countries to attain that result, success will be, in addition to its utility, an object of just national pride." Other goals in the redesign, he said, were to "facilitate the intercourse" between the two houses of Congress and "materially to add to the architectural effect of the building." In all of these particulars, Meigs had performed spectacularly.[47] Davis then submitted Meigs's report, dated October 23, which covered the same ground but in much more detail. Both reports were printed in the *Congressional Globe*, December 6, the day after Congress opened. Meigs pasted in his diary the part where Davis lauded his performance, noting that "it speaks very favorably of my works and conduct."[48]

Davis had just given Meigs Lesson One in how to fight a congressional battle, and Meigs had missed it. The kind words were not there just to make the captain feel good. Davis was announcing that Meigs had his full, unequivocal, and enthusiastic support and that any opponents of Meigs were Davis's opponents. Next, Davis had taken co-ownership of Meigs's redesign, leaving no doubt that he fully endorsed everything that Meigs had done. He wanted details from Meigs because he had already used and approved the big ideas in his own report. Finally, by submitting the report early and in detail—December 1—as part of the first item produced by the new Congress ("House Executive Document No. 1"), Davis was able to benchmark the debate. Anybody who had a problem with the Capitol Extension would have to use his report as the starting point.

It did not take long for the battle to take shape. The enemy this time was Representative Richard Stanton, Walter's former protector. The ostensible source of Stanton's dissatisfaction was the takeover of Capitol construction by the War Department—Stanton's opposition to what he would come to describe as "military rule." But there were probably other motives at work. Stanton doubtless harbored lingering animosity over Davis's attempts in 1850 and 1851 to get his original wing design accepted by the Fillmore administration over House objections. Also, Stanton, a tireless defender of the Capitol Extension who had stood fast during the two years Davis spent in Mississippi, had been completely ignored in the planning for Meigs's redesign. He had returned to Washington to find himself suddenly marginalized on a project he had sponsored from the beginning.

On December 14, Walter wrote a warning letter to Meigs—away from Washington on a two-week trip to visit quarries—reporting that the House had just passed a Stanton-sponsored resolution asking Pierce to provide information on the newly planned alterations to the chamber and asking how much they would cost. Meigs, who had his own sources, noted in his diary that the House had picked its committee chairmen and Stanton had been left off both Public Buildings and Grounds and the Committee on the District of Columbia.[49]

The war, Meigs correctly ascertained, had begun. The "declaration of war," which he had heard about from another Army engineer, was Stanton's unstated determination to get rid of Meigs. The "first act" of war was to get the House leadership to strip Stanton of his committees. This, Meigs wrote, was probably the work of Davis and the mayor of Washington, a leading supporter of Meigs's work on the Aqueduct. The "second act of war," Meigs continued, was Stanton's resolution, which, besides asking for information about the nature and cost of the redesign, also inquired about "the expediency of placing the superintendence under the Commissioner of Public Buildings or some other civil officer." Stanton, Meigs concluded, "has felt the blow" and wanted revenge against Davis—and Meigs.[50]

9

WALTER HAS A NEW IDEA

On January 4, 1854, Democratic senator Stephen A. Douglas of Illinois introduced what was undoubtedly the most ill-advised piece of legislation enacted in the 1850s, and probably one of the worst laws ever passed in the United States. The Kansas-Nebraska Act, as it would come to be called, was designed to formally transform a large chunk of the Louisiana Purchase into a U.S. territory, the first step on the road to statehood. Kansas-Nebraska was important because it straddled any prospective central route for a transcontinental railroad. By the end of the year, it was filled with gunmen, the North was in an antislavery uproar, what was left of the Whig Party had all but disintegrated, the Democrats were paralyzed by bitter internal battles, and a new, vibrant, antislavery Republican Party had emerged. The Act did nothing to promote a transcontinental railroad.

Eighteen fifty-four was the year when the United States began to unravel, a year that the historian Allan Nevins, nearly a century later, labeled simply "Disaster."[1] But it was also the year when construction of the new, enlarged, and increasingly more elegant U.S. Capitol became a truly national goal. Prior to 1854, the Capitol Extension was little more than the curious obsession of a half-dozen lawmakers and bureaucrats, carried forward simply because these few people cared enough to keep it going and were powerful and persuasive enough to obtain the money to do so. But in 1854, Congress ceased suggesting that the project be abandoned because it was too expensive, too pretentious, or simply unnecessary. Instead, lawmakers focused on how it should be accomplished. Should the

War Department keep control of construction? Did the changes made by Secretary of War Jefferson Davis and Engineer in Charge Montgomery Meigs make sense? During debate early in the year, Senator Lewis Cass told his colleagues that he wanted windows, not "lamps burning in the middle of the day."[2] Rhode Island Democrat Charles T. James liked downward ventilation for heating and cooling the chambers, and he thought Meigs had done "all that could be desired."[3] Senator Robert Ward Johnson wondered "how high I am to ascend" when the new basement boilers suddenly exploded.[4] Everyone laughed.

There were many reasons why senators were being less confrontational in their attitudes toward the Capitol in 1854. Under Meigs, construction was advancing so fast that the project was about to become too big to kill except at great expense. Also, Walter's fabulous new Library of Congress had shown lawmakers how a terrible catastrophe could be turned into a thing of beauty if the job were done right. And finally, as many lawmakers had reason to know from personal experience, Davis was not the pliable Fillmore administration. Interfering with the secretary of war could be a humiliating and politically damaging experience, and Davis had left no doubt about the ferocity of his commitment to the new Capitol. The prevailing wisdom, shared by Meigs, among others, held that Davis had instigated the ouster of Richard Stanton as chairman of the House Committee on Public Buildings and Grounds because he did not like Stanton. To get rid of Davis, a Democratic Congress would need to contravene an executive order of the Democratic president. This could be done either by persuading Pierce to change his mind or by enacting legislation to overturn the order. Neither alternative was a task to be undertaken lightly.

But perhaps the main reason the Capitol was becoming popular was that it was one of the few remaining national enterprises that could unite rather than divide Congress. Sectionalism and slavery were poisoning almost every political debate and every candidacy in the country. Everyone may have wanted a transcontinental railroad, but to make it happen, a route needed to be chosen, and picking a route was about picking which part of the country would host the route, and picking a section of the country was about slavery. Tariffs were about sections: should they be high, to protect northern industrial goods produced by free labor, or low, to promote southern agricultural exports produced by slave labor? But politicians, wherever they came from, loved to build things, and they loved legacy. The Capitol project offered an opportunity—perhaps the

Walter's new cast-iron Library of Congress was a fully fireproof triumph. Two tiers of alcoves and three tiers of shelves were connected by iron staircases. Congress supported both the Library and the Washington Aqueduct in part because they felt responsible for the destruction of the old Library, which had burned out of control for lack of a ready supply of pressurized water in the city. (Architect of the Capitol)

only opportunity in 1850s America—for lawmakers to build something permanent and national, "an enduring monument to . . . the honor of our country,"[5] James called it on that January day. Even fiercely proslavery politicians could embrace the effort. As a result of the changes made in 1853, the project had become much more ambitious, and it would become much more expensive in 1854, but Congress supported it without demur—and would continue to do so regardless of who was running it.

That debate—like the debate over what was initially known as the Nebraska territory—was now ready to begin, and Jefferson Davis would play a key role in both dramas. His vision of the new Capitol was well known and meshed seamlessly with Meigs's design changes. His views on Kansas-Nebraska emerged more slowly, but his actions on that question would prove equally decisive.

Douglas's first try at a Kansas-Nebraska bill contained only one clause about slavery: "And when admitted as a State or States, the said Territory, or any portion of the same, shall be received into the Union, with or without slavery, as their constitution may prescribe at the time of their admission."[6] What was not said was whether slavery was to be prohibited in the territory before it became a state. Most interested parties held that it was. Under the Missouri Compromise of 1820, those parts of the Louisiana Purchase, such as Nebraska, that lay above 36 degrees 30 minutes north latitude were free soil.

This interpretation did not sit well with slave state legislators, in particular Missouri Democratic senator David Atchison, the Senate's powerful president pro tempore. Missouri was already bordered on the north and east by free states, and it would be further isolated if Nebraska, on its western border, were to become a free territory. How Atchison and others initially manifested their displeasure to Douglas is not altogether clear, but on January 10 the legislation was reprinted in Washington newspapers with additional words that Douglas said had been omitted from the original because of "clerical error." The new clause said "that all questions pertaining to slavery in the Territories, and in the new States to be formed therefrom, are to be left to the people residing therein, through their appropriate representatives."[7] This was a clear statement of the principle of "popular sovereignty"—that settlers prior to statehood would decide whether to allow slavery, and would do so without preconditions and without federal interference. By implication, the bill now voided the Missouri Compromise. Antislavery northerners were enraged.

But even this was not enough for the southerners, who insisted that the Nebraska bill had to have specific language repealing the Missouri Compromise. Douglas agreed. At the same time, he also decided to modify the bill to create two territories instead of one. The implication of this move was that the Northern piece—Nebraska—would be free while the Southern piece—Kansas—would be a slave state. Northerners hated this, too.[8]

To gain acceptance of what would be the final version of the bill, Douglas would have to weather what he quite accurately described as "a hell of a storm" from the northerners.[9] He needed political cover—the endorsement of the Pierce administration. If Pierce rubber-stamped the Nebraska bill, Douglas could make it a test of party loyalty. Northern Democrats who voted against it would risk the wrath not only of slave-staters, but also of the New Hampshire president.

Pierce was weak. It had taken him less than a year to squander the goodwill that attended his inauguration. Neither northerners nor southerners trusted him on slavery, and his inept efforts to win over competing party factions with patronage had ended up alienating everyone. And finally, since Pierce was a weak man, he easily fell under the sway of the stronger personalities in his cabinet. The strongest of these was Davis, and by the end of 1853, the secretary of war was Pierce's closest adviser.

Davis's presence at Pierce's right hand sent a powerful message to Democrats, since many party northerners regarded him as an outright secessionist. Many policies the president undertook in domestic and, especially, in foreign policy were seen as little more than excuses to expand slavery. Pierce was interested in annexing Cuba, buying a piece of northern Mexico—the logical right-of-way for a southern railroad—and competing with Britain to annex a piece of the Central American isthmus and build a canal across it, and all of these initiatives carried this stigma. Now, if Douglas could arrange it, Pierce would repeal the Missouri Compromise.

And Davis made it happen. By Saturday night, January 21, Douglas had readied his final Nebraska bill and planned to bring it to the Senate floor the following Monday. He needed Pierce's approval, but Pierce did not work on Sundays. So Douglas and a delegation of southern senators, among them Atchison and Hunter, visited Davis on Sunday morning and asked him to intercede with Pierce on their behalf. He agreed. "I went with them to the executive mansion," Davis wrote long afterward, "and, leaving them in the reception room, sought the President in his private apartments and explained to him the occasion for the visit."[10] At Douglas's behest, Pierce wrote and signed a statement saying the Missouri Compromise was "inoperative and void."[11]

Douglas, with Pierce's blessing in hand, reported the measure out of committee on Monday. On Tuesday, before debate began, a self-styled group of antislavery Independent Democrats, led by Ohio senator Salmon P. Chase, Massachusetts senator Charles Sumner, and several antislavery House Democrats, denounced the bill in the Washington weekly National Era. Douglas had created a monster, they said—a "gross violation of a sacred pledge," a "criminal betrayal of precious rights," and part of "an atrocious plot" to transform Nebraska into a "dreary region of despotism, inhabited by masters and slaves."[12]

Douglas, in a bravura display of floor generalship, nonetheless corralled enough votes to pass the bill in the Senate in five weeks. The key question, however, was deliberately left unanswered: When should settlers assert their popular sovereignty and decide whether the territories should be slave or free? Northerners preferred to have it done quickly, before slave owners could get settled. Southerners, not surprisingly, wanted to wait. This and other factors virtually assured that conflict would arise on the Kansas plains. Both sides understood this, and increasingly both sides were prepared for it and may even have welcomed it. The Kansas-Nebraska Act had the dubious distinction of permanently radicalizing public opinion.

The Senate passed the Kansas-Nebraska Act by a vote of 37–14 after a final all-night session March 3. The House, whose membership was weighted more heavily toward the more populous north, needed more time, but passed the bill 113–100 on May 22. Pierce signed it on May 30. By that time northerners had already organized "emigrant aid societies" intent on filling Kansas with free-state settlers. And on July 29, proslavery Missourians organized the Platte County Self-Defense Association, with the avowed purpose of removing the northern emigrants from Kansas, by force if necessary.[13] The battle lines for what was to become "Bleeding Kansas" were thus drawn. In November, voters turned out 66 of the 91 free-state House Democrats who had won election in 1852.[14]

With Davis as his boss and mentor, Montgomery Meigs's stature in official Washington was growing. Early in the year, Davis invited him to a large reception at his house, accompanied him to a dinner attended by Senator Hunter, Joseph Henry, and other notables, and brought him home to take potluck with Varina when both men were working late.[15]

But the early social whirl did not reflect reality. Within a few weeks, the Kansas-Nebraska Act had poisoned the capital's political climate. And very quickly Meigs for the first time had his hands full with Congress. Stanton was stepping up the pressure to end "military rule" for the Capitol Extension. He and like-minded legislators were seeking to take the project away from Davis, and they were serious.

On its face, Davis and Meigs appeared to be well positioned to ride out any tempest that Stanton could create. Alterations to the foundations of the Extension—a prerequisite to building the windowless chambers—

were nearly complete, at a cost of $26,000. In addition, the first floors of the new wings had been finished, and Meigs in 1854 was poised to finish the walls of both buildings as fast as he could lay the bricks and set the marble facing.

The project itself was in no danger. But once Congress had confirmed that the Capitol Extension was both popular and necessary—and this was established by February—the custodianship of the project moved to center stage. Stanton's philosophical argument against the War Department— that military works should be built by the military and civilian works by civilians—was ridiculous on its face. Military engineers were the best trained in the country, and they were cheap. They never had enough redoubts and forts to erect during peacetime, so they were put out on loan for all kinds of civilian jobs: bridge building, road clearing, harbor dredging, and stump pulling from swamps and river bottoms all over the country. Beyond that, the worst that could be said about military control of the Capitol Extension was that it was inefficient or perhaps extravagant— charges that were unproved, unprovable, and almost certainly untrue, given Meigs's prodigious energy and the rapid pace of construction. Furthermore, "extravagant" was no longer a pejorative. For two years, Stanton, among others, had toiled ceaselessly to save the Extension from cost cutters. Now, for the first time, the project was getting all the money it needed and more. With Davis running the show, all the things that had bothered Stanton in the past had been resolved.

Vendetta was the only explanation that made sense. Stanton was known to have been furious when he was ousted as chair of the House Public Buildings and Grounds Committee, and he was sure that Davis was responsible. Also, he could not have been happy when Davis failed to consult him during the 1853 recess about Meigs's planned changes to Walter's original design. On Davis's side, resentment toward Stanton probably originated during the initial stages of the Extension project in 1850–51, when Stanton refused to endorse Davis's original wings plan. This snub festered for two years, until Davis, from his powerful perch at the War Department, decided to seek revenge by arranging for his friends in the House to depose Stanton. But Stanton did not go away, and now Davis was forced to take him on.

Stanton's campaign began in January with a stream of unflattering— and unsigned—newspaper stories and editorials. Meigs had spoiled the Capitol's façade, spent too much money on bricks, and was buying

$30,000 worth of sculpture. Meigs after reading the first accounts, simply remarked in his diary that "the war goes on."[16] Two weeks later, North Carolina representative F. Burton Craige, Stanton's successor as chair of the Public Buildings Committee, told Meigs that he was "satisfied" that Stanton was behind the attacks.[17] Meigs had already figured that out.

Yet, except for expressing an occasional desire to rebut the newspaper charges, Meigs kept quiet. He cultivated Craige as an ally and concluded that Senator Hunter was also "all right."[18] With this kind of support he was ready for whatever came next. Hunter no longer chaired the Senate Committee on Public Buildings, but he had become even more important to Meigs as chairman of the Senate Finance Committee, where he was in charge, among his other duties, of appropriating money for the new Capitol.

Watching quietly on the sidelines and probably grateful to be there was Walter. In a January 3 letter to John Rice he noted that Stanton was "dreadfully opposed to the Capn." He also predicted that "Old Sam Houston" had united with Commissioner Easby "to slaughter Capn. Meigs" in a reprise of the 1852 hearings that Houston had chaired. He repeated this concern in a second letter, this one to his sister Martha, a week later, and on January 13 he and Meigs met with Craige to secure his support for a resolution to rewrite the marble contract so they could pay Rice, Baird & Heebner for thicker stones. Craige told them he thought Stanton was so hostile that he might try to block the measure.[19]

But Walter had misread the threat. Houston had nothing against Meigs. This became apparent to Meigs when he paid a call on Houston at Houston's rooms in Willard's Hotel on January 4. Meigs found Houston unwell, lying on the floor in an upper-story room, covered by a red blanket with his head propped up on a wad of newspaper. He was "pouring out tobacco spit and blasphemies in a mingled stream" while a parade of well-wishers and glad-handers came and went. He "professed a favorable disposition toward me," Meigs wrote in his diary, but Houston was bitter against Walter and "denounced him in unminced terms." Apparently Walter's performance during the 1852 hearings had failed to satisfy Houston, so much so, Houston told Meigs, that "he had nearly abstained from calling upon Jefferson Davis on 1st January" because Davis had not fired Walter.[20]

Meigs, to judge from the tone of his diary, found Houston bizarre and his opinion of Walter inconsequential, but if nothing else, the encounter demonstrated that the Capitol Extension project, now approaching the end of its fourth year, had acquired its own institutional history. Meigs, a relatively new player, may not have known the whole story, but Houston did, and he, unlike Stanton and most of the rest of Congress, was not a Walter booster.

And neither was Davis. But, in defense of both the secretary of war and the senator, anyone knowledgeable about Capitol Extension history could legitimately wonder about Walter's role in Stanton's crusade. During the 1850–51 competition, Stanton and Walter had been allies. Under Pierce, both had been usurped. Now Stanton was trying to get rid of Davis and Meigs. Was he hoping to bring Walter back? And was Walter helping him?

Davis thought so. On January 28 he summoned Meigs to his office and told him he thought Walter was "intriguing" against him. He proposed to write Pierce a note asking for Walter's dismissal. Meigs protested "and I hope satisfied him that Mr. Walter was misjudged in the matter."[21] Davis dropped the subject. Then, two days later, Senator Hunter took Meigs aside and wondered "whether there was any attempt to remove Mr. Walter." Meigs told him about the conversation with Davis, saying "I thought it was a great wrong." Hunter assured Meigs that Walter was "true" to Meigs, and he promised to speak with Davis. Hunter, who had seemed willing to push Walter out the door in 1852, had now become Walter's new Senate champion. Perhaps he, too, was thinking about 1851, when he, like Stanton, had opposed Davis's original wing plan.

Still, the military rule dispute was doing Walter no good. On February 8, Stanton delivered his first floor speech on the subject. The particular object of his displeasure was the practice of putting Army officers in charge of national armories, but his targets were broader. First, the War Department: "I look upon the system of infusing the military men of the country into civil places to the injury of competent mechanics, as a great evil, and shall do all in my power to break up and destroy it," he said. Then, without naming names, he praised Walter to the skies and denounced Meigs as a ham-handed incompetent. "We have, sir, in this country . . . architects and builders, mechanics and artisans, who rank well with the same classes who are to be found anywhere in the world," he said.

And I have seen to my mortification and disgust, some of these men, at
least one with a genius in his profession not surpassed by any of his class
now living, reduced to the class of a mere clerk, draughtsman or servant,
if you please, of one of these military engineers, to record his will, give
form to his crude suggestions, and spend superior talents to make éclat
and fame for his inexperienced but highly favored superior.

And in case his listeners did not understand him the first time, he said it
again, and just as eloquently: "Even your Capitol is under military rule,"
he said. "Why, sir, it is not enough that all these works should be placed
under military control, but you see devised a stupendous plan of bringing
water to this city, at a cost of millions of money, that a military man may
erect a monument to his own fame?"[22]

Meigs absorbed this diatribe with the same dispassion that marked his
reaction to the newspaper attacks, noting only that Walter had reported
Craige's view that Stanton's polemic had been well received, so much so
that it was "probable that all civil works would be taken from us." Walter,
Meigs wrote in his diary, was so "worried and alarmed" by this prospect
that he wanted to write a letter to Hunter to distance himself from Stanton's
views.[23]

Walter at this point was panicking, and with justification. Whether he
liked it or not, or agreed with it, Stanton was painting him as the leading
victim of a War Department that was out of control. Stanton had publicly
proclaimed that Walter's boss and his boss's boss had dreadfully wronged
him and turned him into little more than an indentured servant. Walter,
who still had trouble reading Meigs and had had little or no direct contact
with Davis, now did everything he could to divorce himself from Stanton.
First, he openly discussed Stanton's remarks with Meigs, probably hoping
to inoculate himself against accusations that he was Stanton's stooge. Next,
he decided to contact Hunter, his new patron. Hunter was a powerful senator, a supporter of the Capitol Extension, and, most times, a close associate of Davis. Two days after Stanton's speech, Hunter and Meigs had
dinner with Davis, and Hunter strongly urged Davis not to fire Walter.[24]

Not so easy to understand was Meigs's continued nonchalance, maintained even after the House on February 13 formed a House select committee to investigate military control of government projects and named
Stanton as the chairman. Stanton's bid to take the Capitol away from
the War Department had enough resonance to prompt an investigation.

Walter's fears of a reprise of 1852 seemed to be coming true, but in the House, not the Senate. Meigs had had no experience of 1852, but he went to see Davis, who was enraged and "spoke very contemptuously" of House Speaker Linn Boyd and of Stanton. Still, Meigs himself, writing in his diary, was fatalistic: "If Stanton can beat the Senate and the administration on this question, I can retire with a clear conscience and be quite as well paid as I am now and have much less labor and responsibility."[25]

This, in fact, was Meigs's refuge. Waging a war to the death with Congress was a task far above his stature as a lowly Army captain. He was enjoying his job and wanted to keep it, but he had not yet, apparently, developed the proprietary obsession that had gripped both Walter and Davis—and Stanton—long ago. The Capitol was still an "assignment" to Meigs, so he would sit tight and see what happened. And if Congress dumped him and the War Department, he would simply escape to private business, where he could fulfill his other career goal—making a lot of money.

And this was the strength of "military control." Both Stanton and Davis knew—and accepted—that a changing of the guard at the Capitol Extension no longer involved the surgical removal of a Walter or a Meigs. Military control was a conflict between Stanton and Davis. Nothing would happen to Meigs unless Davis lost that war. Until then, Meigs was free to get on with his job.

And he did. Meigs's first order of business was to get his marble resolution passed so he could pay Rice, Baird & Heebner for the monolithic columns and for the bigger blocks of stone he was using for the facing of the new wings. These changes would add $148,000 to the cost of the job. Even so, and despite Stanton's fulminations against military rule, the resolution passed easily in the House on February 15—two days after Stanton's denunciation—and in the Senate five days later.[26] Next, Meigs wanted a new appropriation. For this he needed to cultivate Craige and Delaware senator James Bayard, the new chairman of the Senate Committee on Public Buildings. Meigs wrote Craige a long letter on January 14, explaining the changes he had made in the original plan and the reasons for them, and followed it a month later with a similar letter to Bayard. His basic theme was that the new design "will add hundreds of years to the durability of the building," and for that it would be "well worth its cost."[27] The new

Capitol promised continuity and permanence in an uncertain world. It was an argument that would gain strength as times grew more desperate.

Meigs's third concern was something he largely kept to himself, although he may have discussed it with Davis. After signing a contract with Thomas Crawford to provide the pediment sculpture for the Senate's East Portico, he had begun thinking about decorating the interior of the new wings. Walter had been told merely to match his interiors to those of the original Capitol, and he and Fillmore had assumed that they would be finished with clean, whitewashed walls, hung with occasional oil paintings. Meigs had a very different, and in one respect a very specific, idea. On January 12 he wrote a letter to Emanuel Leutze, a German-American artist living in Dusseldorf, Germany, who had recently gained fame and stature for his painting *Washington Crossing the Delaware*. Meigs told Leutze that "some of the rooms" in the Extension needed decoration, and wondered, "are there American artists capable of executing a fresco painting of large size," including, presumably, Leutze.[28]

About the same time he contacted the former two-term congressman Gouverneur Kemble, a well-known art connoisseur and armorer who built cannon for the Army in his foundry across the Hudson River from West Point. Kemble's reply to Meigs, dated February 16, 1854, was discouraging: "I am not surprised at your reluctance" to settle for "any inferior work of art" for the Capitol, he said, but if Meigs was determined to hire American artists, he would be disappointed. "We must admit," Kemble added, "that in painting and sculpture, if not in architecture, we are still behind the great masters of Europe."[29]

To get a second opinion, Kemble put Meigs in touch with the expatriate artist John G. Chapman in Rome, whose *Baptism of Pocahontas* hung in the Capitol Rotunda. Chapman proved even less enthusiastic than Kemble, particularly about fresco painting, which he dismissed as a "lower art form."[30] The three men conducted an ongoing discussion about Capitol artwork for most of the rest of the year.

Meigs continued to press for information about fresco. The reason for his persistence is not clear, but it probably had much to do with the medium's endurance. Fresco requires that paint be applied directly to wet plaster, so that when it dries completely, the pigment literally becomes part of the wall or ceiling, lasting as long as the building that hosts it.[31] As far as Meigs was concerned, fresco, like a monolithic column, was forever.

The United States quite likely had no true frescoes in the 1850s, and

Meigs had never been to Europe and thus had never seen one.[32] But he had an abiding interest in art, probably acquired during his days at West Point when he, like all cadets, learned to draw in order to produce accurate pictures of battlefield terrain in the days before photography. Under the tutelage of resident artists Seth Eastman, Charles Leslie, and Robert Weir, many cadets—among them Jefferson Davis and Ulysses S. Grant—created works of surprising talent and intricacy. Meigs was "more than competent" in landscape, watercolor, and technical drawing, as the art historian Barbara Wolanin, curator for the Architect of the Capitol, has pointed out, but more important, "he had great confidence in his own judgment and taste."[33] He was never reluctant either to express his own opinions or to seek those of an Everett, a Kemble, or a Chapman. And if he did not know something, or wanted to know more, or needed ideas, Davis would buy him the books he asked for. During one foray to New York in early 1857 he paid $510 for a copy of *Galeries Historiques de Versailles*.[34]

Meigs continued to gather information about art and decoration and to build the infrastructure he would need to provide it, but he was careful not to get ahead of himself—or his handlers. In mid-January, he wrote Craige a confidential letter telling him that Pierce had approved Crawford's pediment design. He sent along Crawford's photographs, but he cautioned Craige not to mention the pediment because he did not want "to be besieged by every workman who ever made a bust and who therefore thinks himself qualified to undertake a work of this kind." Only one artist in ten thousand is worthy of the job, Meigs said.[35] This letter, written a full six weeks after Meigs put Crawford on contract, was probably designed in part to curry favor with Craige by turning him into a trusted insider worthy of handling confidential information without blabbing it around. Also, however, it was a good way to assess Congress's attitude toward the interior decoration of the Capitol generally and its willingness to spend the extra money it was going to cost.

Still, Meigs proceeded slowly. In early April he wrote a long letter to Crawford discussing progress on the pediment and addressing Crawford's apparent wish to provide sculpture for the House portico. Meigs asked him to slow down: "I shall expect to call upon you for many things as they arise," Meigs wrote, "but I do not feel at liberty yet to recommend to the President to give a second commission of this magnitude to the same artist."[36]

Reticence was probably a good idea, for three weeks later, Meigs had a new problem, this time with the pediment sculpture. Davis, on reexamining it, had noted that Crawford's *America*, the tableau's central figure, was wearing a liberty cap, a soft, narrow cloth hat worn lengthwise, used in classical antiquity to identify freed slaves. It had been resurrected as a symbol of freedom during the American and French revolutions. "Mr. Davis, the Secretary," Meigs noted in his diary on April 20, "does not like the liberty cap."[37]

The sculptor Thomas Crawford proposed the figure of *America* as the center-piece of the Senate pediment sculpture he entitled *Progress of Civilization*. *America*'s floppy cloth hat is a liberty cap, classical symbol of a manumitted slave. Secretary of War Jefferson Davis opposed the cap, but it remained in the final design. (Architect of the Capitol)

Meigs heard Davis's full assessment of liberty caps before sending an awkwardly written letter to Crawford four days later. Davis "does not like the cap that Liberty introduces into the composition," he said. "American liberty is original and not the liberty of the freed slave, and [Davis said] that the cap so universally adopted and especially in France [where] slavery has spasmodic struggles for freedom—is derived from the Roman custom of liberating slaves thence called freedmen and [they are] allowed to wear this cap." He told Crawford that he had not been fully aware of the historical context until learning of it from Davis. Now he said, "I think it my duty to communicate these observations to you that you may give them proper consideration."[38] On April 27, Meigs wrote to Crawford a second time, noting that he had just spoken to Davis, who had again mentioned the liberty cap. And once again Meigs simply passed the information on without making a specific recommendation.[39]

At first glance, Meigs's reaction to all this seems peculiar. Davis's remarks, as related by Meigs, appear to be unequivocal. Davis did not like the liberty cap and wanted it removed. Meigs certainly had the authority to order Crawford to get rid of it, and the compliant Crawford could have done so—and probably would have done so—if Meigs had simply decreed it. But he made no changes at this time.

There are two obvious explanations, both of which may be true. First, Meigs was no supporter of slavery, and thus at odds with Davis on the most important subject facing the country. Slavery had never come up in matters relating to the Capitol Extension—until now. Perhaps Meigs thought that by sending Crawford a mushy response, the sculptor might ignore Davis's wishes and leave the liberty cap alone. Meigs could thus achieve his own wish without endangering the Davis relationship. This course, however, was a dishonorable one, especially for Meigs as an Army officer, for it shifted the burden of decision making to Crawford, his subordinate, and enabled Meigs to deflect blame from himself if Davis subsequently took him to task.

The second explanation suggests prudence rather than evasion. By the end of April, the Senate had approved the Kansas-Nebraska Act, but debate was raging in the House. Passage of the House bill was coming closer, and the national mood was turning bleaker by the day. It was impossible to predict what the political climate would be in three months, let alone a year. For Meigs the overriding priority was to continue building the Capitol Extension. If Davis was gone next year, maybe liberty caps would come into vogue. What would Davis's successor say if he saw that Meigs had been doing Davis's political bidding? In this context, equivocation—better, perhaps, simply to call it stalling—was the best course.

The contest of wills between Stanton and Davis began in earnest on February 15, when Stanton, in his capacity as select committee chairman, asked Davis to provide lists of all military officers of the engineer and ordnance corps who were working on civilian public works. He enclosed a long list of construction jobs: lighthouses, armories, post offices, customhouses, river and harbor facilities—and the Aqueduct and the U.S. Capitol. How many officers were assigned, what were their names, where were they, how long had they been there, and how much were they paid?[40]

Davis took a look at this and bucked it to the president so he could have the request formally cleared—an obvious bureaucratic delaying tactic whose likely purpose was simply to irritate Stanton. Finally, on February 25, Davis sent Stanton his lists. He noted at the end of his cover letter, however, that "there are other officers of the Army employed upon works of a civil character, but not being of the corps specified by you, I do not include them in this report."[41]

Thus ended the first skirmish—an exchange of ranging shots designed principally to establish the order of battle. The conflict would be neither short-lived, nor polite. Stanton had opened with a lawyerly menu of seemingly innocuous but in fact pernicious requirements. He wanted simple information, but to obtain it, Davis had to ransack his records and produce an immense report, only a fraction of which would ever be used by congressional investigators. Davis stalled as long as possible before complying, then deliberately thumbed his nose at Stanton by reminding him that he could have had even more names if he had phrased his request properly.

Stanton then tried out Walter, asking him to provide the select committee with a set of original drawings of the Capitol Extension. Walter told John Rice that "people who live by annoying others are attacking the Capn. almost as hard as they did me last winter." He said he was doing "every thing in my power" to help Meigs and Davis "keep things as they are," but he was not confident. "Politics are hard to manage," he said, and if Stanton succeeded, Walter would try to ensure that the Capitol stayed under War Department control. "I want that to remain as it is," he added.[42]

Walter would not touch Stanton's request for designs, passing it instead to Meigs, who sent a set of drawings to Stanton.[43] This exchange told Stanton that he could not back-channel documents from Walter, and that everything he told Walter would get back to Meigs and inevitably find its way to Davis.

So on March 9, six days after the Senate passed the Kansas-Nebraska Act, Stanton sent Davis a list of sixty-one questions and requests for information relating to military involvement in civilian projects. These ranged from the reasonably straightforward (Why was the Capitol Extension put under military control? Why was Meigs selected as chief engineer?) to the preposterous (Please provide copies of all the expenses and invoices for the waterworks and the Capitol Extension).[44]

The 1854 construction season opened the same day Stanton mailed out the questions, and Meigs for the following week was probably preoccupied with putting his bricklayers back to work and taking delivery of eighteen hundred barrels of cement from the nearby Potomac Kilns.[45] On March 20, however, he visited Davis, who had had plenty of time to think about the select committee investigation and was "very much incensed against Stanton and denounces him unsparingly."[46] Stanton had gotten Davis's attention.

The next phase began the following day. Stanton, ignoring Davis's initial brush-off, had asked for the names of all officers, regardless of corps, working on civilian projects. Most of these, Davis replied, were doing railroad surveys for other cabinet departments and being paid by them. Davis told Stanton that these expenditures were none of Davis's business and that Stanton should contact the individual departments if he wanted to know the officers' salaries. Davis did not provide a list of the departments.[47]

Davis followed up on March 27, replying to a Stanton request for copies of "certain papers" from the ordnance department. Davis, getting a bit snottier with each exchange, told Stanton that his request was so massive that compliance would take "many months" and "interfere with the duties of this office." The War Department had an annual copying allowance, but it would not suffice. Davis suggested that Stanton summon the chief of ordnance and ask him to bring along the originals. Or, he added sweetly, Stanton could get a special appropriation to make copies for himself. Figure on seven thousand pages at a cost of $1,200.[48]

Meigs, meanwhile, worked on the answers to his Stanton questions for

nine days before handing in the final installment to Davis on March 31. It
had been an altogether bleak month, and Walter, for one, saw little sign of
improvement: "Nothing new here," Walter wrote to the ironmaker Charles
Fowler in New York, "but snow and rain and slush and mud, hard words,
threatened duels, people looking daggers at one another, and other amuse-
ments of the kind too numerous to mention."[49] It was not clear whether he
was talking about the Stanton investigation or the increasingly vitupera-
tive House debate on the Kansas-Nebraska Act, or both.

On April 18, Davis submitted his responses to Stanton's sixty-one
questions—another report well over a hundred pages long. At this point
Davis did not even try to be civil. Question 13 asked how the original Extension plans had been changed. Davis replied that the original plans were
"imperfect" and pointed Stanton to his 1853 annual report if he wanted
details. Question 14 asked why changes had been made in the "basement"
of the Extension. Davis replied that "basement" was not the right word.
He was talking about the "cellar." The "basement" was the first floor. Question 35 asked why there were not enough military jobs for the engineers.
Davis said that he needed all his engineers during a war, but had to keep
them busy during peacetime so they would stay in the service. This, he
suggested without saying so, was a stupid question, but it took him ten
pages to answer it.[50]

Most of the questions and answers, apart from the barbs, were predict-
able, but there were some departures. The committee asked Davis a large
number of detailed questions about Meigs's difficulties with the brick contracts the previous year. It also asked whether there was dissension among
the workers because of "arbitrary and vexatious requirements" imposed
by Meigs.[51] Of all the questions in the list, only these suggested that Walter may indeed have coached Stanton. Walter in his diary had commented
extensively on Meigs's failure to heed Walter's warnings about the bricks.
He had also expressed resentment at the resignation of his assistant, Clement West, apparently because Meigs refused to allow draftsmen to earn
extra money on the side.

Walter, however, moved quickly to put himself in the clear, filing a
memorandum with Meigs on May 1 describing a conversation he had had
with Stanton over information on the brickwork that had appeared in a
newspaper article. Stanton denied that Walter had had anything to do
with the news story. But he also told Walter that he had shown the answers to the sixty-one questions to every House member who asked to see

them, and that he planned to continue doing so. Any congressman, he suggested, could have leaked the report to the press.[52]

Regardless of Walter's role, however, the suspect questions suggested that while the select committee was supposedly focused on the War Department, Stanton was also interested in taking Meigs down. Davis would have realized this, and his suspicions may have prompted him to provide an unusual answer to Stanton's Question 12—how had Meigs gotten the job? Davis wrote that he could have picked anyone, but "the importance of the edifice and the desire that it should have any advantage which science and professional experience could bring to make it stand unnumbered years, caused me to designate the officer by selection." He said he had consulted with General Totten and had picked Meigs "because I found in his experience in construction, his character, his standing in the corps of engineers, his attainments and taste, satisfactory assurance of his entire fitness for the position." Either Davis had spent a lot more time talking with Totten than the record showed, or his answer was an outright lie. Totten had designated William Rosecrans to do the Extension, switching to Meigs only after he decided that the Aqueduct was not going to monopolize Meigs's time. The decision appeared to have been Totten's. As to Meigs's "attainments," these were nonexistent. There was nothing special about Meigs to suggest that Davis would have found him more attractive than anyone else. Rather than reviewing the actual circumstances relating to Meigs's hiring, Davis in Question 12 probably wanted to signal to Stanton, yet again, that Meigs had Davis's complete confidence, concluding that "my estimate of his merit has been increased, and my highest anticipation realized."[53] To get at Meigs, Stanton would have to get past Davis.

Stanton pressed forward in May, pushing on Davis's bureaucratic wall. Stanton requested copies of "certain drawings" of the Extension, Meigs told Davis on May 17, along with a "perspective view" of what the Capitol might look like upon completion. Meigs passed Stanton's letter along, accompanied by a suggested reply in which he offered to make the copies but would not be able to provide the perspective drawing immediately because such a drawing did not exist. He could prepare it, but he would need extra time.[54]

He was being too cooperative. The letter he finally sent to Stanton May 20 had Davis's fingerprints all over it. Stanton, Meigs said in a short note, could get nothing from his office without permission from the secretary of war.[55] Stanton apparently immediately countered, reminding Meigs that the drawings, by the 1851 law that authorized the Extension, were in the custody of the Architect of the Capitol Extension, who worked directly for the president of the United States with no involvement from the War Department. In his May 23 reply, penned the day after the House passed the Kansas-Nebraska Act, Meigs did not contest Stanton's views. Instead, he simply took refuge once again in military protocol: "The committee will . . . see," he said, "that so far as the President chooses to commit the work to my charge, and to communicate all his orders in relation to it to me through the Secretary of War—I can look nowhere else for orders than to the Secretary."[56] He was respectful, careful not to give offense, and utterly unhelpful.

Sometime in 1854, and probably much earlier, Thomas Walter began thinking about an innovation that would transform the Capitol Extension and, as he certainly would have understood, guarantee his place in history. In May he started to draw it, and on May 29, the day before President Pierce signed the Kansas-Nebraska Act into law, he made a brief entry in his diary: "Worked at design for dome of Capitol."[57]

Charles Bulfinch's dome, made of wood covered with copper sheathing, had survived for twenty-five years as the Capitol's premier eyesore. The dome was too tall and too ugly, but Congress could not figure what to do about it, so it endured, much like the House's meeting hall echo chamber, a puzzle without a solution.

But just as Meigs used the Capitol Extension as an occasion to gamble on a radical redesign for the Senate and House chambers, Walter proposed a dramatic new look for the Capitol's exterior. Two things had happened since Bulfinch that made a new dome both more desirable and more achievable. Most important for Congress—as focused as ever on having the biggest of everything—the Extension made the old dome suddenly too small. For years it had towered over the Capitol, attracting unwanted attention. But now, with the two new wings extending horizontally on either side, it looked more like a pimple than an outsized sore thumb. The new Capitol needed a bigger top. Big, when trying to close a deal on Capitol Hill, was good.

Second, it was now possible to build a more solid, permanent dome than the rotting fire hazard perched there now. The Rotunda's Aquia sandstone could not be expected to support any kind of masonry dome without a massive and prohibitively expensive rebuilding of the old Capitol foundation. At the same time, there was no possibility of making another slapdash affair out of lumber, tar paper, and sheet copper. Davis, Meigs, and Walter had long ago decided to have done with half measures on the cheap, and Congress by 1854 had finally decided to agree with them.

The key was cast iron. It was much lighter than masonry and almost as durable if tended properly. Once the design was complete, the pieces could be cast easily and mounted quickly. Workers at the Capitol could put the whole thing up in a couple of seasons, another good thing for the U.S. Congress, where patience was not a virtue. With cast iron, Congress could not only have it big, they it could have it now.

Walter knew about domes. In 1838, Girard College had sent him to Europe to look at architecture, and Walter had filed a report describing St. Peter's in Rome, the Pantheon in Paris, and St. Paul's in London. He was most impressed with the Pantheon, which he described as "the most beautiful specimen of Architecture in Paris." The other two left him cold architecturally, except for their domes. St. Peter's " 'swells vast to heaven' with a majesty and grandeur," he wrote, while St. Paul's produced "a most agreeable effect."[58] Also, as the Architect of the Capitol historian William C. Allen has remarked, all three domes shared a basic design: a drum on the bottom, a ribbed cupola on top, and a lantern, or tholus, as a "crowning element."[59] Walter's design, with a peristyle of Corinthian columns forming the lower drum, most closely resembled St. Paul's.

Walter also knew about cast iron, as he had proved the previous year with the highly praised Library of Congress. The dome was a much bigger job, but the basic principle was simple. Since the dome would have no structural function, it could be placed atop the foundation to rest there like an inverted cup. It would be massive, a hundred feet higher than the old dome, and it would be gorgeous. The dome would transform the new Capitol from the rambling horizontal "hacienda" that Borland had scorned in 1852 into an immense presence dominating the Washington skyline. The capital city in 1854 may still have been unwholesome jerkwater, a crossroads in the middle of nowhere, but the new Capitol, as envisioned by Davis, Meigs, and Walter, would offer a glimpse of what the city—and the nation—could become. Now Walter was adding the crowning touch.

Walter at first seemed offhanded about his new project. He did, however, show it to Meigs, who was anything but dismissive. "Mr. Walter has made a sketch for a new dome to be about 100 feet higher than the present dome," Meigs wrote in his diary on May 31. "It is a good one," he added perfunctorily. Then enthusiasm began to creep into his prose. He launched a quick critique of what was wrong with the design, noting that the lower part "looks too much like a drum," a defect he also saw in the Pantheon and St. Paul's.[60]

But that was trivial. He knew what was important: "The height of 240 feet gives a very good finish to the building," he wrote with laudable clarity. "It is enough to make it appear one whole, the dome serving as a crown and collecting the whole into one grand composition." And unlike the European cathedrals, whose domes were all off center, "our composition . . . should have the advantage of them . . . for ours will be exactly in the center." Finally, he said, the new dome was about as big as it could be for "the base we have to build on," but "I think we might have a little more height by raising the drum more." In three long paragraphs, Meigs had gone from "Mr. Walter's design," to what "I" think is wrong with it, to how "we" might fix "our composition." He was fully committed.[61]

10

THE ALIEN MENACE

By the middle of 1854, anyone who worked at the U.S. Capitol or lived in Washington knew that the quirky and intimate, yet uncomfortable and frequently unpleasant meeting house where Calhoun, Webster, and Clay had jousted for so many years would never again be the same. The new Capitol had abandoned republican simplicity in favor of a new idea: that a great nation needed and deserved a seat of government emblematic of its greatness.

Jefferson Davis had begun this metamorphosis with an assist from Millard Fillmore. Davis had insisted that the new Capitol spread out from its north and south ends. Instead of a blockier, more fortresslike Capitol with a new Eastern Front, he envisioned a more expansive Capitol that would jolt a first-time visitor with its extent and immensity.

Next came Thomas Walter, who translated Davis's vision into a working design. He was assisted by Daniel Webster, who suggested that the two new north and south wings be attached to the old Capitol by covered corridors. This gave the new Capitol an uninterrupted line—a more sweeping effect that enhanced the visual impact still further. The new Capitol was no longer three separate buildings in a row. It was now one enormous building, more than 250 yards long.

Then Montgomery Meigs arrived. By installing a hundred new monolithic marble columns on all four sides of the new wings, he ensured that a first-time visitor would not be able to tell that the Capitol had ever been in three pieces. Meigs also made the walls thicker, both literally and figuratively adding substance to the Capitol, which was strong and would endure, just like the nation it served. And by giving the new Senate and House wings their own staircases and porticoes, the Capitol announced that it had become so big that one entrance was no longer enough.

Finally, in mid-1854, Walter designed a new Dome to unify the whole structure. It was a tour de force. First of all, it got rid of Bulfinch's dome, an ugly affair made of wood and copper sheathing. Second, the new Dome was an engineering marvel. The old Capitol could not support a masonry dome of any kind, so Walter decided to make the new Dome out of cast iron. It would be the biggest cast-iron structure in the country—maybe in the world.

And finally, the new Dome would be the perfect architectural finishing touch. Cast iron was so easy to shape and so light in weight that Walter and Meigs could tune the design however they wanted, molding the Dome until it accommodated both the old Rotunda on which it perched and the rest of the new building—just so. Done properly, it would balance the new Capitol both horizontally and vertically. The finished Capitol would, like the nation it embodied, last forever.

Walter's letters and diaries offer no hint of how, when, or why he decided to design a new Dome. A brief diary entry in late May simply notes that he was working on the design, something that he had never mentioned before.

Still, Walter's inspiration was logical. Once Meigs and Davis had agreed on the monoliths, the two new pediments, and the heavier facing for the exterior walls, Walter would have known that a new Dome was almost an aesthetic imperative. It was the only thing the design lacked, and not having it was unthinkable. The dilemma was how to build it. The Library gave Walter the answer. Then he simply had to draw it.

Walter showed Meigs the drawing in late May. Meigs liked the idea but was initially guarded in his enthusiasm. "I think that Mr. Walter's design for a dome is generally good," he wrote in his diary, "but that it will want a good deal of studying to make it as good as it ought to be. It is too much frittered and too much cut up."[1]

Walter broke his own silence on July 20, 1854, in a letter to his friend Charles Fowler, the New York founder who had provided the cast iron for the new Library and who had a good chance to cast the Dome if Walter's plan went forward. Somewhat breathlessly he described his "magnificent Dome," asserting that "every member of Congress who has seen it is enthusiastically in its favor, and is ready to vote the supplies whenever asked—will cost half a million at least—such a design was never made by your friend—the drawing is 7 feet long—I wish you could see it."[2] The new Dome, it appeared, was a sensation.

Ever since Meigs and Walter had come together, there had been a competitive undercurrent in their relationship. Both were single-minded, driven men. Walter, born talented but working-class, had never known any other way to get ahead. Meigs, ambitious yet still largely unknown, wanted desperately to make his mark. For most of the year that they had worked together, the rivalry had lain dormant, but the Dome catalyzed it like nothing that had come before or would come afterward.

Before the Dome, Meigs had spent most of his own creative genius thinking about ventilators, heating systems, and acoustics, but once his new foundation was built, his pediments and columns funded, and his scientifically designed Senate and House chambers approved, he was increasingly shifting his sights to decoration—to the sculpture and painting of the Capitol Extension. These endeavors, like the new chambers, would be central to his legacy.

But now Walter had played the ace of trumps. It would not be the wings, porticoes, chambers, or art that would forever define the Capitol. It would be the Dome. Meigs was dazzled by Walter's achievement, but he never admitted it. Instead, he manifested his excitement by critiquing the design privately in his diary, and then by "studying domes." Meigs could never match Walter's coup; but maybe he could change Walter's design to make it better. Or make it right. Or perhaps make it his. This rivalry would inspire brilliant innovations and distinctive features of the new Capitol. It would also lead to a prolonged display of small-minded selfishness by both men.

At this juncture there were probably no two individuals better qualified to build the new Capitol than Meigs and Walter. For reasons of politics more than anything else, Walter's reputation had been badly buffeted in 1852, and he had been supplanted by Meigs as the project leader the following year. But Walter in 1854 had recouped much of his stature. The Library had helped, and the Dome would help even more.

Meigs was an engineer by profession, trained to build forts, harbors, bridges, and aqueducts. But he was also a polymath, an endless tinkerer and innovator, with boundless vision and self-confidence. In September 1854 he designed a new style of sash fastener for the windows of the Capitol Extension and set out to patent it. "I believe it is the best I have ever seen," he wrote in his diary with his characteristic candid arrogance.[3] If he did not understand architecture, it was close enough to engineering that he could learn. If he did not understand aesthetics, he could learn that, too. In January 1854, Meigs was honored with membership in the American Philosophical Society, the country's premier gathering place for leaders in science and the humanities. And in early 1855 he would be invited to join the informal "Saturday Club"—a weekly gathering of Washington's great scientific minds, led by the Smithsonian's Joseph Henry and Alexander Dallas Bache of the Coast Survey. Meigs would remain a member for the rest of his life.

Meigs and Walter had very different personalities. Walter was a chronic gossip, full of interesting tidbits and insights about the foibles and intrigues of the powerful. He was close friends with his contractors, but sometimes arbitrary and insensitive with his own family.[4] Meigs, aloof and serious, had none of Walter's small-talking, glad-handing skills, the want of which he felt in mid-1854, with Stanton and his allies attacking him almost daily in the newspapers or on the floor of Congress. Meigs would learn them, and quickly, and he had time to learn because Davis gave him cover. And despite whatever suspicions they may have harbored secretly toward one another, Meigs and Walter in 1854 were united in fighting congressional efforts to disrupt the project. Walter, who had firsthand experience of Congress's wrath, offered Meigs moral support, intelligence, and sympathy.

By the time a beautiful late spring started to turn into a brutal Washington summer, Meigs, despite his protectors, was taking some political hits. At the end of May, Congress refused to vote extra money for the Aqueduct, and he was forced to shut the project down until he could get funding for the upcoming fiscal year. Two weeks later, Stanton ripped into Meigs on the House floor, wondering, as he had in his earlier speech, how a military officer had gotten control of a project that ought to be administered by an architect. The difference in Stanton's approach this time, however, was that he heaped praise on the "distinguished architect, Mr. Walter," by name.[5]

"The design of the Capitol, in all its beautiful proportions and elaborate details, is [Walter's], and no one can take from him the honor of its conception," Stanton continued, implying that Meigs was trying to steal the credit for Walter's design. "The military engineer neither liked his plans nor his economy; and when he assumed control, he commenced a complete revolution in all things."[6] These changes—the new chambers, the monoliths, the new pediments—had all been seconded, or at least not opposed, by Walter, but Stanton ignored this detail. He was trying to take down Davis, and Meigs was the available target.

Meigs had to endure Stanton's summer of abuse without help from Davis, whose only child, Samuel, not yet two years old, died three days before Stanton's speech. This loss hit Davis very hard, and "for many months afterward" he "walked half the night, and worked fiercely all day," Varina Davis recalled years later. "A child's cry in the street well nigh drove him mad."[7] He had no time, at that moment, for Meigs.

Nevertheless Meigs battled back, learning as he went along. He became expert at bureaucratic obfuscation, bucking Stanton's document requests up the line to Davis, where they would be certain to die. He could also, however, take pity on his adversaries by doing them an occasional good turn. During one dispute over documents, Meigs tactfully suggested to Stanton that while he was not authorized to provide him with the material, there was no point in applying to Davis, "for it will merely put him (Davis) into a passion, and that will do no good." Instead, he told Stanton, send the request directly to Pierce, where it might have a better reception.[8]

Meigs never speculated in his diary about whether Walter was being disloyal to him. And Walter returned his trust. In mid-June, with Davis in mourning and Stanton exploding rhetorical fireworks almost daily, Walter invited Meigs to his home for a quiet dinner.[9] Later in the year, Walter and Meigs amicably disagreed over the design for the doors of the eastern entrances to the new wings. Walter's design is "magnificent," Meigs wrote in his diary, "but I prefer to have the door fill the entire archway. He prefers to have the semicircle filled with glass." Walter "will make a drawing to fill the whole," Meigs added, "and we will decide the question."[10] In the end they split the difference. There was no glass, but there was an archway, as Meigs wanted. But the archway was a bronze tympanum mounted above the rectangular doors favored by Walter.

Despite the apparent ease of the relationship, it is still reasonable to ask whether Walter was collaborating with Stanton to undercut Meigs. Stanton had been Walter's closest political ally ever since the project began, and in his conflict with Davis he continued to tout Walter's virtues. If Walter was trying to use the military rule dispute to hasten Meigs's departure and reinstate himself, he could not have had a better advocate.

Also, it was clear from Walter's diary that he harbored resentments against Meigs—not so much for supplanting him, but on policy differences, particularly for Meigs's veto of Clement West's outside drafting jobs, and his refusal to heed Walter's advice on the brick contract. Later in 1854, Walter again complained in his diary about Meigs's refusal to seek his advice on a design for the House chamber ceiling, which Meigs wanted to make out of glass squares in a cast-iron frame. Meigs "knows nothing of the principles of trussing," Walter wrote, "and this is an interference with my professional duties, which I cannot consent to."[11]

This would be a source of tension for years to come: Meigs's boundless confidence in his own—untrained—architectural skills and judgment and Walter's resentment that Meigs did not seek his advice. Each man suspected that the other was trying to grab all of the credit. And for all their differences in age, background, and training, the two were in many ways cut from the same template. Meigs's naked ambition is a thread that runs unchecked through his diary for years. But Walter was just as obsessed with his own accomplishments, if not more so. At the end of 1853, Meigs agreed, at Walter's insistence, to add the clause "these plans were prepared by the accomplished architect, M. Thomas U. Walter" to Meigs's annual report on the new design of the House and Senate chambers. That way, Walter's name would appear in the congressional record.[12] Meigs would later remark that Walter insisted on signing all of the drawings coming out of his office, no matter who had done the drafting.[13] And Walter's chief assistant, August Schoenborn, who revered Walter, would in a memoir written decades later claim that the Dome was "my design," even though Walter consistently represented it as his own.[14] The truth of this assertion cannot be proved and seems doubtful, but it is clear that Walter's assistants frequently had a hand in his work and that he seldom acknowledged it. Meigs was not the only Capitol builder with an inflated ego.

Given the competitive tension between Meigs and Walter, it would not be unreasonable to assume that Walter privately celebrated Stanton's praise and the boost it gave to his professional and congressional standing. But he had also become politically savvy enough to know that Stanton had little hope of winning a victory against Davis and the entire Pierce administration.

Meigs, however, was not so sure. Despite the injustice—or at least the hyperbole—of Stanton's attacks, Meigs in June 1854 wrote in his diary that he was far from confident that the House's "general confidence in my ability" would enable him to withstand "this feeling against military officers being put in charge of these works."[15] Meigs also made clear, however, that his devotion to the Capitol was beginning to supplant his commitment to a military career. Should the War Department lose control of the Capitol project, he mused in his diary, there would not be enough decent Corps of Engineers jobs to go around. "I shall be tempted to leave the Army," he confessed, and return as a civilian "to complete these great works."[16]

Even money, always a problem for Meigs, could not pry him away. In June, Meigs got two plum job offers: one to dig the Chesapeake and Ohio Canal for the state of Maryland at an annual salary of $3,500, nearly twice what he was earning at the Capitol; and the second to run a North Carolina lead mine for $5,000 per year. He turned them both down: "I was in charge of the . . . architecture and the greatest work of a civil engineer in the country," he wrote in his diary. "I preferred finishing that for nothing to going to take a similar work for a good salary."[17]

And in this, too, Meigs and Walter had reached the same pass. Both were obsessed by the Capitol. In August 1854, Walter wrote a letter to his second son, Thomas, broke in San Francisco, telling him that he would no longer be able to send him funds. Walter had given up his private practice, he explained, and "things are not as they were when you left. People think that I am getting rich because I have a salary of $4,500, but such is not the case—the high price of living in Washington, the support of your grandpa and aunts . . . and what I have sent to you and [older brother] Robert have amounted to more than my entire salary for the last two years."[18] The truth was that despite his protestations of poverty, Walter still had plenty of money invested. But he had put the rest of his career on hold. His devotion to the Capitol was not up for discussion.

In early August, the House passed a $750,000 appropriation for the Capitol Extension for 1855—everything that Meigs and Davis had requested—and left Meigs in charge. Stanton was defeated. It was Meigs's first political victory, but he knew there was still plenty of congressional opposition to the War Department's control of the Capitol.

In addition, any relief that Meigs might have felt was soon overtaken by a new challenge to his stewardship. This one was an outgrowth of the larger and increasingly intractable dispute over slavery that in 1854 would radically change the national political landscape. Passage of the Kansas-Nebraska Act had enraged the antislavery North, with most of the hatred directed toward the Democratic Party and its pro-South "doughface" president, Franklin Pierce. The Whig Party, already riven by the slavery debate and weakened by the deaths of Clay and Webster in 1852, was dissolving. Two new political actors were emerging. The Republican Party, formed in July 1854 by disillusioned northern Whigs, apostate northern Democrats, and Free-Soilers from the 1840s, was anti-Kansas-Nebraska and antislavery. The second player—the one that directly concerned Meigs—was the Know-Nothings. Founded in New York in the late 1840s as the Order of the Star Spangled Banner, the movement was an anti-immigrant, anti-Catholic, antislavery and pro-temperance organization. Its initial impulse appears to have been a reaction to the enormous influx of immigrants to the United States—2,900,000 between 1845 and 1854, peaking at 400,000 in 1854.[19] A vast number of these were Irish Catholics, and the Democrats hastened to make them party loyalists.

The order stoked its nativist zeal by tapping Protestant America's distrust and distaste for Roman Catholicism as a corrupt, ritualistic Old World religion. It was a popular view.[20] The order also piqued popular interest because it was a secret society, not a declared political party. Folklore had it that members, once initiated, were instructed never to acknowledge their participation, and, if asked, were simply to say "I know nothing." By 1854 the term and the movement had taken root in the country's political consciousness.[21] Sympathizers could use "Know-Nothing Toothpicks," smoke "Know-Nothing Cigars," and wash with "Know-Nothing Soap."[22]

The Know-Nothings had perhaps fifty thousand members when the Kansas-Nebraska Act was passed in May 1854. Over the next five months, however, the historian Tyler Anbinder has calculated that the movement grew to a million, and what had been a fringe, albeit vigorous, movement suddenly became a key national antislavery, America-first political force.[23] The new membership was fueled primarily by antislavery Whigs, vaguely nativist and looking for a new home as their own party disappeared. In the South, Whig unionists, marginalized in a climate increasingly dominated by hard-line states' rights Democrats, rallied to the Know-Nothing cause. The Know-Nothings mostly nominated candidates from within existing parties, but in many cases did not identify them by name. As a result, establishment officeholders—Democrat or Whig—were running scared and espousing their own nativism, bringing further ugliness to politics.

Racism was endemic in 1850s America, and the vast majority of white citizens, North and South, took for granted that blacks were inferior. Know-Nothingism went further. When the Know-Nothings warned that foreigners were driving down wages and taking jobs away from real God-fearing Protestant Americans, or that there were too many Catholics in the government and too many Irish idling in the street, committing crimes, and going to Papist schools, many Americans believed them.

Meigs would feel this pressure keenly and immediately. With Davis's concurrence, he had from the beginning followed a hiring policy that ignored both political affiliation and nationality. Recent arrivals were working on the new Capitol in practically every capacity. The German immigrants August Schoenborn and his brother Henry were Walter's top draftsmen. The Italian sculptor Francis Vincenti was Meigs's leading modeler for ornamentation. The foreman of bricklayers was a Scot. Immigrants were working in most of Meigs's craft shops, especially as stonemasons and carvers, both for Meigs and for Provest & Winter, the marble finishing contractors.

None of this escaped the notice of Meigs's enemies in Congress, who were looking for new ways to exert influence over the project and at the same time proclaim their nativist credentials. What better way to insinuate their own constituents into the Capitol workforce than by forcing Meigs to get rid of the people with the foreign names?

Meigs had his own complaints about foreigners. Provest & Winter, in particular, were beset by work stoppages that caused frequent delays in marble setting and construction. Meigs blamed these job actions on immigrant-dominated craft guilds, and they tried his meager patience, prompting him on one occasion to "damn these foreign rascals" in his diary.[24]

Work crews at the Capitol Extension made an incredible racket, and none were noisier than the marble finishers, with their hammers, saws, and sanders. Congress periodically forced the crews to move operations down the road, but the final work had to be done on-site under makeshift canvas sunshades. (Architect of the Capitol)

To his credit, however, Meigs never let his managerial frustration interfere with his hiring practices. He wanted the best workers he could find, regardless of ethnicity, religion, or politics. And he greeted the advent of Know-Nothingism with pugnacious disdain, leaving little doubt that he intended to fight the movement's incursions at every step. On June 5 he voted for the first time in his life, intent on helping John W. Maury win a second term as mayor of Washington. Maury, an activist dedicated to the development of Washington as a national city, was a tireless promoter of the Aqueduct and a steadfast Meigs booster. He was running against John T. Towers, on whom "all the Know-Nothing force is concentrated," Meigs wrote in his diary. Towers won.[25]

In September, the Pennsylvania Whigs dumped three-term representative Joseph R. Chandler, a longtime supporter of Walter, Meigs, and the Capitol Extension but also a Catholic, and decided to run a Protestant in his place.[26] Then, on Election Day, reaction to the Kansas-Nebraska Act took a devastating toll on northern Democrats, who saw their share of the House of Representatives collapse from 91 seats to only 25 and the party as a whole lose the House majority. One happy outcome for Meigs was the defeat of Stanton in Kentucky's Tenth District—a border-state Democrat ousted by a Know-Nothing. Stanton would be back in late 1854 for the lame duck session, but then he would be gone. The 1854 election effectively marked the end of the Democrats as a national party. For the rest of the decade the party would be dominated by southerners.[27]

The new Congress would not sit until late 1855, but its two-thirds majority, composed of Whigs, Republicans, Know-Nothings, and others, was largely antislavery.[28] This bloc would come to be called simply the "Opposition," for the Know-Nothings' predilection for secrecy and the multiple allegiances of some the members made it difficult to put a label on some of the lawmakers.

But it was clear that the country was choosing up sides.

Despite the political upheavals, Meigs made enormous progress on the Capitol in 1854—with plenty of help from immigrants. He pressed forward with elaborate plans for decorating and finishing the new wings, and in May he began discussing a variety of finishing touches with Vincenti, his in-house sculptor. He had Vincenti draw a series of sketches for the fountain that would bring Aqueduct water to the Capitol, then chose one and had Vincenti make a clay model of it. On August 8, Meigs rode across the river into Maryland to a tobacco plantation, stole a leaf, and took it to Vincenti, who copied it. "I shall tomorrow tell him to make a plaster mold of the capital for the vestibules," he noted in his diary.[29] The capital would have carvings of corn, cherry, tobacco, and magnolia—"entirely American plants," he boasted, but an Italian-born craftsman would make many of the designs.[30]

In October he heard about a pair of Boston companies who made ornaments of papier-mâché, which he wanted to use to finish the cast-iron and glass ceilings of the Senate and House chambers. These decorations, he reasoned, would be light, more durable than plaster, and easier to make than ornaments of any other material. He asked the two companies to send him catalogues, but in the interim he saw the work of the French immigrants Ernest and Henri Thomas in New York, and in December he hired them to provide ornaments and decorations made to look like stone. He would use this *carton pierre* for moldings, panels, pendants, and rosettes for both ceilings.[31]

He also wrote to the British firm of Minton, Hollins & Co., asking for a catalogue of their encaustic tiles. These ceramics were not glazed, but were instead made of colored clays shaped into the desired pattern before baking. The design could not be worn away, scuffed, or chipped, because it was maintained through almost the entire thickness of the tile. Meigs had read about encaustic tiles in an architectural journal a few years earlier and wondered if Minton still made them.[32] They did, and Meigs would use the tiles to spectacular effect in the new Extension's corridors, vestibules, and ceremonial rooms.

Meigs during the year made multiple field trips searching for art, artists, artisans, and ideas. On a visit to West Point in August he spent the day with Robert Weir, who had taught drawing to Meigs and to a vast number of the cadets who would serve as officers in the Civil War, for both North and South. Weir's *Embarkation of the Pilgrims* hung in the

Encaustic tiles provided spectacularly patterned floors throughout the new Capitol. This mosaic outside the Vice President's Room on the second floor of the new Senate wing epitomized the "higher style" opulence favored by Meigs and Jefferson Davis. (Architect of the Capitol)

Capitol Rotunda, but although Meigs saw "many beautiful sketches and drawings," he did not commission anything.[33] On a visit to New York in November, Meigs, already an admirer of the German-born painter Emanuel Leutze, saw Leutze's *Washington Rallying the Troops at the Battle of Monmouth* and was smitten all over again: "I wish I had it for the grand stairway in the Capitol Extension," he lamented in his diary. "The man who could paint that is quite able to paint for the walls of our people's palace."[34]

A few days later he toured the Brevoort House, on Fifth Avenue between Eighth and Ninth streets, and was impressed with the painting and decoration of the hotel's 140 rooms, of which "no two ceilings are alike."[35] He visited the decorative painter, German immigrant Emmerich Carstens, and offered him a job at the Capitol for $1,200 per year. "I wish I could employ Leutze by the day to paint upon our walls some historical pictures, but his pride would probably prevent his coming into such an engagement," he wrote in his diary. "And I should have all Congress on my back if I were to contract with him for a painting to be hung up."[36]

So he settled for Carstens, who turned out to be a lifetime appointment, working as head of decorative painting in the Capitol for four decades. And Meigs even got his way on Leutze in the end, successfully prevailing on the Lincoln administration to hire him for $20,000 to paint *Westward the Course of Empire Takes Its Way* for the grand staircase on the western side of the House wing.

In early August, Thomas Crawford sent Meigs photographs of the figures he was modeling for the Senate pediment. There was no news on either *America* (the central figure) or her cap, but Crawford provided pictures of four of the other figures. In all, the pediment would have thirteen sculptures of human figures, along with some accompanying landscape. The pediment on one side of *America* would represent the early days of the continent, while the other side would feature contemporary motifs. Altogether, *Progress of Civilization* would be sixty feet long and twelve feet tall at the apex of the triangle where *America* stood. Crawford had sent photographs of three contemporary figures—schoolmaster, schoolboys, and a mechanic—and the Indian boy from the early America tableau.

Meigs took these to Davis, who admired the modern figures, "but at once objected, justly, to the Indian boy," Meigs wrote in his diary. "His face was not the face of an Indian, nor his hair the hair of an Indian."[37] The boy,

An Indian and Indian boy by Thomas Crawford. Meigs admired these Senate
pediment figures but was frustrated by Crawford's insistence on sculpting Indians with features that made them look like Europeans in costume. (Architect of
the Capitol)

who was supposed to represent a youthful hunter, looked more like a naked nine-year-old Alpine shepherd with a dead animal slung over his
back. Meigs early on had suspected that Crawford's knowledge of Indians
was either flawed or nonexistent, and had suggested that he find some
books on the subject and look at the illustrations. Crawford apparently
had not followed these instructions. This, and Crawford's inaction on the
liberty cap, suggested that the artist was perhaps not as tractable as he
seemed.

It was, however, also quite possible that Crawford ignored Meigs's
wishes simply because he could not figure out what they were. By 1854

clerks were copying perhaps half of Meigs's correspondence before sending it out, but the letters to Crawford—always several pages long—were written in Meigs's abominable scrawl. One can readily imagine Crawford, his wife, and others of Rome's English-speaking community sitting around Crawford's kitchen table trying to decipher exactly what it was Meigs was asking.

Meigs seemed unaware—perhaps willfully unaware—of the puzzlement and exasperation this caused. His wife, Louisa, whose own handwriting was hardly crystal clear, may have given him a pass, but his children almost certainly did not. Their letters, even at a very young age, show uniformly elegant penmanship, standing as a silent rebuke to the sins of the father.[38]

Meigs's August 9 letter to Crawford (five painful-to-decipher pages) opened by praising the artist's efforts, noting that Davis "expressed his admiration of the grace and beauty of the figures generally." The schoolmaster, he added, "very much pleases my little boy." However, he continued, "the Secretary, myself and all those to whom I have shown the photographs . . . make one criticism—that you have not caught the Indian countenance." He suggested again that Crawford find a copy of Thomas McKenney's *History of the Indian Tribes of North America*, which had "portraits of chiefs, children and papooses," and make the necessary adjustments. "I presume you will be anxious," he said, that the viewing public not take the Indian boy "for a white man." Meigs appeared to have made something of an effort to write clearly in the letter's early stages, but by page three the text was nearly unreadable.[39]

Overall, Meigs and Crawford continued to enjoy a warm relationship. In September, Meigs sent Crawford a design of the doorway he wanted for the new Senate wing and asked Crawford to design a set of bronze doors to fill the space.[40] A month later Meigs attended a dinner party at the home of General Totten, where the general's daughter Kate told him about a recent trip to Rome and how "delighted" Crawford was to be sculpting *Progress of Civilization*. Crawford told Kate that the job not only enhanced "his standing as an artist," Meigs wrote in his diary, but "it is lucrative." Meigs went on to note that it was "natural" that Crawford "should think well of my taste and judgment, as he has from me the best order he has ever had."[41]

By October, Meigs was able to pat himself on the back for what he considered "a good year's work."[42] The brickwork for the Capitol's new wings was almost complete, although setting of the new, heavier marble facing lagged far behind because of slow deliveries of stone.[43] Provest & Winter had about two hundred stonecutters working on the project and needed more, and altogether Meigs had kept between five hundred and six hundred men on the job for most of the year. The first-floor masonry had been entirely completed, and Meigs in September had moved the Capitol Extension construction office from the Adams Express Building, two blocks from the Capitol, into finished rooms on the first floor of the new House wing.[44] Riggers had begun to lay iron bed plates for the roofs of both wings, and roofing itself would soon commence. The walls of the Senate and House chambers were at their full height, and in late November, Meigs took his young son into the vacant new House chamber— unroofed and without doors—to test the acoustics. "I could talk with Monty the whole length of one side of the Hall without any necessity of raising my voice," he exulted, although he admitted he could hear echoes when he clapped his hands. This would improve, he reasoned with typical confidence, "when the ceiling is in place."[45]

With all this under way, Meigs predicted that in the coming year he would finish the wings and begin construction of the east porticoes of the new wings. Up to now, he said in his annual report to Davis, $2,350,000 had been appropriated for the Capitol Extension.[46] More important, at the moment he still had $1,082,130.67 of it to tide him over until the end of the year and get him into the next season.[47] The Capitol Extension was in excellent financial shape.

On Saturday, November 4, shortly after arriving at his office, Meigs was summoned to the War Department. Davis's chief concern at that moment was probably the Tuesday general election and the grim toll the Kansas-Nebraska Act was going to exact from his party. This did not dim his firm wish that proslavery settlers win the battle for Kansas, as his correspondence with Missouri's David Atchison, leader of the proslavery movement and a Davis friend since childhood, made clear. Atchison, a sitting U.S. senator, told Davis his followers were willing to "shoot, burn and hang" without trial anyone who got in their way. Davis, a sitting cabinet secretary, was apparently willing to let him do it.[48]

The subject that Davis wished to discuss with Meigs that morning, however, was something else entirely: why Walter should be fired, or at least stripped of the title of architect and demoted to draftsman. The two men talked about it for nearly an hour.

Davis's argument, Meigs wrote in his diary, was that the Capitol as designed by Walter "was imperfect and would have been a failure" if Meigs had not stepped forward to change the plan "in all its most important parts." Davis said Meigs was a better architect than Walter, and "he had always thought that my reputation would be injured by Walter's presence." He had once let Meigs talk him out of getting rid of Walter, "but now, he thought, was a time to act."

Meigs neither agreed nor disagreed with Davis's assessment. He instead described in detail the collegial relationship he and Walter enjoyed: "that he sketched after we had discussed the general style first together; that I criticized his design, it was modified, then again submitted to me, sometimes many different sketches made before one satisfactory was hit upon." But as far as apportioning credit was concerned, Meigs told Davis, the inescapable fact was that "Walter had designed the outside of the building, which was what the world would look upon." Anyone who seriously analyzed the Extension would see Meigs's role, but "I knew that I should not from the people get all I deserved." Meigs said he "preferred losing some of what was mine to exposing myself to the accusation—unjust, but with some appearance of justice—of having tried to take what was justly another's."

What he told Davis was that even if he wanted to dump Walter, he could not figure out how to do it without losing face. He knew Walter "would be governed by no delicacy and would take all the world would allow him, whether he deserved it or not," Meigs continued. "This was his character and his weakness." That said, however, Walter was "very skillful, more so than any other architect that I knew, more so than anyone who would take his place, submissive and willing to be guided by me in all things and the best assistant I could get, best for my own pleasure, best for the success of the work."

In the end Davis succumbed once again, and Walter was saved. Davis, Meigs wrote, "must feel that he was in a curious condition, urging a man to take a great advantage and being resisted." He was grateful "for Mr. Davis' kindness towards me and his high estimate of my abilities as an engineer and architect . . . and still more grateful for his yielding his wishes in this matter to my own."[49]

Meigs had reached a watershed moment. The first time Davis had tried to fire Walter, the conversation had focused on Walter's loyalty or betrayal in the opening days of the military rule dispute. This time, the rising professional rivalry between Meigs and Walter, unspoken in January, was put on the table. Davis was intensely loyal to Meigs—his man—and had stood by him throughout the year's early travails. It is also quite likely that he was impressed by Meigs's energy, his organizational skills, and his audacity in redesigning the new Senate and House chambers.

It seems clear that in this instance, Davis's motives were transparent. He believed that Walter's continued presence on the project was robbing Meigs of his just reward and thought something should be done about it. For Meigs, still young and striving to make a name for himself, to be singled out for such unmitigated praise by such a powerful man, even after more than a year on the job, must have been heady stuff. Davis and Meigs, both arrogant and vain about their own judgment and skills, had spent a good deal of their meeting sneering at Walter for being inappropriately vainglorious and a publicity hound—without ever acknowledging their own similar weaknesses. Meigs was the man who was having his name spelled out in cast iron in mountings for the Aqueduct's staircases and who intended to leave autographed medallions in the Capitol masonry for archaeologists to find a thousand years hence.

In January, Meigs had highlighted Walter's loyalty and professional expertise as a means of heading off Davis's intentions. By November, Walter's usefulness had become the tag-end consideration. The first things to know about Walter in November, in Davis's telling, were that he was not as good an architect as Meigs, that by his mere presence he was depriving Meigs of the limelight, that he was grabbing all the credit he could, and that he was an unpleasant, petty person.

This was a conversation that Meigs, given his own tendency toward vainglory, did not need to have, and the consequences were immediately apparent. On November 8, he ordered some books from New York on architectural ornaments, remarking in his diary that they would offer enough ideas so that "I could make out a system of decoration for the Extension without Mr. Walter's help."[50] Meigs, now with conscious forethought, was undertaking projects designed to exclude Walter. In relocating the chambers and devising new heat and vent systems in 1853, he had magnanimously acknowledged Walter as a full partner. Then, in 1854, he had, perhaps unconsciously, ignored Walter in designing the chamber ceilings, thus incurring Walter's unspoken wrath. Now, after the

Davis meeting, and perhaps having taken Davis's misgivings about Walter to heart, he was intent on finding new ways to assert his presence and put Walter in the shadows.

In this endeavor, however, Meigs had the same disadvantage he had had in 1853. Just as Walter had asserted authorship of the new wings by making the original design, he had struck first in 1854 by designing the new Dome. Whatever happened in the future, the public would regard the Dome, like the wings, as Walter's idea, Walter's design, and a defining feature of the new Capitol. Walter had already immortalized this vision in the gigantic seven-foot rendering that was now hanging on the wall outside the project's new first-floor offices. Senators and congressmen returning for the December 4 session of Congress could for the first time imagine the splendor of the finished product, complete with new wings, new porticoes, and the beautiful Dome. And to enhance the effect, Walter had filled the East Front foreground of the drawing with carriages, horsemen, and elegantly dressed ladies and gentlemen going about their business. Not only could members see what the completed building would look like—they could put themselves in the picture.

Walter's rendering of the new Capitol Dome was seven feet long and caused a sensation in Congress when lawmakers got their first glimpse of what their building might finally become. Walter tacked the drawing to the wall outside his office, and within months, Meigs had secured funding to begin the project. (Architect of the Capitol)

Meigs learned how powerful this image could be on December 12, when he escorted a half-dozen House members on a tour and showed them the Dome design. "I spoke of it as a thing to be done sometime hereafter and as separate from the Capitol Extension," he wrote in his diary. The members asked how much it would cost, and Meigs replied that he had not made an estimate but "supposed $200,000." The members asked "why not do it at once," Meigs said, and he replied that "if they saw fit to order it, I should be proud and glad to build it myself."[51]

Nine days later Walter told Meigs he had been talking with one senator sympathetic to the Capitol who "wishes to have the new dome begun." Walter, Meigs wrote in his diary, "feels not disposed to encourage this." But "I told him if they wished it, I should like to have it done, for I wish to have the credit and the pleasure of building this dome." Walter balked: "He says that he feels as if all this work was taking brains, and he would not live forever, that we have enough now on hand," Meigs wrote. "For my part, I want to build a great dome, and I hope that this one is the one for me . . . It would be something worth doing."[52]

This, of course, was the other side of Montgomery Meigs. He was vain, arrogant, ambitious, and envious of others' success, no matter how much he tried to hide it. But anyone willing to endure these tedious traits would also get the other Meigs: the energy, the drive, the intellect, and the prodigious talent. In building the new Dome, he would not only get the "credit," which was tremendously important to him, but also feel the "pleasure" of having figured out how to do something that no one else had ever done before in precisely the same way. "The cranes and cupolas and planing machines and the other tools necessary for its construction would be a constant source of occupation and delight to me,"[53] Meigs wrote. He was through talking about the Dome. He was ready to build it. Walter could join him. Or not.

The next day Meigs made his pitch in a letter to Maryland senator James A. Pearce, who, as chairman of the Senate Library Committee, was the man in charge of art and decoration for the Capitol as well as of any architectural modifications to the original building. Meigs's appeal was elegantly understated: "We have in this office a design for a cast iron dome to replace the wooden eye sore which now covers the Rotunda," Meigs wrote. Everybody who had seen it, had "expressed satisfaction with it," and most "wish to have it constructed at once." He asked Pearce to add $200,000 to next year's Capitol Extension appropriation. He suggested that the bill language should authorize replacement of the "present wooden dome by a suitable fireproof structure."[54]

Meigs spent most of Christmas week thinking about the Capitol and, especially, the Dome. On Christmas Eve, Meigs took stock of his relative penury, but decided it was a privation he was more than willing to endure because of the prestige that came with building the new Capitol.[55] On Christmas Day, he began looking at domes in books. He found both St. Peter's and St. Paul's "ungraceful" and concluded he could "make a better one than either."[56] The next day he sketched a design that he decided was "a better outline than the one Mr. Walter and myself settled upon before." And, just as important, he wrote in his diary, by surpassing Walter's efforts, the drawing would fulfill his "wish to have something to do with this design myself." The biggest problem he discerned was that the foundation of the old Capitol Rotunda was not wide enough to support the Dome he wanted to build. With a bigger foundation, "I should get a greater span than anyone."[57]

On December 29, he showed the sketch to Walter, who, predictably, thought his own design was better. "It was evident that he is disgusted that I should attempt such a thing as design a dome," Meigs wrote in his diary. "He wishes to have all the credit to himself, and he will always claim all the credit of all the design of the Capitol, plans and all, I suppose, hereafter."[58]

Then, perhaps prompted by his conversation with Davis, he listed all the resentments that seethed within him. Walter's designs for the interior of the Capitol were drawn by Schoenborn at Meigs's direction. "The arrangement of the rooms is mine," he continued. "The form of the ceiling is mine. The style of decoration is that which I directed." And the "mere details of leaves, etc." could have been drawn just as easily by Schoenborn or any other draftsman as by Walter. And though Walter drew the masonry flowers and leaves, the motifs were "only adopted after having been subjected to my criticism and approval after alteration to make them suit my taste in almost every instance." In sum, he said, echoing Davis, "the design is quite as much, if not more, mine than his."

As for the Dome, "which he will call his," Meigs wrote, "it is very different from what he first proposed." The current design "was far the most beautiful. And for its construction he followed my hints. Yet he would never allow that I had the least claim of any merit in this design." And now, Meigs had designed a Dome that he thought was "much better than the other." But regardless of whether Meigs built his own Dome, he concluded, he would never get his "proper share" of the credit. Walter "has assumed the whole merit," he wrote in his diary. "I am getting tired of it."[59]

11

"A LIVELY OLD MAN WITH A VERY RED NOSE"

Three days after Christmas 1854, an elderly sculptor, aptly named "Mr. Stone," visited the Capitol to see Captain Montgomery Meigs, his fellow vestryman at St. John's Episcopal Church.[1] He brought an acquaintance with him—an Italian immigrant artist who had recently returned from Mexico, where he had been painting a church. The artist was short—probably no more than five feet six inches tall—with a full, dark beard and a ready laugh. Meigs, describing the encounter in his diary that evening, could not remember the name, but he was "a lively old man with a very red nose, either from Mexican suns or French brandies."[2]

The Italian artist told Meigs he had studied at a famous academy in Rome, where he had worked on a number of big projects. Alas, he had run afoul of the government, been imprisoned, and been forced to leave Italy in 1852. He wanted to paint something for the Capitol. He was good, he told Meigs, and he painted in fresco, *true* fresco. There was no one else in America who did it. Much of this conversation, Meigs recalled, was carried on in "bad French" with an occasional assist from a fellow Italian brought along as a translator. Meigs did not seem particularly impressed, but the artist could have known Thomas Crawford, which counted for something. He also knew that Meigs never hired anyone without seeing samples, which presented something of a problem in that none of his relevant work—mostly paintings on walls and ceilings—was portable. So he offered to do a small job for Meigs on spec, and, if Meigs liked it, maybe they could strike a deal.

The Italian émigré Constantino Brumidi came to work at the Capitol in 1854 and, except for occasional absences, stayed for more than twenty years. This gifted artist and meticulous craftsman's frescoes, designs, and skill with optical illusion transformed the interior of the new Capitol into a national showpiece. (Library of Congress)

Meigs had been hunting for a fresco painter for a year without success, and he also needed somebody with the skills and experience to set an artistic standard for the decoration and ornamentation of the Capitol's new wings. He had not had the courage—or, more likely, the money—to get Leutze, the German-American whose work he so admired, and while Carstens was good for decorative work, he did not have the background or training for the epic treatments that Meigs envisioned. Maybe the Italian could do it. Meigs offered him a lunette—a half-moon-shaped space—on the wall of his own office. Paint an allegory, he said, "supposing that the room might be occupied by the Committee on Agriculture at some future day."

The man agreed, but he had a hotel and a church to do first. He would be by in March to paint the lunette. Too late, Meigs warned. Congress will be adjourned by March, so if the artist wanted to show off what he had done, he had better come earlier. "Upon this," Meigs wrote, "he laughed and said that the church would be there always." He would paint Meigs's wall first.[3]

Meigs had just met Constantino Brumidi, then forty-nine. As he had claimed, Brumidi had had serious political problems in his homeland. But there was no denying his impeccable artistic credentials. Born in Rome to a Greek father and an Italian mother, he began his studies at the Accademia di San Luca, Rome's leading art school, when he was thirteen. He learned painting under the neoclassical historical and religious artists Vincenzo Camuccini and Filippo Agricola. His sculpture teachers were the neoclassicist Antonio Canova and Bertel Thorwaldsen, Canova's Danish disciple. His earliest known work was part of a Vatican Palace restoration painted in 1840, and during the following years he did several portraits—historical and contemporary—of popes and other Roman Catholic clergy. He painted his first frescoes at the Palazzo Torlonia, home of a prominent Roman banking family, but it was the dome and ceiling of the new Capella della Madonna dell'Archetto that won him critical plaudits in 1851.

This acclaim did him little good, however, for by then he was in jail. The Vatican government of Pope Pius IX, recently returned from exile, had indicted him for stealing Church treasures from convents and monasteries during the European upheavals of 1848–49, when Rome had a brief fling with republican government. Brumidi, a captain in the civic guard during the republican period (Crawford was also a guardsman), said he had taken the artworks for safekeeping so they would not be stolen by French soldiers sent to garrison the city prior to the pope's return. Brumidi had statements from several prominent monks attesting to his innocence. He was sentenced to eighteen years in prison but pardoned after a few months. He emigrated almost immediately, leaving his wife and two children in Italy, and arrived in New York on September 18, 1852. In November he filed for U.S. citizenship, and never looked back.[4]

Brumidi would turn out to be everything Meigs valued as an artist and a professional. He was hugely talented in a wide range of disciplines. Besides true fresco and oil, Brumidi also used a variety of other methods to make elaborate patterns over large surfaces, and was well versed in tempera, using white glue as a binder for pigments painted on dry plaster. He could paint trompe l'oeil cameo portraits and relief designs made to look like moldings. And although he was trained as a classicist, he was comfortable with U.S. history themes, American Indians, and modern machinery and inventions. For the Capitol, Brumidi would paint a steamship, a railroad, factories, a generator, Cyrus McCormick's reaper, the transatlantic cable, and at least six portraits of George Washington. Anything Meigs wanted, Brumidi could do.[5]

Also, Brumidi, like Crawford, was not particularly temperamental, a good trait to have with Meigs looking over his shoulder. And, like both Meigs and Walter, he worked fast. He did not need to be motivated, pushed, or coddled. And finally, also like Meigs and Walter, he loved the building: "My one ambition and my daily prayer," he once said, "is that I may live long enough to make beautiful the Capitol of the one country on earth in which there is liberty."[6]

Meigs knew none of this on January 25 when Brumidi returned to the Capitol with an oil for his lunette. His subject was "Cincinnatus called from the plow" to defend ancient Rome from invasion. It was a perfect theme, since many Americans regarded Washington as their Cincinnatus—another aristocratic farmer who dropped everything to lead the colonists to freedom. More important to Meigs, who remembered Brumidi's name this time, the sketch "is good and shows skill in drawing and composition and coloring, much greater than I expected." Brumidi needed a bit of time to finish his cartoons, he told Meigs, then he would begin.[7] Because fresco was painted on wet plaster, it had to be done section by section, like pieces of a jigsaw puzzle. The cartoon was the full-scale rendition on paper of the future fresco. When the artist was ready to paint, wet plaster was applied to the wall at the site of the relevant section, and the artist would replicate that section of the cartoon on the plaster.

Meigs saw Brumidi's cartoon on February 12, and he did not like it. "I did not think he had carried out the promise of his sketch," he wrote in his diary. The figures are "carelessly drawn." The priest "is too short for his head." Some parts were drawn in black-and-white. "I pointed out some defects, which he did not seem to be quite pleased at my doing," Meigs wrote. "I told him that he would have many critics, as the American painters would all look with jealousy at him and at his works and that they would find all the fault they could."[8]

Brumidi brushed off Meigs's objections and began wetting down the plaster on the wall. A week later he began to paint. Meigs was transfixed. Brumidi mixed "his palette very deliberately" and used "common artist colors," Meigs wrote in a long diary entry that attested to his fascination with the process and with the artist. Brumidi cut the pigment with lime paste, then applied the paint thickly. "The color did not seem to sink in as quick as I had expected." Would the sky be too blue? Meigs asked. No, Brumidi replied, "he feared rather that it would prove too light, 'troppo chiaro.'" Brumidi started at 10:30 a.m. on February 19 and was still at work when Meigs left the office at 4:00 p.m., anxious "to see the changes which drying will make."[9]

The following day Brumidi outlined his next section, while the completed parts of the first "begin already to come out with much more force and clearness than they did at first," Meigs wrote. It was like oil painting, Meigs noticed. If Brumidi did not like what he had done, or wanted to deepen the color, he could paint the same surface as many times as he wished, as long as the plaster remained wet.[10]

By February 21, Meigs was sold. "The work has much force," he wrote. "The mortar seems to set very hard, and it will make a durable wall, and the picture will be as durable as the wall itself." He had also begun to realize that his fears about jealous American artists had—at least for the moment—been unfounded. Instead, he appeared to have staged a public relations coup. First by accident, then by design, lawmakers began dropping by Meigs's office to watch Brumidi's progress. Stephen A. Douglas appeared with a constituent, Meigs wrote, and was "delighted to have the opportunity to explain it to his friend, who had seen the frescoes of Rome."[11]

Brumidi's arrival was the first major event of what would be a spectacular year of innovation and accomplishment for Meigs. He was managing perhaps a dozen original projects simultaneously, many of which required not only engineering or artistic skills, but also exceptional political sophistication and judgment.

On January 25, the same day Brumidi presented his oil sketch, Meigs wrote a detailed plan for ventilating the new Senate and House chambers.

The Senate, he calculated, could accommodate 3,042 people between the chamber and the galleries, an enormous number relative to the capacity of the intimate chamber in the old Capitol. Each person would occupy 30 square feet of floor space in the chamber or gallery, and each one would need 11,000 cubic feet of fresh air per hour to be comfortable—24 tons of fresh air per hour in all. The House, with a capacity of 4,309, needed 32 tons per hour. Meigs figured he needed a five-horsepower engine to run the Senate fans and a seven-horsepower engine for the House. He gave the specifications to Senator Charles T. James of Rhode Island, a steam engineer, who promised a floor speech to allay other senators' fears that their new, windowless meeting hall might turn out to be an oven.[12]

Others of Meigs successes were based on even riskier gambles. In mid-February he set his chief stonecutter, Francis Vincenti, to sculpt the bust of Be sheekee, or Buffalo, chief of Wisconsin's La Pointe Chippewa. Be sheekee and the chiefs of several other Midwestern tribes had come to Washington for treaty negotiations, causing a sensation in a city where few people had ever seen an Indian leader in full ceremonial costume, complete with feather headdresses and tribal markings. Seth Eastman, another of Meigs's West Point art instructors, had tipped Meigs that Be sheekee had "one of the best Indian heads he has known," Meigs wrote in his diary, and Eastman was right: "He is a fine-looking Indian, with character strongly marked."[13]

Vincenti, who may never have seen an Indian in his life, in five days completed a magnificent bust in clay, infusing Be sheekee's craggy face with remarkable power and dignity. "I think I will have it put into marble and placed in a proper situation in the Capitol as a record of the Indian culture," he wrote. The marble bust was carved in 1856—probably by Vincenti himself, who after his brief flirtation with artistic greatness, went back to yeoman stonework.[14] The bust of Be sheekee went on permanent display at the Capitol the moment Vincenti finished it.

Meigs continued to scout other artists and artisans and to hire those he liked. On February 12 he met Randolph Rogers, a young Rome-based sculptor who had come to Washington in hopes of winning a commission at the Capitol. His works "show talent," Meigs wrote in his diary, and he sent Rogers an encouraging letter.[15] The next day Rogers asked if he could submit a design for one of the doors of the Capitol. Meigs told him to send a sketch, and, "if I thought it suitable," he would send it to Davis, who, he predicted confidently, "would be guided by my opinion in the matter."[16]

Less than two weeks later, Meigs approved Rogers's design for bronze doors leading from the old Capitol to the new House wing. The theme was the life of Columbus, in nine panels, "a fine subject with great variety of costume and scenery," Meigs wrote in his diary. He also suggested that Rogers might want to think about the frieze he was planning for the interior of the Rotunda once the new Dome was finished. This immense project, a band of relief sculpture around the Rotunda's entire circumference, would be three hundred feet long.[17] On May 24, Meigs formally recommended that Davis agree to Rogers's proposal for the Columbus doors at a commission of $10,000. "Mr. Rogers is young—full of ambition, self-reliant," Meigs told Davis. "I believe that from careful study from the life, he has the ability to make a great work."[18] Three days later Davis accepted the proposal.

By the first week in March, Brumidi had been at work for a fortnight, and Meigs was completely persuaded that he had found the artist he sought. In his monthly progress report to Davis, he noted that "a fresco painter" had been working on "a specimen" in his office, destined to become the House Agriculture Committee Room. It "promises to be very beautiful," Meigs said.[19] By March 14, Brumidi had finished everything in the lunette but the head of a boy in one corner of the picture. He made the clever suggestion—apparently with a bit of prompting from Louisa Meigs—that the captain bring his young son, Monty, to the Capitol so he could put his portrait into the painting with Cincinnatus. This was accomplished the following day.[20]

It had taken Brumidi a month from the first brushstroke to the finished lunette, a fact that did not go unnoticed by Meigs. On March 20, four days after completion, Davis, probably at Meigs's invitation, came to see the fresco for himself, and authorized Meigs to hire Brumidi for $8 per day, which was more than Meigs was getting as a still-impoverished army captain.[21] Still, Meigs was happy to pay the price for what Brumidi could do. On March 30, Brumidi proposed four allegorical paintings for the ceiling above Cincinnatus, and Meigs immediately agreed.[22]

Meigs soon hired another Italian. Frederick Casali, the translator who had accompanied Brumidi on his first visit to the Capitol, was, it turned out, a modeler and caster, from life or from drawings, capable of working in bronze and other metals. On April 18, he showed Meigs a mold he had made for a snake that Brumidi wanted to draw for one of his cartoons. Meigs asked Casali to cast the snake in zinc, and Casali produced a "beautifully executed" figure the following day.[23]

Detail of Brumidi's decoration of the House Agriculture Committee Room, with a panel of his ceiling fresco overhanging his lunette *Cincinnatus Called from the Plow*. Brumidi painted the lunette fresco as a free sample of his work, finishing it within a month. Meigs hired him on the spot. (Architect of the Capitol)

Casali became the designer and modeler for decorative door handles, doorknobs, and other ornaments, four of them cast from an increasingly varied collection of live snakes captured by Meigs and his sons John and Monty and by the Aqueduct crew in the woods near Great Falls. Meigs did not explain his special fondness for serpents, but they were certainly versatile: they could be twisted into almost any shape.

Meigs's enthusiasm for this new hobby was boundless. On April 27 he and Monty cornered and captured two blacksnakes, each about five feet long, by whacking them with clubs. "I secured them both alive, though one of them was disabled by a blow which broke his back and disfigured him a little," Meigs wrote that night. The next day he let the snakes run loose in his office, and the uninjured one "struck in most vicious manner

Frederick Casali cast this bronze doorknob for the House of Representatives from a snake given to him by Meigs. Snakes could be easily twisted into many shapes, and Meigs kept a supply of live ones, including poisonous copperheads and rattlesnakes, in his office. (Architect of the Capitol)

at everyone who approached him."[24] The two blacksnakes became the bronze handles for the east doors leading into the new chamber of the House of Representatives.

That was only the beginning. On May 22, with the weather heating up, the Aqueduct team gave Meigs his first copperhead.[25] A week later John Meigs, a thirteen-year-old just as bright and willful as his father, caught another five-foot blacksnake with his bare hands, deeply impressing the Aqueduct's Irish laborers.[26] By June, Meigs was putting some of his trophies into his office chandelier to see what they would do. One jumped down, but most slithered upward, winding themselves around the gas pipe, from where they could survey everything that went on below them. Then, in December, when the snake season should have been over, one of Meigs's Aqueduct foremen sent him two boxes "containing 3 or 4 black snakes and a striped snake and 4 copperheads. I turned the whole of them this evening into the box with the rattlesnake. It looks like a pandemonium."[27]

The project that obsessed Meigs beyond all others, however, was the Capitol Dome. He was relentless in his efforts to lobby and cajole Congress into letting him build it. Walter had designed the Dome and Davis had approved it, but at this point in his career on Capitol Hill, getting Congress to support the new project was Meigs's job. He could call on Davis when he needed a political club to beat down recalcitrant opponents, but he was the man in charge—both for building the Capitol and for the politics.

His first task was to get congressional permission for the new project. He could dip into his reserves to finish the working drawings, place orders for any new machinery he might need, and make some sample castings to show would-be contractors what he intended to do, but the new Dome was not part of the Capitol Extension. It would be separate. He would need new authorizing legislation to begin it, and new money to build it.

Walter had tacked his Dome drawing to the wall outside the Extension offices, and congressional interest began to percolate as soon as lawmakers returned for the start of the new session in late 1854. The winners from the November balloting would not take office for a year, so Meigs would still have a Democratic majority in both Houses, even though many Democratic members, including Stanton, were lame ducks, headed for retirement when Congress shut down in mid-1855.

On January 10, Senator Pearce of Maryland promised Meigs he would vote for the Dome. On the fifteenth, Whig congressman John L. Taylor offered to lobby Burton Craige, the chairman of the House Committee on Public Buildings and Grounds, to make a floor speech in support of it.[28] Finally, on the twenty-third, Meigs sent Pearce a draft amendment authorizing $425,000 for the Dome and asking him to hook it on to the Capitol Extension funding bill.[29] Pearce tried this out, but legislating a new government project on an appropriations bill and paying for it at the same time was a dicey stratagem. The Senate, wary of funding something new without debating it, stripped out Pearce's amendment before passing the Extension bill on January 25.

This setback meant that Meigs would have to take his chances in the House, where Representative Richard H. Stanton, lame duck or not, waited once again to reprise the case against "military rule." Stanton opened his offensive January 27—two days after Senate passage of the Extension funding. Stanton had induced the Baltimore *Sun* to run an article praising the Walter Dome design "to the skies," Meigs wrote. *The Sun* insisted that if Walter—and by implication, not Meigs—were allowed to build it, the Dome would rival Michelangelo's masterpiece at St. Peter's. In his diary on January 27, Meigs scolded himself for not taking the time to "work up" his own Dome design "and see whether I cannot make it better than Walter's."[30] His jealousy was starting to interfere with his good sense. It was obvious that Meigs did not have time to compete with Walter, and he probably could not have bested him under any circumstances. He said as much a few days later in a conversation with Pearce: "I told [Pearce] that it was drawn by Walter, that 9/10 of it was his entirely; that he had changed some parts of it to suit me, particularly the lantern [the light chamber on top of the Dome], but that the design was his almost entirely."[31] Meigs would never summarize the genesis of the Dome more truthfully or give a more accurate description of his professional relationship with Walter.

Stanton's assault continued. Unsigned opinion columns in the Washington *Daily Union* on January 31 and February 6, probably written, or at least planted, by Stanton, praised Walter and condemned Meigs. Rhode Island senator Charles James advised Meigs to respond, and Meigs, still relatively unperturbed, wrote a diplomatic letter to the editor: "Capt. Meigs and Mr. Walter are both devoting their whole time and energies to the completion of this great building." Both "believe that the result will be satisfactory to the public and such as will do no discredit to themselves, and they expect to continue to act together harmoniously, satisfied to accomplish this great work and determined not to be set at variance by the attempts of injudicious friends to exalt either at the expense of the other."[32] Meigs also noted in his diary that the attacks were once again upsetting Walter, who was refusing to speak to Stanton. Meigs told Walter to "keep cool" and ignore the articles—his letter was all the response that was necessary.[33]

Meigs's detachment may have seemed odd, given his own insecurities and resentments, for the issues that he vetted with Pearce and the *Daily Union* were issues that profoundly troubled him: Who did more of the work? Who got more accolades? However, the vitriol that increasingly poisoned his solitude and his private conversations with Davis about Walter had not invaded his public statements. Meigs recognized that his partnership with Walter fueled the project. Meigs admired Walter even as he railed privately against Walter's selfishness and self-promotion. Walter thanked the heavens for Meigs's ability to cope with the politics even as he privately ridiculed the captain's incessant meddling and his arrogance.

The other reason Meigs could ignore Stanton was that Stanton's cause was going nowhere. This became apparent on February 20, during House debate on the Capitol Extension appropriation, when Stanton rose to denounce Meigs's presence on the project as "an encumbrance" that "serves only to embarrass the architect."[34] Whig representative Edward Dickinson of Massachusetts rose to shred this argument. Summarizing for his colleagues, he described Stanton's select committee investigation as "a farce." It is "time to make some demonstration against the daily introduction of this political humbug," Dickinson said. The House passed the appropriation, leaving Meigs in charge.[35]

All this, however, was only a prelude to the main event, which came two days later when the House reconvened to debate the new Dome. Here again, Stanton spoke first, but his priorities had changed. Instead of another diatribe, he simply introduced legislation providing $100,000 for a new Dome, built "upon the plan designed by T. U. Walter." Members were suspicious. Did this measure come out of a committee? No, Stanton said, "it comes recommended by a necessity which every gentleman who examines the subject must see." The current dome may have been all right for the original building, he said, but it will be too "squatty" once the Extension is complete. Walter "has designed a Dome, the plan of which I have seen, and which commends itself to my judgment; and which all who have seen it say is most beautiful and perfect."[36]

One member complained about "useless expenditures." Others were still suspicious. Did the amendment mean Walter would direct the building of the new Dome? Members had no appetite for revisiting the military rule debate yet again. Stanton replied that he knew Walter and Meigs had no disagreement about the Dome, and if members thought the bill favored Walter, he would strike the language they found objectionable. The important thing, he continued, was that both Meigs and Walter "believe the design is practicable, that it is necessary to the perfection of the building, and that without it the building would be imperfect." Meigs and Walter, he concluded, "desire this appropriation." Stanton, it seemed, had completely changed his tune. But the legislation was anything but a sure thing. The vote ended in a 70–70 draw. New Hampshire Democrat Harry Hibbard, chairing the debate, then voted aye.[37] As far as the House was concerned, Meigs and Walter could build the Dome.

Meigs was ecstatic, but suspicious. He wondered if Stanton had sponsored the amendment because he wanted to make sure that Walter's design was approved before the new Congress—without Stanton—came in and adopted a design by Meigs. Also since the new Dome would be part of the original Capitol, and not part of the Extension, did Stanton expect its construction to come under the purview of the commissioner of public buildings rather than Meigs?[38]

What Meigs did not wonder about, at least according to available records, was why the vote was so close. With Stanton surrendering on military rule, and the question of government extravagance having largely been overtaken by events—the Capitol was too far along to stop construction—the way should have been clear for easy passage.

Congress, however, was coping with the relatively new imponderable of Know-Nothingism. The incumbent survivors of the 1854 election—including northern Democrats—would have had a tough time voting for the Capitol Dome. Who wanted to be associated with Meigs and his polyglot gang of German draftsmen, Italian stonemasons, Irish ditchdiggers, and other assorted recent arrivals? Stanton and Hibbard, luckily for Meigs, were both lame-duck Democrats with nothing to lose.

So Meigs may have been right in his suspicions, but for the wrong reason. Stanton may have pushed the Dome forward when he did because he thought there were enough lame ducks in the waning days of the 33rd Congress willing to vote their conscience. The incoming Congress, which would not convene until December, was top-heavy with Know-Nothings and might refuse to fund it because of Meigs's immigrants. Why take that risk?

And as for Stanton himself, he seemed to have no hidden agenda beyond making sure that the Dome got built. The House adjourned on March 4, and on March 8, escorted by Walter, Stanton appeared at the Extension offices. He and Meigs had never met. Stanton appeared nervous, and Meigs "did not feel very easy" himself. Walter introduced the two men, then took Stanton into the office to see Brumidi's lunette. He was delighted with it. Henceforth, he promised, he would support Meigs.[39]

Maybe it had not been personal after all—at least in regard to Meigs. Davis had bounced Stanton from his chairmanship and defeated him in the war over military rule. Once Stanton had moved beyond these bitter losses, he had perhaps been able to see that the project, despite everything, was in good hands. More important, after the Senate had declined to fund the Dome, Stanton may have seen that by changing from an opponent to an advocate in the waning days of the 33rd Congress, he could finally make the vital contribution to the Capitol Extension that had eluded him for five years.

Meigs had also been right about a possible bureaucratic power play to move him aside. But the culprit was not Stanton. It was Commissioner of Public Buildings Benjamin B. French, who came to Meigs's office two days after the House vote to talk about the Dome. French expected to build it, Meigs wrote in his diary, "that is, to spend the money and have Walter make the calculations and do the work." Meigs immediately pushed back. He told French that he, Meigs, had gotten the money from Congress, and that Congress wanted him to do the job. Meigs spent the rest of the day writing letters and lobbying lawmakers.[40] He was not subtle. He asked Senator James A. Bayard, chair of the Committee on Public Buildings, to amend the Dome appropriation to stipulate that the money was "to be expended under the direction of the President of the United States," which would put the Dome, like the Extension, in Pierce's hands.[41] The amendment was added.

As it turned out, Meigs need not have worried. The Senate passed the Dome appropriation on March 4, and Stanton dropped in to make a point of telling Meigs, with some relish, that French was "very much put out" to have lost control of the project.[42]

With the Dome project in hand, Meigs had reached his apogee. On March 28, Pierce invited him and Walter to a private dinner to "talk over the whole matter of the public buildings."[43] On April 3, Meigs wrote Davis asking for formal orders to begin tearing down the old dome and building the new one, putting to rest any questions "as to my authority." Davis issued the orders the following day, and three weeks later he also put Meigs in charge of the construction of a new extension for the General Post Office. Walter, Meigs's collaborator on both of the new projects, was euphoric—no new money, he told his father-in-law, but "Congress has added greatly to my labors as well as complimented me."[44]

On May 11, Meigs wrote a long letter to Thomas Crawford in Rome. He talked first about money, then about the Senate pediment, then about "young Mr. Rogers" and his Columbus doors. Then he talked about the $100,000 Congress had given him as a down payment to spend on "this Dome of cast iron." The cupola, he said, "is to be surmounted by a statue 14 feet high. Suppose you make a sketch for it." Do not draw Washington, he cautioned. "We have too many" of him. Crawford should think of something else.[45]

On July 12, a Crawford sketch arrived in the mail. It was the "very graceful and very beautiful . . . draped figure of a female," Meigs wrote in his diary. Crawford called her *Freedom*. She was fifteen feet tall, with eyes modestly downcast. Her right hand rested on the hilt of a sword, from which hung the shield of the United States. Cradled in her left arm was an olive branch. She wore a laurel wreath in her hair. It was to be executed in bronze. Meigs was enchanted.[46]

It was four months before Meigs sat down with Davis to talk about *Freedom* and about art in general. Davis was spending much of his time closely monitoring events in Kansas, where violence between proslavery gunmen and well-armed antislavery settlers threatened to escalate. He was also trying to figure out a strategy for Democrats to recover from the electoral debacle of the previous November. But for the Capitol Extension and the new Dome, Davis could always find time.

Meigs and Davis had much to discuss. During the summer, sculptor Hiram Powers, who had earlier disdained Meigs's offer to design one of the new Capitol's eastern pediments, wangled $25,000 from Congress to produce a piece of sculpture for the new Capitol. Powers's congressional patrons had apparently discussed their interest in Powers with Davis, who then asked Meigs about it. On July 27, Meigs sent Davis copies of all his correspondence with Powers, along with a cover letter assuring Davis that he had nothing against Powers, and "should be very much gratified now to receive from Mr. Powers an intimation that he was willing to put his talent at the disposal of his country" and do the House pediment.[47]

Instead of a pediment sculpture, however, Powers sent Congress the model of an allegorical female figure he called *America*. Powers had apparently realized the gaffe he had committed two years earlier by ignoring Meigs and was trying to recoup by using friends in Congress to find him a place of privilege in the new Capitol. It seemed, in fact, that he was trying to displace Crawford as the sculptor of the Dome statue. On October 11, Meigs went to Davis to figure out what to do. He brought along the sketch of Crawford's *Freedom*. There was a bit of hemming and hawing, but Davis's key decision was that he preferred Crawford's statue. As for Powers, Davis had the perfect bureaucratic answer: since Congress had appropriated the money especially for him, Powers should do what he thought best and speak with Congress about it.[48] Powers had not chosen to deal with Meigs or Davis directly, so Davis was under no obligation to deal with him. Powers soon abandoned his plan to sculpt *America* and eventually earned most of his commission with statues of Benjamin

Franklin and Thomas Jefferson, one for the Senate and the other for the House, at $10,000 apiece.

Meigs consulted with Davis on a regular basis—usually by mail—throughout 1855. The trust between the two men was such that Meigs felt confident enough to make even important decisions virtually on his own—putting Brumidi to work, encouraging Randolph Rogers, inquiring about encaustic tiles and papier-mâché ornaments—and informing Davis about his activities only when he was actually ready to spend the money. Davis, as far as can be ascertained, never turned him down. In fact, as their relationship developed, it became clear that Davis and Meigs were of one mind about beautifying the Capitol. Brumidi, encaustic tile, papier-mâché, and the fancy decorative painting that was Emmerich Carstens's specialty would not produce the simple, stark neoclassical interior envisioned by Walter and Fillmore. Instead, the new Capitol's ornamentation and decoration would be much more elaborate—and quite unlike what most lawmakers expected.

In addition to art, Meigs also had no hesitation in asking Davis for favors. When he was lobbying to take over the Post Office Extension, Davis was the first person he contacted. Now that the battle for military rule was over, Meigs wrote in a February 22 letter, he wanted to show Congress how good a job he—and by implication, Davis's Army Corps of Engineers—could do if he used government workers under his own direct supervision instead of contractors, with their "clumsy, slovenly" habits.[49] It was an argument designed to appeal to Davis's sense of service pride even as it enabled him to put another large-scale construction project under his control.

Davis excelled in this kind of bureaucratic empire building, and as a major figure in the Pierce administration, he wielded immense power. Not as apparent—except to those, like Meigs, who knew him well—Davis was also a technological innovator with the same kind of curious, scientific mind that Meigs displayed. It was an uncommon trait for a career politician of his experience to possess, and it led to several unusual initiatives, which, of course, included the Capitol. To help these along, Davis had an annual War Department budget of nearly $20 million—roughly one-third of the entire government.[50] If he wanted something, he could buy it.

Davis's greatest impact as a technologist probably derived from his desire to transform the U.S. Army into a larger, more supple force. He was opposed to the practice of allowing officers to take root for years in postings they found agreeable. He also successfully lobbied for the creation of four additional regiments and added a fifth year of instruction at West Point for cadets who needed extra time to master the curriculum. His chief innovation, however, was his decision to abandon the use of smoothbore muskets in favor of rifles. "The superiority of the grooved, or rifle, barrel and elongated ball, in range and accuracy of fire, has long been known," he wrote in his 1854 report. "Yet the difficulty of loading this weapon has hitherto, for most military purposes, counter-balanced its advantages." There were, he said, two possible solutions: breech-loaded rifles, which posed technical problems "not yet overcome," and the use of an oblong ball that was small enough to load but expanded to fill the barrel when the rifle was discharged. This Minié ball, named for the French captain who invented it, was, like the breech-loader, undergoing testing. Armories, he said, would make no more muskets.[51]

The muzzle-loading rifle, introduced by Davis as secretary of war, became the principal weapon of the Civil War. The Minié ball gave foot soldiers the ability to load quickly and hit targets routinely at distances of several hundred yards. Frontal assaults—the essence of smoothbore warfare—turned into lethal bloodbaths when charging soldiers came up against entrenched rifle-carrying defenders. Hundreds of thousands of men would die or have their limbs shattered in the Civil War, most of them because of fearsome wounds inflicted by the new rifles and their Minié balls.

Throughout his tenure at the War Department, there was little, if any, evidence that Davis used his cabinet post in any way to prepare the South for a coming conflict. He wanted a better U.S. Army with better-paid, better-armed, and better-educated officers and men, no matter where they came from. In 1854, responding to a suggestion that he use his office to establish a "southern military academy," Davis wrote that if such an institution were "intended for the education of southern youths exclusively, I fear the tendency would be to create and increase sectional jealousies." Davis's own experience, he said, had shown that "bringing together young men from all parts of the country, at a period of life when they imbibe lasting impressions," created "friendships among northern, southern, eastern, and western youths, remembered in after years."[52]

This was Davis at his most unionist, still comfortable with his sweeping national vision even as he embraced proslavery partisanship—receiving letters from David Atchison threatening murder in Kansas Territory and never saying nor doing anything to discourage him.

The crisis in Kansas developed slowly. On the day the Kansas-Nebraska Act was signed, there were fewer than eight hundred white settlers in Kansas Territory. By the spring of 1855, there were eight thousand, and almost 50 percent were Missourians.[53] These were largely "border ruffians," proslavery gunmen who set up their Kansas headquarters in Leavenworth. By the end of 1854 these early arrivals were balanced by significant numbers of well-armed northern settlers, who built the town of Lawrence. Besides a shared interest in land, both sides also understood they were involved in a crusade. "Come on then, Gentlemen of the Slave States," antislavery senator William H. Seward said in a speech following House passage of the Kansas-Nebraska bill. "Since there is no escaping your challenge, I accept it in behalf of the cause of freedom. We will engage in competition for the virgin soil of Kansas, and God give the victory to the side which is stronger in numbers as it is in right."[54]

On November 29, 1854, a proslavery candidate was elected territorial delegate to Washington, winning overwhelmingly with help from hundreds of Missourians who crossed the border on Election Day. In March 1855, elections for a territorial legislature were held, and proslavery candidates got 5,427 votes out of more than 6,000 cast, even though there were only 2,905 eligible voters in Kansas.[55] The new legislature immediately began passing proslavery laws, prompting the free-staters to form their own government and approve an antislavery constitution. By year's end, the Kansans had divided into armed camps, a free-stater had been killed, and an invasion of Lawrence was threatened.

Besides the deepening morass in Kansas, the Pierce administration in 1855 also had to confront its declining political fortunes. The midterm elections had wrecked the Democrats in the North, put the national party in the hands of southern militants like Davis, and given a huge boost to the Know-Nothings and the increasingly robust Republicans. The Know-Nothings, however, now formally renamed the American Party, failed in midyear to reach agreement on slavery, causing northerners to abandon their national meeting. No sooner had the Know-Nothings moved into the mainstream than they started to fall apart.[56]

Nativism, however, did not wane, but instead appeared to strengthen. On May 18, a fire burned down part of Meigs's blacksmith shop, prompting him to fire the three watchmen who had been posted as guards during the night. When he reported the incident to Pierce and Davis, telling them he needed to hire new watchmen, "the President begged me not to appoint any of these miserable Know-Nothings." Meigs told Pierce he thought he could manage "to steer clear of them," but, he wrote in his diary later that day, "I find it is not so easy." It turned out that Samuel Champion, a longtime Walter loyalist and the highly regarded foreman of the blacksmith shop, had become a Know-Nothing leader. This exasperated Meigs, now militantly anti-Know-Nothing, but he refused to capitulate to Democrats—including the president of the United States—who importuned him to purge his ranks of Know-Nothings. When several prominent Washingtonians demanded that he sack Champion, he told them "I would make no political removal; that if the President or the Secretary chose to remove any man under my direction, they had the right," Meigs wrote in his diary. "If they should insist upon my taking a political part, I should resign my charge."[57] Davis backed him unequivocally. Under no circumstances should he let politics influence his hiring practices.[58]

With his Dome appropriation in hand and the new Congress expected back in December, Meigs continued to negotiate with Crawford over *Freedom*. He had sent back Crawford's original design, asking him to add a pedestal between the statue itself and the top of the tholus, or lantern, that would crown the Dome.[59] With Davis having all but approved Crawford's initial sketch, the revision probably seemed to Meigs to be a simple matter. Leave *Freedom* intact, simply adding the transitional element.

A photograph of the new design arrived on November 16, but instead of a revision, Crawford had sculpted a completely different statue. This *Freedom* was an ethereal figure, less substantial than the first, yet at the same time more beautiful and quietly elegant. Her right hand rested on the hilt of a sheathed sword, like the right hand of the first *Freedom*, but the olive branch was gone. The left hand of the new *Freedom* hung down at her side, grasping a laurel wreath and holding the shield of America. She stood on a spherical pedestal bearing the motto E PLURIBUS UNUM.

The biggest difference between the two *Freedoms*, however, was that the new one wore a liberty cap, the same symbol of manumission that

Davis had vetoed for the central figure of *America* in Crawford's pediment design. Meigs noted this gaffe immediately, but he waited until November 25 to write to Crawford in Rome, preparing him for the worst. The statue, he said, is "lighter and better fitted" to be perched on the tholus: "I will bring it to the notice of the Secretary," he said, "though I anticipate some objection to the cap."[60] Crawford offered no explanation of why he had changed the design so radically, nor did Meigs ask him. And Meigs was not quick to seek a ruling from Davis. That could wait until next year.

12

BLEEDING KANSAS

On the day Congress appropriated $100,000 for the Capitol Dome, Captain Meigs was hardly ready to build it. Walter, struggling to finish the final drawings, by mid-1855 had nine full-time draftsmen working for him, and twelve by year's end. Meigs's most important task was figuring out how to organize the project. Dismantling Bulfinch's external dome, made of wood and sheathed in copper, was the first task, and a fairly simple one. Meigs would build scaffolding around it and have his carpenters rip it apart.

Getting rid of the inner dome, made of stone and brick with some wood at the top, was trickier. For this, Meigs decided on an unorthodox approach. Instead of building scaffolding from the floor of the Rotunda, he decided to erect a single hundred-foot wooden tower in the exact center of the room. The floor was not strong enough to support the tower by itself, so he would extend a pair of timbers from one side of the room to the other, crossing them in the center at right angles. The tower would be placed on the joint. The timbers, anchored at either end to the Rotunda foundation, would ensure that the foundation would bear most of the weight. Once the tower was in place, Meigs would build platforms at different levels to enable workers to reach the inner shell of the old dome and pull it down.

Constructing the new Dome was a different matter altogether. It would be built to a height of three hundred feet above the base of the Capitol. Lifting multiton chunks of cast iron to such an altitude was a daunting, dangerous task. Meigs was keen to avoid scaffolding if at all possible.

The solution presented itself during the summer of 1855, when Meigs had a visit from the New York–based distributor for German-born engineer John A. Roebling, of Trenton, New Jersey, a widely known bridge designer and manufacturer of wire rope. Meigs, who seldom saw an innovation he did not like, was interested in using wire rope for a variety of purposes at the Capitol, including sash cord for windows, but the visit of Roebling's agent gave him another idea. He would mount an additional eighty-foot wooden pillar—a giant mast—atop his wooden tower and affix another eighty-foot timber to the mast as a boom. Using this derrick, he could pick up the cast-iron pieces and lift them into position for workers to bolt into place. With the derrick, he could tear down the old dome and cover the opening with a temporary waterproof wood and canvas roof. The tower would poke through, and the Dome workers would be above the canvas on a wooden platform that would surround the pillar like a crow's nest, moving upward as construction progressed.[1] This was possible because Meigs intended to use heavy-gauge wire rope to stabilize the pillar. Cables would run from the pillar to immense cement blocks sunk in the Capitol grounds on both sides of the building—like stepping a mast.

In a September 16, 1855, letter to Roebling, Meigs asked for a price list for his wire rope. He told Roebling he had already bought some wire from the distributor, "but I prefer always to deal at manufacturers' prices."[2] Roebling, destined to earn renown for designing the Brooklyn Bridge, was apparently unimpressed by Meigs's initial overture, for it took nearly a month for Meigs to reach Roebling and close the deal, and at least another month before he started getting deliveries: "Send the wire rope . . . as soon as possible," Meigs importuned on October 15, probably stamping his feet in frustration.[3] On September 21, 1855, when his workmen ripped away the first sheet of copper from Bulfinch's outer dome, Meigs remarked in his diary that "this day is an era."[4]

Once the old domes—inner and exterior—were down, Meigs's final preparatory task was to rig a temporary cover, both to keep the rain out and to ensure that the workers on the platform above would not be dropping wrenches, hammers, and other lethal bits of hardware onto the lawmakers, visitors, and vendors constantly milling about far below.

Meigs worked this out at the end of 1855, building a roof made of

Instead of constructing the new Dome from precarious scaffolding, Meigs built a sturdy timber tower on the floor of the Capitol Rotunda and extended it through the roof, crowning it with a mast that rose high into the air. (Architect of the Capitol)

wood with rafters radiating downward at an angle from the tower like the ribs of an umbrella and anchored at the Rotunda's edge. Boards were nailed on top of the rafters, and a painted, waterproof canvas top was stretched over the boards.[5] The tower rose through the roof and another platform was built above it for the ironworkers.

Doing all this at once—it took about three months—was messy. Once the copper sheathing came off the outer dome, the workers had to wait until more height was added to the tower. The high-altitude boom derrick was not yet built, but the crews were able to use a hoist rigged with Roebling's wire rope to lower the outer dome's old timbers to the ground. There they burned them in a boiler to make steam for the hoisting engine. Meanwhile, inside the Rotunda, workers choked on billowing clouds of dust as the lath, plaster, and masonry of the inner dome came down.[6]

But it worked. Meigs got all three jobs done without damage or serious injury either to his own people, to passersby, or to the old Capitol. On De-

By anchoring the top of the mast with wire rope, Meigs was able to rig a boom derrick that could lift cast-iron sections of the Dome for workers to bolt into place. Crews worked from a movable wooden platform that rose upward on the tower as the Dome grew in height. (Architect of the Capitol)

cember 7, Bulfinch's dome was gone, the watertight roof was up, and the platform was built.

Meigs had also made substantial progress on the Capitol Extension, and by the end of 1855, senators and House members could begin to anticipate the moment when they might actually move into their new offices. The walls of both new chambers had reached their full height, Meigs reported in October, and most of the other interior walls were up to the third (top) floor. All the roof trusses were finished, and many interior rooms had received a first coat of plaster. The exterior walls for the first floor were finished, and most of the East Front marble facing had been set, although delays in marble deliveries were slowing progress somewhat. On the first floor of the new House wing, his office "is now being painted in fresco," Meigs reported in closing. "This will enable Congress to see a specimen of this, the highest style of architectural decoration. It is the most appropriate and beautiful mode of finishing the building, and it will afford a field for the talents of artists never before offered in this country."[7]

On Wednesday, December 3, 1855, four days before Meigs cleared out the last of the old dome rubble, the 34th U.S. Congress convened. It had been elected more than a year earlier, during the aftermath of the Kansas-Nebraska Act, and while the Democrats retained a substantial majority in the Senate, they had been decimated in the House, where a nonunified "opposition" composed of Whigs, Know-Nothings, old Free-Soilers, and newly minted Republicans held two-thirds of the seats.

It was the opposition's job to elect a Speaker, and they finally got it done after two months on February 2, 1856, when Nathaniel Banks, an antislavery member from Massachusetts, nominally a Know-Nothing but with strong links to the Republicans, won on the 133rd ballot on a plurality vote of 103–100.[8] Meigs described Banks as "a man of ability," but remarked, "I do not believe that he is as much moved in his public actions by the desire to do his duty to the public as by a desire to elevate Mr. Banks."[9]

Official Washington was in a bad mood. Congressional comity, which had frayed badly during the Kansas-Nebraska debate, was strained further once the 34th Congress began. Political parties were losing their national identity, and every transaction seemed to be poisoned by the issue of slavery. Democrats were mostly southerners, while the Republicans were virtually all northerners. The American Party professed a national following, but disagreement over slavery was wrecking it just as surely as it had wrecked the Whigs. Members greeted announcement of Banks's election with both cheers and hisses on the House floor, followed by an immediate dispute over the legality of the balloting. Lewis D. Campbell, an Ohio Whig turned Know-Nothing and a staunch Banks supporter, gave voice to the thought that nagged everyone's mind: Would there be a "dissolution of the Union" if Banks were seated? "If I thought my heart was capable of cherishing [such a] sentiment," he scoffed, "I would . . . tear it out and cast it to the dogs."[10]

Banks's election settled nothing. It was an election year, and a presidential year, which guaranteed even more grandstanding and confrontation. The sour mood continued outside official meetings, as southern hostess Virginia Clay-Clopton noted much later in memoirs. "The representatives of the two antagonistic sections seldom met," she wrote. "Even at the entertainments given at the foreign legations and at the houses of famous Washington citizens, this opposition . . . was carefully considered in the sending out of invitations in order that no unfortunate *rencontre* might occur between uncongenial guests."[11]

The winter of 1855–56 was a particularly brutal one in Washington and all along the East Coast. Harbors froze and mail service stopped. Meigs tied runners to the wheels of his buggy and took his children for sleigh rides in the woods. Walter bought himself a coach and rented a slave to drive it. The owner wanted to sell the slave to Walter—"your man Bacchus (we call him John)," Walter wrote—but Walter was afraid of being "tied to him." He had nothing against slavery—"on the contrary, I think it a good institution"—but he planned to send the coachman back to the owner.[12] Walter's eldest son, Robert, recovering from a disastrous business venture in Kentucky, was about to get married in Indiana, and Walter bought him a farm for $600 cash. His second son, Thomas, wrote for the first time in a year from San Francisco and asked for $200, and Horace was a twenty-year-old sailor aboard a merchant whaler, deciding to go to sea after threatening to kill his previous employer. Walter's newest son, Gardiner, who would also be his last, was eleven months old and thriving.

After holding on to Thomas Crawford's second *Freedom* design for two months, Meigs on January 11 passed it along to Davis, who politely replied, first, that the design "impresses me most favorably. Its general grace and power, striking at first view, has grown on me as I studied the details." But, predictably, he did not like the cap, which seemed "inappropriate to a people who were born free and would not be enslaved." Instead, he suggested gently, "Why should not armed liberty wear a helmet" to celebrate "her cause triumphant?" He would not insist, however, but would leave the final judgment to Crawford, adding, "I certainly would not venture, on a question of art, to array my opinion against his."[13]

Which is exactly what he had done. Meigs passed a copy of the Davis letter along to Crawford. Again, as with Davis's earlier complaint about the cap on Crawford's *America* pediment figure, Meigs provided another soft cover letter, noting that Davis "does leave the matter to your own judgment."[14] Crawford thus had another opportunity to make a controversial decision on his own, even though Davis had made his wishes known.

Meigs may have been ducking responsibility or simply stalling, but in 1856 there was another reason to be careful. Davis was in his last year as the secretary of war, and he would not be part of the next president's cabinet. What Meigs knew for certain in early 1856 was that someone else would be calling his tune next year, and that he was going to be on his

The statue of *Freedom*, first and second designs, by Thomas Crawford. Meigs
and Davis were pleased with the first design but asked Crawford to add a pedestal. Instead, Crawford sent a drawing of a completely different statue, which
included not only a pedestal but also a liberty cap. Davis wanted a helmet instead. (Architect of the Capitol)

own. He would want to present the new secretary with a record unsullied
by politics. If *Freedom* showed up without a liberty cap, let the record
show that Davis and Crawford had made the decision.

In fact, although Meigs did not know it at that moment, Davis had already planned his exit. In the late spring of 1855 he visited Mississippi to
attend the state Democratic Party convention, where he had shaken all
the necessary hands and made all the necessary promises.[15] These efforts
paid off on January 19, 1856, when Mississippi's state legislature elected

him a U.S. senator. On March 4, 1857, once the next president was inaugurated, Davis would reclaim the Senate seat he had abandoned in 1851. Davis's election occurred three days after he ruled on Crawford's second *Freedom*. He and Meigs were close, but while Meigs, the protégé, routinely told Davis about his aspirations and sought his help, there is no evidence that Davis, the mentor, confided in Meigs. Davis's election did mean that Meigs would have another powerful and important friend on Capitol Hill. Still, it would not be the same as having Davis for his direct boss.

The winter was also brutal in Kansas Territory, but while it may have kept people indoors, it did nothing to ease tensions between the free-state and proslavery factions. On January 15, Topeka-based antislavery settlers elected their own state officials despite efforts by Missouri-based gunmen to disrupt them. One free-stater was ambushed and killed with a hatchet. Then, on January 24, President Pierce raised the ante, branding the Topekans as "revolutionary," declaring the proslavery territorial government legitimate, and blaming Kansas's violence on an abolitionist-led "propaganda emigration" designed to inflame tempers.[16] In February, Pierce issued another proclamation making federal troops available to repress lawbreakers. The free-state legislature gathered in Topeka, inaugurated its officers, and decided to resist the territorial government.

On March 12, Senator Stephen Douglas issued a report condemning the Topekans, suggested that Kansans hold a convention to write a state constitution, and recommended increasing money for law enforcement. A Senate Republican minority report called for a free Kansas under the Topeka constitution and accused Democrats of promoting "the subjugation of white freemen" so that "African slavery may succeed."[17] In the House, Speaker Banks sent a three-man delegation—two Republicans and a Democrat—to Kansas on a fact-finding mission. On March 17, Douglas introduced a statehood bill for Kansas. Three days later, Senator William H. Seward, now a Republican, introduced a bill calling for Kansas statehood under the Topeka constitution. On April 9, Seward in a floor speech compared Pierce to King George III.[18]

Next month the violence began. On May 8, the first-term congressman Philemon T. Herbert of California sat down in the dining room at Willard's Hotel shortly after 11:00 a.m. and ordered breakfast. His waiter, Jerry Riordan, brought some food but told Herbert that full breakfast service had ended. Herbert did not welcome this news and chased Riordan from the room, ordering him either to "go and get some breakfast, you damned scoundrel you!" or to get lost altogether, "you damned Irish son of a bitch!" Accounts differed. Herbert then turned to a second waiter, Thomas Keating, made the same demand, got the same result, and screamed the same insult.

Keating, rather than leave the room, apparently turned his back on Herbert and went about his business. At that point, Herbert rose from his table and attacked Keating. Witnesses, depending on their bias, claimed either that Keating, a brawny two-hundred-pounder, had first turned to Herbert and sneered at him "You are a damned son of a bitch!" or that Herbert, without provocation, mugged Keating from behind, slugging him in the throat with his fist. A chair-swinging, plate-throwing brawl ensued, with Herbert and William H. Gardiner, his would-be breakfast companion, facing off against Keating and Keating's brother Patrick, another restaurant employee.

The melee ended suddenly and terribly when Herbert pulled a derringer from his pocket, pointed it at Thomas Keating's chest, and squeezed the trigger. Keating died within two minutes. Herbert's partisans said that half the dining room staff—all of whom were Irish except the French cook—were wrestling with Herbert and that he shot in self-defense. Keating supporters said Herbert grabbed Keating by the back of the coat, spun him around, pressed the pistol against his chest, and waited three cold-blooded seconds before pulling the trigger. Herbert, accompanied by Gardiner, left the dining room with the pistol in his hand.[19]

Violence and death at Washington's most fashionable hotel were big news, but the story also had a number of sidebars that kept it in the headlines. The implications of the ethnic insults were self-evident during the heyday of the Know-Nothings. The brawl either proved the truth of what the Know-Nothings were saying about the disorderly, profane Irish, or it showed how easily Know-Nothing intolerance could provoke a capital crime. Newspapers also quickly found out that Herbert was an Alabama-born blueblood and an avid secessionist who had been kicked out of the University of Alabama for stabbing a fellow student. The New York Times, for one, lamented that Herbert, for whatever reason, "found it necessary to assail at all one whose station was so far beneath his own."[20] In the increasingly militant North, this sentiment had coded significance for the struggle in Kansas: like the free-state settlers there, Keating, a white workingman, had been assaulted—and killed—by an agent of the slave power.

Meigs, for one, was disgusted with Herbert. "This is one example of the evil of carrying weapons," Meigs wrote in his diary.[21] Meigs was even more scandalized a week later when Herbert appeared on the House floor. "How he can sit there with the guilt of murder upon his hands, in the face of his fellowmen, I do not see."[22]

Herbert was eventually acquitted on a self-defense plea, but by that time his sins had been trumped by a string of new outrages. The first of these began when Senator Charles Sumner, a Massachusetts abolitionist, for three hours beginning May 19 and ending May 20 delivered a white-hot floor speech that came to be known as "The Crime Against Kansas," accusing the Pierce administration and specifically the South of hijacking democracy in Kansas in order to force slavery down the throats of peaceful, freedom-loving settlers.

Sumner was forty-five, a physically imposing, pugnacious demagogue and very little else. He had no legislative expertise and no particular following. Varina Davis, who kept her knife-edged wit sheathed most of the time, probably described him as well as anyone: "He was a handsome, unpleasing man, and an athlete whose physique proclaimed his physical strength," she wrote many years later. "His conversation was studied but brilliant," she added, yet he was more interested in listening to himself than pleasing his listeners. He "prepared himself with great care for these conversational pyrotechnics," Varina added, favoring "set pieces" on subjects he had read up on. He "once gave me quite an interesting résumé of the history of dancing."[23]

"The Crime Against Kansas" was filled with classical and historical imagery, literary references, and analogies that detonated in explosions of outrage. Sumner repeatedly and exuberantly violated the Senate's unspoken rule against personal attacks, focusing on South Carolina's aging senator Andrew Butler, coauthor with Douglas of the Kansas-Nebraska Act. Butler was recovering from a stroke and was not even in the Senate chamber for Sumner's diatribe. The stroke had left Butler with slurred speech and what Sumner termed "loose expectoration," caused by Butler's inability to swallow. Butler and Douglas together were the Don Quixote and Sancho Panza of Kansas, Sumner said. But instead of Doña Dulcinea,

Butler "has chosen a mistress to whom he has made his vows, and who, though ugly to others, is always lovely to him, though polluted in the sight of the world is chaste in his sight—I mean the harlot, slavery." Pierce was guilty of "imbecility," and Douglas was a "noisome, squat and name-less animal."[24]

Michigan's venerable Lewis Cass, like Sumner a northern Democrat, rose immediately after Sumner finally finished to denounce "the most un-American and unpatriotic" speech "that ever grated on the ears of this high body."[25] This may have been a hard case to make, given some of the other dreadful things that senators had said over the years, but Cass had made a point. The Senate was losing its restraint.

The next day, as if to demonstrate the truth of Sumner's words, a gang of southern rights thugs invaded Lawrence, Kansas, the headquarters town of the free-state movement, burned the free-state governor's house, and wrecked the offices of two antislavery newspapers, dumping the type into the Kansas River. They battered the Free State Hotel with cannon fire and looted it, taking all the whiskey and emptying the wine cellar. The townspeople did not resist, and only one person was killed, a proslavery man hit by a falling brick. Still, the "Sack of Lawrence" immediately en-tered northern folklore as yet another criminal outrage against the rights of free settlers.[26]

Back in Washington the following day, Sumner sat at his desk in the Senate chamber after the Senate adjourned, franking copies of his speech to send to constituents. "I was entirely absorbed," he later wrote, until a tall, slim man approached his desk and addressed him by name.[27]

"I have read your speech over carefully," the man said. "It is a libel on South Carolina, and Mr. Butler, who is a relative of mine."[28] Before the man had finished speaking, he raised a heavy cane made of gutta-percha, a tropical resin, and brought it down on Sumner's head. Sumner, stunned, nonetheless rose from his seat, ripping his desk from its moorings. His attacker pursued him, grabbing the stumbling Sumner by the coat to hold him upright while he clubbed him repeatedly.[29]

The attacker was South Carolina congressman Preston S. Brooks, a cousin of Butler's, come to avenge his kinsman and the South for Sumner's insults. Brooks originally had wanted to challenge Sumner to a duel, but his friend and fellow South Carolina representative Lawrence M. Keitt, told him that Sumner did not deserve such honorable treatment. A can-ing or flogging was called for. Brooks, frail and lame from an old hip wound, ordinarily used the cane to help him walk, and while he may have intended a perfunctory attack designed to inflict pain and humiliation, he could not stop once he had begun. He hit Sumner perhaps thirty times, Brooks wrote later, and "toward the last he bellowed like a calf."[30] He stopped only when his cane broke.

The damage was further compounded by the presence in the Senate chamber of Keitt, who threatened Kentucky senator John J. Crittenden with his own cane when Crittenden tried to intervene. "Let them alone, God damn you!" Keitt is alleged to have yelled.[31]

Sumner was carried from the chamber, and was unable to return to the Senate for two and a half years because of recurring nightmares and headaches. Northerners were appalled. *The New York Times* called the attack "another exemplification of the arrogance and overbearing insolence" of the "slave power," and "part of the great plot of fraud and violence and wrong enacting on a larger stage in Kansas."[32]

The reaction in the South was quite different. Both Brooks and Keitt resigned their House seats in July, and both were promptly reelected in August. Southerners regarded Sumner as a dangerous radical and a bully who had gotten exactly what he deserved. Admirers sent Brooks new canes and held testimonials in his honor. Jefferson Davis, invited to one of these dinners in October, declined, but did so in an open letter to "South Carolina Citizens" offering "my sympathy with the feeling that prompts the sons of Carolina to welcome the return of a brother [South Carolinian], who has been the subject of vilification, misrepresentation and persecution, because he resented a libelous assault."[33] Brooks died of a lung ailment six months after the caning.

The climax of that bloody May began just before midnight on May 24, two days after Brooks attacked Sumner. Eight riders, armed with pistols, long guns, and short, two-edged broadswords, arrived at James Doyle's cabin on the banks of Pottawatomie Creek south of Lawrence. They were led by a rawboned man with iron-gray hair and remarkably cold eyes. He was John Brown, then fifty-six, a militant abolitionist who during a varied life had plied many trades, none of them successfully. That night he became a terrorist. Four of the riders were his sons.

Brown was looking for Allen Wilkinson, another Pottawatomie settler, who, like Doyle, was proslavery but owned no slaves. Doyle said he would tell Brown where Wilkinson lived. Brown then took Doyle prisoner along with his two eldest sons, and marched them out of the cabin and into the woods. There the band summarily chopped up father and sons with broadswords, killing all three. Brown did not use a sword, but shot James Doyle as he lay on the ground. It is unclear whether he killed Doyle or was simply making sure.

Next was Wilkinson, who also lived along Pottawatomie Creek. When Brown arrived and demanded that Wilkinson leave with him, Wilkinson explained that his wife was sick with measles. Brown did not care about the wife. The neighbors would take care of her. He marched Wilkinson 150 yards down the road, where one of the younger Browns killed him with a sword and cut him up. Then the riders stopped at the home of James Harris, who knew Brown. Harris managed to convince the riders that he had nothing to do with the proslavery movement, but William Sherman, a guest in the Harris house, did not give the right answers. His body was found the next day. His skull had been cleaved open in two places.[34]

The Pottawatomie massacre marked the end of innocence for the free-state movement. Up to then, the antislavery settlers, generally acting with restraint, had created a convincing image of themselves as simple white folk beset by proslavery thugs who were denying them basic rights as American citizens. That was over now. And not only had Brown ruined the narrative, he had taken the violence to a new level. He and his men were not stuffing ballot boxes, stealing booze from hotel bars, or roughing up the occasional sodbuster. They had murdered five people, and done it in such a way that nobody could mistake their intent. Proslavery settlers emptied out of the Pottawatomie Creek valley practically overnight, and free-staters, fearing retribution, were not far behind. This was "Bleeding Kansas."

Meigs missed practically all of this. On May 22, after attending a funeral, he returned home "much fatigued," and the next day he could not get out of bed. He stayed home for six weeks, enduring "the severest illness I have had since my childhood." He described the ailment in his diary as a "typhoid form" of fever and nervous discomfort, so dangerous that it brought visits from his mother, father, and brother John from Philadelphia. He was unable to do any work beyond signing a few checks every day. He weighed a robust 198 pounds when he was struck down. When he made his next diary entry in early July, he weighed 176 pounds, and he figured he had probably bottomed out at 168 pounds.[35]

By the time Meigs returned to work on July 2, the political ambience in the country had changed. Pierce, a weak president reeling from multiple blunders, had failed to win renomination from the beleaguered Democrats, who, at their June convention, had picked career politician James Buchanan as their candidate. Davis was still a formidable figure in the White House, but by mid-1856 he was easier to ignore, like a guard dog protecting an abandoned house. Worse from Meigs's standpoint, a large number of Meigs's House supporters, most of them Democrats and most of them reliable votes in support of public works, had been deposed after the 1854 elections—from their committee chairmanships, if not from Congress altogether. The committees were now in the hands of the majority "opposition," whose aims were often unclear but who uniformly had no love for Pierce, the Democratic Party, or anything it had done. The Capitol was fair game.

In late February—even before that bloody May and Meigs's illness—the Capitol builders had gotten their first taste of the new Congress. Ohio's Lewis Campbell, the new chairman of the House Ways and Means Committee, asked Meigs and Davis how much the new Dome was going to cost.

Meigs and Walter discussed it. Even a year after getting the first $100,000 Dome appropriation, they were still working up the design details and had not yet dared to speculate publicly on what the total cost might be. Walter, based on his Library experience and an analysis of the per-pound price of cast iron, had given Meigs a rough estimate of $1.5 million a few weeks earlier. Since then, iron had dropped to 6 cents per pound, Walter said, and, pressed for information by Campbell, he now believed the job could be done for $945,000. "I told him he had better think again before sending this in," Meigs wrote in his diary. Walter stuck by the new figure. "I do not endorse the estimate," Meigs wrote, and he refused to pass it along to the committee until they heard it from Davis. Campbell, anticipating a very large number, joked to another committee member, "I will take 10 per cent upon the cost and retire from Congress."[36]

Campbell followed this up May 8 with a request to Davis to know the weight of the new Dome and whether the walls of the old Capitol could bear it. Meigs again consulted with Walter, who estimated the Dome would weigh 15 million pounds. Meigs noted in his diary that this worked out to a load on the Rotunda foundation of 10,000 pounds per square foot, child's play for the Capitol's Aquia sandstone, which broke at 755,000 pounds per square foot.[37] His engineering was right. But in this instance, his political instincts had forsaken him. For the layman, a weight of 15 million pounds sitting on top of the old Capitol was almost impossible to imagine. On hearing about it, presumably from Campbell, Senator Robert M. T. Hunter, one of the project's most enduring allies, stormed into the Extension office, convinced that the Dome would crush the Rotunda walls.

All of this, however, was but an introduction to the main event, which began in July, as Meigs emerged from convalescence. Summer was the high season not only for Capitol construction, but also for congressional appropriations. Meigs needed another $750,000 for the Extension and $100,000 for the Dome to tide him over for the remainder of the fiscal year. Once more, he would have to fight to get it.

Meigs's main antagonist this time was Edward Ball, an Ohioan and the chair of the House Committee on Public Buildings and Grounds. Ball was a Whig with a hint of Know-Nothing, and he would later become a Republican. Most of all, he was militantly anti-Democrat and, in an election year, was doing his best to smear the Pierce administration however he could. He did not like the way the War Department was handling the new Capitol, he said. It was poorly planned, over budget, ugly, pretentious, and being built by third-rate foreigners scavenged from the poorhouse.

Ball had laid the groundwork for serious opposition early in the year. In April he had let it be known that he was not enthusiastic about military supervision of public works. He also wondered why Meigs had not come to see him.[38] Speaker Banks also weighed in. He "had nothing against Captain Meigs," he told John B. Blake, the commissioner of public buildings, but "these officers of the Army never did accomplish anything."[39]

Meigs had made a pair of serious mistakes. It was an unpardonable bureaucratic blunder for him to have ignored for two months the new House Speaker and the new chairman of his House authorizing committee. Whatever he might have felt about their politics, he needed the goodwill of both men.

One reason for miscalculation may have been that he was blinded by his own rising celebrity. Beginning in late 1855, Meigs, who in previous years had manifested virtually no enthusiasm for any social event, suddenly found himself on guest lists. The principal reason was undoubtedly that he was an Army officer and thus by definition apolitical and acceptable in any company in Washington's highly charged social atmosphere. Also, refurbishing the Capitol was a noble and increasingly fashionable cause, and one of the few things government was doing that was not turning into a disaster. Finally, and not to be ignored, Meigs in 1856 was probably Washington's biggest employer, with 1,260 men working for him on three enormous public works projects.[40]

In the first three months of 1856, Meigs was a man about town as never before. He dined or attended receptions hosted by the antislavery senator Hamilton Fish of New York, the Washington banker George Riggs, and Davis, among others. He rubbed elbows with virtually the entire Pierce cabinet, with his savant friends Joseph Henry and Alexander Bache, with his longtime patron General Totten, and with noted visitors, including the British author Willliam Makepeace Thackeray and William H. Aspinwall, the builder of the Panama Railroad. He was always careful to note in his diary which of these social companions were hugely wealthy (Fish, Riggs, and Louisiana senator John Slidell) and whether he had had a good time (generally speaking, yes).[41]

What Meigs had apparently forgotten as spring began, however, was that most of the wining and dining had occurred during the prolonged hiatus between the convening of Congress and the election of the Speaker. Once Banks was in place, it was time for business, and Meigs would pay a price for his neglect of the new leadership. His ego had interfered with his good sense. This would not—by a long shot—be the last time he made that mistake.

On May 19, Ball introduced a set of resolutions calling on Pierce to account for every dollar spent on the Capitol Extension and the Dome and requesting an estimate of how much more would be needed before the projects were finished. Ball wanted to know about everything. What had been bought, and for how much—bricks, marble, draft animals, vehicles, plant and equipment, wages. How many people had worked at the Capitol, including the names of everyone but day laborers. How much had workers been paid?

A week later, with Congress still traumatized by the attack on Sumner and by John Brown's bloodbath on Pottawatomie Creek, Ball detailed his complaints about the Capitol. He started with an old saw: he esteemed the public buildings but was opposed "to all expenditures which add nothing to the strength, or convenience, or true beauty of these edifices." Then he moved to another evergreen: the Capitol was too expensive, he continued, and, no offense against Meigs, but the Capitol Extension was built like a fort. And he finished with current affairs: there were two shops filled with Italian and German sculptors just making pediment statuary, a "ridiculous feature" in which "our republican government is made to play the poor part of a wretched imitator of the broken-down monarchies in the Old World." Further, Congress had been told the Dome would cost $100,000, and Meigs now reported that it would cost $945,000, Ball said. He wanted an explanation, and without it, "I will never vote another dollar of appropriations to be expended in the construction of civil architecture under military superintendence." Ball concluded by condemning the Pierce administration for championing the new Capitol, another manifestation of the president's incompetence, and promising that things would change. Just wait until November.[42]

These were harsh words, but for all the rhetorical fireworks, it was unclear exactly what Ball wanted beyond the ouster of the War Department from public works. The Extension was more than half finished, and there was absolutely no chance of stopping work. Four rooms in the new House wing were ready to be turned over to the Speaker in May, and the first room in the new Senate would be finished in July.[43] As for the Dome, Meigs had deliberately and wisely hastened to dismantle Bulfinch's work so the new Congress would have no chance for second thoughts; doing nothing was not an option. Finally, even though Ball wanted to get rid of the War Department, and by implication Meigs, he behaved in a remarkably straightforward and transparent manner. He and Meigs got to know each other, and Ball took care to warn Meigs, either through mutual acquaintances or personally, whenever he planned to denounce military rule or criticize Meigs's performance.[44]

Ball's actions suggested that the attacks were primarily partisan jabs aimed at the Democratic Party and the Pierce administration. Ball would not run again in 1856, but he showed up as a Republican delegate to the national convention that nominated Lincoln in 1860. And as an antislavery congressman speaking in the midst of the horrific events of May 1856, his animus toward Pierce knew no bounds. Ball was chairman of the

House Committee on Public Buildings and Grounds, and if he wanted to hurt Pierce—and Davis, his slave-power factotum—Meigs was his logical target.

Regardless of motive, Ball caused Meigs considerable anxiety. No sooner had Meigs risen from his sickbed than he began to compile the information the House had demanded. He had a tough political problem to solve. He needed new money to keep his projects going, but to get it, he had to estimate how much they were going to cost, and in early July 1856, he had no idea.

It took him a month to finish the analysis, and the result was shocking. The Extension was going to cost much more than Walter had estimated five years earlier, and "far beyond my expectations," a fact he noted in his diary on August 6.[45] He was so worried about the discrepancy that he wrote Davis a long letter of explanation. Walter's original 1851 estimate, he noted, had been "carefully made," and had predicted that the Extension could be built for $2,675,000. Meigs had hoped that by using machinery, trimming the labor force, and watching his materials more closely he could make a "better and more durable building" for that price. This had not worked out. Meigs now estimated the Extension would cost an additional $2,835,183.34—bringing the total cost of the Extension to more than twice Walter's estimate. Extravagance had made the difference. Instead of bricks, Meigs had paved the corridors with "beautiful and durable" encaustic tiles; instead of wood, he had used iron for the door and window frames and jambs; instead of whitewash, he had used paint on the interior walls. He had put fireproof iron roofs on the wings and built iron ceilings for the new chambers. He had used heavier, more expensive marble for the exterior facing and marble monoliths for the outside columns. This was all costly, he said, but the biggest new expenses were the outside porticoes and stairways he had added to Walter's original design. These would cost $51,126 in extra labor and add more than a million dollars to the total cost of the Extension.[46]

All that said, Meigs apologized for nothing. "I have labored faithfully and diligently to construct this building in such a manner that it would last for ages," he wrote. He needed $750,000 for the Extension and $100,000 for the Dome to finish out the fiscal year.[47]

Davis summoned Meigs on August 13 and took him to the White House to plot strategy. Pierce would personally ask for the $750,000 in a special message to Congress, enclosing Meigs's new estimate without explanation, hoping to roll the Senate, where there was a solid Democratic majority and plenty of Democrat friends. Meigs spent the rest of the day briefing Senator James A. Pearce, a faithful Senate supporter who would handle the Extension request on the Senate floor.[48] Senator Hunter, another friend of the Capitol Extension, was the overall floor manager for the bill that included Capitol funding.

The Senate debated the Capitol's future on August 14 and 15, and Meigs won nearly everything. On the first day, the Senate, in a nearly unanimous vote, killed a Ball-inspired proviso that would have transferred the superintendence of public works from the War Department to the Interior Department. The next day, the Senate voted the full $750,000 to continue Extension construction and $100,000 for the Dome, with support from northerners and southerners of all parties. The Senate did not vote immediately on the $500,000 Meigs had asked for the Aqueduct.

It was clear from the Senate debate, possibly for the first time, that the new Capitol had fully seized the imagination of Congress as a symbol of national achievement and greatness. Proslavery supporters included Senators James M. Mason of Virginia, Robert Toombs of Georgia, and Pearce of Maryland. Illinois Democrat Stephen A. Douglas, the author of the Kansas-Nebraska Act, compared Walter's Dome to the best of Europe and said he could find "no dome, or model for a dome, that excels the one which has been prepared here."[49]

Delaware's John M. Clayton, a former secretary of state under Whig president Zachary Taylor and a cosponsor of the Kansas-Nebraska Act, said "I do not care whether the money is $500,000 or $5,000,000," adding that "I will vote the money that will make it worthy of this Republic. If Athens would have a Parthenon, a great Republic like ours may well have a Capitol."[50]

And finally, the Capitol had become an indispensable source of confidence in increasingly troubled times. New York's William H. Seward, the Senate's only overt Republican and a leading antislavery advocate, acknowledged that he had had little enthusiasm for the Capitol Extension when it was first proposed in 1850 but had voted for it then because "weak and idle and foolish men were talking about the dissolution of this Union, as if it were a thing not merely possible, but a thing that was imminent."

"I seized upon the Extension," he continued, to show "the country and mankind that this Union was not to be dissolved." Now, he said, he wished to continue, so that "the weak, the incredulous and even the desponding may take heart if they see the Congress of the United States expending $2,000,000 to enlarge and complete the National Capitol, in this hour when these apprehensions are again renewed."[51] The following day, the House defeated Ball's proviso and passed the Extension and Dome appropriations without debate.

Only the $500,000 Aqueduct appropriation went down, tacked on to an Army bill that the opposition House majority refused to pass because of disagreements with the administration about the use of federal troops in Kansas. A joint Senate-House conference committee gave Meigs $250,000 to pay bills and mothball the Aqueduct until a new round of funding. For now, work on the project would have to stop.

Nonetheless, Meigs felt vindicated and was elated. On September 13, three weeks after his appropriations passed, Meigs wrote to Poole & Hunt, the Baltimore firm that was making many of the iron fixtures for the Capitol, instructing that his name be inscribed on "every piece of cast iron they may send to me." A second note went to Samuel Champion, the Capitol's metalworking foreman, telling him to stamp Meigs's name on every finished "bar, board or clamp" coming out of the smith shop.[52] Two days after that he sent a long, officious letter to Joseph Henry at the Smithsonian complaining about a recent Henry research paper entitled "The Science of Sound in Public Buildings" in which Henry, "unintentionally," Meigs was sure, suggested that Meigs had been told to consult with Henry and Alexander Bache before preparing the acoustical plans for the new Senate and House. The paper appeared to assign "to Prof. Bache and yourself all the credit of the authorship of the plans." He wished the record to be corrected, because "you will remember that I am the sole author of the plans in question."[53] Henry made the correction.[54]

As his stock rose, Meigs began to see Walter in a lesser light. His complaints—still confined to his diary—were somewhat more frequent and more contemptuous. Walter—five years after designing the Extension, four years after rebuilding the Library, two years after unveiling the Dome, and a year after Stanton, his mentor, had gone away—was losing luster in Meigs's eyes. Walter was "little able to understand" the engineering behind Meigs's heating system, disposed to adopt the views of the last person who spoke with him, and "insolent in success and servile in defeat."[55]

If Walter, like Meigs, harbored resentment or contempt, there was little indication of it. In almost daily correspondence with the marble contractor John Rice in Philadelphia and the iron contractor Charles Fowler in

New York, he gossiped about Washington, about the Capitol, and about his friends' prospects for further work—especially Fowler's hopes to supply the cast iron for the Dome. Walter seldom commented on Meigs, except to soothe his friends when they did not get paid on time. Meigs tended to let bills pile up and pay them all at once. He was always in arrears to someone.

Walter did let his guard down occasionally, but usually in good humor, and never with disloyalty. In an April 12 letter to Alexander Provest, the marble finishing contractor, he noted that Congress was threatening to cut funding for the Aqueduct and "the Capt. has his hands full with it." But "don't forget that man is a *vivacious* animal," he wrote, and had taken "about 60 congressmen" on an excursion to Great Falls aboard the project's packet boat, which, he told Provest gleefully, was named the "*M. C. Meigs*."[56] In late July, in a much more revealing letter to Provest, he noted that Ball was giving Meigs a terrible beating on military rule, and that Meigs "had better quit the War Department and make a man of himself." He continued, "I am as great an admirer of the military as any man, but I don't want them to tread on my toes."[57] Which was exactly what Meigs had been doing to him for the last three years.

On April 21, 1856, Crawford sent a photograph of what would be the final version of *Freedom*, the statue to be placed on the pinnacle of the new Dome.[58] The statue was nearly two feet taller than the earlier versions, standing 18 feet 9 inches. Like the second statue, this *Freedom* rested her right hand on the hilt of a sword, while her left hand, holding a wreath, covered the shield of America.

Everything else, however, was different. The new *Freedom* was quite hefty, broad in the shoulders and wearing a heavy dress, fringed at the bottom in what appeared to be the style of an Indian princess, although the drapery above the hem cascaded in folds of a more classical style and the figure had no Indian features. The most unusual aspect of the statue, however, was the headdress. The liberty cap was gone, per Davis's wishes, replaced by a crest of feathers and a bird's head. This, Crawford said in a letter accompanying the photograph, was a "bold arrangement . . . suggested by the costume of our Indian tribes."[59] The bird, purported by Crawford to be an eagle, looked more like a rooster with its mouth open.

Final design for the statue of *Freedom* by Thomas Crawford. The statue was taller and heavier than the previous versions. Crawford replaced the liberty cap with an unusual headdress composed of an eagle's head topped with feathers. (Architect of the Capitol)

But Meigs liked it. "I think he [Crawford] has much improved it in design," he wrote in his diary, adding that the figure is both "more graceful and more vigorous" than the first two *Freedoms*. "The figure is dignified, full of grace and beauty." Davis, too, was "very much pleased" when he saw it, Meigs wrote, and he told Meigs that the statue "fulfills every condition."[60] Meigs wrote a letter to Crawford to close the deal, and Crawford in early August came for a visit to Washington. Later in the year Crawford, working with his usual dispatch, told Meigs he would have the plaster model of *Freedom* ready in January 1857.

The only member of the Capitol triumvirate who did not much care for the final *Freedom* was Walter, but he did not say so overtly until many years had passed. In 1864, in response to a senior House member's desire to get rid of the headdress, Walter told him that it should not be removed, since Crawford had intended the statue to be the way it was. That said, however, Walter did acknowledge that he had always regarded the headdress as "a very objectionable feature of the figure."[61] In 1856, however, it was certainly not in his best interest to say so.

Besides art and politics, Meigs spent much of 1856 on finishing up rooms in the new wings, installing mantelpieces and more fresco and decorative painting, laying more encaustic tile, and painting the House chamber in rich, vibrant colors. All of these flourishes were aimed at preparing the new wings for the House and Senate to take possession in the not too distant future.

He also wanted to complete the high-altitude derrick he planned to use to build the new Dome and to prepare the Dome foundation on the Capitol Rotunda. These two tasks were linked and required the resolution of one unusual problem: Meigs and Walter, early in their planning, realized that the cast-iron Dome, in order to give architectural balance to the new Capitol, would have to have a larger circumference than the old Capitol Rotunda could provide. The Rotunda, quite simply, was too small.

The initial solution, embodied in Walter's early drawing but not carefully thought out, was to build a new attic floor atop the old Capitol and rest the Dome on that. The load would be borne by the old Rotunda walls and foundation and the central East Front Portico.

Sometime in early 1856, however, Meigs, or Meigs and his German-born engineering assistant Ottmar Sonnemann, had a different idea.[62] They would mount thirty-six pairs of heavy iron brackets at ten-degree intervals around the entire circumference of the old Rotunda. The brackets would stand on the Rotunda walls on the inside and be cantilevered outward, creating midair shelves on which to rest the thirty-six hollow iron columns that formed the circular peristyle—the lowest and widest level of the new Dome. The columns would thus form a drum, which would jut out from the old Rotunda wall to give extra breadth to the finished Dome. Meigs and Sonnemann spent much of the year working out the details, and by September 17, Meigs had figured out that each set of brackets would weigh 7,336 pounds.[63] The columns would weigh 11,475 pounds apiece and would look immense, although they bore no appreciable weight themselves.[64]

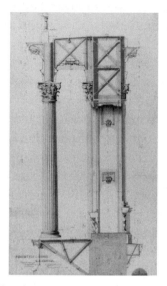

Needing a larger base for the new Dome, Meigs devised brackets that allowed the Dome peristyle columns to cantilever outward from the old sandstone foundation. The brackets accommodated a Dome wide enough to give the new Capitol aesthetic balance without major structural modification to the old building. (Architect of the Capitol)

Meigs had contracted with Poole & Hunt of Baltimore in April for the peristyle columns, and in October he accepted their bid for the brackets, which, the company told him, would be less expensive than Meigs had anticipated because they needed to weigh only 5,100 pounds.[65] By September 24, Meigs had begun to dismantle the upper masonry of the old Dome to bring it to the level where he would attach the brackets. To do this, he needed his Dome derrick to be fully operational. Once the scaffolding tower had poked through the temporary roof, Meigs rigged a platform on which he mounted the eighty-foot mast and the eighty-foot boom he would use as a crane. By the end of September, the crane was working exactly as Meigs hoped it would—plucking 3,500-pound blocks of Aquia sandstone from the upper walls of the Rotunda and lowering them gently to the ground, untouched by human hands.[66]

Meigs, exultant whenever his innovations worked, immediately made a crony of "Mr. Hunt" of Poole & Hunt and wrote him a long letter about the wonders of Roebling's wire rope.[67] He explained the derrick to Davis in numbing detail, and he asked the foreman of his bricklayers to compute how much money he could save by hoisting bricks with a steam engine instead of carrying them by hand. (The answer: $1.25 per thousand by hand, on a cool day, versus 23 cents per thousand with the hoist.)[68]

Meigs's other pioneering innovation for 1856 was industrial photography. At a meeting of the Saturday Club late the previous year, he had seen a demonstration of how to make photographs using the relatively new wet collodion process. The photographer used a glass plate that was coated with a combination of gun cotton and ether. The prepared plate had to be exposed and developed before the collodion dried. Once completed, the process left a negative image on the glass from which the photographer could make as many prints as desired.[69] Meigs immediately realized that the new technique had tremendous labor-saving implications for his projects. Walter kept a half-dozen draftsmen constantly busy making duplicate drawings for contractors, foremen, artisans, and congressional committees. If he used photography instead, Meigs wrote in his diary, the same task "can be done for a small sum," and copies could be made endlessly.[70]

Meigs was hooked. Ten days after the Saturday Club meeting, he ordered some books on photography. On January 26, 1856, he told Davis about his plans, and two days later, he wrote to Davis asking him to authorize the purchase of photographic equipment. His office, he told Davis, held several hundred drawings of everything from large-scale architectural treatments to details of individual ornaments. "To reduce them is very expensive and tedious," he wrote. "By the photographic process they can be accurately and much more cheaply copied."[71] Davis agreed, and in April, Meigs bought $242.43 worth of cameras and gear from Anthony's National Daguerrean, Photographic and Ambrotype Depot in New York. On May 13, one of Meigs's Saturday Club friends introduced him to photographer John Wood, and Meigs hired him the following day.[72] By August, Wood, who would serve as the Capitol's in-house photographer for the next five years, was routinely producing usable reductions of Walter's designs and detail drawings.[73]

He also put Wood to work copying some of the artistic renderings of the Capitol, and on August 22 Wood brought him a "beautiful reduction" of one of Walter's perspective drawings of the new Dome. Meigs showed

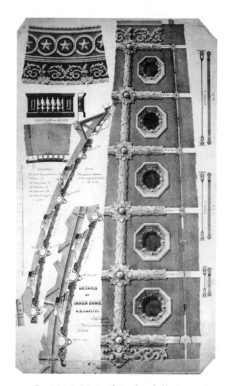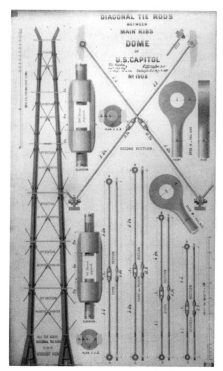

In 1856, Meigs hired a full-time photographer to take pictures of detail drawings prepared by Walter's office for the Capitol Extension. Instead of making
copies by hand for shop foremen and crew chiefs—a painstaking and expensive
process—Meigs could make as many prints as he wished. (Architect of the Capitol)

it to Senators Douglas and Seward, who asked him for copies. The next
day he also had copies made for Senator Pearce and for the wife of Alabama senator Percy Walker. Wood then started making photographs of
the Capitol itself, recording the changes in the building even as they were
made.[74]

Meigs had helped launch what was probably the United States' first
successful large-scale experiment in industrial photography. He had also
found out that photography could be a mammoth public relations triumph. In coming years he would make a special effort to hand out prints
to favored public officials and assemble gift packs for his friends and
patrons.

On February 7, 1857, Meigs sent a packet of photographs to Davis as
mementos "of the connection he had with this, one of the great buildings
of the world." Davis wrote back, "You are not mistaken in supposing

that [these photographs] would be of interest to me. I shall not fail to remember that whatever the pride and satisfaction I may feel in consequence of that connection [to the Capitol and to Meigs's other public works] will be mainly attributable to your having been put in charge of them."[75]

13

A NEW HOUSE OF REPRESENTATIVES

Nobody had better qualifications to be president of the United States than James Buchanan. He had four decades of experience in government—in the House of Representatives and the Senate representing his state of Pennsylvania, in the diplomatic corps, and as secretary of state under James K. Polk. Over the years he had acquired several nicknames, all of which bore the same unfortunate adjective. Some knew him as "Old Buck," or the "Old Squire." He called himself "the Old Public Functionary."[1] But never mind. In 1856, at age sixty-five, it was his turn.

The Democrats in 1856 needed a national candidate who could win northern states. Pierce and Illinois senator Stephen A. Douglas, the first-tier contenders, were tainted because of their identification with the Kansas-Nebraska Act. No southerner had a chance. On the seventeenth ballot the delegates to the Democratic Party convention, meeting in Cincinnati, nominated Buchanan. Pennsylvania was a big border free state with plenty of electoral votes. Buchanan's home was in Lancaster, just north of the Maryland state line; he was sympathetic to the South and had owned slaves.

The Democrats appeared to have chosen well. Buchanan won the election handily, defeating Republican candidate John C. Frémont, "the Pathfinder," a handsome western explorer with no political experience and little discernable political talent, and former president Millard Fillmore, running for the southern wing of the American Party as a nominal Know-Nothing. Buchanan received 174 electoral votes to 114 for Frémont and

8 for Fillmore, who won Maryland. Democrats also rode Buchanan's coat-tails to win back the majorities in both Houses of Congress.

Both Buchanan's victory and the Democrats' nationwide resurgence, however, were illusions. Buchanan had won all the southern states plus California, Illinois, Indiana, New Jersey, and Pennsylvania. The American Party/Know-Nothings were finished, but the Republicans, stepping into the national spotlight for the first time, had won eleven free states with a nonentity as a candidate. They had no southern following, which did not bode well for national unity. But if they could flip Pennsylvania and an-other of Buchanan's free states in 1860, the White House was theirs.

And nothing about Buchanan's election offered an escape from the morass into which the country was sinking. Pierce, in the summer of 1856, traumatized by the rising bloodshed in Kansas, had sent San Fran-cisco mayor John Geary, a no-nonsense Mexican War veteran, to serve as territorial governor and had put federal troops at his disposal. Geary pac-ified Kansas—or at least forced a truce—by warning both the free-staters and the proslavery forces that things would go hard for anyone who opposed him. Both sides cooled off, but Kansas still had two govern-ments, neither of which was legitimate, two hostile ideologies, and two fiercely opposed visions of its future. Buchanan's victory did nothing to fix any of this.

Inauguration Day dawned cold and misty. Buchanan was greeted on Cap-itol Hill by a Congress exhausted after an all-night session prior to ad-journment. A bleary-eyed Captain Montgomery Meigs stood in the Senate chamber looking out a window at the festivities. With the exception of one brief nap, he had spent most of the previous twenty-four hours shut-tling back and forth between House and Senate, hustling for votes to get the appropriations he wanted. He had won everything he had asked for: $900,000 for the Capitol Extension, $500,000 for the Dome, and $200,000 for the Post Office Extension. He had also been granted $1 mil-lion to restart work on the Washington Aqueduct after a year's hiatus. In all, with what was left over from 1856, he had access to an extraordinary $3,687,000, more than he had ever had to spend on his projects at one time. He was in excellent shape to welcome the incoming administration, "and being in the Senate at the time of the adjournment," he wrote in his diary, "I stayed to see the inauguration ceremonies."[2]

In 1857, Meigs planned to complete the House of Representatives. Heavy construction on both new wings of the Capitol Extension, he had reported the previous November, was now finished. The exterior marble had reached the top of the third floor, roof trusses had been installed, and window casings and door frames—all of cast iron—had been mounted. The last big job—cutting openings and beginning construction of the connecting corridors between the new wings and the old Capitol—would begin in the spring, when Congress was in recess. Most of the other Extension work during the year would be finishing—painting, mounting mantelpieces and other fixtures, decorating, and buying and installing furniture and carpets. He would focus on completing the new House chamber so members would never again have to scream to be heard. Meigs's plan, although he did not promise it in his report, was to have the House ready in time for the first session of the 35th Congress, opening on December 7, 1857.[3] And while the Capitol no longer had a dome, the boom derrick was in place, and Meigs planned to start mounting the brackets for the peristyle columns when the weather moderated.

Meigs had expected about twenty-five thousand people to show up for the swearing-in and had built a wooden platform to cover the blocks of marble lying in the yard just in front of the Eastern Portico where much of the crowd would stand. The platform cost $1,200 but would keep people from scuffing the stone and chipping pieces off it, and he could make good use of the lumber once the ceremony ended.[4]

Meigs was also interested to see what John Wood, his photographer, could do with the ceremony. He had built a stage on the south edge of the platform so Wood could have an unimpeded view of the Capitol steps and get a photograph of the swearing-in.[5] The picture that Wood eventually produced, somewhat unevenly exposed but nicely framed and clearly recognizable as the Capitol façade, would be the first known photograph of a presidential inauguration.

Buchanan's chief domestic worries were to settle Kansas's future and to attempt to resolve the slavery question. He hoped to get help from the Supreme Court, which had before it the case of a slave, Dred Scott, residing in Missouri. Scott was suing for his freedom on grounds that by once living in Illinois and in the free territories of Minnesota and Wisconsin, his master had forfeited the right to keep him in bondage. Ultimately, how-

The first presidential inauguration ever photographed: James Buchanan takes office, March 4, 1857, by John Wood. Meigs set up a platform so Wood would have an unobstructed view of the East Portico. The beginnings of the Dome construction can be seen on the upper corner of the Rotunda, just above the ceremony. (Architect of the Capitol)

ever, the case had little to do with Dred Scott. A solid majority of justices agreed that Scott, being a slave, had no standing to bring suit against anyone. In short, slaves were not citizens.

Later generations would rightly find this aspect of the case particularly appalling, but at the time, the country—and in particular Buchanan—was far more interested in the Court's decision on whether Congress had the right to prohibit slavery in territories, as it had done through the Missouri Compromise in Minnesota and Wisconsin when Dred Scott lived there. Although the Kansas-Nebraska Act had effectively voided the compromise, the issue of excluding slavery by congressional mandate had never been brought before the Court.

The nine justices, if they chose to rule broadly in the Dred Scott case, could make that judgment now. Buchanan desperately wanted such a ruling, and he wanted the ruling to say that Congress could not prohibit slavery in the territories. That way, he concluded, things would quiet down not only in Kansas but everywhere else. Settlers, Congress, and the North would all have to respect the Court's decision.

Even before his inauguration, he had begun to lobby the Court surreptitiously, urging the justices to make a broad ruling and suggesting that they issue the finding he wanted. This was patently unethical and a violation of the separation of powers, but Buchanan found a receptive audience among the justices. While the majority were southerners, only one was a states' rights hard-liner, and the rest, including Roger B. Taney, the eighty-year-old chief, were moderates with no particular fondness for slavery. But these moderates were desperately worried about the survival of the union. They were anxious to find an antidote to the poison that was dividing the country, and they thought that by taking slavery out of the hands of Congress they would strip the issue of its political force and the din would subside.[6]

The fix was in. As Buchanan stood on Meigs's platform waiting to be sworn in, he was seen to exchange a few words with Taney. Then he made his speech. Slavery in the territories was "a judicial question," he said, that should be settled by the Supreme Court, "before whom it is now pending." A decision is imminent, he said, and to whatever the justices decide, he continued, "I shall cheerfully submit."[7]

Two days later, Taney read out the Court's 6–3 decision. The majority included the five southern justices and Pennsylvanian Robert C. Grier. Scott, Taney said, was not a citizen and had no standing to sue. Blacks, "for more than a century, had been regarded as beings of an inferior order," and "they had no rights which the white man was bound to respect." On the other question, Taney said the Missouri Compromise, by excluding slavery from any territory north of 36 degrees 30 minutes north latitude, violated the Fifth Amendment because it denied a citizen the right to bring his property—including slaves—into territories, even though that citizen had broken no law.[8]

Buchanan had gotten everything he wanted. But the results were not what he had anticipated. The North was infuriated and traumatized. Republicans were convinced of a Buchanan–Supreme Court conspiracy. Fears that slavery would spread across the country and set off more

Kansas-style conflagrations helped provoke an economic panic later in the year. In Kansas, settlers in June elected delegates to a constitutional convention to be held in Lecompton in September. Free-staters boycotted the vote.

Meigs had little personal experience with Buchanan and apparently had made no effort to contact him or his inner circle after the election. This was a grave mistake, which Meigs certainly should have been smart enough to avoid. Walter had barely survived Pierce's arrival in 1852. Robert Mills had been marginalized by Fillmore two years earlier, and even the patrician Bulfinch had been retired by Andrew Jackson. Now Meigs, with $3,687,000 to spend, was in the crosshairs of a new administration, and he did not seem to realize it.

Meigs's only pre-inauguration contact with Buchanan had occurred in early 1857, when the president-elect had visited Meigs's office to leave him a copy of a letter he had received from Edward Everett claiming that Meigs had promised Hiram Powers $25,000 if Powers prepared a "colossal" *America* for the Capitol. Buchanan told Meigs he did not understand what Everett was talking about and asked him to explain. Meigs at this point was fed up with Powers, who had been trying for three years to undo the mistake he had made by refusing to sculpt figures for the Senate pediment. Instead of approaching Meigs, Powers had been back-dooring him, using Everett, and now Buchanan, to plead his cause. Meigs was sick of him, and dismissed him in his diary as a money-grubber out to swindle the country.[9] He told Buchanan what he knew of the *America* exchanges, and found that Buchanan had no interest in getting tangled up with Powers.[10]

Meigs, who still needed a sculptor for the House pediment, broached the subject with Crawford, even though he had never been enthusiastic about having the same sculptor do both porticoes. Then, early in February 1857—again, just before Buchanan's inauguration—he learned that Crawford was terminally ill. He had undergone an operation to remove a tumor over his eye, but the tumor turned out to be a malignant cancer. "They say he can hardly live long," Meigs wrote. He felt "great regret," he wrote. Crawford "will leave behind him an imperishable monument" in the Senate pediment. Meigs had all the pediment figures, and thought that Crawford had made "small models" for his door. As for *Freedom*,

Crawford had expected to finish the plaster model "60 days from his last letter," which meant that it was due any day. Meigs would cross his fingers.[11]

Crawford's illness—he would die on October 10, 1857—meant that Meigs had no fallback plan for the House, but early in the year he became very interested in the work of the New York sculptor Erastus Dow Palmer, whose marble *Indian Girl* was earning wide praise in art circles. Meigs saw the statue at a Palmer exhibition in January 1857 and remarked on "a talent I have seen no evidence of before." He sent his friend the New York senator William H. Seward a drawing of the House pediment and asked Seward to find out if Palmer wanted the job.[12] Palmer came to Washington on February 24 to talk it over, and he told Meigs that $20,000, Crawford's fee for the Senate pediment, was not enough, because he intended to cut all the stone himself. Meigs scoffed at this idea. The job would take forever.[13] There was no deal.

Palmer, like Powers, reconsidered, but unlike Powers, he made a serious pediment design and sent it to Meigs, who was not enamored of it but had been sufficiently impressed with Palmer's work that he wrote him an encouraging letter. Palmer replied almost immediately. He would do the job for $25,000, and he had already thought of some changes that he could make in his original design.[14]

For the next six months Palmer worked on his pediment drawings. From August onward, Meigs, at times accompanied by Palmer, tried without success to gain an audience with either Buchanan or Secretary of War John B. Floyd. On November 4, Buchanan and Floyd finally came to Meigs's office for a look. Both were almost inarticulate, according to Meigs's diary account. Buchanan said it "pleased him better as he studied it more," and Floyd said that it "seemed to be a copy of Crawford's."[15] Eleven days later, Floyd sent Palmer a letter saying he did not want the sculpture. Palmer, more worn out than disappointed, asked Meigs to pay him $1,000 for his time, and Meigs agreed.

By that time, Meigs had taken the measure of both Buchanan and Floyd, and he was no longer surprised at either their procrastination or their indifference. But earlier in the year, when he had a chance to make a good first impression, he had not taken advantage of it. Davis tried to help him before the inauguration, writing a letter to Buchanan to invite him to visit the War Department so he could take a tour of the Capitol and become "acquainted with Capt. Meigs, whose conduct of the Capitol Extension is worthy of high praise."[16] He also told Buchanan that Meigs was a Pennsylvanian—obliquely suggesting that Meigs might be a Buchanan supporter. He further mentioned that Meigs was the son of the prominent and well-connected Philadelphia physician Charles D. Meigs, someone Buchanan probably knew. Davis had made all the right gestures. It was Meigs's job to follow up.

He tried, but only after a fashion. The day after the Dred Scott decision, Meigs called at the War Department, hoping to attend the investiture of Floyd as secretary of war and to meet both Floyd and the president. Arriving early, Meigs inquired whether there was going to be a ceremony and was told none was planned. He left the building, only to find out that the president had arrived a half hour after his departure.[17] Meigs tried to find Floyd the next day but only caught up with him five days later, on March 12, when he saw him for ten minutes before a cabinet meeting. Floyd, a former governor of Virginia, was a "fine-looking man of large size," Meigs remarked in his diary, but not particularly impressive.[18] He would not see Floyd again until the end of April, and he did not meet Buchanan until May 4, waiting in an anteroom for two hours until Buchanan invited him in with "a number of others, all brought in together to get rid of them."[19]

It would be the Washington Aqueduct that would define Meigs's relationship with his new masters. This immense project had been closed down for seven months since the money had run out in the summer of 1856. Getting it started again was a mammoth task. Meigs had laid off workers and let contracts lapse, and now, with a million dollars to spend, he was in a fever to get started. His diary for the first half of 1857 describes almost daily trips to Great Falls, to Little Falls, to his tunnels, and to the site of the new Cabin John Bridge, which, when completed in 1864, would be the longest single-span masonry bridge in the world. He was buying up rights-of-way, taking bids, and letting contracts for most of the year, and for long stretches during the first six months of the Buchanan administration he had time for little else.

All this was an even better reason to cultivate Buchanan. Simply by having control over so much money, he was the focus of attention for all kinds of grifters and potential competitors. Some, if not all, of these Johnnies-come-lately were sure to have excellent relations with influential people in the new White House. Meigs, for all practical purposes, knew no one.

Finally, and perhaps most important, Meigs was still a serving military officer answering to the War Department, but he could no longer count on the unwavering support of the secretary of war. Davis had protected Meigs and his public works from the usual Washington plundering and patronage seeking, but Floyd was a complete unknown. And after a ten-day special session immediately following Buchanan's inauguration, Congress went home for the summer and fall. Walter in 1851 and Meigs in 1853 had used similar prolonged honeymoons to ingratiate themselves with Fillmore and Pierce. This time, however, all of Meigs's friends were in Congress. Recess meant that for half a year he would have to fend for himself.

He soon found out that business was not going to be as usual. He did not get his first written communication from Floyd until April 6, and this was simply to pass on a constituent complaint about one of Meigs's watchmen, whom the petitioner described as a "violent" Know-Nothing.[20] So much for turning a blind eye to politics in the Capitol workforce.

Then, a bit over a week later, two men, apparently sent by Floyd, or with Floyd's blessing, showed up in Meigs's office to "notify" him as a "courtesy" that they intended to displace Samuel Champion—another Know-Nothing—as the master blacksmith for the Capitol Extension. "They did not ask my influence," Meigs wrote in his diary, "as they understood that I would not exert any influence in such an affair." Meigs told the pair that he made his own hires and would oppose them. Then he wrote a letter to Floyd outlining his labor practices.[21] He would do his best to cooperate with the administration on patronage hires, but he would not displace a good worker like Champion without professional cause, and he would reserve the right to veto someone's recommended protégé if he could not do the work.

Two days after the blacksmiths tried to strong-arm him, the former Democratic congressman Charles J. Ingersoll, a Philadelphian who was also the father-in-law of one of Meigs's sisters, came to see the new Capitol. He was "very old" (seventy-six), Meigs wrote, "but is a vigorous man yet." Ingersoll summed up the picture that was starting to come into focus for Meigs: "He says that he would not be surprised if Mr. Buchanan was to turn me out of my employment as he had been so long used to providing for politicians and the temptation is so great, with the immense disbursements which I have to take care of."[22]

Ingersoll's observations about the power of money to stimulate interest in public works proved correct almost immediately. Meigs printed the contracts for the Aqueduct on April 21, but even before he sent them out for bids, he received a letter from his father warning him of a Pennsylvania-based plot to push him aside and take over the entire project.[23] The next day, an independent contractor already working at the Aqueduct told him that a Pennsylvania group had offered to buy him out. "They could do anything with Mr. Buchanan," they told the contractor, and they planned to oust Meigs and install their own engineer.[24]

The culture of Washington was changing fast. Instead of Pierce, the recovering alcoholic from New Hampshire with the grief-stricken wife, Washington now had Buchanan, the consummate insider, an aging bon vivant whose social calendar was managed by Harriet Lane, his razor-sharp niece, a woman of elegant poise and sophistication. Pierce's White House had been so joyless and dark that the president spent his off-hours wandering around the neighborhood looking for friends to visit. To judge from Meigs's diary, the Buchanan White House was beset constantly by throngs of petitioners, bureaucrats, and cronies, all waiting endlessly for an opportunity to get something from the boss.

What all this meant for Meigs, as Ingersoll had pointed out, was that for the next four years, if he lasted that long, he would be picking his way through a jungle of incompetents, opportunists, and outright scoundrels. Many of them were sent to him either directly or indirectly by Buchanan or, much more often, Floyd. Meigs never demonstrated that either of his bosses was corrupt—that they were colluding with crooks in return for kickbacks. But they definitely liked to deal patronage—to do a favor for a friend and expect a future favor in return—and to Meigs, it amounted to the same thing. His unwillingness to play this game eventually led him to distrust Buchanan. His relationship with Floyd, except for brief holidays, would always be dreadful.

In April, General Totten, now Meigs's highest-ranking friend at the War Department, told Meigs that Floyd was asking about public works and suggested that Meigs seek him out and brief him.[25] Meigs tried but got nowhere. Floyd was away from his office and had not read any of Meigs's correspondence.[26] And when Meigs on May 5 finally sat down to explain his cost estimates for the Aqueduct, Floyd said he had "no time to look at them." Meigs was enraged.[27]

Two days later, at a ceremony in his office, Meigs opened the Aqueduct

John B. Floyd, successor to Jefferson Davis as secretary of war, was a patronage politician and an intriguer, too inept to be a true scoundrel but powerful enough to cause incessant trouble for Meigs, who grew to loathe him. (Library of Congress)

bids and read them. It took him six and a half hours, and the meeting was attended by more than fifty petitioners, representing individuals, large firms, and consortia interested in single contracts, bundles of contracts, and pieces of contracts. Two firms were bidding the entire job, including a group headed by George Lauman, a hard-bitten dealmaker from Pennsylvania. Meigs immediately knew that Lauman was the contractor that was trying to take him down. He found the Lauman group's bids credible and reasonable, but he said nothing to them during the meeting.[28]

The next day, Lauman returned to the Capitol for a private session with Meigs. He did not believe that his employees would be able to work alongside government employees, he said, so he had bid the whole job in order to take it out of the government's hands entirely. He did not mention any planned move to get rid of Meigs, who remained noncommittal. He doubted whether Lauman and his colleagues would be able to fulfill the contract, except perhaps by hiring away Meigs's entire workforce—which was probably what Lauman intended to do.[29]

Meigs took the bids to Floyd, who had no idea how to decipher the different jobs, estimates, and proposals but nevertheless wondered why

Meigs was not interested in employing "one or two" large firms. This told Meigs that Lauman had indeed visited Buchanan and, perhaps, Floyd. For three weeks Floyd puzzled over the Aqueduct paperwork, summoning Meigs on several occasions to explain, only to dismiss him because he was too impatient or too busy to pay attention.[30]

Meigs finally sent the paperwork to Buchanan, who invited him in for a chat on May 23 and accepted Meigs's simple recommendation: give the individual contracts to the lowest bidder. He told Meigs he would not exert political influence on the project. Meigs, to his surprise, had carried the day. He and the president "parted good friends," he wrote later. "He is a quicker man than Floyd in understanding anything. Clear head and quick apprehension."[31]

Floyd told Meigs in June that he intended to have "certain Know-Nothings" fired from the public works, and Meigs got him to back off by pointing out that as a serving military officer, he, Meigs, had no right to fire anyone for his political beliefs. If Floyd wanted someone to go, he would have to fire him himself, and do it in writing. The orders were not forthcoming.[32]

But Floyd kept after him. When Champion, the Know-Nothing smith shop foreman, suddenly died of pneumonia, Meigs appointed a replacement the same day, calculating, no doubt, that if Floyd's goal was to make vacancies so they could be filled with patronage appointments, Champion's death would be a golden opportunity. Meigs took care to slam the door shut even as it opened.[33]

In mid-October, however, after Floyd started railing against Know-Nothings to William Bryan, Meigs's deputy in charge of the Aqueduct, Meigs began to lose his temper—but not in public. Floyd was "a two-pennies politician" and a "contemptible fellow," Meigs wrote in his diary. He thinks "more of prosecuting a Know-Nothing than of the value of the government work."[34] Three days after that, Floyd ordered Meigs to fire an alleged Know-Nothing engineer and replace him with another one acceptable to Floyd. Meigs was furious, but he complied. Bryan wielded the axe, but he immediately found the dismissed man an equivalent job with an Aqueduct contractor. When an enraged Floyd found out about this, he forced Meigs to fire Bryan.[35] Floyd, Meigs wrote, is "a man of no principle."[36]

Besides the running battle over job patronage, squabbling continued over the Aqueduct contracts. Meigs notified the winning May bidders of their good fortune, and when some of them failed to sign their contracts in time, he suggested to Floyd that he make an offer to the next-lowest bidder. Instead, Floyd, probably at Buchanan's behest, wanted to rebid all of the outstanding jobs. "There was a good deal of excitement in Pennsylvania about this," Floyd told Meigs, "and the President thought it of importance." Meigs doubted whether Floyd could handle another full-scale round of bidding. "The fact is," he wrote, "the Secretary is not up to his place."[37]

Meigs sent a letter to Buchanan to make his case, but on June 16, Buchanan confirmed that while "my fixed purpose" is that construction of the Aqueduct "shall be done in the best manner and consistent with this upon the most economical terms," he preferred contractors and wanted a second round of bidding.[38] Meigs did not find this response reassuring, fearing that Buchanan was in thrall to the still-hovering Lauman group.[39] Meigs met with Buchanan two days later, and although he thought the meeting was "satisfactory," his earlier confidence in Buchanan had vanished.[40]

The stalemate endured until July 27, when Floyd came for a visit to the Capitol, toured the Extension and the shops, "and was very pleasant and agreeable." Meigs gave him a packet of photographs, and Floyd suddenly told him not to bother about a second round of bidding. Meigs should do the rest of the job on a day's-work basis. Meigs could not tell whether Floyd had suddenly decided that Meigs was right. More likely, he, and perhaps Buchanan, realized that the contracts were too complicated for them to decipher. Whatever the reason, Meigs wrote in his diary, "I have apparently gained the whole of the battle."[41]

No sooner had he celebrated this happy outcome, however, than he learned of a new plot against him. The administration, according to a newspaper report, was going to fire him as superintendent of the Capitol Extension and replace him with another engineer. Was this why Floyd had been so nice to him? A few days later his father sent Meigs a letter describing similar rumors emanating from Philadelphia. Meigs decided then to play his trump card. On August 8 he sent Davis a letter describing the "political influence and intrigue" that had plagued him and relating the "rumors" of his imminent departure from the Capitol.[42]

Davis, who was in Mississippi during the recess, replied from Brierfield on August 23, enclosing a copy of a letter to Floyd in which he noted that "I have heard that it is urged upon you to relieve Capt. Meigs" at the Capitol Extension. This would be a bad idea, he said, "since the manner in which the work had been conducted furnishes sufficient evidence of the capacity, zeal and integrity of the officer in charge." Davis told Floyd that his own experience with Meigs was "a most gratifying connection," and "I doubt" that anyone Floyd might pick could compete with Meigs in knowledge and expertise. "I am sure you will not fail" to keep him in place, Davis said, and finished by promising to take "a continued interest in the great national work of which I have written."[43] Davis did not yet know Floyd, but Floyd could be sure that when it came to the Capitol Extension, Davis would make his presence felt.

Davis also referred to the imminent completion of the House of Representatives and the innovations Meigs had used in its construction. If the new House "should fulfill the expectations," Davis wrote, "it will be a great triumph for American science and probably contribute much to the transaction of business." But if things did not work out as planned, and Floyd had fired Meigs, people would quite likely think—and Meigs would probably say publicly—that if he had remained in charge, there would have been no problems. The implied message was that Meigs—and Davis—would blame Floyd for any shortcomings.[44]

The veiled threat may have been leveled at Floyd, but Davis's letter also underscored how much Meigs had riding on the new House. With Davis's acquiescence and active support, Meigs had taken a series of breathtaking gambles, wagering that his judgment—in acoustics, ventilation, decoration, and art—would satisfy 235 monstrous egos, none of whom had ever experienced anything like what Meigs was going to show them. They would see it, hear it, feel it, and smell it all at once, and Meigs would stand or fall on their verdict. The new House may have been a manifestation of Meigs's overweening arrogance, but it also showed remarkable courage. Even as preparations accelerated through 1857, Meigs never took a step back. Instead, he embraced the responsibility and refused to give it up.

When the House moved into the new chamber, Meigs would finally get a ruling on all his engineering experiments: Could members hear? Would the ventilation system work in the summer? Would the heating system work in the winter? Would twelve hundred gaslights be better—and safer—than chandeliers? Could members be comfortable in a large meeting hall with no windows and sunshine filtered through glass skylights?

And then there were the artwork and decoration. Walter and Fillmore had taken the safe road of stark neoclassicism: uncluttered blank space that could be filled in later as members saw fit. Davis and Meigs had taken the dangerous road: ornate decorations and ornamentation, designed, drawn, crafted, and painted under the direction of immigrants. Like it or not, there was no turning back.

Meigs had never publicly explained his artistic vision for the Capitol, but his goals had been clear since he started hunting for a fresco painter in 1854, and any lawmaker who cared could see enough by mid-1857 to know what was intended. For Meigs, the Capitol was less a meeting hall than a cathedral—an enduring and unforgettable monument to the greatness, not only of God and the Republic, but also of Montgomery C. Meigs.

He liked American themes in classical formats, and he was particularly partial to elaborate patterns and ornate decoration in the Pompeian style. With Brumidi in-house, he had started to implement his preferences, and he had gotten away with it up to this moment—and virtually without a serious challenge—because Jefferson Davis unfailingly backed him up. Nevertheless, complaints about Meigs's copycat European artwork and how it was corrupting republican virtue had never gone away.

Davis, in fact, had addressed this undercurrent of discontent in his last report to Congress as secretary of war. The document, submitted on December 1, 1856, was a marvel of defiant circumlocution whose basic message was that Davis and Meigs had chosen a "higher style of finish" for the new Capitol because Congress had asked for it. In fact, nothing specifically about the style of the new Capitol interior had ever been debated in Congress, and the decisions about fresco painting, encaustic tiles, papier-mâché decoration, sculpture, and the statue of *Freedom* were made at Meigs's initiative in consultation with Davis and with no one else. Brumidi's Cincinnatus lunette could perhaps have been considered a "specimen," but Meigs's other artistic innovations, once accepted by Davis, were accomplished facts and were announced as such. After glossing over this technicality, Davis made an even more brazen assertion. The extra cost to fulfill Congress's wishes for the Capitol Extension would be $2,100,000, "with the understanding that it was the will of Congress that the higher style of finish should be introduced into the whole building." Meigs now had the legacy he needed.[45]

And he pushed forward. He had first described these efforts—and the politics behind them—in an unusually frank and revealing 1855 letter to the historical painter Thomas P. Rossiter, an American living in Paris. Meigs did not even know Rossiter, who had inquired about the possibility of painting something for the new Capitol. Meigs could not help at the moment, he said, since Congress had not authorized him to commission individual works.

What he could do and had started to do, however, was put sculpture in the pediment of the Senate portico, paint the walls with frescoes and trompe l'oeil moldings and arches, and garnish the metalwork with papier-mâché ornaments. All this, however, was not "art work," he insisted, but integral to the Capitol's structure. He could paint frescoes on the walls and call it house painting. The moldings and arches were "finishing," and the pediment was part of the façade of the building itself. The political rationale for the frescoes, he told Rossiter, was thus made simple: "I ventured upon this as being part and parcel of the walls," Meigs wrote. "I thought I could support it as being part of the building."[46]

Given the constraints under which Meigs worked—tight money, his inability to buy individual works of art, and his own impatience—Constantino Brumidi was the very definition of what Meigs could do. He might be foreign-born, but Meigs did not care. He painted "walls" and worked for day wages as a government employee.

And Brumidi did that work gloriously well. After completing the Cincinnatus lunette, he took a full year to finish the rest of the House Agriculture Committee Room. On the ceiling, the four seasons were portrayed as classical figures—Flora for spring, Ceres for summer, Bacchus for autumn, and Borcas for winter—seated on clouds and served by cherubs. The four panels were divided by white "carved relief moldings," which were in fact illusionistic paintings made to look like sculptures of cherubs, garlands, and shrubbery, their forms shaded as if by light coming from the windows. Opposite Cincinnatus, Brumidi had painted Israel Putnam, the American Cincinnatus, being called from the plow to join the revolution. In facing lunettes on the other two walls were trompe l'oeil cameo portraits of Washington and Jefferson. Below Washington was a farmer harvesting wheat with a sickle; below Jefferson was a farmer using Cyrus McCormick's modern reaper. The lower walls were decorated with gilded moldings, all of which were illusions.[47]

By early 1856, Meigs knew that the room he called "the painted chamber" was going to be a sensation. Visitors allowed to watch Brumidi at work were hugely impressed. When he heard that Speaker Banks was belittling the Army's ability to handle public works, Meigs mused in his diary about how he would hand Banks the key to the chamber, "then let his committees fight for it."[48] And when he did turn over the chamber, on April 11, 1856, he noted that "whatever committee takes possession of it will have a hard time with the public who throng to see it."[49] By September the clerk of the House had a guard on duty to handle the crowds.

Regardless of what the Know-Nothings and the "republican austerity" advocates said, Meigs's style of Capitol artwork—colorful, complicated, rife with fascinating optical illusion—was a phenomenal success. Meigs hastened to take full advantage. By the spring of 1856, Brumidi was designing the Senate Reception Room, the Senate Naval Affairs Committee Room, the Senate corridors, and the ceiling of the new House chamber.[50] These rooms, Meigs promised in his end-of-the-year report, would be finished in "the same style of decoration, so far as possible," as the House Agriculture Committee Room. In all, between Brumidi and other artists, he had nine decorative art projects under way.[51]

The Palmer affair had probably told Meigs as much as he needed to know about the Buchanan administration's interest in art at the Capitol Extension. There would be no House pediment sculpture in the foreseeable future. But Buchanan's indifference also meant that Meigs had a virtually free hand to undertake whatever projects he deemed worthwhile, as long as they were, by Meigs's definition, "structural." Even before Buchanan's inauguration, he had started searching for artists to decorate the rooms that Brumidi would never have time to paint. Never tortured by doubt, Meigs in this quest could be counted on to make a judgment quickly and follow it up with a brisk decision. John McNevin's historical paintings were "full of spirit and energy," but "I fear he would be careless in his drawing." He was not hired. Sculptor Chauncey Ives's work was "tolerably well done." His statue of Roger Sherman would be placed in the old House chamber. Baltimore sculptor William Rinehart showed "talent and skill," and Meigs hired him on the spot. He would complete Crawford's unfinished bronze doors. Fridolin Schlegal brought portraits Meigs deemed "very fine" and "some sketches which were very bad. I do not think much can be done with him." James Walker, not yet forty in 1857, had been living in Mexico City during the Mexican War and joined the U.S. Army during the war's climactic battles. "His sketches are as full of life and knowledge as any battle pieces I have ever seen," Meigs wrote. He hired Walker to paint *Storming of Chapultepec* for the Senate, which more than a century later would send it to the Marine Corps Museum.[52]

In late 1856 Brumidi began painting the ceiling of the new House chamber, a lattice of cast-iron rafters with panels of glass to allow light to enter the room. The glass panels were inscribed with the seals of the states. Brumidi proposed bold colors—red, blue, and yellow—augmented with gilding and gilt bronze. Meigs was wary at the outset that the ceiling would be too fancy for the use of the building, he wrote in his diary.[53] But he was quickly won over. Brumidi had used "much more gilding than I intended, and the effect is most magnificent," he wrote. "I am not too sure that it is not too gorgeous, but I begin to think that nothing so rich in effect has ever been seen this side of the Atlantic."[54]

Meigs never wavered. The job was finished in June 1857 and the scaffolding came down. Brumidi immediately set to work on what were to be several fresco panels along the walls of the chamber. The first painting, to the left of the Speaker as he sat at his desk, depicted the British surrender at Yorktown and was entitled *Cornwallis Sues for Cessation of Hostilities Under the Flag of Truce.*

This, too, was a daring move, for Meigs had entrusted the first painting in the new chamber to an immigrant. Brumidi was clearly aware of what the Know-Nothings and malcontents were saying behind his back. At the same time, he was obviously proud to have been entrusted with painting such a significant work. When the House opened in December, lawmakers would notice the inscription on the strap of General Washington's dispatch case: "C. Brumidi, artist citizen of the U.S." Brumidi was naturalized on November 12.[55]

As the year wore on, preparations for the grand opening proceeded smoothly, although there were glitches. An epic hailstorm on the twenty-first of June broke more than two thousand windows on the Capitol grounds, including several of the skylight panels in the roof of the House.[56] In September, the clerk of the House appeared in Meigs's office to announce that he was ready to lay the carpets. Meigs told him icily that until he was finished with the chamber and handed the key to the Speaker, the carpets and everything else were none of the clerk's business. When the clerk told Meigs that he would have to take a "hostile attitude" toward Meigs if he did not change his mind, Meigs told him to get lost.[57]

On November 30, Meigs turned on the chamber's gaslights for the first time, and the effect was "brilliant." On December 6, the boilers were lit for the entire House wing. On the following day, Meigs told Floyd the House was finished, and Davis stopped by Meigs's office to tell him how pleased he was. On December 9, Meigs invited Davis, Senators Seward and Pearce, Joseph Henry, and Alexander Bache to give the acoustics a test. "We tried the voices in all parts," he wrote. "We tried the lighting." Everything worked perfectly. On December 10, Louisa Meigs came in at dusk "and sang a verse or two" in the new chamber. "The effect of her magnificent and rich voice in this great chamber was beautiful," Meigs wrote. "She says it is perfectly easy to sing in. The voice fills without effort the whole space."[58]

The Hall of Columns, on the first floor at the south entrance of the new House of Representatives. When the encaustic tiles eventually wore out, they were replaced with a simple design in black and white marble. (Architect of the Capitol)

By opening day, many members, newspapermen, and sundry critics had already seen the chamber and issued opinions. Previews of the venti-

lation, heating, acoustics, and especially the lighting were generally favorable. The Washington *Evening Star* described a December 12 visit to the
darkened hall as "grim, forbidding, Plutonic." But then, the *Star* continued,
"at a signal, as if a higher power had said, 'let there be light,' the hall was
suddenly filled with a flood of the richest golden rays; every tongue was
loosened, and the walls of the great room fairly rang with shouts of delight."[59] On December 14, Arkansas representative Edward A. Warren, chair
of a committee appointed to assess the new chamber's readiness, reported
a "dry atmosphere" and a room "warm, well-lighted and ventilated." Tests
of the acoustics "found very little reverberation," and not only could the
Speaker be heard in every part of the room, but members could be heard
by the Speaker no matter where they stood. The committee recommended
that the House move to its new chamber "as soon as possible."[60]

That took place on December 16, only nine days after the session
opened. On balance, an optimistic Meigs wrote two days later, "there was
far less trouble and complaint than I expected."[61] But it was not an unmitigated success. During the run-up to the grand opening, Meigs had been
able to control access to the chamber, either touting its virtues to reporters
who wanted to like it because it made a better story, or listening to his
wife, to Davis, and to Bache and Henry, his two collaborators in the
1853 acoustical study, complimenting him. For anyone who wanted ammunition to attack him later, there was plenty.

Trouble began immediately when reporters discovered that they no
longer had access to the House floor but were instead confined to ten seats
installed behind the Speaker's desk—not a good plan, since there were
about five dozen accredited newspeople covering Congress. Since reporters tended to be both vocal and aggressive, members hastened to placate
them, spending their first day of debate discussing how they might appropriate a section of third-floor gallery for their use. The *Pennsylvania Inquirer* of December 17 urged members to move quickly. If they did not,
the *Inquirer* threatened baldly, they "will assuredly get the worst of it in
the long run."[62] Meigs, who was both friendly to reporters and knowledgeable about using them, had blown this one completely.

The touchiest subjects, however, were of course the painting and decoration. Benjamin Brown French, the former commissioner of public
buildings and no friend of Meigs, echoed the ambivalence of several critics who were impressed with the hall but not quite sure that they should
be. French called it "a gorgeous affair" on December 4, but "too much so

for my taste." The ceiling "is magnificent," but he found much of the rest of the gilding "tawdry and out of place, worthy only of a theatre, lager beer saloon, or steamboat cabin!" By December 20, overt criticism had became fashionable, and French branded the chamber "the most dismal place I have ever seen for a Public Body to meet in."

Still, Meigs could be thankful that he had achieved his principal goal, and French acknowledged it: "There is no question that it is a better room for meeting in than the old hall."[63]

14

THE FEUD

On December 19, 1857, a *New York Herald* reporter told Captain Meigs that an unnamed "party from Philadelphia" was "working against" him by putting nasty stories about the new House in the *Herald* and other publications. Meigs was unworried. Certain that he knew who was after him, he wrote confidently in his diary, "I was prepared to beat them."

Maybe Meigs was thinking about the Lauman group, but what he almost certainly did not know was that Thomas U. Walter was doing everything he could to get Meigs fired. After toiling in Meigs's shadow for almost five years, Walter wanted Meigs gone, and he had been working toward that goal virtually from the moment Buchanan took office.

Summoned that December day by Speaker James L. Orr to discuss the new House chamber, Meigs found that Walter was also at the meeting. Meigs knew that Walter did not like his downward ventilation system for the new chamber—mostly, Meigs suspected, because he did not understand it. Sure enough, members soon asked about the vents. Meigs replied that he was more certain than ever that the system would be a success. Someone mentioned that downward ventilation had proved to be a disaster in the British House of Commons. Meigs explained that a "system of quackery" had been used there. Any objections to his own design, he said, were being raised by "persons who had not scientific knowledge enough to understand the matter." He stared at Walter as he said this.

Forced to respond, Walter told the committee that he had never agreed with Meigs on downward ventilation. Yes, Meigs answered, he knew that.

Meigs's response betrayed no agitation, but inside he was furious at what he considered to be Walter's effrontery. He was "tempted to say," he wrote later, "that as he (Walter) had nothing to do with it, it was entirely un-called for in him, my assistant, to express his opinion to the committee."[1]

For Meigs and Walter, the brief argument marked the first public dis-play of an animosity that had been simmering dangerously for months. Their dispute was serious, embracing the two critical issues that faced them as they moved into the final phases of Capitol construction: Who would get to finish the project? And who would earn lasting fame for cre-ating the new Capitol? The skirmish in the Speaker's office was the last time for two years that Meigs and Walter would jointly participate in a formal meeting, and one of the last times, to judge by journals and letters, that they would ever speak to each other face-to-face.

The roots of their resentment were not difficult to discern. For Meigs, ambitious yet insecure, Walter had been an asset, even a godsend, during his early days on the project. Walter was a quick worker and a proven ex-pert, not only with architectural design but also in knowledge of building techniques, materials, and suppliers. Meigs's three biggest contracts—for marble, marble finishing, and cast iron—were with firms originally hired by Walter. Meigs had known that he needed Walter, and he had been quick to shield him from Davis's wrath. Walter had generally served him well.

But things had recently changed for Meigs. Walter's Dome design, in particular, had provoked awe and envy. But Walter's very skill made Meigs jealous in a way he could not always control. Driven to make his own mark on the Capitol, Meigs had been trying to outdraw or outdesign Wal-ter ever since the Dome, and he undoubtedly kept Walter away from his artistic projects lest he give Walter another chance to outdo him.

Shoving Walter to the margin became progressively easier to do, for by December 1857, Walter's expertise was no longer as necessary as it had once been. Walter had presented the Dome design three and a half years earlier, and since then, Meigs had taken control of both the Extension and the Dome with increasing confidence. His boom derrick and foundation brackets for the Dome were brilliant solutions to difficult problems. The daringly elaborate artistic style he was using in the Extension was his alone—and seconded by the unflinching support of Secretary of War, and now Senator, Jefferson Davis.

Walter's attitudes toward Meigs had followed a similar course. Un-justly accused of malfeasance in 1852, he had been demoted and forced to serve for more than four years as the assistant to an army officer twelve years his junior. At first he had welcomed Meigs as a buffer, protecting him from political pressures and the conniving of disgruntled contractors. But those pressures had waned, and the stout defense that Meigs—and Davis—had provided for him during the Pierce administration was no longer as necessary as it had once been. Walter chafed at Meigs's imperious ways and reveled in Meigs's difficulties with the new secretary of war, John Floyd, and the Buchanan administration. As early as May 1857, he was privately predicting that Meigs's power was "at an end."[2]

The change of administration had given Walter his chance. It is not clear whether he simply wanted Meigs to go away or whether he also set out, as soon as Buchanan arrived, to regain control of the project. But by the summer, he was working toward both goals. Meigs had not seen Walter's downfall in 1853 or Robert Mills's downfall two years before that, and he did not realize how vulnerable he could become. Meigs, a military man, liked structure, and Davis, also a military man, had provided it. Floyd was not a military man but a politician, and he, like Buchanan, saw Meigs's job as a political plum. The nature of the game had changed, and Meigs was slow to learn the rules. Walter, by contrast, already knew how to play.

All the elements of their rivalry and impending breakup were on display in Orr's office. Nothing enraged Walter more than to be ignored or dismissed as "not a man of science." Walter had been fighting for respectability his entire life, and in 1857, intent on raising the standards and stature of his profession, he had been named the first vice president of the new American Institute of Architects, of which he was a principal founder.

And nothing enraged Meigs more than to have a subordinate challenge him outside the chain of command. It did not matter to Meigs so much whether Walter believed in downward ventilation. Reasonable people could disagree. What rankled was that he often said so—to Hunter, to the House committee, and apparently to anyone else who cared to listen.

Also noteworthy during the brief exchange was the inability of either man to understand the other's motives. The day after the meeting in the Speaker's office, Meigs had a conversation with Joseph Nason, the contractor who had helped him with the Extension's ventilation and heating system, and told him that Walter "had not the right to claim the credit" for it.[3] Meigs by this time had become obsessed with getting recognition for his accomplishments, and he was convinced that Walter was trying to cheat him at every step. Walter's ambition, however, went further than Meigs realized. He did not want to take credit for the ventilation system; he wanted lawmakers not to like it so they would get rid of Meigs.

Walter's mistake was his refusal to see beyond Meigs's straitlaced arrogance and self-aggrandizement. Three days after the meeting in Orr's office, Walter wrote a sarcastic letter to the marble contractor John Rice in Philadelphia, saying that Meigs was off "explaining his greatness and the unimportance of somebody else—he is vain to an extent amounting to insanity, bitter and vindictive."[4] What Walter had forgotten was that Meigs was an Army officer, and therefore imperious almost by definition. His self-assurance and by-the-book rectitude may have rankled Walter, but it kept much more powerful men than Walter from meddling with the project. The Lauman group had been looking for a chink in Meigs's armor for nine months and had gotten nowhere. Meigs took care of his people.

By mid-December 1857, the two men had been competing with and misunderstanding each other for some time. The rivalry, along with Davis's open pocketbook, had fostered a climate of aggressive and spectacular creativity during the Pierce years, resulting in a building that even now so dominated the Washington landscape that it had come to define the city, the federal government, and even the nation itself. But the positive energy was turning sour.

Meigs had spent the first months of the Buchanan administration focused on the Aqueduct—restarting the project, trying to explain it to the president and Floyd, and fending off challenges from the Lauman group and others eager to seize control. During the same period, Walter was quietly mustering allies and joining forces with several influential Philadelphia Democrats intent on ousting Meigs from the Capitol. The key member of the group appears to have been the former Democratic congressman William H. Witte, a political operator who served as the go-between for the other plotters.[5] These included, besides Walter, Pennsylvania senator William Bigler, a former state governor and a close Buchanan ally; John Rice, the Capitol's marble supplier; and his brother, William Rice, publisher of the *Pennsylvanian*, a Democratic Party mouthpiece. Later, Pennsylvania representative Thomas B. Florence, also a Democrat, would join in.

The plan was straightforward. Buchanan and Floyd were political animals, and the intriguers were politically powerful men who would

The East Front of the Capitol in 1857, showing the boom derrick built by Montgomery Meigs to hoist pieces of cast iron into position on the new Dome. The feud between Meigs and architect Thomas U. Walter virtually halted construction a year after this photo was taken, idling the derrick and leaving the Dome unbuilt. (Architect of the Capitol)

persuade Buchanan and Floyd to fire Meigs. Walter on October 2 wrote a short letter to Witte describing a "pleasant interview this morning with our friend" (probably Floyd, or perhaps Bigler), saying "there is no difference of opinion between us in reference to the matter you and I were talking about." The "thing," he wrote, "will positively be done, and the only question is as to time."[6]

Walter's interest in the plot was obvious: he wanted Meigs out or his authority sharply limited. The motives of the other conspirators were unclear, but they most likely were simply intent on patronage. They wanted to get rid of the incorruptible Meigs and use his projects to further the interests of their Pennsylvania friends, whoever they might be. It was possible that the Lauman group and the Walter intrigues were linked. One of the Lauman group principals was John W. Forney, a former clerk of the House of Representatives, a Buchanan acolyte, and a career newspaperman

By the time workers began to build the connecting corridors between the new wings (left) and the old Capitol (right) in the late 1850s, broken and unused stone from almost a decade of construction littered the Capitol grounds. (Architect of the Capitol)

who had owned and edited the *Philadelphian* before William Rice took it over.[7] Forney soon broke with Buchanan over Buchanan's soft stance on slavery, but in mid-1857 he, like Witte and Bigler, was a premier political fixer in the Pennsylvania Democratic Party. Walter was a natural fit for the group because of his own ambition, his close ties to John Rice, and—most important to the other participants—his access to documents and inside information that could help the others make the case against Meigs to Buchanan and Floyd. The Capitol project would be Walter's reward.

Another possibility, first suggested by the Meigs biographer Russell F. Weigley, put John Rice at the head of the conspiracy because of Meigs's insistence on monolithic column shafts, which the Lee quarry, it turned out, could not provide. This shortcoming first came to Meigs's attention in late1856. Charles Heebner, Rice's on-site partner, all but confessed in a letter that Lee did not have big enough blocks of white marble for the monoliths.[8] Meigs refused either to accept drums or to rewrite the marble contract, and by September 1857 he and the company had reached an impasse. Meigs privately decided to import monoliths of Carrara marble from Italy and, under the contract, charge Rice and Heebner the difference in price.[9] In November, Rice and Heebner said they would supply the monoliths—probably from Italy—for $1,700 apiece. The marble contract fixed the per-column price at $1,400.[10]

Before Meigs told the partners he would not pay the extra $30,000—$300 per column for 100 columns—he decided he ought to speak with Floyd. This conversation was a disaster. Not only did Floyd refuse to understand what Meigs wanted to do, he made a counterproposal: Why not use granite for the columns instead of marble? Meigs delicately suggested that granite would not have a "good effect" on a marble building, and told him that it would add as much as six years to the time it would take to complete the Capitol and $2 million to its price. "What an absurdity! What folly!" he wrote in his diary that night.[11]

The column question remained unresolved throughout 1857, but Meigs by the end of the year was convinced that Rice wanted him unseated in order to avoid having to forfeit money on the marble contract. Rice thus had a "direct interest" in getting Meigs out of the way and putting "some suppler man in my place."[12]

Besides the columns, Rice may also have had other business complaints about Meigs. In early May 1857, he told Walter that Meigs was slow to pay for marble deliveries, prompting Walter several times during the next several months to urge Meigs's clerks to move faster when Rice and Heebner's bills came due.[13] Eventually his meddling earned a comparatively mild rebuke from Meigs, who told Walter that disbursements were none of his business. Walter agreed, replying in a similar tone that he had simply made inquiries because Rice was asking him about money all the time.[14] Either this was another example of contractor irritation with Meigs's dilatory bill-paying habits, or Rice was financially strapped for some reason and urgently needed cash. In either case the incident was also noteworthy for the artificial courtesy displayed by both Meigs and Walter. Meigs at that point—September 1857—was seriously quarreling with Rice over the columns and did not like Walter's cozy relationship with him. And Walter was already seriously involved in plotting Meigs's departure.

It is difficult to determine Floyd's role in these machinations. As in the concurrent Aqueduct case, every player in Walter's efforts to supplant Meigs was a Pennsylvanian. The conspirators already had the connection to Buchanan, so Floyd was superfluous—a Buchanan appendage from Virginia with whom they might or might not have been acquainted. During the Aqueduct affair, Floyd came across as an uninformed buffoon, but in the early days of the Rice-Walter plot he apparently played a more significant role. As secretary of war, Floyd would be the one to fire Meigs, and Walter was trying to meet with him to make the case. His efforts, however, were just as futile as Meigs's, and he gave up in the fall.[15] Witte, however, apparently had better luck, and convinced Walter that Floyd was going to fire Meigs by the end of the year. Increasingly excited, Walter wrote Rice on October 19, "the thing is coming into focus quite rapidly."[16] This was followed on October 22 with "the thing will be accomplished without difficulty."[17] Then, in a postscript to a letter dated December 8, Walter told Rice that "Meigs is here, just from the Dept. and says *the order was issued this morning!!*"[18]

Unfortunately for Walter, the order did not oust Meigs, though it looked fairly tough. Sent from Floyd to Meigs on December 4, it noted that "vastly increased expenditures" on the Capitol, and "the large sums you ask for the future," required that Meigs submit to closer monitoring of his disbursements:

> No contract or order for any work upon the buildings under your charge is hereafter to be made for any alteration or work upon any plan differing from the original plan adopted, nor is any change in the original plan to be made except upon a distinct proposition for such change of plan, concurred in and approved by the architect and authorized by the Department.[19]

Meigs handled this assault with aplomb. He could "cheerfully conform" to the order, he replied to Floyd on December 9, since he intended to make no modifications to the plans. He noted that expensive changes to Walter's 1851 design had certainly been made, but that the Pierce administration had promulgated them in 1856. This harked back to Davis's annual report that year, in which he asserted that Congress had approved a "higher style" for the Capitol. He would certainly consult Walter if there were disagreements, he continued silkily, if not altogether truthfully, since "we have always conferred frankly and fairly." Also, he added, he knew of "no architect whom I would be willing to see replace Mr. Walter, personally or professionally, in assisting me."[20]

Despite his confidence, Meigs at Christmastime wrote a pair of quick notes to Davis apprising him of his suspicions of Walter's plotting against him and his supposed designs on Meigs's job. Davis paid Buchanan a visit and reported back on the last day of 1857. Buchanan had assured Davis that no one had suggested taking Meigs off the Capitol, but only of relieving him at the Post Office and the Aqueduct. He went further, promising Davis that he would not do anything about Meigs without talking to Davis first.[21]

The battle lines were now evident. Walter had Floyd's ear, and Floyd did not like Meigs. Meigs had Davis's ear, and Davis did not like Walter. Both men were extremely important to Buchanan—Floyd as a trusted associate, Davis as a pillar of the Democratic Congress. It was a standoff.

This tawdry saga showed Walter at his worst. Like most successful architects of his day, he was by necessity also a schemer, accustomed to courting jobs among the moneyed class by working contacts and outsmarting rivals. It was not enough in Walter's world simply to be talented, because prospective clients—like Jefferson Davis—often did not respect his profession. To succeed, Walter not only had to be good, he had to be a hustler. He had abundantly demonstrated this skill during the Capitol competitions of 1850 and 1851, and he was trying to use it again now. He had resented for some time what he regarded as Meigs's usurpation of his design prerogatives, and with the arrival of the Buchanan administration, he had a chance, at a minimum, to get Meigs ousted and reclaim the authority he had lost in 1853. It was, however, a risky game. Meigs was ethically unassailable. His stewardship of the Capitol was an open book—no bribes, no favors, no corner cutting, no wasted money. Yet Walter had made common cause with a group of conspirators who wanted to get Meigs fired almost assuredly because he could not be blackmailed or otherwise manipulated into cooperating with their special interests. Walter was no bribe-taker either, and had escaped the travails of 1852 virtually blemish-free. Yet one might have wondered, as 1857 drew to a close, what, if anything, he had promised John Rice should he win the power struggle. Rice had plenty to gain by having a friend in charge at the Capitol, and Walter would have plenty to offer. Walter had walked right up to the edge of what could be ethically justifiable, and may have stepped over.

The cheap shiftiness of Walter's activities, however, does not dismiss the legitimate reasons that Walter had to mistrust Meigs and even to fear him. Meigs, Walter believed, was stealing his legacy, and, he wrote in early 1858, "we have got completely at war."[22] As time passed, Walter would have even more reason to worry about Meigs.

There was no doubt that Meigs had an obsession about getting "credit" for everything he worked on. It had grown gradually. Davis, when he was intent on firing Walter in late 1854, had presented most of the arguments that Meigs would eventually make to justify his encroachments. Davis warned that Walter would take credit for Meigs's achievements. It was Meigs, he said, who had rescued the original design from disaster, Meigs who was the real architect—and a better architect than Walter—and Meigs who had changed the design "in all its important parts." Meigs was a fellow West Pointer, an elite professional with an elegant pedigree. Walter was a parvenu who had gotten lucky with a couple of good ideas.

The Meigs of 1854 had had the good sense to point out to Davis the flaws in this argument. Walter had designed the building's exterior, he told Davis, and regardless of what Meigs or Davis thought, Walter was going to get the credit. Walter had been there at the beginning, and Meigs had not.[23] That exchange should have closed the debate forever, but less than two months later, Meigs was drawing domes in his office because "I wish to have something to do with this design myself."[24]

The skirmishing continued over the new Capitol's interior decoration, this time with Walter chafing that he had no voice in the artistic decisions. In May 1857, Walter complained to Meigs that Brumidi had altered some architectural features in the new Senate wing without telling him, thus weakening an archway. Meigs told him there was no structural danger, but Walter wrote in his diary that "such things ought at least to be the subject of consultations with the arch[itect]."[25]

Walter's resentment may have seemed petty, but it was not. To think, as Meigs tried to convince himself, that Walter had no artistic sense was absurd on its face. And worse, failing to discuss art and decoration with Walter—probably the only other person on earth with a complete vision of the project—shortchanged the effort. Meigs was behaving stupidly, almost viciously: "His taste is nothing," Meigs said of Walter in a letter to a Philadelphia acquaintance late in 1857. Walter "hates" painting and sculpture "as rival arts, and taking, when used in building, the attention from the architect to the painter or sculptor," he wrote. "He says they are not arts, that architecture is the only art, and that Michelangelo was a humbug and no artist."[26]

Meigs was also increasingly indulging his desire to stamp—literally, in many cases—his own name all over his public works: on the steamboat that plied the Potomac between Washington and the Aqueduct, on assorted cornerstones and plaques, even on engraved pieces of sheet copper tucked into pillars and foundations where only archaeologists or wreckers would ever see them. In February 1858 he wrote his name in wet stucco inside Tunnel C of the Aqueduct.[27] In March he stuck two dozen copper plates bearing his name in the masonry around the Aqueduct's bridge number 3. These, he wrote in his diary, "will keep clean and legible for centuries and, if ever dug up, will show their intention and meaning."[28] A few days later he put up a stone inscription bearing his name at bridge number 1.[29] On April 3, he ordered an inscribed cornerstone inserted in the underwater masonry at Great Falls.[30] On August 2, 1858, he put a copper plate inside the northeast corner of the new Senate portico at the Capitol and another one under the west front of the Post Office Extension.[31] He had been inserting metal plates and bits of cast iron bearing his name for years in the Capitol's masonry and fixtures.

At the same time, Meigs was deliberately and gratuitously impugning Walter's character. In 1855, Meigs acknowledged to Senator James A. Pearce of Maryland, one of his staunchest supporters, that "9/10" of the Dome design was Walter's, then, almost as an afterthought, added that Walter "was a vain man without proper strength of character."[32] Even if this assertion were true, Meigs had no business making it to a U.S. senator. Similar letters and exchanges followed, usually acknowledging Walter's contributions but then dismissing them by making sure his listener or reader understood that anything Walter had done, he had accomplished under Meigs's supervision and guidance. His December 9, 1857, letter to Floyd praised Walter lavishly, then abruptly shifted to a long ode to his own brilliance for the job he had done on the House chamber. "I cannot but feel that I have achieved a great success," he concluded.[33]

Sometime in late December 1857 or early January 1858, Meigs made the mistake that turned the animosity in evidence at the Speaker's office into an open feud.

Walter had drawn the original architectural plans for the Capitol Extension in 1851. After Meigs decided to move the new Senate and House chambers into the centers of their respective wings, Walter produced a second, revised, set of "original" drawings in 1853—the ones that Davis would three years later christen the "higher style" plans. These were signed by Walter, Pierce, and Davis. Sometime at the end of 1857, Meigs added an inscription to this second set of drawings: "Original Revised Plan—By Capt. M. C. Meigs, U.S. engineer," the inscription read, "adopted by the President of the U.S. 27 June 1853."[34]

Walter spotted the change in mid-January 1858 and sent Meigs two "Dear Sir" letters. The first, dated January 19, noted that a photographic copy of "my design" of the second floor of the new Senate wing now bore "certain lettering" that "implies that the revised plan was devised by you, which you well know was not the case." Similar lettering, he continued, had been inscribed on others of "my designs for the alterations of the original plans." He asked "respectfully" that the lettering be removed "and the drawings be returned to my office."[35]

The following day, Walter sent a second letter. Meigs, it appeared, had ordered John Wood to destroy the glass plate negatives of the plans that did not bear the new inscription. "Your motive for doing so cannot be misunderstood," Walter wrote. "You will please stop all further proceeding in reference to the photography of these drawings and return them to my office, that I may have them restored to the condition they were in when approved by the President."[36]

Meigs was enraged. Walter's claim to be the author of the design changes to the Capitol was "preposterous," he wrote in his diary. Walter had no connection with the "great features" of the new Senate and House chamber designs other "than by making the drawings under my direction, in obedience to my orders in accordance with principles which I first announced, and which he did not and does not understand." The rooms were "completed by me, on my responsibility, in a style of architecture which I ordered, with his help as a draftsman only, in truth, though I have always given him the title of architect in order to give him as high a position as I could." Walter's assertions were "impudence—for I can call it by no other name."[37]

He replied to Walter in an immense letter on January 21. He defended his actions by reviewing his original appointment, in which Pierce in 1853 had taken not only disbursement authority away from Walter, "but

all other authority whatever," and placed it in Meigs's hands. This "changed
your position," he told Walter, "and deprived you of all authority, except-
ing such as I might confide to you as my assistant." Over the years, he
continued, Davis had expressed a desire to get rid of Walter, but Meigs
had "resisted his wish." Walter had himself several times thanked Meigs
for keeping him on.

After all this, Meigs continued, "I am at a loss to understand how you
can so far forget your position as to call upon me to return certain drawings to your office." Walter could not "expect me to again entrust them to
you when you avow a desire to erase from them the descriptive legend
which I have caused to be put upon them." He said he would not return
the drawings because he now knew of "the steps you were taking" to deny
him the credit he was due. This, Meigs continued, was a fine way to repay
"five years of kindness and protection, during which you held the position
and the advantages which you now abuse, solely through my influence
and protection."

Then Meigs told a preposterous lie: "The world does not care a fig
whether you, or I, or another made, drew, prepared, designed—call it
what name you will—the plans for the Extension of the Capitol." And he
finished with the thought that probably should have informed both men
months earlier, but which would never be seriously considered: "There is
room in such a work for all the industry, knowledge and ability of both
of us."[38]

By examining the facts—disputed by neither Meigs nor Walter—the
quarrel that began here can be seen first, and most benignly, as a misunderstanding. Neither man believed for a minute that "the world does not
care a fig" about who designed the Capitol. Each was trying to ensure that
he got the credit that was due him, and each was convinced that the other
was trying to steal all the credit. Altering the drawings was the proof that
both men were right. Seen from Walter's point of view, the analogy of
William Allen, architectural historian for the Architect of the Capitol,
seems most apt. Meigs, Allen has written, was like "an editor-in-chief at
a newspaper, who consults with writers, approves certain things, and
changes or disapproves others. While the final product reflects his management and style, the byline still carries the author's name."[39] Walter had
made the original plans and had revised the plans to reflect Meigs's wishes.
Meigs demanded changes, but the original framework was still Walter's.

Meigs, however, had a different view, equally reasonable. He regarded the new Capitol as would a business entrepreneur or, perhaps more aptly in this case, a military commander. Meigs was the boss. He paid the bills, assumed the responsibility, hired the employees, and supervised the work. He deserved to take the credit, but he was also in line to take the blame. It was his job, win or lose. In defending his actions, Meigs would repeatedly cite his original 1853 orders, in which Pierce and Davis had given him total control of the Capitol Extension. He was right to claim credit, he insisted, because he was in charge. Furthermore, Meigs saw himself as a brilliant designer in his own right—one who had made a fundamental change in the Capitol by moving the chambers. Also, although Meigs did not say so, engineering in 1857 had greater cachet than architecture. Meigs was a professional, trained at a professional school. Walter was an artisan who had acquired additional skills.

From their different perspectives, both men could make convincing cases. There were, however, several additional considerations, all of which reflect badly on Meigs and ultimately make Walter the wronged party.

First of all, Meigs, as he so adamantly insisted, was the boss. So if he considered it appropriate that he sign the plans, why did he not insist on signing them when they were first presented in 1853? Once he had made the decision not to sign, he was honor-bound—as the boss—to stick by it. In failing to do so, he abused his position.

Second, Walter had the title of architect, but he held no authority. Meigs could talk about all the favors he had done for Walter—protected him from Davis, kept him on after the 1852 trial—all of which were true. On the other hand, Walter could, and did, do many things for Meigs beyond mere drawings and designs. He helped Meigs with intelligence during Stanton's "military rule" assault, defended Meigs in disputes with disgruntled contractors and lawmakers, and provided the project with a marvelous Dome design. Being the boss did not mean that Meigs's favors had any greater valence than Walter's favors. Walter may have ended up betraying Meigs to the Buchanan administration, but Meigs, in signing Walter's designs ex post facto and slandering Walter before the likes of Senator Pearce, had violated a hallowed precept of military leadership— one that he would have recognized. He wanted "loyalty up" from Walter, but did not always give "loyalty down" in return.

Finally, when Meigs altered the drawings, he did so without telling Walter or anyone else. Given the rancor and paranoia that were already infecting the relationship, one could easily imagine Walter's panic when he first saw the altered plans. If Meigs was so certain he was right, he should have announced his intentions and inscribed the drawings in full daylight. His actions suggest that he himself was not altogether comfortable with what he had done.

The feud, from January 1858 forward, would be direct and no-holds-barred. In its way it would be a noble contest, fought openly and with great tenacity by both men. And once the final breach occurred over the altered drawings, the principals understood that only one could survive.[40]

They were well matched. With Davis out of the cabinet, Meigs had been considerably weakened. He had no serious support in the Buchanan administration, and he was almost totally alienated from Floyd, his immediate boss. Floyd believed in patronage and made deals. Meigs thought he was stupid and corrupt and viewed him with a contempt that he could not always hide. Meigs's relationship with Floyd was further complicated because he was trying to get Floyd to give his eldest son, John Rodgers Meigs, now sixteen, an at-large appointment to West Point. John did not make it in 1857, causing Meigs to remark in his diary, "I cannot help thinking that had I been a more ready tool to give jobs to his [Floyd's] friends, I might have succeeded in obtaining this."[41] It is almost impossible to imagine the two men ever achieving a modus vivendi.

Meigs's weakness in the administration brought him within political reach of Walter, who had joined a plot whose goals, beyond getting rid of Meigs, were unclear. After its failure, while Walter would still be able to count on Bigler and Witte for help to advance his agenda—and to protect himself—he needed to find his own friends. He turned to the new administration for help, correctly identifying Floyd as the key link in Meigs's chain of command.

With little or no backing from Floyd or the White House, Meigs's power base shifted to Congress. His primary supporter, of course, was Davis, and Meigs did not hesitate to lean on Davis whenever new threats arose. The same day Meigs responded to Walter's accusations about the altered plans, he wrote Davis a long letter enclosing all of the Walter correspondence and copies of the drawings, both altered and unaltered. He reviewed his claim that the new Senate and House chambers were his designs, and outlined his concerns that Walter "must think he has backers," including, perhaps, Floyd. But Davis could trump all this, for "in a question of this kind," Meigs said, "no evidence can be so conclusive as that of the fountain from which the authority of both parties was derived." He asked Davis to intercede once again to set things right.[42]

Walter, as Meigs suspected, was working the administration. On that same day, January 21, Walter had seen Floyd and had handed him two extraordinary documents. The first was a draft order from Floyd to Meigs, written by Walter and clearly meant to substitute for the vague directive that Floyd had mailed to Meigs six weeks earlier. The new one directed Meigs "to submit to the architect of the U.S. Capitol, all the designs you may have adopted for the painting, sculpture, and other ornamentation of the Capitol Extension, also copies of all contracts, agreements, orders and directions you may have entered into or given for work yet to be done." Meigs was "further directed not to proceed with any part of the work, which has not had the official sanction of the architect, without his approval."

The second document was a draft letter from Walter to Meigs, also dated January 21. It complained that "most of the painting and ornamentation is decided on without my knowledge" and insisted that this must stop, because "all designs of architectural forms must, of course, be made in reference to light, and shade, and color, hence if it is proper for me to design the forms, it is proper for me to say how they should be painted." Meigs, the letter said, must submit his designs for Walter's approval so that Walter would have "an opportunity to put a stop to some of the most objectionable and expensive ornamentation that has ever been attempted in a public building."[43]

Walter was attempting a coup d'état. Frustrated by the Philadelphia conspiracy and evidently tired of operating from behind the scenes, he was apparently trying to win his prize with one bold frontal attack, and he thought he had made his case: "the tables are about turning," he exulted in a letter to John Rice.[44]

In fact, Floyd saw Walter's initiative as not only presumptuous but even damaging to the administration. On January 25, when Davis made another pilgrimage to the White House to press Meigs's case, Buchanan remarked that Walter "had behaved in an insubordinate manner" and might have to be fired.[45] It was not clear from the conversation exactly what Walter had done, and Davis did not pursue it, but Davis's visit took place only four days after Walter had delivered his two takeover documents.

Walter was not discouraged. He waited until February, then tried again. This time he was even more forceful. He brought another draft to Floyd, in which Floyd was to tell Meigs that "the interests of Government require" that he devote his full attention to the Washington Aqueduct. "It has been deemed expedient to relieve you" of all responsibility for the Capitol Extension, the Post Office Extension, and the new Dome, the draft continued, "and to place the same under the immediate control of the Architect, whose sole duty it will be hereafter to report directly to this Department."[46] This order, if Floyd had signed it, would have banished Meigs from the Capitol altogether.

And still nothing happened. Meigs heard almost daily rumors about Walter's maneuvers, but he could confirm nothing. Davis, Pearce, and others reported holding conversations with Buchanan and Floyd to defend Meigs, but the tribulations of the Capitol Extension had no resonance in the White House. As Davis's December meeting with Buchanan showed, the president's last briefing about Meigs's affairs appeared to have occurred during the Lauman group controversy the previous summer.

By February 26, Walter's latest surge of euphoria had dissipated as he finally began to realize that he had stuck his neck out too far and too early and now risked beheading. "I am completely worried out with the continued unpleasantness of my position and the prospect of things never being any better," he wrote in a letter to Rice. But nothing will happen for months, he concluded. "The cabinet will not act in any way until the Kansas question is settled."[47]

Walter was right. Buchanan, as a result of his own ineptitude and that of his predecessor, had little time for the Capitol because he was trying desperately to force-feed an unpopular and misguided statehood policy to the settlers in Kansas and to get his allies in Congress to vote for it. He had started down this path during his inaugural address in March 1857, seeking to end the "long agitation" over slavery by having the federal government ensure "every resident inhabitant the free and independent expression of his opinion by his vote." This would be simple, he said, for "nothing can be fairer than to leave the people . . . to decide their own destiny for themselves."[48] Settlers would vote on whether to have slavery in Kansas or not, and that would be the end of it. The Dred Scott decision was supposed to depoliticize the slavery question even further.

None of this worked out. Dred Scott enraged the North generally and left the factions in Kansas more polarized than before. Then, on June 15, 1857, Kansas held elections for a constitutional convention, which free-staters boycotted, fearing another round of fraudulent balloting. As a consequence, the proslavery settlers won a huge majority of the convention seats. This ensured that the constituent assembly, when it sat in September, would not be representative of the territory's overwhelmingly free-state population, although it had been legally elected.[49]

After this inauspicious beginning, Buchanan's statehood initiative probably should have been scrapped, but Kansans—and the president—pressed on. The convention met for a few days in the town of Lecompton, Kansas, in early September, then adjourned for a month while Kansas held more elections—this time for a new territorial government. The free-staters participated in this one, but the voting in early October at first looked like a close win for the proslavery forces. Then the territorial governor found that returns from a town near the Missouri border included a fifty-foot-long list of voter names written in the same hand and apparently lifted in its entirety from a directory of residents of the city of Cincinnati, Ohio. The Kansas governor voided these results and other fraudulent returns, thus giving the free-staters control of the incoming legislature.[50]

So when the Lecompton convention resumed on October 19, Kansas had a free-state government and a proslavery constituent assembly. The question facing the convention was whether to submit their proslavery draft constitution to a referendum by the voters or simply send it to Washington. The assembly wanted nothing to do with an up-or-down referendum, but agreed to a compromise. Kansans on December 21 would vote on the constitution's slavery provisions alone. If voters rejected them, slavery would be prohibited in Kansas, but slaves already in the territory would remain slaves and would be allowed to stay in the state. And one other thing: the referendum would be supervised by the convention president. The choice would be between unrestricted slavery and some slavery. Buchanan supported both the referendum and the Lecompton constitution.[51]

Things simply got worse. The free-staters boycotted the referendum, and the slavery provisions were approved by a vote of 6,266–567. The Lecompton constitution—with no restrictions on slavery—was on its way to Washington. Then, on January 4, 1858, the free-staters held their own, unauthorized referendum. "No constitution" got 10,226 votes, and the Lecompton constitution, with or without slavery provisions, got 162.[52]

Buchanan's situation was now hopeless. The Lecompton constitution was a patently absurd document that did not reflect the views of the vast majority of Kansans. Buchanan, however, had endorsed it, and he had no legal reason to disallow it since no laws had been broken in drafting it. Furthermore, if he rejected it, he would alienate the entire southern wing of the Democratic Party, which, by the end of 1857, was about all the Democrats there were. Pierce may have been a doughface by choice. Buchanan had no other option.[53]

Northern Democrats were in deep trouble. Stephen A. Douglas, Buchanan's chief rival as party kingpin, had a tough Senate reelection campaign in 1858 and needed to get away from Lecompton; otherwise Illinois might get rid of him, making his expected bid for the presidency in 1860 all but impossible. When Douglas visited Buchanan on December 3, 1857, to explain why he would not support Lecompton, the meeting did not go well. Buchanan had decided to make the Lecompton constitution a test of party loyalty, and at one point he apparently told Douglas that he, like Andrew Jackson, would destroy any Democrat who decided to oppose a Democratic president on an issue of such signal importance. To which Douglas delivered his storied rejoinder: "General Jackson is dead."[54]

Yet Buchanan persisted. On February 2, 1858, he sent the Lecompton constitution to both houses of Congress along with a message urging its adoption. He expected to win in the Senate, where Democrats enjoyed a solid majority, but in the House he needed 118 votes and could count perhaps 100. He would have to find the rest with patronage and threats.[55]

The Meigs-Walter altered-drawings affair came to light right in the middle of all this. Both men expected their battle to be resolved in favor of one or the other, but Buchanan and Floyd had Kansas to think about. This was probably a blessing for both Meigs and Walter, for different reasons. Walter had made the mistake of trying for a knockout before Floyd was ready to help him. He had overreached and needed to lie low for a while. The Lecompton debate allowed him to fade back into the shadows.

For Meigs, no news would turn out to be good news. He had asked the administration to choose between him and Walter, and he thought Buchanan would choose him because he had Davis's support. This was not necessarily a sound assessment. Davis was a staunch supporter of Lecompton, and Buchanan certainly needed all the help he could get. Alienating him on a trivial matter like the Capitol Extension would make no sense. But Floyd was one of Buchanan's most loyal subordinates and would be humiliated, and perhaps even have to resign, if Buchanan dipped his fingers into the Capitol mess. Buchanan undoubtedly did not want to make a decision about Meigs and Walter, and Lecompton gave him an excellent reason to duck it.

The Lecompton debate immediately turned nasty. House members baptized their new chamber with its first dustup a little after midnight on February 6, 1858, during an all-night session.

Pennsylvania Republican Galusha A. Grow stood up on the Democratic side of the chamber to lodge an objection. South Carolina Democrat Laurence M. Keitt, Preston Brooks's accomplice during the Sumner attack, yelled at Grow to "return to your own side of the Hall." There are many versions of what was said next, but all agree that Grow then told Keitt something to the effect that "every man has a right to stand where he pleases." Keitt then called Grow a "black Republican puppy." To which Grow retorted, according to the journalist Benjamin Perley Poore, "Never mind. I shall occupy such place in this Hall as I please, and no negro-driver shall crack his whip over me."

Grow and Keitt rushed at each other, prompting about two dozen members, equally divided between North and South, to join the melee. Somebody—not Grow, according to Poore—knocked Keitt down, and the fighting became even more frenzied. Wisconsin Republican Cadwallader C. Washburn seized Mississippi Democrat William Barksdale by the hair and swung his fist, only to have Barksdale's wig come off in his hand. This caused the free-for-all to dissolve into gales of laughter, prolonged in part, Poore said, because Barksdale, "in the excitement of the occasion," put his wig back on "wrong-side foremost."[56]

The next day, it was the turn of the Senate, still meeting in the old chamber where Foote had pulled a gun on Benton during the 1850 compromise debate. Davis took Maine Republican William Pitt Fessenden to

The first brawl in the new House of Representatives occurred only two months after its grand opening. More than two dozen members from free and slave states joined in a general melee on February 6, 1858, during debate over the future of Kansas. (Library of Congress)

task for scoffing at southern threats to secede if Lecompton failed to pass. Instead of displaying bombast and barroom brawl, Davis, true to form, was icily threatening and deliberately insulting. He decried the "miserable slang" that Fessenden had used to describe Buchanan, and Fessenden's "malignant purposes" in denouncing "southern institutions." Fessenden, he suggested, was "a man who [so] little regards the union" that he would "perpetuate a joke on the hazards of its dissolution." An unfazed Fessenden, just as hardheaded as Davis, mounted a spirited counterattack, earning a draw. It was only a preliminary skirmish, but more fireworks were to come.[57]

Davis missed most of them. A few days after his exchange with Fes-

senden, he was stricken with a sudden and violent attack of facial neuralgia. He was totally incapacitated for nearly two months and would be
unable to participate meaningfully in the Lecompton debate, showing up
only to vote. So for Meigs, as for Walter, the Lecompton debate would
keep Buchanan and Floyd occupied, buying Meigs some time until Davis
returned.

If he returned. "Mr. Davis has been dangerously sick," Meigs wrote in
his diary on February 25. "They were much alarmed about him. He is now
said to be a little better. I do hope and trust that his life will be spared."
Davis, he continued, "is a valuable man," and not only to Meigs. Davis
"has learned by experience to know that the interest of this country, both
South and North, is union, and can do much towards softening the feeling
which now looks towards disunion among Southern men."[58] Many things
would happen to make Meigs repudiate these words.

15

MEIGS UNDER SIEGE

As winter changed to spring in early 1858, Captain Montgomery C. Meigs found himself fighting a multi-front war. He was fending off challenges not only from Thomas Walter but also from would-be Aqueduct and Post Office contractors, aggrieved American artists who had missed out on jobs at the new Capitol, and congressmen upset at the bold colors and elaborate decoration in the new House. They wanted, yet again, to free the Capitol from "military rule."

What allies Meigs had in Congress were preoccupied with the rancorous debate over Kansas and the Lecompton constitution. And once that was over, Congress would adjourn and members would go home for the long summer, leaving Meigs even more at the mercy of his boss, Secretary of War John B. Floyd, who was shifting from petulant irritation toward active opposition. Meigs was forced to focus on his own survival.

Walter, frustrated by failed plots to oust Meigs, had only become more intransigent. Late in January, as part of their bitter exchanges over the altered Capitol drawings, Walter told Meigs in a letter that he had never been his assistant but was "always in full and independent charge" of Capitol architecture. Meigs, Walter said, "was appointed for the purpose of relieving him from certain onerous [administrative] duties."[1]

After that, Walter simply refused to let Meigs have any more drawings, and he moved his office, draftsmen, and designs to rooms on the third floor of the old Capitol, while Meigs was now quartered in new offices two blocks from the Capitol grounds. On March 4, Meigs found that Walter had been giving foremen and artisans working drawings without first getting them signed by Meigs.[2] And on March 12, Walter wrote what may have been his first letter ever to Brumidi, probably Meigs's most faithful employee, telling him to stop gilding the galleries of the new Senate chamber because he was ruining the architectural montage: "You will confer with me before proceeding any further," he wrote.[3]

Meigs was predictably enraged by all this. Complaints to Walter availed him nothing, and he had no expectation of help from Floyd, whom he now regarded as an unequivocal Walter supporter. So he wrote to Buchanan directly. The work could no longer "be properly carried on by me" unless Walter followed orders, he said. He told Buchanan about Walter's refusal to move to the project office and about Meigs's demands for drawings and Walter's refusal to hand them over. "He leaves my letters unanswered," Meigs continued, "and violates rules which have been in force ever since I have been in charge of the work." Walter "is no longer of any assistance to me," and Meigs could no longer "continue to give orders to be disobeyed." He concluded: "I must therefore wait your decision."[4]

There was no decision. Even in less complicated times than 1858, the idea that the president of the United States would be called upon by an Army captain to referee such a dispute must have seemed the ultimate in petty distraction. But it would not be the last time that either Meigs or Walter would importune Buchanan. In fact, officials at the highest levels of government—Floyd and Senators Davis, Pearce, and Bigler, among others—would repeatedly lay the Meigs-Walter feud on Buchanan's desk in hopes that the man Walter described with false affection as "the old gentleman" might make up his mind.

Whereas Walter began to succumb to a mix of frustration and resignation, Meigs was learning how to cope. He could not bully or intimidate Walter, but by the spring of 1858 he had learned to restrain himself so that his tantrums had subsided into simmering but generally well-controlled rage. He had been slow to grasp the dangers that a new administration posed for a low-level appointee like himself, but he was fully aware of them now.

He had also come to recognize that inertia could be the bureaucrat's best friend. If nothing else worked, he was prepared to outlast Walter—and Buchanan, and Floyd, if it came to that. To this end he was scrupulously careful not to compromise his greatest strength: he had done nothing wrong. If Buchanan and Floyd were running an honest administration, they had no reason to get rid of him. If they did so without a reason, they would have to justify it to Congress; and Meigs and, he hoped, Davis would make sure that they had a very hard time.

Meigs paid meticulous attention to the written record, and any time Floyd wanted him to do something questionable, he made sure that Floyd put it on paper. Integrity was part of Meigs's makeup, but in a protracted struggle like the one at hand, it was also a weapon. Meigs would do Floyd no favors. If Floyd wanted Meigs to get rid of a Know-Nothing watchman, fire a disobedient engineer, or hand over Aqueduct construction to a single bidder, Meigs demanded that Floyd send him an order in writing, and he made sure that Floyd knew—in writing—when Meigs disagreed with him. In November 1858, a sympathetic contractor confirmed to Meigs that Floyd had been trying to award the Aqueduct contract to the Philadelphia-based Lauman group, but could not fix it because Meigs refused to go along. Floyd told the contractor that Meigs "was so damned honest" that he could find nothing to use for leverage.[5]

But Floyd never stopped trying. During the winter of 1858, Floyd asked Meigs to hire pet contractors to lay pipe for the Aqueduct and to provide lumber and groceries and other consumables for the project. Next, Meigs learned that his Floyd-appointed assistant was seeking to displace him at a salary of $6,000 per year, guaranteed for life.[6] When none of these schemes bore fruit, Floyd on January 25, 1858, told Meigs to bid the Aqueduct contracts again in order to give his friends another shot at the pot of gold.[7]

Perhaps the most bitter Meigs-Floyd face-off was over the ventilation contract for the new Post Office Extension. It started in late 1857, when Charles Robinson, a Virginia dentist, would-be contractor, and Floyd crony, wrote a letter to Meigs seeking to install heating and ventilation at the Post Office. He proposed to build the system on the same terms as those prescribed for the Capitol Extension, and he suggested peremptorily that Meigs forward his letter "immediately to the Secretary of War." Even before Meigs could respond, Robinson passed the same proposal straight to Floyd, and three days after that, Floyd instructed Meigs to award the contract to Robinson.[8]

Meigs was not amused. He had planned to use the Capitol's heating and ventilation contractors, Nason & Dodge of New York, to do the Post Office. The firm had earned Meigs's respect for its innovation and creativity, and it "had the highest reputation in the country," he told Floyd in a letter. Also, Joseph Nason, like Brumidi and Provest, the marble finisher, had become one of a handful of trusted associates whom Meigs consulted regularly when he needed advice. Nason, in short, was a professional used to handling one-of-a-kind jobs. Floyd insulted Meigs's intelligence if he thought Robinson could compete.[9]

Floyd was upset by Meigs's resistance, so he simply swapped the front man, telling Meigs that Robinson had planned to get a Baltimore firm, Lapsley & Thomas, to actually do the work, and ordering Meigs to give the contract to them directly. With direct orders in hand, Meigs could stall no longer. On March 10, he notified Lapsley & Thomas that they were in and told Nason & Dodge they were out.[10] On July 8, Meigs received a telegram from New York congressman Dan Sickles, who suspected that Nason & Dodge—his constituents—had gotten a raw deal. He planned to ask for an investigation.[11] The Post Office heating and ventilation system would remain the subject of endless wrangling between Meigs and the War Department for the next eighteen months, and it would play a pivotal role in bringing the Meigs-Walter dispute to a close.

By the beginning of spring 1858, Meigs and Walter had reached an impasse. Walter refused to give up his drawings, and Meigs refused to examine them in Walter's renegade headquarters. Meigs regarded the drawings as stolen government property, and he maintained that by visiting Walter's "cockloft" office on the third floor of the old Capitol he would legitimize both the theft and Walter's unauthorized move. Instead, he demanded that Walter surrender to him all the drawings and plans, without exception. Once that had been accomplished, he told Walter in a letter, "such drawings as may be necessary to enable you to prepare further drawings of work will be again placed in your hands."[12]

The biggest loser in the dispute was the Capitol. By the middle of spring, the cast-iron columns of the Dome peristyle had been set and the Dome's inner brick wall had been raised to the same level. The next step, however, was to begin building the Dome proper, and that would proceed at a snail's pace unless Walter turned over the working drawings, which, of course, he was unwilling to do. Neither would budge.

Floyd refused to interfere. The "skill and taste of Mr. Walter could not be spared," he told Meigs during a contentious two-hour meeting in September, and if Walter and Meigs could not get along, that was Meigs's problem.[13] A month later, Floyd wrote Meigs a brief note telling him that if he wanted drawings, he should "call upon" Walter to get them.[14] If Floyd could not find a reason to fire Meigs, maybe he could force him to quit. Meigs, in a letter, promptly "called on" Walter to hand over the drawings. Walter refused.

Meigs's chief task at the Capitol Extension in 1858 was to finish the new Senate chamber in time for the next session of Congress in December. There were dozens of tasks to complete, and designs had already been prepared for many of them. Meigs mustered his corps of decorators, artists, and finishers for jobs ranging from installing decorative bronze railings on the stairways to choosing the carpet and upholstering the seats in the Senate visitors' gallery.

And for Constantino Brumidi, 1858 was to be a spectacular year. Designs that Brumidi had proposed for the new Senate in some cases more than two years earlier began to take shape. He started work on the first floor of the new Senate on the Military Affairs Committee Room—Davis's committee—and also began decorating the Senate Library and the Senate Receiving Room, both on the second floor.

Brumidi's second room, following his success with Cincinnatus in the House, was that of the Senate Naval Affairs Committee, which he had begun in 1856. Within the overall design—in the Pompeian style— Brumidi had painted eight gods and goddesses in fresco for the ceiling and used oil paint for maidens on the wall panels.[15] The room was overwhelming, ablaze with bold colors and embellished with a profusion of false columns and other trompes l'oeil. Once the art was finished in midyear, Meigs, like a proud father, posted a sign inside. "The decorative paintings of this room are a specimen of the manner in which the ancient Greeks and Romans ornamented their splendid buildings," the note said. "*America*, with the sea divinities, are painted on the ceiling in real fresco."[16]

Brumidi's tour de force for 1858, however, was the network of first-floor Senate hallways that would come to be known as the Brumidi Corridors. The six passages were divided into bays—piers and arches that leaped upward from one side of the corridor, across the vaulted ceilings, and down to finish on the opposite side. They were decorated in symmetrical patterns, but these were interspersed with paintings, trompe l'oeil moldings and sculptures, and geometrical and natural designs of all kinds. Brumidi laid out the general plan, then he and others began to fill in the blank spaces. The corridors would eventually depict one hundred different species of birds.[17] There were vines, mice and squirrels, gods and goddesses, shields and weapons, the signs of the zodiac, and, eventually, portraits of Columbus, Franklin, Adams, Jay, Monroe, and Robert Fulton, among many others.

The Brumidi Corridors, U.S. Senate wing, first floor. Brumidi provided the original design and worked on the corridors—among other projects—for the last twenty years of his life. Many other artists added decorations or painted lunettes over the following hundred-plus years. (Architect of the Capitol)

Besides Brumidi's montage of panels, faux moldings, and trompe l'oeil "relief sculpture," the corridors also featured hundreds of detail patterns and images such as this eagle with the American shield. (Architect of the Capitol)

What made this explosion of Senate artwork still more remarkable was that it took place even as Meigs was moving to meet another wave of attacks from Congress over precisely this work. Meigs got his first whiff of trouble in early February when Representative George Taylor, an obscure first-termer from New York, introduced a cryptic bill to create a "commission" to finish the Capitol.[18] This had echoes of the efforts during the "military rule" dispute to push Meigs off the project, but whatever its purpose, Meigs was sure that "someone" other than Taylor was behind it. He suspected that Walter or Floyd was trying to do him mischief.[19]

Meigs decided to ignore the bill. He was convinced that the new House was a success, especially after several members told him that they liked it better once they got used to it. So confident was Meigs of the House's utility and beauty that he sent packets of commemorative photographs to Buchanan, Floyd, and former president Millard Fillmore. He also sent photos to be archived at West Point and at New York's Astor Library. He did not convey, either in his diary or in his letters, any hesitation or doubt about sending Brumidi to paint the Senate corridors in brilliant primary colors. And although some House members may have denounced the artwork, Meigs probably felt safe in disdaining these complaints as harmless political pop-offs. The massive numbers of visitors to the House Agriculture Committee Room had told him that the "higher style" he and Davis had chosen for the Capitol was a crowd-pleaser.

It was only in midspring 1858 that Meigs may have realized his haste in dismissing the threat of Taylor and his commission. Late in April, more than two months after the last round of member complaints about the new House had died down, the *New York Express* suddenly printed a long, unflattering appraisal of the chamber as "not much superior to many concert or lecture rooms" built "in provincial towns of no greater importance than Rochester, Syracuse, Buffalo or Chicago." And "far more to be condemned," the *Express* continued, "not a single American artist has been employed to fill the panels, still vacant, with appropriate painting." The décor, the *Express* concluded, felt "tawdry," like a Philadelphia saloon.[20]

The *Express* followed this salvo with a May 1 column signed by "Americus" and listing 74 artists and painters doing ornamental and decorative work for the Capitol, with "but 12 that can, by possibility, be pleaded as Americans."[21]

Then, on May 17, the *New York Tribune* issued a long screed in the same vein. The "best artists in the country" had "asked to be employed upon the Capitol," the *Tribune* said, but "without an exception, their applications have been rejected." Instead, the work was being supervised by "an Italian whose reputation is little better than that of a successful scene painter, and who employs under him a crowd of 60 or 70 foreign painters, chief among them Italians and Frenchmen." While acknowledging the engineering accomplishments and overall stewardship of the Capitol, the newspaper said, the *Tribune* blamed Meigs for hiring this "crowd of needy foreigners."[22]

On March 23, the Senate, as expected, voted 33–25 to grant statehood to Kansas under the Lecompton constitution. But despite months of arm-twisting and patronage promises, Buchanan could not get Lecompton through the House. On April 1, the House effectively killed it, passing, by a vote of 120–112, a substitute bill giving Kansans another opportunity to approve the constitution before it became law. As long as legitimate voters voted, and the votes were properly counted, such a "resubmission" virtually guaranteed that Lecompton would be rejected. The initiative was dead unless the administration and its congressional allies could put together some sort of a compromise that both the Senate and House would support. The deadlock lingered on Capitol Hill for another pressure-filled month of threats and sectional rage.

Eventually lawmakers produced the compromise, with House conferee William H. English, a Buchanan Democrat from an antislavery district in Indiana, as the leading author.[23] The "English Bill," as it came to be known, contrived to resubmit the Lecompton constitution to Kansans on a technicality. The territorial legislature, in writing Lecompton, had requested more than 23 million acres of government land—more than six times what new states were usually allotted. The English Bill cut the grant sharply, thus requiring the constitution to be revoted. An affirmative vote would admit Kansas as a state with less government land, but with the Lecompton constitution otherwise intact. A negative vote would say nothing about slavery but would kill Lecompton and leave Kansas as a territory until some future time. This solution gave Buchanan's southern friends a face-saving way to lose in Kansas without compromising their stance on slavery. On April 30, the bill passed both houses of Congress: the Senate voted 31–22, the House 112–103. On August 2, Kansans held an uncorrupted referendum on the land grant and rejected the Lecompton constitution by a vote of 11,300–1,788. Kansas would remain a territory.

Lecompton marked the first time the South had ever lost a major vote on slavery.[24] This did not augur well for Congress's slave-state minority, whose strength—especially in the House—was eroding steadily as immigrants swelled the northern population. Worse, through his take-no-prisoners approach to Lecompton, Buchanan had completed the sectional sundering of the Democratic Party, the only strong national political force in the country. He had given northern Democrats two unpalatable choices: oppose the constitution and be cast into the political wilderness by the Buchanan administration and the party's dominant southern wing, or support Lecompton and risk annihilation in the November elections. Both of these outcomes came to pass. Stephen A. Douglas, who led the apostates, also happened to be the party's leading presidential possibility for 1860, and the best, and perhaps only, hope the Democrats had of finding a leader who could keep the nation from coming completely unglued. But the South hated him after Lecompton.

Douglas's defection paid off in the short term when he won reelection in a closely contested race against Abraham Lincoln, a Republican lawyer from Springfield. But the Democrats took a fearful beating in the House, where they lost 21 seats in the North and 34 seats overall. They held their majority in the Senate, but the House in 1859 would have a Republican plurality. And there were no Republicans from the south in either house of Congress. The country was so badly divided that reconciliation was beginning to look impossible.

On May 17, more than one hundred American artists sent a petition to both houses of Congress asking that they be allowed to form an "art commission" to oversee the decoration of "the noble structures now being reared by the nation for the nation's use." The commission was to be composed of "those designated by the united voice of American artists" and would serve as "channels for the distribution of all appropriations to be made by Congress for art purposes."[25]

This, then, was the punch line of all the murmurings about art over the winter and early spring. There was no Floyd-Walter cabal. Rather, it was a maneuver by American artists—frequently snubbed or ignored by Meigs during the past few years—to take control of the Capitol artwork. The petitioners, unable to change Meigs's opinion of their own skills and talents, decided to see if they could simply shove Meigs out of the way.

The power struggle that ensued benefited no one. Meigs did not have money to spend on "paintings" or "statues" per se, and thus no commissions to offer for individual works. What he had decided to do, and what he had gotten away with up to now, was to hire decorative and ornamental artists and craftsmen to finish the Capitol on a day's-work basis, paying them out of annual appropriations in much the same way he would pay housepainters. If the hired hands painted beautiful frescoes and elegant murals, that was well within his mandate, he reasoned. The walls had to be painted with something. Rogers's doors and Crawford's sculpture were also part of the building and thus subject to the same rules.

Whenever someone applied to Meigs for a commission to produce a discrete work of art, Meigs for the most part told the aspirant to seek an appropriation from Congress. This is what Hiram Powers had done, and Powers, with his money in hand, was free to carve a statue of anything Congress would accept. What he could not do, without Meigs's permission, was put a statue on top of the new Dome. Meigs considered the statue to be part of the structure of the Capitol, and that was his domain.

The artists were, however, correct in their view that Meigs, in building the new Capitol, had not always been helpful in advancing the cause of American art. This was not due to a failure of patriotism. Meigs had consistently sought the best art available—that Congress would pay for. This had led him to hire American sculptors exclusively to do the most important jobs in the new Capitol. And he had also tried to hire Americans to help with the decorative and ornamental work, but few were qualified. By comparison, Meigs's immigrants worked cheaply, and they knew what they were doing.

Where Meigs had left himself vulnerable was in not hiring American portrait and historical painters. Quite simply, Meigs hardly ever found one that he liked. When he did—as in the case of James Walker and *Storming of Chapultepec*—he was willing to have the artist paint a large canvas and willing to call the work "decoration" and pay for it out of his appropriation. But for the most part, as the petitioners knew, the Capitol's frescoes and murals, including those with American themes, were being painted by immigrants, and there were many people in Congress who resented it.

This was the opening the artists hoped to exploit. Still, they had little to gain, since Meigs had no power to hire them for the jobs they coveted—painting and sculpting individual works of display art. The artists did manage, however, to create more trouble for Meigs by rekindling old grudges and reviving old questions about his taste, his arbitrary decisions, and military rule. The artists had primed Congress's ill will with sneering newspaper polemics about Meigs's judgment and Brumidi's brothel-style décor. Now, with the petition, they had given Congress a vehicle for action.

It was not long in coming. On May 19, during debate on the upcoming year's Capitol Extension appropriation, Illinois Republican Owen Lovejoy summed up congressional resentment toward Meigs in a few nasty sentences: "If you want a monument of military architecture, look at the meretricious and garish gilding of these walls." The House Agriculture Committee Room, he said, should have had "some paintings that would represent the agriculture of the present time." Instead, the painters had chosen Putnam, "a revolutionary reminiscence," and Cincinnatus, while overhead "we have pictures of Bacchus, Ceres, and so on, surrounded with cupids, cherubs, &c., to the end of heathen mythology."[26]

With this as an introduction, American Party representative Humphrey Marshall of Kentucky then offered an amendment to the appropriation to create a presidentially appointed art commission. No part of the Capitol appropriation would be spent "upon the embellishment or decoration of the Capitol Extension, either by painting or sculpture, in the panels or niches of the Senate or House, or in the pediments of the porticoes, or in the finish of the halls, committee rooms, or passages," unless the expenditure was approved by a commission, appointed by the president and "composed of three distinguished artists, citizens of the United States," who would choose "such designs as shall be adopted for the embellishment of the Capitol Extension."[27] A few days later, Marshall succeeded in adding this measure as a "proviso" to the regular Capitol appropriation.

Meigs immediately sought out Marshall, who assured him that his purpose was not to get Meigs fired.[28] Next, on May 24, he met with New York representative George Taylor and learned that Taylor's February legislation, as Meigs suspected, had inspired the Marshall proviso. He also learned that Taylor was a great friend of the New York sculptor Henry Kirke Brown, whose proposal for a House pediment sculpture had been turned down by Meigs in 1856.[29] The other ringleader in the commission proposal was Horatio Stone, whom Meigs categorically disdained as someone "who calls himself a sculptor."[30] Like disappointed contractors, the spurned artists were now seeking revenge.

The next thing Meigs did on May 24 was prepare a substitute for Marshall's proviso. Instead of prohibiting Meigs from decorating anything in the Capitol without the art commission's permission, Meigs asked Congress to appropriate $1 million for the Capitol Extension, no strings attached, and a further $50,000 with which the Joint Library Committee of Congress would buy individual paintings and sculpture for the Capitol. This would kill the commission, yet give the artists what they appeared to want. Meigs sent copies of the substitute to his best friends in the Senate—Pearce, Seward, and, of course, Davis, who had returned full time to the Senate three weeks earlier and was steadily regaining strength. He asked Davis to introduce the substitute on the Senate floor, noting that an undoctored Marshall proviso "would be held to be a censure upon me."[31]

Davis embraced his assignment. On May 28 he began a carefully choreographed floor procedure designed to kill the commission with kindness. His accomplices were Pearce, Seward, and possibly Robert M. T. Hunter. The Senate version of the Capitol appropriation asked for $750,000 for the Capitol Extension, with the Marshall proviso as a rider. Davis on the Senate floor asked for $1,185,183.34, which he described as the exact sum needed both "for the completion" of the Capitol Extension and for a $50,000 art fund for works to be commissioned by the Library Committee.

Then Hunter, who as Finance Committee chairman had written the Senate bill, said he would offer $750,000 for the Extension but did not want to go higher. He did not see any need at all to deal with the art money. Seward then suggested that the Senate split the legislation. Appropriate $1 million for the Extension, and deal with the art question separately. Davis agreed to this, and then Pearce also agreed.[32] The idea was to get Meigs his Extension money and leave the art commission to be funded at a later date, if at all.

Davis, anticipating dissent, also wanted to "correct an error which is creeping into the popular mind," he said. Works of art were not being bought for the Capitol with congressional appropriations, so there was no point in adopting the proviso, because there was no money for an art commission to spend. The frescoes, ornamentation, and sculpture were part of the construction.[33]

This was a risky point to make, because it unnecessarily raised the core complaint that many senators had with Meigs. Vermont Republican Jacob Collamer did not like the frescoes and the fancy ornamentation in the House chamber, he said, and wanted to know who had authorized them. Davis said the House Agriculture Committee Room had been decorated as a sample, and although Congress never offered an opinion "in any vote," he acknowledged, colleagues had shown their approval in "every other form."

Collamer was not mollified. He had no particular objection to appropriating money for painting, but what he really cared about was that the Senate not end up, like the House, as a "Joseph's coat."[34] Collamer's remarks had shifted the debate away from the Capitol appropriation, which was the object of Davis's opening gambit, and focused it on the far more contentious topic of Capitol décor and, by implication, Davis's and Meigs's stewardship of the project.

Davis, of course, could not let this challenge go unanswered, and so he began a mild argument with Collamer over artistic style. He was soon interrupted by Seward, however, who tried to put the debate back on track. Art, Seward said, "is a matter of taste, and our tastes differ naturally." The primary task in building the new House was to create a chamber in which members could hear each other, he continued, and the outcome was an unqualified success. Once the main purpose was accomplished, he said, something had to be put on the ceiling and the walls, and "the process of embellishment" had worked wonderfully—even though that was just his opinion.[35]

Then Sam Houston rose. He and Davis had never been friends, and Houston had a gift for provoking Davis, which, on this occasion, he seemed fiendishly eager to do. He asked first "who are the sculptors that are employed in the shanties out there," referring to the stonemasons who were carving Crawford's marble pediment figures from the plaster models Crawford had sent from Italy. Houston had seen the "goddess Liberty" (whose actual name was *America*), and although he was no expert, he thought she was "in anguish—drawn back in the most ungraceful and ungainly attitude for a lady." This drew a laugh. "It appears to be in torment; and had it been physical, I should have imagined that it really had a boil under the arm." More laughter. Furthermore, instead of bare feet with sandals, the figure wore "a very formidable pair of russet brogans." The Indian mother, he added, "has a little papoose in her arms, and its little head is sticking out like a terrapin's." Still more laughter. The "little neck, without the least curve or grace, is very stiff, like an apple on a stick."[36]

Houston continued in the same vein, to the amusement of his colleagues. Then Davis, nasty and sneering, rose in rebuttal. The figures described by Houston were pediment components, not stand-alone statues.

Indian mother and child on the Senate East Portico pediment. Crawford's shortcomings in his portrayal of Indians earned guffaws in the Senate and ridicule from Senator Sam Houston, who described the child's head as "an apple on a stick." (Architect of the Capitol)

Houston did not know this, and "turned his imagination loose." And had he known the figures were sculpted by Crawford, an American, he never would have criticized them.

Houston, undaunted, then wondered "how any man, unless he was under the influence of a diseased brain, could ever have fancied that a pair of brogans were becoming, and incorporated necessarily with heathen mythology."

Houston's "wit is out of place," Davis retorted, "particularly as it is practiced on a dead artist of such eminent character." Houston, still unruffled, said he was criticizing the sculpture, not the artist.

The figures were not, Davis continued, from heathen mythology.

What about the goddess of Liberty? Houston asked.

"You did not even stop to learn the name of the thing, or the distance at which it was to be viewed," Davis replied, now thoroughly enraged.

Houston, clearly thrilled with the setup lines Davis was feeding him, said he was not interested in learning about it: "I was satisfied that it was some unfortunate lady that had fallen into great bodily agony," he said. "I should like to know what lady has commended herself to the consideration of the Government, in a national point of view . . . that has worn brogan shoes."[37]

Davis had lost his focus along with his temper, and he apparently realized it, for he let Houston ramble on for a while to the continued amusement of his colleagues. Eventually Hunter intervened, read Davis's amendment asking for $1,185,183.34, and said he would not support it. Davis lost on a close vote. Then Seward suggested that the Senate vote on the $750,000 without the art commission proviso. Davis and Pearce quickly agreed, and the proviso, by acclamation, was dropped altogether. The $750,000 appropriation passed a few days later. This had probably been Davis's original intention, and it would have been consummated much more quickly if he had not let Houston sidetrack him. But in the end he had gotten Meigs a victory in the first round. Now it was the House's turn.

Davis at this point in his congressional career was finding himself in an increasingly awkward position. The Senate, as far back as 1850, had regarded him as a staunch defender of slavery and southern rights, probably willing to dissolve the union in order to protect his beloved Mississippi. This conviction had inevitably grown as the decade progressed, for the Senate, like the rest of the country, had become increasingly polarized. Northerners suspected that Davis wanted to increase the size of the regular army so Buchanan's doughface administration could use troops to help proslavery settlers in Kansas. What the northerners had forgotten was that Davis had long advocated a larger army, believing it necessary for a growing and powerful nation.

In fact, in the late 1850s, despite the increasing antipathy between North and South, Davis's unionist leanings were as strong as ever. Another of his particular concerns was the curriculum at his alma mater, West Point, and in 1857 he had written Buchanan about his wish to improve cadet education in traditional drawing room pursuits such as writing, literature, languages, and the classics. "To train the men who are at the head of armies to maintain the honor of our flag, and in all circumstances to uphold the Constitution," he wrote Buchanan, "requires a man above sectional prejudices, and intellectually superior to fanaticism."[38] It was this same impulse that drove Davis to champion a larger and more imposing U.S. Capitol.

But late the same year, in a remarkable speech in Mississippi, Davis switched gears completely. He spoke about how the South had purged itself of soft-liners, who had either headed north or come back to the southern fold after deciding that slavery was a "positive good." What was needed now, he continued, was to "build up on a durable basis the independence of the South." Southerners should promote home education and encourage the establishment of more southern schools equipped with southern-trained teachers, and textbooks written by "competent southern men." If successful, "the south might avoid the abolition position introduced through this channel."[39] The South, he recognized with what could almost be characterized as despair, was isolated, backward, and dependent on the industry and erudition of its sworn enemies. The solution that would allow the South to maintain its individuality and its way of life was to isolate itself even further—or perhaps become independent. So much for rising "above sectional prejudices."

And by 1858 he was hearing from other southerners with even more radical ideas. In the middle of his illness in April, with the Lecompton controversy at its height, he received a "Dear Jeff" letter from an old West Point colleague. "You and I have long been apart," the letter said. *"The day may not be far off when we shall be brought together in the effort to throw back the threatened aggressions of those who assail us, under the idea that the South is weak."* Circumstances were worsening, the letter continued, but *"I do not despair* of seeing the Southern people yet awakening to the necessity of uniting in a more compact alliance, making them *more to be appreciated as friends—more to be dreaded as foes."*[40]

Back in the days when Davis had first sworn fealty to both Jackson and Calhoun, the distinction between unionism and states' rights had been blurry enough to accommodate two kinds of patriotism. But now this comfortable gray area had become a bright line, increasingly impossible to straddle. Davis was smart enough to know that his own stands—on Kansas-Nebraska and Lecompton—had contributed to the political segregation that was now denying him the privilege of living in two worlds. He would have to choose, and his choice would matter, because he had become that important. With these pressures increasing almost daily, it is not surprising that Davis in 1858 would undergo another epic bout of neuralgia, or allow Houston to provoke him over a trivial matter.

And only ten days later he became embroiled in a ridiculous argument with a fellow southerner, Louisiana senator Judah P. Benjamin, over the purchase of breech-loading rifles for the Army. So incensed did Benjamin become at Davis's sneering replies to his questions that he challenged Davis to a duel. The next day, Davis, realizing what a fool he had made of himself, apologized profusely to both Benjamin and the rest of his colleagues.[41] He suffered during debates from "an infirmity" that caused him to get into "controversies which partake more or less of a personal character," he said in a surprising flash of self-knowledge. "I regret it whenever it occurs."[42] His icy reserve had deserted him once again, and he had lost control of himself. He was also losing control of his environment, and he knew that, too.

With only a few days left before adjournment, the House on June 7 finally debated the Capitol Extension appropriation, using the Senate's bill—without the art commission—as its starting point. Taylor immediately tried to add the commission proviso: "We have expended already thousands of dollars on this contemptible decoration," he said. "There is no economy, no taste; and we pay this enormous amount absolutely to disgrace the country." He said that while he had nothing against the architecture, he thought that "Captain Meigs is unfit to direct the decoration of this Capitol."[43] He made the House take three votes on different versions of the proviso, and lost by a wider margin each time, to his growing irritation. More versions were offered by other members, and these were voted down as well. Meigs could take heart. There was no interest whatsoever in turning the commission proviso into a referendum on his job performance.

Finally Humphrey Marshall, a cooler head than Taylor, stood up. He had "no desire, sir, to attack the engineer who has charge of this work," he said. "Although, I do not consider him a Phidias, or a Michael Angelo, I do not want to attack him." Marshall then offered his old, uncluttered proviso, and it was accepted.[44] The art commission was approved.

Four days later, after conferees had met, both houses of Congress passed the bill. Meigs got enough money to finish the Aqueduct and $710,000 for the Capitol Extension. The proviso had been watered down so that it did not interfere with decorative painting or structural sculpture. The only thing Meigs was going to lose was a bit of Walker's salary. "Upon the whole," Meigs concluded in his diary, "I have had a good measure of success."[45]

Otherwise 1858 continued to be a grim year for Meigs and for Walter. Their deadlock, if anything, worsened as time passed. Walter carefully watched Meigs's art troubles in Congress, figuring that the Marshall proviso, if successful, would require Meigs's resignation out of "common decency and self-respect."[46] When this failed to happen, Walter focused on Congress's impending adjournment. Once Davis and Meigs's other Senate friends were out of town, he decided, Floyd would take action. At the end of May, Witte, Walter's ally, told him that Floyd planned "to ship Meigs" the day after the gavel fell. "I believe the matter is already forced and his successor indicated," Walter said in a letter to Rice.[47]

But this prediction, like Witte's other insider plots, did not come true. Instead, by the time Congress adjourned on June 14, Floyd was the one in deep trouble with Congress. On June 1, the House came within five votes of censuring Floyd for his bumbling role in selling a frontier military reservation to a developer for a fraction of its value.[48] And in the Senate, Seward on June 11 opened the investigation into Floyd's decision to hand the Post Office heating contract to his crony Robinson, the Virginia dentist.[49] By June 22, Walter rated the chances of getting rid of Meigs as "very slim."[50]

The inactivity and suspense took their toll on Walter. He blamed the feud for the halting progress on the Extension and the virtual work stoppage on the Dome. On several occasions he appeared ready to resign. He lost faith in Floyd and lost confidence in his own tactics. In September he told Rice he would have to either hand over his drawings to Meigs or quit: "I cannot justify myself before Congress or before the world if I hold on any longer."[51]

Walter also had family problems. His third son, Horace, had secretly married a girl Walter regarded as little better than a streetwalker, and after a few months working for Rice in Philadelphia, he told Walter he wanted to come to Washington. Walter suggested instead that Horace dump the wife and go gold mining in Australia. He offered to pay his passage. A couple of months later Horace wrote again, this time talking about becoming a policeman and building a house. Walter reminded him that he did not know how to build a house and had no money. A month after that,

Horace was broke again. He decided to take the wife and join his elder brother, Robert, who was married and living on a farm in Indiana.[52]

This seemed at first a harmless idea. Robert had begun the year badly, going into debt as a storekeeper in partnership with his brother-in-law, but in February he had been appointed the local postmaster. This sinecure was about the best Robert could hope for, given his modest skills, but somehow it did not work out, and in a sharp reversal of fortunes he was arrested in August for grand larceny and sent to jail for two years. In the next few months Walter learned that Robert still owed $500 on the store, had a lien on his farmhouse, and had not paid back wages to a farmhand. He had turned to thievery to fix his financial woes and been caught burgling houses with a local gang. He had left his wife and daughter with nothing.[53] Horace and his wife, also penniless and friendless, arrived in Indiana at that moment. Horace sent a shipment of lumber to Rice's building supply business in Philadelphia, then asked Walter to send him some money so he could open a store. Walter agreed, but told him, "this must now stop."[54]

Meigs did not lose his job when Congress adjourned, but Floyd, even under duress, could still frustrate Meigs. In August, Floyd told Meigs that he categorically would not buy Italian marble for the monolithic columns, and he sent Meigs on a tour of American quarries to find out which of them could supply the needed monoliths. This "wild goose chase," as Meigs termed it in his diary, predictably yielded nothing.[55] Nonetheless Floyd instructed him to ask for bids. He got six offers, none of them particularly impressive. Only one bidder, John Connolly of Baltimore County, Maryland, could provide monoliths, Meigs noted, but Connolly's marble, although "similar in composition to the Lee marble," was "not equal to it in beauty."[56] On December 18, Meigs recommended to Floyd yet again that he buy Italian monoliths and urged him to deal with Rice and Heebner.[57]

As the end of the year approached with no discernable thaw in the Meigs-Walter dispute, Floyd finally began to understand that the Capitol project was grinding to a halt. Meigs referred to the effects of the feud in his annual report to Floyd in November. His men had spent much of 1858 decorating and finishing the interior of the new Senate wing—the chamber, committee rooms, and interior corridors—with the hope of a grand opening in December. This date was going to slip, however, because of his inability to coordinate with Walter, which caused delays "not necessary for me to recount. They were beyond my control."[58] As far as the Dome was concerned, serious work had virtually stopped after the peristyle columns were mounted: "I should be pleased to be able to report a greater progress in this work," Meigs wrote in a separate report, "but the want of cordial cooperation on the part of the architect associated with me has much interfered."[59] This nasty dig was either another effort by Meigs to ensure that his views were placed on the record, or it was simply spite, or perhaps both.

Cast-iron column on its way to be mounted on the Dome peristyle. Congress worried that the cast iron would be too heavy for the sandstone of the original Capitol to support. Meigs and Walter repeatedly explained that the iron weighed only a fraction of what a stone dome would weigh. (Architect of the Capitol)

Meigs was not telling Floyd anything he did not know. By the summer of 1858, Meigs and Walter were barely communicating at all. Both found it more convenient to use Floyd as an intermediary, a role that must have irritated Floyd beyond endurance. In September, Walter discovered that Meigs had submitted a design by Brumidi for the vice president's chair in the new Senate chamber. Walter, furious that Meigs had usurped his prerogatives with this "hideous affair," told Floyd he "was insulted by such proceedings, and could stand it no longer."[60] A week later Walter submitted his own designs for all the officers' chairs—vice president, clerks, and official reporters.

Floyd had no standing to make aesthetic judgments, but there were signs that he also genuinely liked Walter's work. He said as much to Meigs during a long meeting in mid-September, then told Meigs, as Meigs wrote in his diary, that Walter was "to make designs which I was to execute."[61] Floyd probably meant this remark simply as a hope that both Meigs and Walter should do what they did best, but Meigs suspected that Floyd had finally decided to make him Walter's subordinate. Meigs exploded like a rocket, penning a four-page screed to Floyd denouncing Walter.[62]

By this time, Floyd, after two years of incompetence, was finally trying to assert himself in a constructive way. A week after the furniture tantrums, he asked Colonel Robert E. Lee, a fellow Virginian and one of the most highly regarded officers in the Army, to form a "board" with another officer to "determine and approve the designs and plans which might be sent to them by Mr. Walter," and to direct Meigs "to execute them if approved," Meigs wrote in his diary. Lee, who knew Meigs and had worked with him two decades earlier on the Mississippi River, invited Meigs for a visit at his War Department offices, where he listened to a long Meigs jeremiad. After this, Lee, not surprisingly, did not want anything to do with the new Capitol or Floyd's board. He advised Meigs not to be "troublesome or obstinate."[63]

The Robert E. Lee encounter marked the end of Floyd's efforts at diplomacy. Meigs spent the rest of the year, even as he rushed to complete the Senate and the Aqueduct, enduring a series of petty humiliations and dodging bureaucratic traps. When Walter refused to turn over the Capitol drawings after Meigs formally demanded them, Floyd took no further action. In late October, Meigs wrote Floyd a letter acknowledging that Walter's chair designs had been accepted over his and promising to "endeavor, by beauty of material and workmanship, to make some amends for the poverty of the design."[64] On November 8, Floyd's office sent him a demand from Walter that Meigs pay back wages to one of his draftsmen, which Meigs had refused to do on grounds that he had fired the man.[65] Then, on the following day, Floyd asked Meigs for all his payrolls since his arrival on the project as well as many of his other records. Meigs, knowing that his paper trail was his most important asset in any showdown with Floyd, appealed to Buchanan directly, calling the records "my private property." The following day, Floyd sent him a letter saying the payrolls would not be necessary.[66]

On November 23, Meigs in his diary admitted "I have felt discouraged." The "continual torment," he said, had "deprived me of the interest with which I have heretofore carried out the work."[67] But he had no intention of quietly bowing out. He was too bloody-minded and absolutely sure of the rightness of his position. He had long ago decided that Floyd was a fool, a view that he had recently extended to include Buchanan. While he may have complained frequently in his diary of being wronged, he never cried about it, either in public or in private. Now, although he had reached a point where he felt "discouraged," it was not because his handlers did not like him, or because he thought he had done something wrong. He was upset because the accursed Floyd was taking the joy out of the job. He was no longer having fun.

16

SWAN SONG

Captain Montgomery C. Meigs rode out to the Aqueduct on New Year's Day 1859, and missed the president's big White House reception. It was a Saturday, cloudy but unseasonably warm and lovely. He stopped first at the downstream reservoir in Georgetown, then continued on to the upstream reservoir at Little Falls, on the District line. There had been rain, and water was starting to sluice into the pipes at Georgetown, heading toward the city. Up at Little Falls, a stream of water three feet deep was coming down the conduits from the Potomac at Great Falls, ten miles away. Meigs had his engineers secure the valves so the workmen could plug leaks and give the whole system a last look. But he had seen enough. It worked. "Upon this New Year's Day, I have first passed water through my Aqueduct," he exulted that night in his diary; "6 years and two months I have been at work upon it."[1]

He had no time to rest. On Monday he wanted to use the Aqueduct to bring water to the West Front fountain on the Capitol grounds, and on Tuesday the Senate planned to move into its new chamber. These were historic moments, both for the city of Washington and for the country as a whole, and Meigs, who was adding a double exclamation point to his own career, did not want anything to go awry.

On December 23, he had moved his desk and most of his office into the unfinished Senate in order to be closer to the action at the Capitol. He had worked late into Christmas Eve with Jefferson Davis, brainstorming Davis's new idea for arranging the gallery seats. On Christmas Day he had gone to church, then returned to the Capitol, "putting down carpets in the galleries and lining the backs of the seats with cotton flannel before putting on the damask."[2] By the twenty-ninth he was satisfied he would meet the January 4 Senate deadline. This was fortunate, because he had to spend most of that day haggling with the Supreme Court. The justices were happy to be moving into the old Senate chamber, but hungry for extra territory in the Senate Extension. Arguing with them was tiresome.[3]

Meigs spent the night at his home in downtown Washington and rode up to Georgetown the next morning. He found the crew panicking. Pipes were out of alignment at the downstream reservoir and water would not flow properly. Meigs told the men to make a crooked connection and worry about the alignment later, then continued on to Little Falls, where he rode around the receiving reservoir for the first time. The water had reached a depth of nearly 142 feet in spots, and the man-made lake was filling nicely. He spent the night there. "The men worked with a will," he wrote in his diary, and by dawn on January 3, joints and valves were all in place and the thirty-foot throttle valve controlling the flow of water into the reservoir was fully mounted. "We then gave 3 cheers, and the men went to breakfast," Meigs wrote. He rode back to Georgetown then, and a little before 7:30 a.m. opened the four-foot conduit to let water into the distributing reservoir. It took two hours to rise high enough so that a casual passerby would know it was something other than a muddy pond, but Meigs waited until 10:00 a.m. before opening the stopcock to charge the twelve-inch pipe that sent the water on its way to the Capitol.[4]

Now he was racing against time. It would take several hours for the water to reach the fountain. But he had to get to the Capitol by noon to meet with the Senate's ad hoc Committee on Arrangements, which was planning the move to the new chamber the following day. At 10:30 a.m. he crossed his fingers, abandoned the reservoir, rode the three and a half miles to his H Street home, changed clothes, ate breakfast, and took a carriage to the Capitol. The committee was already in the new chamber when he arrived. Its members had taken formal possession, arranged the desks and chairs, and handed the keys to the Senate officers, and they were now discussing ceremonies and procedures for the following day. Meigs joined the discussion and was hard at work when a messenger found him at 2:30 p.m. The water was coming, the messenger said, and would reach the fountain in a few minutes.

"I could not then leave the committee," Meigs wrote in his diary, "but

I said to Mr. Davis, 'I have a message which will please you.'" He suggested that he and Davis go to the windows on the West Front and take a look. "Mr. Davis shook my hands with a warm 'Congratulations,'" and, together with Jacob Collamer and a few other senators, he and Meigs marched into the Library and stepped to the windows. "The water did not keep us long waiting," Meigs wrote. "It soon began to bubble up from the jet."

That went well, and at 4:30 p.m. Meigs ordered the stopcock opened all the way. "A magnificent column of water" spurted up twenty or thirty feet into the air. Nevertheless, Meigs was a bit disappointed. The four-and-a-half-inch nozzle was too wide, he concluded. He told his crew chief to swap it out overnight for a one-and-a-half-inch nozzle.[5] That would get him a hundred-foot geyser, he figured, "or probably more."[6] With Meigs, bigger, stronger, heavier, or, in this case, higher, was always better. He went home for a rest. He had been up for thirty-three hours.

The West Front fountain shortly after water first arrived from the Washington Aqueduct. The figure standing on the fountain is labeled "Meigs," and the photograph was probably taken after he had a chance to shrink the fountain aperture so the water would shoot high in the air. (Architect of the Capitol)

At noon on January 4, the Senate gathered in the old chamber for the last time. The desks had already been moved out, but cane chairs had been distributed throughout the empty room, and senators and visitors crowded in, spreading out over the Senate floor and up the stairs and onto the narrow overhanging balcony. Both Meigs and Walter were there, undoubtedly standing apart from each other. Davis, as head of the Committee on Arrangements, was in charge of the ceremonies, but he was also bearing witness to the completion of another phase of the project that he had set in motion almost exactly a decade earlier. The unseasonable weather had broken, and a soft snow fell outside.[7]

The ceremonies of "departure and arrival" would be hosted by two Kentuckians. John J. Crittenden, seventy-one, was the Senate's longest-serving member, an illustrious former Whig, a two-time attorney general, and a former state governor. John C. Breckinridge was the vice president of the United States and the presiding officer of the Senate. He was a political prodigy who, at thirty-six, had been barely old enough to run for vice president and was the youngest person ever to hold the office. It fell to Crittenden to say goodbye to the old chamber. He was brief, recalling Calhoun, Webster, Clay, and others "whose fame is not surpassed" and the words they had spoken "within these walls."[8]

Breckinridge then stood before the milling crowd to deliver a longer and more passionate ode to the strength and durability of the United States and how the "proofs of stability" were embodied in the Capitol.[9] Then he led his colleagues to their new lodgings.

A few years later, those who had attended the ceremony might marvel at the subsequent choices of its two leading participants. Crittenden, a unionist to the last, would die a U.S. congressman in 1863, a few weeks after the Battle of Gettysburg. Two of his sons were officers in the U.S. Army, one of them a general, and a third son was a Confederate general. Breckinridge ran for president in 1860 as the candidate of the southern Democrats and was expelled from Congress at the end of 1861 as a southern sympathizer from a state that did not secede. He joined the Confederate Army, fought at Chickamauga, Chattanooga, the Shenandoah, New Market, and Monocacy, and rose to the rank of brigadier general. He served under Jefferson Davis as the Confederacy's last secretary of war.

Newspaper reviews of the new Senate chamber were generally more restrained than those that had greeted the opening of the new House

The new Senate chamber, fairly soon after it opened in 1859. Each senator had his own desk, and desks were grouped on either side of a central aisle—majority party on one side, opposition on the other. (Architect of the Capitol)

chamber a year earlier. One account, printed in both *The New York Times* and the Baltimore *Sun*, pronounced the Senate "light and graceful," predicting that "when the dust of a few sessions shall have taken the gloss off it," there "can be little doubt this new chamber will be found every way more fitting than the old." The floor was covered with 1,700 yards of carpet—flowers on a purple background, and "not unpleasing," the article continued, although had there not been such a rush, "red stars on a buff ground" would probably have worked better. Seats in the balcony galleries—six hundred in all—were "upholstered in drab damask, rather too blue in tone for good effect." The reviewer was far more taken with the two grand stairways leading to the third-floor galleries, one of Tennessee marble, the other of white marble "of extreme purity." They were still unfinished, but far enough along to reveal the "magnificence of the design."

On the accessories and decorations the reporter hedged. The vice president's desk—Walter's design, Meigs's workmanship—got high marks. It was "a modest table of mahogany, as unlike as possible to the marble bar on which the Hon. [House] Speaker pounds." All of Brumidi's corridors and committee rooms, the article reported diplomatically, "are decorated" but "incomplete." The rooms were "paved with encaustic tiles" and had arched ceilings decorated with geometric patterns and heraldic devices. "The walls are covered with trellis-work of flowers and foliage, on which cupids and native American birds, beasts and creeping things are ascending and descending, with more or less resemblance to nature."[10]

The article noted that decoration had begun for the president's "apartment" off the Senate floor but said little else about it. Brumidi would finish this room, to be used by the president during ceremonial visits, in 1859 and 1860, and it would be the most lavishly decorated space in the Capitol. Every inch from floor to ceiling of what would come to be called the President's Room would be covered with paintings or richly colored designs and moldings, much of it optical illusion designed to look three-dimensional. Four Madonna-like figures representing legislation, religion, executive authority, and liberty would gaze down from the ceiling, along with historical paintings of Columbus, Franklin, Amerigo Vespucci, and the Pilgrim leader William Brewster. Every bit of wall space would be filled with paintings, mirrors, or geometric patterns, all of it woven together in a symmetry of fantastic complexity and trompe l'oeil. The tile floor offered an elaborate circular design, centered beneath an enormous chandelier that at night made the entire room shimmer.[11]

One probable reason Meigs managed to escape the vituperation and occasional ridicule that had greeted his House chamber as tasteless and overdone was that official Washington—from Breckinridge on down—needed to feel good about something after the dreadful events of 1858. In spite of everything, as Breckinridge noted in his speech, the city was growing, the country was growing, and the horizon—if one did not dwell on the slavery debate—seemed unlimited. The Capitol symbolized this dream—a dwindling hope that people did not want to abandon.

Walter, too, partook of this Indian summer. So pleased was he with the progress of his project and the accompanying celebration that he forgot, at least for the day, to hate Meigs. "We have the water at last—it was let into the pipes yesterday and all the public buildings are now using it," he wrote early on January 4 in a letter to his wife. "The fountain at the Capitol is playing—the people seem very much pleased," and Meigs is "about as busy as a nailer." Later in the day he added to the letter. The Senate ceremony was "most beautiful and appropriate," with "not one word said that was objectionable." Walter walked with the senators to the new chamber, and he noted that "every seat in the galleries was filled," adding that "scores of the senators congratulated me."[12]

There were other likely reasons why Meigs enjoyed relatively mild treatment from his critics. He had given the Senate a somewhat more muted décor than the House, a politic decision that was probably deliberate. Also, and perhaps most important of all, Meigs had extremely powerful friends in both of the principal Senate factions: Davis among the southern Democrats, Seward among the Republicans. Even better, Davis and Seward, against all odds, were good friends. During Davis's 1858 illness, Seward had checked on him "daily, and sometimes oftener," Varina Davis recalled much later.[13] With a pair of allies like these, it would have been next to impossible for Senate dissenters to put any meaningful pressure on Meigs.

Once Davis returned to health in mid-1858, he quickly rose to a level of power and influence greater than anything he had ever attained in politics, even during his days as Pierce's secretary of war. When the dust settled after the Lecompton constitution debacle, he had emerged as a key leader—perhaps *the* leader—of the southern Democrats in Washington. This was important, for the southern Democrats were all Buchanan had left after Lecompton. William Bigler, the Pennsylvania senator, may have been Buchanan's congressional errand boy, but Davis was the congressional power broker.

Helping Buchanan was a role that Davis neither sought nor necessarily filled. As Buchanan drifted into his third year, his presidency was in such a shambles that it made no sense for any independent actor to link fortunes with him. But Davis was someone that others respected. He had given little recent evidence of being a proslavery fire-eater, and beyond slavery, he had a remarkable and respected grasp of national affairs and an ability to produce learned debate on any theme that might arise—from Atlantic fisheries to breech-loading rifles or the Capitol Extension.

And on rare occasions, he could see into the future. Six days after

Breckinridge led the way to the new chamber, the Senate met to decide how it should be used: how senators should behave during debates, and who should be allowed on the floor. Davis was a hard-liner. As far as he was concerned, the Senate should be closed to everyone but senators. "This is a place for deliberation, for action," he said. "Let the spectators be in the gallery; let silence be in the chamber." If senators wanted to chat with each other or third parties, they should do it in the new retiring room next door. That was why it was there, he argued. Also, diplomats no longer needed special seating. They could sit in the roomy new galleries. And finally, he said, he wanted to make sure that senators knew about the President's Room, "very convenient to the chamber." He doubted whether the president himself would use it more than once a year, "if that often," but it would keep cabinet secretaries at bay.[14]

The President's Room, on the second floor of the U.S. Senate, was perhaps the most sumptuously decorated space in the Capitol. It was intended for the president to use when signing bills, but when the president was elsewhere, senators used it to meet their guests. (Architect of the Capitol)

Davis whittled down the proposed list of people to be allowed in, but he lost the argument on the president, the cabinet, and the diplomats. What he had successfully accomplished, however, was to provide a template for the privilege and exclusivity of the Senate, articulating protocols that in time would define it. For Davis, function should follow form. The new chamber strengthened the Senate in the same way that the new Capitol strengthened the entire country. His colleagues were not yet fully ready for such senatorial exclusivity—which some might call snobbery— but for Davis the added gravitas was essential for the deliberative body of a great nation. The United States was great, and would become greater. Senators should act accordingly. And eventually they would.

Such visions of a national future seemingly without limit, anchored in the same unabashed optimism that had prompted Davis to propose a bigger Capitol in 1850, made him a formidable man, especially in the murky twilight of antebellum America. People hungered for hope when, increasingly, there was none.

But optimism carried risks, as Davis would discover. As he convalesced before returning to Congress in 1858, he had confided in a letter to former president Franklin Pierce, then traveling in Europe, that he wished to avoid Mississippi's "malarial exposure" and did not plan to go home in the summer or early fall.[15] This was probably a wise decision. Just out of bed, according to one reporter, he was "a pale, ghastly looking figure, his eye bandaged with strips of white linen passing over the head, his whole aspect presenting an appearance of feebleness and debility."[16] Once Congress adjourned, his doctor advised, he should move out of Washington "to a higher latitude, for a month or two."[17]

So he and Varina took their two children, Margaret and Jefferson, Jr., born in 1857, and went to New England for four months. Beginning with an impromptu July 4 onboard address to fellow passengers on the ship heading north, Davis gave at least six speeches to various audiences during his vacation. In all cases, newspaper accounts recorded that he was received with cheers, applause, and affection. He clearly owed part of his success to natural charm and political instincts. In Portland, Maine, on July 9, he was at his unionist best, invoking the sense of shared purpose that inspired the American Revolution: "Has patriotism ceased to be a virtue?" he asked. "And is narrow sectionalism no longer to be counted a crime?"[18] And at the Maine state fair in Augusta in September, he noted that while "Yankee is a word once applied to you as a term of reproach," the Mainers, at least in his experience, "have made it honorable and renowned."[19]

Like his audiences, he, too, wanted to believe that the country's widening sectional divide was still bridgeable. "Shall narrow interests, shall local jealousies, shall disregard of the high purposes for which our union was ordained, continue to distract our people and impede the progress of our government?" he asked the delegates to the Maine state Democratic convention in August.

"No, no!" they answered, and applauded. "Thanks for the answer," he said. "Let every American heart respond, no."[20]

At Faneuil Hall in Boston in October, Davis described abolitionism as "a brawler" and told his audience that all "we of the South" ever wanted was to perform the duties of states and enjoy their rights as outlined by the Constitution and "made for our mutual protection"; surely no one could argue with that. Again he was applauded.[21]

And then, in late fall, he went home to Mississippi. His constituents had read about his trip from reprints of stories that had run in northern newspapers. Where the northerners had seen sunshine—wanted to see sunshine—the home folks had seen betrayal. Davis had to defend himself.

In a long speech in November to the Mississippi legislature, Davis behaved almost as if he were on trial, unjustly accused of sins he had not committed. He confronted his critics in their own den, explained that he had done nothing wrong, and described his actions without apology.

He had gone north for his health, he said, and given his political positions, he had expected to be "left in loneliness." Instead, "courtesy and kindness met me." The Republican papers had given him a hard time, and "their assaults did not surprise me," he added. But then he found these assaults "echoed" in southern papers—attacking him for cozying up to the enemy. This, "I will confess, did pain me." But what was he supposed to do—meet New England's kindness with abuse? He acknowledged that he had never advocated secession, but should Mississippi decide to leave the union, he expected to be withdrawn from Washington. And if he ever adopted a "feeling of hostility" toward the union, he would resign.[22]

It was vintage Davis. First he put on his unionist, optimist's hat—the northerners' wishful thinking about him had prompted at least some of his own wishful thinking about them. But then he put on his southern rights hat. He spoke of Lecompton and the disastrous midterm election just concluded. Abolitionists will control the House of Representatives at the end of the coming year, he said, but Buchanan would veto whatever they tried to pass. There were, however, no guarantees for 1860. Should there be an abolitionist president, Mississippians would have to decide whether the government should "pass into the hands of your avowed and implacable enemies." A Republican in the White House is entitled "to no respect," he said. Should it happen, southerners should look to what he termed—without saying the word "secession"—"the last remedy."[23]

And then Davis returned to Washington for the beginning of the Buchanan administration's last act. It was a grim time. The new Senate and House chambers, with their ample visitors' galleries, drew bigger crowds than ever, even as the words spoken there grew ever more contentious and insulting. Members frequently threatened one another in speeches and nearly came to blows. Abolitionist Republicans and slaveholding southern Democrats by 1859 had virtually nothing left to talk about, and when the daily shouting match had stopped, shared resentment subsided outside the Capitol into cold correctness. "There was an unspoken feeling of avoidance" that induced colleagues to dodge one another and stick with their own kind, Varina Davis wrote years later. "Unconsciously all tentative subjects were avoided by the well-bred of both sections."[24]

Still, the Buchanan years were also noteworthy for a long list of memorable social events, parties, and delicious scandals that northerners and southerners alike would recall fondly for decades afterward. It was the last Neroesque gasp of a world that would never again be the same, and the celebrants, it seemed, knew it. "The hidden fires of the coming revolution were smoldering at the Capitol," the pro-Republican journalist Benjamin Perley Poore later wrote, but "even when Lent came, instead of going to church in obedience to the chimes of consecrated bells, society kept on with its entertainments."[25]

In 1859, the year's main event came in February—a spectacular farewell ball thrown at Willard's Hotel for the hugely popular British ambassador, Francis Lord Napier, and his wife, Elizabeth, whose two-year posting was ending. New York's William Seward was credited with organizing the party, but the cost was probably shared. Invitations tactfully included a list of party "managers" so guests would know that whatever their politics, there would be someone famous at the ball who shared their views. Davis was a manager, along with Senator James M. Mason, a southern-rights Virginian. Seward and Senator Henry Wilson, a fire-breathing Massachusetts abolitionist, were also managers, as were the tarnished Douglas and Crittenden, the border state conciliator.[26] Buchanan, vexed with Napier over a diplomatic matter, pleaded a head cold and ducked the party, but most of his cabinet attended. It was perhaps the last time that Washington's elite put aside their personal and political grudges for one last evening of glitter. "In a word," *The New York Times* reported, "all that Washington holds of gay, gallant and distinguished, thronged Willard's Hotel tonight."[27]

Society's last gasp took place a bit over a year later when the celebrated Baroness Bodisco, the former Harriet Williams of Georgetown, married British Army captain Gordon Scott at St. John's Church. In 1838, as a sixteen-year-old schoolgirl and an already legendary beauty, Harriet had caught the attention of Count Alexander de Bodisco, the Russian ambassador, who was fifty-three. Despite the initial objections of Harriet's parents, the two were married, and they lived happily together until the count died in 1854. The baroness, spectacularly titled and moneyed, was a top-tier Washington socialite during widowhood, but she waited six years before remarrying.

The ceremony at St. John's, an Episcopal church on Lafayette Square, close by the White House and attended frequently by Meigs, was the high point of the social season, with Buchanan tapped to give away the bride. Now approaching the age of forty, the baroness, though still attractive, was, according to Virginia Clay, the wife of Alabama senator Clement C. Clay and another well-known hostess, no longer the "sylph" she had once been. The wedding, on May 29, 1860, presented an interesting dilemma, Clay continued, for "the plumpness of the stately bride and the President's ample figure, made the walk, side by side, almost an impossible feat." Buchanan solved this problem by "tactfully" allowing the baroness to precede him to the chancel, where Scott awaited her.[28]

In 1859, nobody was more attached to Davis than Meigs. The two men had built the new Capitol together for six years. They had made crucial and controversial decisions about where to locate the new chambers, how to heat and ventilate them, and how to ensure the best possible acoustics. They had thickened the Capitol's skin, making the building not only more impressive but also stronger—a monument for posterity. They had lavished attention on fancy artwork and ornamentation and had tenaciously defended their "higher style" before critics in Congress, in the press, and in the art world. Only Walter had an institutional memory that matched theirs, and they had tried to cast him into the wilderness. For Meigs, the falling-out with Walter had complicated origins—healthy competition deteriorating to mutual jealousy and distrust. For the patrician Davis, however, Walter was simply unworthy—a commoner masquerading as a peer, a clever draftsman with pretensions as an artist. And by 1859 he was also the enemy of the army engineer, still young at forty-two, to whom Davis had given a spectacular opportunity and who had used it to produce the building that Davis had envisioned ten years earlier.

Meigs could not have had a more powerful or more loyal friend, and he knew it. When his dispute with Walter turned bitter in 1858, Meigs asked Davis to make his case to Floyd. And when it looked as though Meigs might be ousted during the recess that year, he wrote to Davis in Maine asking him yet again to intercede with Buchanan. Davis wrote back in September: in "obtaining justice for you," he said, he thought it would be better to see Buchanan in person, and since he was about to leave New England, he would visit the White House on his way home to Mississippi.[29]

Davis arrived in late October, saw both Floyd and Buchanan, and invited Meigs over to his house to brief him. Floyd had admitted to Davis that he sometimes found Meigs "disagreeable" and would already have gotten rid of him "if he had someone to put in his place." He told Davis that Meigs habitually violated the chain of command by ignoring Floyd and making overtures directly to Buchanan. Davis calmed Floyd down, then went to see Buchanan.

That conversation had started badly, with a mealymouthed Buchanan telling Davis that he had not at first believed that a military officer could handle public works, but that he now knew that "nobody could question the ability or the integrity" of Meigs.

"Well, in God's name, Mr. President," Davis replied, going on the offensive. "What [more] can you ask for in a public officer than ability and integrity?" Davis told Buchanan that he, Davis, "had a very great responsibility in connection with the Extension of the Capitol" and that he had always been able to answer his critics "so long as the works were being properly conducted." But Walter's insubordination had brought construction almost to a standstill. Either Walter or Meigs had to go. Davis "would not pretend to judge for the President," he told Buchanan, but he certainly knew what he would do "if he had any authority."

And then came his final word. Davis wanted to support the administration on its new Capitol policy, "as upon other questions." He had delayed his departure for Mississippi so he could "urge the proper settlement" of the Meigs-Walter controversy, a dispute, he had pointed out, that was not just about the Capitol Extension. It was personal for Davis, and it had broader policy implications. Buchanan, Davis suggested, might want to keep that in mind.[30]

When Davis returned in December for the opening of Congress, he called again on Buchanan to find out about Walter, but Buchanan told him that he had to defer to his secretary of war, and Floyd "had some feeling on the subject."[31] The lines had now been officially drawn. Davis had enough influence to keep Meigs from being axed, but not enough to get rid of Walter.

Davis had made sure that he would endure as Meigs's good shepherd. He chaired the Senate's Military Affairs Committee, which gave him license to meddle in Floyd's affairs as much as he wished. Additionally, he had himself appointed to the Committee on Public Buildings and Grounds, giving him direct oversight over the Capitol and over Meigs's other public works. From this perch—the same pair of jobs he had held in 1850—he had the political leverage both to put a check on Floyd and to protect Meigs. It was Davis who prepared the Senate's report on the new chamber. And it was Davis who managed the transition as chair of the Committee on Arrangements.

In November 1858, Meigs's eldest son, John, had reapplied to West Point, and Davis agreed to write a letter of recommendation, as he had done the previous year. Just to make sure Davis got it right, John Meigs sent him a sample letter along with his own letter to Buchanan. West Point candidates seeking at-large appointments—the only kind available to residents of the District of Columbia—had to apply directly to the president.

Although the elder Meigs undoubtedly helped him write the letters, John's precocious bravado marked him not only as his father's son but also as an aggressive self-promoter in his own right. In his letter to Buchanan, John noted that his father had "zealously" pursued his duties in building the Capitol and other public works, but "his pay is not sufficient to allow him to give me such an education as I think I can make good use of, and I wish to relieve him of my expense as soon as possible." John reviewed the revolutionary credentials of his forebears, and noted that his grandfather, Dr. Charles Meigs, "is a staunch Democrat." His other grandfather, of course, was Commodore John Rodgers, so "our family is thus not unknown in the history of the country." He finished by listing endorsements and recommendations from a wide selection of senators and other political worthies.[32]

In March 1859, John found out that he had been rejected again. By early June, Meigs had learned that John would have won an appointment "but for the obstinacy of one man," who, Meigs was certain, was Floyd.[33] On June 23, however, he found out that "2 or 3" of Buchanan's at-large appointees had failed their entrance examinations. Meigs wrote to Buchanan and was invited to the White House. Buchanan told him that he liked John, but that Floyd had indeed blocked him. Meigs told him that Davis had promised to write a note to Floyd to remind him that John was Commodore Rodgers's grandson. Buchanan bridled at this plan, which he said would "do harm." Instead, he suggested that Meigs go directly to Floyd.[34]

Two days later, Meigs appeared before Floyd, hat figuratively in hand. Despite the disgust and humiliation he must have felt, he kept his wits about him. He had prepared his request in writing, and he offered to read it aloud because his handwriting was so bad. The letter was straightforward but not confrontational, although it expressed the hope that Meigs's differences with Floyd would not interfere with his son's hopes. Its effect on Floyd, however, was almost volcanic. "Captain Meigs, I can never forgive, to one who knows so well its meaning, official discourtesy," Floyd thundered. "To any other man I could, but not to you. When a man like you does such a thing, it means something."

Meigs, to whom this outburst was apparently not altogether unforeseen, said he had meant no disrespect, then told Floyd how his failure to act on Meigs's complaints about Walter had caused "grievous injury." This opened a long and apparently ugly conversation, the nub of which was Floyd's outrage that Meigs had written directly to Buchanan to introduce John, bypassing the chain of command. Because of this slight, Floyd told Meigs, he had opposed the appointment "and would have sacrificed his position in the cabinet had the appointment been made."

Meigs was undaunted. He had written to Floyd the previous year, he said, and gotten nowhere, so he had not bothered this year because "I thought it useless." Floyd said he had never seen any application from Meigs in either year. To this Meigs did not reply directly. Instead he told Floyd, fairly abruptly, that at-large West Point appointments were none of Floyd's business. They were presidential appointments, not secretary of war appointments. Anybody who wanted one asked the president for it. Floyd had no cause to complain.

Floyd then changed the subject. "He said I had entirely misconceived him, misunderstood him," Meigs wrote. "That I had set myself to thwart him in everything." They argued further, about how Meigs had "oppressed" Walter, and about Meigs's refusal to do Floyd's bidding. Meigs said he was not disobedient. He always complied, he added, "if the order was insisted upon." Gradually he seemed to make progress, apparently by refusing to back down and by tying his adversary into rhetorical knots. Finally Floyd told him that John's path was still blocked, because he and Buchanan had standby cadet candidates waiting to fill two of the open appointments and the third failed candidate was to get a second chance at the test. Still, Floyd said, capitulating finally, he would no longer stand in John Meigs's way should an opening eventually appear.[35]

And on August 31, it did. West Point sent Meigs a note telling him that the third candidate had failed again. Meigs wrote a letter to Buchanan with a copy to William Drinkard, the acting secretary of war. Floyd was ill and out of town. On September 5, the West Point superintendent officially notified Meigs that John had been accepted. Drinkard suggested Meigs go to the White House to receive the news directly from Buchanan. The president handed him the appointment, telling him that "Floyd had behaved handsomely in this matter." He wished Meigs well and sent him on his way with the admonition that while he appreciated that Meigs expressed his opinions "strongly and fully" in his dealings with Floyd, he wished that he would "use some conciliatory language."[36] Meigs apparently managed to keep his mouth shut on his way out the door, probably by gritting his teeth.

Father and son quickly packed, and by 3:30 p.m. the same day, they were on the train to New York. Twelve hours later they checked into the Fifth Avenue Hotel on Washington Square and went to bed. The next day they visited Central Park, walked down Broadway, visited a museum, and got on the Hudson River train, arriving at West Point by 7:30 p.m. On

September 7, John took his physical and sat for his exams at 5:00 p.m. Meigs "spent a very pleasant day" touring the campus and talking to old professors. John passed the exams effortlessly.[37]

Despite this hard-won triumph, it was safe to say that by mid-1859, Jefferson Davis was the only reason Meigs still held his job. Opening the valves of the municipal water supply and the move to the new Senate chamber were the high points of the year for Meigs, and they would be his last high points at the Capitol. His dispute with Walter was now more than a year old. He still had no new designs, and no way to undertake anything ambitious. Work on the Dome was virtually halted. The Rotunda remained headless above the peristyle, and Meigs's celebrated derrick spidered idly in the sky waiting for something to lift. Congress started to empty out in March, and another long and merciless recess loomed, leaving Meigs virtually friendless among his opponents. All the problems that had tortured him the previous year still lingered, including the Post Office heating and ventilation system, the procurement of monolithic columns for the Extension, and the endless wrestling match over the funding and contracts at the Aqueduct. Davis, who remained in town through the spring, went to Buchanan to renew the pressure over the Walter affair but got nowhere.

In June 1859, Meigs found out that Floyd planned to turn over the finished parts of the Aqueduct to the Interior Department and appoint another Army engineer to manage them. Infuriated that this was being done behind his back, he contacted Davis, who immediately went to see Buchanan once more. Meigs subsequently learned that the order had been suspended "for a time," but the suspension turned out to be just a stay of execution.[38] In August, Meigs turned over the finished sections of his waterworks with reasonably good grace.

The monolithic columns dispute resumed in late 1858 and continued throughout 1859. In this, through no fault of their own, Walter and Meigs turned out to be in complete agreement. Both believed that the columns should be purchased in Italy by Rice and Heebner under the existing marble contract. But after Floyd insisted late in 1858 that the columns had to be American, this hoped-for arrangement fell apart. This left Rice, Heebner, Meigs, and Walter wondering what would happen next.

Floyd temporized. In the early spring of 1859 he sent Meigs a letter essentially blaming him for the delay. When Meigs opened the second round of bids the previous December, Floyd had thought that the Rice-Heebner marble contract was "practically void." Now, he said, he had found out that it was not, so the bids had to be thrown out and new action taken. What he planned next was unclear, but Meigs suspected that he wanted to declare the contract in forfeiture. This was an incredibly bad idea, Meigs wrote in his diary, because only Meigs had the power to annul the contract, and besides, the columns were part of the Lee marble contract, and the quarry was still supplying blocks for the exterior of the Capitol Extension.[39]

At the end of April, Floyd sent Meigs to visit the Lee quarry and John Connolly's quarry outside Baltimore. Meigs found Lee in bad shape, almost played out and unable to supply columns in fewer than four pieces. Connolly, on the other hand, had four monoliths quarried and ready to go, and he had plenty of marble beyond that. The difficulty here, as Meigs had told Floyd previously, was that the Connolly marble was "of inferior quality," neither "as fine" nor as beautiful as the Lee marble. In addition, Connolly wanted $1,550 per column, $150 more than Rice and Heebner wanted to charge for the Italian columns.[40] This was a terrible price.

On May 13, Floyd directed Meigs to declare the Rice-Heebner contract void and sign a contract with Connolly. Meigs did not do anything immediately about Connolly, knowing that Rice and Heebner would almost certainly make a claim against the forfeiture and win a hefty settlement on the grounds that they could fulfill the letter of the contract with purchases from Italy. Floyd, still ill, was in Virginia and out of touch. Meigs got on a train and immediately went to Philadelphia to meet with Rice, who, as expected, formally protested the annulment. Two days later, Buchanan summoned Meigs to the White House. He was in a bad mood because Floyd was out of town and Philadelphia businessmen were upset. Meigs handed Buchanan the monolith correspondence; the president read it and agreed with Meigs that the Lee contract could be legally annulled only by Meigs, and that the Extension still needed Lee marble. What was to be done?

Meigs said nobody had made a mistake yet, since he had not signed Connolly up. Buchanan then "suspended" Floyd's order "for further consideration."[41] For most of the next month, Meigs traveled all through the northeast, visiting quarries and once again finding nothing that could compete with the Italian marble. On June 22, he sent Floyd a letter ranking the marbles he had seen. Connolly, outside Baltimore, was coming into focus as the preferred choice. His stone was only fourth-best in quality, Meigs said, but it was first in availability. It would take years to get any of the other quarries in shape to cut a hundred monoliths. Connolly could do the work as fast as the Italians—if he focused on it.

More important, Meigs told Floyd, he had found a way to fix the contract mess. He suggested that Floyd allow Rice and Heebner to handle the purchases of the American monoliths under the existing contract. He had checked with the Lee partners, and they were happy to do it.[42] Eight days later, Floyd accepted the deal. Meigs had managed to save Floyd from himself.

Aside from this brief interlude, however, virtually anything that Meigs tried to do was made either hopelessly complicated or simply impossible because of the feud with Walter. This was especially apparent in the bureaucratic wrangle that had begun in 1858 over the heating and ventilation contract for the Post Office Extension and was destined to continue throughout the year and into 1859. Despite having grudgingly agreed to give the contract to Lapsley & Thomas, Floyd's handpicked Baltimore company, Meigs was in no hurry to implement it. Soon after the deal had been struck, the contractors, not surprisingly, began to complain to Floyd about Meigs's lack of cooperation. By early fall, 1858 they had begun asking Floyd to intercede with Meigs so they could get the Post Office plans and begin designing the piping and ductwork. Floyd told Meigs to get the plans from Walter, prompting Meigs to ask Walter for all plans for all the public works. This, once again, got to the heart of the Meigs-Walter dispute: he who had custody of the drawings had control of the project. Walter, of course, refused to hand over the drawings. Drinkard, the assistant secretary of war standing in for Floyd, finally, on November 18, ordered Walter to furnish plans for the Post Office cellar so that Lapsley & Thomas's boilermakers could build and site the furnaces.[43]

Another two months limped by, until Meigs in early January 1859 complained to Floyd in a long letter that the work on the Post Office, the Capitol Extension, and the new Dome simply could not go forward unless he could get Walter's drawings. In this letter, signs also emerged that Meigs had begun to realize that his Post Office foot-dragging and insistence on having the plans were becoming tiresome to his superiors. Walter had turned out to be just as stubborn as Meigs, and Floyd and Drinkard liked Walter and did not like Meigs.

In the middle of January, Meigs's appropriations once again ran out and he started to lay people off. He asked Floyd to request an "advance" from Congress, but Floyd ignored him.[44] In early March, the new appropriation went through, but the Aqueduct was not funded. New construction there—and much still needed to be built—once again had to be stopped, and Meigs began buttoning up everything except the Cabin John Bridge.[45] Failure to fund new Aqueduct construction had a particularly pernicious effect on Meigs's activities once Floyd handed operational control of the completed parts of the project to another officer. Meigs, in effect, had nothing to work on.

On March 5, Walter sent pay certificates via Floyd for Meigs to pay some of his draftsmen. He signed the certificates "Architect of the New Dome," among his other titles. Meigs refused to make the payment on grounds that Walter had never been granted such a designation.[46] In the middle of March, Floyd ordered Meigs to fire Emmerich Carstens, the German-born foreman of the decorative painters whom Meigs had hired in 1856, offering no reason (he would be rehired after Floyd's departure).[47] On March 19, Floyd, on the strength of Walter's certificate as Architect of the New Dome, ordered Meigs to pay the draftsmen. "I grow weary of all this," Meigs wrote in his diary. "It is too much worry, and worry, not work, wears out a man."[48]

The first shipments of heating and ventilating equipment from Lapsley & Thomas, now known as Henry F. Thomas & Co., arrived for the Post Office early in the year. Meigs was slow to pay, and the contractors complained. Floyd in early April ordered Meigs to give Thomas & Co. what they asked. Meigs protested to Floyd that Thomas was charging far above the industry standard—$2,000 too much. Floyd on April 16 ordered Meigs to pay it anyway.[49] Meigs was losing every battle, but his paper trail was still immaculate.

In late July, Henry Thomas wrote to Floyd saying he was losing money because the company had no orders. Drinkard sent the note to Meigs, who replied on July 30. He was unhelpful, almost insubordinate: "Having no plans, I can give no orders," he wrote. "Whatever is to be done, when the plans of the building shall be restored to me and made available for study, will have to be done by myself in the intervals of other duties."[50] Drinkard chose not to take offense. Instead, Walter and Meigs embarked on another massive review of their power struggle, each providing Drinkard with enormous letters accompanied by piles of supplementary documents.

Neither man expected to win. Walter understood that Floyd was a frail reed, "so sick from a nervous condition that anything which upsets him puts him in a tailspin," he told Rice, and "nothing upsets him more than the Meigs situation."[51] Meigs, for his part, was simply wearing down. He had managed to weather one summer of discontent, but this one was even worse.

On September 22, Drinkard wrote to Meigs commenting on the latest round of polemics. It was true that Floyd the previous year had authorized Meigs to ask Walter for any drawings he needed. However, he continued, this did not mean, as Meigs had asserted repeatedly, that Meigs could "*permanently*" (italics in original) take the drawings. To be clear, he said, "the secretary deemed that the rooms in the Capitol occupied by the architect were the proper depository for the drawings, and intended that they should remain there." With this understanding, Drinkard concluded, Meigs could have anything he wanted.[52] Two days later, Drinkard and his wife had dinner with Walter and Amanda at Walter's house.

Walter, it appeared, had gotten his way. Drinkard's letter had removed the ambiguity that had guided Meigs's behavior for nearly two years. Meigs was not to be the custodian of the drawings, and if he needed some, he had to get them from Walter. It was, for Meigs, the ultimate insult.

"I am as capable of understanding a written order of the Secretary of War, as the chief clerk or the acting secretary," Meigs replied on September 23. He once again reviewed—briefly—his mandate to control the drawings. "My official rights cannot be explained away by any knowledge Mr. Drinkard may have of the desires or purposes of the Secretary of War," Meigs continued. He expected to "hear again from the department."[53] He waited more than a month for Floyd to return to Washington and catch up on his correspondence. Floyd's reaction was unmistakable.

"The conduct of Captain Meigs . . . manifesting such flagrant insubordination, and containing language both disrespectful and insulting to his superiors, is reprehensible in the highest degree," Floyd wrote in commenting on the letter. "The spirit that dictated it is manifested throughout this correspondence, and shows a continuous insubordination that deserves the strongest censure."[54]

Meigs had finally given Floyd the ammunition he needed, and on

November 1, 1859, Floyd formally relieved him as Engineer in Charge of the Capitol Extension, the Dome, and the Post Office Extension. He named Captain William B. Franklin, of the Topographical Engineers, to succeed him. Davis was out of town on recess, but he would not have been able to help even if Meigs had asked him. Meigs did not need to be told that back talk to a superior, from a military officer, was unacceptable behavior.

On November 2, Meigs called his workers together, read his orders, and thanked everyone. His men were not to worry: "After the envies and jealousies of the day are past, justice will be done to the skillful artists whose hands have aided me," Meigs said. "I leave the work with confidence in the unbiased verdict of the American people, who will, I doubt not, in time, set the seal of their approbation upon it."[55]

17

TYING OFF LOOSE ENDS

Thomas Crawford died in London on October 10, 1857, of an inoperable brain tumor over his left eye. He was forty-four, and was survived by his wife, Louisa, and four children. It was no surprise. Six months earlier, a dispatch in the art journal *The Crayon* recounted how he had begun to have headaches the previous September during his visit to the United States and had complained that his eyes were bothering him. He had gotten steadily worse despite the best efforts of doctors in three countries.

Crawford had stopped in Washington during that U.S. trip to meet Captain Meigs, check on the progress of his pediment sculptures, and talk over his plans for completing *Freedom Triumphant in War and Peace*, as she was now known, the figure that would crown the Capitol atop the new Dome. Meigs had had no inkling that there was anything wrong, and Crawford had returned to Rome predicting confidently that he would finish the plaster model of *Freedom* by early 1857.

He had done that, but he had grown increasingly ill in the process, suffering from headaches, nausea, vomiting, and periodic paralysis on his right side. Doctors in Rome could neither diagnose his ailment nor treat him, so he had gone to Paris. There he learned that he had a cancerous tumor, and that there was no cure.[1] He returned to Rome for a short while, but the pain became too much to endure, so he traveled to London in the hope that surgery might help. In August, Meigs received two letters from James Clinton Hooker, a Rome-based banker who had recently been in London. "Within the past few weeks," Hooker wrote, "all hopes of Mr.

Crawford's ever being able to resume his labors have passed away." Crawford had been blind for three months, with no possibility of regaining his eyesight. Surgery had released the pressure inside Crawford's skull, and the pain had finally abated, but "the duration of his life is quite uncertain." Any further work on the House pediment of the Capitol's East Front, or on other projects Crawford might have discussed with Meigs, was of course out of the question. However, Hooker had spoken to Louisa Crawford, who told him that her husband wanted to cast *Freedom* at the Royal Bavarian Foundry in Munich.[2] What did Meigs think?

Meigs had already exchanged letters with Crawford about the Munich foundry, and in his final letter to the sculptor in April 1857 had told him of "the importance of making this statue in this country," especially given the Know-Nothing fervor of the moment. It would not play politically to cast such an important symbol overseas, he told Crawford. He knew that Munich was generally regarded as the finest foundry in the world, but Crawford's death had not changed the politics.

So on April 19, 1858, Louisa Crawford, who had stayed in Rome to clean up her husband's affairs, had the plaster *Freedom* stowed aboard the bark *Emily Taylor* at the Tuscan port of Livorno. It would be sent to New York, with intermediate stops. The full-scale model was in six pieces, packed in individual crates. Once in the United States, the pieces were to be cast separately and bolted together. When *Freedom* was finished, it would stand 19 feet 6 inches tall and weigh 15,000 pounds.

The voyage did not go well. Four days out of Livorno the *Emily Taylor* started to leak. The crew pumped the water and continued under way for a month, in and out of Mediterranean ports, where the seas were relatively calm. But on May 19, the ship stopped for repairs at Gibraltar, undoubtedly anticipating heavier going during the Atlantic crossing. Almost everything aboard was unloaded and temporarily warehoused, including the six Livorno crates. Shipyard workers were patching and caulking the *Emily Taylor*'s hull until the end of June.

The reloaded and repaired ship ventured into the ocean on June 26. Buffeted immediately by gales and heavy seas from the northwest, the repairs worked loose. Leaks began July 1, and by the twelfth, the *Emily Taylor* was taking on a foot of water per hour. The crew pumped steadily to stay ahead, and started tossing cargo overboard to lighten the load. First to go were 117 bales of rags and 48 crates of citrus fruit. The next day another 133 bales of rags departed.

Nothing helped. The *Emily Taylor* steamed onward, but two weeks later, sixteen inches of water was filling the hold every hour. The captain decided "for the general safety" to put into Bermuda, and the ship limped into port on July 29. The *Emily Taylor* was emptied once again and examiners took a look. The ship was immediately condemned and sold.[3]

Meigs did not learn the full details of this ordeal for nearly a year, but on Christmas Eve 1858 he received news that four of his crates had arrived in New York aboard the bark *G. W. Horton*, which had been sent to Bermuda to pick up what remained of the *Emily Taylor*'s cargo.[4] On January 29, 1859, agents in New York advised Meigs that the remaining two crates, which had been too big for the *Horton*, were expected aboard another ship. This was apparently accomplished without incident, and on March 9, the agents told Meigs that all the crates had left New York for Georgetown aboard the schooner *Fairfax*. But the *Fairfax* carried only three crates. In early April 1859, nearly a year after Louisa Crawford had loaded them, the other three crates reached the harbor at Georgetown. Meigs did not formally take delivery until June and had to pay $1,972.05 in extra shipping charges. "Many thanks for the trouble occasioned you in this small matter," the agents wrote Meigs in an oddly worded letter July 23. "We hope any further shipment may come in some more fortunate vessel."[5]

The crates were moved to the Capitol, and Meigs prevailed on the Speaker of the House to put the old chamber off-limits so they could be opened and the model assembled there.[6]

By that point, however, Meigs was worried mostly about getting his son John into West Point and trying to keep his job. Five months after the statue's arrival, he was relieved of his Capitol post.

Figuring out how to cast *Freedom* was only one piece of unfinished business that Meigs left behind when Floyd dismissed him at the end of October. Before *Freedom* could be mounted, the Dome had to be finished, and nothing had been built above the peristyle for well over a year. Also, decisions needed to be made about future artwork: what kind would be allowed, who would paint or sculpt it, who would pay for it. Although Congress had approved the appointment of a three-member art commission, nothing had been done about it. And finally, the Extension still needed a hundred monolithic marble columns, and while everyone fi-

The plaster model of Crawford's statue of *Freedom* was uncrated and assembled in mid-1859 in the abandoned old House chamber. It stayed there until the following year, when it was cast in bronze. (Library of Congress)

nally knew where they would come from, and how they would be paid for, Floyd had not yet closed the deal.

What had been resolved, however, at least for the moment, was the convoluted politics of Capitol construction. In the immediate aftermath of Meigs's dismissal, the newspapers conducted a series of postmortems. The Philadelphia *North American and United States Gazette* attributed Meigs's departure to "the want of cordial agreement between his views and those of the War Department."[7] *The New York Times* described a confusing dispute over a payment to Emory, the granite contractor, involving Meigs, Emory, Walter, and Floyd, and ending with Meigs's refusal to obey a direct order.[8] *The New York Herald* said Meigs had lost, or perhaps helped himself to, "something like $50,000" from the construction fund.[9]

Over time the *North American*'s view, with some modification, sure to please Meigs, would become the accepted version: honest Meigs had fought corrupt Floyd for two and a half years until he finally got fed up. This story was accurate as far as it went, but it ignored the climax. It was certainly true that Meigs and Floyd did not like each other, but Meigs was prepared to outwait Floyd, and Floyd, blocked by Davis, could do nothing about it. What pushed Meigs over the edge was the decision by William Drinkard—Floyd's deputy—to revisit the dispute between Meigs and Walter over custody of the drawings for the Capitol and the Post Office. Meigs's reasoning in this regard—that access to individual plans meant he should have control of all plans—had been questionable from the beginning, and Drinkard had finally called him on it. Meigs then lost his temper, thus giving Floyd the opening he needed. Meigs had not disobeyed an order; he had been insubordinate and rude to Drinkard.

So Walter won. By taking the plans and locking them up in a third-floor aerie in the old Capitol, he had driven Meigs to distraction and finally forced him to make a mistake. Within days of Floyd's discovery of the Drinkard exchange, Meigs was gone.

In the short run, this was probably a good thing for all concerned. Meigs had chosen an unwavering, doctrinaire path in the feud with Walter, which had won him only a deadlock by the middle of 1858, when work on the new Dome all but stopped. He had become increasingly ineffective as the Buchanan administration evolved, and in the end he was spending altogether too much time petitioning for redress and worrying about whether Walter was authorized to call himself "Architect of the New Dome." By November 1859, he had built the United States a new Senate and House of Representatives, brought running water to the U.S. Capitol and Washington, D.C., and obtained a presidential appointment to West Point for his eldest son. "I feel less regret than I thought I should," Meigs wrote in his diary on October 31, 1859, when he learned of his imminent firing. Despite having been "tormented" unmercifully, he had "completed, so far that no man can claim them, many great works."[10]

Besides, he was not altogether gone. He was still a captain of Engineers in good standing, and he was still in charge of building the unfinished segments of the Aqueduct. He was readily available to resume his previous duties should fortune reverse itself.

Floyd, whose own fortunes did not look overly bright, nonetheless managed to handle the transition with a certain deftness. He had not, as Walter hoped, handed the project to the architect. Instead, he named another Army captain, William B. Franklin, to replace Meigs. In so doing he ensured bureaucratic continuity and maintained the confidence that Congress had in the integrity, if not the artistic judgment, of the army to finish their building.

Franklin was seven years younger than Meigs, with a similarly impeccable pedigree. He had graduated from West Point in 1843, first in his class, and was an up-and-comer working in Washington when Floyd tapped him. He, like Meigs, was a member of the Saturday Club, and he had made all the right moves in a very delicate situation, making sure to tell Meigs of Floyd's interest in hiring him, keeping Meigs informed of the courtship as it unfolded, and disclaiming any personal interest in the outcome.

Most important for Floyd, choosing Franklin neutralized Davis, thus all but eliminating the possibility that Meigs might make a comeback. Davis had put the Capitol in the hands of the War Department in 1853 so that he could keep a close watch on the project and have someone in charge who was well trained, above reproach, and directly beholden to him and under his protection. He could hardly fault Floyd for doing the same thing. Meigs had transgressed, and Floyd had relieved him and installed his own man. Had Floyd chosen to replace Meigs with one of his Virginia cronies, or, worse, with Walter, Davis would have been enraged. But with Franklin in charge, Davis had no excuse to complain.

Walter had gotten at least part of what he wanted: Meigs was gone. Yet he took no great pleasure in the victory. In short notes to his father-in-law, to John Rice, and to Charles Fowler, the New York iron manufacturer, he announced simply that "Meigs is at last removed." Walter would now handle the architecture without interference. "This has been a long warfare," he wrote. "I am glad it is over."[11] On November 3, Walter spent more than two hours with Franklin, showing him his office, drawings, and designs. Franklin, Walter told Rice, was "kind, affable, gentlemanly, liberal in his views and determined not to interfere with any body's rights."[12]

Walter, however, may have overstated his enthusiasm. August Schoenborn, Walter's longtime assistant, would write much later that Walter came to describe Franklin as "a big, fat, lazy man."[13] This may have been true, but it was also necessary to remember that Walter, for the last seven years, in both good times and bad, had been living in a cauldron. The obsession that drove him in designing and building the U.S. Capitol and in hanging on to his own job when it was unjustly threatened was a trait that he shared with only one man—Montgomery C. Meigs. For someone like Walter, anyone of lesser intensity would quite likely appear lazy.

Early in 1859, before Meigs's departure, Walter had written a short letter to his friend Fowler, the cast-iron manufacturer, catching him up on the desultory progress of Capitol construction. He also let Fowler know that he had completed a new design for the Dome, "to the very apex," that would "be ready to go ahead as soon as they give me a chance."[14]

Walter needed a new Dome design because Crawford's final statue of *Freedom*, as Crawford had warned Meigs in early 1856, was going to be about nineteen feet tall—three feet taller than his first two *Freedom*s. This meant that the Dome, as Walter had originally designed it, would be too tall. To obtain the artistic balance he sought, the altitude of the top of the statue had to be in harmony with the rest of the building. Also, a taller, bulkier statue meant that he would need a stronger platform to support it.

Fortunately, cast-iron construction made the needed modification a relatively easy matter, and with Dome construction at a virtual standstill, Walter in early 1859 had plenty of time to modify his design. Walter dropped the summit of the Dome seventeen feet and changed its shape from an ellipsoid to a hemisphere. In doing this, he made the top wider and even more substantial, giving the seven-and-a-half-ton *Freedom* a wider, firmer base.

Walter also redesigned the inner dome. From the Rotunda down below, visitors would see a lower, more intimate ceiling, 180 feet above the Rotunda floor. It would be shaped like an inverted cup with the bottom cut out. Above the hole, called an oculus, Walter planned to suspend a huge concave fresco mural, like the underside of an umbrella, from the top of the outer dome, forty feet above the oculus. Without knowing that the oculus was there, viewers would simply see the mural as an extension of the inner ceiling itself. The fresco would be illuminated by sunlight coming through the windows of the outer dome and projected upward by mirrors.[15]

It is doubtful that Meigs ever saw this design. Walter created it during the absolute nadir of their personal relationship, and he almost certainly kept it locked away in the attic office, where Meigs refused to go. Also, of

To accommodate Crawford's outsized statue of *Freedom*, Walter had to design a lower dome. He also redesigned the inner dome, opening the top and adding an "umbrella" on the underside of which Brumidi would paint a monumental fresco mural to crown the Rotunda. (Architect of the Capitol)

course, the new design invited the same sort of meddling that had befallen the drawing of the original Dome. It served as yet another example of Walter's creative genius—a brilliant solution to a problem that he had identified and Meigs had missed. Walter, almost paranoid about his artistic legacy, would not have wanted Meigs anywhere near the revised Dome plans.[16]

Within a month of Meigs's departure, however, Walter had shown the design to Franklin, and undoubtedly also to Floyd, who ordered Franklin to seek bids—finally—for the Dome and for its framing. Franklin, after only a month on the job, sent a letter to Janes, Fowler, Kirtland & Co., successors to Janes, Beebe, soliciting bids for two separate contracts.[17]

The company responded the following day. It made two offers, but then, unsolicited, made "another proposition." Having seen the Dome plans, the company found it difficult to determine which part would be performed under which contract. Accordingly, it offered to finish the entire Dome—skin, trusses, and installation—on a single contract for one price of 7 cents per pound. The company noted that this was a penny higher than the Dome work they were currently doing, but "when we come to the spherical part of the Dome" the cost would be higher, and it would become even more expensive as the height rose. Still, "in view of our knowledge of the work, the facilities we now have for doing it, and our pride to complete what we have begun, we have offered the whole at the low price of seven cents."[18]

Franklin notified Floyd of the two contract bids and informed him of the unsolicited proposal. He recommended accepting their bid for the skin at 6 cents per pound, but told Floyd he could get a better deal for the trusses in an open competition. He also noted that he had asked a second firm to make offers, but the company had declined.[19] On December 5, Floyd instructed Franklin to accept Janes, Fowler's seven-cent proposal for the whole job.[20] The following day, Franklin agreed, taking care, however, to note in a letter to the company that Floyd had "directed me to accept your offer." He was just as nervous about Floyd as Meigs had been.[21]

This contract was worth around $300,000, by Franklin's estimate, a substantial commitment for its time.[22] Floyd had awarded it without competitive bidding on a proposal made by Janes, Fowler, the lone bidder, and without Franklin's recommendation. Meigs, who probably heard about this sequence of events from Franklin during a Saturday Club meeting, was outraged. Janes, Fowler were "very skillful persons and very reliable," he wrote in his diary that Saturday night, but they had almost certainly gotten a sweetheart deal from Floyd. Meigs had been paying Janes, Fowler 6 cents per pound, and he calculated that the company, at 7 cents per pound, would be getting "a clear gift of $110,000 of public money." The contract was "in direct violation of the law," he wrote. "Does not someone make money out of this?"[23]

Franklin, probably now worried that the government was being cheated, began a protracted negotiation with Janes, Fowler over contractual details: Who was going to build scaffolding and hoist the cast pieces into place? Who was going to tear down the temporary roof once the job was finished? Whose machinery would be used? During this same period, Meigs probably also spoke with Davis, for the Senate Committee on Public Buildings and Grounds, of which Davis was a member, called for all the correspondence related to the Dome contract. The committee received the information from Franklin in February 1860 and submitted it for the record in early March.

The committee printed the Janes, Fowler interchange without recommendation. Franklin's accompanying commentary was every bit as meticulous as anything ever produced by Meigs, showing that the negotiations were conducted amicably. Janes, Fowler was unfailingly polite, gave ground to Franklin on many points, and assumed the cost of scaffolding and hoisting. This obligation, Franklin said in the covering letter sent to the Senate, justified the 7-cents-per-pound base price.[24] The deal appeared reasonable and above reproach. Two questions, however, remained, out of curiosity, if nothing more. How did Janes, Fowler think up the idea of a one-price-fits-all contract, and why did Floyd choose to accept it?

If there were intrigues, Walter certainly could have been involved. Besides John Rice, Charles Fowler was one of Walter's closest friends. Walter had known Fowler for years and had routinely confided in him ever since he began work on the Capitol Extension. Janes, Beebe had done the iron-work for the new Library, and Fowler was, if not the first, certainly one of the first persons to learn in 1854 that Walter had designed a cast-iron Dome for the Capitol. Walter constantly provided Fowler with inside information and gossip to keep him apprised of the Capitol's progress and of the prospects for new jobs. He and Fowler and their families had been social friends for years. And more recently, Walter's second son, Thomas, had taken a job in a Fowler business venture as a broker overseeing guano-collecting expeditions to the Swan Islands in the Caribbean. This had gone well for most of 1859, but a year later, Thomas was looking for something else to do. He, at least, had some money. Robert was finally out of jail, but broke, while Horace's experiment in storekeeping had ended in bankruptcy.

There is no evidence that Walter ever used his insider knowledge to bilk the government, but it is reasonable to ask whether, in this case, he helped his friend formulate a plan to win the Dome contract at 7 cents. He was probably close enough to Floyd at this point to lobby him, and on January 20, 1860, he wrote Fowler that there was a "tempest" because Floyd had offered the no-bid contract. Walter had been in conference with Franklin and Floyd, who had assigned him the job of persuading Fowler to accept conditions that would make the contract palatable to Congress.[25]

Still, there was nothing in Franklin's report to the Senate to suggest that Janes, Fowler had any motive other than the one they put forth: that it was more convenient for them to do the whole job at one price. The company also had credibility for fair dealing in its other work for the Capitol. Even Meigs acknowledged that. Certainly Janes, Fowler was not fronting for a Virginia dentist.

And finally, although none of the principals could know it at the time, Floyd's iron contract would turn out to be a brilliant stroke of luck for the future of the Capitol. When Floyd finalized the agreement on February 15, the United States was just fourteen months away from the beginning the bloodiest war in its history. Iron would become scarce, and it would be hard to obtain for any purpose other than cannonballs—unless the client already held a contract.

Besides the Dome, Franklin's report also provided an update on the ongoing saga of the monolithic columns, which remained just as contentious and confusing as it had been for the past several years. Like both Meigs and Walter before him, Franklin had concluded that the United States did not have a white marble quarry that could furnish enough high-quality stone for a hundred monoliths in a reasonable period of time. Rice and Heebner had provided him with six specimens from which to choose, and Franklin had told Floyd in a January 7, 1860, letter that none of the quarries represented could do the job in less than four years, and the best quarry might need seven years. "It is my opinion," he told Floyd, "that the time required in all of these cases is too great."[26]

He repeated this argument in his cover letter to the Senate committee, but added two bits of information that he had neglected to mention to Floyd. If Rice and Heebner bought Italian instead of American marble, he wrote, all hundred columns would be on hand within eighteen months, "and the building can be completed in three years." If American quarries were used, the additional cost in labor and time would be $100,000.[27]

Franklin had made the project's last plea for Italian marble, apparently without telling Floyd and in defiance of Floyd's categorical refusal to buy it. For Franklin, still trying to establish himself, it was an odd gamble. Why irritate the boss after only four months on the job? The likely reason was that everyone who knew about the project, regardless of personal grudges, agreed that Italian marble was the best alternative. Franklin was probably getting reinforcement for this view from Meigs at the Saturday Club, and he was certainly hearing the same story at the office from Walter. In December, Walter had told Rice that "we have the Senate committee just as we want it." Committee chairman Jesse Bright, a southern sympathizer from Indiana, "will do any thing that Davis wants," Walter wrote, "and Davis is crazy for Italian."[28]

Walter, however, had once again let his enthusiasm outrun his good sense. Everyone—Davis, Meigs, Walter, Rice and Heebner—may have been arrayed against Floyd for a year, but Floyd had not budged on this. He had Know-Nothing xenophobia on his side, still a powerful weapon, especially in the jingoistic House. Italian marble might be the cheapest, quickest, and best, but it was still Italian. Buying it would be a very tough vote to take in the poisonously partisan Congress of 1860.

One thing appeared clear, however, from this interminable conflict: Floyd almost certainly had a private deal going with John Connolly. Every time Meigs, Rice and Heebner, and now Franklin had made a survey of the available marble, Connolly had emerged as the best of a bad lot. His stone was coarse, plain, and streaked with black mica that showed an inclination to decompose in bad weather. But Connolly had a lot of it; it was nearby; and it came in very big pieces.

And Connolly was very aggressive in pushing his case. Within a week after submitting his report, Franklin had received instructions from Floyd to sign a contract with Connolly for one hundred columns at Connolly's proposed price of $1,550 per column. Franklin stalled. There was no money at the moment, he told Floyd. Also, Rice and Heebner had agreed to provide columns for $1,400 apiece, a price that Connolly at one point had accepted. Now Connolly was asking more. This was not the right way to go.[29]

Floyd backed off, telling Franklin he could offer the contract at the price he thought proper. Franklin on April 3 notified Connolly that he would buy columns for $1,400 apiece. Connolly promptly threatened legal action, a gesture that Franklin flicked aside. He reminded Connolly of his earlier offer to do the job for $1,400 per column: "In my opinion, you will have no legal rights in this matter."[30]

The participants had now achieved the same degree of belligerent deadlock that had confounded Meigs the previous year. Floyd wanted to breach the Rice and Heebner contract and hire Connolly on the spot. Connolly wanted his price, knowing that with Floyd ruling out foreign marble, his stone was the only credible alternative. Franklin refused to pay him what he asked because, like Meigs, he understood that doing so would leave the government open to a lawsuit.

Then Davis stepped in. During Senate debate on June 11, Davis offered legislation to appropriate $47,000 to buy thirty-four monoliths from Rice and Heebner, at the same time stipulating that the government itself could use no appropriated funds to buy columns. The amendment passed by acclamation.[31]

Franklin had warned Floyd on March 7 that Congress would be unhappy with him if he ignored an apparent "desire on its part" to resolve the column affair with new legislation. Now Davis had provided the new legislation, and in doing so he had dealt Floyd—and the Buchanan administration—a brisk slap in the face. Davis's proposal simply meant that only Rice and Heebner could buy columns, and they were to have $47,000 to purchase thirty-four of them. That came out to a bit less than $1,400 per column. Connolly would sell to Rice and Heebner at the price they had negotiated with Meigs, or he would not sell at all.

Apparently neither Connolly nor Floyd caught on immediately. Franklin wrote Floyd an urgent note on July 3, letting him know that Connolly had showed up at the Capitol with two columns and left them in the front yard. Now there was another one at the train station, and nine more ready to ship. Under the Davis proviso, Franklin—as the government—could not pay for them, so what should he do?[32] No answer was forthcoming, so Franklin wrote again on July 30. There were now five columns on the grounds.[33]

Finally Floyd gave up, for Franklin on August 18 formally ordered thirty-four columns from Rice and Heebner and notified them that "six are already on the grounds." He would pay Rice and Heebner for the six, and he expressed hope "that you will be able to furnish them all during the fiscal year."[34]

And that appeared to be the end of it. There was one last protest from Connolly, prompting Walter to write to him in early September. Connolly should close a deal with Rice and Heebner immediately, Walter said, or prepare for the possibility that the rest of the columns would be coming from Italy.[35]

Thomas Walter (third from right with full beard) and Jefferson Davis (standing next to him) watch as a monolithic column is hoisted into place on the East Front of the Senate. Davis would leave Washington less than two months later to become the president of the Confederacy. (Architect of the Capitol)

By September, this argument had teeth. Floyd's days were numbered—the Buchanan administration would be gone in six months. Connolly needed to accept what was offered, and accept it quickly, or he would be arguing with new people who might not behave charitably toward the disgruntled crony of a discredited secretary of war. On November 6, 1860, Franklin reported to Floyd that Connolly had delivered sixteen columns, of which eight or ten would be in place by the end of the year. Connolly was now quarrying his twenty-second column, and if things went according to plan, all one hundred columns "should be delivered during this fiscal year and the next."[36]

Things would, of course, never again go according to plan. On the day that Franklin signed his report, the United States elected the Republican Abraham Lincoln of Illinois to be its sixteenth president. The Democratic Party had finally fractured, with the northerners choosing Stephen A. Douglas as their candidate and the southerners choosing Vice President John C. Breckinridge. The newly formed Constitutional Union Party, composed of now-homeless Whigs and Know-Nothing remnants, nominated former Tennessee senator John Bell. There was little suspense during the campaign, since Lincoln, with massive support in the more populous North, was expected to win a plurality easily, which he did. Not a single southern state voted for him.

Throughout this chaotic and dangerous year, the Capitol project never lost its allure, and it could even be said that interest—among northerners and southerners alike—was never higher. Except for the Dome and the porticoes on the four sides of the Extension, the new Capitol was almost finished. Congress could see what it had, and by 1860, members were concentrating on making it perfect. Everyone, it seemed, had a stake. Early in the year the Senate Committee on Public Buildings and Grounds wanted to make sure, once again, that the new Dome—estimated at 7.4 million pounds of iron—would not crush the old Capitol. Franklin did the math and found that the iron would exert only 1/56 of the pressure required to destroy the foundation (when the Dome was finished, it actually weighed nearly 9 million pounds).[37] In June, Senator Bright suggested that the Supreme Court be given $45,000 to defray the cost of moving into the old Senate chamber. That was too much, senators said, so a bidding war began. The first amendment offered $5,000. It lost. The next offered $20,000. It, too, went down. The third, for $25,000, was quickly endorsed by Bright, and the gavel came down.[38]

The appropriations debates moved quickly, and with an unaccustomed air of impatience, conveying a congressional wish to settle the Capitol's important matters and get rid of the rest, and to do it all quickly. Davis effortlessly carried the day on the columns because Congress did not trust Floyd, who was the subject of ongoing investigations into his handling of the Post Office Extension ventilation and misuse of Indian trust bonds. It wanted the columns but did not want the project to be bogged down in suspect deals. The same was true of the Dome. Congress wanted to know if Janes, Fowler had behaved honorably, and once satisfied that they had, they blessed the iron contract.

For the new art commission, however, there was little but contempt. The commission had been established by Congress in 1858 to oversee the selection of display art in the Capitol, but little had happened since. It took Buchanan until the spring of 1859 to name the commissioners. They were the portrait painter James R. Lambdin of Philadelphia, the landscape painter John F. Kensett from New York, and Henry Kirke Brown, the New York sculptor whose pediment design Meigs had spurned for the House portico.

In a long July 1859 letter to the sculptor Randolph Rogers, whose Columbus doors were being cast in Munich, Meigs had predicted the commission would end in disaster. The commissioners had no money to solicit designs, let alone buy art, and "under the law seem to hold only a veto power or power of approval." If it had been up to Meigs, and if Crawford had lived, the frieze along the interior of the new Dome would already have been partly finished, Meigs wrote. "Now, with this committee of artists . . . and various other obstructions, I do not know when, or if ever, in my lifetime, it will be accomplished."[39]

Finally, on February 22, 1860 the commission submitted its report. It had obviously been crafted to appeal to House xenophobia, but the commissioners had apparently forgotten that it also had to pass muster in the Senate, and there it was doomed. The report was polemical and pompous, and the Senate already had a monopoly on those attributes. It did not need to be told what to do.

The report noted that building a Capitol was a unique experience for any nation, and that as "patriots" the commissioners had a responsibility "to see to it that no taint of falsity is suffered to be transmitted to the future upon the escutcheon of our national honor in its artistic record." The only way to ensure this was to have American artists provide American art, and the commission outlined what art should be underwritten by Congress and where it should go: Columbus in the Rotunda, legislative history in the chambers, judicial history in the Court, and maybe Adams and Jefferson, the first two vice presidents, flanking the desk of the Senate's presiding officer.[40]

The Senate looked this over on June 11 and disposed of it in about a half hour. Senator Robert Toombs of Georgia introduced an amendment to kill the commission, and Senator Pearce condemned its work in a few devastating sentences. After eight months, the commissioners had produced "a little report of about seven pages" criticizing the work up to now, making a number of recommendations, and transmitting "their" beliefs on what should go where, Pearce said. They wanted $3,000 each per year in salary, plus some equipment, office space, messengers, "and so on." He stopped, then began again: "I think that this little product . . . admonishes us that it is scarcely worth while to continue this art commission," which, he reminded his colleagues, had been forced upon them by the House. What about paying them $3,000 each in severance and telling them to go away?

Wisconsin Republican James R. Doolittle said that sounded like a good idea and made a motion to vote on Pearce's suggestion. But then Davis interrupted: "What ought we to pay them for?" Other senators chimed in. Nobody in the Senate had asked the commissioners to prepare such a report. The Senate owed them nothing. Toombs then told Doolittle his motion was out of order, and Doolittle withdrew it. Moments later the commission—at least in the Senate—was dead.[41]

The commissioners fared better in the House, where the debate was more about protecting homespun American values than about treading on congressional prerogatives. New York Republican Charles Beale introduced an amendment restoring the commission, and the House did so, then sent the amended bill back to the Senate, which refused to pass it. Conferees met to discuss differences and issued their report on June 20. The Senate prevailed, and the commission was, indeed, dead.[42]

These debates, given the time at which they took place, were remarkably free of rancor, in contrast to the pervasive resentment and outright hatred that gripped Congress for much of the year. The Capitol undoubtedly won approval in part because it was one thing—perhaps the only thing by mid-year—on which lawmakers from both sections could still agree. The Capitol did not belong to either the North or the South; funding it did not give an economic advantage to either section; and the building was no longer seriously controversial from an aesthetic point of view. Building things was what politicians liked to do, and there it was.

But on another level, the Capitol, more than ever for lawmakers, had become in 1860 a national rallying point—a vision of what might have been. The Capitol was a national promise, something to hold on to in a time of acute distress. "I shall never hesitate," Georgia representative Joshua Hill said during the 1860 debate to fund the Capitol, "whenever a proper appropriation is called for, for the completion or the embellishment of the Capitol of my country, to vote for it with pleasure."[43] Hill would resign from Congress in 1861 after Georgia seceded.

This ability to invoke the virtues of national pride and at the same time espouse rabid sectionalism was an unusual talent that Jefferson Davis had displayed for most of his political career. But he was not the only one to practice it.

By the late summer of 1859, Meigs's workmen had assembled the six pieces of Crawford's plaster model of *Freedom Triumphant in War and Peace* in the old House chamber so that members of Congress, tourists, and casual visitors could imagine what the Capitol might look like when the finishing touch had been added. Since there was no Dome at that moment on which to mount *Freedom*, Meigs had little incentive to have it cast immediately. The plan favored by both him and Walter was eventually to give the job to the Ames Manufacturing Co. of Chicopee, Massachusetts, regarded at the time as the most sophisticated metal foundry in the country.

But sometime in the latter part of 1859, sculptor Clark Mills, who had opened a bronze foundry on the Bladensburg Road, inside the district line, decided to lobby for the job himself. Mills was no amateur. His equestrian statue of Andrew Jackson in Lafayette Square was one of the first public monuments ever erected in the capital, and the first bronze statue cast in the United States. Its unveiling in 1853 was a celebrated public event. Meigs, after his firing late in 1859, had visited the foundry to see the casting of a Mills equestrian statue of Washington, which he dismissed as "very rough," "badly finished," and unworthy of a contract.[44] Fortunately for Mills, what Meigs thought no longer mattered.

Mills was born in New York but had settled in South Carolina as an adult before moving to Washington. He was famous and apparently quite well connected to South Carolina's political establishment. Walter discovered this in January 1860 and wrote a quick note to J. A. Ames in Chicopee, another of his contractor friends. Mills, Walter wrote, had prevailed on the South Carolina congressional delegation—six congressmen and two senators—to visit Floyd "in a body" to "intercede with him in reference to the statue for the Dome." Walter told Ames he had gone to see an "embarrassed" Floyd, who was fully aware that Walter, Franklin, and the art commission wanted Ames to make the statue.[45] Three weeks later, Walter wrote again to say that he thought Mills was going to get the job. While Floyd was still embarrassed, Walter wrote, the "outside pressure" exerted by the South Carolinians was so great that he would have to "give in."[46]

And he did. Mills got Floyd's approval and proposed to make the statue for $25,000. He eventually did it for about $20,000, using copper from Lake Superior and tin bought in New York.[47] Casting began in June 1860, five months before Lincoln's election.

South Carolina's two senators withdrew from the Senate within five days of Lincoln's victory. South Carolina's House delegation "retired" en masse four days before Christmas and the day after South Carolina became the first state to leave the union. South Carolina may have bred the most militant secessionist movement in the country, but its elected officials, before abandoning Washington, had ensured that its favorite son would cast the statue that crowned the U.S. Capitol.

South Carolina's secession signaled the beginning of the breakup of the union, but the final slide toward civil war had begun more than a year earlier and had continued inexorably throughout 1860 and into 1861.

The catalytic event, felt throughout the country, but even more powerfully in Washington because it was so close by, was the takeover of the federal armory at Harpers Ferry, Virginia, by John Brown. Meigs in his diary in mid-October 1859, noted "a strange riot" at the armory. "The report at first was that the Negroes had risen, and that the abolitionists had taken the place."[48] This turned out not to be the case, but it was certainly what Brown, whose band of broadsword-wielding zealots had killed five proslavery settlers on the Kansas plains in 1856, had hoped would happen. On the evening of October 16, 1859, he and twenty-one accomplices—sixteen white and five black—attacked Harpers Ferry and took over the federal armory, arsenal, and rifle works there with the intention of inspiring a slave revolt.[49]

The raid stalled, however, for, once inside the armory, Brown and his men simply waited for something to happen. Brown's men killed a train station baggagemaster—a black man—by mistake, and one of Brown's black followers was shot and killed by locals. Brown moved his men and hostages to a fire engine house to make a last stand. Skirmishing with militia and townspeople continued all day on October 17 until Colonel Robert E. Lee arrived late in the evening with a detachment of marines. After brief and fruitless negotiations at dawn the following morning, the marines stormed the engine house. One marine and two of Brown's men were killed, and Brown himself suffered several bloody sword wounds.

Had Brown himself been killed, the episode would probably have enjoyed a few days of headlines and been forgotten. Instead, during his incarceration and trial, and in the days leading up to his execution on December 2, Brown behaved with such solemn dignity and courage that he and his cause held the country spellbound.

"I believe that to have interfered as I have done . . . in behalf of His despised poor, [is] no wrong, but right," Brown said in his celebrated final statement to the court that convicted him. "Now, if it is deemed necessary that I should forfeit my life for the furtherance of the ends of justice, and mingle my blood further with the blood of my children and with the blood of millions in this slave country whose rights are disregarded by wicked, cruel and unjust enactments, I say let it be done."[50]

John Brown was instantly transformed into a national symbol. In the North he became a martyr to the antislavery cause. Bells tolled in northern cities on the day he died. Prayer meetings were held, and citizens hung black crepe from their windowsills. In the South, he was an agent of evil, leader of what Jefferson Davis labeled "a murderous gang of Abolitionists" who "come to incite slaves to murder helpless women and children."[51] Southerners in the immediate aftermath of the raid combed their communities looking for coconspirators, meting out beatings and worse to suspect blacks, expatriate white northerners, and other interlopers.[52]

Most important, John Brown confirmed how far apart the two sections had grown. If John Brown was a hero in the North and a dangerous cutthroat in the South, then there was nothing further to discuss.

The new Congress convened on December 5, 1859, three days after Brown's hanging. The Democrats still controlled the Senate, with a comfortable 13-vote majority. In the House the Republicans held a plurality of 109 seats, but they needed 119 to elect a Speaker. It took nearly two months, almost as long as it had in 1856, before Representative William Pennington, an innocuous first-term Republican from New Jersey, took the chair. This protracted struggle was notable for the large number of armed congressmen and senators who attended the debates. One near-riot began when a pistol fell from a member's pocket by accident, prompting colleagues to ready their own weapons for the anticipated shoot-out. "The only persons who do not have a revolver and a knife," wrote Senator James H. Hammond of South Carolina, "are those who have two revolvers."[53]

The age of accommodation was over.

For Jefferson Davis, 1860 was the year when he found it no longer possible to be a slaveholding states' rights southerner and a believer in the union at the same time. For much of the year he tried to escape this trap, but in the end he could not. And when he finally had to choose, he did what he had always said he would do. He chose Mississippi and abandoned the United States.

Davis and other non-"fire-eaters" in Congress knew that the only way to avoid the disintegration of the union was to figure out a way that the Democrats could find another compromise presidential candidate— preferably a northerner—and win the election. Then they could kick the slavery conundrum down the road for another four years, hoping a solution might turn up. Davis's favorite was Franklin Pierce, and he told Pierce in late 1859 that Pierce was preferred "above all others" in Mississippi.[54] If a Republican were elected president, Davis and other non-fire-eaters knew, southern states were certain to secede.

Davis throughout the year was in the forefront of efforts to find a solution to the Democrats' dilemma. There is much disagreement about what he intended, for although his proposals offered an escape, they also helped cause the rift that ultimately split the party. Many canny southern leaders, committed to secession, wanted the split. Davis may or may not have been one of them.

The leading Democratic presidential aspirant as 1860 began was

Stephen A. Douglas, but he had alienated the South, first by refusing to support the Lecompton constitution and again in 1858 by articulating the so-called "Freeport Doctrine" during his debates with Lincoln. Douglas held that while the Dred Scott decision guaranteed that slavery could not be prohibited in U.S. territories, slavery, as a practical matter, would never take root unless a territorial government passed laws to protect it. If it did not, no slave owner would dare bring slaves into the territory. This stance, a careful circumlocution crafted for Illinois Democrats, was seen in the South as essentially a repudiation of the Dred Scott decision. Southern Democrats hated Douglas for taking this position and would never support his presidential candidacy.

So Douglas had to be gotten out of the way if the national party was to endure. The Senate leadership—dominated by southern Democrats—bounced Douglas from the chairmanship of the Committee on Territories, a gross insult, and southerners began attacking him and the Freeport Doctrine. Davis was Douglas's antagonist in two January floor debates. Douglas contended that senators had conspired to take away his chairmanship at a time when he was ailing. Davis, with characteristic venom, brushed this complaint aside. First of all, he said, Douglas "certainly has no right to say there is any disposition here to 'double team' on him." Douglas "magnifies himself" in making this assertion. Davis was not buying the illness excuse, either. He was ready, he said, to debate Douglas "man-to-man, at any time."[55]

On February 2 and March 1, Davis presented his response to Freeport, offering a set of seven resolutions reaffirming the core tenet of Dred Scott—the right of citizens to take their property, including slaves, into territories. If experience showed that neither the territorial government nor the courts were willing to protect the settlers' slave property, the resolutions said, "it will be the duty of Congress to supply such deficiency." The resolutions recognized, as Douglas did, that the Dred Scott decision would be useless if territorial governments refused to enforce it, but they demanded that Congress provide redress if necessary.

The historian David Potter, later echoed by Michael F. Holt, has described these resolutions as a "federal slave code," designed to marginalize Douglas and demand an ideological commitment to Dred Scott by northern Democrats.[56] Seen in this light, the resolutions appeared, practically speaking, as a guarantee that the party would split, for northerners would never vote for them.

William J. Cooper, a Davis biographer, has offered a different interpretation. Instead of trying to split the party, Cooper maintained, Davis wanted to "build a bridge over the chasm." Dred Scott made it legal to take slaves into the territories. Congress was bound to protect slave owners' rights—but only at some unspecified time in the future, and only if other remedies were shown to be ineffective. With this, Cooper said, Davis hoped to kill Douglas's candidacy. Then the party could pick a palatable national candidate.[57]

The historian William W. Freehling has taken something of a middle position. He acknowledged that convention delegates from the North would never accept the Davis resolutions. He also argued that Davis knew this and did not want the resolutions included in the national platform. What occurred, however, was that the Alabama secessionist William Yancey used the Davis resolutions for his own ends. Seeking to "lure moderates to the extreme," Freehling wrote, the Alabama state party, with Yancey's guidance, issued an ultimatum: the Democrats' national platform must "explicitly" endorse congressional protection of slavery in territories. If it failed to do so "in substance," the Alabamans would withdraw from the convention. The moderate Davis resolutions were the "substance" that Yancey sought.[58]

Thus the Davis resolutions, either deliberately or unwittingly, became the tool that broke the Democrats apart. The delegates convened in Charleston in April, and after five days of deliberation they issued a majority report and a minority report on slavery in the territories. The majority report, written by southerners on the Platform Committee, included the Davis language calling for congressional protection. The minority report, issued by Douglas's supporters, gave the Supreme Court the obligation to determine how territorial governments and Congress should enforce Dred Scott. When delegates voted to adopt the minority report, Alabama, six other southern delegations, and part of an eighth abandoned the convention. The split was consummated. The different factions subsequently nominated Douglas and Breckinridge, thus all but assuring a Republican victory.

"If northern men insist upon nominating Douglas we must be beaten, and with such alienation as leaves nothing to hope for in the future of nationality in our organization," a pessimistic Davis wrote to Pierce in June. "I have never seen the country in so great danger and those who might protect it seem to be unconscious of the necessity."[59]

Davis spent most of the rest of 1860 issuing warnings to both friends and adversaries. At the same time, however, he was remarkably willing and able to continue defending the new Capitol, his role in building it, and his wishes for its completion. In June, with Republicans intent on investigating Floyd for corruption, Davis spoke several times on behalf of the departed Meigs to exonerate him from any past wrongdoing, prompting Meigs on June 13 to write a short note of appreciation: "I cannot too warmly thank you for your vindication of my conduct in yesterday's debate," he said. "I shall preserve this debate and transmit it to my children."[60]

A week later, during debate on Capitol appropriations, Davis once again came to Meigs's defense, relating, apparently from memory, the entire history of Meigs's quest for monolithic columns. Questions about the Connolly contract, which were part of the Republican case against Floyd, had nothing to do with Meigs, Davis said. Meigs had never recommended either Connolly's quarry or its inferior marble, which, he predicted, "would exfoliate" if brought to the "sharp edges" and "deep relief" that the Lee marble could accommodate. His—and Meigs's—recommendation was to buy Italian, Davis reminded his colleagues. And by refusing to do so, "you have to diminish the style, and at last to disgrace the building by putting up an inferior building, merely in order that you may keep the name of American."[61]

With the election of Lincoln, a Republican, Davis's worst fears had come true. Congress reconvened in early December, but the Republicans were in no mood to make deals. "The argument is exhausted," wrote Davis and several other southerners in a December 14 letter addressed "To Our Constituents." Republicans, they continued, "are resolute in the purpose to grant nothing that will or ought to satisfy the South." The letter called on southerners to organize "a confederacy—a result to be obtained only by separate state secession."[62]

In a last effort to save the union, Congress on December 20 formed a "Committee of Thirteen" to find a solution, which Davis joined. The committee's proposal, elaborated by John J. Crittenden, called for a constitutional amendment to extend the Missouri Compromise line to the Pacific

Ocean. Davis was willing to accept the proposal, but Republicans on the committee remained adamantly opposed.[63] On December 31, the committee reported that it was unable to make a decision.

And that was all. South Carolina had already seceded, and Mississippi followed on January 9, 1861. Ten days later, Davis received official notification of the decision. On the morning of January 21, he went to the U.S. Capitol for the last time.

Crowds had mobbed the corridors and the galleries. Davis, in great pain from another attack of facial neuralgia, picked his way carefully to his desk, taking care not to jostle those who stood in his way. "There brooded over this immense crowd a palpitating, expectant silence," Varina Davis recalled. "Curiosity and the expectation of an intellectual feast seemed to be the prevailing feeling," she added, but "we felt blood in the air."[64]

Davis's remarks were brief. He had received official notification of Mississippi's decision to leave the union, he said, and "under these circumstances, of course, my functions are terminated." Mississippi had "justifiable cause" to secede, and Davis agreed with the decision. But even if he had not, he added, "I should still . . . have been bound by her action." He was, before anything else and ultimately, a Mississippian. "I am sure I feel no hostility toward you," he said, nor did the people of Mississippi. "I hope and they hope for peaceable relations with you, though we must part."

"Mr. President and senators," he concluded, "having made the announcement which the occasion seemed to me to require, it only remains for me to bid you a final adieu."[65]

18

FREEDOM'S CAP

It had been cold that week. Just the day before, December 1, the temperature at dawn was 23 degrees with a howling wind. Thomas U. Walter had had only two pieces of the statue left to install, but he had to wait for a bit. It was hard enough, even on a good day, to get his riggers to climb to the little scaffold above the Dome nearly three hundred feet overhead. Some of them needed a shot of whiskey before they went up there—really not a good idea. Walter had put a stop to that, but even so, it was a constant struggle to find skilled workers who could handle the heights. Especially in the middle of a war.

The wind had died down, and in the afternoon the riggers had hooked *Freedom*'s upper torso to the derrick and hoisted it up the side of the Capitol, past the peristyle, past the sloping cupola of the Dome, and perhaps thirty feet into the air before lowering it gently into position and bolting it to the rest of the statue.[1]

Now came the final act. It was Wednesday, December 2, 1863, a chill, bright morning, about as good as Walter could hope for. He had put ads in the local papers to let people know that the final piece of *Freedom*, the head with its eagle headdress, would be winched up and mounted at noon. He had, however, sent out no invitations, planned no elaborate ceremony, scheduled no speeches. He was not fond of big, splashy spectacles, he had said. Maybe it was his Baptist parsimony, grown more pronounced these last few years. Or maybe it was the endless months of rage and despair.

The Union Army had won big victories at Vicksburg and Gettysburg the previous summer, but there was no joy in Washington, no sign, at least as far as Walter could see, that this conflict would ever end. Reporters had clamored for interviews, but he had given none. He had told his men that the statue would be completed as part of "everyday work." There would be no shouting and no waving of hats. He would not be on the platform, he said. August Schoenborn, who had been there from the beginning, would represent him.[2]

This is not to say that Walter was indifferent. He had spent most of his time closeted in the office for the past several days, "all excitement," he confessed in a letter to Amanda.[3] He had invested twelve years of his life in the U.S. Capitol, helped it grow from a wooden-domed glorified town hall into a seat of government proud enough to rival any in the world. He had begun lifting the bronze pieces of the statue into place a week ago, and despite occasional delays for inclement weather, the statue would be in place in time for the opening of the new Congress the following Monday.

It was the great achievement of his life, and he knew that. Over those twelve years, the country had changed, Washington had changed, and Walter had changed—from a vaguely pro-South apologist who owned a slave into a bitter foe of the Confederacy and slavery who in 1862 had embraced the opportunity to hire a black youth as a paid messenger. And while he had built the Capitol for himself, for the nation, and for posterity, he told his son that he had also built it as a testament to the tenacity of Abraham Lincoln and his government. Walter scarcely knew Lincoln, if he knew him at all. But he had written Thomas more than a year earlier that "no honor is too great for this administration." He wished to "add a ray of glory, in the way of art, to the brilliancy that will surround it in the history that is to [be] hand[ed] down to future times," he wrote. "I will sacrifice any thing in reason to do it."[4]

Lincoln, ill at the White House, did not appear at the Capitol that day. But people came. Thousands of them. They began arriving at midmorning to stand in the muck on what remained of the grounds in front of the eastern façade. They stood among the storage sheds and machine shops that crouched near the building. They dodged the uncollected windblown trash that skittered among heaps of junk, derelict marble boulders, and piles of unused bricks. Their feet squelched in the muddy wheel ruts and skid marks that scarred what was left of the lawn.[5]

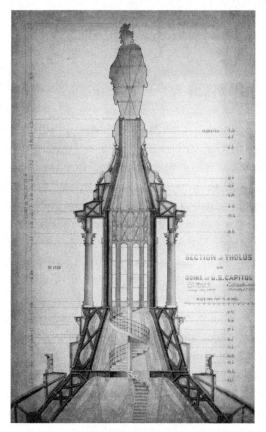

Walter's drawing of the central tholus (lantern) of the Capitol with *Freedom* atop the new Dome. His vision was realized when his team bolted the last piece of the statue in place on Wednesday, December 2, 1863. (Architect of the Capitol)

Shortly after noon, Walter told the riggers to engage the winch, and the last piece of *Freedom* began to rise. Walter went to his office and began a letter to Amanda, peeking out the window periodically to watch the proceedings. Charles Fowler, the supplier of cast iron for the Dome, had been in town the previous week, but had left. He was nervous and afraid: the scaffold would break; the statue would be too heavy and destroy the Dome.[6] Something would surely go wrong.

At 12:25 p.m. it was over. "I have succeeded in putting on the head of the statue without accident," Walter told Amanda. "Her ladyship looks placid and beautiful."[7] As soon as the head was bolted in place, the riggers raised the U.S. flag above the Dome, the crowd cheered, and an artillery battery began a salute—one gun for each of the thirty-five states, including those that had seceded. When the battery had finished, the salute was repeated at twelve forts around the city. It took some time.

Thomas U. Walter had traveled a long road since Lincoln's election set in motion the bloody events that preceded *Freedom*'s investiture atop the Capitol. The things that had mattered four years ago—the iron contract, the art commission, the wall painting, the immigrant workers—had long been forgotten. The Capitol, too, had for a time been deemed irrelevant, but Walter fixed that. Through political acumen, help from his friends, and his own tenacity, he had made his historical statement.

When the war began, Walter had been pro-South and conservative. He blamed "the insane North" for disturbing his world, he told Fowler on December 29, 1860, and had nothing against slavery.[8] He had seen nothing good in Lincoln's election. He had warned his ne'er-do-well third son, Horace, that a "dissolution of the union is more than probable" and urged him to move to the far West and become a farmer.[9] A month later, work on the Capitol stopped. On December 15, 1860, Walter wrote to his eldest son, Robert, "I believe the country is doomed."[10]

He was not, however, unremittingly pessimistic. Shortly after the election, still anticipating a successful end to his work in Washington, he paid $5,700 for a lot in Philadelphia's Germantown section, where he planned to build his dream house.[11] The day after Christmas 1860, he wrote an upbeat letter to Charles Fowler in New York. Not only were people working again at the Capitol, but the second tier of iron on the Dome had been completed and the riggers were getting ready to raise the derrick.[12]

Still, there was no denying he was fearful. Walter had risen from modest beginnings, mastering a hostile world to become one of the premier architects in the country. He did not like change. So confident was he of his future that in late 1858 he had purchased his house servant, John Keith, from Keith's owner for $730, being careful to ask for legal title so he could "recover him should he run away."[13] With his own slave and his lot in Germantown, he was as respectable as anyone he knew.

One thing Walter did not have to worry about on that day in December 1863 was Montgomery Meigs, who no longer had anything to do with the Capitol. But by the end of 1863, Meigs had already served for two and a half years as Brigadier General Montgomery C. Meigs, Quartermaster General of the U.S. Army. He was a member of Lincoln's inner circle and one of the most powerful men in Washington.

Meigs owed his success to toughness, courage, intelligence, and his refusal to compromise his hostility to the Buchanan administration and to Secretary of War John B. Floyd. Before the war started, all he had wanted was to get his jobs back at the Capitol and Aqueduct. But when the war began, he aimed higher.

After his dismissal from the Capitol in late 1859, Meigs had done his best to undercut Floyd from behind the scenes. Meigs prodded Congress through his mentor, Jefferson Davis, to broaden its investigations into Floyd's handling of public works contracts for the Dome and the Post Office. He was honestly concerned that Floyd was going to ruin the Capitol through cronyism and other corrupt practices. But Meigs also wanted vindication and recognition for his achievements, a list that seemed to lengthen the more he thought about them. He had built the Capitol Extension, but he also convinced himself that he had designed it. And by helping to modify the new Dome, he convinced himself that he had designed that as well.

The final face-off between Meigs and Floyd had begun at midyear 1860. Meigs had been off the Capitol project for months but was still in charge of the Aqueduct, and he estimated that he could finish construction with a $500,000 appropriation. Even though there was water at the Capitol and several other Washington locations, Meigs still had bridges to complete, tunnels to dig, and piping to lay. Floyd, however, did not request funds for the project, and without money, Meigs would have to shut down the works, leaving him with nothing to do.

Meigs brought his problem to the attention of his Senate friends—Robert Toombs of Georgia, and of course Davis. Toombs in June offered an amendment to the civil appropriations bill, providing $500,000 "according to the plans and estimates of Captain Meigs." The money should be administered by "an officer of the corps of Engineers, not below the rank of captain, and having experience in the design of bridges and aqueducts." The language applied to no one but Meigs, and it was intended to bypass Floyd and ensure that Meigs got the money and the job.[14]

This was a risky ploy, because it encroached upon executive privilege, inviting a rebuke from President Buchanan. But Davis made the case on the Senate floor. He praised Meigs at length, acknowledged that the amendment applied to Meigs, and argued that Congress remained within its rights as long as it did not name the designated individual in the legislation. He did not think the War Department would take offense, for none was intended. If that were the case, he said, "my support could not be obtained." The measure passed.[15]

Buchanan both signed the bill and took offense. He signed, he wrote in a cover letter, only because he "deemed it impossible that the Congress could have interfered" with his right to order any army officer "to any duty" he wished.[16] He would do what he wanted with Meigs and would not ask permission. Before a month had elapsed, Floyd had appointed a new supervisor for the Aqueduct—an officer junior to Meigs—and made Meigs the disbursing officer. These moves kept Floyd within the letter of the new law even as he transformed Meigs into a paper pusher.

Meigs was furious. He fired off a letter to Buchanan, complaining that Floyd's orders were contrary to the new law, and thereby illegal.[17] Buchanan consulted with the attorney general, who ruled that Meigs had no grievance. Meigs wrote again to Buchanan and received an icily polite reply in return. Despite "sincere good feeling toward yourself," Buchanan said, the discussion was over. There would be "no more direct correspondence between us on this subject." Meigs's last letter was returned unopened.[18]

A few weeks later, Meigs got into two trivial fights with Floyd, refusing to pay one of his successor's new hires and then refusing to reimburse an Army officer's travel expenses because the trip had nothing to do with the Aqueduct.

Floyd had had enough. In late September, he relieved Meigs at the Aqueduct and sent him to Fort Jefferson, on the Dry Tortugas, a set of seven remote desert islands in the Gulf of Mexico seventy miles west of Key West, Florida. He was supposed to work on the fortifications. It was apparently the worst duty Floyd could think of.

The entire sequence, from appropriation to banishment, took only three months and had a scripted feel. Davis and Meigs—both of them skilled bureaucrats—should have known that having Congress prescribe personnel decisions for the executive branch was not a good idea. It would have been far better for Davis to try the tactics that had served him and Meigs so well in the past—visit Buchanan at the White House and quietly get him to help Meigs and finesse the Floyd dispute. Instead, Davis chose confrontation, and he got the rest of the Senate—which had little love for

Buchanan and still less for Floyd—to go along. Meigs's fate, at that point, was all but foretold.

It is not clear why Davis miscalculated. Perhaps he simply wanted to go on record, along with his colleagues, in praising Meigs and attesting to his competence. Or Davis may have decided this was the only way to guarantee one last favor for his protégé before his own likely departure. By the time the appropriation reached the Senate floor, the Republicans had named Lincoln as their presidential candidate and the Democrats were a week away from decomposing.

Meigs, apparently, thought the new legislation would work, and he was outraged when it did not. And he was unrepentant. When General Totten, a faithful supporter and counselor for two decades, suggested to Meigs that he might want to swallow his pride in his last petty disputes with Floyd, Meigs was adamant: "What would you do if the secretary ordered you to cut your own throat?" Meigs asked. "To disobey an unlawful command of a superior is undoubtedly lawful."[19]

Not even the posting to the Tortugas cooled Meigs's fury or his confidence in his swift return to Washington. With Buchanan at twilight and a Republican candidate with good prospects for November, nothing was forever. "He thinks it is not very probable that he will remain in the Tortugas for any length of time," his wife, Louisa, wrote to her sister in late September.[20]

Walter took no official note of Meigs's departure for Florida. Also unremarked was Floyd's resignation on December 29. Congress had already nearly censured Floyd for his role in selling an Army frontier outpost to a developer at bargain prices, and had asked him to explain the contracts for the monolithic columns and the Dome iron. The Seward-ordered investigation of the heating and ventilation contracts at the Post Office was almost completed, as was another investigation into illegal sales of more than $2.5 million in Indian trust bonds held by the War Department.[21] Floyd ostensibly resigned because he disagreed with Buchanan's decision to reinforce federal troops at Fort Sumter, in Charleston, South Carolina. In fact, Floyd had become much more trouble than he was worth. His successor was Joseph Holt, an antislavery Kentuckian who had been Buchanan's postmaster general.

In early January 1861, with only two months left in office, Buchanan was incapable of stopping the country from unraveling. Four states seceded by January 10 and three more by February 2. Buchanan's view was that while states had no right to secede, the federal government had no authority to force them to remain in the union. This was a prescription for national paralysis.

On February 18, still more than two weeks before Lincoln's inauguration, delegates meeting in Montgomery, Alabama, from seven seceded states formed a provisional government of the Confederate States of America and made Jefferson Davis their president. Three days earlier, Walter had blithely written to his second son, Thomas, in Norfolk, Virginia, congratulating him on a successful guano expedition and predicting that "very soon" things would "settle down" and the country would begin an unmatched era of prosperity. "Before the year is out, the states will be again united."[22] And then, on February 27, Walter wrote a short note to Fowler. Meigs had returned to Washington and was "doing his best" to once again take charge of the Capitol Extension and the new Dome.[23]

Walter was right. Meigs had traveled overland to Florida, sampling the militancy of the southern states during the run-up to the November elections. Once in the Tortugas, he had mounted a lobbying campaign, warning of the weakness of the federal garrisons he had seen along the way and seeking reinforcements and armament for Fort Jefferson and Fort Taylor in Key West—preparing the outposts in case southern state militias tried to take them over. He heard nothing from Buchanan or Floyd, so he wrote directly to Winfield Scott, the commanding general of the Army. Scott sent him what he needed.[24]

On January 28, Holt, the new war secretary, brought Meigs back to Washington. Southern sympathizers were leaving the Buchanan administration in droves, and with a month left in office, the president was finally stiffening his spine. While everyone else in government had been wringing his hands, Meigs had anticipated a complicated logistical problem—fortifying isolated federal military facilities—and implemented a solution in less than four months. Holt needed him, and Lincoln would need him even more.

Meigs got Holt's letter on February 12, 1861, and reached Washington on the twentieth. His stock had never been higher. Holt recounted how Floyd had dismissed Meigs's requests for men and guns to defend "some heap of rocks." But Floyd in his turn had been swept aside when Scott appeared, waving Meigs's reports and declaiming on "the great importance of holding" the Tortugas.[25]

Meigs—probably at his own request, although his diary did not make this clear—immediately took over as supervisor of the Aqueduct. He was not feeling charitable. His successor was given orders to succeed him once again—on the Dry Tortugas. At the Saturday Club on February 23, Alexander Dallas Bache asked him if he intended to reclaim the Capitol, to which Meigs replied, "Of course." He would give Franklin a few days to resign, and if that did not work, he told Bache, "I should myself apply my powers of persuasion to bring it about." Bache suggested obliquely that Franklin might want to stay on and that Meigs was now "in a position to be generous." Meigs did not know what he was talking about.[26]

On Monday, Franklin sent an emissary to Meigs to inform him that he would be happy to finish building the Cabin John Bridge in those moments he could spare from the Capitol. Meigs sent Franklin a note describing "the true view of the case." Not only would Franklin not be building the bridge, he was finished at the Capitol as well.[27]

Franklin refused to cooperate, pointing out in a letter that getting rid of him would be a "great injury to himself" because everyone would say he had been "put in the place by a dishonest Secretary of War" and "turned out by an honest" secretary. Meigs immediately went to Secretary Holt and told him about all the injustices he had endured. He was somewhat sympathetic to Franklin, suggesting that Holt make him supervisor of the Treasury Department Extension. He drew up the orders, and Holt signed them.[28]

On February 28, at noon, Meigs met Franklin and took charge of the Capitol for the first time in sixteen months. At 12:15 p.m. Walter appeared. "Good morning, Captain Meigs," he said, "I have called to pay my respects to you." It was the first time Walter had spoken to Meigs in more than a year. The meeting, he said later in a letter to Charles Fowler, was extremely uncomfortable. "He looked daggers at me, and gave a grunt, gnashing his teeth."[29]

Three days later, Walter heard from Meigs. It was not good news: "Being satisfied that your continuance upon the public buildings in my charge, the Capitol Extension, Post Office Extension, and New Dome will not conduce to the public interests," Meigs wrote, "I have the honor to inform you that your services are dispensed with from this date."[30]

Fortunately for Walter, Meigs had left it too late. Holt would probably

With Meigs gone, construction of the Dome resumed. This photograph of the
West Front, taken from Pennsylvania Avenue, shows the peristyle finally
capped. The Civil War was about to begin. (Architect of the Capitol)

have fired Walter in a moment on Meigs's say-so, but Holt's time had run
out. Walter received Meigs's note on March 4, and that same day, even as
he wrote feverish letters seeking help, Lincoln was being sworn in at the
Capitol's Eastern Portico beneath the unfinished Dome.

"Have received the dismissal, am answering it now," Walter told John
Rice. His only chance, he said, was to ask the incoming secretary of war,
Simon Cameron, a Pennsylvanian, to intercede on his behalf. Walter asked
Rice to come to Washington and to bring with him former congressman
Henry D. Moore, a state Republican Party leader with close ties to Cam-
eron. "Meigs is busy night and day to make an immediate and strong im-
pression" on Cameron, Walter wrote. "No time to be lost."[31]

And it worked. Walter temporized in a note to Meigs, reminding him
yet again that he had no authority to fire him since Walter held a presidential appointment. His employment "depends upon the will of the President of the United States, and is no way at your disposal."[32]

On March 14, Cameron countermanded Meigs's dismissal of Walter
and directed him "not to interfere with Mr. Walter in the performance of
his official duties until the question as to his continuance on the public
works shall be decided by the President."[33] An ecstatic Walter dashed off

Abraham Lincoln took office on March 4, 1861, below the still-unfinished
Dome. Meigs tried to fire Walter in the Buchanan government's last days, but
time ran out. Lincoln's inauguration, significant in so many ways, marked the
final confrontation between the Capitol's engineer and its architect. (Library of
Congress)

notes to a dozen friends and relatives and sent a relieved thank-you note
to "my dear Moore" in Harrisburg.[34]

Meigs would not give up. He immediately protested the decision to
Cameron in an encyclopedic letter recounting the entire history of the
feud and the reasons why Walter's original appointment by President Fillmore was no longer valid. The letter was remarkably tone-deaf. Like Floyd,
Cameron was a lifetime political operative with questionable ethics, but
he was neither stupid nor a Democrat. Almost by definition he cared
nothing for the bureaucratic moves made by his predecessors. And as a
brand-new secretary of war with a major civil conflict looming before
him, the last thing he needed was a low-ranking army engineer trying to
steamroll him into firing the Architect of the Capitol Extension over an
ancient dispute.

Finally, in an even more impolitic move, Meigs rested his case on directives issued by the Pierce administration's "Secretary of War"—Jefferson Davis. These he cited repeatedly, along with the "urgent remonstrances of the Secretary, who repeatedly warned me of his [Walter's] character." He noted his own generosity in keeping Walter on. It apparently never occurred to Meigs that under current circumstances, Cameron might view Walter as a hero and see Meigs as the lapdog of a doughface president and a national traitor.[35] Cameron was unmoved.

For a fortnight, Walter and Meigs were back in their old stalemate. On the eve of civil war, they had turned the clock back to 1858.

Walter spent his time cultivating Cameron as his new protector, while Meigs tried to induce Cameron to void the Dome iron contract that Walter and Franklin had worked so hard to obtain. On March 28, Walter reported to Rice that Meigs was a ubiquitous nuisance.[36]

And then, suddenly, Meigs was gone. The Lincoln administration had better things to do than referee a fight over public works, and it had a more important job for Meigs. On March 29, Secretary of State William H. Seward summoned Meigs to a confidential meeting with Lincoln. The president wanted to reinforce both Fort Sumter, in Charleston harbor, South Carolina, and Fort Pickens, off the coast of Florida near Pensacola. Both were threatened by Confederate forces. Scott did not want to take immediate action and risk provoking hostilities that did not yet exist. What did Meigs think? the president asked. Could relief expeditions to the beleaguered forts be successfully carried out? They could, Meigs replied. Lincoln told him he would be in touch with him in the next few days.[37]

Seward, who was rapidly becoming one of Lincoln's closest advisers, had been a solid Meigs supporter during his Senate days and was now the only powerful friend Meigs had in the new administration. Lincoln needed help crafting a policy for his forts, and Seward, obviously, had suggested he speak with Meigs. Then, instead of excuses, Meigs had offered solutions. Meigs did not yet know it, but Seward had set him on the path that would redefine his career. Walking home from the White House, Seward told Meigs he was "much gratified at the result of this interview."[38] Meigs had apparently passed a crucial test.

On Sunday morning, March 31, Meigs returned to Seward's house with one of Winfield Scott's aides to discuss the forts. He and the aide were told to figure out a way to hold Fort Pickens and to bring the plan to the White House by 4:00 p.m. They arrived at 2:30 p.m. and briefed Lincoln on a seaborne relief mission to Pickens. Lincoln told them to show the plan to Scott: "'Tell him,' says the President, 'that I wish this thing done and not to let it fail.'"[39]

Three days later, Meigs left secretly for New York, charged with organizing the relief expedition as its engineering and logistics officer. On April 7, he was at sea aboard the steamship *Atlantic*, along with 399 soldiers, including sappers, engineers, and an artillery company—and seventy-three horses. On April 13, the *Atlantic* reached Key West and picked up some extra howitzers and ammunition. It set out for the Tortugas the following day. Meanwhile, in Charleston, also on April 13, army major Robert Anderson surrendered Fort Sumter after a day and a half of bombardment, and Lincoln called for seventy-five thousand volunteers. The Civil War had begun.

The *Atlantic* stayed one night in the Tortugas, reached Pensacola on April 15, and reprovisioned and reinforced Fort Pickens without interference. By the twentieth, Meigs had a thousand troops inside Fort Pickens. Word of the Sumter surrender reached him on April 21, and two days later, he and the *Atlantic* began the return trip to New York, arriving on May 1.[40]

From *Harper's Weekly*, July 27, 1861, two months after the beginning of the war. The drawing of the Dome is accurate, but the artist has charitably removed the clutter from the grounds. The stub of the Washington Monument can be seen in the distance next to the river on the left side of the Washington Canal. (Architect of the Capitol)

When the war began, Capitol construction came to a halt. Meigs, still nomi-
nally in charge, shut down the public works under his command in May 1861.
Walter immediately started plotting to resume the project. (Architect of the
Capitol)

In Washington, Walter spent early April waiting uneasily for the war
everyone knew was coming. "My family feel insecure and nervous here,"
he wrote to Rice on April 8. Meigs had left his brother-in-law, Captain
John N. Macomb, in temporary charge of the Capitol, and he "seems to be
all we could wish," Walter told Rice.[41] But construction had virtually
stopped while the capital held its breath. On April 11, Walter went to Philadelphia, intending to leave his family there. Hostilities began two days
later.

Lincoln's call for volunteers set off massive and immediate changes in
the capital. The city was a Union citadel surrounded mostly by enemies.
With Virginia widely expected to secede (it did so on April 17), northerners began leaving the city en masse, and everyone expected a southern
invasion momentarily. The armory at Harpers Ferry was seized by Virginia militia and burned to the ground. Northbound highways and rail-

roads were jammed. Military sentries guarded public buildings around the clock. Residents with telescopes could see the Confederate Stars and Bars waving above the Marshall House, a saloon across the Potomac in Alexandria. The Sixth Massachusetts Regiment, the first reinforcements sent to Washington, had to fight its way through an angry mob of southern sympathizers in Baltimore. Four men were killed and thirty-one wounded.[42]

Walter returned to Washington on Tuesday, April 16, to find a company of soldiers "quartered in our office, much to my annoyance." He told contractor Alexander Provest, the marble finisher, that the "noise and the tumult, and the music and the pipe smoke daily interfere with my personal comfort." Marble finishers and most of the other workers were "soldiering" and no work was getting done.[43] Three days later he wrote to his eldest son, Robert, in Omaha that the Capitol "is to be turned into a barracks."[44]

Local militiamen took possession of a couple of Senate committee rooms, and two companies of Pennsylvania volunteers arrived April 18 to be installed in the House chamber.[45] The next evening the Sixth Massachusetts arrived, bloodied from the Baltimore fighting. Doorkeeper Isaac Bassett welcomed them and opened the Senate chamber. The troops camped in the galleries while their colonel converted the Vice President's Room into his headquarters.[46] Within a few days, the House chamber was taken over by the Seventh New York, and the Rotunda was housing the Eighth Massachusetts.[47]

Walter and Amanda began packing up on April 20. "The citizens [are] in a panic," he wrote in his diary on the twenty-second. "All are moving who can get away."[48] The next day, he took the family to Philadelphia, stayed a week, and then returned to Washington. His slave, John Keith, was still at home, but half the houses in the city were shuttered. "They say that it is the safest place in the country, but who cares for safety in such a place as this," he wrote in a letter to Amanda.[49]

The Capitol became a halfway house for incoming troops. As each regiment received orders and departed, it was replaced by another. Very soon the soldiers wore out their welcome. Bassett, happy to welcome the Sixth Massachusetts, was appalled when he caught the Ellsworth Regiment of the New York Zouaves, a gang of hard-nosed Manhattan firefighters, ripping up a desk on the Democratic side of the Senate chamber with bayo-

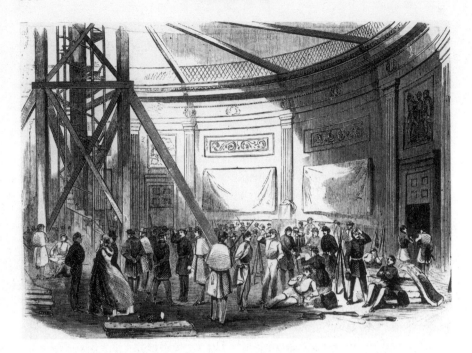

Union troops began arriving in Washington as soon as the war began, but with the city unprepared to garrison large numbers of soldiers, units bivouacked in the Capitol, creating an enormous mess and using the Rotunda for muster and conversation. (Architect of the Capitol)

nets. It was not the desk Jefferson Davis had used, Bassett explained.[50] The New Yorkers also rigged ropes from the cornice of the unfinished Dome and amused themselves by swinging back and forth above the Rotunda. Troops in both chambers spent their days conducting mock debates and shouting obscenities at each other from the galleries.[51]

"There are 4,000 [soldiers] in the Capitol, with all their provisions, ammunition and baggage," Walter wrote to Amanda on May 3. "The smell is awful." Every "hole and corner is defiled," he wrote.[52] Bassett reported soldiers arriving with armloads of ham and bacon, finding a vacant room, and dropping the meat on the floor.[53] Kitchens were set up in the basement, along with a string of bakeries, and the odors of cooking food and baking bread eddied through the corridors.[54] Smoke venting from West Front chimneys invaded the Library and spread soot through the stacks: "I am pained to see a treasure . . . that money cannot replace—receiving great damage," wrote Librarian of Congress John G. Stephenson later in

The troops drilled incessantly on the Capitol grounds, producing a din of shouting and drumming that made it almost impossible for anyone to work in the
buildings. As soon as one unit moved out, another arrived to take its place.
(Library of Congress)

the year. "There is no remedy except in the removal of the circle of bakeries that hems us in."[55]

On May 8, Walter wrote to Amanda that "things are more unpleasant
here every day." The Senate chamber was contaminated with lice, and "every street, lane and alley is filled with soldiers."[56] Walter had not seen
Meigs, but he was worried that Meigs's triumph in reinforcing Fort Pickens would give him such stature in the Lincoln administration that "it will
be impossible to restrain him."[57]

Despite everything that had happened, Meigs was still in charge of the
Capitol, and Walter was once again anticipating his own departure. This
time he was right, but not for the reason he expected. On Wednesday,
May 15, Meigs suspended work on the Capitol for the duration of the war.
Walter left for Philadelphia the following day. "I am so tired of war and so

disgusted with this place, and so vexed at the defilement of my works that I don't think I will make any further resistance," he told Amanda.[58] Aside from the Dome, Walter still had plenty to do: there were columns to mount, porticoes to complete, and staircases and flagging to build. But in April 1861, while there were still able-bodied men available for the Capitol, there was nowhere for them to work.

Meigs returned to Washington on May 3. He immediately went to the State Department, where Seward complimented him on his success at Fort Pickens and sent him to the White House to brief Lincoln and most of the cabinet on his trip. That night at supper Seward told him he wanted to make him a general. On May 6, Meigs wrote in his diary that Treasury Secretary Salmon P. Chase had told him that the army was being reorganized and that Meigs was going to be used "largely" in it. Postmaster General Francis Blair first asked him if he wanted to become a major general and a few days later told him the administration was trying to get him put in command of the entire army, apparently to replace Scott.[59]

These were heady moments, but on May 10, Seward cooled him off. The cabinet had agreed to make Meigs a colonel and put him in the field. Meigs, somewhat dismayed after the big buildup, went to see Blair, who, Meigs wrote, was "disgusted" with Seward's decision.

Meigs was fairly certain what he wanted. He was appalled by the logistics breakdowns that had brought bakeries and bivouacs to the Capitol and most of the rest of Washington: "They had better make me Quartermaster General than to keep up the present rotten system," Meigs wrote that night in his diary. "I do not think I can stand this. I fear that I am growing ambitious. I thought I desired only to be useful, but I feel the breakdown too much."[60] He had not yet, apparently, communicated this wish to anyone, but he was evidently getting ready to plant it in the mind of one of his cabinet friends when he had the chance.

On May 14, Seward told Meigs that the administration had decided to give him a regimental command. Meigs turned it down. He would rather be an engineer. Seward, he wrote, "seemed disappointed." The next morning he rode out on Aqueduct business to the Georgetown reservoir, where a messenger found him. He was to call on Seward immediately. "As I was sitting a fast horse, I turned his head to the city and let him run, which he did with a vengeance," Meigs later wrote. He was at the State Department in twelve minutes.

The president was "much concerned" that Meigs had refused to accept a colonelcy, Seward said, so what exactly did Meigs want? Meigs told him he only wished to be more useful, rather than less useful as a troop commander. He would "not refuse" a position as "a general officer—a Brigadier," he added quickly, but it would have to be something better than being a captain of Engineers. Then he went to see Blair, who told him "he thought I would have to take the place of the Quartermaster General, for I could be useful to him." Meigs told Blair that the administration needed to decide what they wanted to do.[61]

On May 15, anticipating that he would soon have a new job, Meigs suspended work on the Capitol. On June 13, Lincoln promoted Meigs to brigadier general, retroactive to May 14, and appointed him quartermaster general of the United States Army, a job he would hold for the next twenty-one years.

Walter's resolve to leave Washington and have nothing further to do with the Capitol lasted for as long as it took him to join his family in Germantown. He was bored and getting angry. Sometime in the spring or summer of 1861, he either freed John Keith, or Keith ran away. It was time to choose sides, and Walter did so. In June, Walter learned that his middle son, Thomas, now living in Virginia, had repudiated his debts in the North and effectively thrown in his lot with the Confederacy, "a traitor to his country and to his family," Walter wrote in a letter to John Rice. Later in the year, Thomas was rumored to have joined a Confederate rifle company, and "should such be the case," Walter wrote, "I shall never again acknowledge him as belonging to me."[62] Meanwhile, Horace, the third son, volunteered for the union cavalry in Nebraska, and Robert would later volunteer in Indiana.

Walter wanted, more than anything else, to resume work on the Capitol. He left for Washington in the first days of July in order to press his case when Congress convened a special session on Independence Day. Work on the Capitol Extension had stopped completely, but the session nevertheless had one happy result even before it started: it forced the soldiers out and allowed a cleanup, though not enough to erase all the traces of damage. If Walter needed to show why it was a bad idea to leave the Capitol untended, the building told the tale. By July 6, he was nosing around trying to line up support for resuming construction. His accomplices were Rice, who had come to Washington for a couple of days, and Fowler, who had met them there. "We are putting our heads together in reference to future operations," he wrote in a letter to Amanda. "My present impression is that we will put things into a better shape than they have ever been before."[63]

Later, however, in a note to Rice, who had returned to Philadelphia, he was more pessimistic. "Meigs has the War Dept. under his thumb," he said, and was determined to keep the Capitol on ice. Walter planned to draw up a proposal to "transfer the works from the War [Department] to the Interior" Department and show it to Lincoln.[64] If he was successful, Meigs would be gone for good.

Walter went back to Germantown after Congress adjourned to work on Dome drawings and think about what to do next. But it was Fowler who had made the decisive move. On the day Meigs suspended work on the Capitol, there were 1.3 million pounds of Dome castings on the ground waiting to be hoisted up and bolted into place.[65] To stop then would have meant dismantling all the Janes, Fowler company workshops and stowing the iron somewhere in Washington or taking it back to the foundry in New York. Instead, Fowler made a crucial decision to keep working, gambling that construction would formally resume and that the company would be paid. "I am nearly ready for you with the remaining plans," Walter wrote in a short note to Fowler in August, "and if you are really going on with the work, I will complete them and bring them with me in a few days."[66]

Dome construction did not proceed rapidly after Meigs suspended operations in May 1861, but it did proceed, and it was vital in establishing the earnest intentions of Walter and his three contractor accomplices— Fowler, Rice, and Alexander Provest. By August 10, Fowler had made his case to Vermont senator Solomon Foot and Massachusetts representative Charles R. Train, chairmen of the Public Buildings and Grounds committees of the Senate and House respectively. They had then gone to see Meigs, who told them he could not spare any money for the Capitol. Finally they went to Cameron, who agreed to recommend that construction be resumed.[67]

Nothing changed immediately, but the political climate was ripening. In November 1861, Meigs, still officially in charge, submitted what would be his last annual report for the Capitol Extension. He used most of it to tout his own accomplishments: "The building has been in use for some years, and has realized all that I undertook to accomplish in regard to light, warmth, ventilation, and fitness for debate and legislation," Meigs wrote. "The health of the legislative bodies has never been better." The new chambers have conducted more business in a shorter time, he said, and the acoustics were flawless. The "spacious galleries" attracted crowds of people during the prewar hearings, and the audience "were able to hear the words of those who then debated the greatest questions discussed in our Congress since the revolution." He noted that troops had used the Capitol as a barracks, but "the little injury done by them to the walls has been repaired."[68]

A few days later, Interior Secretary Caleb Smith submitted his report on the old portion of the Capitol, still under his charge. He told a much different story. He would need "more than the ordinary appropriations for repairs," he said, and he wanted the basement bakery operation dismantled and moved "to some other locality, where it may be conducted without injury to the national Capitol or annoyance to its occupants."[69]

Foot followed this up on December 17 with a resolution calling on the Army to explain why the bakeries continued to operate. On December 21, Benjamin Brown French, the new commissioner of public buildings, wrote Foot to tell him that it was going to cost $7,800 to clean up and repair the old Capitol, not including the bakeries. The commissary general of the Army admitted that he had not asked for permission to build the bakeries, but maintained that it was wartime and he did not need permission. The bakeries could not be moved, the commissary general said, because it would be too inconvenient and costly. This, French said, was absurd. The Army could use a nearby abandoned gasworks and accomplish the move "in a single week."[70]

The Army had made several unfortunate mistakes. With the arrogance typical of many military bureaucrats during wartime, the commissary general had trivialized civilian complaints and taken refuge in knee-jerk obfuscation. This was not a good idea when the civilian complainers were members of Congress. And Meigs, with his grotesquely self-serving report, had insulted congressional intelligence. He had obviously not visited the Capitol for months, had paid no attention to it, and had not even bothered to brief himself on the damage that had occurred. Meigs, always so meticulous, clearly had no time to spare for the public works still nominally under his care. He could not have made a worse gaffe. Solomon Foot, in addition to his chairmanship, was the Senate president pro tempore.

Meigs paid dearly. On March 5, 1862, Foot introduced Senate legislation transferring Capitol construction to the Interior Department. The debate, on March 5 and 24, dusted off many of the old complaints that had enriched the congressional discourse in years past. What business did the army have building civilian structures? Why does the Capitol need such fancy decoration? Why does the chamber have no windows? Was this just another episode in the endless power struggle between Walter and Meigs?

Several things had changed, however, since the old days. Nobody in either the Republican-dominated Congress or the Lincoln administration had a stake in the old arrangements except Meigs. Maryland senator James A. Pearce was still nominally in the Senate, but he was ailing and powerless as a southern sympathizer. He would be dead by the end of the year. Many of those who had remained in Congress since the beginning of the project had never liked the Extension. Moving the chamber to the middle of the building, John Hale noted, was about as useful as putting "a mousetrap in a pot."[71]

And Meigs, who once owed his job at the Capitol to Jefferson Davis, was doomed in 1862 for the same reason. Being Davis's man now was like having the endorsement of Satan. The Pierce administration had given the project to the War Department simply "to gratify the personal pride and ambition of Jefferson Davis," Foot said, and it "was continued in the War Department only to gratify the rapacity of John B. Floyd."[72] Lincoln may not have cared about Meigs's antecedents, but Congress had a longer memory.

Walter wanted to take over, but did not want Meigs's supporters to know it, so he left the lobbying to Fowler. In between the two Senate sessions, however, he outlined the strategy that he thought would win the prize: first, Interior, not the War Department, was the Capitol project's natural home, and it would still have been there if not for that "atrocious wretch, Jeff. Davis"; second, the War Department did not want the Capitol; third, the Interior Department did; and finally, a transfer to the Interior Department would mean resumption of Capitol construction, a major morale booster during wartime.[73]

Foot and his supporters made all of these arguments and added others. The building was taking a beating from billeted troops and from the weather and needed to be protected, and quickly. Foot had nothing against Meigs, but the War Department could not give the Capitol the attention it deserved.[74]

Less obvious, but probably also true, Meigs may have had "a laudable ambition to distinguish himself by the completion of all of these works," as Chairman Train remarked during the House debate, and "it would be a nice little entertainment for the decline of his life." However, Train asked, "are we to suffer loss" until then because "Meigs would not allow Walter to complete the building?"[75]

Finally, Congress in 1862 displayed an urgency it had lacked during peacetime. By 1862, Jefferson Davis's vision of the Capitol as a symbol of nationhood was finally being realized: "Sir, we are strong enough yet, thank God, to put down this rebellion and to put up this our Capitol at the same time," Foot said on March 25. "And when the rebellion shall have been suppressed—as suppressed it soon will be; when this war shall have been terminated . . . and when this union of ours shall have been restored . . . it will furnish a fitting and appropriate occasion to celebrate that welcome event by crowning the American Capitol with the statue of the Goddess of Freedom."[76] The joint resolution passed in both houses with fewer than ten votes in opposition. Lincoln signed it into law on April 16, and Smith put Walter back in charge.

Walter stayed in a hotel for two weeks, then moved to a boardinghouse while he looked for a home to rent. After eleven years on the job he knew exactly what needed to be done, and after eleven months of enforced idleness he was practically exploding with energy. On May 3 he formally ordered Janes, Fowler back to work. On May 4, he paid Fowler for the iron that had been installed during the suspension. On May 16 he rehired August Schoenborn, and the next day he hired Orlando Bouri, an Italian, as the foreman of painters for the Dome, advising him that he had to sign a loyalty oath to the United States before beginning work. Walter required four coats of lead-based paint on the iron pieces as they were put in place and two more coats of lead, inside and out, once the Dome was completed. Also on May 16, Walter told Caleb Smith that James Walker, working on spec like Fowler, had finished *Storming of Chapultepec* and wanted $3,380, the balance of his commission. Walker had not paid his

With Walter in charge, construction resumed in 1862. His major tasks as the war dragged on were to finish the Dome and the Senate and House East Front Porticoes. (Architect of the Capitol)

rent in three years, his landlord was about to sell the painting to cover the arrears, Walker was facing eviction, and the painting was a "creditable work of art," he told Smith. Walter did everything but demand the money.[77]

On May 8, Walter sent Smith a comprehensive status report. Following Congress's instructions, he focused only on what was needed to repair damage suffered by the Capitol and to protect it from further harm. The only way to comply with this directive, he said with Meigsian audacity, was to finish the Dome and the entire exterior of the Capitol Extension.

All the porticoes and steps still needed to be built. There was $205,000 worth of marble lying on the grounds, picking up stains as it waited to be set in place. Granite steps needed to be built on the West Front. Flagging needed to be completed on the west terraces. And then there were the accursed columns. Connolly, as both Meigs and Walter had feared, was dragging his feet. Of the one hundred columns needed, Connolly had delivered only thirty-two, of which eleven had been set.

Inside, there was considerable water damage caused by seepage through cracks and crevices around the unfinished porticoes. Plaster was decaying in places and falling off the wall. Many stucco ornaments were already destroyed and others were heavily damaged. The only way to fix this—once again—was to stop the leaks by completing the outside of the Extension as quickly as possible.

The Dome was in better shape. During the hiatus, Janes, Fowler had extended the framing upward until only one more tier was needed to reach the level of the lantern. Finally, there were four outstanding art contracts, including Walker's. Both Randolph Rogers and the Crawford estate had bronze doors being cast in Munich. And Meigs in 1861 had finally prevailed upon Congress to commission Emmanuel Leutze to paint *Westward the Course of Empire Takes Its Way* for $20,000.[78]

Early in June, Walter, Amanda, and Walter's young children moved into a rental house about eight blocks southeast of the Capitol. Walter acknowledged to a friend that it was "dirty and inconvenient," and Amanda and the children eventually decamped for Philadelphia, where they would spend most of the next two years.

At this point Washington bore little resemblance to the modest prewar city of sixty thousand people. By 1863 the population had exploded to two hundred thousand. Washington was a noisy, raucous army town. Housing was at a premium and services were inadequate, sporadic, or nonexistent. No one collected the garbage or disposed of sewage. Enormous numbers of soldiers were constantly tramping in and out of the city. A stream of heavily loaded wagons chopped up the streets, raising clouds of dust in dry weather and stirring oozing, fetid pools of mud and slime when it rained. Teamsters were forced to use the sidewalks until those fell apart as well. Gangs of juvenile marauders roamed the alleys, frightening the residents, burglarizing houses, and making trouble.[79] Young vandals pitched stones "as big as hen's eggs" through Walter's bathroom windows, breaking all of them. Neighbors dumped sewage and garbage in the vacant lot next to his house.[80] In the summer of 1863 a mad dog suddenly appeared in the kitchen, then fled to the cellar, where a servant clubbed it to death.[81]

Walter ignored his discomforts and grew more militant as the war progressed. After the battle of Second Bull Run in late August 1862, the army requisitioned the Capitol as a hospital. "Poor fellows, what they must suffer!" Walter wrote in a letter to Alexander Provest, in marked contrast to his reaction when the troops inconvenienced him the previous year. "One thousand beds have been put up. It does not interfere with our work in the least, and I think the move is a good one."[82] After the battle of Antietam three weeks later, however, he moved to temporary offices in the front yard, overwhelmed by the smell, but he never stopped working. In November, Caleb Smith asked him to put a black youth to work on the project, and Walter told him he could "make him useful in the running of errands, making fires or in connection with this office." He suggested paying the boy day laborer's wages—a dollar a day.[83]

His grown sons continued, mostly, to bewilder or enrage him. Robert, the eldest, was in a good phase, serving as a Union Army sergeant in Kentucky. His third son, Horace, purportedly wounded at Fort Donelson, returned with his wife to Pennsylvania, where he soon went broke again, and by November, Walter had found out he was a deserter—"I can only forget it by forgetting you," he wrote.[84] Except that Horace in December 1862 was caught burglarizing a jewelry store and asked Walter to stand his $3,000 bail.[85] Walter refused. He did, however, contribute $50 for a lawyer, who sprang Horace and got him back in the army as a private soldier.

Walter directed his most scathing rebuke, however, toward his second son, Thomas, who had been listed as killed during First Bull Run but who had apparently simply been discharged from the Confederate Army for an unnamed "heart disease."[86] Thomas was somehow able to send a letter to Walter in the summer of 1862 touting the virtues of the Confederacy. Walter in August replied with a salvo of Baptist fury. "Pandemonium has been let loose upon us, but Mr. Lincoln, and his constitutional advisers have met the hydra-headed monster, and fall it must," Walter wrote. "There can be no secession in this country. The traitors must be swept out with the broom of destruction." It would be better to make the "South a desert than let a single traitor live to sow his pestiferous seeds abroad in the land." He urged Thomas to "repent" and take a loyalty oath. Only then would he "let bygones be bygones."[87]

Through all this personal upheaval, the work continued, and Walter's energy seemed to intensify. He relentlessly pushed marble contractor John Rice to get Connolly to provide more columns more rapidly, and when he had columns, he was after Rice's partner, Charles Heebner, to send him pedestals from the quarry in Lee, Massachusetts, so they could be mounted. In early 1863 he noted in a letter to the partners that the first 34 columns had been ordered two years earlier but he had received only 29. He had asked for 26 more, and nothing happened: "it is useless to issue any new orders," he wrote.[88] Nevertheless, he maintained the pressure, and by late 1863 he had 46 columns, enough to complete the East Senate Portico.

His goal was to install the statue of *Freedom* on July 4, 1863, but Janes, Fowler was having a terrible time finding enough men to build the Dome at the pace Walter demanded. In April 1863, Walter admitted to Fowler that "our 4th of July frolic is no go."[89] It was at that point that he probably decided to target the opening of Congress as the date for the ceremony. The Dome "could easily employ four times as many (men) as we have," Walter reported to Congress in late 1863, "and the added difficulty of finding men who can, under any circumstances work at so great a height from the ground, has also tended to retard the progress of the work. These difficulties cannot be overcome."[90]

On August 18 1862, Walter contacted Constantino Brumidi, who was working on a church in Philadelphia, with a proposal to make "a picture 65 feet in diameter, painted in fresco on the concave canopy over the eye of the New Dome of the U.S. Capitol." The canopy, designed by Walter more than three years earlier, would hang just beneath the exterior dome so that a viewer standing in the Rotunda could see the painting by looking up through the inner dome oculus. It would look like the ceiling of the inner dome, even though the inner dome and the canopy were separate pieces. Three weeks later, Brumidi wrote back. He chose the apotheosis of George Washington as his theme. Washington would sit on a cloud with allegorical figures on either side and thirteen women in a circle around the canopy representing the original thirteen sister states. Six occupational groups would be painted around the border—War, Science,

Marine, Commerce, Manufactures, and Agriculture. Walter and French accepted the design, on the condition that Brumidi drop his fee from $50,000 to $40,000. The deal was finalized early in 1863.[91]

Unbeknownst to Walter, this arrangement had received a helping hand from Meigs, who, a month after work resumed on the Capitol, had written Secretary Smith a letter recommending Brumidi as "an artist of great experience and of great ability." Although Brumidi "has suffered from the cliques and jealousies which have beset the works of the Capitol," he "has himself behaved with modesty and propriety and attended laboriously to his duties."[92]

It was a handsome endorsement, but it also showed that no matter how much Meigs and Walter hated each other, their views on taste, style, and substance were more alike than either would have cared to admit. Walter was a neoclassicist, while Meigs favored the more ornate "higher style," but they both knew good work—and bad—when they saw it. Whether it was their enthusiasm for *Storming of Chapultepec*, their contempt for Connolly and his second-rate columns, or their mutual admiration for Brumidi, they were almost always of the same mind. Walter had kept his distance from Brumidi—Meigs's man—during the Meigs years, but even before Brumidi began the *Apotheosis*, Walter had hired him to decorate his Germantown house and invited the artist and his wife to live there while he painted.[93]

On June 1, 1862, Walter, Benjamin Brown French, and Caleb Smith drove out the Bladensburg Road with Clark Mills to see the finished statue of *Freedom Triumphant in War and Peace*. "It is a magnificent figure and exceedingly well done," French wrote in his diary. Smith accepted the statue, and Mills made plans to bring it to the Capitol. There it was assembled on the East Lawn and placed on a temporary pedestal, Walter said in a report to Congress, "in order that the public may have an opportunity to examine it before it is raised to its designed position."[94]

In November 1863, in preparation for its final installation, the statue was disassembled and "pickled" piece by piece in an acid solution to encourage what Walter called "a slight oxidation," thereby producing "a rich and uniform bronze tint which will never change."[95]

It was during this long process that Philip Reid became the only slave known to have worked on the new Capitol. Reid, in his late thirties, was owned by Mills, who bought him, Mills said, "because of his evident talent in the foundry business."[96] At some point, when Mills needed to disassemble or reassemble the statue, Reid stepped in after an Italian worker, believing that he was the only person available who could do the job, refused to proceed unless his wages were increased. The earliest account, from the *New York Tribune* of December 10, 1863, said Reid intervened when the statue was first bolted together for display on the Capitol lawn. Five years later, S. D. Wyeth, in a book entitled *The Federal City: Ins and Abouts of Washington*, cited Mills's son as saying that Reid took the plaster model apart, presumably when it was being removed from the old House chamber and taken to the Mills foundry for casting. Reid used a block and tackle, and inserted a hook in the iron eye at the top of the statue; "the rope was gently strained repeatedly" until the statue began to pull apart, at which point Reid and Mills were able to begin to unbolt the individual pieces.[97]

The workers—either Mills and Reid, or Walter's day's-work federal employees—disassembled *Freedom* for pickling in late October 1863. On November 19, the job was done.[98] The first piece was bolted into place the week of November 22. And on November 30, Walter wrote to the Interior Department asking the secretary to arrange for an artillery salute. *Freedom* would rise on schedule.

On the day that *Freedom* took its place atop the Capitol, Jefferson Davis, president of the Confederacy and the man who had chosen the statue's design, was in Richmond, Virginia, sorting out the disastrous aftermath of the Chattanooga campaign. In a series of battles beginning November 24, 1863, Union forces under General Ulysses S. Grant had driven the Confederate Army from Tennessee, opening the deep southern heartland to northern invasion. In a speech at the opening of the Confederate Congress, Davis acknowledged that "our success in driving the enemy from our soil has not equaled our expectations," but "his progress has been checked," and the Confederate Army was "in all respects in better condition than at any previous period of the war."[99] His presidency, and his rebellion, had less than seventeen months to endure.

Some 460 miles west of Richmond, Brigadier General Montgomery C. Meigs, Davis's former protégé and the man who had built most of the Capitol Extension and a good part of the new Dome, was in an ebullient

The winter of 1863–64. The statue of *Freedom* is in place, but scaffolding still surrounds the tholus. The Senate portico is all but complete, with work still to be finished on the stairway. (Architect of the Capitol)

mood. He had been coordinating Union supply lines from Chattanooga since September and, like Davis, was unaware that the statue had been mounted. According to his wife, Louisa, however, he was having a grand time in the field. He had "forgotten all about rheumatism," Louisa wrote in a letter to her sister. He "takes long rides of 20 or 30 miles a day without fatigue, and, in fact, feels, he says, as if he could ride 100 without inconvenience."[100]

On December 2, Meigs "rode up Lookout Mountain with Gen'l Grant, Gen'l [John] Logan, Gen'l [John] Rawlings and others," he wrote in his diary. There he started "a covey of partridges, and with my pistol shot three of them."[101]

EPILOGUE

Major General Montgomery C. Meigs received a letter from Varina Davis late in June 1865. She had always impressed him—"a very agreeable woman of great sprightliness and wit," as he had once described her, "with much intelligence."[1]

She wrote on behalf of her husband, Jefferson Davis, the imprisoned former president of the Confederacy and Meigs's former patron. The army was holding him as a traitor at Fortress Monroe in Hampton Roads while the government tried to figure out what to do next. That was about as much as Meigs knew about Davis.

"Plead for me," Varina Davis had written, "that I may be allowed if not to see, then to correspond with my husband." Reports of his treatment by army jailers "harrow me," she said, and she asked Meigs to "tell me what you know of Mr. Davis' health."

She was in Savannah and not allowed to leave Georgia. She wanted to come north, she continued, to get her "unacclimated little children" away from "this unhealthy climate" while "my scanty means suffice for the purpose." She also wanted to take her older children to Europe in order to put them in school there. But she promised to return "if required as a witness" in Davis's trial. "I will bind myself not to do anything prejudicial to your government," she wrote. "Please answer by telegram. I have been three weeks in suspense."[2]

Meigs did not record his immediate reaction to the note, but he had little sympathy for the South, or for its women, generally. "Let the rebels

Major General Montgomery C. Meigs, quartermaster general of the Union Army. Still trim in his mid-forties, Meigs by the end of the war had become one of the most important men in Washington. (Library of Congress)

take care of their own widows," he had written a week earlier. "They have filled [the North's] hands with [its] own."[3]

Only two and a half months had elapsed since Lincoln's assassination, and the North was also trying to absorb the appalling story of the Andersonville prison, where nearly thirteen thousand Union prisoners had died of starvation and disease in only fourteen months. A military tribunal, meeting in secret, was about to sentence four of the Lincoln conspirators to death, and they would hang on July 7. Prosecutors at the trial had said there was "positive proof" that Davis could have planned the assassination with help from his secret agents in Canada and their hired killers.[4] The chasm separating the South from what Varina Davis called "your government" had never been deeper.

For the past four years, Meigs had probably had as much to do with the destruction of the Confederacy as any other man alive. When Sherman marched on Atlanta, Meigs had supplied him. When Grant crossed the Rapidan to pound Lee's army to a pulp, Meigs had supplied him, too. Meigs had sat on the inner councils of the Lincoln administration and had routinely met with cabinet officers and the army high command. On April 15, he had been in the Petersen boardinghouse opposite Ford's Theatre watching Lincoln die. On April 20, he had organized the viewing of Lincoln's body in the Capitol Rotunda, and early the next day he joined the honor guard that took Lincoln to the train station for his final trip home to Springfield, Illinois.[5]

Meigs also had additional, personal demons. Nine months earlier, his eldest son, Lieutenant John Rodgers Meigs, had been killed in the Shenandoah Valley by three gunmen that young Meigs apparently thought were Union soldiers.

Attached as an engineer officer to General Philip Sheridan's forces, Lieutenant Meigs and two orderlies at dusk on October 3, 1864, spotted three other horsemen riding ahead of them on the Swift Run Gap Road near the town of Dalton, Virginia. According to Army dispatches, the three men, wearing slickers in drizzly weather, pulled their horses to the side of the road and stopped. Then, as Meigs and the orderlies approached, the gunmen pulled revolvers, grabbed the bridles of Meigs's horse and the horses of his companions, and opened fire. Meigs was shot twice, in the forehead and left side of the chest, apparently dying instantly. One orderly abandoned his horse, jumped a fence, ran into the woods, and eventually made it to General George Armstrong Custer's nearby headquarters to report what had happened. The second orderly was never seen again.

A patrol sent to investigate found Meigs lying on his back, "one arm partially raised, the other extended by his side." Official dispatches quoted the orderly as saying that Meigs thought the three horsemen were "our men," and that he "distinctly heard Lt. Meigs say twice 'I surrender,' but they kept on firing." Based on the orderly's statement, Sheridan's chief of staff, Colonel G. A. Forsyth, who led the search party, concluded that the gunmen were irregulars and that "poor Meigs was murdered."[6]

General Meigs learned of this on the night of November 6, 1864, when Secretary of War Edwin M. Stanton appeared outside his house and asked him to come out into the street so he could tell him the news.[7] Young John, for whom so many strings had been pulled so he could get into West Point, had graduated first in his class. His father took it hard. "Dear Mont grieves for him," Louisa Meigs wrote in a letter to her sister, "but has so much pride in remembering what he was and so much patriotism which encourages him to remember the holy cause in which our happiness was sacrificed that he does not give way to despondency."[8]

It would be suggested later that the death of John Rodgers Meigs was what turned the father into such a fierce and irreconcilable opponent of the defeated South, but that was not the case. Meigs's hatred had begun early and never waned. Nothing enraged him more than disloyalty and duplicity. He had shown this in his prolonged—and as yet unresolved—feud with Thomas U. Walter over the building of the Capitol. His bright-line morality had hurt him in the Walter affair, but during the Civil War it made him a ferocious and implacable enemy. And from the beginning he reserved his greatest hatred for fellow West Point graduates such as Jefferson Davis and Robert E. Lee.

"No man who ever took the oath to support the Constitution as an officer of our army or navy a graduate of West Point a member of Congress or Cabinet & who has since actively engaged in rebellion in any civil or military station should escape without loss of all his goods & civil rights & expatriation," Meigs wrote in 1862. "The leaders should be put formally out of the way if possible by sentence of death executed if ever caught."[9]

This view undoubtedly contributed to his decision in the spring of 1864—months before John Rodgers Meigs's death—to convert part of Lee's Arlington, Virginia, estate into a national military cemetery. He wanted to make sure that the early arrivals were buried close to the mansion.[10] The setting was more beautiful there, and if the graves were close to the doorstep, Lee would never live there again. By the end of the war, there were five thousand Union dead at Arlington. John Rodgers Meigs's final resting place was within a hundred feet of Robert E. Lee's rose garden.

After he received the letter from Varina, Meigs went to Stanton for advice on how he should reply. Stanton, as hard-line as Meigs, if not more so, left it up to him: "He thinks of the starvation of 10,000 men at Andersonville under the orders of Jeff Davis," Meigs wrote.[11] His own attitude toward Jefferson Davis remained unchanged. He did not care that Davis had done him countless good turns in the past, or even that Davis had twice written letters of recommendation for his son's West Point applications. He noted that he had some sympathy for Varina Davis, though he would not even write her name: "Poor woman, she has been guilty of great crime," he wrote. "She set on this husband of hers, but I feel pity for her present condition. Even the blood of my son slain by her husband's hired murderers does not shut up my compassion."[12] But he never answered her.

Jefferson Davis had left Richmond, the Confederate capital, on the night of April 2, 1865. That morning, General Ulysses S. Grant had broken through Lee's lines at Petersburg and was chasing down the remnants of the Army of Northern Virginia. Davis took a train southwest to Danville, Virginia, intending to set up an interim headquarters, gather his troops, and continue the war. Lee was supposed to withdraw to the south and join him there.

But Lee never made it. Grant was squeezing him on all sides, and Lee ran out of options. He surrendered at Appomattox on April 9. When Davis confirmed the news, he boarded another train and took his government to Greensboro, North Carolina. There, on April 13, his advisers told him that his remaining forces east of the Mississippi River could not survive.

Davis persevered for another month as a fugitive. He took his cabinet, an armed escort, and what remained of the Confederate treasury and headed for the Gulf Coast, intending to go west to Texas, either overland or by ship, and join up with loyal forces there to carry on the war.

Varina and the children had left Richmond ahead of him and were heading southward in the same general direction. But as Union troops swept in, Confederate forces were surrendering or joining ad hoc gangs of pillagers. Davis had left the Confederate gold with loyal cavalry units, but he was afraid that Varina's slow-moving wagons would prove an irresistible target for the marauders. He and his remaining escorts overtook Varina on May 7.[13]

The last of his luck ran out on May 10, in the pine woods of south central Georgia near the town of Irwinville. Gunfire awakened him that morning. Union cavalry had invaded the Confederate encampment. During the melee, Davis emerged from the wagon he shared with Varina wearing a waterproof cloak and a shawl she had thrown over his shoulders. If he hurried, Varina told him, he might be able to reach the woods and escape before the soldiers discovered him. She directed a maid to pick up a bucket and a mop and walk with him as if they were going to a nearby stream. The cavalry was not fooled. A trooper rode up and ordered him to surrender. He did.

Davis, ridiculed in the northern press for trying to escape by pretending to be a woman, wrote much later that he had thrown back the cloak when the trooper accosted him, intending "to put my hand under his foot, tumble him off on the other side, spring into his saddle and attempt to escape." Suddenly, however, Varina appeared, threw her arms around her husband, and entreated the trooper not to shoot. His planned stratagem had "depended on instantaneous action," he wrote, but with Varina holding him, "the opportunity had been lost."[14]

His captors looted the camp and the fugitives' belongings, then took the prisoners to Macon, Georgia, Savannah, and Hilton Head, South Carolina, where they were put aboard a ship and sent north. Davis was taken ashore at Fortress Monroe, and Varina was sent back to Savannah. Throughout this ordeal, both Davis and Varina frequently mentioned how badly they were treated—robbed, jeered at, treated roughly, and subjected to "annoyances such as military *gentlemen* never commit or permit."[15]

On the day that Meigs read Varina Davis's letter, Jefferson Davis was lodged in a dank cell built into the outer wall of Fortress Monroe. The windows were barred, the door was secured from the outside, a light was kept burning at all times, and an armed guard was stationed inside the cell with Davis. His furniture included a hospital bed, a chair, a table, and a small chest for personal belongings. He had been shackled for a few days shortly after he was brought to the fort on May 19—probably not only to prevent escape, but to discourage suicide attempts. Stanton soon put a stop to this. Davis by the end of June was in reasonably good health and was eating hospital food. He had not heard a word from Varina.[16]

Davis spent nearly two years at Fortress Monroe, and his treatment improved over time. He was moved into dry rooms with a fireplace of his own. He began corresponding directly with Varina in August 1865, and in May 1866 she joined him at the fort. By the fall of 1865, no one seriously believed that Davis had had anything to do with Lincoln's assassination, but on May 8, 1866, the "state prisoner" Davis was indicted for treason. He was never tried but was instead released on $100,000 bail on May 11, 1867, exactly two years after his capture. In December 1868 he was included in a general amnesty.

For the last twenty-two years of his life, Davis traveled and lived in Canada, Europe, and various places in the United States, sometimes with Varina, sometimes alone. His marriage suffered some bad patches caused by illness, the deaths of two sons, and rumors that Davis was having affairs with Virginia Clay, the wife of former U.S. and Confederacy senator Clement Clay, and Sarah Dorsey, a childhood acquaintance of Varina's. The truth of these reports was never established.

Jefferson Davis was imprisoned at Fortress Monroe immediately after the war, with a twenty-four-hour guard on suicide watch. His conditions improved after it became clear that he had had nothing to do with President Lincoln's assassination. (Library of Congress)

Davis never returned permanently to Brierfield, but he tried to rekindle its prosperity as an absentee landlord using free labor, with little success. In 1869 Davis accepted an offer to become the president of a Memphis-based life insurance company, a job that brought him a degree of financial stability until he resigned during the Panic of 1873. For most of the rest of his postwar life he was strapped for money, and at times he was nearly destitute.

Even before his release from prison, however, Davis was regarded throughout the South as a martyr to what came to be known as the "Lost Cause"—the view that the South had done nothing wrong in the run-up to the war but had merely defended states' rights against a powerful aggressor whose huge advantages in population and resources had been too much to overcome. Davis, for most of his postwar years, did not actively embrace the Lost Cause, but he did not need to. His imprisonment ennobled him, as did his refusal to repudiate his principles and his refusal to blame others for the South's defeat.

In late 1877, Sarah Dorsey invited Davis to settle at Beauvoir, her estate on the Gulf Coast near Biloxi, Mississippi, to write his memoirs.

Varina joined him there the following year, and she and Sarah, despite a rocky beginning, eventually became friends. Sarah died of cancer in 1879 and bequeathed Beauvoir to the Davises. They lived there for the next ten years.

In 1881 Davis cemented his place in the Lost Cause with publication of his memoir, *The Rise and Fall of the Confederate Government*, a fifteen-hundred-page, two-volume polemic whose avowed purpose, he wrote, was "from historical data to show that the Southern States had rightfully the power to withdraw from a union into which they had, as sovereign communities, voluntarily entered."[17]

Davis never returned to Washington after the war. He never saw the completed Capitol Extension, the new Dome, or the statue of *Freedom Triumphant in War and Peace*—all built from designs he approved. He almost certainly never knew that Lincoln had been signing bills in the President's Room of the Capitol—sumptuously furnished in Davis's "higher style"—at the moment when an aide told him in early March 1865 that General Lee had proposed a peace conference. Lincoln sent word to Grant not to bother unless Lee planned to surrender.

But Davis never forgot about the Capitol. In March 1888, in a letter to the editor of the *New York World*, he took exception to an item that "asserts that in 1855 I 'claimed that a statue with a Liberty cap on the dome of the Capitol for a people half-free & half-slave was a menace to the South.'" Davis insisted he had a different objection: that the liberty cap, as the emblem of a freed slave, was inappropriate since "our people were born free and had maintained their freedom." The final statue, he asserted, substituted "a crown of feathers" (in fact, it was an eagle's head). The aim, he explained, was to make the image "appropriate to our Aborigines, and the figure as thereby becoming typical of America."[18]

Nearly a year later, Davis wrote to U.S. senator John H. Reagan, a Texan who had served as the Confederacy's postmaster general, to complain that a recent Senate publication, in its discussion of the new Capitol, had "omitted all reference" to the circumstances surrounding the statue's design and construction. He included a draft memorandum, apparently intended to be substituted for page 153 of the offending report. Davis's amendment identified "Meiggs" as the superintendent and Walter as his "draftsman," both of them working "under the direction of the Secretary of War."[19]

Jefferson Davis died in New Orleans on December 6, 1889, and was buried in Metairie, Louisiana, in the Army of Northern Virginia cemetery there. In 1893, Varina directed that the casket be exhumed and reburied at Hollywood Cemetery in Richmond, Virginia. Shortly after Davis's death, Varina moved to New York and became a newspaper columnist. In 1902 she sold Beauvoir to a group called the Sons of Confederate Veterans for $10,000. She scandalized the South not only by moving to the North, but also by becoming a close friend of Julia Dent Grant, the widow of Ulysses S. Grant. She lived comfortably in residential hotels until her death, in 1906, of pneumonia at the age of eighty.

For Thomas Walter, the eagle sitting atop *Freedom*'s head, which Davis so emphatically described as a "crown of feathers" evocative of "our Aborigines," was the one flaw in an otherwise lovely piece of art. He called it a "buzzard," and he wished it had never become part of the statue.[20]

He was not alone. Griping about Crawford's headdress began almost as soon as *Freedom* had been assembled on the Capitol grounds in the summer of 1862. During House debate in early 1863, Republican Robert McKnight of Pennsylvania offered a proviso to get rid of the statue's "nondescript ornament" before "the same is elevated to its position on the apex of the Capitol Dome." But McKnight, although he was a member of the Committee on Public Buildings and Grounds, had not done his homework. He was unaware that Crawford was dead, for he wanted the eagle removed "under the direction of the sculptor."[21] And he did not have the votes for his proviso, for he was ruled out of order on the grounds that he was trying to legislate on an appropriations bill. This practice, officially frowned upon, was in fact enthusiastically embraced whenever a majority of members agreed with the legislation. Clearly the House was not of one mind.

A year later, with the statue already in place, Representative John H. Rice of Maine, the chairman of the Public Buildings and Grounds Committee, tried again, asking Walter exactly what it would take to get rid of the eagle. He wanted to know, first, whether the headdress was "in accordance with the original's design." It was, Walter replied, if the "original" design was understood to be the one approved by Jefferson Davis. Walter sent Rice all the correspondence relating to the earlier designs and the freedom cap. Next, Rice asked, could the crest be removed, and what would it cost? Walter said he could do it for $300, although it would be complicated. The statue's head weighed 2,700 pounds, and the scaffolding would have to be reconstructed.

Then Rice asked whether it was "advisable" to remove the crest. "To this inquiry, I may be permitted to say that I have always considered it a very objectionable feature of the figure; but the removal of it alone would leave the statue imperfect as a work of art," Walter replied, and "the idea of leaving the head bare could not be entertained for a moment." The integrity of the figure demanded a head ornament, he continued. "If, therefore, the crest were removed, it would be necessary to substitute one of a different design, or a wreath, as in Mr. Crawford's first sketch, or some other crowning feature." This would mean remodeling the head and recasting the entire upper part of the figure, a project that would take months and cost thousands of dollars.

"I am decidedly of the opinion that the crest on the statue should be suffered to remain without alterations," Walter concluded. "It is now precisely as it came from the hands of one of the most distinguished artists our country has ever produced and he is no more among the living." Walter did not like *Freedom*'s strange headgear, either, but he was unwilling to deface the statue in order to change it.[22]

With the installation of *Freedom*, Walter's work began to draw to an end. By late 1864, the Senate East Portico was finally completed. Crawford's pediment sculpture had been mounted, and stairs and columns—all monolithic—were installed. The exterior of the Dome had been painted and the interior was nearly finished, although it was ever more difficult to find anyone willing to work on the high-altitude catwalks.[23] Walter had taken delivery of nineteen monolithic column shafts during the previous year, but still needed thirty-five more to finish the East Front. The Rogers doors had been installed between the old House chamber and the new House wing, and the Crawford doors were being cast by James T. Ames in Chicopee, Massachusetts.[24] Work on the East Front House Portico was going slowly owing to the near impossibility, he told Congress, of finding ships to bring the Lee quarry marble down from Bridgeport. Still, he expected the job would be finished in 1865.

Meigs, once the Capitol project had been transferred to the Interior Department, never communicated with Walter and never interfered with the Capitol alterations. Although Walter and Meigs both continued to live in Washington, and to work within a short carriage ride of each other, they apparently never had any personal contact during the war. Meigs was in the Rotunda all day when Lincoln was lying in state, but Walter, who hated ceremonies and large public gatherings, did not attend.

Walter contacted Meigs only once. "It occurred to me," he wrote in October 1864, on learning of the death of John Rodgers Meigs, "that it would be grateful to you to have whatever reminiscences of your son may have been left in this office; I therefore send you herewith all the negatives and impressions pertaining to your family, which are to be found in the photographic rooms connected with these works."[25]

Meigs did not visit the Capitol until the beginning of 1864, after he returned from Chattanooga. His laconic diary entry for Sunday, January 10, notes that he went to church in the morning, and in the "afternoon to look at Capitol statue on Dome; effect good." He also went inside the building to see what had happened. "Bronze doors of Rogers in place," he wrote; "not as good a work as I had hoped."[26]

Besides the finishing Capitol touches, Walter at war's end had new projects under way. In response to fresh complaints about Meigs's House chamber heating and ventilation system, Walter hired Joseph Henry to make a new study. In late 1863 he ordered a pair of water tanks installed in the air ducts so that he could run steam coils through them to increase the humidity in the House chamber. This was a stopgap, designed to "appease" the members "until we come to more philosophical conclusions."[27] He did not remind Congress that Henry had been involved in the study that had approved the original Meigs system.

Walter in 1864 also began converting the old House chamber into an exhibit hall where individual states could place sculptures of their choosing. The old chamber had been sorely used since the new wing had opened. Though it retained its tiered floors and a few pieces of display art, it had been largely given over to street vendors peddling souvenirs and food to tourists. Walter had enough chunks of white marble lying around the grounds to level the floor and tile it, varying the pattern by interspersing the white squares with black ones. By the end of the year, "National Statuary Hall" was almost finished, and would cost $20,000.[28]

The most spectacular of the Capitol's ongoing jobs, however, was the completion of Constantino Brumidi's *Apotheosis of Washington*, high over the Rotunda floor above the oculus. Brumidi's design had been approved, and he had been under contract for the *Apotheosis* since March 1863, but

he had been forced to mark time for nine months, waiting for Janes, Fowler to finish casting the iron canopy and put it in place. Besides the iron, Brumidi also had to cope with the quirks of John P. Usher, the prickly interior secretary who had replaced an ailing Caleb Smith at the end of 1862. Usher stopped work on the fresco for two months in 1863 until he decided that the painting was part of the Capitol's structural design and did not need its own appropriation. Then he stopped paying Brumidi for several months after Brumidi finished the cartoons for the fresco.[29]

Once Brumidi finally got going in December 1864, the whole job took him only eleven months. During that time, the war was won, Lincoln was killed, and his body was displayed in the Rotunda. Brumidi may have used the faces of Jefferson Davis, Confederate vice president Alexander H. Stephens, and Robert E. Lee to depict the villains in the group of figures denoting "War" on the fresco's edge. These were only vague likenesses; there could be no doubt, however, that the figure representing Samuel F. B. Morse in the "Science" group was in fact Thomas U. Walter. Brumidi also painted Meigs in the "Commerce" group, but Meigs had him remove the portrait, perhaps because the god Mercury appeared to be handing him a bag of gold.[30]

Apotheosis of Washington, by Constantino Brumidi, 1865. From the floor of the Rotunda it is impossible to tell that the mural hovers over the open oculus. In the center of the painting Washington rises to heaven, encircled by maidens (facing page). Six groups line the outer rim of the mural, including "War" just below Washington. (Architect of the Capitol)

Once the *Apotheosis* was finished, it was clear that the Know-Nothing scare was long over. Brumidi, once criticized as a ham-handed Italian second-rater, got uniformly spectacular reviews, and Meigs and Walter, still miles apart in their personal relations, agreed enthusiastically with the accolades. The fresco was "most agreeable and beautiful," Meigs wrote. He doubted "whether anyone not well acquainted with the construction of such edifices as the Dome could determine by the mere use of his eyes the form and position of the surface which is painted."[31]

Walter praised the work as "a decided success" and "far better than the great painting . . . in the eye of the dome of the Pantheon at Paris." That painting, he said, "is 170 feet above the floor, while *Apotheosis* is ten feet higher and contains one-third more surface."[32]

Brumidi finished the *Apotheosis* at the end of 1865. From that time until 1877, he worked sporadically at the Capitol, painting mostly individual works and filling in lunettes in designs he had made years earlier. In 1877 he came back full time to undertake the *Frieze of American History*, a three-hundred-foot band of sculpturelike trompe l'oeil paintings around the interior of the new Dome just above the Rotunda walls. Brumidi designed twenty of these scenes, each of them 8 feet 4 inches tall, beginning with the arrival of Columbus and ending with the California

Gold Rush. When he started work he was seventy-two and suffered from a variety of physical problems. He had reached *William Penn and the Indians*, the tenth scene, in the summer of 1879 when the edge of his chair slipped off his scaffold and nearly threw him to his death. Brumidi hung on to the rung of a ladder for fifteen minutes until help came. Soon he was back at work—he even came back to paint the next day—but he was growing ever more feeble. He died in February of the following year.[33]

In January 1865, Walter began making a design to expand the Library. With an appropriation of $160,000 in hand, he solicited bids from a number of iron firms, and his friend Charles Fowler, perhaps not surprisingly, got the job. Fowler had begun demolition of part of the old Library in May, less than a month after Lincoln's death.

The assassination brought Andrew Johnson to the White House, and of course brought a new set of challenges for holdover government employees like Walter. Former Iowa senator James Harlan became Johnson's interior secretary; Walter met him on May 16 and was favorably impressed. He also noted in a letter to Amanda, however, that the ever-present Benjamin Brown French, the commissioner of public buildings, might be plotting his overthrow.[34] On May 22, he told Amanda that French was going to replace him as superintendent at the Capitol, and on May 25, Harlan issued the order. French told Walter he intended to appoint Walter's onetime assistant Edward Clark to replace him. Clark was the supervising architect of the Post Office Extension. "I am, of course, taken all aback, and must study what is best to be done, and how it is best to do it," Walter told Amanda. "My present impression is that I will resign tomorrow, to take effect Jun. 1."[35]

On May 26, Harlan stopped work on the Library and voided the Fowler contract, apparently worried that the procedures Walter had followed in awarding it were somehow illegal. Walter, who had carefully kept Usher informed as the process unfolded, resigned the following day: "I have cut loose from a work that has occupied all my energies and skill for 14 years, and I naturally feel the occasion to be one of no ordinary interest," he wrote Amanda on May 29. "I am glad that I took time by the forelock and stood upon my dignity."[36]

Then Walter left for Germantown. Since completion of the Dome, he had spoken frequently of retirement in letters to Amanda and others. He seemed well satisfied as he departed, but no sooner had he arrived in Philadelphia than he began writing to his friends telling them that his resignation was still pending and setting forth the terms under which he would be willing to return to work. He even visited Washington on a scouting trip in early July, but learned nothing. On July 10, however, President Johnson formally accepted his resignation.[37]

Walter, still vigorous at sixty-one, intended to retire to his beautiful new house in Germantown and live off his investments. This plan worked out fairly well until late 1872, when he lost all his money in stock speculation during the run-up to the Panic of 1873. He was forced to sell the Germantown house, move downtown, and go back to work. He took a job as an architect for the Pennsylvania Railroad and later worked as an architectural assistant during design and construction of the Philadelphia City Hall. He served as president of the American Institute of Architects for ten years beginning in 1877 and never ceased submitting designs and bidding jobs in Washington.

In good times and bad, his three eldest sons continued dunning him for money. Robert fought with distinction with Sherman throughout the Atlanta campaign and joined Grant for the final breakout at Petersburg. When the war ended, he decided to see if he could make some money buying cotton in the South, but by the autumn of 1865 he was back in Indiana with a wife, four children, and no money. He tried farming again, then went back to teaching and achieved a measure of stability.

Thomas forswore the Confederacy in late 1863, took the loyalty oath, and opened a photography business in Norfolk, Virginia, under Union protection. He went broke when the war ended and the soldiers left, and tried unsuccessfully to recoup by going back into guano shipping. Then he tried something else but lost everything again in 1874. He asked Walter to bankroll him in a new venture, but Walter did not have the money. Thomas moved to Baltimore in the 1880s but failed there as well, eventually returning to Norfolk and his photography studio.

Horace and his father finally had a full reconciliation in 1869 after Horace got a job with a shipping company. He moved with his family to San Francisco and served as a shipboard purser. In 1873, with Walter's business ventures falling apart, Horace suggested he come west and move in with him. A year later, however, he lost his job and moved to Monterey to start another business. His wife and children showed up in Philadelphia in early 1876, Walter said, "in a destitute condition."[38]

Meigs served as Army quartermaster general until his retirement in 1882. He built himself a home at Vermont Avenue and N Street, with a workshop and a lathe in the basement where he could tinker with do-it-yourself projects and visit with old friends including General Sherman. It was Sherman who, during his march from Atlanta to the sea, received a dispatch from Meigs, took a look at it, and remarked, "The handwriting of this report is that of General Meigs, and I therefore approve of it, but I cannot read it."[39] Meigs, ever the early adopter of new technology, in 1874 bought himself a typewriter, and for a brief, glorious interlude he used it to write his diary. After a few weeks, however, he began to notice that his speed was not improving, and the project was doomed.

Upon retirement, he was able to realize one of his lifelong dreams, becoming the architect of a substantial public work: the new Pension Office Building, later to become the National Building Museum. This immense project, built in the Italian Renaissance style out of 15 million bricks, was known as "Meigs's Old Red Barn." At the time of its construction, either Sherman or General Sheridan is reported to have remarked, "too bad the damn thing is fireproof." *The Washington Post*, however, in 1959 probably best captured its essence: "Whatever its use, the American Institute of Architects has designated it as an example of architecture worth saving— not for its gracefulness, but for its crazy mixed-up distinction."[40]

In 1875, with Congress showing interest in extending the Capitol still further, Meigs wrote a letter to Vermont senator Justin S. Morrill, chairman of the Joint Committee on Public Buildings and Grounds. Expansion, he said, was a bad idea because Walter's design was perfect as it stood. Morrill passed the note on to Walter, and the ice began to thaw.[41]

In March 1882, Walter noted in a letter to Meigs that "in years gone by we have had our differences, but I am happy to say they have left no traces of vindictiveness on my mind." He hoped, he said, that Meigs felt the same way, and he was "desirous to join you in forgetting whatever of the past may have once disturbed our intercourse, and in mutually promoting the interest of science and art as best we may."[42] By late April, the two men had exchanged ideas on the building of a new Library—a building apart from the Capitol—which both agreed was a good idea. Meigs sent some serious sketches, and Walter promised to "go to work with all diligence, to get up a design in semblance with the grand conception you have sketched in your letter." He added, "I confess to an apparent neglect not answering your letter before, but it contained so much material for thought, that I did not feel like being in a hurry."[43] In late 1883, while on a short visit to Washington, Walter noted that he "spent the evening with Gen. Meigs," and the next day he visited with Meigs and his daughter, Loulie.[44]

Walter died at the age of eighty-one in 1887. In a note to Amanda, Meigs described him as "the first of American architects, and to this day no one has excelled him in taste and knowledge of his profession."[45] Meigs died five years later, at age seventy-five. The funeral was held at St. John's Church on Lafayette Square, and the casket was then placed on a caisson and escorted by a cavalry detachment to the cemetery at Arlington.[46]

The completed West Front of the U.S. Capitol, seen from Pennsylvania Avenue during or immediately after the Civil War. (Architect of the Capitol)

Despite his affinity for honorifics, Thomas U. Walter never actually held the title he most coveted. He has it now. His portrait, as fourth Architect of the Capitol, today hangs in the Architect's office. Montgomery C. Meigs, so concerned about his legacy that he had his name carved in stone, stamped in sheet copper, wrought in iron, and hidden away in countless nooks and crannies of his beloved Capitol, need not have worried. His portrait today is in the Western Expansion Corridor on the first floor of the House, and in 2001, the U.S. Congress published the translation of his shorthand diaries, a priceless chronicle of his years as engineer in charge of the Capitol Extension. And although Jefferson Davis abandoned Washington in January 1861, never to return, the state of Mississippi made sure he was remembered. His statue stands today in National Statuary Hall, the old House chamber where bedlam, thanks to him, no longer reigns.

NOTES

PROLOGUE

1. U.S. Library of Congress, Papers of Montgomery C. Meigs, reel 12. Handwritten diary entry, June 30, 1860.
2. Ibid., typewritten diary entry for July 14, 1874.
3. For Meigs's description of the hoisting apparatus, see Meigs to Davis, Nov. 26, 1855, National Archives, *Letters Received by the Secretary of War*, Registered Series 1801–1870, M-221, reel 176.
4. Tyler Anbinder, *Nativism and Slavery: The Northern Know Nothings and the Politics of the 1850s* (New York: Oxford University Press, 1992), ix.
5. See, for instance, Meigs to Davis, March 2, 1854, in U.S. Congress, Architect of the Capitol, Montgomery C. Meigs, *Letterbooks*, RG 40, series 40.1, reel 31.
6. Montgomery C. Meigs, *Capitol Builder: The Shorthand Journals of Montgomery C. Meigs, 1853–1859, 1861*, ed. Wendy Wolff (Washington, D.C.: U.S. Government Printing Office, 2001), 350.
7. Ibid., 332.
8. Ibid., 66.
9. Ibid., 332.
10. Meigs to Davis, Jan. 11, 1856, *Letterbooks*.

1. "CONGRESS HOUSE"

1. Constance McLaughlin Green, *Washington, Village and Capital, 1800–1878* (Princeton, N.J.: Princeton University Press, 1962), 183.
2. Holman Hamilton, *Zachary Taylor, Soldier in the White House* (New York: Bobbs-Merrill, 1951), 177. See also William W. Freehling, *The Road to Disunion*, vol. 1: *Secessionists at Bay* (New York: Oxford University Press, 1990), 487. Freehling suggests that eighty thousand of the Californians were recent immigrants.

3. For a description of Houston's outfits, see e.g. Oliver Dyer, *Great Senators of the United States Forty Years Ago (1848–1849)* (New York: Robert Bonner's Sons, 1889), 166–67. References to Houston's habit of carving wooden hearts are many. See e.g. Virginia Clay-Clopton, *A Belle of the Fifties: Memories of Mrs. Clay of Alabama, Covering Social and Political Life in Washington and the South, 1853–1866* (New York: Doubleday, Page and Co., 1905), 99–100.

4. Christian F. Eckloff, *Memoirs of a Senate Page (1855–1859)*, ed. Percival G. Melbourne (New York: Broadway Publishing Co., 1909), 5.

5. Robert Mills to the Senate and House of Representatives, Feb. 22, 1850, in Robert Mills, *The Papers of Robert Mills 1781–1855*, ed. Pamela Scott (Wilmington, Del.: Scholarly Resources, 1990), microfilm, reel 10, item 2731A.

6. See Green, *Washington*, 4–7, for a description of the District and its hopes for commercial success.

7. William C. Allen, *History of the United States Capitol: A Chronicle of Design, Construction, and Politics*, Senate Document 106-29, 106th Congress, 2nd session (Washington, D.C.: U.S. Government Printing Office, 2001), 8.

8. Ibid., 10.

9. Green, *Washington*, 7–9.

10. Ibid., 183.

11. Alexis de Tocqueville, *Democracy in America*, ed. J. P. Mayer (New York: Harper Perennial, Harper and Row, 1988), 469.

12. See Allen, *History*, 16–21, for a description of the competition.

13. See ibid., 23–25, for a description of the cornerstone ceremony and early infighting over the design.

14. Ibid., 46.

15. Ibid., 50.

16. Ibid., 61–62, 77.

17. Ibid., 60.

18. Ibid., 72.

19. Ibid., 98–99.

20. Ibid., 100.

21. Latrobe's wife quoted in Allen, *History*, 123.

22. See Allen, *History*, 127–28, for background on Bulfinch.

23. Ibid., 133–34.

24. Ibid., 137.

25. Ibid., 133–44.

26. Quoted in Allen, *History*, 145.

27. Allen, *History*, 166.

28. Information on the dimensions of the Capitol at the end of the Bulfinch era can be obtained from the Architect of the Capitol website, aoc.gov/cc/capitol/capitol_construction.cfm.

29. Ibid.

30. See Allen, *History*, 174, for a description of the public outrage. For concerns about

weight, see H. Paul Caemmerer, *A Manual on the Origin and Development of Washington* (Washington, D.C.: U.S. Government Printing Office, 1939), 321.

31. Green, *Washington*, 171–72.
32. R. W. Liscombe, *Altogether American: Robert Mills, Architect and Engineer, 1781–1855* (New York: Oxford University Press, 1994), 158.
33. Isaac Bassett, Isaac Bassett Papers, U.S. Senate (microfilm), box 20, folder F, 157–58.
34. Eckloff, *Memoirs*, 5–6.
35. U.S. Congress, House of Representatives, *Documentary History of the Construction and Development of the United States Capitol Buildings and Grounds*, H.R. Report 646, 58th Congress, 2nd session (Washington, D.C.: U.S. Government Printing Office, 1904), serial 4585, 409.
36. Ibid., 410.
37. Ibid., 408–409.
38. Ibid., 421.
39. Ibid., 422.
40. Ibid., 424–30.
41. U.S. Congress, Senate, "Message from the President of the United States, to the two Houses of Congress at the Commencement of the First Session of the Thirty-First Congress," Report of the Secretary of the Interior, December 24, 1849, Senate Executive Doc. 1, pt. 2, 31st Congress, 1st session, serial 550, 3.
42. Charles Dickens, *American Notes* (New York: Modern Library, 1992), 156–61.
43. Green, *Washington*, 72, 112.
44. Ibid., 160.
45. Donald E. Press, "South of the Avenue: From Murder Bay to the Federal Triangle," *Records of the Columbia Historical Society* (Washington, D.C.: Historical Society of Washington, D.C.), vol. 51, 1984, 51.
46. Clay-Clopton, *Belle*, 28, 42.
47. Jesse J. Holland, *Black Men Built the Capitol* (Guilford, Conn.: Globe Pequot Press, 2007), 29.
48. Green, *Washington*, 183.
49. Ibid., 215. See also Russell F. Weigley, *Quartermaster General of the Union Army* (New York: Columbia University Press, 1959), 58.
50. Green, *Washington*, 160.
51. Ibid., 209–11.
52. Ibid., 183.
53. See Green, *Washington*, 183. In 1840 the city had a slave population of 1,713, or 7 percent of the total. In 1850, the number of slaves had risen to 2,113, but in an era of explosive urban growth generally, this was only 5.3 percent of the total population.
54. Ibid., 184–91. Green contrasts in detail the generally positive evolution of race relations in the city during the period with the reluctance of whites to participate in the debate.
55. Hamilton, *Zachary Taylor*, 21–23.
56. Ibid., 23, 60–61.

57. See e.g. George F. Hoar, *Autobiography of 70 Years*, vol. 1 (New York: Charles Scribner's Sons, 1903), 147–52, for a discussion of Taylor's initially poor reception in Massachusetts. Also, for Washington elites underestimating Taylor, see Benjamin Perley Poore, *Perley's Reminiscences of Sixty Years in the National Metropolis*, vol. 1 (Philadelphia: Hubbard Brothers, 1886), 349, 357.

58. Zachary Taylor to Jefferson Davis, July 27, 1847, in Jefferson Davis, *The Papers of Jefferson Davis*, vol. 3: *1846–1848*, ed. James T. McIntosh, Lynda Lasswell Crist, and Mary S. Dix (Baton Rouge: Louisiana State University Press, 1981), 198–204.

59. Lawrence A. Gobright, *Recollections of Men and Things at Washington, During the Third of a Century* (Philadelphia: Claxton, Remsen and Hafflefinger, 1869), 101–102.

2. PLANTING THE SEED

1. Mills to Jefferson Davis, May 1, 1850, in Robert Mills, *The Papers of Robert Mills 1781–1855*, ed. Pamela Scott (Wilmington, Del.: Scholarly Resources, 1990), microfilm, reel 10, item 2735C.

2. R. W. Liscombe, *Altogether American: Robert Mills, Architect and Engineer, 1781–1855* (New York: Oxford University Press, 1994), 257–58.

3. Robert Mills to the Senate and House of Representatives, Feb. 22, 1850, in Mills, *Papers*, reel 10, item 2731A.

4. Constance McLaughlin Green, *Washington, Village and Capital, 1800–1878* (Princeton, N.J.: Princeton University Press, 1962), 136–37.

5. William C. Allen, *History of the United States Capitol: A Chronicle of Design, Construction, and Politics*, Senate Document 106-29, 106th Congress, 2nd session (Washington, D.C.: U.S. Government Printing Office, 2001), 180.

6. Liscombe, *Altogether American*, 171.

7. Ibid., 187.

8. Ibid., 206–12.

9. Mills to Senate Committee on Public Buildings, Mar. 9, 1846, in Mills, *Papers*, reel 10, item 2488.

10. Ibid.

11. In U.S. Congress, Architect of the Capitol, vertical files, *Architects: Robert Mills: Magazine and Journal Articles*, Robert Dale Owen, "Hints on Public Architecture" (Cambridge, Mass.: Da Capo Press [reprint], 1978). See also Allen, *History*, 182.

12. David M. Potter, *The Impending Crisis: 1848–1861* (New York: Harper and Row, 1976), 97.

13. For a description of Calhoun's final appearance, see Allan Nevins, *Ordeal of the Union*, vol. 1: *Fruits of Manifest Destiny, 1847–1852* (New York: Charles Scribner's Sons, 1947), 280–81. For a discussion of the effect of this speech and the Webster and Seward speeches that followed, see Michael F. Holt, *The Fate of Their Country: Politicians, Slavery Extension, and the Coming of the Civil War* (New York: Hill and Wang, 2004), 73–74.

14. Quoted in Nevins, *Ordeal of the Union*, vol. 1, 288.

15. Holt, *Fate of Their Country*, 73; Potter, *Impending Crisis*, 102.

16. William C. Davis, *Jefferson Davis: The Man and His Hour* (New York: HarperCollins, 1991), 12.

17. For a discussion of Davis's split political personality, see William J. Cooper, Jr., *Jefferson Davis, American* (New York: Alfred A. Knopf, 2000), 112.

18. Varina Howell Davis, *Jefferson Davis, Ex-President of the Confederate States of America: A Memoir by His Wife in Two Volumes*, vol. 1 (New York: Belford Co., 1890), 462. See also Robert Barnwell Rhett, *The Death and Funeral Ceremonies of John Caldwell Calhoun* (Columbia, S.C.: A. S. Johnson, 1850), 33.

19. Cooper, *Jefferson Davis*, 29–30.

20. Ibid., 33, and William C. Davis, *Jefferson Davis*, 28.

21. Cooper, *Jefferson Davis*, 33.

22. Quoted in William C. Davis, *Jefferson Davis*, 33.

23. Cooper, *Jefferson Davis*, 46–47.

24. Quoted in Holman Hamilton, *Zachary Taylor, Soldier of the Republic* (New York: Bobbs-Merrill, 1941), 101.

25. William C. Davis, *Jefferson Davis*, 52–53.

26. See William C. Davis, *Jefferson Davis*, 66–70 for the charges and details of the court-martial.

27. Jefferson Davis, "Autobiography of Jefferson Davis," *Bedford's Magazine*, Jan. 1890, reprinted in full in Jefferson Davis, *Jefferson Davis, Constitutionalist: His Letters, Papers and Speeches*, ed. Dunbar Rowland, multivolume set, vol. 1 (Jackson, Miss.: S. J. Little and Ives, Company, 1923), xx.

28. Davis to Sarah Knox Taylor, Dec. 16, 1834, in Jefferson Davis, *Private Letters 1823–1889*, ed. Hudson Strode (New York: Harcourt, Brace and World, 1966), 10–11.

29. For a description of the wedding and Davis's brief marriage, see Cooper, *Jefferson Davis*, 70–72.

30. Ibid., 76.

31. Varina Davis, *Jefferson Davis*, vol. 1, 171–72.

32. Cooper, *Jefferson Davis*, 86–88.

33. Ibid., 91.

34. Varina Davis, *Jefferson Davis*, vol. 1, 191.

35. Ibid.

36. Cooper, *Jefferson Davis*, 99.

37. Varina Davis, *Jefferson Davis*, vol. 1, 199.

38. Cooper, *Jefferson Davis*, 107.

39. Varina Davis, *Jefferson Davis*, vol. 1, 212.

40. Davis to Port Gibson (Miss.) *Correspondent*, June 3, 1846, in Rowland, vol. 1, 46.

41. Jefferson Davis, *The Papers of Jefferson Davis*, vol. 2: *1841–1846*, James T. McIntosh, ed. (Baton Rouge, La.: Louisiana State University Press, 1974), 642; Cooper, *Jefferson Davis*, 126.

42. Cooper, *Jefferson Davis*, 132–40.

43. See Joan E. Cashin, *First Lady of the Confederacy: Varina Davis's Civil War* (Cambridge, Mass.: Harvard University Press, 2006), 44–52, for a detailed discussion of Varina's relationship with Joseph Davis.

44. Davis to Varina, Dec. 10, 1846, in Jefferson Davis, *The Papers of Jefferson Davis*, vol. 3: *1846–1848*, ed. James T. McIntosh, Lynda Lasswell Crist, and Mary S. Dix (Baton Rouge: Louisiana State University Press, 1981), 93–95.

45. See e.g. Zachary Taylor to Davis, July 27, 1847, in *Papers of Jefferson Davis*, vol. 3, 198–204.

46. For accounts of the Battle of Buena Vista, see Cooper, *Jefferson Davis*, 149–54, and William C. Davis, *Jefferson Davis*, 150–58.

47. Quoted in Cooper, *Jefferson Davis*, 155.

48. All references are found in Jefferson Davis, *Jefferson Davis, Constitutionalist*, vol. 1. Polk to Davis, May 19, 1847, 73; Davis to Polk, June 20, 1847, 86; Albert Brown to Jefferson Davis, Aug. 10, 1847, 92; and Davis to Brown, Aug. 15, 1847, 92–93.

3. JEFFERSON DAVIS LOSES ONE AND WINS ONE

1. U.S. Congress, House of Representatives, *Documentary History of the Construction and Development of the United States Capitol Buildings and Grounds*, H.R. Report 646, 58th Congress, 2nd session (Washington, D.C.: U.S. Government Printing Office, 1904), serial 4585, 443.

2. Ibid.

3. William J. Cooper, Jr., *Jefferson Davis, American* (New York: Alfred A. Knopf, 2000), 183.

4. Benjamin Perley Poore, *Perley's Reminiscences of Sixty Years in the National Metropolis*, 2 vols. (Philadelphia: Hubbard Brothers, 1886), vol. 1, 342.

5. Jefferson Davis, *Jefferson Davis, Constitutionalist: His Letters, Papers and Speeches*, ed. Dunbar Rowland, multivolume set (Jackson, Miss.: S. J. Little and Ives, Company, 1923), vol. 1, 349, 357.

6. Isaac Bassett, Isaac Bassett Papers, U.S. Senate (microfilm), box 19, folder A, 8.

7. Zachary Taylor to Jefferson Davis, Aug. 16, 1847, in Jefferson Davis, *The Papers of Jefferson Davis*, vol. 3: *1846–1848*, ed. James T. McIntosh, Lynda Lasswell Crist, and Mary S. Dix (Baton Rouge: Louisiana State University Press, 1981), 208–15.

8. In Rowland, ed., *Jefferson Davis, Constitutionalist*, vol. 1, 191–98.

9. Ibid., 220, Davis to John J. Crittenden, Jan. 30, 1849. During and after his presidency Taylor remained a surprisingly enigmatic figure. Davis's respect, loyalty, and admiration contrast markedly with the views of Taylor's contemporary adversaries, who regarded him as little more than a semiliterate bumpkin. But see William W. Freehling in *The Road to Disunion*, vol. 1: *Secessionists at Bay* (New York: Oxford University Press, 1990), 491, who argues that all this "misses the point," and that Taylor was a nationalistic southern Whig interested in revitalizing the fortunes of the party. Michael F. Holt, in *The Political Crisis of the 1850s* (New York: W. W. Norton and Co., 1983), 73–74, goes a step further, describing Taylor's presidency as a conscious effort to transform the Whigs into a "Taylor Republican Party," with himself at its center.

10. Holman Hamilton, *Zachary Taylor, Soldier in the White House* (New York: Bobbs-Merrill, 1951), 237.

11. Jefferson Davis, *The Papers of Jefferson Davis*, vol. 4: *1849–1852*, ed. Lynda L. Crist,

Mary S. Dix, and Richard E. Beringer (Baton Rouge: Louisiana State University Press, 1983), 62–70.

12. Quoted in Fred. J. Maroon, *The United States Capitol* (Washington, D.C.: Maroon Editions, 1993), 115.

13. Bassett, Papers, box 19, folder B, 30–38.

14. Quoted in Maroon, *Capitol*, 115.

15. For descriptions of Clay during the debate, see Poore, vol. 1, 363, and Oliver Dyer, *Great Senators of the United States Forty Years Ago (1848–1849)* (New York: Robert Bonner's Sons, 1889), 22–25.

16. For the Davis speech in its entirety, see Rowland, ed., *Jefferson Davis, Constitutionalist*, vol.1, 263–307. The views expressed here closely reflect those in Freehling, *Road to Disunion*, 499. It is hard to regard Davis's southern position as anything more than what would be called at a later time a "deal-breaker." Insisting on an extension of the Missouri line, thus guaranteeing more territory for slavery, was a position northerners would never accept. By drawing the southern position so starkly, Davis effectively halted the debate in its tracks before it had fairly begun. Davis's biographer William J. Cooper, Jr., noted in a conversation with the author, however, that extending the Missouri line was for Davis a significant concession. While this is certainly the case, one searches in vain for Davis's thoughts on how to get there.

17. Ibid., 411.

18. Quoted in Lawrence A. Gobright, *Recollections of Men and Things at Washington, During the Third of a Century* (Philadelphia: Claxton, Remsen and Hafflefinger, 1869), 115.

19. David M. Potter, *The Impending Crisis: 1848–1861* (New York: Harper and Row, 1976), 103; Michael F. Holt, *The Fate of Their Country: Politicians, Slavery Extension, and the Coming of the Civil War* (New York: Hill and Wang, 2004), 71–73.

20. Quoted in Allan Nevins, *Ordeal of the Union*, vol. 1: *Fruits of Manifest Destiny, 1847–1852* (New York: Charles Scribner's Sons, 1947), 319.

21. U.S. Congress, *Documentary History*, 430–31.

22. Ibid., 433.

23. Ibid., 434.

24. Ibid., 435–37.

25. Quoted in Nevins, *Ordeal*, vol. 1, 330.

26. Poore, vol. 1, 377–78.

27. See Hamilton, *Zachary Taylor*, 388–89. Taylor's sudden death poses two intriguing and unanswerable questions. David Potter (*Impending Crisis*, 118) wonders without success whether Taylor would have rolled the dice: used military force to bring the Texans and, thus, the South to heel, and whether the South would have acquiesced or gone to war to prevent him from doing so. Second, what did Clay hope to accomplish? There is no reason to doubt that Taylor would have vetoed Clay's compromise. What then? In this context, Taylor's death was, for Clay, a gift.

28. Varina Davis to her mother, July 10, 1850, in Jefferson Davis, *Private Letters 1823–1889*, ed. Hudson Strode (New York: Harcourt, Brace and World, 1966), 62.

29. U.S. Congress, *Documentary History*, 438.

30. Ibid., 439.

31. Ibid., 440.

32. Potter, *Impending Crisis*, 107–108.

33. Rowland, ed., *Jefferson Davis, Constitutionalist*, vol. 1, 435.

34. *New York Herald*, Sept. 6, 1850.

35. Ibid.

36. *New York Tribune*, Sept. 9, 1850.

37. Senate Proceedings, Sept. 16, 1850, *Congressional Globe*, 31st Congress, 1st session, 1829–30.

38. U.S. Congress, *Documentary History*, 441.

39. Ibid.

40. Ibid., 442.

41. Ibid., 443–45.

4. THE CONTEST

1. *National Intelligencer*, Oct. 7, 1850.

2. For details of Walter's background, see "Minority Report," Mar. 1852, in Robert Mills, *The Papers of Robert Mills 1781–1855*, ed. Pamela Scott (Wilmington, Del.: Scholarly Resources, 1990), reel 11, item 2965B. See also James M. Goode, "Architecture and Politics: Thomas Ustick Walter and the Enlargement of the United States Capitol, 1850–1865," dissertation submitted to the Faculty of the Graduate School of Arts and Sciences of George Washington University, Dec. 6, 1994, vol. 1, 5–16.

3. Thomas U. Walter, "Autobiographical Sketch," Jan. 8, 1873, Thomas Ustick Walter Collection, Archives of American Art, Athenaeum, Philadelphia, roll 4143.

4. Glenn Brown, *History of the United States Capitol*, 2 vols. (Washington, D.C.: Government Printing Office, 1902), vol. 2, 192–93.

5. For details of Walter's trip to Washington, see diary entries for Sept. 28 and Oct. 1, 1850, Walter Collection, roll 4133. For Walter's enduring desire for La Guaira payment, see, for instance, diary entry for Oct. 9, 1883, Walter Collection, roll 4143.

6. Ibid., roll 4133.

7. Ibid.

8. William C. Allen, *History of the United States Capitol: A Chronicle of Design, Construction, and Politics*, Senate Document 106-29, 106th Congress, 2nd session (Washington, D.C.: U.S. Government Printing Office, 2001), 190–91.

9. Ibid., 189.

10. Ibid.

11. Diary entries for Nov. 22–30, 1850, Walter Collection, roll 4133.

12. Mills, *Papers*, reel 10, item 2480.

13. Ibid., reel 11, item 2796C.

14. Ibid.

15. Ibid.

16. Diary entries for Dec. 2–4, 1850, Walter Collection, roll 4133.

17. Ibid., Dec. 13–21, 1850.

18. Mills, *Papers*, reel 11, item 2995B. This is from a petition to Congress written by

Charles Cluskey several years later, probably in 1856, in an attempt to press his case for compensation as designer of the cast-iron dome (a spurious claim). He makes reference to the many-times-weekly meetings after February 1, but he undoubtedly refers to the December and January schedules. After the first week in February, all the action moved to the White House.

19. "Washington" to Millard Fillmore, Jan. 26, 1851, in Millard Fillmore, *Papers*, Buffalo and Erie County Historical Society, Buffalo, N.Y. (microfilm).

20. Allen, *History*, 192.

21. Note in a locked book, Jan. 30, 1851, *The Papers of Joseph Henry*, vol. 8: *Jan. 1850– Dec. 1853*, ed. Marc Rothenberg (Washington D.C.: Smithsonian Institution Press, 1998), 134.

22. U.S. Congress, House of Representatives, *Documentary History of the Construction and Development of the United States Capitol Buildings and Grounds*, H.R. Report 646, 58th Congress, 2nd session (Washington, D.C.: U.S. Government Printing Office, 1904), serial 4585, 446.

23. Davis to Millard Fillmore, Feb. 9, 1851, Walter Collection. See also Jefferson Davis, *The Papers of Jefferson Davis*, vol. 6: *1856–1860*, ed. Lynda Lasswell Crist and Mary Seaton Dix (Baton Rouge and London: Louisiana State University Press, 1983), 676.

24. Ibid.

25. See Mills, *Papers*, reel 11, item 2995B, for Cluskey's report, which is undated but was probably written in the mid-1850s. For Walter's observations, see diary entry for Feb. 20, 1851, in Walter Collection, roll 4133.

26. Mills, *Papers*, reel 11, item 2995B.

27. See, for instance, C. F. Anderson to Fillmore, Mar. 14, 1851, in Fillmore, *Papers*, in which Anderson appears to be presenting his bona fides to someone he does not know. See also Robert Mills to Millard Fillmore, May 3, 1851, in Mills, *Papers*, reel 11, item 2860, in which Mills refers to "meeting you" that morning.

28. Diary entry for Feb. 12, 1851, Walter Collection, roll 4133.

29. Mills, *Papers*, reel 11, item 2995B.

30. Ibid.

31. Walter to Fillmore, Feb. 21, 1851, Fillmore, *Papers*.

32. See Henry D. Moore to Fillmore, Feb. 25, 1851, confirming the meeting. Moore was a Whig congressman from Pennsylvania. Fillmore, *Papers*.

33. *National Intelligencer*, Mar. 7, 1851.

34. Mills to Taylor, Feb. 26, 1851, Fillmore, *Papers*.

35. Ibid., C. F. Anderson to Fillmore, Mar. 14, 1851.

36. Henry D. Moore to Fillmore, Mar. 19, 1851, Fillmore, *Papers*; diary entry, Mar. 20, 1851, Walter Collection, roll 4133.

37. Mills, *Papers*, reel 11, item 2995B.

38. Walter to Fillmore, Apr. 7, 1851, Fillmore, *Papers*.

39. Diary entry for Apr. 12, 1851, Walter Collection, roll 4133.

40. See, for instance, R. W. Thompson to Fillmore, Mar. 22, 1851, and A. B. Young to Fillmore, Apr. 16, 1851, Fillmore, *Papers*.

41. Mills, *Papers*, reel 11, item 2995B.

42. Diary entry for Apr. 20, 1851, Walter Collection, roll 4133.

43. Joseph R. Chandler to Fillmore, Apr. 23, 1851, Fillmore, *Papers*.

44. Diary entry for Apr. 27, 1851, Walter Collection, roll 4133.

45. Ibid., May 1, 1851.

46. A. B. Young to Fillmore, May 2, 1851, Fillmore, *Papers*.

47. Ibid., C. B. Cluskey to Fillmore, May 2, 1851.

48. Ibid., Robert Mills to Fillmore, May 3, 1851.

49. Diary entries for May 6–8, 1851, Walter Collection, roll 4133.

50. A. B. Young to Fillmore, May 19, 1851, Fillmore, *Papers*.

51. Ibid., W. Hickey to Fillmore, May 31, 1851.

52. Ibid., Thomas McCleland to Fillmore, May 17, 1851.

53. Goode, "Architecture and Politics," vol. 2, 350–51.

54. Diary entry for June 11, 1851, Walter Collection, roll 4133.

55. Allen, *History*, 196.

56. Lawrence A. Gobright, *Recollections of Men and Things at Washington, During the Third of a Century* (Philadelphia: Claxton, Remsen and Hafflefinger, 1869), 118–19.

57. Allen, *History*, 200.

58. Gobright, *Recollections*, 121.

59. U.S. Congress, *Documentary History*, 447.

5. THOMAS U. WALTER IN CHARGE

1. See Thomas U. Walter, Thomas Ustick Walter Collection, Archives of American Art, Athenaeum, Philadelphia, multiple microfilm rolls. Virtually any short sampling of Walter's letters will give a flavor of the tribulations constantly roiling the Walter family. For one summary of family affairs see Walter to Thomas Walter, Feb. 3, 1856, in Walter Collection, roll 4137, in which Walter has not heard from his second son in over a year and hears from him now only because Thomas needs $200.

2. U.S. Congress, House of Representatives, *Documentary History of the Construction and Development of the United States Capitol Buildings and Grounds*, H.R. Report 646, 58th Congress, 2nd session (Washington, D.C.: U.S. Government Printing Office, 1904), serial 4585, 465.

3. See James M. Goode, "Architecture and Politics: Thomas Ustick Walter and the Enlargement of the United States Capitol, 1850–1865," dissertation submitted to the Faculty of the Graduate School of Arts and Sciences of George Washington University, Dec. 6, 1994, vol. 1, 2–9.

4. William C. Allen, *History of the United States Capitol: A Chronicle of Design, Construction, and Politics*, Senate Document 106-29, 106th Congress, 2nd session (Washington, D.C.: U.S. Government Printing Office, 2001), 195.

5. Diary entry for June 23, 1851, Walter Collection, roll 4133.

6. Turpin C. Bannister, "The Genealogy of the Dome of the United States Capitol," *Journal of the Society of Architectural Historians*, vol. 7, Jan.–June, 1948, 17.

7. See diary entries for July 2–Nov. 4, 1851, Walter Collection, roll 4133.

8. Bannister, "Genealogy," 18.

9. Architect of the Capitol to President of the United States, July 29, 1851, in U.S. Congress, *Documentary History*, 449–50.

10. Philip Reid was the only slave known to have worked on the Capitol Extension. For an account of his role in preparing the statue of *Freedom* for its place atop the Capitol Dome, see chapter 18.

11. Architect of the Capitol to President of the United States, July 29, 1851, in U.S. Congress, *Documentary History*, 449–50.

12. For Mills's contention that he devised the winning Capitol design, see e.g. Robert Mills to Franklin Pierce, Mar. 1, 1853, in Robert Mills, *The Papers of Robert Mills 1781–1855*, ed. Pamela Scott (Wilmington, Del.: Scholarly Resources, 1990), reel 12, item 3033; for Cluskey's claim to be the designer of the cast-iron dome, see ibid., reel 11, item 2995B; for Anderson's lingering court case against Walter, ultimately dismissed only months before the Civil War ended, see items beginning in the middle of 1864 and ending on Feb. 8, 1865, in Walter Collection, rolls 4141 and 4142.

13. See U.S. Congress, Senate, "Report of the Select Committee to Investigate Abuses, Bribery, Fraud," S. Report 1/1, 33rd Congress, special session, Mar. 22, 1853, serial 688, 133, 171, 179.

14. Walter to William Easby, Commissioner of Public Buildings, May 31, 1852, in Thomas U. Walter, *Records of the Architect of the Capitol: Letterbooks of Thomas U. Walter*, U.S. Congress, Architect of the Capitol.

15. Varina Howell Davis, *Jefferson Davis, Ex-President of the Confederate States of America: A Memoir by His Wife in Two Volumes*, vol. 1 (New York: Belford Co., 1890), 465.

16. Reuben Davis, *Recollections of Mississippi and Mississippians* (Boston and New York: Houghton, Mifflin and Co., 1890), 315–16.

17. Varina Davis, *Jefferson Davis*, vol. 1, 466.

18. William J. Cooper, Jr., *Jefferson Davis, American* (New York: Alfred A. Knopf, 2000), 217.

19. Varina Davis, *Jefferson Davis*, vol. 1, 470.

20. U.S. Congress, *Documentary History*, 454.

21. The organization of the workforce can be extrapolated from a number of sources, including witness testimony in U.S. Senate, "Report of the Select Committee." For a good summary of this information, see Goode, "Architecture and Politics," vol. 2, 204–10.

22. Wages are estimated by examining witness testimony in U.S. Senate, "Report of the Select Committee." See also Goode, "Architecture and Politics," vol. 2, 363–64, for an 1858 wage table.

23. U.S. Congress, *Documentary History*, 452.

24. Ibid., 553.

25. Ibid., 464, message from the president of the United States transmitting the report of the architect for the Extension of the Capitol, Feb. 12, 1852.

26. Ibid., 451, Walter to Fillmore, Sept. 13, 1851.

27. U.S. Senate, "Report of the Select Committee," 140–41.

28. Diary entry for Oct. 22, 1851, Walter Collection, roll 4133.

29. U.S. Congress, *Documentary History*, 558.

30. U.S. Senate, "Report of the Select Committee," 141.

31. Ibid., 142.

32. Walter to Alexander H. H. Stuart, Dec. 27, 1851, in Walter, *Letterbooks*.

33. U.S. Senate, "Report of the Select Committee," 142–43.

34. Walter to John Rice and John Baird, Jan. 13, 1852, in Walter, *Letterbooks*.

35. U.S. Congress, *Documentary History*, 454.

36. Ibid.

37. Ibid., 456–57.

38. *National Intelligencer*, Dec. 25, 1851, quoted in William Dawson Johnston, *History of the Library of Congress*, vol. 1: *1800–1864* (Washington, D.C.: Government Printing Office, 1904), 275–76.

39. Benjamin Brown French, *Witness to the Young Republic: A Yankee's Journal, 1828–1870*, ed. Donald B. Cole and John J. McDonough (Hanover, N.H.: University Press of New England, 1989), 223.

40. Johnston, *Library of Congress*, 276–77.

41. August Schoenborn, quoted in Bannister, "Genealogy," 18.

42. Meehan to Boyd, Dec. 25, 1851, in Johnston, *Library of Congress*, 277–78.

43. *National Intelligencer*, Dec. 25, 1851, in ibid., 276–77.

44. Easby to Walter, Dec. 27, 1851, quoted in ibid., 280.

45. Walter to Easby, Dec. 26, 1851, quoted in ibid., 280–81.

46. Walter to Alexander H. H. Stuart, Nov. 11, 1852, in Walter, *Letterbooks*.

47. Walter to Easby, Jan. 27, 1852, quoted in Johnston, *Library of Congress*, 288–91.

48. Bannister, "Genealogy," 3.

49. Siegfried Giedion, *Space, Time and Architecture: The Growth of a New Tradition*, 5th ed. (Cambridge, Mass.: Harvard University Press, 1967), 174.

50. See John Gloag and Derek Bridgewater, *A History of Cast Iron in Architecture* (London: George Allen and Unwin Ltd., 1948), 192–98.

6. SHARKS IN THE WATER

1. Diary entry for Jan. 1, 1852, in Thomas U. Walter, Thomas Ustick Walter Collection, Archives of American Art, Athenaeum, Philadelphia, roll 4133.

2. U.S. Congress, House of Representatives, *Documentary History of the Construction and Development of the United States Capitol Buildings and Grounds*, H.R. Report 646, 58th Congress, 2nd session (Washington, D.C.: U.S. Government Printing Office, 1904), serial 4585, 459.

3. See ibid., 469–71.

4. Diary entry for Jan. 16, 1852, Walter Collection, roll 4133.

5. U.S. Congress, *Documentary History*, 461.

6. Ibid., 462.

7. Ibid., 463.

8. See diary entries beginning Feb. 11, 1852, Walter Collection, roll 4133.

9. U.S. Congress, Senate, "Report of the Select Committee to Investigate Abuses, Bribery, Fraud," S.Rep. 1/1, 33rd Congress, special session, Mar. 22, 1853, serial 688, 12.

10. U.S. Congress, *Documentary History*, 468–69.

11. Ibid., 469.

12. Ibid.

13. Ibid., 470.

14. Ibid.

15. Ibid.

16. Ibid., 470–71.

17. Ibid., 471–76.

18. Ibid., 497.

19. Ibid., 498.

20. Ibid., 499.

21. Ibid., 500.

22. Ibid., 501.

23. Ibid., 505.

24. Ibid., 509.

25. Ibid., 510–14.

26. Ibid., 516.

27. Ibid., 507.

28. Ibid., 508.

29. Ibid., 521.

30. Ibid., 522–23.

31. Ibid., 524.

32. For the list of bidders, see William Dawson Johnston, *History of the Library of Congress, vol. 1: 1800–1864* (Washington, D.C.: Government Printing Office, 1904), 294.

33. Walter to Alexander H. H. Stuart, Secretary of the Interior, June 26, 1852, in Thomas U. Walter, *Records of the Architect of the Capitol: Letterbooks of Thomas U. Walter*, U.S. Congress, Architect of the Capitol.

34. Walter to Provest & Winter, July 3, 1852, ibid. For examination by Stanton and Hunter, see U.S. Senate, "Report of the Select Committee," 167.

35. Walter to Samuel Strong, July 24, 1852, in Walter, *Letterbooks*.

36. Ibid.

37. U.S. Senate, "Report of the Select Committee," 80.

38. Ibid., 13.

39. Ibid., 144.

40. Ibid., 15, 92–95.

41. Ibid., 123–25.

42. Ibid., 173.

43. Ibid., 99; see also Walter to Alexander H. H. Stuart, Secretary of the Interior, June 7, 1852, in Walter, *Letterbooks*.

44. U.S. Senate, "Report of the Select Committee," 114.

45. Ibid., 126.

46. Ibid., 16.
47. Ibid., 102–11.
48. Ibid., 177.
49. Ibid., 107.
50. Ibid., 151–52.
51. Ibid., 176.
52. Ibid., 181.
53. Diary entry for Feb. 17, 1853, Walter Collection, roll 4133.
54. Ibid., Feb. 19, 1852.
55. U.S. Congress, *Documentary History*, 568.
56. Ibid.
57. Ibid., 570–71.
58. Ibid., 572.
59. Ibid., 584.

7. JEFFERSON DAVIS RETURNS

1. Benjamin Perley Poore, *Perley's Reminiscences of Sixty Years in the National Metropolis*, 2 vols. (Philadelphia: Hubbard Brothers, 1886), vol. 1, 428–29.
2. U.S. Congress, Senate, "Report of the Select Committee to Investigate Abuses, Bribery, Fraud," S.Rep. 1/1, 33rd Congress, special session, Mar. 22, 1853, serial 688, 146.
3. For a slightly more positive assessment of Pierce, see Michael Holt, *Franklin Pierce* (New York: Times Books, 2010), 1–4. Holt acknowledges Pierce's flaws but argues that his mistakes derived principally from his desire to hold the Democratic Party together in the absence of robust opposition from the declining Whigs.
4. Varina Howell Davis, *Jefferson Davis, Ex-President of the Confederate States of America: A Memoir by His Wife in Two Volumes* (New York: Belford Co., 1890), vol. 1, 474.
5. Joan E. Cashin, *First Lady of the Confederacy: Varina Davis's Civil War* (Cambridge, Mass.: Harvard University Press, 2006), 60.
6. Varina Davis, *Jefferson Davis*, vol. 1, 474–75.
7. For samples of the "newspaper war," see *Southern Press*, Feb. 12, 1852, in Jefferson Davis, *Jefferson Davis, Constitutionalist, His Letters, Papers and Speeches*, ed. Dunbar Rowland, multivolume set (Jackson, Miss.: S. J. Little and Ives, Company, 1923), 10 vols., vol. 2, 117; also *Yazoo Democrat*, Feb. 18, 1852, ibid., 126–30.
8. Poore, *Reminiscences*, vol. 1, 418. See also Michael F. Holt, *The Political Crisis of the 1850s* (New York: W. W. Norton and Co., 1983), 119. The Whigs were fatally divided along sectional lines by 1852, and Holt notes that southern Whigs regarded Scott as "a lackey of Seward" and the party's antislavery northerners.
9. Pierce to Davis, Dec. 7, 1852, in Rowland, ed., *Jefferson Davis, Constitutionalist*, vol. 2, 177.
10. Varina Davis, *Jefferson Davis*, vol. 1, 476.
11. Pierce to Davis, Jan. 12, 1853, in Rowland, ed., *Jefferson Davis, Constitutionalist*, vol. 2, 178.

12. Varina Davis, *Jefferson Davis*, vol. 1, 477.

13. William C. Davis, *Jefferson Davis: The Man and His Hour* (New York: HarperCollins, 1991), 225.

14. Varina Davis, *Jefferson Davis*, vol. 1, 551.

15. U.S. Congress, House of Representatives, *Documentary History of the Construction and Development of the United States Capitol Buildings and Grounds*, H.R. Report 646, 58th Congress, 2nd session (Washington, D.C.: U.S. Government Printing Office, 1904), serial 4585, 552.

16. Walter to Alexander H. H. Stuart, Dec. 28, 1852, in Thomas U. Walter, *Records of the Architect of the Capitol: Letterbooks of Thomas U. Walter*, U.S. Congress, Architect of the Capitol.

17. For excerpts from the debate, see William Dawson Johnston, *History of the Library of Congress*, vol. 1: *1800–1864* (Washington, D.C.: U.S. Government Printing Office, 1904), 295–97.

18. For copies of all the letters, see U.S. Congress, Architect of the Capitol, vertical files, *Robert Mills*.

19. Walter to His Excellency the President of the United States, Mar. 9, 1853, in Walter, *Letterbooks*.

20. U.S. Senate, "Report of the Select Committee," 10–15.

21. Ibid., 10.

22. Ibid., 18.

23. Ibid., 19.

24. Ibid., 19–20.

25. Ibid., 24.

26. U.S. Congress, *Documentary History*, 585.

27. Benjamin Brown French, *Witness to the Young Republic: A Yankee's Journal, 1828–1870*, ed. Donald B. Cole and John J. McDonough (Hanover, N.H.: University Press of New England), 240.

28. The cause-and-effect relationship is seldom cited explicitly, since Pierce gave the order, but see next note.

29. Jefferson Davis, *The Rise and Fall of the Confederate Government*, 2 vols. (Richmond, Va.: Garrett and Massie, Inc., 1881), vol. 1, 21. This is a clear statement that Pierce drove the decision to put Davis in charge of the Capitol, but since the statement is made by Davis, it has more force than it merits.

30. McClelland to Davis, Mar. 19, 1853, National Archives, *Records of the Office of the Chief of Engineers, Public Works and Buildings in the District of Columbia*, RG 77, entry 278, "Vouchers, Financial Statements and Lists of Papers Relating to the Washington Aqueduct," box 1.

31. Ibid.

32. Ibid.

33. Ibid. Rosecrans bore Totten no ill will, and may never even have known that Totten had tapped him for the Capitol job. He retired later in 1854, only to return to uniform during the Civil War. His performance as a field general was mixed, but his chief drawback was that he quarreled with both Secretary of War Edwin M. Stanton

and General Ulysses S. Grant, the two most important superiors in his chain of command. He later had a long political career, serving as a U.S. congressman from California from 1881 to 1885. He died in 1898.

34. Ibid.

35. Totten to Davis, Mar. 28, 1853, National Archives, *Letters, Reports, Statements Sent to the Secretary of War and Congress*, RG 77, vol. 7, 478.

36. Montgomery C. Meigs, *Capitol Builder: The Shorthand Journals of Montgomery C. Meigs, 1853–1859, 1861*, ed. Wendy Wolff (Washington, D.C.: U.S. Government Printing Office, 2001), 67. See also Russell F. Weigley, *Quartermaster General of the Union Army* (New York: Columbia University Press, 1959), 51.

37. Weigley, *Quartermaster*, 67.

38. Ibid., 52.

39. Meigs, *Capitol Builder*, 34, 42, 51, 58, 94.

40. Totten to Secretary of War Charles M. Conrad, Feb. 14, 1853, National Archives, *Records of the Office of the Chief of Engineers*, general correspondence 1787–1870. RG 77, entry 8, "Letters, Reports and Statements Sent to the Secretary of War and Congress 1836–68," vol. 7, NM 19, 469.

41. See Rowland, ed., *Jefferson Davis, Constitutionalist*, vol. 2, 194–95.

8. ENGINEER IN CHARGE

1. Montgomery C. Meigs, *Capitol Builder: The Shorthand Journals of Montgomery C. Meigs, 1853–1859, 1861*, ed. Wendy Wolff (Washington, D.C.: U.S. Government Printing Office, 2001), 102.

2. Typewritten diary entry for July 14, 1874, in Montgomery C. Meigs, Papers of Montgomery C. Meigs, U.S. Library of Congress, Manuscript Division, reel 12.

3. See, e.g., diary entries for May 17, 1853, and Dec. 27, 1853, in Meigs, *Capitol Builder*, 6, 35.

4. Ibid., 121.

5. Ibid., 67.

6. See Russell F. Weigley, *Quartermaster General of the Union Army* (New York: Columbia University Press, 1959), 21–22, and David W. Miller, *Second Only to Grant: Quartermaster General Montgomery C. Meigs* (Shippensburg, Pa.: White Mane Books, 2000), 4–5.

7. Meigs, *Capitol Builder*, 67–68.

8. Miller, *Second Only to Grant*, 12–13.

9. Diary entry for Apr. 5, 1853, in Walter, Thomas U., Thomas Ustick Walter Collection, Archives of American Art, Athenaeum, Philadelphia, roll 4133; Meigs to Davis, Apr. 5, 1853, in Meigs, Montgomery C., *Letterbooks*, Mar. 1853–Oct. 1859, 1861, U.S. Congress, Architect of the Capitol.

10. Meigs to Davis, Apr. 8, 1853, Meigs, *Letterbooks*.

11. Diary entry for Apr. 14, 1853, Walter Collection, roll 4133.

12. Meigs, *Capitol Builder*, 5.

13. Meigs to Walter, Jan. 21, 1858, in Meigs, *Letterbooks*.

14. Walter to Richard Gardiner, June 27, 1853, Walter Collection, roll 4133.

15. Walter to Richard Gardiner, Feb. 22, 1854, Walter Collection, roll 4136.
16. See, e.g., Davis to John B. Floyd, National Archives, RG 107, Letters Received by the Secretary of War, microfilm 221, roll 183, f/w/ p-22 (91).
17. M. C. Meigs, "On Acoustics and Ventilation, with Reference to the New Halls of Congress, May 1853," in *The Civil Engineer and Architect's Journal*, vol. XVII, no. 242, May 1854, 161–63.
18. For Meigs's obsession with inscriptions, see e.g. Miller, *Second Only to Grant*, 23; William C. Allen, *History of the United States Capitol: A Chronicle of Design, Construction, and Politics*, Senate Document 106-29, 106th Congress, 2nd session (Washington, D.C.: U.S. Government Printing Office, 2001), 282; diary entries for Mar. 23 and Apr. 3, 1858, in Montgomery C. Meigs, *The Shorthand Diaries of Montgomery C. Meigs*, unabridged transcription, U.S. Congress, Architect of the Capitol, undated; Meigs, *Capitol Builder*, 643.
19. Meigs to Davis, Apr. 15, 1853, National Archives, *Records of the Office of the Chief of Engineers*, "Records Relating to Work on the Capitol Extension and Washington Aqueduct," RG 77.
20. Meigs, "On Acoustics and Ventilation," 161–63.
21. Meigs, *Capitol Builder*, 7.
22. Davis to Bache and Henry, May 20, 1853, National Archives, *Records of the Coast and Geodetic Survey*, RG 23, vol. 1, 471.
23. Meigs, *Capitol Builder*, 14.
24. Ibid., 15; see also U.S. Congress, House of Representatives, *Documentary History of the Construction and Development of the United States Capitol Buildings and Grounds*, H.R. Report 646, 58th Congress, 2nd session (Washington, D.C.: U.S. Government Printing Office, 1904), serial 4585, 585.
25. Rice, Baird & Heebner to Meigs, Sept. 28, 1853, National Archives, *Records of the Office of the Chief of Engineers*, Records Relating to Work on the Capitol Extension and Washington Aqueduct, RG 77, file C-278.
26. Meigs to Rice, Baird & Heebner, Aug. 4, 1853, in Meigs, *Letterbooks*.
27. Meigs to Davis, Dec. 29, 1853, ibid.
28. Meigs to Everett, July 7, 1853, sent as an enclosure in Meigs to Davis, June 27, 1855, ibid.
29. Everett to Meigs, July 12, 1853, ibid.
30. Meigs to Thomas Crawford, Aug. 18, 1853; Meigs to Hiram Powers, Aug. 21, 1853, ibid.
31. Powers to Meigs, Sept. 28, 1853, ibid.
32. Meigs, *Capitol Builder*, 24.
33. Meigs to Crawford, Nov. 30, 1853, Meigs, *Letterbooks*.
34. Meigs to Crawford, Dec. 27, 1853, ibid.
35. Meigs to Crawford, Dec. 29, 1853, ibid.
36. Meigs to Davis, Apr. 18, 1853, ibid.
37. Meigs to Davis, Apr. 23, 1853, ibid.
38. Meigs, *Capitol Builder*, 6.
39. Ibid., 5.

40. Davis to Meigs, July 22, 1853, U.S. Congress, Architect of the Capitol, vertical files, *Capitol Extension.*

41. Meigs to Maj. W. D. Frazer, Army Corps of Engineers, N.Y., Aug. 2, 1853, in Meigs, *Letterbooks.*

42. Meigs, *Capitol Builder,* 16.

43. Ibid., 17.

44. Diary entry for Sept. 25, 1853, Walter Collection, roll 4133.

45. Diary entry for Oct. 29, 1853, Walter Collection, roll 4133.

46. Walter to My Dear Father, Nov. 11, 1853, Walter Collection, roll 4136.

47. U.S. Congress, *Documentary History,* 585–86.

48. Meigs, *Capitol Builder,* 35.

49. Meigs, *Capitol Builder,* 32.

50. Ibid.

9. WALTER HAS A NEW IDEA

1. Allan Nevins, *Ordeal of the Union,* vol. 2: *A House Dividing, 1852–1857* (New York: Charles Scribner's Sons, 1947), 78.

2. U.S. Congress, House of Representatives, *Documentary History of the Construction and Development of the United States Capitol Buildings and Grounds,* H.R. Report 646, 58th Congress, 2nd session (Washington, D.C.: U.S. Government Printing Office, 1904), serial 4585, 598.

3. Ibid., 599.

4. Ibid., 605.

5. Ibid., 602.

6. Quoted in Nevins, Ordeal, 94. Also see Michael F. Holt, *The Fate of Their Country: Politicians, Slavery Extension, and the Coming of the Civil War* (New York: Hill and Wang, 2004), 99–101, in which Holt outlines his view that Douglas (and later Pierce) undertook Kansas-Nebraska as a measure that would unite fractious Democrats in the absence of coherent Whig opposition around the themes of Western expansion, homesteading, and a transcontinental railroad.

7. Holt, *Fate of Their Country,* 101. Also see David M. Potter, *The Impending Crisis, 1848–1861* (New York: Harper and Row, 1976), 159.

8. Holt, *Fate of Their Country,* 102.

9. William W. Freehling, *The Road to Disunion,* vol. 2: *Secessionists Triumphant, 1854–1861* (New York: Oxford University Press, 2007), 62.

10. Jefferson Davis, *The Rise and Fall of the Confederate Government,* 2 vols. (Richmond, Va.: Garrett and Massie, Inc., 1881), vol. 1, 25.

11. Michael F. Holt, *Franklin Pierce* (New York: Times Books, 2010), 77.

12. Michael F. Holt, *The Political Crisis of the 1850s* (New York: W. W. Norton and Co., 1983), 152–53.

13. Potter, *Impending Crisis,* 199–200.

14. Holt, *Political Crisis,* 150.

15. Montgomery C. Meigs, *Capitol Builder: The Shorthand Journals of Montgomery C.*

Meigs, 1853–1859, 1861, ed. Wendy Wolff (Washington, D.C.: U.S. Government Printing Office, 2001), 41, 48, 51, 54.

16. Ibid., 44.

17. Ibid., 50.

18. Ibid., 44.

19. Walter to Rice, Jan. 3, 1854; Walter to My Dear Sister, Jan. 10, 1854; Walter to Rice, Jan. 13, 1854, in Thomas U. Walter, Thomas Ustick Walter Collection, Archives of American Art, Athenaeum, Philadelphia, roll 4136.

20. Meigs, *Capitol Builder*, 42. But see Houston to Walter, Feb. 24, 1859, and Walter to Houston, Feb. 25, 1859, in Walter Collection, roll 4139. After spending the better part of two years in the early 1850s trying to hound Walter from the Capitol, Houston asked him to design a prefabricated wooden house to be shipped to the Texas plains. The house (never built) was to be "made in the cheapest manner to be permanent and durable."

21. Ibid., 51.

22. House Proceedings, *Congressional Globe*, Feb. 8, 1854, 33rd Congress, 1st session, 381.

23. Meigs, *Capitol Builder*, 54.

24. Ibid.

25. Ibid., 55.

26. U.S. Congress, *Documentary History*, 607–608.

27. Meigs to James A. Bayard, Feb. 16, 1854, in Montgomery C. Meigs, *Letterbooks*, Mar. 1853–Oct. 1859, 1861, U.S. Congress, Architect of the Capitol.

28. Meigs to Emanuel Leutze, Jan. 14, 1854, ibid.

29. Gouverneur Kemble to Meigs, Feb. 16, 1854, U.S. Congress, Architect of the Capitol, vertical files, *Montgomery C. Meigs*, "Role in Art Program."

30. John Chapman to Kemble, Feb. 28, 1854, ibid.

31. For a description of fresco technique, see Barbara A. Wolanin, *Constantino Brumidi: Artist of the Capitol* (Washington, D.C.: U.S. Government Printing Office, 1998), 25–30.

32. Ibid., 25.

33. Ibid., 52.

34. Meigs to Davis, Feb. 25, 1857, in Meigs, *Letterbooks*.

35. Meigs to F. Burton Craige, Jan. 14, 1854, ibid.

36. Meigs to Thomas Crawford, Apr. 4, 1854, ibid.

37. Meigs, *Capitol Builder*, 66.

38. Meigs to Crawford, Apr. 24, 1854, in Meigs, *Letterbooks*.

39. Ibid., Apr. 27, 1854.

40. R. H. Stanton to Jefferson Davis, Feb. 15, 1854, National Archives, *Letters Received by the Secretary of War*, Registered Series, 1801–1860, microfilm 221, roll 169, S-96 (78).

41. Davis to R. H. Stanton, Feb. 25, 1854, National Archives, *Records of the U.S. House of Representatives, 33rd and 34th Cong.*, RG 233, vol. 83.

42. Walter to Rice, Feb. 21, 1854, Walter Collection, roll 4136.

43. Meigs to Stanton, Feb. 28, 1854, in Meigs, *Letterbooks*.

44. Davis to Stanton, Apr 18, 1854, National Archives, *Reports to Congress from the Secretary of War, 1803–1870*, microfilm 220, roll 4, vol. 8, 134–78.

45. Meigs, *Capitol Builder*, 59.

46. Ibid., 61.

47. Davis to Stanton, Mar. 21, 1854, National Archives, *Records of the U.S. House of Representatives, 33rd and 34th Cong.*, RG 233, vol. 83.

48. Davis to Stanton, Mar. 27, 1854, National Archives, *Reports to Congress from the Secretary of War*, microfilm 220, roll 4, vol. 8, 127.

49. Walter to Charles Fowler, Mar. 30, 1854, Walter Collection, roll 4136.

50. Davis to Stanton, Apr. 18, 1854, *Reports to Congress from the Secretary of War*, microfilm 220, roll 4, vol. 8, 134–78.

51. Ibid.

52. Walter memorandum, May 1, 1854, in Meigs, *Letterbooks*. See also Meigs, *Capitol Builder*, 68.

53. Davis to Stanton, Apr. 18, 1854, *Reports to Congress from the Secretary of War*, 134–178.

54. Meigs to Stanton, May 17, 1854, in Meigs, *Letterbooks*.

55. Meigs to Stanton, May 20, 1854, ibid.

56. Meigs to Stanton, May 23, 1854, ibid.

57. Diary entry for May 29, 1854, Walter Collection, roll 4133.

58. William C. Allen, *The Dome of the United States Capitol: An Architectural History*, Senate Document 102-7, 102nd Congress, 1st session (Washington, D.C.: U.S. Government Printing Office, 1992), 15.

59. Ibid.

60. Meigs, *Capitol Builder*, 75.

61. Ibid., 73–74.

10. THE ALIEN MENACE

1. Montgomery C. Meigs, *Capitol Builder: The Shorthand Journals of Montgomery C. Meigs, 1853–1859, 1861*, ed. Wendy Wolff (Washington, D.C.: U.S. Government Printing Office, 2001), 76–77.

2. Walter to Charles Fowler, July 20, 1854, in Thomas U. Walter, Thomas Ustick Walter Collection, Archives of American Art, Athenaeum, Philadelphia, roll 4137.

3. Meigs, *Capitol Builder*, 112.

4. See e.g. Walter to Horace Walter, Aug. 6, 1853, in Walter Collection, roll 4136. After his third son, Horace, apologized for running away from school, Walter promised retribution: "I am your master. I shall do my duty fearlessly after finding which that duty is from the word of God."

5. U.S. Congress, House of Representatives, *Documentary History of the Construction and Development of the United States Capitol Buildings and Grounds*, H.R. Report 646, 58th Congress, 2nd session (Washington, D.C.: U.S. Government Printing Office, 1904), serial 4585, 611.

6. Ibid., 612.

7. Varina Howell Davis, *Jefferson Davis, Ex-President of the Confederate States of America: A Memoir by His Wife in Two Volumes* (New York: Belford Co. 1890), vol. 1, 534–35.

8. Meigs, *Capitol Builder*, 74.

9. Ibid., 78.

10. Ibid., 110.

11. Diary entry for Aug. 18, 1854, Walter Collection, roll 4133.

12. U.S. Congress, *Documentary History*, 588.

13. Meigs to Walter, Jan. 21, 1858, in Montgomery C. Meigs, *Letterbooks*, Mar. 1853–Oct. 1859, 1861, U.S. Congress, Architect of the Capitol.

14. Turpin C. Bannister, "The Genealogy of the Dome of the United States Capitol," *Journal of the Society of Architectural Historians*, vol. 7, Jan.–June 1948, 24.

15. Meigs, *Capitol Builder*, 79.

16. Ibid.

17. Ibid., 82.

18. Walter to Thomas Walter, Aug. 19, 1854, Walter Collection, roll 4137.

19. Tyler Anbinder, *Nativism and Slavery: The Northern Know Nothings and the Politics of the 1850s.* (New York: Oxford University Press, 1992), 3.

20. Ibid., 45–46. See also David M. Potter, *The Impending Crisis: 1848–1861* (New York: Harper and Row, 1976), 251.

21. Anbinder, *Nativism and Slavery*, 21.

22. Ibid., 52.

23. Ibid., 43.

24. Meigs, *Capitol Builder*, 90.

25. Diary entry for June 5, 1854, in Montgomery C. Meigs, *The Shorthand Diaries of Montgomery C. Meigs*, unabridged transcription, U.S. Congress, Architect of the Capitol, undated.

26. Diary entry for Oct. 12, 1854, ibid.

27. Potter, *Impending Crisis*, 251. See also Michael F. Holt, *The Political Crisis of the 1850s* (New York: W. W. Norton and Co., 1983), 155–65, for a discussion of the havoc created by the Know-Nothings for both Whigs and Democrats in the 1854 election.

28. Ibid., 239.

29. Meigs, *Capitol Builder*, 74.

30. Ibid., 97.

31. Meigs to Thomas Brothers, Dec. 21, 1854, in Meigs, *Letterbooks*. See also William C. Allen, *History of the United States Capitol: A Chronicle of Design, Construction, and Politics*, Senate Document 106-29, 106th Congress, 2nd session (Washington, D.C.: U.S. Government Printing Office, 2001), 248.

32. Meigs, *Capitol Builder*, 114.

33. Diary entry, Aug. 26, 1854, in Meigs, *Shorthand Diaries* (unabridged).

34. Meigs, *Capitol Builder*, 144.

35. Ibid., 145.

36. Ibid., 146.

37. Ibid., 96.

38. See e.g. Meigs's handwritten letters and those of sons John Rodgers Meigs and Montgomery Meigs and daughter Louisa Meigs Forbes, in Montgomery C. Meigs, Papers of Montgomery C. Meigs, U.S. Library of Congress, Manuscript Division, addition 1, family papers 1799–1971, reels 1 and 2.

39. Meigs to Crawford, Aug. 9, 1854, in Meigs, *Letterbooks*.

40. Meigs, *Capitol Builder*, 114.

41. Ibid., 136.

42. Ibid., 129.

43. Ibid., 87.

44. Ibid., 111.

45. Ibid., 152.

46. U.S. Congress, *Documentary History*, 617–18.

47. Meigs, *Capitol Builder*, 129.

48. Quoted in William W. Freehling, *The Road to Disunion*, vol. 2: *Secessionists Triumphant, 1854–1861* (New York: Oxford University Press, 2007), 72–73.

49. Meigs, *Capitol Builder*, 140–42.

50. Ibid., 144.

51. Ibid., 164.

52. Ibid., 173.

53. Ibid., 174.

54. Meigs to James A. Pearce, Dec. 23, 1854, in Meigs, *Letterbooks*.

55. Meigs, *Capitol Builder*, 176.

56. Ibid., 176–77.

57. Ibid., 178.

58. Ibid., 183.

59. Ibid.

11. "A LIVELY OLD MAN WITH A VERY RED NOSE"

1. Barbara A. Wolanin, *Constantino Brumidi: Artist of the Capitol* (Washington, D.C.: U.S. Government Printing Office, 1998), 52. Meigs never identified "Mr. Stone" by his first name, but he is almost certainly sculptor Horatio Stone, a longtime Washington resident and no favorite of Meigs, although, as Wolanin points out, there was at least one other artist "Stone" in the D.C. area who could have been a sculptor.

2. Montgomery C. Meigs, *Capitol Builder: The Shorthand Journals of Montgomery C. Meigs, 1853–1859, 1861*, ed. Wendy Wolff (Washington, D.C.: U.S. Government Printing Office, 2001), 180.

3. Ibid.

4. Wolanin, *Brumidi*, 15–22, 239.

5. Ibid., 10–12.

6. From D. Fry Smith, *Thrilling Story of the Wonderful Capitol Building and Its Marvelous Decorations* (n.p. 1911), quoted in Wolanin, *Brumidi*, 9.

7. Meigs, *Capitol Builder*, 209.

8. Ibid., 222.

9. Ibid., 228–29.

10. Ibid., 230–31.

11. Ibid., 232.

12. Ibid., 210.

13. Ibid., 229.

14. Ibid., 232.

15. Ibid., 221. See also Meigs to Randolph Rogers, Feb. 16, 1855, in Montgomery C. Meigs, *Letterbooks*, Mar. 1853–Oct. 1859, 1861, U.S. Congress, Architect of the Capitol.

16. Meigs, *Capitol Builder*, 226.

17. Ibid., 252.

18. Ibid., 272. See also U.S. Congress, Architect of the Capitol, vertical files, *Doors: Bronze*.

19. Meigs to Davis, Mar. 5, 1855, in Meigs, *Letterbooks*.

20. Meigs, *Capitol Builder*, 250.

21. Ibid., 252.

22. Ibid., 258.

23. Ibid., 265.

24. Ibid., 266–67.

25. Ibid., 271.

26. Ibid., 273.

27. Ibid., 339.

28. Ibid., 204.

29. Meigs to Sen. J. A. Pearce, Jan. 23, 1855, in Meigs, *Letterbooks*.

30. Meigs, *Capitol Builder*, 212.

31. Ibid., 217.

32. Meigs to the *Union*, Jan. 31, 1855, in Meigs, *Letterbooks*.

33. Meigs, *Capitol Builder*, 215.

34. U.S. Congress, House of Representatives, *Documentary History of the Construction and Development of the United States Capitol Buildings and Grounds*, H.R. Report 646, 58th Congress, 2nd session (Washington, D.C.: U.S. Government Printing Office, 1904), serial 4585, 621.

35. Ibid., 621–27.

36. Ibid., 991.

37. Ibid., 991–92.

38. Meigs, *Capitol Builder*, 233.

39. Ibid., 245–46.

40. Ibid., 236–37.

41. Meigs to Bayard, Feb. 24, 1855, in Meigs, *Letterbooks*.

42. Meigs, *Capitol Builder*, 245.

43. Ibid., 256.

44. Walter to Richard Gardiner, Mar. 9, 1855, in Thomas U. Walter, Thomas Ustick Walter Collection, Archives of American Art, Athenaeum, Philadelphia, roll 4137.

45. Meigs to Crawford, May 11, 1855, in Meigs, *Letterbooks*.

46. Meigs, *Capitol Builder*, 289.

47. Meigs to Davis, July 27, 1855, in Meigs, *Letterbooks*.

48. Meigs, *Capitol Builder*, 323.

49. Meigs to Davis, Feb. 22, 1855, National Archives, *Records of the Office of the Chief of Engineers, 1853–1857*, "Records Relating to Work on the Capitol Extension and Washington Aqueduct," RG 77, file C-192.

50. William C. Davis, *Jefferson Davis: The Man and His Hour* (New York: HarperCollins, 1991), 252.

51. Jefferson Davis, *Jefferson Davis, Constitutionalist: His Letters, Papers and Speeches*, ed. Dunbar Rowland, multivolume set, vol. 2 (Jackson, Miss.: S. J. Little and Ives, Company, 1923), 410–12.

52. Ibid., vol. 2, 350.

53. Nicole Etcheson, *Bleeding Kansas: Contested Liberty in the Civil War Era* (Lawrence: University Press of Kansas, 2004), 29.

54. Quoted in David M. Potter, *The Impending Crisis: 1848–1861* (New York: Harper and Row, 1976), 199.

55. Etcheson, *Bleeding Kansas*, 59.

56. See Michael F. Holt, *The Political Crisis of the 1850s* (New York: W. W. Norton and Co., 1983), 170–73, for a discussion of the implosion of the Know-Nothings.

57. Meigs, *Capitol Builder*, 288.

58. Ibid., 294.

59. William C. Allen, *History of the United States Capitol: A Chronicle of Design, Construction, and Politics*, Senate Document 106-29, 106th Congress, 2nd session (Washington, D.C.: U.S. Government Printing Office, 2001), 253.

60. Meigs to Crawford, Nov. 25, 1855, in Meigs, *Letterbooks*.

12. BLEEDING KANSAS

1. See Meigs to Davis, Nov. 26, 1855, National Archives, *Letters Received by the Secretary of War*, Registered Series 1801–1870, microfilm 221, roll 176, f/w M-326 (83).

2. Meigs to Roebling, Sept. 16, 1855, in Montgomery C. Meigs, *Letterbooks*, Mar. 1853–Oct. 1859, 1861, U.S. Congress, Architect of the Capitol.

3. Meigs to Roebling, Oct. 15, 1855, ibid.

4. Montgomery C. Meigs, *Capitol Builder: The Shorthand Journals of Montgomery C. Meigs, 1853–1859, 1861*, ed. Wendy Wolff (Washington, D.C.: U.S. Government Printing Office, 2001), 315.

5. Meigs, *Capitol Builder*, 321.

6. Ibid., 333.

7. U.S. Congress, House of Representatives, *Documentary History of the Construction and Development of the United States Capitol Buildings and Grounds*, H.R. Report 646, 58th Congress, 2nd session (Washington, D.C.: U.S. Government Printing Office, 1904), serial 4585, 628–29.

8. See, e.g., Michael F. Holt, *Franklin Pierce* (New York: Times Books, 2010), 92–93, for Republican pleasure with the result. See also David M. Potter, *The Impending Crisis: 1848–1861* (New York, Harper and Row, 1976), 256, 256n.

9. Meigs, *Capitol Builder*, 340, 363–64.

10. House Proceedings, *Congressional Globe*, Feb. 2, 1856, 34th Congress, 1st session, 340.

11. Virginia Clay-Clopton, *A Belle of the Fifties: Memories of Mrs. Clay of Alabama, Covering Social and Political Life in Washington and the South, 1853–1866* (New York: Doubleday, Page and Co., 1905), 27.

12. Walter to L. B. Hardin, Feb. 19, 1856, in Thomas U. Walter, Thomas Ustick Walter Collection, Archives of American Art, Athenaeum, Philadelphia, roll 4137.

13. U.S. Congress, *Documentary History*, 997.

14. Meigs to Crawford, Jan. 16, 1856, in Meigs, *Letterbooks*.

15. Davis left Washington on May 26, 1855, arrived in Jackson on June 2, and returned to Washington on June 25. See Jefferson Davis, *The Papers of Jefferson Davis*, vol. 5: *1853–1855*, ed. Lynda Lasswell Crist and Mary S. Dix (Baton Rouge: Louisiana State University Press, 1985), 108, which describes Davis's presence at the state Democratic convention June 4–5 in Jackson: "His friends got possession of the convention and managed every thing in their own way . . . every possible opportunity was given Davis to make an impression—He made it." See also Davis to Collin S. Tarpley, Dec. 19, 1855, ibid., 147–50. The Mississippi legislature returned Davis to the Senate on Jan. 19, 1856.

16. Nicole Etcheson, *Bleeding Kansas: Contested Liberty in the Civil War Era* (Lawrence: University Press of Kansas, 2004), 91.

17. Ibid., 97.

18. Ibid.

19. There are several accounts of this brawl. See e.g. *The New York Times*, May 12, 1856, and July 14, 1856, for an early description of the incident followed by a recounting of Herbert's trial with detailed, and often contradictory, testimony by individual witnesses.

20. Ibid., May 12, 1856.

21. Meigs, *Capitol Builder*, 395.

22. Ibid., 397.

23. Varina Howell Davis, *Jefferson Davis, Ex-President of the Confederate States of America: A Memoir by His Wife in Two Volumes*, vol. 1 (New York: Belford Co., 1890), 557–58.

24. Appendix to the *Congressional Globe*, 34th Congress, 1st session, 529–30, 532, 536.

25. Ibid., 544.

26. James A. Rawley, *Race and Politics: Bleeding Kansas and the Coming of the Civil War* (Philadelphia: J. B. Lippincott, 1969), 132–33.

27. Quoted in Thomas Goodrich, *War to the Knife: Bleeding Kansas, 1854–1861* (Mechanicsburg, Pa.: Stackpole Books, 1998), 120.

28. Ibid.

29. William W. Freehling, *The Road to Disunion*, vol. 2: *Secessionists Triumphant, 1854–1861* (New York: Oxford University Press, 2007), 82.

30. Goodrich, *War to the Knife*, 120.

31. Freehling, *Road to Disunion*, 82.

32. *New York Times*, May 24, 1856.

33. Davis to South Carolina Citizens, Sept. 22, 1856, in Jefferson Davis, *The Papers of Jefferson Davis*, vol. 6: *1856–1860*, ed. Lynda Lasswell Crist and Mary S. Dix (Baton Rouge: Louisiana State University Press, 1989), 44.

34. This description of the Pottawatomie massacre is taken from primary sources quoted in Goodrich, *War to the Knife*, 123–28, and from accounts in Etcheson, *Bleeding Kansas*, 109–10, and David S. Reynolds, *John Brown, Abolitionist* (New York: Alfred A. Knopf, 2005), 170, 171–73. Reynolds (170) describes the broadswords as "two-edged" and "inscribed with eagles . . . reportedly left over from a failed filibustering scheme to take over Canada."

35. Meigs, *Capitol Builder*, 400–401.

36. Ibid., 374–75.

37. Ibid., 377.

38. Diary entry for Apr. 1, 1856, in Montgomery C. Meigs, *The Shorthand Diaries of Montgomery C. Meigs*, unabridged transcription, U.S. Congress, Architect of the Capitol, undated.

39. Meigs, *Capitol Builder*, 385.

40. Ibid., 337.

41. Ibid., 342, 355; diary entries for Jan. 17, Jan. 24, and Mar. 3, 1856, in Meigs, *Shorthand Diaries* (unabridged).

42. U.S. Congress, *Documentary History*, 631–41.

43. Meigs to Davis, May 23, 1856, and Meigs to Hunter, July 31, 1856, in Meigs, *Letterbooks*.

44. See e.g. Meigs, *Capitol Builder*, 405, 413; also diary entries for May 16 and 17, 1856, in Meigs, *Shorthand Diaries* (unabridged).

45. Meigs, *Capitol Builder*, 413.

46. U.S. Congress, *Documentary History*, 657–59.

47. Ibid.

48. Meigs, *Capitol Builder*, 418.

49. Senate Proceedings, Aug. 15, 1856, *Congressional Globe*, 34th Congress, 1st session, 2149.

50. Ibid., 2147.

51. Ibid.

52. Meigs, *Capitol Builder*, 431.

53. Meigs to Joseph Henry, Sept. 15, 1856, in Meigs, *Letterbooks*.

54. Joseph Henry, *The Papers of Joseph Henry*, vol. 9: *Jan. 1854–Dec. 1857*, ed. Marc Rothenberg (Washington, D.C.: Smithsonian Institution Press, 2002), 395n.

55. Meigs, *Capitol Builder*, 383, 400.

56. Walter to Alexander Provest, Apr. 14, 1853, Walter Collection, roll 4137.

57. Ibid., July 29, 1856.

58. Meigs, *Capitol Builder*, 391.

59. Quoted in William C. Allen, *History of the United States Capitol: A Chronicle of Design, Construction, and Politics*, Senate Document 106-29, 106th Congress, 2nd session (Washington, D.C.: U.S. Government Printing Office, 2001), 255.

60. Meigs, *Capitol Builder*, 391–92.

61. Walter to John H. Rice, Chairman of the Committee on Public Buildings and Grounds, House of Representatives, April 20, 1864, in Thomas U. Walter, *Records of the Architect of the Capitol: Letterbooks of Thomas U. Walter*, U.S. Congress, Architect of the Capitol.

62. Allen, *History*, 230.

63. Meigs, *Capitol Builder*, 433.

64. Meigs to Jefferson Davis, May 6, 1856, in Meigs, *Letterbooks*.

65. Meigs, *Capitol Builder*, 441, 443.

66. Ibid., 433–34.

67. Meigs to Poole & Hunt, Apr. 9, 1856, in Meigs, *Letterbooks*.

68. A. B. McFarlan to Meigs, June 21, 1856, ibid.

69. For a description of the wet collodion process, see Wayne Firth, "Montgomery C. Meigs and Photography at the Capitol," in William C. Dickinson, ed., *Montgomery C. Meigs and Building of the Nation's Capital* (Athens: Ohio University Press, 2002), 129.

70. Meigs, *Capitol Builder*, 351.

71. Meigs to Davis, Jan. 28, 1856, photocopy of letter, in U.S. Congress, Architect of the Capitol, "A Chronology of Photography at the United States Capitol," 2005, 6.

72. Meigs, *Capitol Builder*, 396.

73. Firth, "Photography at the Capitol," 129.

74. Meigs, *Capitol Builder*, 423.

75. Ibid., 481.

13. A NEW HOUSE OF REPRESENTATIVES

1. See David M. Potter, *The Impending Crisis: 1848–1861* (New York: Harper and Row, 1976), 260, for "Old Public Functionary." See Benjamin Perley Poore, *Perley's Reminiscences of Sixty Years in the National Metropolis*, 2 vols. (Philadelphia: Hubbard Brothers, 1886), vol. 1, 505, for "Old Buck." See William W. Freehling, *The Road to Disunion*, vol. 2: *Secessionists Triumphant, 1854–1861* (New York: Oxford University Press, 2007), 107, for "Old Squire."

2. Montgomery C. Meigs, *Capitol Builder: The Shorthand Journals of Montgomery C. Meigs, 1853–1859, 1861*, ed. Wendy Wolff (Washington, D.C.: U.S. Government Printing Office, 2001), 495.

3. U.S. Congress, House of Representatives, *Documentary History of the Construction and Development of the United States Capitol Buildings and Grounds*, H.R. Report 646, 58th Congress, 2nd session (Washington, D.C.: U.S. Government Printing Office, 1904), serial 4585, 660–62.

4. Meigs, *Capitol Builder*, 484.

5. Ibid., 495.

6. See Freehling, *Road to Disunion*, 109–22 for a detailed discussion of the intrigues surrounding the Dred Scott decision.

7. Quoted in Potter, *Impending Crisis*, 287. See also Michael F. Holt, *The Political Crisis of the 1850s* (New York: W. W. Norton and Co., 1983), 200–203.

8. Ibid. See also *Impending Crisis*, 275–76, for a discussion of Taney's reasoning.

9. Meigs, *Capitol Builder*, 484.

10. Ibid., 491.

11. Ibid., 477.

12. Ibid., 463.

13. Ibid., 491–92.

14. Ibid., 504.

15. Ibid., 538.

16. Davis to James Buchanan, Feb. 2, 1857, in Jefferson Davis, *Jefferson Davis, Constitutionalist: His Letters, Papers and Speeches*, ed. Dunbar Rowland, multivolume set (Jackson, Miss.: S. J. Little and Ives, Company, 1923), vol. 3, 110.

17. Meigs, *Capitol Builder*, 497.

18. Ibid., 498–99.

19. Ibid., 507.

20. Ibid., 501.

21. Ibid., 503.

22. Ibid., 504.

23. Diary entry for Apr. 23, 1857, in Montgomery C. Meigs, *The Shorthand Diaries of Montgomery C. Meigs*, unabridged transcription, U.S. Congress, Architect of the Capitol, undated.

24. Ibid., Apr. 24, 1857.

25. Meigs, *Capitol Builder*, 505–506.

26. Ibid., 506.

27. Diary entry for May 5, 1857, in Meigs, *Shorthand Diaries* (unabridged).

28. Ibid., May 7, 1857.

29. Ibid., May 8, 1857.

30. Ibid., May 25, 1857.

31. Ibid., May 23, 1857.

32. Ibid., June 8, 1857.

33. Ibid., May 25, 1857.

34. Ibid., Oct. 13, 1857.

35. Ibid., Nov. 7, 1857.

36. Ibid., Nov. 6, 1857.

37. Ibid., June 8, 1857.

38. Ibid., June 16, 1857.

39. Ibid.

40. Ibid., June 18, 1857.

41. Ibid., July 27, 1857.

42. Meigs to Davis, Aug. 8, 1857, in Montgomery C. Meigs, *Letterbooks*, Mar. 1853–Oct. 1859, 1861, U.S. Congress, Architect of the Capitol.

43. Meigs, *Capitol Builder*, 528–29.

44. Ibid., 529. The relevant sentence reads, "The responsibility would be removed by a change of the constructing engineer and neither Capt. Meigs or his advisers would probably feel that it would have failed to succeed if left in his charge until completion."

45. U.S. Congress, *Documentary History*, 664.

46. Meigs to Thomas P. Rossiter, Nov. 8, 1855, in Meigs, *Letterbooks*.

47. For a detailed description of the House Agriculture Committee Room, see Barbara A. Wolanin, *Constantino Brumidi: Artist of the Capitol* (Washington, D.C.: U.S. Government Printing Office, 1998), 54–59.

48. Meigs, *Capitol Builder*, 385.

49. Ibid., 389.

50. Wolanin, *Brumidi*, 63.

51. U.S. Congress, *Documentary History*, 662.

52. Meigs, *Capitol Builder*, 466, 480, 534, 542.

53. Ibid., 441.

54. Ibid., 446.

55. Wolanin, *Brumidi*, 91.

56. Meigs, *Capitol Builder*, 513.

57. Ibid., 530–31.

58. Ibid., 548–54.

59. Washington, D.C., *Evening Star*, Dec. 13, 1857.

60. House Proceedings, Dec. 14, 1857, *Congressional Globe*, 35th Congress, 1st session, 31–32.

61. Meigs, *Capitol Builder*, 557.

62. *Pennsylvania Inquirer*, Dec. 17, 1857.

63. Benjamin Brown French, *Witness to the Young Republic: A Yankee's Journal, 1828–1870*, ed. Donald B. Cole and John J. McDonough (Hanover, N.H.: University Press of New England, 1989), 288.

14. THE FEUD

1. Montgomery C. Meigs, *Capitol Builder: The Shorthand Journals of Montgomery C. Meigs, 1853–1859, 1861*, ed. Wendy Wolff (Washington, D.C.: U.S. Government Printing Office, 2001), 558–59.

2. Walter to Amanda Walter, May 20, 1857, in Thomas U. Walter, Thomas Ustick Walter Collection, Archives of American Art, Athenaeum, Philadelphia, roll 4138.

3. Meigs, *Capitol Builder*, 560.

4. Walter to John Rice, Dec. 22, 1857, Walter Collection, roll 4138.

5. See, e.g., Walter to William H. Witte, Oct. 2, 1857, ibid.

6. Walter to Witte, Oct. 2, 1857, ibid.

7. For mention of John Forney, see diary entry for July 2, 1857, in Meigs, *Shorthand Diaries* (unabridged).

8. Meigs, *Capitol Builder*, 454.

9. Ibid., 526. By this time John Baird appears not to have been an active partner in the marble firm. It is not clear whether the company retained the name Rice, Baird & Heebner or changed it, but from this point (and perhaps earlier) all decisions seem to have been made by Rice and Heebner.

10. Ibid., 539.

11. Ibid., 539–40.

12. Ibid., 566.
13. See, e.g., Walter to Rice, May 1, 1857, Walter Collection, roll 4138.
14. Walter to Meigs, Sept. 7, 1857, ibid.
15. Walter to Rice, Oct.12, 1857, ibid.
16. Walter to Rice, Oct. 19, 1857, ibid.
17. Walter to Rice, Oct. 22, 1857, ibid.
18. Walter to Rice, Dec. 8, 1857, ibid.
19. Meigs, *Capitol Builder*, 553.
20. Meigs to Floyd, Dec. 9, 1857, in Montgomery C. Meigs, *Letterbooks*, Mar. 1853–Oct. 1859, 1861, U.S. Congress, Architect of the Capitol.
21. Meigs, *Capitol Builder*, 564, 571.
22. Walter to M. E. Harmstead, Jan. 30, 1858, Walter Collection, roll 4138.
23. Meigs, *Capitol Builder*, 140–41.
24. Ibid., 178.
25. Diary entry, May 4, 1857, Walter Collection, roll 4133.
26. Meigs, *Capitol Builder*, 568.
27. Diary entry for Feb. 16, 1858, in Meigs, *Shorthand Diaries* (unabridged).
28. Ibid., Mar. 23, 1858.
29. Ibid., Mar. 27, 1858.
30. Ibid., Apr. 3, 1858.
31. Meigs, *Capitol Builder*, 643.
32. Ibid., 217.
33. Meigs to Floyd, Dec. 9, 1857, in Meigs, *Letterbooks*.
34. Meigs to Walter, Jan. 21, 1858, ibid.
35. Meigs, *Capitol Builder*, 582–83.
36. Ibid., 583.
37. Ibid., 583–84.
38. Meigs to Walter, Jan. 21, 1858, in Meigs, *Letterbooks*.
39. William C. Allen, *History of the United States Capitol: A Chronicle of Design, Construction, and Politics*, Senate Document 106-29, 106th Congress, 2nd session (Washington, D.C.: U.S. Government Printing Office, 2001), 228.
40. See e.g. Meigs to Davis, Jan. 21, 1858, in Meigs, *Letterbooks*; Walter to M. E. Harmstead, Feb. 5, 1858, in Walter Collection, roll 4138.
41. Meigs, *Capitol Builder*, 603.
42. Meigs to Davis, Jan. 21, 1858, in Meigs, *Letterbooks*.
43. Copies included in Walter to Rice, Jan. 21, 1858, Walter Collection, roll 4138.
44. Ibid.
45. Meigs, *Capitol Builder*, 588.
46. Draft letter, Floyd to Meigs, Feb. (no date) 1858, Walter Collection, roll 4138.
47. Walter to Rice, Feb. 26, 1858, ibid.
48. Text of Buchanan's inaugural address is available on Bartleby.com website, Great Books Online, www.bartleby.com/124/pres30.html.
49. For a detailed discussion of the Lecompton fiasco and Buchanan's dilemma, see

David M. Potter, *The Impending Crisis: 1848–1861* (New York: Harper and Row, 1976), 301, 313–15, 318–19.

50. See William W. Freehling, *The Road to Disunion*, vol. 2: *Secessionists Triumphant, 1854–1861* (New York: Oxford University Press, 2007), 133, for a description of the election and its aftermath.

51. Ibid., 134.

52. Ibid., 138.

53. See Michael F. Holt, *The Political Crisis of the 1850s* (New York: W. W. Norton and Co., 1983), 205–206, for a discussion of the damage to the Democratic Party.

54. Ibid., 316; Freehling, *Road to Disunion*, vol. 2, 138.

55. Holt, *Political Crisis*, 204.

56. This account is taken largely from Benjamin Perley Poore, *Perley's Reminiscences of Sixty Years in the National Metropolis*, 2 vols. (Philadelphia: Hubbard Brothers, 1886), vol. 1, 534–35. But see also Reuben Davis, *Recollections of Mississippi and Mississippians* (Boston and New York: Houghton, Mifflin and Co., 1890), 372, and Freehling, *Road to Disunion*, vol. 2, 139–40.

57. Jefferson Davis, *Jefferson Davis, Constitutionalist: His Letters, Papers and Speeches*, ed. Dunbar Rowland, multivolume set (Jackson, Miss.: S. J. Little and Ives, Company, 1923), vol. 3, 169–73.

58. Meigs, *Capitol Builder*, 601.

15. MEIGS UNDER SIEGE

1. Montgomery C. Meigs, *Capitol Builder: The Shorthand Journals of Montgomery C. Meigs, 1853–1859, 1861*, ed. Wendy Wolff (Washington, D.C.: U.S. Government Printing Office, 2001), 589–90.

2. Meigs to Walter, Mar. 4, 1858, in Montgomery C. Meigs, *Letterbooks*, Mar. 1853–Oct. 1859, 1861, U.S. Congress, Architect of the Capitol.

3. Walter to Brumidi, Mar. 12, 1858, in Thomas U. Walter, Thomas Ustick Walter Collection, Archives of American Art, Athenaeum, Philadelphia, roll 4138.

4. Meigs to Buchanan, Mar. 22, 1858, in Meigs, *Letterbooks*.

5. Diary entry for Nov. 24, 1857, in Montgomery C. Meigs, *The Shorthand Diaries of Montgomery C. Meigs*, unabridged transcription, U.S. Congress, Architect of the Capitol, undated.

6. Ibid., Jan. 24, 1858.

7. Ibid., Jan. 25, 1858.

8. U.S. Congress, Senate, "Message of the President of the United States, communicating in compliance with a resolution of the Senate, information in relation to the heating and ventilating of the Capitol extension, the Post Office Department, etc.," Senate Exec. Doc. 20, 36th Congress, 1st session, Jan. 26, 1860, serial 1031, vol. 9, 93–94.

9. Ibid., 96–99.

10. Ibid., 100–101.

11. Ibid., 105.

12. Meigs to Walter, Oct. 7, 1858, in Meigs, *Letterbooks.*

13. Meigs, *Capitol Builder*, 653.

14. Floyd to Meigs, Oct. 4, 1858, in Meigs, *Letterbooks.*

15. Barbara A. Wolanin, *Constantino Brumidi: Artist of the Capitol* (Washington, D.C.: U.S. Government Printing Office, 1998), 67–68.

16. Ibid.

17. Ibid., 76.

18. U.S. Congress, House of Representatives, *Documentary History of the Construction and Development of the United States Capitol Buildings and Grounds*, H.R. Report 646, 58th Congress, 2nd session (Washington, D.C.: U.S. Government Printing Office, 1904), serial 4585, 669.

19. Meigs, *Capitol Builder*, 594.

20. *New York Express*, Apr. 26, 1858.

21. Ibid., May 1, 1858.

22. *New York Tribune*, May 17, 1858.

23. David M. Potter, *The Impending Crisis: 1848–1861* (New York: Harper and Row, 1976), 323. See also Michael F. Holt, *The Fate of Their Country: Politicians, Slavery Extension, and the Coming of the Civil War* (New York: Hill and Wang, 2004), 121–22.

24. William W. Freehling, *The Road to Disunion*, vol. 2: *Secessionists Triumphant, 1854–1861* (New York: Oxford University Press, 2007), 141.

25. House Proceedings, *Congressional Globe*, May 17, 1858, 35th Congress, 1st session, 2546.

26. U.S. Congress, *Documentary History*, 670–71.

27. Ibid., 672.

28. Meigs, *Capitol Builder*, 617.

29. Ibid., 343, 618; see also Meigs to Davis, Mar. 20, 1856, in Meigs, *Letterbooks.*

30. Meigs, *Capitol Builder*, 616.

31. Meigs to Davis, May 24, 1858, in Meigs, *Letterbooks.*

32. *Documentary History*, 674–76.

33. Ibid., 676.

34. Ibid., 677–78.

35. Ibid., 679.

36. Ibid.

37. Ibid., 681.

38. Davis to Buchanan, June 19, 1857, in Jefferson Davis, *Jefferson Davis, Constitutionalist: His Letters, Papers and Speeches*, ed. Dunbar Rowland, multivolume set (Jackson, Miss.: S. J. Little and Ives, Company, 1923), vol. 3, 116.

39. Memphis, Tenn., *Daily Appeal*, Sept. 8, 1857.

40. Thomas F. Drayton to Davis, Apr. 9, 1858, in Rowland, ed., *Jefferson Davis, Constitutionalist*, vol. 3, 216.

41. For a detailed account of this incident, see "The Benjamin Affair," *Harper's Weekly*, June 19, 1858, 390.

42. Senate Proceedings, *Congressional Globe*, June 9, 1858, 35th Congress, 1st session, 2822–23.

43. U.S. Congress, *Documentary History*, 691–92, 699.

44. Ibid., 701.

45. Meigs, *Capitol Builder*, 629.

46. Walter to My Dear Wife, May 20, 1858, Walter Collection, roll 4138.

47. Walter to Rice, May 31, 1858, ibid.

48. House Proceedings, *Congressional Globe*, June 1, 1858, 35th Congress, 1st session, 2595–604.

49. Diary entry for June 11, 1858, in Meigs, *Shorthand Diaries* (unabridged).

50. Walter to Rice, June 22, 1858, Walter Collection, roll 4138.

51. Ibid., Sept. 6, 1858.

52. Walter to My Dear Son, Feb. 8, 1858; Walter to My Dear Son Horace, Apr. 21, 1858; Walter to My Dear Wife, May 31, 1858, ibid.

53. Walter to Robert Walter, Jan. 11, 1858; Walter to my Dear Son Robert, Feb. 13, 1858; Walter to My Dear Daughter, Aug. 20, 1858; see also Walter to My Dear Son Horace, Sept. 7, 1858, and Walter to Martin Harmstead, Sept. 28, 1858, ibid., roll 4139.

54. Walter to Harmstead, Sept. 28, 1858; Walter to Horace Walter, Dec. 26, 1858, ibid.

55. Meigs, *Capitol Builder*, 648.

56. Meigs to Floyd, Dec. 18, 1858, in Meigs, *Letterbooks*.

57. Meigs, *Capitol Builder*, 685.

58. Meigs to Floyd, Nov. 15, 1858, in Meigs, *Letterbooks*.

59. Meigs to Floyd, Nov. 15, 1858, ibid. (separate letter).

60. Walter to Rice, Sept. 7, 1858, Walter Collection, roll 4139.

61. Meigs, *Capitol Builder*, 653.

62. Meigs to Floyd, Sept. 16, 1858, in Meigs, *Letterbooks*.

63. Meigs, *Capitol Builder*, 655–56.

64. Meigs to Floyd, Oct. 25, 1858, in Meigs, *Letterbooks*.

65. Meigs, *Capitol Builder*, 673.

66. Ibid., 674–75.

67. Ibid., 679.

16. SWAN SONG

1. Montgomery C. Meigs, *Capitol Builder: The Shorthand Journals of Montgomery C. Meigs, 1853–1859, 1861*, ed. Wendy Wolff (Washington, D.C.: U.S. Government Printing Office, 2001), 691.

2. Ibid., 687.

3. Ibid., 688.

4. Diary entry for Jan. 2–3, 1859, in Montgomery C. Meigs, *The Shorthand Diaries of Montgomery C. Meigs*, unabridged transcription, U.S. Congress, Architect of the Capitol, undated.

5. Meigs, *Capitol Builder*, 691.

6. Diary entry for Jan. 4, 1859, in Meigs, *Shorthand Diaries* (unabridged).

7. *New York Times*, Jan. 5, 1859.

8. Meigs, *Capitol Builder*, 795–97.

9. Ibid., 797–805.

10. *New York Times*, Jan. 4, 1859. See also Meigs, *Capitol Builder*, 805–807.

11. For a description of the President's Room, see Barbara A. Wolanin, *Constantino Brumidi: Artist of the Capitol* (Washington, D.C.: U.S. Government Printing Office, 1998), 116–21.

12. Walter to My Dear Wife, Jan. 4, 1859, in Thomas U. Walter, Thomas Ustick Walter Collection, Archives of American Art, Athenaeum, Philadelphia, roll 4139.

13. Varina Howell Davis, *Jefferson Davis, Ex-President of the Confederate States of America: A Memoir by His Wife in Two Volumes*, vol. 1 (New York: Belford Co., 1890), 580.

14. Senate Proceedings, *Congressional Globe*, Jan. 10, 1859, 35th Congress, 2nd session, 288–90.

15. Davis to Franklin Pierce, Apr. 4, 1858, in Jefferson Davis, *Jefferson Davis, Constitutionalist: His Letters, Papers and Speeches*, ed. Dunbar Rowland, multivolume set (Jackson, Miss.: S. J. Little and Ives, Company, 1923), vol. 3, 214.

16. Quoted in William J. Cooper, Jr., *Jefferson Davis, American* (New York: Alfred A. Knopf, 2000), 289.

17. Varina Davis, *Jefferson Davis*, vol. 1, 584.

18. Speech in Portland, Maine, July 9, 1858, in Rowland, ed., *Jefferson Davis, Constitutionalist*, vol. 3, 275.

19. Speech in Augusta, Maine, Sept. 1858, ibid., 305.

20. Speech in Portland, Maine, Aug. 24, 1858, ibid., 285.

21. Speech in Boston, Oct. 11, 1858, ibid., 319.

22. Speech before the Mississippi legislature, Nov. 16, 1858, in ibid., 339–46.

23. Ibid., 346–58.

24. Varina Davis, *Jefferson Davis*, vol. 1, 574.

25. Benjamin Perley Poore, *Perley's Reminiscences of Sixty Years in the National Metropolis*, 2 vols. (Philadelphia: Hubbard Brothers, 1886), vol. 1, 524.

26. See "Facsimile of the Card of Invitation to Napier Ball," *Harper's Weekly*, Mar. 5, 1859, 153.

27. *New York Times*, Feb. 19, 1859.

28. Virginia Clay-Clopton, *A Belle of the Fifties: Memories of Mrs. Clay of Alabama, Covering Social and Political Life in Washington and the South, 1853–1866* (New York: Doubleday, Page and Co., 1905), 32, 34.

29. Meigs, *Capitol Builder*, 660.

30. Ibid., 669–70. See also diary entry for Oct. 27, 1858, in Meigs, *Shorthand Diaries* (unabridged).

31. Meigs, *Capitol Builder*, 684.

32. John Rodgers Meigs to Davis, no date (but probably Nov.), 1858, Papers of Montgomery C. Meigs, Library of Congress, Manuscript Division (microfilm).

33. Meigs, *Capitol Builder*, 721.

34. Diary entry for June 23, 1859, in Meigs, *Shorthand Diaries* (unabridged).

35. Meigs, *Capitol Builder*, 723–26.

36. Ibid., 739–41.

37. Diary entries for Sept. 5–7, 1859, in Meigs, *Shorthand Diaries* (unabridged).

38. Diary entry for June 20, 1859, in ibid.

39. Meigs, *Capitol Builder*, 709–10.

40. Ibid., 713–14.

41. Ibid., 716–18.

42. Meigs to Floyd, June 22, 1859, in Montgomery C. Meigs, *Letterbooks*, Mar. 1853–Oct. 1859, 1861, U.S. Congress, Architect of the Capitol.

43. U.S. Congress, Senate, "Message of the President of the United States, communicating in compliance with a resolution of the Senate, information in relation to the heating and ventilating of the Capitol extension, the Post Office Department, etc.," Senate Exec. Doc. 20, 36th Congress, 1st session, Jan. 26, 1860, serial 1031, vol. 9, 118.

44. Meigs to Floyd, Jan. 13, 1859, in Meigs, *Letterbooks*.

45. Meigs, *Capitol Builder*, 703.

46. Meigs to Floyd, Mar. 5, 1859, in Meigs, *Letterbooks*.

47. Meigs, *Capitol Builder*, 706.

48. Ibid., 708.

49. U.S. Congress, Senate, "Message of the President," 147–51.

50. Ibid., 158.

51. Walter to Rice, Apr. 27, 1859, Walter Collection, roll 4139.

52. U.S. Congress, Senate, "Message of the President," 181.

53. Ibid., 181–82.

54. Ibid., 182.

55. Meigs speech, Nov. 2, 1859, in Meigs, *Letterbooks*.

17. TYING OFF LOOSE ENDS

1. "Foreign Correspondence, Items, Etc.," *The Crayon*, June 1857, in U.S. Congress, Architect of the Capitol, vertical files, *Thomas Crawford*, "Periodicals."

2. James Clinton Hooker to Meigs, Aug. 22, 1857, Aug. 27, 1857, U.S. Congress, Architect of the Capitol, vertical files, *Thomas Crawford*, "Correspondence."

3. Tappan & Starbuck to Meigs, June 29, 1859, U.S. Congress, Architect of the Capitol, vertical files, *Works of Art, Statues: Capitol and Grounds*, "Freedom, by Thomas Crawford, Shipment."

4. Tappan & Starbuck to Meigs, Dec. 24, 1858, in Montgomery C. Meigs, *Letterbooks*, Mar. 1853–Oct. 1859, 1861, U.S. Congress, Architect of the Capitol.

5. Tappan & Starbuck to Meigs, July 23, 1859, U.S. Congress, Architect of the Capitol, vertical files, *Works of Art, Statues*.

6. William C. Allen, *History of the United States Capitol: A Chronicle of Design, Construction, and Politics*, Senate Document 106-29, 106th Congress, 2nd session (Washington, D.C.: U.S. Government Printing Office, 2001), 292. See also Montgomery C. Meigs, *Capitol Builder: The Shorthand Journals of Montgomery C. Meigs, 1853–1859, 1861*, ed. Wendy Wolff (Washington, D.C.: U.S. Government Printing Office, 2001), 739.

7. *North American and United States Gazette*, Nov. 4, 1859.

8. *New York Times*, Nov. 10, 1859.

9. *New York Herald*, Nov. 7, 1859.

10. Meigs, *Capitol Builder*, 751.
11. Walter to R. H. Gardiner, Nov. 2, 1859, in Thomas U. Walter, Thomas Ustick Walter Collection, Archives of American Art, Athenaeum, Philadelphia, roll 4139.
12. Walter to Rice, Nov. 3, 1859, ibid.
13. Turpin C. Bannister, "The Genealogy of the Dome of the United States Capitol," *Journal of the Society of Architectural Historians*, vol. 7, Jan.–June, 1948, 19.
14. Walter to Fowler, Mar. 2 1859, Walter Collection, roll 4139.
15. Allen, *History*, 288.
16. Ibid., 289.
17. U.S. Congress, Senate, "Letter from the Superintendent of the Capitol Extension to the Chairman of the Committee on Public Buildings and Grounds in Relation to the Dome and Porticos of the Capitol," Senate Misc. Doc. 29, 36th Congress, 1st Session, Feb. 29, 1860, serial 1038, 39–40.
18. Ibid., 40–41.
19. Ibid., 42.
20. Ibid., 43.
21. Ibid.
22. Ibid., 4.
23. Meigs, *Capitol Builder*, 763–64.
24. U.S. Senate, "Letter from the Superintendent," 4.
25. Walter to Fowler, Jan. 20, 1860, Walter Collection, roll 4139.
26. U.S. Senate, "Letter from the Superintendent," 145–46.
27. Ibid., 7–8.
28. Walter to Fowler, Dec. 17, 1859, Walter Collection, roll 4139.
29. Franklin to Floyd, Mar. 7, 1860, in Meigs, *Letterbooks*.
30. Franklin to Connolly, Apr. 12, 1860, ibid.
31. U.S. Congress, House of Representatives, *Documentary History of the Construction and Development of the United States Capitol Buildings and Grounds*, H.R. Report 646, 58th Congress, 2nd session (Washington, D.C.: U.S. Government Printing Office, 1904), serial 4585, 765.
32. Franklin to Floyd, July 3, 1860, in Meigs, *Letterbooks*.
33. Franklin to Floyd, July 30, 1860, ibid.
34. Franklin to Rice, Baird & Heebner, Aug. 18, 1860, ibid.
35. Walter to Rice, Sept. 11, 1860, Walter Collection, roll 4139.
36. Franklin to Floyd, Nov. 6, 1860, in Meigs, *Letterbooks*.
37. U.S. Senate, "Letter from the Superintendent," 1–2.
38. U.S. Congress, *Documentary History*, 758–65.
39. Meigs to Rogers, July 23, 1859, in Meigs, *Letterbooks*.
40. U.S. Congress, *Documentary History*, 743–49.
41. Ibid., 755–57.
42. Ibid., 780.
43. Ibid., 768.
44. Diary entry for Dec. 28, 1859, in Montgomery C. Meigs, *The Shorthand Diaries of*

Montgomery C. Meigs, unabridged transcription, U.S. Congress, Architect of the Capitol, undated.

45. Walter to J. Ames, Jan. 1, 1860, Walter Collection, roll 4139.

46. Walter to J. Ames, Jan. 20, 1860, ibid.

47. Allen, *History*, 308.

48. Meigs, *Capitol Builder*, 745.

49. For a detailed account of the Harper's Ferry raid, see David S. Reynolds, *John Brown, Abolitionist* (New York: Alfred A. Knopf, 2005), 306–28.

50. *New York Times*, Nov. 3, 1859.

51. Senate Proceedings, *Congressional Globe*, Dec. 8, 1859, 36th Congress, 1st session, 61–62.

52. William W. Freehling, *The Road to Disunion*, vol. 2: *Secessionists Triumphant, 1854–1861* (New York: Oxford University Press, 2007), 213–14.

53. Quoted in David M. Potter, *The Impending Crisis, 1848–1861* (New York: Harper and Row, 1976), 389.

54. Davis to Pierce, Sept. 2, 1859, in Jefferson Davis, *Jefferson Davis, Constitutionalist: His Letters, Papers and Speeches*, ed. Dunbar Rowland, multivolume set (Jackson, Miss.: S. J. Little and Ives, Company, 1923), vol. 4, 93.

55. Ibid., 131–32.

56. Potter, *Impending Crisis*, 403. See also Michael F. Holt, *The Political Crisis of the 1850s* (New York: W. W. Norton and Co., 1983), 205–206.

57. William J. Cooper, Jr., *Jefferson Davis, American* (New York: Alfred A. Knopf, 2000), 305–306.

58. See Freehling, *Road to Disunion*, vol. 2, 275–87.

59. Davis to Pierce, June 13, 1860, in Rowland, vol. 4, 496.

60. Meigs to Davis, June 13, 1860, in Montgomery C. Meigs, Papers of Montgomery C. Meigs, U.S. Library of Congress, Manuscript Division.

61. Rowland, ed., *Jefferson Davis, Constitutionalist*, vol. 4, 536–38.

62. "To Our Constituents," Dec. 14, 1860, in Jefferson Davis, *The Papers of Jefferson Davis*, vol. 6: *1856–1860*, ed. Lynda Lasswell Crist and Mary S. Dix (Baton Rouge: Louisiana State University Press, 1989), 377.

63. Cooper, *Jefferson Davis*, 319–20.

64. Varina Howell Davis, *Jefferson Davis, Ex-President of the Confederate States of America: A Memoir by His Wife in Two Volumes* (New York: Belford Co., 1890), vol. 1, 696–97.

65. Rowland, ed., *Jefferson Davis, Constitutionalist*, vol. 5, 40–44.

18. FREEDOM'S CAP

1. Walter to My Dear Wife, Dec. 1, 1863, in Thomas U. Walter, Thomas Ustick Walter Collection, Archives of American Art, Athenaeum, Philadelphia, roll 4141.

2. Walter to Capt. C. R. Thomas, Dec. 2, 1863, in Thomas U. Walter, *Records of the Architect of the Capitol: Letterbooks of Thomas U. Walter*, U.S. Congress, Architect of the Capitol.

3. Walter to My Dear Wife, Dec. 1, 1863, Walter Collection, roll 4141.

4. Walter to My Dear Son Thomas, Aug. 16, 1862, ibid., roll 4140.

5. Margaret Leech, *Reveille in Washington, 1861–1865* (New York: Harper and Bros., 1941), 279.

6. Walter to My Dear Wife, Dec. 1, 1863, Walter Collection, roll 4141.

7. Ibid., Dec. 2, 1863.

8. Walter to Fowler, Dec. 29, 1860, ibid., roll 4140.

9. Walter to Horace Walter, Nov. 16, 1860, ibid.

10. Walter to Robert Walter, Dec. 15, 1860, ibid.

11. Walter to John Rice, Dec. 16, 1860, ibid.

12. Walter to Charles Fowler, Dec. 26, 1860, ibid.

13. Walter to Dr. W. P. Schuster, Dec. 21, 1859, ibid., roll 4139.

14. Senate Proceedings, *Congressional Globe*, June 12, 1860, 36th Congress, 1st session, 2868.

15. Ibid., 2870.

16. Quoted in Harry C. Ways, *The Washington Aqueduct, 1852–1992* (Washington, D.C.: U.S. Army Corps of Engineers, 1996), 39.

17. Quoted in David W. Miller, *Second Only to Grant: Quartermaster General Montgomery C. Meigs* (Shippensburg, Pa.: White Mane Books, 2000), 59–60.

18. Ibid., 60–61; see also Ways, *Aqueduct*, 39.

19. Quoted in Russell F. Weigley, *Quartermaster General of the Union Army* (New York: Columbia University Press, 1959), 106.

20. Louisa to Nannie, Sept. 21, 1860, in U.S. Congress, Library of Congress, Rodgers Family Papers, part I, box 8.

21. See U.S. Congress, House of Representatives, *Abstracted Indian Trust Bonds*, H.R. Report 78, 36th Congress 2nd session, Feb. 12, 1861, serial 1105.

22. Ibid., Walter to Thomas Walter, Feb. 15, 1861, Walter Collection, roll 4140.

23. Walter to Fowler, Feb. 27, 1861, ibid.

24. Weigley, *Quartermaster*, 125.

25. Montgomery C. Meigs, *Capitol Builder: The Shorthand Journals of Montgomery C. Meigs, 1853–1859, 1861*, ed. Wendy Wolff (Washington, D.C.: U.S. Government Printing Office, 2001), 771.

26. Ibid., 772.

27. Ibid.

28. Ibid., 773.

29. Walter to Fowler, Mar. 1, 1861, Walter Collection, roll 4140.

30. Meigs to Walter, Mar. 6, 1861, ibid.

31. Walter to Rice, Mar. 4, 1861, ibid.

32. William C. Allen, *History of the United States Capitol: A Chronicle of Design, Construction, and Politics*, Senate Document 106-29, 106th Congress, 2nd session (Washington, D.C.: U.S. Government Printing Office, 2001), 310–11.

33. Letter from Simon Cameron, Secretary of War, Mar. 14, 1861, in U.S. Congress, Architect of the Capitol, vertical files, *Montgomery C. Meigs*, "General."

34. Walter to Moore, Mar. 14, 1861, Walter Collection, roll 4140.

35. Meigs to Cameron, Mar. 16, 1861, in Montgomery C. Meigs, *Letterbooks*, Mar. 1853–Oct. 1859, 1861, U.S. Congress, Architect of the Capitol.

36. Walter to Rice, Mar. 28, 1861, Walter Collection, roll 4140.

37. Diary entry for Mar. 29, 1861, in Montgomery C. Meigs, *The Shorthand Diaries of Montgomery C. Meigs*, unabridged transcription, U.S. Congress, Architect of the Capitol, undated.

38. Ibid.

39. Meigs, *Capitol Builder*, 776.

40. Diary entries for Apr. 4–23, 1861, in Meigs, *Shorthand Diaries* (unabridged).

41. Walter to Rice, Apr. 8, 1861, Walter Collection, roll 4140.

42. Leech, *Reveille*, 61, 80.

43. Walter to Provest, Apr. 16, 1861, Walter Collection, roll 4140.

44. Walter to Robert Walter, Apr. 19, 1861, ibid.

45. Leech, *Reveille*, 58–59.

46. Isaac Bassett, Isaac Bassett Papers, U.S. Senate (microfilm), box 21, folder B, 8H–8M.

47. Leech, *Reveille*, 66–67.

48. Diary entry for Apr. 22, 1861, Walter Collection, roll 4134.

49. Walter to Amanda, May 2, 1861, ibid., roll 4140.

50. Bassett, Papers, box 21, folder B, 8H–8M.

51. Leech, *Reveille*, 67, 73.

52. Walter to Amanda, May 3, 1861, Walter Collection, roll 4140.

53. Bassett, Papers, box 21, folder B, 8H–8M.

54. Leech, *Reveille*, 68.

55. U.S. Congress, House of Representatives, *Documentary History of the Construction and Development of the United States Capitol Buildings and Grounds*, H.R. Report 646, 58th Congress, 2nd session (Washington, D.C.: U.S. Government Printing Office, 1904), serial 4585, 788.

56. Walter to Amanda, May 8, 1861, Walter Collection, roll 4140.

57. Walter to Amanda, May 4, 1861, ibid.

58. Walter to Amanda, May 10, 1861, ibid.

59. Diary entries for May 5–9, 1861, in Meigs, *Shorthand Diaries* (unabridged).

60. Ibid., May 10.

61. Ibid., May 15.

62. Walter to Rice, May 8, 1861; Walter to Horace Walter, Dec. 25, 1861, Walter Collection, roll 4140.

63. Walter to Amanda, July 6, 1861, ibid.

64. Walter to Rice, July 8, 1861, ibid.

65. U.S. Congress, *Documentary History*, 1022.

66. Walter to Fowler, Aug. 1, 1861, Walter Collection, roll 4140.

67. Walter to Henry Moore, Aug. 10, 1861, ibid.

68. U.S. Congress, *Documentary History*, 785.

69. Ibid., 787.

70. Ibid., 787–89.

71. Ibid., 795.

72. Ibid., 799.

73. Walter to Fowler, Mar. 17, 1862, Walter Collection, roll 4140.

74. U.S. Congress, *Documentary History*, 791.

75. Ibid., 807.

76. Ibid., 802.

77. Walter to Caleb Smith, Secretary of the Interior, May 17, 1862, in Walter, *Letterbooks*.

78. Walter to Smith, May 8, 1862, ibid.

79. Constance McLaughlin Green, *Washington, Village and Capital, 1800-1878* (Princeton, N.J.: Princeton University Press, 1962), 244-57.

80. Walter to Amanda, June 28 and July 22-25, 1862, Walter Collection, roll 4140.

81. Walter to Olivia, June 11, 1863, ibid., roll 4141.

82. Walter to Provest, Sept. 2, 1862, ibid., roll 4140.

83. Walter to Smith, Nov. 14, ibid., roll 4141.

84. Walter to Horace Walter, Nov. 22, 1862, ibid.

85. Walter to Lucas Hirst, Mar. 5, 1863, ibid.

86. Walter to Olivia, June 20, 1862, ibid., roll 4140.

87. Walter to Thomas Walter, Aug. 16, 1862, ibid.

88. Walter to Rice, Baird & Heebner, Jan. 10, 1863, in Walter, *Letterbooks*.

89. Walter to Fowler, Apr. 20, 1863, Walter Collection, roll 4141.

90. U.S. Congress, *Documentary History*, 1025.

91. Barbara A. Wolanin, *Constantino Brumidi: Artist of the Capitol* (Washington, D.C.: U.S. Government Printing Office, 1998), 125-26.

92. Meigs to Caleb Smith, Secretary of the Interior, June 5, 1862, in U.S. Congress, Architect of the Capitol, vertical files, *Montgomery C. Meigs*, "Role in Art Program."

93. Walter to Brumidi, Feb. 25 and Mar. 30, 1863, Walter Collection, roll 4141.

94. U.S. Congress, *Documentary History*, 1023.

95. Ibid.

96. Jesse J. Holland, *Black Men Built the Capitol* (Guilford, Conn.: Globe Pequot Press, 2007), 5.

97. S. D. Wyeth, *The Federal City: Ins and Abouts of Washington* (Washington, D.C.: Gibson Bros., 1865), 194-95.

98. Quoted in Allen, *History*, 325.

99. William J. Cooper, Jr., *Jefferson Davis, American* (New York: Alfred A. Knopf, 2000), 468-69.

100. Louisa to Nannie, Nov. 28, 1863, Rodgers Family Papers, part I, box 8.

101. Diary entry for Dec. 2, 1863, in Montgomery C. Meigs, Papers of Montgomery C. Meigs, Library of Congress, Manuscript Division, container 5, reel 12.

EPILOGUE

1. Montgomery C. Meigs, *Capitol Builder: The Shorthand Journals of Montgomery C. Meigs, 1853-1859, 1861*, ed. Wendy Wolff (Washington, D.C.: U.S. Government Printing Office, 2001), 670.

2. Varina Davis to Montgomery Meigs, June 17, 1865, in U.S. Secretary of War, *Official Records of the War of the Rebellion* (Washington, D.C.: U.S. Government Printing Office, 1880), series 2, vol. 8, 666.

3. Quoted in David W. Miller, *Second Only to Grant: Quartermaster General Montgomery C. Meigs* (Shippensburg, Pa.: White Mane Books, 2000), 264.

4. *New York Times*, June 29, 1865.

5. Diary entries for Apr. 15, 20, and 21, 1865, in Montgomery C. Meigs, Papers of Montgomery C. Meigs, Library of Congress, Manuscript Division, container 5, reel 12.

6. The circumstances of Lieutenant Meigs's death have been a matter of contention since it took place. The official account appears to show unequivocally that Meigs was gunned down by rebel partisans who he believed were Union soldiers. This view was certainly shared by General Meigs throughout his life, and this is the view presented here, since it reflects what was known and believed by Meigs at the time. For a thorough presentation of the official dispatches, see G. A. Forsyth, Harrisonburgh, Va., to Lt. Col. J. H. Taylor, Oct. 4, 1864; Forsyth to My Dear Gen., Oct. 4, 1864; Capt. James R. Hosmer to Maj. Gen. M. C. Meigs, Oct. 4, 1864; G. A. Custer to Major Russell, Oct. 4, 1864; Gen. Philip Sheridan to Lt. Col. J. H. Taylor, Oct. 5, 1864; and Maj. Gen. M. C. Meigs to John N. Macomb, Oct. 10, 1864, in U.S. Congress, Library of Congress, Rodgers Family Papers, part I, box 8. For Meigs's own interpretation of the event, see his diary entry for Oct. 6, 1864, in Meigs, Papers, container 5, reel 12. Different versions of the Confederate view—that young Meigs was killed by regular soldiers on a legitimate scouting patrol—can be found in a number of locations. See, for instance, arlingtoncemetery.net/jrmeigs.htm for an exhaustive investigation written in 1925.

7. Miller, *Second Only to Grant*, 241.

8. Louisa Meigs to Nannie Rodgers Macomb, Nov. 27, 1864, Rodgers Family Papers, part I, box 8.

9. Miller, *Second Only to Grant*, 90–91.

10. Robert M. Poole, *On Hallowed Ground: The Story of Arlington National Cemetery* (New York: Walker and Company, 2009), 61–62.

11. Quoted in Russell F. Weigley, *Quartermaster General of the Union Army* (New York: Columbia University Press, 1959), 325.

12. Ibid.

13. For a detailed account of Davis's flight and capture, see William J. Cooper, Jr., *Jefferson Davis, American* (New York: Alfred A. Knopf, 2000), 521–34.

14. See Varina Howell Davis, *Jefferson Davis, Ex-President of the Confederate States of America: A Memoir by His Wife in Two Volumes*, vol. 2 (New York: Belford Co., 1890), 637–39. For newspaper accounts of the capture, see e.g. Secretary of War Edwin M. Stanton's official news release, which describes how Davis "hastily put on one of his wife's dresses" to aid his escape, in *The New York Times*, May 15, 1865.

15. Varina Davis, *Jefferson Davis*, vol. 2, 640.

16. Ibid., 653–54.

17. Jefferson Davis, *The Rise and Fall of the Confederate Government*, 2 vols. (Richmond, Va.: Garrett and Massie, Inc., 1881), vol. 1, vii.

18. Davis to the Editor of the *World*, Mar. 15, 1888, in Tulane College, New Orleans, La., Davis Collection.

19. Davis to John H. Reagan, Feb. 28, 1889, Jefferson Davis Project, Rice University, Houston, Texas.

20. William C. Allen, *History of the United States Capitol: A Chronicle of Design, Construction, and Politics*, Senate Document 106-29, 106th Congress, 2nd session (Washington, D.C.: U.S. Government Printing Office, 2001), 326.

21. U.S. Congress, House of Representatives, *Documentary History of the Construction and Development of the United States Capitol Buildings and Grounds*, H.R. Report 646, 58th Congress, 2nd session (Washington, D.C.: U.S. Government Printing Office, 1904), serial 4585, 820.

22. Walter to J. H. Rice, Apr. 20, 1864, in Thomas U. Walter, *Records of the Architect of the Capitol: Letterbooks of Thomas U. Walter*, U.S. Congress, Architect of the Capitol.

23. U.S. Congress, *Documentary History*, 1026.

24. Ibid., 838–40.

25. Walter to Meigs, Oct. 14, 1864, in Thomas U. Walter, Thomas Ustick Walter Collection, Archives of American Art, Athenaeum, Philadelphia, roll 4141.

26. Diary entry for Jan. 10, 1864, in Meigs, Papers, container 5, reel 12.

27. Walter to My Dear Mr. Briggs, Dec. 14, 1863, Walter Collection, roll 4141.

28. Walter to Benjamin Brown French, Jan. 20, 1865, ibid.

29. Barbara A. Wolanin, *Constantino Brumidi: Artist of the Capitol* (Washington, D.C.: U.S. Government Printing Office, 1998), 127.

30. Ibid., 129–30.

31. Ibid., 131.

32. Ibid.

33. Ibid., 165–66.

34. Walter to My Dear Wife, May 16, 1865, Walter Collection, roll 4142.

35. Walter to My Dear Wife, May 25, 1865, ibid.

36. Walter to My Dear Wife, May 29, 1865, ibid.

37. Walter to Alexander Provest, July 10, 1865, ibid.

38. Walter to Robert Walter, Feb. 24, 1876, ibid., roll 4143.

39. In typewritten biography, U.S. Congress, Architect of the Capitol, vertical files, *Montgomery C. Meigs,* "Biographical."

40. *Washington Post*, Dec. 4, 1959.

41. James M. Goode, "Architecture and Politics: Thomas Ustick Walter and the Enlargement of the United States Capitol, 1850–1865," dissertation submitted to the Faculty of the Graduate School of Arts and Sciences of George Washington University, Dec. 6, 1994, vol. 2, 322.

42. Walter to Meigs, Mar. 29, 1882, Walter Collection, roll 4143.

43. Walter to Meigs, Apr. 26, 1882, ibid.

44. Diary entries, Oct. 9–10, 1883, ibid., roll 3135.

45. Goode, "Architecture and Politics," 323.

46. Miller, *Second Only to Grant*, 289–90.

SELECTED BIBLIOGRAPHY

BOOKS

Allen, William C. *The Dome of the United States Capitol: An Architectural History*. Senate Document 102-7, 102nd Congress, 1st session. Washington, D.C.: U.S. Government Printing Office, 1992.

——. *History of the United States Capitol: A Chronicle of Design, Construction, and Politics*. Senate Document 106-29, 106th Congress, 2nd session. Washington, D.C.: U.S. Government Printing Office, 2001.

Anbinder, Tyler. *Nativism and Slavery: The Northern Know Nothings and the Politics of the 1850s*. New York: Oxford University Press, 1992.

Brown, Glenn. *History of the United States Capitol*, 2 vols. Washington, D.C.: U.S. Government Printing Office, 1902.

Caemmerer, H. Paul. *A Manual on the Origin and Development of Washington*. Washington, D.C.: U.S. Government Printing Office, 1939.

Cashin, Joan E. *First Lady of the Confederacy: Varina Davis's Civil War*. Cambridge, Mass.: Harvard University Press, 2006.

Clay-Clopton, Virginia. *A Belle of the Fifties: Memories of Mrs. Clay of Alabama, Covering Social and Political Life in Washington and the South, 1853–1866*. New York: Doubleday, Page and Co., 1905.

Cooper, William J., Jr. *Jefferson Davis, American*. New York: Alfred A. Knopf, 2000.

Davis, Jefferson. *Jefferson Davis, Constitutionalist: His Letters, Papers and Speeches*. Edited by Dunbar Rowland. Multivolume set. Jackson, Miss.: S. J. Little and Ives, Company, 1923.

——. *The Papers of Jefferson Davis*. Vol. 2: *1841–1846*. Edited by James T. McIntosh. Baton Rouge: Louisiana State University Press, 1974.

——. *The Papers of Jefferson Davis*. Vol. 3: *1846–1848*. Edited by James T. McIntosh, Lynda Lasswell Crist, and Mary S. Dix. Baton Rouge: Louisiana State University Press, 1981.

——. *The Papers of Jefferson Davis.* Vol. 4: *1849–1852.* Edited by Lynda Lasswell Crist, Mary S. Dix, and Richard E. Beringer. Baton Rouge: Louisiana State University Press, 1983.

——. *The Papers of Jefferson Davis.* Vol. 5: *1853–1855.* Edited by Lynda Lasswell Crist and Mary S. Dix. Baton Rouge: Louisiana State University Press, 1985.

——. *The Papers of Jefferson Davis,* Vol. 6: *1856–1860.* Edited by Lynda Lasswell Crist and Mary S. Dix. Baton Rouge: Louisiana State University Press, 1989.

——. *Private Letters 1823–1889.* Edited by Hudson Strode. New York: Harcourt, Brace and World, 1966.

——. *The Rise and Fall of the Confederate Government.* 2 vols. Richmond, Va.: Garrett and Massie, Inc., 1881.

Davis, Reuben. *Recollections of Mississippi and Mississippians.* Boston and New York: Houghton, Mifflin and Co., 1890.

Davis, Varina Howell. *Jefferson Davis, Ex-President of the Confederate States of America: A Memoir by His Wife in Two Volumes.* New York: Belford Co., 1890.

Davis, William C. *Jefferson Davis: The Man and His Hour.* New York: HarperCollins, 1991.

Dickens, Charles. *American Notes.* New York: Modern Library, 1992.

Dyer, Oliver. *Great Senators of the United States Forty Years Ago (1848–1849).* New York: Robert Bonner's Sons, 1889.

Eckloff, Christian F. *Memoirs of a Senate Page (1855–1859).* Edited by Percival G. Melbourne. New York: Broadway Publishing Co., 1909.

Etcheson, Nicole. *Bleeding Kansas: Contested Liberty in the Civil War Era.* Lawrence: University Press of Kansas, 2004.

Freehling, William W. *The Road to Disunion.* Vol. 1: *Secessionists at Bay, 1776–1854.* New York: Oxford University Press, 1990.

——. *The Road to Disunion,* Vol. 2: *Secessionists Triumphant, 1854–1861.* New York: Oxford University Press, 2007.

French, Benjamin Brown. *Witness to the Young Republic: A Yankee's Journal, 1828–1870.* Edited by Donald B. Cole and John J. McDonough. Hanover, N.H.: University Press of New England, 1989.

Giedion, Siegfried. *Space, Time and Architecture: The Growth of a New Tradition.* 5th ed. Cambridge, Mass.: Harvard University Press, 1967.

Gloag, John, and Derek Bridgewater. *A History of Cast Iron in Architecture.* London: George Allen and Unwin, Ltd., 1948.

Gobright, Lawrence A. *Recollections of Men and Things at Washington, During the Third of a Century.* Philadelphia: Claxton, Remsen and Hafflefinger, 1869.

Goodrich, Thomas. *War to the Knife: Bleeding Kansas, 1854–1861.* Mechanicsburg, Pa.: Stackpole Books, 1998.

Green, Constance McLaughlin. *Washington, Village and Capital, 1800–1878.* Princeton, N.J.: Princeton University Press, 1962.

Hamilton, Holman. *Zachary Taylor, Soldier in the White House.* New York: Bobbs-Merrill, 1951.

——. *Zachary Taylor, Soldier of the Republic.* New York: Bobbs-Merrill, 1941.

Henry, Joseph. *The Papers of Joseph Henry*. Multivolume set. Washington, D.C.: Smithsonian Institution Press, vol. 3 (Jan. 1836–Dec. 1837), Nathan Reingold, ed., 1979; vol. 7 (Jan. 1847–Dec. 1849), Marc Rothenberg, ed., 1996; vol. 8 (Jan. 1850–Dec. 1853), Marc Rothenberg, ed., 1998; vol. 9 (Jan. 1854–Dec. 1857), Marc Rothenberg, ed., 2002.

Holland, Jesse J., *Black Men Built the Capitol*. Guilford, Conn.: Globe Pequot Press, 2007.

Holt, Michael F. *The Fate of Their Country: Politicians, Slavery Extension, and the Coming of the Civil War*. New York: Hill and Wang, 2004.

———. *Franklin Pierce*. New York: Times Books, 2010.

———. *The Political Crisis of the 1850s*. New York: W. W. Norton and Co., 1983.

Johnston, William Dawson, *History of the Library of Congress*. Vol. 1: *1800–1864*. Washington, D.C.: Government Printing Office, 1904.

Leech, Margaret. *Reveille in Washington, 1861–1865*. New York: Harper and Bros., 1941.

Liscombe, R. W. *Altogether American: Robert Mills, Architect and Engineer, 1781–1855*. New York: Oxford University Press, 1994.

Maroon, Fred. J. *The United States Capitol*. Washington, D.C.: Maroon Editions, 1993.

Meigs, Montgomery C. *Capitol Builder: The Shorthand Journals of Montgomery C. Meigs, 1853–1859, 1861*. Edited by Wendy Wolff. Washington, D.C.: U.S. Government Printing Office, 2001 (unabridged diary cited below).

Miller, David W. *Second Only to Grant: Quartermaster General Montgomery C. Meigs*. Shippensburg, Pa.: White Mane Books, 2000.

Nevins, Allan. *Ordeal of the Union*. Vol. 1: *Fruits of Manifest Destiny, 1847–1852*. New York: Charles Scribner's Sons, 1947.

———. *Ordeal of the Union*. Vol. 2: *A House Dividing, 1852–1857*. New York: Charles Scribner's Sons, 1947.

Poole, Robert M. *On Hallowed Ground: The Story of Arlington National Cemetery*. New York: Walker and Company, 2009.

Poore, Benjamin Perley. *Perley's Reminiscences of Sixty Years in the National Metropolis*. 2 vols. Philadelphia: Hubbard Brothers, 1886.

Potter, David M. *The Impending Crisis: 1848–1861*. New York: Harper and Row, 1976.

Rawley, James A. *Race and Politics: Bleeding Kansas and the Coming of the Civil War*. Philadelphia: J. B. Lippincott, 1969.

Reynolds, David S. *John Brown, Abolitionist*. New York: Alfred A. Knopf, 2005.

Rhett, Robert Barnwell. *The Death and Funeral Ceremonies of John Caldwell Calhoun*. Columbia, S.C.: A. S. Johnson, 1850.

Tocqueville, Alexis de. *Democracy in America*. Edited by J. P. Mayer. New York: Harper Perennial, Harper and Row, 1988.

Ways, Harry C. *The Washington Aqueduct, 1852–1992*. Washington, D.C.: U.S. Army Corps of Engineers, 1996.

Weigley, Russell F. *Quartermaster General of the Union Army*. New York: Columbia University Press, 1959.

Wolanin, Barbara A. *Constantino Brumidi: Artist of the Capitol*. Washington, D.C.: U.S. Government Printing Office, 1998.

Wyeth, S. D. *The Federal City: Ins and Abouts of Washington*. Washington, D.C.: Gibson Bros., 1865.

ARTICLES

Bannister, Turpin C. "The Genealogy of the Dome of the United States Capitol." *Journal of the Society of Architectural Historians*, vol. 7, Jan.–June 1948.

"The Benjamin Affair." *Harper's Weekly*, June 19, 1858.

Davis, Jefferson. "Autobiography of Jefferson Davis." *Bedford's Magazine*, Jan. 1890.

Firth, Wayne. "Montgomery C. Meigs and Photography at the Capitol," in Dickinson, William C., ed., *Montgomery C. Meigs and the Building of the Nation's Capitol*. Athens, Ohio: Ohio University Press, 2002.

Meigs, M. C. "On Acoustics and Ventilation, with Reference to the New Halls of Congress, May 1853," in *The Civil Engineer and Architect's Journal*, vol. XVII, no. 242, May 1854.

Owen, Robert Dale. "Hints on Public Architecture," Da Capo Press (reprinted), 1978. In Architect of the Capitol, vertical files: *Architects: Robert Mills: Magazine and Journal Articles*.

Press, Donald E. "South of the Avenue: From Murder Bay to the Federal Triangle." *Records of the Columbia Historical Society*, Historical Society of Washington, D.C., vol. 51, 1984.

DOCUMENTS

Bassett, Isaac. The Isaac Bassett Papers, U.S. Senate (microfilm).

Fillmore, Millard. Papers. Buffalo and Erie County Historical Society, Buffalo, N.Y. (microfilm).

Goode, James M., "Architecture and Politics: Thomas Ustick Walter and the Enlargement of the United States Capitol, 1850–1865." Dissertation submitted to the Faculty of the Graduate School of Arts and Sciences of George Washington University, Dec. 6, 1994, vols. 1 and 2.

Meigs, Montgomery C. *Letterbooks*, Mar. 1853–Oct. 1859, 1861. U.S. Congress, Architect of the Capitol (archive and microfilm).

———. The Papers of Montgomery C. Meigs. Library of Congress, Manuscript Division (microfilm).

———. *The Shorthand Diaries of Montgomery C. Meigs* (unabridged transcription). U.S. Congress, Architect of the Capitol, undated (digitized manuscript).

Mills, Robert. The Papers of Robert Mills 1781–1855. Edited by Pamela Scott. Wilmington, Del.: Scholarly Resources, 1990, Microfilm.

National Archives. RG 107. *Letters Received by the Secretary of War*, Registered Series, 1801–1870 (microfilm 221).

———. RG 77. *Letters, Reports, and Statements Sent to the Secretary of War and Congress*, vol. 7.

———. RG 23. *Records of the Coast and Geodetic Survey*, vol. 1.

———. RG 77. *Records of the Office of the Chief of Engineers*, General correspondence 1787–1870, Letters, Reports, and Statements Sent to the Secretary of War and Congress 1836–68, entry 8.

———. RG 77. *Records of the Office of the Chief of Engineers, Public Works and Buildings in the District of Columbia*, Vouchers, Financial Statements, and Lists of Papers Relating to the Washington Aqueduct, entry 278.

———. RG 77. *Records of the Office of the Chief of Engineers*, Records Relating to Work on the Capitol Extension and Washington Aqueduct.

———. RG 107. *Records of the Secretary of War 1820–1861*, letters received (microfilm 221, roll 183).

———. RG 233. *Records of the U.S. House of Representatives, 33rd and 34th Cong.*, vol. 83.

———. *Reports to Congress from the Secretary of War, 1803–1870* (microfilm 220, roll 4, vol. 8).

U.S. Congress. Architect of the Capitol. "A Chronology of Photography at the United States Capitol," 2005 (pamphlet).

U.S. Congress, Architect of the Capitol, vertical files, including journal and newspaper articles, transcriptions, research notes, and other materials by topic. Specific files consulted:

> *Capitol Extension*
>
> *Doors: Bronze*
>
> *Library of Congress*
>
> *Montgomery C. Meigs* (five files)
>
> *Robert Mills* (three files)
>
> *Thomas Crawford* (four files)
>
> *Works of Art, Statues, Capitol and Grounds*

U.S. Congress. House. *Documentary History of the Construction and Development of the United States Capitol Buildings and Grounds*. H.R. Report 646, 58th Congress, 2nd session. Washington, D.C.: U.S. Government Printing Office, 1904 (serial 4585).

———. "Abstracted Indian Trust Bonds." H.R. Report 78, 36th Congress, 2nd session, Feb. 12, 1861 (serial 1105).

U.S. Congress. Library of Congress. Rodgers Family Papers.

U.S. Congress. Senate. "Letter from the Superintendent of the Capitol Extension to the Chairman of the Committee on Public Buildings and Grounds in Relation to the Dome and Porticos of the Capitol." Senate Misc. Doc. 29, 36th Congress, 1st session, Feb. 29, 1860 (serial 1038).

———. "Message of the President of the United States, communicating in compliance with a resolution of the Senate, information in relation to the heating and ventilating of the Capitol extension, the Post Office Department, etc." Senate Exec. Doc. 20, 36th Congress, 1st session, Jan. 26, 1860 (serial 1031, vol. 9).

———. "Message from the President of the United States to the two Houses of Congress at the Commencement of the First Session of the Thirty-First Congress," Report of the Secretary of the Interior, Dec. 24, 1849, Senate Exec. Doc. 1, pt. 2, 31st Congress, 1st session, Dec. 24, 1849 (serial 550).

———. "Report of the Select Committee to Investigate Abuses, Bribery, Fraud," S. Report 1/1, 33rd Congress, special session, Mar. 22, 1853 (serial 688).

U.S. Secretary of War. *Official Records of the War of the Rebellion*. Washington, D.C.: U.S. Government Printing Office, 1880.

Tulane College, New Orleans, La., Davis Collection.

Walter, Thomas U., *Records of the Architect of the Capitol, Letterbooks of Thomas U. Walter*. U. S. Congress, Architect of the Capitol, multivolume set.

————. *Thomas Ustick Walter Collection*, Archives of American Art, the Athenaeum, Philadelphia (microfilm).

NEWSPAPERS

Congressional Globe (Washington, D.C.)
The Crayon (New York)
Daily Appeal (Memphis, Tenn.)
Daily National Intelligencer (Washington, D.C.)
The Daily Union (Washington, D.C.)
Democrat (Yazoo City, Miss.)
Evening Star (Washington, D.C.)
New York Express
The New York Herald
The New York Times
New York Tribune
North American and United States Gazette (Philadelphia)
Pennsylvania Inquirer (Philadelphia)
Southern Press (Jackson, Miss.)
Standard (Columbus, Miss.)
The Sun (Baltimore)
The Washington Post

WEBSITES

Architect of the Capitol: aoc.gov
Arlington Cemetery: arlingtoncemetery.net/jrmeigs.htm
Great Books online: Bartleby.com

ACKNOWLEDGMENTS

I first became interested in the U.S. Capitol in the 1990s, when I wrote about Congress for *The Washington Post*. I worked from a desk in the third-floor Senate Press Gallery and took advantage of my press pass to wander the halls and byways of the building whenever I had the chance. I first made the acquaintance of Jefferson Davis, Montgomery C. Meigs, and Thomas U. Walter in 1998, when I wrote a story about the Architect of the Capitol's plans to renovate the cast-iron dome. I had a sense of the innovation and creativity they had used to build the modern Capitol, and I always intended to return to the story once the renovation had begun. Alas, Congress set aside the project after the events of September 11, 2001, and instead focused on building the Capitol Visitor's Center.

I had all but forgotten about the Capitol by 2008, when I met Thomas LeBien, my editor and publisher at Farrar, Straus and Giroux. I was writing magazine stories at the time and trying to sell him a book on a completely different subject. That project interested him not at all, but he suggested I think about some of the other stories I had written over the years, and we agreed to stay in touch. Within hours of that meeting, the lightbulb went on. Why not write about the Capitol? It seemed perfect, and Thomas also thought so. The result is *Freedom's Cap*.

Over two years of research and writing I have been the beneficiary of help and encouragement from a large number of people who cheerfully provided me with everything from tactful research suggestions to overnight lodging. I cannot thank them enough.

Architect of the Capitol Stephen T. Ayers and his staff made archives, files, books, records, photographs, architectural drawings, and office space available to me during countless visits. Barbara A. Wolanin, the curator for the Architect, served as my good shepherd throughout. She found the records I needed, told me which records I was missing, and provided those as well. On her advice I applied for and received two very welcome research grants from the Capitol Historical Society. I thank the Historical Society president,

Ronald Sarasin, and Don Kennon, vice president in charge of the fellowship program, for their generosity during hard economic times.

Also at the Architect's office, curators Jennifer Blancato, Ann Kenny, and Pamela Mc-Connell and writer-editor Eric Paff were all helpful and unfailingly cheerful. Chief of Photography Michael Dunn did yeoman work gathering most of the pictures that appear in the book. James B. Myers, chief of the records management and archives branch, let me clutter up his office for weeks on end while I read the Meigs and Walter correspondence. Archivist Andria Fields helped me navigate these immense letterbooks and sympathized with me as I puzzled over Meigs's cuneiform-like handwriting.

I would also like to thank William C. Allen, architectural historian for the Architect of the Capitol (now historian emeritus), for advice and counsel on numerous occasions. No one knows more about the Capitol than Bill and Barbara, and both of them read and critiqued the manuscript, keeping me from making dreadful mistakes and offering advice, much of which I took.

I also spent a great deal of time at Rice University in Houston, where the Jefferson Davis Project is headquartered. Lynda Crist, editor of the Jefferson Davis papers, and assistant editor Suzanne Scott Gibbs taught me how to use their prodigious archive, found me whatever else I needed from the Rice library, helped me with footnotes, sourcing, and even computer repair, and let me work so late that I once almost got locked in the library overnight.

The Davis biographer William J. Cooper, historian emeritus at Louisiana State University, offered counsel at several points in the project and encouraged me to pursue one of the central themes of *Freedom's Cap*: Jefferson Davis's remarkable ability to espouse a stronger, more powerful federal union even as he steadfastly proclaimed the inviolability of states' rights. Bill also read the manuscript, offering welcome corrections and urging interpretive changes, which I mostly, but not always, accepted. Any errors in this regard are mine.

Special thanks are due to the historian Catherine Clinton, of Queen's University, Belfast. It was Catherine, a longtime friend and author of many, many books, who introduced me to Farrar, Straus and Giroux. It would be safe to say that there quite likely would have been no book if not for her. Catherine told me what to read, whom to contact, and how to verse myself in the complexities of 1850s politics. She read the manuscript and critiqued both style and sourcing, a thankless but much needed task.

At Farrar, Straus and Giroux, Thomas LeBien provided unflagging encouragement and superb editing. I would also like to thank Assistant Editor Dan Crissman, designer Abby Kagan, and, especially, copyeditor Emily DeHuff, who fixed errors (so many I could not count) not only of style, but also of substance.

In Washington, I stayed for weeks on end at the home of old friends Tom and Mary Edsall, who live about five minutes from the Capitol, and also begged lodging with former neighbors and eternal friends Joe Oppenheimer and Edie Fraser and with Nils Bruzelius, my former editor at the *Post*, and Lynne Weil, also denizens of Capitol Hill. In Houston, Ann Jackson and her daughter Ginny put up with my comings and goings for several weeks. Ann went to a ballgame with me and may even have enjoyed it.

Finally I owe huge debts to my spouse, Carla Robbins, and to my daughter, Annie. I did much of the writing and editing while Annie studied in the next room. She laughed at my technological shortcomings, fixed the computer, and listened to me mutter and curse without complaint. Carla, quite simply, is the best editor I know. She hammered me mercilessly for sloppy thinking, empty-calories writing, and organizational blunders, and without her clean insights, encouragement, and carefully rationed praise, I would probably still be muddling through the manuscript.

INDEX

Page numbers in *italics* refer to illustrations.

Abert, John James, 23–25, 83

abolitionism, 5, 57, 65, 327, 328; Harpers Ferry raid, 358–60; Kansas slave debate and, 233, 235–38; Pottawatomie massacre, 237–38; of Washington, D.C., slave trade, 57, 65–67

acoustics, 11, 20, 23–25, 143, 153–54, 200, 266, 385; House, 11, 17, 18, 20, 23–24, *24*, 25, 32, 33–34, 35, 55, 63, 107, 161, 200, 266, 271, 272, 329; in Meigs-Davis plan, 151, 153–54, 245, 266, 271, 272, 329; Senate, 55, 60, 329

Adams, John, 16, 103, 301

Adams, John Quincy, 21

Agricola, Filippo, 208

Alabama, 362, 372

Allen, William C., 86, 183, 286

altered-drawings affair, 285–89, 292, 296

American Institute of Architects, 276, 409, 410

American Philosophical Society, 188

American Revolution, 6, 19, 73, 176, 270, 326

Ames, J. A., 358, 404

Ames Manufacturing Co., 357–58, 404

Anbinder, Tyler, 192

Anderson, Charles, 74, 78, 80, 81, 82, 93

Anderson, Robert, 377

Andersonville prison, 395

Antietam, 390

Appomattox, Lee's surrender at, 399

Aqueduct, *see* Washington Aqueduct

Aquia sandstone, 15, 21, 25, 92, 182–83, 240, 249

architects, 14–21, 33, 34, 67, 137, 276, 283; altered-drawings affair, 285–88; early, 14–21; 1850–51 Capitol design contest, 69–87; lack of, 22; Meigs-Walter rivalry, 148–51, 159–62, 170–73, 184, 186–91, 200–205, 216, 245–46, 274–90, 296–300, 313–17, 329–39, 344–47, 372–76, 386, 392, 398, 404–405, 410–11; *see also specific architects and buildings*

Arizona, 25

Arlington cemetery, 398, 411

Army, U.S., 50, 129, 131, 137, 140, 147, 321; control of Capitol project, 136–44, 145–62, 164, 168–73, 178–82, 240, 242,

Army, U.S. (*cont.*)
  260–66, 287, 345, 384–86; Jefferson
  Davis as technologist for, 221–23;
  Montgomery Meigs as quartermaster
  general of, 383, *396*, 410; Mexican War,
  44–47, 129; rifles, 50–51, 222, 312; *see
  also* War Department
Army Bureau of Topographical Engineers,
  23, 35, 40, 60, 61, 117–18, 136, 339
Army Corps of Engineers, 40, 117–18,
  136, 138, 139, 143, 221
art and decoration, 4, 5, 60, 90, 97, 103,
  131, 156–57, 174–78, 187, 193, 195–99,
  202–14, 219–21, 266–70, 289, 297,
  300–10, 323, 330, 346, 387–93;
  Congressional commission on, 304–10,
  312, 342, 355–56, 358; frescoes and
  murals, 206–10, 212, *213*, 229, 248,
  267–70, 283–84, 300–301, *301*,
  302–303, 305, 307, 323, 355, 391–92,
  405–406, *406*, 407, *407*, 408; "higher
  style," 196, 221, 267, 272–73, 302, 323,
  330, 392, 402; Library of Congress, 103,
  132; lost in 1851 fire, 103; Marshall
  proviso, 306–10, 312; Meigs plan for,
  174–78, 187, 195–96, *196*, 197–99,
  202–14, 224–25, 231–33, 243, 246–48,
  258–59, 266–70, 272–73, 283–84, 297,
  300–10, 312–17, 323–24, *325*, 330,
  340–42, *342*, 357, 392, 402, 405; statues
  and pediments, 156–57, 174–76, *176*,
  177, 187, 197–98, *198*, 199, 219–20,
  224–25, 231–32, *232*, 233, 242, 246–47,
  247, 248, 258–59, 268, 269, 283–84,
  307–309, *309*, 355–58, 365–67, *367*, 368,
  402–404; *see also* frescoes and murals;
  painting; statues and sculpture; *specific
  artists, works, methods and materials*
art commission, 304–10, 312, 342,
  355–56, 358
Aspinwall, William H., 241
Astor Library, New York, 302
Atchison, David R., 133, 166, 167, 200, 223
Atlanta, 396, 410

Bache, Alexander Dallas, 131, 154, 158,
  161, 188, 241, 245, 271, 272, 373
Badger, George E., 115
Baird, John, 101, 441n9
Ball, Edward, 240–46
Baltimore, 129, 336, 379
Baltimore *Sun*, 215, 322
Banks, Nathaniel, 230, 233, 240, 241, 269
Barksdale, William, 293
basement, 26
Bassett, Isaac, 23, 50, 56, 379, 380
Bayard, James, 173, 219
Beale, Charles, 356
Bell, John, 354
Benjamin, Judah P., 312
Benton, Thomas Hart, 58, 66
Be sheekee, 211
Bigler, William, 277, 278, 279, 288, 324
Billinghurst, Charles, 28
bird decorations, 301, *301*, 323
blacksmiths, 122, 224, 261
Blair, Francis, 382, 383
Blake, John B., 240
Bleeding Kansas, 5, 168, 220, 223, 233,
  235–38, 254
bluestone, 97, 113, 117–18, 134
Bodisco, Baroness, 329
Bogardus, James, 105
Borland, Solon, 110, 114–19, 125, 133–37,
  155, 158, 183
Borland investigation, 121–26, 132–38,
  149, 150, 154–55; report, 134–38, 149
Boston, 19, 154, 327
Boyd, Linn, 103, 133, 173
brackets, 248–49, *249*, 255, 275
Breckinridge, John C., 321, 323, 325,
  354, 362
breech-loading rifles, 222, 312
Brewster, William, 323
brick, 21, *91*, 158–59, 169, 179, 199–200,
  241; contracts, 97, 98, 120, 123, 158–59,
  180, 190; hoisting, 250
bricklayers, 71, 158–59, 179, 193, 250
bridges, 227; cast iron, 105; masonry, 260

Brierfield, 42–43, 46, 51, 96, 128, 130, 401

Bright, Jesse, 351, 354

bronze, 212; casting of *Freedom* statue, 341, 357–58, 392–93; door handles and knobs, 212–14, *214*; doors, 199, 212, 269, 355, 389, 404, 405; foundries, 341, 355, 357–58, 389; railways, 300; statues, 220

Brooklyn Bridge, 227

Brooks, Preston S., 236–37, 293

Brown, Albert, 47

Brown, Henry Kirke, 306, 355

Brown, John, 237, 358–60; Harpers Ferry raid, 358–60; Pottawatomie massacre, 237–38, 242

Brown's Hotel, 27

Brumidi, Constantino, 206–207, *207*, 208–10, 221, 267–70, 297, 299, 300–303, 306, 315, 405–408; *Apotheosis of Washington*, 346, *347*, 391–92, 405–406, *406*, 407, *407*, 408; Capitol frescoes, 206–10, 212, *213*, 218, 267–70, 283, 297, 300–301, *301*, 302–303, 306, 323, 347, 391–92, 405–406, *406*, 407, *407*, 408; Cincinnatus lunette, 209, 212, 267, 306; *Cornwallis Sues for Cessation of Hostilities Under the Flag of Truce*, 270; death of, 408; *Frieze of American History*, 407–408; House Agriculture Committee Room, 212, *213*, 268–69, 302, 306; Senate corridors, 300–301, *301*, 302, 323

Bryan, William, 264

Buchanan, James, 129, 239, 253–54, 372; Capitol project and, 258–66, 269, 383, 343–54; Jefferson Davis and, 324–34, 370; inauguration of, 254–56, *256*, 257; Lecompton debate and, 290–95, 303–304, 311; Montgomery Meigs and, 258–66, 269, 276–82, 288–90, 296–302, 316–17, 331–39, 344, 369–71; as patronage politician, 261–65, 292; slave debate and, 256–58, 279, 290–95, 303–304, 310, 328

Bulfinch, Charles, 19–21, 24, 33, 35, 37, 55, 89, 258; dome, 20–21, 61, 103, 182, 186, 226–29, 242; Rotunda plan, 19–21, 61, 73, 79

Butler, Andrew, 235–36

Cabin John Bridge, 260, 337, 373

Calhoun, John C., 10, 33, 36, 38–39, 44, 49, 51–52, 54, 55, 185, 321

California, 9, 25; annexation, 56; statehood, 53, 58–59, 61, 65, 66

Cameron, Simon, 374–76, 384

Campbell, Archibald, 138

Campbell, Lewis D., 230, 239

Campbell, William, 46

Camuccini, Vincenzo, 208

Canova, Antonio, 208

Capitol, U.S., 3, 9–10, *10*, 11; beginnings of, 11–30; Buchanan inauguration, 254–56, *256*, 257; early plans, 14–21; 1850–51 design contest, 69–87; of 1851, 88–91, *91*, 92–106; of 1852, 107–24; of 1853, 124–44, 145–62; of 1854, 163–84, 185–205; of 1855, 206–25, 226–31; of 1856, 230–52; of 1857, 253–56, *256*, 257–73, 274–84; of 1858, *279*, 284–95, 296–317; of 1859, 318–39, 342–50; of 1860, 350–64, 369–71; of 1863, 365–67, *367*, 368; as hospital, 390; Library fire, 102–104, 165; as source of national pride, 357; space problem, 11, 36; symmetry, 24, 35, 60; wartime, 365–68, 373–74, *374*, 375, *375*, 376–77, *377*, 378, *378*, 379–80, *380*, 381, *381*, 382–88, *388*, 389–94, *394*, 403–408, *411*; wings designs, 35–36, 37–38, 59–64, 67–68, 69–87, 88–106, 107–24, 151–56; War of 1812 and, 17–18, *18*, 97; *see also* Capitol Extension; Dome, Eastern Extension; East Front; House chamber; Rotunda; Senate chamber; *specific architects and sections*; West Front

Capitol Extension: altered-drawings affair, 285–89, 292, 296; Army control of, 136–44, 145–62, 164, 168–73, 178–82, 240, 242, 260–66, 287, 345, 384–86; Congressional debate and funding, 48, 59–64, 67–68, 70–87, 101–102, 108–19, 124–25, 132–34, 161–62, 173, 188–92, 200, 204, 214–20, 239–46, 254, 267, 304–10, 312, 352–57, 363, 384–89, 403–404; cornerstone ceremony, 86–87, 90; custody of drawings, 296–97, 299–300, 316, 336–38, 344–46; early proposals, 14–30; 1850–51 design contest, 69–87; of 1851, 88–91, *91*, 92–106; of 1852, 107–24; of 1853, 124–44, 145–62; of 1854, 163–84, 185–205; of 1855, 206–25, 226–31; of 1856, 230–52; of 1857, 253–56, *256*, 257–73, 274–84; of 1858, *279*, 284–95, 296–317; of 1859, 318–39, 342–50; of 1860, 350–53, *353*, 354–64, 369–71; of 1863, 365–67, *367*, 368; foundations, 96–97, 107, 108–19, 126, 132, 134, 143, 148–49, 150; Greek Cross plan, 34–36, 75; House chamber opening, 270–73; Interior Department control of, 386–87, 404; Meigs-Davis plan, 151–52, *152*, 153–62, 168–84, 185–205, 206–25, 226–52, 253–95, 296–317; Meigs dismissed from, 339, 343–45, 369; Meigs as supervisor of, 139–44, 145–62, 163–84, 185–205, 206–25, 226–52, 253–95, 296–344; Meigs-Walter rivalry, 148–51, 159–62, 170–73, 184, 186–91, 200–205, 216, 245–46, 274–90, 296–300, 313–17, 329–39, 344–47, 372–76, 386, 392, 398, 404–405, 410–11; military rule dispute, 168–73, 178–82, 287; Mills proposals, 31–38, 58, 59–64, 67–68, 73–76, 79, *79*, 80; photography of drawings, 250–51, *251*, 252; Senate chamber opening, 321–22, *322*, 323–26; slavery debate and, 176–77; Walter-Fillmore plan, 70–72, 77–87, 88–106, 107–24, 151, 155–56, 276; wartime, 365–68, 373–74, *374*, 375, *375*, 376–77, *377*, 378, *378*, 379–80, *380*, 381, *381*, 382–88, *388*, 389–94, *394*, 403–408, *411*; West Front fountain, 318–20, *320*, 323; wings designs, 35–36, 37–38, 59–64, 67–68, 69–87, 88–106, 107–24, 151–56; *see also* acoustics; art and decoration; brick; columns; construction; dome; façade; foundations; funding; heating; labor; lighting; marble; roofs; stone; ventilation; windows; wings; wood

carpenters, 96, 123, 133, 135

carpets, 107, 153, 154, 255, 270, 300, 319, 322, *322*

Carstens, Emmerich, 197, 207, 221, 337

carvings, 195

Casali, Frederick, 212–14; snake door handles and knobs, 212–14, *214*

Cass, Lewis, 29, 52, 68, 110, 129, 164, 236

cast iron, 3–4, 104–106, 119, 186, 243, 346; brackets, 248–49, *249*; Civil War use of, 350; contracts, 119, 249, 275, 348–50, 371, 376; dome, 183–84, 186–87, 203–205, 226–29, 239–40, 246, 248–50, 299, 315, *315*, 346–50, 354–55, 365–68, 384, 421n18; dome peristyle columns, 248–49, *249*, *278*, 299, 315, *315*; fixtures, 243, 245; Library, 104–106, 119, *165*, 183–84, 186, 349; load-bearing, 105, 315; stamped with Meigs's name, 153, 202, 245, 284

Catholicism, 4, 192–94

ceilings, 195–96; iron, 243; ornamentation, 195–96, 202–203, 205, *213*, 269, 270, 300–301, *301*, 323

cement, 97, 179; contracts, 97

chairs, 153, 315–36, 318–19, 320–21, 322; upholstery, 300, 319, 322; vice president's, 315–16

Champion, Samuel, 122, 224, 245, 261, 264

Chandler, Joseph R., 72, 77, 80, 83, 110

Chapman, John G., *Baptism of Pocahontas*, 174

Chase, Salmon P., 167, 382

Chattanooga, 321, 393, 394

Chesapeake and Ohio Canal, 191

Chickamauga, 321

China, 105

cholera, 12

Civil and Diplomatic Appropriations Bill, 48, 68

Civil Engineer and Architect's Journal, The, 153

Civil War, 50, 51, 196, 321, 365–99, 402, 427n33; beginning of, 377–82; end of, 399; events leading to, 358–64, 371–72; iron used in, 350; muzzle-loading rifle and, 222

Clark, Edward, 90, 408

Clarke, John H., 69, 79

Clay, Clement C., 329, 400

Clay, Henry, 10, 21, 37, 52–54, 55, 129, 185, 192, 321; compromise debate and, 52–54, 58–59, 61–62, 65–66, 94, 95, 419n27; as snuff user, 56

Clay, Virginia, 230, 329, 400

Clayton, John M., 244

Cluskey, Charles B., 25–26, 77, 80–85, 93, 421n18

Cluskey report, 25–27, 80

Cobb, Howell, 63, 64

Collamer, Jacob, 307–308

Colorado, 25

Columbus doors, 212, 219, 355, 404

columns, 155, 249, 249, 255, 279–80, 299, 382; dome peristyle, 248–49, 249, 278, 299, 315, 315; monolithic marble, 155, 160–61, 185, 243, 255, 279–80, 314–15, 334–36, 342–43, 350–53, 353, 354, 355, 363, 371, 389, 391, 404; sandstone, 155

Committee of Thirteen, 363

compromise debate, 36–37, 52–54, 56–59, 61–62, 64–67, 94, 95, 127, 419n27

Confederate Army, 321, 390, 393, 399, 403

Confederate States of America, 363, 366, 372, 383, 390, 393, 395, 399

Congress, 4, 5, 9–11, 17–18, 30, 44, 137, 351; art commission, 304–10, 312, 342, 355–56, 358; Borland investigation, 121–26, 132–38, 149, 150; Capitol improvement debate and funding, 48, 59–64, 67–68, 70–87, 101–102, 108–19, 124–25, 132–34, 161–62, 173, 188–92, 200, 204, 214–20, 239–46, 254, 267, 304–10, 312, 352–57, 363, 384–89, 403–404; compromise debate, 36–37, 52–54, 56–59, 61–62, 94, 95, 127, 419n27; dome appropriation, 214–20, 239–46, 254; early Capitol construction and, 17–19, 21–25, 26; 1850–51 Capitol design contest and, 69–87; 1854 elections, 194–95, 218, 223, 239; 1856 elections, 230; 1858 elections, 292, 304; events leading up to Civil War, 358–64; Floyd investigation, 348–50, 355, 363, 369, 371; Kansas-Nebraska Act, 163–68, 177, 180, 182, 192, 223, 230, 256; Know-Nothingism, 192–95, 218, 223–24; Lecompton debate, 290–94, 294, 295, 296, 303–304, 311, 361; Marshall proviso, 306–10, 312; McNair committee, 108–19; Montgomery Meigs and, 158–62, 164, 170–73, 188, 193, 203–204, 214–20, 239–46, 267, 277–82, 288–89, 296, 313, 385–90; Mills proposals and, 31–18, 59–64, 67–68, 73–76, 79–80; Omnibus Bill, 58–59, 65–67; slavery debate, 50–54, 56–59, 64–67, 164–68, 177, 192, 195, 233–38, 255–57, 290–95, 303–304, 310, 328, 358–64, 419n16; Thomas Walter and, 89–90, 94, 105, 108, 125, 188, 203–204; Wilmot Proviso, 51, 53, 56

Congress House, 13

Congressional Globe, 62–63, 161

Connecticut, 98

Connolly, John, 314, 335–36, 351–54, 389

Connolly marble, 314, 335–36, 351–54, 363, 389

Constitution, U.S., 56, 327

Constitutional Union Party, 354

Constitution Avenue, 27

construction, 14; accusations of kickbacks
and fraud, 4, 109, 120–26, 132–37;
altered-drawings affair, 285–89, 292,
296; Army control of, 136–44, 145–62,
164, 168–73, 178–82, 240, 242, 260–66,
287, 345, 384–86; cast iron, 104–106,
119, *165*, 193–84, 186, 203–205,
226–29, 239–40, 346; Congressional
debate and funding, 48, 59–64, 67–68,
70–87, 101–102, 108–19, 124–25,
132–34, 161–62, 173, 188–92, 200, 204,
214–20, 239–46, 254, 267, 304–10, 312,
352–57, 363, 384–89, 403–404;
cornerstone ceremony, 86–87, 90;
custody of drawings, 296–97, 299–300,
316, 336–38, 344–46; dome, 226–28,
228, 229, *229*, 239–30, 248–49, *249*,
250, *256*, 275, *278*, 299, 315, *315*, 334,
342, 346–50, 354–55, 365–68, *374*, *375*,
377, *378*, 384, 388, *388*, 389, 391, *394*;
early, 14–30; of 1851, 88–91, *91*,
92–106; of 1852, 107–24; of 1853,
124–44, 145–62; of 1854, 163–84,
185–205; of 1855, 206–25, 226–31; of
1856, 230–52; of 1857, 253–56, *256*,
257–73, 274–84; of 1858, *279*, 284–95,
296–317; of 1859, 318–39, 342–50; of
1860, 350–53, *353*, 354–64, 369–71; of
1863, 365–67, *367*, 368; final phases of,
275; foundations, 90, 96–97, 107,
108–19, 126, 132, 134, 143, 148–49,
150; Interior Department control of,
386–87, 404; Latrobe supervision,
16–19; Meigs-Davis plan, 151–62,
168–84, 185–205, 206–25, 226–52,
253–95, 296–317; Meigs as supervisor
of, 139–44, 145–62, 163–84, 185–205,
206–25, 226–52, 253–95, 296–344,
382–89; Meigs-Walter rivalry, 148–51,
159–62, 170–73, 184, 186–91, 200–205,
216, 245–46, 274–90, 296–300, 313–17,
329–39, 344–47, 372–76, 386, 392, 398,
404–405, 410–11; mess and noise, 89,

91, 107, 127, 158, 228, *229*, 366;
removal of old dome, 226–29, 242;
shoddy, 16–17, 120, 135; Walter-
Fillmore plan, 70–72, 77–87, 88–106,
107–24, 151, 155–56, 276; War of 1812
and, 17–18, *18*, 97; wartime, 365–68,
373–74, *374*, 375, *375*, 376–77, *377*,
378, *378*, 379–80, *380*, 381, *381*,
382–88, *388*, 389–94, *394*, 403–408,
411; *see also* acoustics; architects; art
and decoration; brick; Capitol
Extension; cast iron; contracts;
foundations; heating; labor; lighting;
marble; *specific contractors and
materials*; stone; ventilation

contest, Capitol design (1850–51), 69–87

contracts, 97–101, 109, 131, 134–35, 158,
180, 260–65, 275, 279–82, 289, 389;
accusation of kickbacks and fraud,
120–26, 132–37; Aqueduct, 260–65,
280–82, 296, 298, 334, 369–70; brick, 97,
98, 120, 123, 158–59, 180, 190; cast iron,
119, 249, 275, 348–50, 371, 376; dome,
249, 348–50, 371, 376; Floyd corruption
and, 348–50, 355, 363, 369, 371; granite,
343; lumber, 97; marble, 97–101, 110,
120–21, 134–35, 154, 158, 174, 275,
279–80, 299, 314, 334–36, 350–54, 363,
371, 391; one-price-fits-all, 349–50;
pediment sculpture, 174; Post Office,
298–99, 313, 334, 336–37, 371;
ventilation and heating, 276–77, 298–99,
313, 334, 336–37, 371; *see also* art and
decoration; construction; *specific artists,
contractors, materials, and services*

Cooper, James, 125

Cooper, William J., 362

copper, 21, 26, 358; dome, 34, 182, 226,
227, 228; plates stamped with Meigs's
name, 152–53, 284

cornerstones, 284; ceremony, 86–87, 90;
inscribed with Meigs's name, 284

corridors, 151, 196, 255, *279*; Brumidi,
300–301, *301*, 302, 323; decoration,

196, *196*, 243, 269, 300–301, *301*, 302, 314, 323; in Meigs-Davis plan, 151, *152*

corruption, 4, 120–26, 146, 262, 282; Borland investigation, 121–26, 132–38, 149, 150; construction abuses and kickbacks, 4, 109, 120–26, 132–37; John Floyd charged with, 343–44, 348–50, 355, 363, 369, 371

Corwin, Thomas, 77

craft guilds, 193

Craige, F. Burton, 170, 173, 175, 215

crane, 249

Crawford, Louisa, 341, 342

Crawford, Thomas, 6, 156–57, 174, 197–99, 206, 208, 209, 219–20, 305, 308–309, 355, 357, 389; *America*, 157, 176, *176*, 177, 197, 232, 308; Capitol work, 157, 174–76, *176*, 177, 197–98, *198*, 199, 219–20, 224–25, 231–32, *232*, 233, 246–47, *247*, 248, 308, *309*, 340–42, *342*; death of, 340–42, 403; *Freedom* (plaster model), 340–42, *342*, 357–58, 393; *Freedom* (first version), 219–20, 224, *232*; *Freedom* (second version), 224–25, 231–32, *232*, 233; *Freedom* (final version), 6–7, 246–47, *247*, 248, 258–59, 267, 346, *347*, 365–67, *367*, 368, 392–93, *394*, 402, 403–404; illness of, 258–59, 340–41; pediment designs, 174, 175–76, *176*, 177, 197–98, *198*, 199, 219–20, 232, 308, *309*, 404; *Progress of Civilization*, 157, 176, 197–99

crime, 27, 28, 389–90

Crittenden, John J., 52, 66, 97, 110, 237, 321, 329, 363

Cuba, 5, 167

Custer, George Armstrong, 397

Custis, George Washington Parke, 62

custody of drawings, 296–97, 299–300, 316, 336–38, 344–46

Davis, Jefferson, 5–7, 30, 31, 38, *39*, 40–41, 127, 174, *353*, 357, 376, 406, 418*n*9, 437*n*15; background of, 39–41; James Buchanan and, 324–34, 370; Capitol project and, 5–6, 31–32, 37–38, 48–49, 58–59, 67–68, 69–72, 87, 101, 116, 127–32, 136–44, 148–62, 163–86, 196, 200–23, 231–33, 243, 251, 285, 287, 307–10, 324–26, 329–31, 345, 349, 352, 363, 387, 402, 427*n*29; as congressman, 44, 45; death of, 402–403; education of, 39–40, 42; 1850–51 Capitol design contest and, 69–87; events leading up to Civil War and, 359–64; facial neuralgia of, 95–96, 295, 311, 312, 326, 364; gubernatorial campaign, 95–96; imprisoned at Fortress Monroe, 395, 400, *401*; legacy of, 412; marriage to Knox, 40–42, 95; marriage to Varina, 43–45, 46, 49, 400–401; Montgomery Meigs and, 5–7, 140, 142–45, 148–62, 168–86, 189, 200–205, 220–21, 231–33, 243, 243, 251, 259–60, 265–67, 271, 275, 282, 283, 288–90, 293, 295, 307–10, 318, 320, 329–31, 334, 339, 363, 369–71, 386, 395–96, 398; Mexican War and, 44–47, 49, 51; military career, 40–41, 44–47; military rule dispute and, 168–73, 178–82, 287; Mississippi secession and, 364; personality of, 6, 41–43, 50, 150, 326; physical appearance of, 39, 40, 49; Franklin Pierce and, 127–28, 136–37, 167, 221; postwar life, 139, 399–403; as president of the Confederacy, 321, 372, 393, 395; resolutions, 361–62; *The Rise and Fall of the Confederate Government*, 402; as secretary of war, 39, 127–32, 136–45, 148–62, 167–86, 200–23, 232–33; as senator, 31–32, 37, 39, 47, 48–59, 65–67, 94–95, 131, 233, 237, 282, 293–95, 307–12, 321, 324–34, 360–64; slavery debate, 38, 43, 49, 50–54, 56–59, 65–67, 128, 177, 310–12, 324, 327–28, 357, 360–62, 419*n*16; Richard Stanton and, 94, 162, 164, 168–73, 178–82, 218,

Davis, Jefferson (*cont.*)
  400; Zachary Taylor and, 40–42, 44–47,
  51–54, 62; as a technologist, 221–23;
  unionism of, 38, 41–42, 50–54, 131,
  222–23, 310–12, 327; Thomas Walter
  and, 94, 148–51, 171, 200–205, 330
Davis, Jefferson, Jr., 326
Davis, Joseph, 39, 43, 46, 127
Davis, Margaret, 326
Davis, Samuel, 130, 189
Davis, Varina Howell, 43–44, 45, *45*, 46,
  49, 95, 96, 128, 130, 131, 189, 235, 324,
  326, 328, 364, 395, 398, 399, 400, 403
day's work, 91–92, 96, 158, 265, 305, 390,
  393
decoration, *see* art and decoration
Democratic Party, 5, 43–44, 52, 73, 77, 95,
  127, 129, 148, 150, 163, 166–68, 192, 195,
  218, 230, 239, 242, 277, 292, 304, 324,
  328; 1856 presidential election, 253–54;
  1860 presidential election, 354, 360–63;
  Philadelphia Democratic plot against
  Meigs, 277–82; split of, 354, 360–62
derrick, 4, 6, 227, *229*, 248, 249, 250, 266,
  275, *278*, 334, 368
desks, 123, 153; Senate, 54, 55, 60, 320,
  322, 323, 379–80; vice president's, 323
Dickens, Charles, 55; *American Notes*, 26
Dickinson, Daniel S., 58
Dickinson, Edward, 217
Dimmick, Milo, 112
disease, 12, 42
District of Columbia, 12, *12*, 113, 18, 29, 38
Dome, 3, 6, 26, 79, 182–84, 203–205, 212,
  214–20, 226–29, 255, 290, 313, 339;
  brackets, 248–49, *249*, 255, 275;
  Bulfinch, 20–21, 61, 103, 182, 186,
  226–29, 242; cast iron, 183–84, 186–87,
  203–205, 226–29, 239–40, 246, 248–50,
  299, 315, *315*, 346–50, 354–55, 365–68,
  384, 421*n*18; contracts, 249, 348–50,
  371, 376; construction, 226–28, *228*, 229,
  229, 239–30, 248–49, *249*, 250, *256*, 275,
  278, 299, 315, *315*, 334, 342, 346–50,

354–55, 365–68, *374, 375, 377, 378*, 384,
  388, *388*, 389, 391, *394*; copper, 34, 226,
  227, 228; derrick, 4, 6, 227, *229*, 248,
  249, 250, 255, 275, *278*, 334, 368;
  Freedom installation, 365–67, *367*, 368,
  391, 392, *394*, 403–404; fresco mural
  (*Apotheosis of Washington*), 346, *347*,
  391–92, 405–406, *406*, 407, *407*, 408;
  funding, 214–20, 239–46, 254; Meigs,
  204–205, 215–16, 275; Mills, 60–61;
  peristyle columns, 248–49, *249*, *278*, 299,
  315, *315*; removal of old dome, 226–29,
  242; revised design, 346–47, *347*,
  348–50; statue, 219–20, 224–25, 231–32,
  232, 233, 246–47, *247*, 248, 305, 340–42,
  342, 346, *347*, 357–58, 365–67, *367*, 368,
  392–93, *394*, 402, 403–404; Thornton,
  14, *15*; Walter, 182–84, 186–88, 203, *203*,
  204–205, 214–20, 226–29, 239, 248–50,
  275, 284, 287, 315, 346–47, *347*, 348–50,
  365–67, *367*, 368, 391; weight of,
  239–40, 315, 354
Doolittle, James R., 356
doors, 211–12, 243; bronze, 199, 212, 269,
  355, 389, 404, 405; Columbus, 212, 219,
  355, 404, 405; frames, 255; snake
  handles and knobs, 212–14, *214*
Dorsey, Sarah, 400, 401, 402
Douglas, Stephen A., 65–66, 94, 129, 133,
  163, 210, 233, 244, 251, 253, 292, 304,
  329, 354, 361–62, 430*n*6; Kansas-
  Nebraska Act and, 165–68
Downing, Andrew Jackson, 99
Doyle, James, 237–38
drapery, 153
Drinkard, William, 333, 336–38, 344
Dry Tortugas, 370–71, 372, 373
Duncan, James H., 112
dysentery, 12

Easby, William, 93–94, 103, 120–25, 132,
  133, 134, 136, 155, 158, 170
Eastern Extension, 35, 59, 70–76, 78;

1850–51 design contest, 70–87; Mills plan, 34–36, 73–76, *79*, 80; Walter plan, 73, 77–78, 81–87

East Front, *10*, 16, 25, 34, 35, 36, 67, 75, 89, 185, 203, 229, 248, *353*, *388*; Greek Cross plan, 34–36, 75

East Portico, *10*, 14, *15*, 21, 22, 26, 126, 156, 174, 255, *256*, *309*, 374, *388*, 391, *394*, 404

Eastman, Seth, 175, 211

economy, 11, 13, 127

Elliot, William, 73–74, 77, 78, 80, 81

encaustic tiles, 196, *196*, 221, 243, 248, 267, *271*, 323

engineers, *see* Meigs, Montgomery C.; *specific engineers*

English, William H., 303

English Bill, 303

Everett, Edward, 156, 258

Ewbank, Thomas, 99

Ewing, Thomas, 26

Extension project, *see* Capitol Extension

façade, 15, 70, 255, *256*, 268; marble, 155; Meigs redesign, 155–56, 160–61; Thornton design, 14, *15*; Walter-Fillmore plan, 155, 156

fans, 151, 211

Fessenden, William Pitt, 293–94

Fillmore, Millard, 32, 64, 70, 107, 108, 126, 129, 141, 185, 253, 254, 258, 261, 267, 302, 375; Capitol project and, 70–71, 77–87, 88–106, 108–26, 128, 132, 151, 155; compromise debate and, 64–66

fire, 28, 224; 1851 Library of Congress, 102–104, 165; proofing, 31, 105, 165; War of 1812, 17–18, *18*

First Bull Run, 390

Fish, Hamilton, 241

floors, 97, 196, *196*

Florence, Thomas B., 112, 113, 277

Florida, 23, 25, 370–71, 372, 376, 377

Floyd, John B., 259, *263*, 292, 386; Capitol project and, 259–66, 277–82, 288–90, 296–302, 314–17, 330–39, 343–55, 358, 369–72; corruption charges against, 343–44, 348–50, 355, 363, 369, 371; William Franklin and, 348–54; Montgomery Meigs and, 259–66, 276–82, 288–90, 296–302, 314–17, 330–39, 343–44, 369–71

Foot, Solomon, 284, 286–87

Foote, Henry S., 58, 66, 94–95, 128, 129

Forney, John W., 278–79

Fort Crawford, 40

Fort Jefferson, 370–71, 372

Fort Pickens, 376–77, 381

Fortress Monroe, 395, 400, *401*

Fort Sumter, 371, 376, 377

Fort Taylor, 372

foundations, 67, 90, 96–97, 107, 108–19, 126, 132, 134, 143, 148–49, 150, 240, 354; McNair investigation on, 108–19; Meigs redesign, *152*, 154, 168; safety inspections, 108–19, 148–49, 150; trenches, *91*, 96–97, 107, 154

fountain, West Front, 318–20, *320*, 323

Fowler, Charles, 119, 180, 186, 245–46, 345, 346, 349–50, 367, 373, 384, 408

France, 4, 14; Revolution, 6, 176, 177

Franklin, Benjamin, 220–21, 301, 323

Franklin, William B., 339, 345–46; as Capitol architect, 345–46, 348–54, 373; John Floyd and, 348–54

free blacks, 6–7, 28–29

Freedom Triumphant in War and Peace, 6–7, 219–20, 258–59, 267, 340–42, 346, 402–404; casting, 341, 357–58, 392–93; final version, 6–7, 246–47, *247*, 248, 258–59, 267, 346, *347*, 365–67, *367*, 368, 392–93, *394*, 402, 403–404; first version, 219–20, *232*; headdress, 246, *247*, 248, 402, 403–404; installation, 365–67, *367*, 368, 391, 392, *394*, 403–404; plaster model, 340–42, *342*, 357–58, 393; second version, 224–25, 231–32, *232*, 233; shipping, 341–42

Freehling, William W., 362
Freeport Doctrine, 361
Free-Soilers, 192, 230
free-state movement, 52–54, 56–59, 61–62, 64–67, 223, 233–38, 254, 258, 291–95
French, Benjamin Brown, 136–37, 219, 272–73, 385, 393, 408
French immigrants, 195
frescoes and murals, 4, 174–75, 187, 206–10, 229, 248, 267–70, 283–84, 300–303, 305, 307, 323, 355; Brumidi, 206–10, 212, *213*, 218, 267–70, 283, 297, 300–301, *301*, 302–303, 306, 323, 347, 391–92, 405–406, *406*, 407, *407*, 408; dome, 346, *347*, 391–92, 405–406, *406*, 407, *407*, 408; techniques, 209, 210; *see also* art and decoration; painting; *specific artists and works*
fugitive slave laws, 53, 58
Fulton, Robert, 301
funding, 4, 18, 21, 24, 48, 59–64, 67–68, 148; Aqueduct, 244, 245, 246, 254, 260, 312, 337, 369–70; Congressional debate and appropriations, 48, 59–64, 67–68, 70–87, 101–102, 108–19, 124–25, 132–34, 161–62, 173, 188–92, 200, 204, 214–20, 239–46, 254, 267, 304–10, 312, 352–57, 363, 384–89, 403–404; dome, 214–20, 239–46, 254; early, 18; Library of Congress construction, 104–106; of 1853, 132–34, 161–62; shortages, 101–102; *see also* contracts
furniture, 54, 55, 60, 123, 153, 255, 300, 315–16, 318–19, 322, *322*, 323, 379–80

garbage, 27, 28
gardens, 37
Gardiner, Richard, 150
Gardiner, William H., 234
gas lighting, 22, 28, 151, 266, 271, 272
Geary, John, 254
General Post Office, 33, 73, 219; *see also* Post Office Extension

Georgetown, 318, 319
Georgia, 5, 396, 410
Georgian style, 14, *15*
German immigrants, 193, 218, 242
Germany, 4, 174, 341
Gettysburg, 321, 365
Girard College, Philadelphia, 72, 72, 154, 183
Gobright, Lawrence, 30, 86
gold, 9, 132
gold leaf bronze, 132
granite, 86, 92, 280, 343
Grant, Julia Dent, 403
Grant, Ulysses S., 175, 393, 396, 399, 402, 403, 428*n*33
Great Britain, 5, 156, 270; cast iron used in, 105; House of Commons, 274; War of 1812, 17–18, *18*, 97
Great Falls, 141, 142, 213, 260, 284, 318
Greek Cross plan, 34–36, 75
Green, Constance McLaughlin, 33
Greenough, Horatio, 22; statue of Washington, 22, 34
Grier, Robert C., 257
Grow, Galusha, A., 293

Hale, John, 386
Hallet, Stephen, 14–15, 33
Hall of Columns, *271*
Harlan, James, 408
Harpers Ferry, Virginia, 378; John Brown's raid at, 358–60
Harris, James, 238
Harry, Philip, 78
Harvard University, 105
heating, 11, 23, 32, 55, 78, 143, 266, 443*n*8; inadequate, 11, 22, 55, 107; in Meigs-Davis plan, 151, 152, 153, 164, 203, 245, 266, 271, 272, 276–77, 329, 405; Post Office contracts, 298–99, 334, 336–37, 371; Senate, 11, 22, 32, 55
Heebner, Charles, 279, 280, 391

Henry, Joseph, 74, 78, 99, 131, 154, 158, 161, 168, 188, 241, 245, 271, 272, 405

Herbert, Philemon T., 233–35

Hibbard, Harry, 217

Hole in the Wall, 22–23

Holt, Joseph, 371–74

Holt, Michael F., 361

hot blast furnace, 105

hotels, 26–27, 28, 233, 328–29

House Agriculture Committee Room, 212, *213*, 268–69, 302, 306, 307

House chamber, 10, *10*, 11, 16, *24*, 32, 63–64, *343*, 357; acoustics, 11, 17, 18, 20, 23–24, *24*, 25, 32, 33–34, 35, 55, 63, 107, 161, 200, 266, 271, 272, 329; art and decoration, 156–57, 174–78, 187, 195–99, 202–13, *213*, 214, *214*, 219–21, 248, 258–59, 266–70, 272–73, 283–84, 300–301, *301*, 302–10; completion of, 266–73; early construction, 14–30; of 185, 88–106; of 1852, 107–24; of 1853, 124–44, 145–62; of 1854, 163–84, 185–205; of 1855, 206–25, 226–31; of 1856, 230–52; of 1857, 253–73, 274–84; of 1858, 284–95, 296–317; of 1859, 318–39, 342–50; of 1860, 350–64, 369–71; fire of 1814, 17–18, *18*; House of Columns, *271*; Meigs-Davis plan, 151–52, *152*, 153–62, 168–84, 185–205, 206–25, 226–52, 253–74, 296–317; Mills proposals, 31–38, 59–64, 67–68, 73–76, 79, *79*, 80; opening of, 270–73; the Oven, 16; pediments and statuary, 156–57, 174–77, 187, 220, 242, 258–59, 269, 306, 405; press on, 271–72; seating capacity, 211; ventilation, 151–54, 210–11, 266, 272, 274–77, 329; Walter-Fillmore plan, 70–72, 77–87, 88–106, 107–24, 151, 155–56, 276; wartime, 373–74, *374*, 375, *375*, 376–77, *377*, 378, *378*, 379–85, 403–408, *411*; windowless, 153–54, 160, 211; wings design, 35–38, 59–64, 67–68, 69–87, 88–106, 107–24, 151–56

House Committee on Public Buildings and Grounds, 24, 25, 31, 60, 64, 67, 68, 77, 94, 110, 113, 160, 162, 164, 169, 215, 240, 243; Capitol design contest, 77–87

House of Representatives, U.S., 3, 10, 35, 328; Capitol improvement debate and funding, 48, 59–64, 67–68, 70–87, 101–102, 108, 114–19, 124–25, 132–34, 161–62, 173, 188–92, 200, 204, 214–20, 239–46, 254, 267, 304–10, 312, 352–57, 363, 384–89, 403–404; Kansas-Nebraska Act, 163–68, 177, 180, 192, 223, 256; Lecompton debate and brawl, 290–94, *294*, 295, 296, 303–304, 311, 361; McNair committee, 108–19; *see also* Congress, U.S.; House chamber

House Ways and Means Committee, 239

Houston, John W., 62, 63, 64

Houston, Sam, 11, 34, 66, 111, 121, 312, 431*n*20; on Capitol decoration, 308–10; Montgomery Meigs and, 121, 170–71

Houston committee, 121–26, 132–38, 149, 150, 154–55; report, 134–38, 149

Humphreys, A. A., 23–24

Hunter, Robert M. T., 37, 59–61, 67–68, 69, 70, 74, 167, 168; Capitol project and, 69–76, 77, 94, 110–11, 116–19, 120, 125, 170–72, 240, 244, 276, 307, 310

Hunter report, 59–62

Illinois, 255, 361

immigrant labor, 4, 28, 29, 90, 193–95, 206–14, 218, 234, 242, 267, 270, 300–303, 304–10, 387, 407

immigration, 4, 192–94

Indians, 40, 211, 246; headdress, 246, *247*, 248; statues of, 197–98, *198*, 199, 211, *309*; treaty negotiations, 211

industrial photography, 250–51, *251*, 252

Ingersoll, Charles J., 261, 262

Interior Department, 244, 334; Capitol construction transferred to, 386–87, 404

Irish immigrants, 192, 193, 218, 234

iron, *see* cast iron; wrought iron
ironworkers, 96, 119
Italian immigrants, 193, 206–10, 218, 242, 387
Italy, 4, 156, 206, 208, 341; marble, 280, 314, 334, 336, 351, 363
Ives, Chauncey, 269

Jackson, Andrew, 21, 23, 33, 38, 44, 133, 148, 258, 292, 357
James, Charles T., 164, 211, 216
Janes, Beebe & Co., 119, 348, 349
Janes, Fowler, Kirtland & Co., 348–50, 384, 387, 389, 391, 406
Jefferson, Thomas, 11, 12, 13, 14, 23, 103, 148; Capitol construction and, 16–17; portraits of, 221, 268
Jenkins Hill, 13
Johnson, Andrew, 408, 409
Johnson, Robert Ward, 164
Joint Library Committee of Congress, 307
Jones, John W., 102–103

Kansas, 163, 166, 245, 254; Bleeding Kansas, 5, 168, 220, 223, 233, 235–38, 254; Lecompton debate, 290–95, 296, 303–304, 311, 361; Pottawatomie massacre, 237–38, 242, 438*n*34; slavery debate, 164–68, 220, 223, 233, 235–38, 256, 257, 290–95, 304–305
Kansas-Nebraska Act, 163–68, 177, 180, 182, 192, 200, 223, 230, 244, 253, 256, 311, 430*n*6
Keating, Thomas, 234–35
Keith, John, 368, 379, 383
Keitt, Lawrence M., 236, 237, 293
Kemble, Gouverneur, 174
Kensett, John F., 355
Kentucky, 39, 52, 54
kickbacks and fraud, 4, 109, 120–26, 132–37, 146, 262, 282; Borland investigation, 121–26, 132–38, 149, 150

King, William R., 126
Kingsley, Nathan, 122, 133
Kirkwood House, 27
Know-Nothings, 4, 192–95, 218, 223–24, 230, 234, 253, 254, 261, 264, 270, 341, 351, 354, 407

labor, 28–29, 91–94, 96, 158–59, 241, 243; accusations of kickbacks and fraud, 119–26, 132–37; American vs. foreign artisans, 302–303, 304–10; day's work, 91–92, 96, 158, 265, 305, 390, 393; hiring practices, 194, 224, 261–65, 304–10, 316; immigrants, 4, 28, 29, 90, 193–95, 206–14, 218, 234, 242, 267, 270, 300–303, 304–10, 387, 407; layoffs, 101–102, 107, 108, 316, 337; patronage hires, 261–65; relations, 93–94, 158–59, 193, 316, 339; shoddy, 16–17, 159; skilled, 4, 28, 92, 96, 206–10; slave, 28, 29, 92, 164, 392–93, 423*n*10; strikes, 158–59; unskilled, 28, 96; wages, 96, 241, 250; wartime, 382, 387, 390; *see also specific types of labor*
Lambdin, James R., 355
Lane, Harriet, 262
Lane, Samuel, 19
Lapsley & Thomas, 299, 336, 337
Latrobe, Benjamin Henry, 16–19, 20, 33, 54, 89
Lauman, George, 263–64, 274, 277, 278, 298
Lawrence, Kansas, 223, 236, 237
leaks, 17, 389
Lecompton debate, 290–94, *294*, 295, 296, 303–304, 311, 361
Lee, Robert E., 148, 316, 359, 396, 398, 399, 402, 406
Lee marble, 98–100, *100*, 101, 120, 155, 279, 314, 335, 336, 363, 391, 404
L'Enfant, Pierre Charles, 13–14, 15, 23, 33, 89
Leslie, Charles, 175

Leutze, Emanuel, 174, 197, 207;
  Washington Crossing the Delaware, 174;
  *Washington Rallying the Troops at the
  Battle of Monmouth*, 197; *Westward the
  Course of Empire Takes Its Way*, 197, 389
liberty caps, 6–7, 176, *176*, 177, 224–25,
  231–32, *232*, 246, 247, 402
Library of Congress, 11, 16, 18, 34, 75, 77,
  89, 102–106, 108, 141, *165*, 380,
  410–11; cast iron construction,
  104–106, 119, *165*, 183, 186, 349; 1851
  fire, 102–104, 165; 1865 expansion, 408;
  Mills plan, 34, 35, 73; ornamentation,
  103, 132; Walter designs, 104–106, 111,
  119, 132, 149, 153, 160, 164, *165*, 183,
  186, 408
lighting, 18, 78, 154, 164; gas, 22, 28, 151,
  266, 271, 272
lime, 97
Lincoln, Abraham, 197, 242, 304, 354,
  361, 363, 366, 368, 371, 386, 402;
  assassination of, 395–97, 400, 405, 406;
  Civil War and, 378, 381; inauguration
  of, 372, 374, *375*; Montgomery Meigs
  and, 369, 376–77, 383, 396
Little Falls, 260, 318, 319
London, 60, 183, 340
Lost Cause, 139, 401, 402
Louisiana, 29
Louisiana Purchase, 5, 163, 166
Lovejoy, Owen, 306
lumber, *see* wood
lunettes, 207, 208, 209, 212, *213*

Macomb, John N., 378
made ground, 97
Madison, James, 17, 18, 19, 103
Maine, 326, 327
malaria, 12, 42, 95
Mall, 13, 20, 22, 26, 33, 37, 50, 62, 85, 89,
  90, 93, 97, 102
mantelpieces, 248, 255
manumission, 176–77, 224–25

marble, 75, 92, 97–101, 110, 111, 120–21,
  154–55, 193, 229, 241, 243, 255, 322;
  commission, 99; contracts, 97–101, 110,
  120–21, 134–35, 154, 158, 174, 275,
  279–80, 299, 314, 334–36, 350–54, 363,
  371, 391; finishing, 120, 246, 275, 299,
  379; hauling, 158; Italian, 280, 314, 334,
  336, 351, 363; Meigs redesign and, 154,
  161, 162, 169, 174, 185–86, 200, 243,
  255, 334–36, 363; monolithic columns,
  155, 160–61, 185, 243, 255, 279–80,
  314–15, 334–36, 342–43, 350–53, *353*,
  354, 355, 363, 371, 389, 391, 404;
  quarries, 92, 98–100, *100*, 101, 155, 162,
  279–80, 314, 335–36, 350–54
Marcy, William L., 129
Marine Band, 66
Marshall, Humphrey, 306, 312
Marshall proviso, 306–10, 312
Maryland, 11, 98, 191, 253, 254
Mason, James M., 244, 329
Masonic ceremony, 15, 22
masonry, *see* marble; sandstone; stone;
  stonemasons
Massachusetts, 98, 119, 147, 327
Masterton-Smith, 99, 101
materials, *see* construction; *specific
  materials*
McClelland, Robert, 132–34, 137–39
McClelland, Thomas, 78, 85–86
McCormick, Cyrus, 268
McKnight, Robert, 403
McNair, John A., 108–14, 123, 134
McNair committee, 108–19
McNevin, John, 269
Meehan, John S., 103, 105
Meigs, Charles J., 147, 260, 332
Meigs, John Rodgers, 213, 214, 331; death
  of, 397–98, 405, 453*n*6; West Point
  appointment, 288, 331–34
Meigs, Louisa Rodgers, 147, 199, 212, 271,
  394, 397
Meigs, Montgomery C., 3–7, 139–43, *143*,
  144, *396*, 406, 434*n*1; altered-drawings

Meigs, Montgomery C. (*cont.*)
  affair, 285–89, 292, 296; ambition of,
  146, 151–53, 187, 190, 204; Aqueduct
  project, 140–42, *142*, 145, 151, 153, 188,
  195, 244, 254, 260–65, 277, 280–82, 284,
  290, 296, 298, 312, 318–20, *320*, 323,
  334, 337, 344, 369–70, 373; as Army
  quartermaster general, 383, *396*, 410; art
  and decoration plans, 174–78, 187,
  195–99, 202–14, 219–21, 224–25,
  231–33, 243, 246–48, 258–59, 266–73,
  283–84, 297, 300–10, 312–17, 323–24,
  325, 330, 340–42, *342*, 357, 392, 402,
  405; attempt to fire Walter, 373–76;
  background of, 147–48; James
  Buchanan and, 258–66, 269, 276–82,
  288–90, 296–302, 316–17, 331–39, 344,
  369–71; Constantino Brumidi and,
  206–10, 212, 218, 267–70, 283, 297,
  300–303, 306, 392; as Capitol
  supervisor, 139–44, 145–62, 163–84,
  185–205, 206–25, 226–52, 253–95,
  296–344, 382–89; celebrity of, 240–41,
  245; Civil War and, 368–69, 376–78,
  381–89, 393–98; Congress and, 158–62,
  164, 170–73, 188, 193, 203–204, 214–20,
  239–46, 267, 277–82, 288–89, 296, 313,
  385–87; custody of drawings, 296–97,
  299–300, 316, 336–38, 344–46; Jefferson
  Davis and, 5–7, 140, 142–45, 148–62,
  168–86, 189, 200–205, 220–21, 231–33,
  243, 251, 259–60, 265–67, 271, 275, 282,
  283, 288–90, 293, 295, 307–10, 318, 320,
  329–31, 334, 339, 363, 369–71, 386,
  395–96, 398; death of, 411; death of son
  John, 397–98; dismissed from Capitol
  project, 339, 343–45, 369; dome
  appropriation, 214–20, 239–46, 254;
  dome design, 204–205, 215–16, 275;
  egomania of, 151–53, 202, 240–41, 245,
  277, 283–84; 1854 construction,
  163–84, 185–205; 1855 construction,
  206–25, 226–31; 1856 construction,
  230–52; 1857 construction, 253–73,
  274–84; 1858 construction, 284–95,
  296–317; 1859 construction, 318–39,
  342–44; John Floyd and, 259–66,
  276–82, 288–90, 296–302, 314–17,
  330–39, 343–44, 369–71; grand opening
  of House chamber, 270–73; hatred for
  South, 398; hiring practices and
  bill-paying habits, 194, 224, 261–65,
  280, 304–10, 316; honesty with money,
  146–47, 282, 343–44; illness of, 238–39;
  legacy of, 412; Lincoln and, 369,
  376–77, 383, 396; military rule dispute
  and, 168–73, 178–82, 287; obsession
  with getting "credit," 283–88; paper trail
  of, 298, 316, 337; Patent Office project,
  142; personality of, 3, 145–46, 151–53,
  188, 204, 277; photography and, 250–52;
  poor handwriting of, 146, 199, 332;
  postwar life, 410–11; press and, 169–70,
  172, 272, 274, 302, 343–44; redesign of
  capitol plan, 151–52, *152*, 153–62,
  168–84, 185–205, 206–25, 226–52,
  253–95, 296–317; relief mission to Fort
  Pickens, 376–77, 381; return to
  Washington, 372–76; Rice-Walter plot
  against, 277–82; salary of, 147; stamps
  his name on public works, 152–53, 202,
  245, 284, 412; Richard Stanton and,
  178–82, 188–90, 215–19; Tortugas
  posting, 370–71, 372, 373; Joseph Totten
  and, 139–44, 181, 262; views on slavery,
  5, 177; -Walter rivalry, 148–51, 159–62,
  170–73, 184, 186–91, 200–205, 216,
  245–46, 274–90, 296–300, 313–17,
  329–39, 344–47, 372–76, 386, 392, 398,
  404–405, 410–11
Meigs, Monty, 213
Mexican Cession, 9, 25, 31, 32, 53, 58, 62
Mexican War, 9, 32, 44–47, 49, 51–52,
  140, 269
Mexico, 25, 30, 44–47, 167
Mexico City, 46
Michelangelo, 215
Michigan, 40

Mills, Clark, 357–58, 393
Mills, Robert, 22, 31–38, 77, 79–80, 83, 93, 133, 136, 154, 258, 276; Capitol Extension proposals, 31–38, 58, 59–64, 67–68, 73–76, 79, 79, 80; dome, 60–61; Greek Cross plan, 34–36, 75; replaced by Walter, 83; wings plan, 35–36, 37–38, 58, 59–64, 67–68, 73–76, 79, 79, 80
Minié ball, 222
Minnesota, 255, 256
Minton, Hollins & Co., 196
Mississippi, 5, 31, 38, 42–43, 45, 46, 87, 94, 128, 232, 310, 326, 360, 401; Davis's gubernatorial campaign, 95–96; legislature, 43, 232–33, 327; secession, 364
Mississippi Rifles, 45–47
Mississippi River, 148, 316
Missouri, 57, 166, 168, 223, 255, 291, 419n16
Missouri Compromise, 53, 57, 58, 166–67, 256, 257, 363; repeal of, 167
moldings, 132, 196, 209, 268, 300, 301
Monroe, James, 19–20, 103, 301
Moore, Henry D., 82, 374, 375, 421n32
Morse, Samuel F. B., 406
mosaics, 196, 196
Mount Vernon, 12, 13
Munich, 341, 355, 389
murals, see frescoes and murals
Murder Bay, 27
muskets, 222
muzzle-loading rifles, 222

Napier, Francis Lord, 328–29
Nason, Joseph, 276–77, 298–99
Nason & Dodge, 298–99
National Era, 167
National Hotel, 27, 66, 74, 129
National Intelligencer, 69, 80, 81, 102, 103
National Statuary Hall, 405
nativism, 223–24
Nebraska, 163, 164–68

Neoclassicism, 15, 73, 267, 392
Nevada, 25
Nevins, Allan, 163
New Hampshire, 127
New Mexico, 25, 53, 62, 65
New York, 70, 119, 140, 154, 159, 197, 342
New York City, 93, 119, 333
New York Express, 302
New York Herald, The, 66, 274, 343
New York Times, The, 234, 237, 322, 329, 343
New York Tribune, 66, 302, 393
New York World, 402
New York Zouaves, 379–80
North, 5, 11, 12, 29, 50; Jefferson Davis in, 326–27; increasing antipathy between South and, 222, 310–11, 358–64, 371–72; press, 327, 399; slavery debate, 163–68, 192, 235–38, 290–95, 303–304, 310, 358–64; see also specific states
North Carolina, 191

Oklahoma, 41
Omnibus Bill, 58, 65–67
ornamentation, see art and decoration
Orr, James L., 274, 276
Oven, the, 16
Owen, Robert Dale, Hints on Public Architecture, 36

painting, 19–20, 22, 60, 90, 97, 103, 174–75, 187, 196–97, 243, 248, 255, 268–70, 283–84, 300–303, 305, 307, 323, 355, 387, 389, 391–92, 405–408; history, 19–20, 22; trompe l'oeil, 209, 268, 300, 301, 323, 407; see also art and decoration; frescoes and murals; specific artists and works
Palmer, Erastus Dow, 259, 269; Indian Girl, 259
Panama Railroad, 241
panels, 196, 301

Panic of 1873, 401, 409
Pantheon, Paris, 183, 184
papier-mâché decoration, 153, 195–96, 221, 267, 268
Paris, 60, 183
Patent Office, 33, 142; wings project, 142, 149
patronage, 108, 122, 131, 167, 261–65, 278–79; Buchanan administration, 261–65, 292
Peale, Rembrandt, "porthole" portrait of Washington, 54
Pearce, James A., 32, 37, 59, 65, 204, 215, 216, 244, 251, 271, 284, 287, 290, 307, 356, 386
pediments, 156–57, 174–77, 187, 197–99, 219–20, 242, 268, 308; statuary, 156–57, 174–76, *176*, 177, 187, 197–98, *198*, 199, 219–20, 231, 242, 258–59, 269, 306, 308–309, *309*, 404
pendants, 132, 196
Pennington, William, 360
Pennsylvania, 98, 112, 253, 254, 277, 278
Pennsylvania Avenue, 13, 26–28, *278*, *374*
Pennsylvania Inquirer, 272
Pennsylvanian, 277
Pension Office Building, 410
Philadelphia, 5, 12, 14, 70, 71, 82, 83, 84, 140, 141, 147, 154, 159, 277, 335, 368, 378, 379, 409; Democratic Party plot against Meigs, 277–82
Philadelphia *North American*, 343
photography, 146, 255, 285; industrial, 250–51, *251*, 252
Pierce, Franklin, 5, 126–30, 132, 148, 160, 223, 239, 253, 254, 261, 262, 277, 326, 360, 376, 386, 426n3, 427n29; Capitol project and, 126–28, 132–44, 154, 157, 162, 171, 175, 219, 242–44, 281, 285, 287; Jefferson Davis and, 127–28, 136–37, 167, 221; slavery debate and, 127–28, 166–67, 182, 233–38; Thomas Walter and, 133–34, 258
Pitman shorthand, 146

Pius IX, Pope, 208
plaster, 195, 229, 389
Plumbe, John, Jr., 10
police, Capitol, 93, 102–103
Polk, James K., 25, 44, 46, 47
Poole & Hunt, 245, 249
Poore, Benjamin Perley, 49, 62, 129, 293, 328
porticoes, 156, 382, *388*, 389, 391, *394*, 404; in Meigs redesign, 156, 160–61, 243, 248
Post Office Extension, 221, 254, 282, 290, 296, 344; ventilation and heating contracts, 298–99, 313, 334, 336–37, 371
Potomac River, 11, 12, 13, 141, 142, 145, 284, 318
Pottawatomie massacre, 237–38, 242, 438n34
Potter, David, 36, 361
Powers, Hiram, 156–57, 220, 258, 259, 305; *America*, 220, 258; *The Greek Slave*, 156; statues of Franklin and Jefferson, 220–21
presidential elections: of 1844, 44; of 1848, 29, 30; of 1852, 108, 129–30; of 1856, 239, 253–54; of 1860, 242, 304, 354, 360–63
President's House, 13, 14, 17, 18, 19, 22, 27, 28; see also White House
President's Room, 323, 325, *325*, 402
press, 56, 66, 129, 234; antislavery, 236; on Capitol project, 169–70, 172, 271–72, 274, 302–303, 321–23, 343–44; Northern, 327, 399; Southern, 327; Whig, 116–17; see also specific publications
prostitution, 27
Protestantism, 109, 147, 192, 193, 194
Provest, Alexander, 120, 246, 299, 379, 384, 390
Provest & Winter, 99, 120, 135, 158, 193, 200

quarries, 92, 98–100, *100*, 101, 162, 279–80, 314, 335–36, 350–54; see also marble; specific quarries
Quitman, John A., 95, 96

racism, 193, 234
railways, 300
Reagan, John H., 402
Reid, Philip, 392–93, 423n10
religion, 4, 192–94
Republican Party, 163, 192, 223, 230, 242, 244, 254, 304, 328, 360; 1860 presidential election, 360–63
restaurants, 22–23
Rice, Baird & Heebner, 98–101, 109–10, 120, 121, 135, 154, 155, 158, 170, 174, 279–80, 314, 334–36, 350–53, 441n9
Rice, John, 98, 101, 119, 178, 245, 277–82, 289, 313, 345, 349, 374, 384, 391; plot against Meigs, 277–82
Rice, John H., 403–404
Rice, William, 277, 279
Richardson, Samuel A., 63, 64
Richmond, 393, 399
rifles, 50–51, 222; breech-loading, 222, 312; innovations, 222
Riggs, George, 241
Rinehart, William, 269
Riordan, Jerry, 233–34
Robinson, Charles, 298, 299, 313
Rodgers, John, 147, 332
Roebling, John A., 227, 228, 250
Rogers, Randolph, 211–12, 221, 305, 355, 389; Columbus doors, 212, 219, 355, 404, 405
Rome, 6, 60, 156, 177, 183, 199, 206, 208, 210, 340
roofs, 97, 200, 228; glass, 151; iron, 105, 243; leaky, 17; rotting, 26; skylights, 151, 266, 270; trusses, 190, 229, 255
Rosecrans, William S., 139, 142, 181, 427n33, 428n33
rosettes, 196
Rossiter, Thomas P., 268
Rotunda, 3, 10, 10, 14, 16, 19–21, 22, 34, 75, 103, 156, 174, 182–83, 186, 197, 204, 205, 226, 256, 334, 346, 379, 380, 380, 391, 397, 405, 407; Bulfinch plan, 19–21, 61, 73, 79; frieze, 212; new dome

construction, 226, 228, 240, 248–50; paintings, 19–20, 22
Royal Bavarian Foundry, Munich, 341, 355, 389

St. Charles Hotel, 27
St. Louis, 148
St. Paul's, London, 60, 183, 184, 205
St. Peter's, Rome, 60, 183, 205, 215
sand, 97
sandstone, 15, 21, 25–26, 75, 92, 155, 182–83, 240, 249
San Francisco, 49, 80, 254
sanitation, 27, 28; lack of, 27, 28, 389; wartime, 389–90
sash fasteners, 188
Saturday Club, 188, 250, 345, 348, 351, 473
scaffolding, 226, 227, 228, 349, 367, 394, 408
Schlegal, Fridolin, 269
Schoenborn, August Gottlieb, 90, 91, 190, 193, 205, 345, 366, 387
Schoenborn, Henry, 193
Scott, Dred, 255–58, 291, 361–62
Scott, Winfield, 46, 129–30, 372, 377, 382
sculpture, see statues and sculpture
secession, 234, 327–28, 358, 360, 363–64, 372, 378
Second Bull Run, 390
Senate, U.S., 3, 10, 32, 35, 48–54; Borland investigation, 121–26, 132–38, 149, 150; Capitol improvement debate and funding, 48, 59–64, 67–68, 70–87, 101–102, 108–19, 124–25, 132–34, 161–62, 173, 188–92, 200, 204, 214–20, 239–46, 254, 267, 304–10, 312, 352–57, 363, 384–89, 403–404; 1850–51 Capitol design contest, 69–87; Kansas-Nebraska Act, 163–68, 177, 192, 223, 256; Lecompton debate, 290–95, 296, 303–304, 311, 361; Marshall proviso, 306–10, 312; slavery debate, 50–54, 56–59, 64–67, 164–68, 177, 233–38,

Senate, U.S. (*cont.*)
  255–57, 290–95, 303–304, 310, 328,
  358–64; *see also* Congress, U.S.; Senate
  chamber
Senate chamber, 10, *10*, 11, 16, 32, 49, *353*;
  acoustics, 55, 60, 329; art and
  decoration, 156–57, 174–78, 187,
  195–96, *196*, 197–99, 202–14, 219–21,
  248, 258, 268, 269, 283–84, 297,
  300–301, *301*, 302–10, 314–17, 323–24,
  325; balcony, 55, 55, 322; completion
  of, 318–21; corridors, 300–301, *301*,
  302, 323; debates, 55, *55*, 56; early
  construction, 14–30, 54–55, *55*;
  1851 construction, 88–106; 1852
  construction, 88–106; of 1853, 124–44,
  145–62; of 1854, 163–84, 185–205; of
  1855, 206–25, 226–31; of 1856, 230–52;
  of 1857, 253–73, 274–84; of 1858,
  284–95, 296–317; of 1859, 318–39,
  342–50; of 1860, 350–64, 369–71; fire of
  1814, 17–18, *18*; heating, 11, 22, 32, 55;
  Latrobe, 16–19, 54, 55, *55*; Meigs-Davis
  plan, 151–52, *152*, 153–62, 168–84,
  185–205, 206–25, 226–52, 253–74,
  296–317; Mills proposals, 31–38,
  59–64, 67–68, 73–76, 79, *79*, 80;
  opening of, 321–22, *322*, 323–26; the
  Oven, 16; pediments and statuary,
  156–57, 174–76, *176*, 177, 187, 197–98,
  198, 199, 219–20, 242, 258, 268,
  308–309, *309*, 404; press on, 321–23;
  seating capacity, 211; snuffbox, 56;
  ventilation, 151–54, 210–11, 329;
  Walter-Fillmore plan, 70–72, 77–87,
  88–106, 107–24, 151, 155–56, 276;
  wartime, 373–74, *374*, 375, *375*,
  376–77, *377*, 378, *378*, 379–85,
  403–408, *411*; windowless, 153–54, 160,
  211; wings designs, 35–38, 59–64,
  67–68, 69–87, 88–106, 107–24, 151–56
Senate Committee on Indian Affairs, 104
Senate Committee on Military Affairs,
  31, 49
Senate Committee on Public Buildings,
  31, 34, 59, 61, 67, 68, 69, 94, 110, 116,
  117, 170, 331, 349, 354; Capitol design
  contest, 69–87
Senate Committee on Territories, 361
Senate Finance Committee, 170
Senate Library, 300
Senate Library Committee, 204
Senate Military Affairs Committee, 331
Senate Military Affairs Committee Room,
  300
Senate Naval Affairs Committee Room,
  269, 300
Senate Reception Room, 269, 300
sewage, 27, 28, 389, 390
Seward, William H., 37, 65, 129, 223, 233,
  244–45, 251, 259, 271, 307, 308, 313,
  324, 328–29, 376, 382, 383
Seymour, David, 113
Sheridan, Philip, 397
Sherman, Roger, 269
Sherman, William Tecumseh, 396, 410
Sickles, Dan, 299
skylights, 151, 266, 270
slavery, 5, 38, 49, 126, 368, 379; Davis
  resolutions, 361–62; debate, 5, 29–30,
  50–54, 56–59, 64–67, 127–28, 164–68,
  177, 192, 220, 223, 233–38, 254–58,
  290–95, 303–304, 310, 328, 358–64,
  419*n*16; Dred Scott case, 255–58, 291,
  361–62; Harpers Ferry raid and,
  358–60; in Kansas, 164–68, 220, 223,
  233, 235–38, 256, 257, 290–95, 303–304;
  Kansas-Nebraska Act and, 163–68, 177,
  180, 182, 192, 223, 256; labor, 28, 29, 92,
  164, 392–93, 423*n*10; Lecompton
  debate, 290–95, 296, 303–304, 311, 361;
  liberty caps and, 176–77, 224–25,
  231–32, *232*, 402; Washington, D.C., 9,
  27, 29, 53, 57, 59, 65–67, 415*n*53;
  Wilmot Proviso, 51, 53, 56
Slidell, John, 241
smallpox, 12
Smith, Caleb, 385, 387, 388, 390, 392, 406

Smith, Frederic A., 141
Smith, Margaret Bayard, 56
Smithsonian Board of Regents, 49
Smithsonian Institution, 26, 31, 37, 50, 99, 245
snake door handles, 212–14, *214*
snuff, 56
Sonnemann, Ottmar, 248
South, 5, 11, 12, 30, 38, 50, 222, 398; agriculture, 164; increasing antipathy between North and, 222, 310–11, 358–64, 371–72; Know-Nothingism, 193; Lost Cause, 139, 401, 402; press, 327; secession, 328, 358, 360, 363–64, 372, 378; slavery debate, 163–68, 192, 235–38, 290–95, 303–304, 310, 358–64; *see also specific states*
South Carolina, 236, 237, 358, 376, 377; secession, 358, 364
Spain, 5
stairways, 243, 322, 382
Stanton, Edwin M., 397, 427*n*33
Stanton, Richard H., 64, 67, 76, 78, 81, 160, 195; Capitol project and, 78, 81–82, 94, 101–102, 110–14, 125, 132, 150, 162, 164, 168–73, 178–82, 188–90, 215–19; Jefferson Davis and, 94, 162, 164, 168–73, 178–82, 218, 400; dome appropriation and, 215–19; Montgomery Meigs and, 178–82, 188–90, 215–19; military rule dispute and, 168–73, 178–82; Thomas Walter and, 81–82, 101–102, 150, 170–73, 178–81, 190, 191
states' rights, 5, 38, 49, 50–51, 115, 311, 401
statues and sculpture, 6–7, 22, 103, 156–57, 174, 187, 197–99, 211, 219–21, 258–59, 268, 269, 283–84, 307, 308, 355–58, 402; dome, 219–20, 224–25, 231–32, *232*, 233, 246–47, *247*, 248, 304, 340–42, *342*, 346, *347*, 357–58, 365–67, *367*, 368, 392–93, *394*, 402, 403–404; of Indians, 197–98, *198*, 199, 211; pediment, 156–57, 174–76, *176*, 177, 187, 197–98, *198*, 199, 219–20,

231, 242, 258–59, 269, 306, 308–309, *309*, 404; *see also* art and decoration; *specific artists and works*
steamboats, 284, 377
steam engine, 105, 211, 250
Stephens, Alexander H., 406
Stephenson, John G., 380
stone, 15, 21, 48, 75, *91*, 92, 105, 200; bluestone, 97, 113, 117–18, 134; broken and unused on Capitol grounds, *279*; contracts, 97–101, 110, 120–21, 134–35, 154, 158, 174, 275, 279–80, 314, 334–36, 343, 350–54, 363, 371, 391; granite, 86, 92, 280, 343; marble, 75, 92, 97–101, 110, 111, 120–21, 134–35, 154–55, 193, 229, 314–15, 322, 334–36, 350–54, 389, 391; quarries, 92, 98–100, *100*, 101, 155, 162, 279–80, 314, 335–36, 350–54; sandstone, 15, 21, 25–26, 75, 92, 155, 182–83, 240, 249; *see also* columns; construction; foundations; sculptures and statues
Stone, Horatio, 306, 434*n*1
stonemasons, 96, 122, 124, 127, 134, 193, 200
Strickland, William, 71
Strong, Robert, 122, 133
Strong, Samuel, 93–94, 96, 120–24, 132, 134, 135, 137, 138
Stuart, Alexander H. H., 86, 90, 96, 97, 99, 103–104, 107, 110, 117
Stuart, Gilbert, portraits of presidents by, 103
Sumner, Charles, 167, 235–37; Brooks attack on, 236–37, 241; "Crime Against Kansas" speech, 235–36
Supreme Court, U.S., 11, 35, 319, 354, 362; Dred Scott case, 255–58, 291, 361–62; early development of, 11, 17
swamp gas, 62
symmetry, 24, 35, 60

Taney, Roger B., 257
tariffs, 164

Taylor, George, 301–302, 306, 312
Taylor, John L., 82, 215
Taylor, Knox, 40–41, 42, 95
Taylor, Zachary, 9, 29–30, 40–41, 42, 44, 49, 58–59, 61–62, 103, 129, 130, 139, 244, 418n9, 419n27; compromise debate and, 51–54, 62; Jefferson Davis and, 40–42, 44–47, 51–54, 62; death of, 62, 73; Mexican War and, 44–47, 51; views on slavery, 29, 30, 51–54
temperance, 192
Tennessee, 393, 394
Texas, 23, 25, 57, 62, 65, 66; statehood, 44
Thackeray, William Makepeace, 241
Thomas, Ernest, 195–96
Thomas, Henri, 195–96
Thomas (Henry F.) & Co., 337
Thompson, Jacob, 63–64
Thornton, William, 14–17, 19; Capitol design, 14–15, 15, 16, 17
Thorwaldsen, Bertel, 208
tobacco chewing, 55, 56, 107
Tocqueville, Alexis de, 14; Democracy in America, 14
toilets, 22, 34
Toombs, Robert, 244, 356, 369
Totten, Joseph G., 99, 139–44, 145, 199, 241, 262, 427n33; Montgomery Meigs and, 139–44, 181, 262
tourism, 127
Towers, John T., 194
Train, Charles R., 384, 387
transcontinental railroad, 163, 164, 430n6
Treasury, 33, 73, 93, 148, 150, 373
trenches, 91, 96–97, 107, 154
Trollope, Frances, 55
trompes l'oeil, 209, 268, 300, 301, 323, 407
Trumbull, John, 19; Rotunda paintings, 19–20
trusses, 190, 229, 255, 348
Tyler, John, 34
typhoid, 12

Uncle Tom's Cabin, 127
unemployment, 28
Union Army, 365–68, 390, 397, 398, 399; in Washington, D.C., 378–80, 380, 381, 381
unionism, 38, 41–42, 44, 50–54, 94–95, 131, 222–23, 310–12, 327
U.S. Coast Survey, 131
United States Gazette, 343
Usher, John P., 406
Utah, 25, 65

Van Buren, Martin, 29, 44
Venable, Abraham W., 102
Venezuela, 72
ventilation, 11, 16, 18, 78, 143, 151, 164, 210–11, 266, 385, 443n8; downward, 151–54, 274–77; inadequate, 16, 55, 107; in Meigs-Davis plan, 151, 152, 153–54, 164, 203, 210–11, 266, 272, 274–75, 329, 405; Post Office contracts, 298–99, 313, 334, 336–37, 371
Vespucci, Amerigo, 323
Vice President's Room, 196
Vicksburg, Mississippi, 44, 365
Vincenti, Francis, 193, 195, 211
Virginia, 11, 12, 378–79; Harpers Ferry raid, 358–60; secession, 378

Walker, James, 269–70, 313, 389; Storming of Chapultepec, 270, 305, 387–88, 392
Walker, Percy, 251
Walker, Amanda, 72, 84, 88, 98, 367, 379
Walker, Gardiner, 231
Walter, Horace, 231, 313–14, 350, 368, 383, 390, 409–10, 432n4
Walter, Irene, 83, 84, 88
Walter, Olivia, 84, 88
Walter, Robert, 231, 314, 349–50, 368, 383, 390, 409
Walter, Thomas Ustick, 70–71, 71, 72, 77–87, 147, 185, 231, 261, 267, 353, 406, 431n20; accused of kickbacks and

fraud, 120–26, 132–37; altered-drawings affair, 285–89, 292, 296; on art and decoration, 247–48, 283–84, 297, 391–93, 407; background of, 71–72; becomes Architect of the Capitol Extension, 86, 90; Borland investigation, 121–26, 132–38, 149, 150, 154–55; Buchanan administration and, 276, 277–95; Capitol designs, 70–72, 77–87, 88–106, 107–24, 151, 155–56, 182–88, 203–205, 214–20, 226–29, 248–50, 274–95, 346–50; cast iron used by, 104–106, 119, *165*, 183–84, 186; Civil War and, 366–68, 372, 378–84, 387–94; Congress and, 89–90, 94, 105, 108, 125, 188, 203–204; custody of drawings, 296–97, 299–300, 316, 336–38, 344–46; Jefferson Davis and, 94, 148–51, 171, 200–205, 330; death of, 411; dome designs, 182–84, 186–88, 203, *203*, 204–205, 214–20, 226–29, 239, 248–50, 275, 284, 287, 315, 346–47, *347*, 348–50, 365–67, *367*, 358, 391; 1851 construction and, 88–106; 1852 construction and, 107–24; 1853 construction and, 124–36; family problems of, 313–14, 349–50, 383, 390, 409–10, 422n1, 432n4; *Freedom* statue and, 247–48, 365–67, *367*, 368, 391, 392, *394*, 403–404; funding debate and, 101–102, 108–19, 125; furniture designs, 315–16, 323; as a hustler, 282–83; legacy of, 412; Library designs, 104–106, 111, 119, 132, 149, 153, 160, 164, *165*, 183, 186, 408; McNair committee and, 108–19; -Meigs rivalry, 148–51, 159–62, 170–73, 184, 186–91, 200–205, 216, 245–46, 274–90, 296–300, 313–17, 329–39, 344–47, 372–76, 386, 392, 398, 404–405, 410–11; military rule dispute and, 170–73, 178–81; opening of Senate chamber and, 323–24; Patent Office project, 149; personality of, 188, 282,

366; Franklin Pierce and, 133–34, 258; postwar life, 408–12; quarry choices, 98–101; resigns from Capitol project, 408–409; salary of, 88, 96, 191; Richard Stanton and, 81–82, 101–102, 150, 170–73, 178–81, 190, 191; views on slavery, 366, 368, 383; wartime Capitol construction and, 378–84, 387–94, 403–408; wings design, 73, 77–78, 81–87, 88–106, 107–24, 151, 155–56, 185–86, 281, 285–88

Walter, Thomas, Jr., 191, 231, 349, 366, 372, 383, 390–91, 409

War Department, 128, 131, 136, 169, 221–23, 240, 242, 244, 260, 316, 384–87; control of Capitol project, 136–44, 145–62, 164, 168–73, 178–82, 240, 242, 260–66, 287, 345, 384–86

War of 1812, 17–18, *18*, 97

Warren, Edward A., 272

Washburn, Cadwallader C., 293

Washington, D.C., 4, 9, 21–22, 26–29, 50, 62, 141, 147; Buchanan-era, 254–56, *256*, 257, 328–29; crime, 27, 28, 389–90; early development of, 11–12, *12*, 13–30; lack of running water, 28, 103, 105, 139–40, 165; L'Enfant plan, 13–14; population, 9, 27–29, 389; slavery, 9, 27, 29, 53, 57, 59, 65–67, 415n53; society, 230, 241, 328–29; War of 1812, 17–18, *18*, 97; wartime, 365–68, 373–74, *374*, 375, *375*, 376–77, *377*, 378, *378*, 379–80, *380*, 381, *381*, 382–88, *388*, 389–94, *394*

Washington, George, 11, 12, 13, 14, 23, 34, 54, 78, 103, 157, 209; Capitol design and, 13–16; portraits of, 22, 34, 54, 268, 270, 391–92, 407, *407*

Washington, Martha, 34

Washington Aqueduct, 140, 141–42, *142*, 145, 151, 153, 165, 178, 188, 195, 213, 214, 244, 254, 260–65, 277, 280–82, 284, 290, 312, 318–20, *320*, 323, 334, 337, 344, 373; contracts, 260–65,

Washington Aqueduct (*cont.*)
280–82, 296, 298, 334, 369–70; funding, 244, 245, 246, 254, 260, 312, 337, 369–70
Washington Canal, 27, 28
Washington *Daily Union*, 216
Washington *Evening Star*, 272
Washington Hotel, 27
Washington Monument, 22, 26, 31, 33, 61, 62, 73, *377*
Washington Monument Society, 22, 61, 62
water, 27; Aqueduct project, 140, 141–42, *142*, 145, 151, 153, 188, 195, 244, 254, 260–65, 277, 280–82, 290, 298, 312, 318–20, *320*, 323, 334, 337, 344, 373; lack of running water, 28, 103, 105, 140, 165
Webster, Daniel, 10, 37, 52, 54, 55, 64–66, 72, 74, 129, 185, 192, 321; Capitol project and, 72, 74, 77, 84–87, 90
Weigley, Russell F., 140, 279
Weir, Robert, 175, 196–97; *Embarkation of the Pilgrims*, 196
West, Clement, 90, 159–60, 180, 190
West Front, 13, 16, 20, 26, 34, 35, 37, 61, 73, 75, 102, 104, 151, *278, 374,* 380, 389, *411*; fountain, 318–20, *320*, 323
West Point, 3, 39–40, 42, 137, 145, 148, 175, 222, 288, 302, 310, 311, 331–34, 345, 397; appointments, 331–34
Whig Party, 9, 29, 36, 43, 46, 61, 72, 73, 77, 108, 116, 122, 126, 129, 155, 163, 192, 193, 230, 354, 418n9, 426nn3, 8
White, Hugh, 63–64
White House, 27, 33, 74, 82, 93, 149; Buchanan, 262, 328–29; Pierce, 262
Wilkinson, Allen, 237–38
Willard's Hotel, 27, 233, 234, 328–29
Wilmot, David, 51
Wilmot Proviso, 51, 53, 56
Wilson, James G., 99, 101
Wilson, Henry, 329

windows, 151, 243; casings, 255; lacking in Meigs redesign, 151–54, 160, 211; sash fasteners, 188
wings, 14; detached, 84–85; 1850–51 design contest, 69–87; Meigs-Davis plan, 151–52, *152*, 153–62, 168–84, 185–205, 206–25, 226–52, 253–95, 296–317; Mills plan, 35–36, 37–38, 58, 59–64, 67–68, 73–76, 79, *79*, 80; pediments added to, 156; Walter plan, 73, 77–78, 81–87, 88–106, 107–24, 151, 155–56, 185–86, 281, 285–88; wartime construction, 373–74, *374*, 375, *375*, 376–77, *377*, 378, *378*, 379–85, 403–408, *411*; *see also* art and decoration; construction; Capitol Extension; House chamber; Senate chamber
wire rope, 227, 228, *229*, 250
Wisconsin, 25, 255, 256
Witte, William H., 277, 279, 288, 313
Wolanin, Barbara, 175
wood, 21, 103–104, 105, 123, 133; contracts, 97; dome, 182, 228; rotting, 26; tower for dome construction, 226, 227, *228, 229, 229*
Wood, James, 113
Wood, John, 250–51, 255, 285; photograph of Buchanan inauguration, *256*
Woodward, Joseph A., 63, 64
wrought iron, 104
Wyeth, S. D., *The Federal City: Ins and Abouts of Washington*, 393
Wyoming, 25

Yancey, William, 362
yellow fever, 12
Young, A. B., 84, 85

zinc, 212

For Carla and Annie